SOCIAL PROBLEMS

social problems:
causes and controls

HOWARD E. FREEMAN

BRANDEIS UNIVERSITY AND RUSSELL SAGE FOUNDATION

WYATT C. JONES

BRANDEIS UNIVERSITY AND VETERANS ADMINISTRATION

RAND MᶜNALLY & COMPANY · CHICAGO

RAND McNALLY SOCIOLOGY SERIES / *Edgar F. Borgatta,*
Advisory Editor

For Lisa and Seth

preface

THERE IS NO SHORTAGE of well-done textbooks that consider the problems of social deviance and disorganization in the United States. What, then, argues for this one? Its timeliness, its attempts at clarity and ease of reading, its format and printing style?

Hopefully, the collaborative enterprise of the authors and publisher has given it these assets. But these are not sufficient to commend its publication; nor are the returns for either authors or publisher high enough to motivate publication of just another social-problems book. Rather, we feel that we have provided a special—we would like to think unique—treatment of deviance and disorganization. How well we have done must be judged by professor and student, but it may be useful to try to set down our objectives.

Most simply put, we have tried to accomplish three things in this book:

To consider a broad spectrum of social problems rather than focus in depth on a relatively few. At the same time we wanted to do more than merely note the facts and figures on the scope of each problem; we have attempted, therefore, to place them in a systematic framework.

To draw on the research literature wherever possible. We have tried, however, not to make the volume either so technical that only advanced students could read it or so statistical that it would bore the reader.

To stress the knowledge available about the causes and current efforts at intervention and amelioration of social problems. Nevertheless, we recognize the lack of definitiveness that exists about the causes and controls of social problems and we have not hesitated to speculate rather freely even when data are skimpy.

Our efforts to accomplish these objectives can be gleaned from glancing at the table of contents and by leafing through this volume. First, we were concerned with the organization of the material. Three introductory chapters set forth our theoretical and methodological stance. We then divide social problems into those that are so pervasive that they affect all age groups in the community and those that are concentrated more or less within age groups. The pervasive problems are considered first. The last part of the book discusses the age-related problems in chapters concerned with stages in the life cycle.

Second, while we wanted to write as nontechnical a volume as possible, we wished to give the reader at least a flavor for the research literature and the scholarly views on which it is based. For this reason, each chapter contains a variety of "documentations"—extracts from various monographs and journals that clarify and amplify the text.

Third, and perhaps most controversial, we have taken a number of stands on what can and should be done in order to intervene and control deviance and disorganization in the United States.

Naturally, we do not expect all professors and students to regard our organization of the volume as optimal. With the exception of the first three chapters of introductory material, we have attempted to make each chapter an independent essay so that the book can be used in a number of different ways consistent with the interests and orientations of teachers and students. We have tried to provide a fairly representative series of references to guide the student in further study and research. We hope that we have been able to meet the needs of students at various levels of academic accomplishment and the interests of professors with different viewpoints and special concerns.

From start to finish, putting this volume together has been an adventure—in part pleasurable and in part painful. We trust the reader will find his use of the book involves only the former.

acknowledgments

There is a risk in singling out individuals by name for their contributions to this volume, since many persons have given us valuable advice and assistance. Nevertheless, there are some to whom we are unusually grateful and whom we would like to thank by name.

Mrs. Linda Waddington at the University of Wisconsin not only typed the first draft but did extensive library research as well. Miss Kathy Grenham of Russell Sage Foundation undertook extensive reference checking and clerical work. Finally, Miss Kathie McConnell of Brandeis University proved invaluable in preparing the final manuscript. We are most grateful to the three of them.

Many of our colleagues have been subjected to our material. Edgar F. Borgatta, our publisher's advisory editor and our close friend, was encouraging and critical in about equal proportions. Stanton Wheeler of Russell Sage Foundation and Yale University and David Mechanic of the University of Wisconsin have been unusually helpful. We are also grateful to the two anonymous readers (whose names we can guess) for the critical reviews they provided and whose thoughts helped greatly in our revision of the manuscript. The institutions we now work for, as well as the University of Wisconsin where one of the authors spent his sabbatical, should be mentioned; in these settings the minds of both colleagues and students and the resources of supply rooms were freely invaded.

A word should be said for our publisher, Rand McNally and Company. Larry Malley, former social science editor and now executive editor of the college department, not only has given freely of his credit card but has been most patient as well as sympathetic to our many requests; we appreciate also his many creative ideas on the book. We are most grateful to Marianne Clark, then head of Rand McNally's college editorial staff, whose advice and encouragement is most appreciated. We owe her a special debt—selecting Mrs. Martha Urban to edit the final manuscript. Mrs. Urban deserves mention not only for her editorial skill but for her tolerance and sense of humor as well. She needed these qualities in abundance to work with us.

It is our book, however, and we take full responsibility for its contents.

HOWARD E. FREEMAN
WYATT C. JONES

Waltham, Massachusetts
September, 1969

contents

PART TWO / PERVASIVE PROBLEMS

SOCIAL PROBLEMS

PART ONE

SOCIOLOGICAL FRAME OF REFERENCE

social problems
and the social order

UTOPIA, Sir Thomas More's conception of the ideal social order, was published in 1516. But man was searching for a utopian community life long before More coined the term, and man is seeking it still. Some philosophers, poets, theologians, and even social scientists, as Barber (1952) notes, still insist that a perfect social system is possible. But it is evident that the contemporary American community is not the prototype of an ideal social order. Rather, we are confronted with so broad a spectrum of social problems that our communities might better serve as dis-utopian models.

In a democracy, every citizen has the privilege, indeed the duty, to hold perspectives on what is right and wrong with his way of life and to strive vigorously for a social system consistent with his values. Many community members in their personal conduct seek to exemplify the values they cherish and to exercise initiative as individuals in order to advance their ideas of a meaningful social life. But individualized action has seldom proved sufficient. Whenever chaotic social conditions have been avoided and where social progress has been advanced, it has been accomplished through the communal behavior of individuals, supporting their leaders who have the ability and opportunity to function as agents of social control and of social change.

the search for utopia

Collective actions to improve community life or specific parts of it have taken many forms: the monastic communities of Christian and Buddhist religious; the Puritan theocracy of the Massachusetts Bay Colony; the various experiments in communalism ranging from the idealistic but short-lived Brook Farm of Emerson and Alcott to the cohesive and productive kibbutzim of modern Israel, to name a few. These and countless other efforts to mold society to a particular moral or philosophical doctrine have met with varying degress of success. While none of these movements should be disparaged completely, it can be fairly said that few have succeeded; most of them have been transitory in time, highly selective of their participants, and subject to divisive forces within and without their boundaries.

It is quite clear that the actions of individuals or isolated groups simply are not sufficient to remedy or even minimize the various social ills afflicting our society. There is great variance and deep conflict about what constitutes a good society. Even in areas about which there is virtual consensus of goals and values—medical care, for instance—intense and serious disagreement exists about the utility and desirability of appropriate mechanisms to achieve these goals. In some cases there is conflict because of different views on the pace at which progress and social change should take place. Indeed, a special problem is presented by the competition for resources and for power and control among the various individuals and groups engaged in the tasks of mediating undesirable social conditions, moderating the deviant behavior of community members, and advancing our society toward a more desirable goal. All of us are familiar with the myriad of public agencies—federal, state, local—that function as regulatory bodies and as agents of social control; of the numerous religiously based groups who choose to attack this or that aspect of social or moral decay; of the many fraternal and social organizations whose good works are grist for the local society page; of the politically motivated who are willing to use both physical aggression and subtle psychological means to establish a social system more consistent with their ideology.

Such contradictory and fragmented activities represent, as much as do our slums, prisons, overflowing mental hospitals, riots, and discriminatory social and economic practices, the inadequacies of our contemporary social order and the extent of corruption and contamination in our society. Consequently, we are turning more and more to science, and particularly to the social science disciplines, in our search for a more utopian way of life. It apparently is the only framework for progressive social change that holds out much hope of success.

the study of social problems

Man has always sought to rationalize his fears and reduce his anxieties about things he does not understand by rendering them explainable. At least in the Western world, a particular system of thought has been used

the etiology of sociology

The success or failure of sociology as a scientific study of society can be gauged according to different conceptions of science. From the practical point of view, the utility of science lies in bringing benefit to mankind. In this perspective, the purpose of social science is to solve social problems and to improve the social scene. This credo has been explicitly formulated by prominent sociologists and propagated through textbooks of sociology which often organize the material of instruction around social problems or with an eye to beneficial applications of sociological principles. From this vantage point, natural sciences, which have produced the X-ray, penicillin, nuclear generators, moon rockets, etc., are resounding successes. By the same standard, however, sociology must be judged a failure to the extent that it has not produced the social equivalents of the X-ray, penicillin, and nuclear generators, not to speak of moon rockets. On a less spectacular level, it is indeed doubtful that sociologists have begun to solve the problems that have received their intense attention: crime, racial strife, juvenile delinquency, mental disorder, alcoholism, drug addiction, rebellions at home and abroad, alienation, and anomie. If we compare the incidence and prevalence of these social disturbances of today with those of the bygone days when sociologists were less numerous and less active, it is not obvious that sociologists have contributed much toward a satisfactory solution of these problems. It is undoubtedly true that the intensity and variety of social problems have multiplied with the growing complexity of society even as sociology has been growing and becoming more active. Nevertheless, this does not vitiate the fact that sociology has been ineffectual with the problems with which it has been grappling. It may also be argued that sociology as a science is a relatively new enterprise, but this is not a sufficient explanation for the lack of success; the late development of sociology as a science is something that requires an explanation itself. After all, the study of man goes back to the days of Aristotle, if not to greater antiquity, as does the study of the physical world. Or, if we compare our society with those which do not benefit from the services of sociological consultants as we know them, Communist China, for example, and even the Soviet Union, it appears that they are no more beriddled with unsolved social problems for the lack of sociologists. (Park, 1967:155.)

to advance understanding and, as a consequence, reduce the underlying distress experienced by community members. This philosophy is commonly known as the scientific method. Notwithstanding the fact that most major breakthroughs in knowledge have raised more questions than they have answered, man's explorations in the physical and life sciences, and the resulting broad knowledge base, leave most individuals convinced of the pragmatic worth of the scientific system of thought. It is only reasonable that, being the intelligent animals that we are, we bring to bear the same system of thought to increase our understanding and reduce our anxiety about social life and the workings of the community.

Man's interest in the social sciences is as old as his interest in the life and physical sciences. We have been concerned with understanding abhorrent behavior and the dynamics of the social order for as long as we have been looking for explanations of heat and light and the functioning of the planetary system. Indeed, man's intense interest in knowing about the mechanisms of psychological gratification probably preceded his attempts to explain physiological processes.

But some people will say we have not gone very far, that our so-called modern methods for treating the mentally ill are little more efficacious than those of prescientific societies, or that our programs for caring for the elderly are no more humane than those that existed before the great civilizations, or that our moral order has not shown any vast improvement during the last ten centuries. (*See* Documentation 1.) There are many explanations for this: The complexity of man's social life is vastly greater than that of his physiological being or his physical world. Moreover, the engineering and technical developments that typically follow breakthroughs in the physical and life sciences have not been achieved in the social sciences. Then, too, the scientific advances in the physical and biological sciences and their resultant engineering developments keep changing the social order so rapidly that scientific discoveries about social life and behavior, and the implementation of action programs based on these discoveries, are made exceedingly difficult.

Nevertheless, while there are still setbacks and barriers to systematic investigation (including man's natural reluctance to having his behavior and ideologies brought into the open and sometimes challenged), this is the era of scientific inquiry into social problems; this is the generation of the social engineer. The direction of activity is apparent and the course of action is clear. The social sciences today represent robust disciplines actively engaged in delving into social processes, and the social engineering based upon their accrued knowledge is now accorded stature and respectability within the social order.

While there are no clear lines between disciplines in the social sciences any more than there are in the life and physical sciences, one of the social sciences—sociology—is concerned primarily with describing and understanding the social behavior and social conditions of community members. Sociology today can be said to dominate the spheres of activity related to the spectrum of difficulties and dilemmas known as social problems. It is of primary influence as the knowledge base for social engineering and for the technical development of programs and procedures related to the amelioration and prevention of these problems. In fact, one definition, or at least one frame of reference, for the discipline of sociology is to think about it as the science of the study of social problems (Becker, 1966).

Implicitly, of course, all of sociology, by virtue of its focus on social processes and the phenomena of group life, has relevance for the solution of community conditions and social behavior that inhibit the functioning of society. But individual social scientists in their work vary in the scope of their activities, in the substantive problems to which they address themselves, and in their views regarding the propriety of the scientist devoting himself to "engineering" problems, that is, to the adaptation and utilization of scientific knowledge for immediate application.

Some sociologists, then, see the primary thrust of the field to be one of developing general theories of social behavior, ones that, at an abstract level, have relevance for the understanding of all social life. Others focus their attention on less abstract problems and are primarily concerned with the development of special theories that explain segments of social life, such theories often being referred to as *middle-range theories* (Merton, 1957). Still others concentrate their efforts on the building of analytic and descriptive bodies of information based on empirical studies. When challenged about the lasting utility of such efforts they argue strongly that only with such bodies of information available is it possible to develop generalizations about social behavior. Some sociologists are primarily interested in developing the technical repertoire of the field and argue vehemently that the refinement of research methods is essential to the general task. Finally, there are some whose interests are in the evaluation of techniques of social change and methods of social intervention whether based upon scientific thought or not (Sheldon and Moore, 1969).

With respect to the substantive concerns, there are a number of different dimensions along which sociologists order their interests. Some are concerned with the application of sociological frames of reference and the scientific method to the analysis of history and even the prehistory of man. Others focus on contemporary aspects of social life but seek out simple or narrow groups for study. These range from laboratory oriented small-group analysts, who literally develop their own social groups for study, to those who select small and sometimes geographically isolated communities for their investigations. This limited approach is justified on the ground that it is possible to examine social processes more fully under simplistic conditions and to derive generalizations—or at least hypotheses—about social life which can later be tested in more complex and realistic situations. Then there are sociologists who focus their work on the highly complex urban community and the aspects of social life within it.

Within the discipline of sociology, individual workers also hold different views on whether, in their role as scientists, it is proper and appropriate for them to become concerned with the technical problems of program development. Some maintain that their responsibility does not include applying their knowledge or, for that matter, even making it widely known outside the circle of their peers. But there are others who feel most strongly that it is the urgent responsibility of the sociologist not only to encourage the use of scientific findings but to engage in the necessary engineering tasks. Indeed, they sometimes argue that the fundamental test of scientific study can be derived only from the sustained application of knowledge and from applied research directed at examining contemporary social problems (Davis, 1964).

In all fields of scientific study, and certainly in sociology, debate on these several issues continues unceasingly. The positions argued are not whether one is superior to another; rather, the debate is usually in terms of degrees of emphasis. Even those sociologists who are social-problems oriented agree that their area of concern needs to be complemented by other sociologists less immediately concerned with the contemporary community. These would emphasize principles that have direct relevance for the present-day community but would not be involved in program development. Thus most sociologists who identify themselves as students of social problems encourage and support a variety of work focuses and stances for persons in their fields.

Nevertheless, students of social problems generally occupy a particular posture on these issues: They reflect an impatience with the development of general theories, primarily because of the long-term investments necessary to this task. They are critical of an overemphasis upon methodological developments that have but limited utility in the study of the contemporary social scene. They are often disappointed with the endless assembling of empirical information which has limited use or which is gathered in ways that prevent integration and comparisons. Rather, they are concerned with the development of special or middle-range theories that have immediate potential relevance for understanding the contemporary situation or aspects of it. They are encouraging about the development of methodological techniques that not only permit reasonably precise work but that have broad adaptability to issues currently being investigated. They are supportive of work directed at the evaluation of programs for the treatment and prevention of current and persistent social problems. Moreover, while they recognize the worth of studying simple groups and social systems and the value of analyzing historical periods and other societies for their own sake, they argue for a concentration of effort on the contemporary community and for broader inquiries into current problems. Finally, they take the position that if they themselves are not willing to engage in the social engineering tasks, it certainly behooves them to encourage and to ally themselves with groups of practitioners who are willing to direct their efforts to this endeavor.

While it is not possible to outline a single profile of the problem-oriented sociologist that would distinguish him from his peers in the discipline, there is reasonable consensus on the thrust of his work in the arena of social problems and agreement that the binding characteristic is the application of the scientific method. The heart of the matter, however, lies in identifying, labeling, and focusing effort on particular social phenomena, particular social conditions, and particular community behavior because they are undesirable—that is, because they are social problems. Of course, workers in all scientific fields face to some extent the question of what is important for study. But establishing criteria for the selection of areas for concentrated effort is not a scientific problem, it is one of values. Clearly each scientist, as an individual community member, is faced with the question of where to direct his efforts: to those areas which interest and challenge him, to those areas which he feels most community members hold as important, or to those areas which some other person or agency has deemed important? The issue becomes even more salient for the sociologist concerned with current social processes and the contemporary social order.

The very labels "social problems," "social pathology," "social disorganization," and "deviant behavior" that are attached to phenomena under investigation point up the problem. Sociologists concerned with social problems are doing research of a general sociological nature. The core of their commitment as scientists is to explicate the phenomena that are the proper domain of their discipline. But the sociologist who regards himself as a student of social problems likewise regards himself as making contributions directed at the control and prevention of social ills. Unavoidably the student of social problems must assume the responsibility for attaching particular importance to any area of inquiry. By the very act of indicating his concern with a certain phenomenon he calls attention to its problematic character for the functioning of the social system. The responsibility is equally severe for those who fail to pay attention to those problems at the heart of society's difficulties or who are stimulated by issues which, on balance, are of a relatively minor importance in the scheme of things. Certainly accusations of bias on both counts have been quite properly lodged at different times against members of the discipline. The danger, as Homans (1950:5) indicates by quoting some unknown novelist, is that the sociologist may become ". . . a man who spends some forty-thousand dollars to find a whore house."

During the more than fifty years that have passed since the earliest text-books on social problems were published (Ellwood, 1910), sociologists have engaged in heated arguments regarding the issue of what is a social problem. Offhand it might seem that criteria for designating certain social behavior or community conditions as social problems are obvious. But there are, at the polar extremes, two rather antagonistic positions with respect to the appropriate criteria. One position identifies social problems or social conditions on the basis of moral and ethical criteria; the other argues for objective and neutral criteria. This volume will advance a third position: the social-policy orientation. But first it may be useful to discuss the moral and objective positions in some detail.

the moral position

For the most part, early sociologists did not question whether the investigation of social problems should be a moral or an objective field of study. Without much criticism they accepted as their bases for judging good and evil a code of morality and a set of ethical standards which were rooted in the Judeo-Christian heritage and confirmed by tradition. Many of these early sociologists were ministers and social workers who turned to sociology in order to advance their theological and philosophic positions regarding right and wrong (Odum, 1951). In fact, one prominent sociologist, Samuel Stauffer, often said of his peers, "Scratch a sociologist and you will find a Methodist minister." Lemert (1951:1) has described the early sociologist as follows:

> Generally speaking, these late nineteenth- and early twentieth-century sociologists grouped together under the heading of "social pathology" those human actions which ran contrary to ideals of residential stability, property ownership, sobriety, thrift, habituation to work, small business enterprise, sexual discretion, family solidarity, neighborliness, and discipline of will. In effect, social problems were considered to be any forms of behavior violating the mores from which these ideals were projected. The mores behind the ideals, for the most part, were those of rural, small-town, and middle class America, translated into public policy through the rural domination of county boards of supervisors and state legislatures, and through the reform activities of humanitarian social workers and Protestant religious federations.

It is evident from the tone of Lemert's remarks that many contemporary sociologists do not hold with the normative views that guided much of the early work of their colleagues in the field of social problems. Were it not for World War II, the subsequent Cold War, the rapid urbanization and industrialization in many parts of the world, and the sweeping economic changes in the United States, the moral view of social problems might no longer be regarded as respectable within the sociological discipline. The current strength of the moral position is related, at least in part, to the increased social consciousness of the physical scientists. As a result of the development and use of the atomic bomb, physicists and other "hard" scientists have become increasingly aware of the social consequences of their scientific investigations. As never before, the accomplishments of the past decades in nuclear research have emphasized the power of the scientist and his responsibilities to the world in which he lives. Many scientists feel very strongly that at this point in the history of science it is the social responsibility of all scientists to support scientific analysis of the social and political problems which so dangerously threaten the existence of science itself (Barber, 1952).

The position of the moralists is that science, and physical science even more than social, has always been engaged in research of value to human welfare. In demonstrating this point, the analogy of medical science is often used. It is commonly held that the basic value premise of medicine is that sickness is undesirable. The scientific objectivity of medical research is rarely questioned. It is equally possible for the study of other types of human ills and social disorders to be scientifically vigorous. The value premise that the social scientist applies to his study of social problems does not render his research unscientific.

At the core of the values that constitute the departure point for most sociologists sympathetic with this position is a belief in the human dignity of man. The infinite worth of the person and the importance of his health and welfare constitute the ultimate criteria for assessing social problems. Sociologists who hold this view explicitly acknowledge the value position they espouse and demand of themselves strict adherence to the canons of science in the actual conduct of their research (Kelman, 1968).

A proportion of the sociological profession contends that the moral identification of social problems impedes the development of a "science" of sociology. They maintain that moral values are not universal and, consequently, a moral definition of social problems really amounts to the advancement of a personal theological position or a position advocated by various social reformers, ranging from social workers to churchmen. Variations in sexual values and practice graphically make this point. For example, unlike in American communities, premarital pregnancy is not considered objectionable in rural Denmark (Christensen. 1960).

patterns of marriage and conception

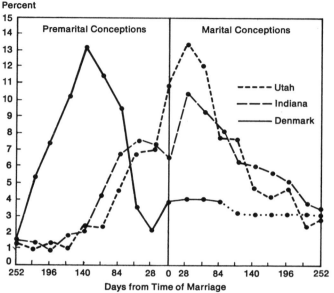

Pregnancy inception as related to time of marriage: a cross-cultural comparison. Data are for births occurring during the first nineteen lunar months of marriage and are expressed as percentages.

It may be noted that, whereas in the Utah and Indiana samples the modal time of conception is one lunar month after marriage, in the Danish sample it is five lunar months *before* the marriage. As a matter of fact the Danish data show many more couples conceiving about five months before the marriage than at any other time; in that culture, therefore, premarital conception coupled with subsequent delayed marriage must be considered as the norm. The Indiana curve is bimodal, with the peak for premarital conceptions at two lunar months prior to marriage—suggesting a tendency to get married as soon as possible after the second menstrual period has been missed and the doctor's positive diagnosis has been given. The Utah curve starts low and moves up regularly until the time of marriage and immediately

thereafter, when it is the highest of all three.

[This] fact . . . is further evidence of Utah's pattern of early conception following the wedding. Of the three cultures, Utah has not only the lowest rates of premarital conception but the highest rate of *early* postmarital conception.

Apparently, in Denmark there is little pressure to hurry marriage merely because of pregnancy. In Indiana the tendency is to marry immediately after the pregnancy is definitely known so as to hide the fact from the public. Couples who have premarital sexual intercourse in Utah, on the other hand, seem to hurry marriage because of that fact alone, without waiting for pregnancy to force them into it (religious guilt is a sufficient sanction once the "law of chastity" has been broken.) (Christensen, 1960:35–36.)

Indeed, as illustrated in Documentation 2, going steady and engagement include rights to sexual intercourse, and pregnancy is viewed as a normal prelude to marriage. Empirically, with the possible exception of incest (and even incest allegedly was prescribed for the pharaohs of ancient Egypt), there are probably no acts of behavior or social conditions that are viewed as undesirable in all communities, at all times.

Moreover, the moral standards that pertain to even small, homogeneous communities are ambiguous and open to various interpretations by different social reformers and experts. It is evident that in large social systems, such as the United States, a moral view of social problems requires not only the acceptance of a particular set of values but also allegiance to a group of experts who define these values as they pertain to particular behaviors or social conditions. Whether medical care for the aged is a social problem, for example, depends upon which group is defining the need. Physicians, or at least the American Medical Association, maintained that aged individuals could solve most of their own medical problems; the political sponsors of Medicare, on the other hand, insisted that the problem was superordinate to the individuals involved and constituted a social problem necessitating legislative action.

Sociologists opposed to or ambivalent about the moral basis of social problems also maintain that scientific inquiry is restricted by the particular interpretation of morality that guides the investigator's evaluation of behavior and social conditions as a social problem: for example, the problem for the teacher or researcher working in an extremely sectarian school that places explicit and doctrinaire limits on fields of inquiry. Those opposed to a moral definition of social problems maintain that in all settings, not just in sectarian schools, the acceptance of moral judgments results in pressures to conform in both their teaching and their research.

In brief, the moral approach to identifying social problems is to define them as behaviors of individuals or conditions within society that threaten or infringe upon established moral values and may be ameliorated or eliminated by appropriate social action on the part of community members. This approach is criticized by some sociologists as semiscientific because it contradicts the ethical neutrality that is supposed to characterize every scientist.

the objective position

Sociologists who reject the moral position do not deny the need for or the right of individuals to engage in value-oriented analysis of social behavior or community conditions. But they do insist that analyses of a moral or ethical character be kept distinct from the scientific work of the sociologist. Cuber and Harper (1951:11), speaking as sociologists, express the position as follows:

> Certainly, of course, someone has the right to advocate or recommend that this or that value position is better or worse than some other one. We, however, do not choose to accept this responsibility.

The solution offered is to treat values as data. In this frame of reference the term *social problems* is restricted to the persistent occurrence of individual or group behavior or the continued existence of social conditions that are contrary to the expressed norms of community members and which community members strive to correct by collective action. This position keeps the sociologist outside the fishbowl, not swimming in it.

At first glance the objective definition may not seem too different from the moral position. The key difference is that community life styles become the pivotal reference points in assessing the congruence of a standard with reality, i.e., empirical rather than ideal values are used. Thus the objective sociologist sees as a social problem any social behavior or community condition that, by virtue of its disparity from accepted standards, evokes a response from community members. This response is frequently referred to as a *sanction*. Sociologists sometimes use the term *norms* or *normative values* to distinguish those standards with concomitant sanctions from the ideal standards or values of the community. For example, the Golden Rule is not a norm, for if man lives by it he does so only for his own sake; failure to do so provokes no social punishment.

Most of the time the sanctions used to bring the individual back into line are carried out by persons intimately involved with the behavior or the conditions viewed as deviating from the normative standards; other community members remain unalarmed and unconcerned. In so-called primitive communities, virtually all deviance is so controlled, and the actions of primary group members usually prove sufficient to maintain the social order. Even in modern urban communities, most deviance is dealt with solely on an informal level. For example, in some factories overproduction is controlled by "binging" (a sharp blow on the upper arm), but it is carried out by the rate-buster's fellow workers (Homans, 1950). Informal sanctions may range from a raised eyebrow to a homemade bomb through the front window. The term *social problem* is usually reserved under this approach for deviance that evokes sanctions of the formal sort: sanctions legitimized by the approval of legal-political bodies such as the state legislature, or quasi-legal groups such as the American Bar Association. Norms associated with formal sanctions are often called *institutional norms*. In some instances formal sanctions are used only as a last resort; this is true regarding most adolescent behavior problems. Other times both formal and informal controls operate as, for example, in dealing with deviant sex conduct. In still other instances the control is almost entirely on a formal level, such as in the case of homicidal acts. These illustrations, of course, refer only to the United States.

This objective approach to social problems does not place emphasis upon the undesirability of behavior and conditions but on the empirical responses of community members to them. The sociologist ascribing to this definition thus becomes the interpreter, not the advocator, of values. The objective approach is quite attractive in many respects. But it, too, has been questioned. One criticism is that it also is based on a moral value, just a different one.

The objective position assumes that community members know what is best for themselves, a position that is debatable. Moreover, the issue is made stronger by the fact that norms do not necessarily reflect the consensual agreement of community members, or even a majority view. A norm does not specify the average behavior expected of individuals or the social conditions under which they live but refers instead to the expectations of a group or groups who hold the power or who have been designated by some portions of the community members—but not necessarily the majority—as the standard setters. Also, the norms and the implementation of sanctions may lag behind community sentiments; hence, the objective approach to social problems is often a conservative one and supports unduly the status quo.

Finally, critics of an objective definition of social problems argue that it curtails the basic function of science, namely, the adjustment of man to his environment. A somewhat outdated example, given today's campus views on sex, may illustrate this criticism. (*See* Documentation 3.) The illustration in Documentation 3, that caressing the breasts evokes more consequences than an all-out sexual attack, may seem trivial. Also, it could be argued that a college campus is not a viable community and that this relationship would not occur if an entire urban center were the unit of analysis. But the point made is rather evident and certainly applicable to our contemporary society: namely, that by objective criteria, white-collar pilfering and expense-account padding are less of a social problem than petty crimes such as pickpocketing; that criminal abortionists are less of a social problem than peeping toms; and that child abuse is less of a social problem than cruelty to animals. This so-called objective definition, then, is also a problematic one, and the sociologist has a major dilemma if he insists upon choosing it over a moral definition, albeit the dilemma is often abstract or theoretical, owing to the fact that there is considerable overlap in the social behavior and conditions identified as social problems by both definitions.

the social-policy position

For a variety of reasons, including the human limitation on the breadth of material about which one individual can be knowledgeable, the subject matter of sociology has become divided into a variety of specialties. These fields are organized about specific content—criminology, industrial sociology, and mental health, to name a few. In virtually every substantive field of sociology there has been considerable concern with the study of existing conditions and behavior and how they deviate from sets of standards. Certain fields, such as criminology, have an inherent social-problems base and virtually all research in these areas is related to deviance and deviants. In others, such as the study of the family, only a part of the research has this social-problems quality, since discontinuities be-

---

DOCUMENTATION 3

the pitfalls of objective criteria

In a study of sexual behavior on a college campus, girls were asked if they had experienced sexual aggression in the form of "petting below the waist" or "attempted intercourse" (Kirkpatrick and Konin, 1957). On the average, they reported 4.2 instances of sexual aggression during the academic year. Undoubtedly, such aggressive action would be regarded as the most serious dimension of the problem. This is not the case, however, if one uses the action which the girl took in response to the "attack" as the objective definition (see Table below, from Kirkpatrick and Konin, 1957:56).

In terms of formal sanctions ("Report to authority"), the boy who attempted intercourse was perfectly safe; the less ambitious the aggressor, the more likely were formal sanctions to be evoked or at least brought to the attention of persons authorized to evoke the formal sanctions.

TYPES OF AGGRESSION AND RESPONSE OF GIRLS

Response	TYPES OF AGGRESSION		
	Petting Above Waist	Petting Below Waist	Attempted Intercourse
Avoidance	37%	25%	31%
Warning to peers	34	21	16
Secrecy	19	46	49
Discussion with aggressor	3	3	4
Report to authority	7	5	0

tween existing conditions and sets of standards constitute only one area of concentration. In all fields of sociology, however, there is considerable attention paid to the strains and conflicts that exist in man's social behavior and social milieu.

It is the position of this book, however, that the study of social problems is not a substantive subfield within the discipline of sociology. Rather, it is a particular approach or attitude that is applicable to all sociological content. The social-policy approach does not emphasize certain types of behavior and conditions over others, or one research method as compared to another. This view of social problems places primary concern upon the discrepancy between what actually exists and the various standards of what should exist and views the resulting discontinuity as somehow dysfunctional to the social order.

> Above all it must be emphasized that the concept of social dysfunction does not harbor an implied moral judgment. Social dysfunction is not a latter-day terminological substitute for immorality, unethical practice, or the socially undesirable. It is an objective concept, not a morally evaluating one. Whether one judges a particular social dysfunction as good or bad, as desirable or regrettable, depends, not on the sociological analysis of the consequences for a particular social system, but upon the further and entirely independent judgment of the moral worth of that system (Merton, 1966:822).

From this perspective, moral and objective definitions are equally relevant as standards for evaluating social behavior and community conditions. Both sets of standards, as well as actual behavior and conditions, represent data germane to the field of sociology, and disparities between reality and these two sets of standards are clearly within the domain of sociological analysis. All areas of social behavior and all types of social conditions represent phenomena that may deviate from moral and objective standards, and these discrepancies are important in understanding social life. The study of social problems, in this frame of reference, is an approach to general sociology, one that places an emphasis upon these discrepancies and discontinuities. It is as valid an approach to understanding social life as one that centers upon formal structure, cultural traditions, or intrapsychic needs. Moreover, the utilization of a social-policy approach is defensible on pragmatic grounds; it aids in understanding sociological phenomena. In other words, it serves an heuristic purpose.

BASIS FOR POLICY VIEW

The organization of the study of social behavior and conditions around a frame of reference that emphasizes discontinuities is partly a response to the pressures of community members who make use of basic sociological research in their occupational and citizen roles. It is naive to maintain that much of scientific research, and particularly social science research, is conducted for its own sake. The emphasis on social discontinuities within various research ventures in sociology and the numerous attempts to integrate these into a field of social problems are clearly related to the values that social scientists hold because they are themselves community members.

Indeed, there is ample evidence that the sociological study of the moral and objective problems in the community does have an impact on community members and influences the way they evaluate and seek to modify existing social behavior and social conditions. Perhaps no single instance illustrates this point as well as the critical role of social science in effecting the antisegregation ruling of the Supreme Court. According to Lee (1954:62–63):

> The educational work done by social scientists over the years since 1896 provided the foundation for the elimination of the Plessy "separate but equal" doctrine. This reference to historical preparation is not to belittle the hard-won accomplishment of Clark and his associates but to help place it in longer perspective. As James Reston commented in *The New York Times,* the "court's opinion read more like an expert paper on sociology than a Supreme Court opinion." These high court decisions constitute a degree of policy-making success beyond anything previously achieved by sociologists in public affairs in this country.

Some social scientists would maintain that, in terms of the actual document developed, Kenneth Clark and his committee moved beyond what is an appropriate activity for scientists, or at least for basic scientists. In practice, there is no clear-cut line between those activities that are "scientific" and those that, while highly desired by one's professional colleagues, are part of one's role as a community member.

Whether or not the sociologist, in his scientific role, feels a commitment to participate personally in effecting social change, most of his efforts are going to have some impact on the community and the social order. A good illustration is Dr. Alfred Kinsey's research in human sexual behavior. Kinsey, a zoologist, contended that he was a basic researcher, not a sexologist, and as such was not prepared to involve himself in the social implications of his findings. But he became involved by virtue of publicly publishing his data. To quote one critical statement:

> The way in which the Report on Women was presented to the public insured its distribution to all females who can read. . . . This result must be what Dr. Kinsey and his associates wished to achieve. But it has brought about a situation which gives me great concern. I am certain that Dr. Kinsey's books contribute materially to the diffi-

the myth of value-free sociology

The problem of a value-free sociology has its most poignant implications for the social scientist in his role as educator. If sociologists ought not express their personal values in the academic setting, how then are students to be safeguarded against the unwitting influence of these values which shape the sociologist's selection of problems, his preferences for certain hypotheses or conceptual schemes, and his neglect of others. For these are unavoidable and, in this sense, there is and can be no value-free sociology. The only choice is between an expression of one's values, as open and honest as it can be . . . and a vain ritual of moral neutrality which, because it invites men to ignore the vulnerability of reason to bias, leaves it at the mercy of irrationality. . . .

It would seem that social science's affinity for modeling itself after physical science might lead to instruction in matters other than research alone. Before Hiroshima, physicists also talked of a value-free science; they, too, vowed to make no value judgments. Today many of them are not so sure. If we today concern ourselves exclusively with the technical proficiency of our students and reject all responsibility for their moral sense, or lack of it, then we may someday be compelled to accept responsibility for having trained a generation willing to serve in a future Auchwitz. Granted that science always has inherent in it both constructive and destructive potentialities. It does not follow from this that we should encourage our students to be oblivious to the difference. Nor does this in any degree detract from the indispensable norms of scientific objectivity; it merely insists that these differ radically from moral indifference. (Gouldner, 1962:212.)

culties encountered by young people in establishing good relations between the sexes. All boys and girls are pathetically anxious to be "normal." A counselor in a university recently stated that many boys he knew felt that they were not actually virile if they could not keep up with the statistics Dr. Kinsey presents of sex experiences for males of their age group (McIntosh, 1954:140).

This position that we have described as the social-policy one views the sociologist concerned with social problems as a third force. It is a view that recognizes elements of both the moral and objective positions, but strongly holds that it is insufficient to limit the field of investigation of social problems by either a set of moralistic values or the popularized reaction of community members.

Rather, the social-policy oriented sociologist argues that he should have a hand in shaping not only the subject matter of the field but also the degree of attention paid to particular problems within the community; and further, that he should be a responsible participant in the social engineering aspects that must follow in order to ameliorate and prevent those conditions and behaviors deemed undesirable.

One point of departure for this position is the recognition in the maturing discipline of sociology of the impossibility of a value-free orientation. (*See* Documentation 4.) The sociologist is a participant in the social life that he seeks to study, in the very communities that he seeks to improve. Perhaps not all will agree with this statement, but at least those sociologists who identify themselves with the "new sociology" argue that it is perfectly proper, indeed critical, for the social scientist to bring his orientation as a sociologist to bear in his superordinate role as a responsible community member (Miller and Riessman, 1968).

A second point of departure represents an even more powerful argument, namely, that the sociologist, by virtue of his full-time preoccupation with the social system, is in a particularly advantageous position to grapple intelligently with the complexities of the social order and to act as a social interventionist, as an agent of social control and social change. The sociologist's role as a scientist is anticipated, projected, and supported by the community because of the very unrest and anxiety occasioned by the problems that face us in community life. It is a declaration that the role of the scientist in a contemporary world is to mediate the problems faced by all of its citizens. As Goode (1967:19) notes:

> Perhaps, by ascertaining both our values and the possible organizations for achieving them, we might learn that the costs of many contemporary patterns are too great. I do not agree with the many critics in sociology who hold that our dominant theory is merely an extended Panglossian commentary, providing this is the best of all possible worlds. Doubtless, whatever is, is possible, and whatever is may have had to be, but we can, I believe, go beyond those powerful laws and demonstrate, as other sciences have before us, that many desirable but presently nonexistent arrangements *are* also possible.

It must be emphasized that the social-policy position does not go unchallenged, but the arguments for it are most persuasive. The very fabric of the social order, the complexities of contemporary life, do not truly allow the sociologist to take any other position, for he is denying the empirical realities that he knows too well if he argues that it is possible for him to be either the handmaiden of the moral activist or a neutral interpreter of the mandates of any collectivity in the community. (*See* Documentation 5.)

RISKS OF THE POSITION

It is important, however, to recognize the risks involved in such a position. Paramount among them is the danger that the social-policy position may lead to a very specialized but nevertheless totalitarian

the new sociology

[A meaningfully new] sociology would begin and end with the advice of Francis Bacon: "I would address one general admonition to all: that they consider what are the true ends of knowledge, and that they seek it not either for pleasure of the mind, or for contention, or for superiority to others . . . but for the benefit and use of life, and that they perfect and govern it in charity. . . ." The meaningfully new sociology would teach its recruits that it is not an indication of scholarly detachment for a sociologist to refuse to indicate which of a variety of alternatives seems most likely, on the basis of available evidence, to contribute to the good society (as defined); it is a cheap avoidance of responsibility. The recruits would also be taught that the so-called apolitical scientist is not *just* irresponsible; he is always a Frankenstein who can quite easily engage in activities that threaten to destroy man himself. As Tom Lehrer puts it with bitter humor, the politically non-committed scientist, having no significant human group loyalties, is motivated by expedience only and can therefore be *expected* to choose the side of the highest bidder regardless of the nature of the job requirements:

"Don't ask me where the bombs come down"—says the ex-Nazi missile expert, now working for the United States—"That's not my department. . . ."

The logical opposite of the apolitical scientist described is not—at least for present purposes—the "political man" who is almost totally lacking in objectivity. Neither is he the teacher who carelessly, and without labeling, presents *evaluations* of facts as if they were *empirical* observations. The politically-responsible sociologist I envisage would cling tenaciously to the generally accepted canons of science. He therefore would not think of supporting or opposing given issues, controversial or not, without having a defensible (i.e., "scientific") basis for his stand. He would, whenever possible—in line with his training and responsibility—insist upon having adequate empirical, and even experimental, knowledge before drawing conclusions. Where such knowledge is lacking—because of the pressure of time or because of the inherent complexities of any given case, as in international affairs—then he would feel that the *minimum* requirement is to be as certain as possible that sources of information are reliable (in accordance with *generally* accepted standards, not Pentagon, pacifist, or other specialist point of view) and that judgments which appear tentatively justified are properly qualified and labeled. (Hoult, 1963:5.)

social system, one in which the expert becomes the determinator of values *and* the director of actions within the community. Fortunately, it is hard to imagine a sociologist becoming a dictator. His work is too highly dependent upon a social system in which others have much to say about the propriety of his discipline. And, of course, other interest groups concerned with the same social problems operate as a check. But it is important to recognize that there could be some risk of this position leading to an unhealthy dominance of the sociologist.

One of the responsibilities of the sociologist who takes this social-policy position is to explicate the ways by which he arrives at his identification of social problems and to formalize the operations by which he makes judgments and assessments of what is right and wrong for society. It is simple to talk in vague terms about social progress, consistency within the social order, the supposed universality of standards, or the will of the community. In perfect form, these would suggest the elaboration of an entirely logical and fundamental life philosophy. But who is to hold that the sociologist is any better equipped for this task, or more efficacious, than the philosopher or other scholars who have wrestled with this central issue of human nature and social conduct throughout the history of man? However, the task cannot be avoided entirely. Sociologists must make their position known, state openly their criteria, and publish their propositions for all to judge. With these limitations in mind, we can move ahead to discuss the identification of social problems.

REFERENCES

BARBER, BERNARD.
1952 Science and the Social Order. Glencoe, Illinois: Free Press.

BECKER, HOWARD S.
1966 Social Problems. New York: Wiley.

CHRISTENSEN, HAROLD T.
1960 "Cultural relativism." American Sociological Review 25(February):31–39.

CUBER, JOHN F. AND ROBERT A. HARPER.
1951 Problems of American Society. New York: Holt.

DAVIS, JAMES A.
1964 "Great books and small groups." Pp. 244–269 in Phillip E. Hammond (ed.), Sociologists at Work. New York: Basic Books.

ELLWOOD, C. A.
1910 Sociology and Modern Social Problems. New York: Century.

GOODE, WILLIAM J.
1967 "The protection of the inept." American Sociological Review 32 (February):5–19.

GOULDNER, ALVIN.
1962 "Anti-Minotaur: The myth of value-free sociology." Social Problems 9(Winter):199–213.

HOMANS, GEORGE C.
1950 The Human Group. New York: Harcourt, Brace and World.

HOULT, THOMAS FORD.
1963 ". . . Who shall prepare himself to the battle?" The American Sociologist 3(February):3–7.

KELMAN, HERBERT C.
1968 A Time to Speak. San Francisco: Jossey-Bass.

KIRKPATRICK, CLIFFORD AND EUGENE KONIN.
1956 "Male sex aggression on a university campus." American Sociological Review 22(February):52–58.

LEE, ALFRED McCLUNG.
1954 "Sociologists in an integrating society." Social Problems 2(October): 57–66.

LEMERT, EDWIN M.
1951 Social Pathology. New York: McGraw-Hill.

McINTOSH, MILLICENT C.
1954 "I am concerned . . ." Pp. 138–142 in Donald P. Geddes (ed.), An Analysis of the Kinsey Reports. New York: Dutton.

MERTON, ROBERT K.
1957 Social Theory and Social Structure. Glencoe, Illinois: Free Press.
1966 "Social problems and sociological theory." Pp. 775–823 in Robert K. Merton and Robert A. Nisbet (eds.), Contemporary Social Problems. Second Edition. New York: Harcourt, Brace and World.

MILLER, S. M. AND FRANK RIESSMAN.
1968 Social Class and Social Policy. New York: Basic Books.

PARK, PETER.
1967 "The Cretan dictum: a functional analysis of sociology." The American Sociologist 2(August):155–157.

ODUM, HOWARD W.
1951 American Sociology. New York: Longmans, Green.

SHELDON, ELEANOR B. AND WILBERT E. MOORE.
1969 Indicators of Social Change. New York: Russell Sage.

CHAPTER 2

the identification
of social problems

TO DEVELOP an adequate frame of reference for the sociological analysis of social problems, the sociologist must examine both the moral values and objective standards of the community. His task is to define, describe, and delimit both types of norms and to assess the departures of actual behavior and conditions from each set of standards.

objective standards

Objective standards may be defined as those norms of the community which demonstrate, in terms of the actions taken, what community members expect from one another. In analyzing objective standards, one is mainly concerned with the institutional norms, i.e., those that are accompanied by formal sanctions. These sanctions are well illustrated in the penalties contained in the laws enacted by the various political jurisdictions. In fact, the legal code reflects the majority, if not all, of the institutional norms. Occasionally, the institutional norms are not directly in the hands of the legal authority, but even here responsibility is usually assigned by some political body. For example, certain actions, such as commitment to a mental hospital for observation, can be taken by the psychiatrist in his treatment of the mentally ill without reference to the courts or other legal authorities. But this responsibility is formally delegated to the physician by the state legislature.

Virtually every aspect of social behavior and community conditions is covered by law or some other institutional norm. However, were all laws on the books to be enforced—that is, sanctions fully implemented—community life would be thrown into chaos. For all practical purposes, many laws operate without sanctions, and community members (including the legal profession) are largely unconcerned when they are violated. At the time of their enactment, most laws probably reflect the views of a substantial proportion of community members regarding the undesirability of certain behavior or conditions. But they cannot be taken at face value to indicate objective norms at any particular point in the life-span of a community (Merton, 1966:812).

Indeed, enacting laws may be a way by which the community seeks to avoid taking action on certain behavior and conditions; in other words, laws may be looked upon as a form of mass psychotherapy designed to minimize concern of community members over an issue. A significant number of laws serve primarily to reduce anxiety. Somehow, if there is a law on the books, people seem less concerned about the matter. One guideline for determining objective standards, therefore, is to consider only those norms, legal and otherwise, whose formal sanctions are actively enforced.

Even this guideline is not always sufficient to distinguish objective standards from moral ones. Many times formal sanctions are brought to bear not because the behavior or condition violates the expectations of all or even most community members but because it is incongruent with the moral standards of a few people in the community. Take gambling,

---

DOCUMENTATION 1

public vs. private morality

In a clinical study of The Village, a small rural community in Kansas, we discovered a systematic inconsistency between the public and private expressions of values about drinking alcoholic beverages. In public people affirmed an "official" morality which held that the drinking of alcoholic beverages was wrong, that The Village was a "dry" town, and that only "bums and other elements of the lower classes" drank. In observations of several thousand events we found no instance in which there was a public violation or rejection of this official morality. The general applicability of our observations was confirmed. . . .

This publicly expressed ideology was not, however, an indication of the private drinking behavior or of the personal sentiments and beliefs of the members of the community. For example, one of the leaders of The Village who had expressed the official morality most directly and forcefully during our first visit to the community was a regular though moderate drinker in his home and within his clique. Similarly, some members of the Women's Christian Temperance Union drank and served alcoholic beverages in their homes. Although some members of the community expressed personal moral beliefs consistent with the official morality, the majority did not feel that there was anything wrong with moderate drinking. Many of our informants recognized this inconsistency and typically expressed the idea that "this town is full of hypocrites: they vote dry and drink wet." (Warriner, 1958:165.)

for example. Legal attempts to curb gambling are viewed unsympathetically by many community members.

> Although illegal, gambling is a form of mass behavior, and has a wide mass appeal. It is associated with leisure, fun, and daring. It is an escape from the drab work routine and from the boredom of leisure time. By its suspense about the unpredictable, it breaks the monotony of routine, and allows time to pass quickly. . . . The thought that everyone has an equal chance to win in gambling reinforces the mass orientation that every participant can be rich. Winning by gambling becomes consistent with this Cinderella myth. This myth of "equality" appeals to the mass because winning is accessible to all, regardless of knowledge, skill, or social class (Weinberg, 1960:272).

Many laws that are actively enforced, at least for a time, are out of sympathy with the attitudes of a majority of community members. (*See* Documentation 1.) In reality such laws reflect not objective, but moral values. Consequently, to determine objective standards one must estimate the responses of community members as well as ascertain whether sanctions are operating to control deviant behavior and discrepant conditions.

moral standards

Moral standards are more difficult to define with specificity. Here the question is not whether the behavior or condition is considered undesirable or evokes a response from the general run of community members, but whether so-called experts consider it appropriate. The great difficulty is that community members have accepted, or at least acknowledged, the competence of a number of different groups of experts to set and enforce moral standards. Unfortunately, these groups do not always agree on what constitutes improper behavior and unallowable community conditions.

At least several important groups of moralists can be identified. Perhaps largest in number, and certainly the oldest, are the leaders of organized religion. In urban communities, these persons are usually the clergy —priests, ministers, and rabbis—although at times a lay member, in his role as a church official, may also be active in setting and enforcing moral standards.

Another important group is composed of health and welfare leaders. Physicians and other medical practitioners are important segments of this group and, in recent years, social welfare specialists such as social work practitioners and applied economists have risen in influence. Those social scientists who believe it appropriate to take upon themselves the task of delineating areas of social problems should also be included in this category. Much of the time, however, these last mentioned have failed to act or act only on a formal level to enforce their standards. An exception is the previously noted activities of sociologists in connection with the school desegregation case.

A final group of persons who set standards are the politicians and others who supposedly reflect the will of the community. They may not always constitute a good index of the objective standards held by community members, but their perceptions of community consensus have important repercussions in the laws and regulations that mold society.

Of course, politicians, churchmen, and other moral leaders in the community do not operate autonomously; they are influenced by the views and values of their constituencies. (*See* Documentation 2.) In this respect, it is necessary to differentiate between a person's role as spokesman for a particular organization or group and his role as an individual community member. All experts have this problem in varying degrees. For example, the academician in most universities is formally protected from having to agree with his university's policies. The rights of academic freedom include publicly expressing one's opinion, and those moral leaders who stem from university backgrounds have considerable freedom and latitude in pronouncing moral standards. But many individuals do indeed represent organizational groups. These include not only religious spokesmen but individuals who are employed in corporate enterprises or are dependent upon political or economic groups in the community for their livelihood or other support. The sources of influence on the moral leaders of this country represent one of the vast unknowns about which information is critically needed if we are ever to understand how the moral norms are initiated and modified and how moral leadership influences social policy.

It should also be pointed out that the experts who have much to do with setting the moral standards often express their views of deviation differently. An interesting transition in this respect has been the shift in the definition of deviation. Where formerly certain conditions or particular behaviors were considered incidences of evil or badness, today they are referred to as problems of illness or sickness.

> Having "advanced" beyond blaming the bad man for his moral depravity, the middle-class investigator proposes to treat him for his sickness. This proposal is emboldened by the optimistic assumption that goodness and health (which includes telling, seeking, and seeing the truth) are reciprocally related. With faith so set, it follows that evil may be cured, like other infirmities, and that an important part of the cure lies in the bad, sick man's taking psychotherapeutic exercises in correct perception—of what he has done, and why, and of how people

The church does not merely support the status quo, nor merely follow the lead of its parishioners in the formulation of its social and economic policy. . . . The church is in fact ahead of . . . its laity on most issues. It is more receptive to social change than its parishioners.

But in supporting social change, the church must proceed cautiously lest its stand offend the collective sentiments of its parishioners. This danger is most acute on issues which bear directly on the distribution of power in society, such as war, labor, government control, and the political role of the church. On these issues parishioners have definite convictions and their self-interest is clearly identifiable. As a result, the church seeks to avoid a head-on collision with the collective will of its laity on these issues. It treads softly and resorts to equivocality in its pronouncements. At the same time, it does not identify completely with parishioner sentiment but includes in its pronouncements reference to the normative principles which an issue involves.

However, on issues of an ideological or moral character, the church finds it less necessary to temper its stand in accordance with the will of its parishioners. There is no solidified collective will of parishioners which can serve as a brake on church policy. Parishioner sentiment on these issues is largely unsettled and divergent, suggesting the lesser importance of these issues for the self-interest of parishioners. As a result, the church has a greater opportunity to exercise its leadership. It can express itself through strong and clear-cut pronouncements.

The church's social policy, then, depends on the nature of the issue and the state of sentiment among parishioners. On issues where parishioner sentiment is relatively homogeneous, and self-interest considerable, the church's ability to deviate from the views of its parishioners is severely limited. It must compromise its policy and accommodate itself to the views of its parishioners. But on issues where parishioner sentiment is relatively unsettled and the church has a definite normative interest, the church is better able to step forth in a firm and decisive manner. (Glock and Ringer, 1956:154-155.)

"really" are as opposed to what he thought they were. . . . Bad actors may not be sick—at least no more so than good men—and, particularly, they may not suffer from perverted perception (Nettler, 1961:291).

Nettler's point has relevance, certainly, for understanding the genesis and identification of social problems. Typically, it is not the role of the expert merely to point his finger at a particular deviation and argue against it; most often he labels it in terms of some ideological or causal category. It is this categorization that marks the discrepant behavior as a critical issue not only for the average community member but also for other experts. Thus definitions of social problems are influenced by those who occupy strategic positions of authority and power and who carry more weight in deciding social policy. As Merton (1966:785) notes:

> There is not a merely numerical democracy of judgment in which every man's appraisal is assigned the same voting power in defining a condition as a social problem. It is a mistaken atomistic notion that each member of society sets about to define social problems for himself and that it is the aggregate of these independent judgments that decides the array of problems in the society and the comparative importance of each problem in the array.

If areas of concern were to be determined by popular vote, certain burning issues, such as the plight of the poor or the status of black citizens, would probably rank rather low. With respect to poverty and race relations, there is evidence of a pervasive moral apathy and political cynicism in the United States. If, as Clark (1965:204) notes, constructive changes were to depend on the profound moral conversion of a majority of Americans, there might be cause for extreme pessimism.

In viewing both objective and moral norms it is often useful to separate the proscriptive dimensions from the prescriptive. (*See* Documentation 3.) A proscriptive norm is a "Don't." It refers to a standard in which the predominant element is negative, directing participants to avoid, abstain, desist, or reject all forms of behavior associated with a particular type of activity—murder, for example. A prescriptive norm, on the other hand, is a "Do." It spells out the types of behavior to which an individual should conform, such as voting in political elections. Perhaps too often students of social problems focus on the proscriptive norms and devote insufficient efforts to the issues that surround conformity to the prescriptive ones. For the social order to function well and maintain a level of stability in community life, it is necessary to examine departures from prescriptive and proscriptive norms (Mizruchi and Perrucci, 1962).

measuring the norms

An obvious approach to measuring norms is to obtain from both community members-at-large and the considered experts or arbitrators of morality an expression of the relevance of discontinuities. In certain areas, such as that of the family, there exist a large number of surveys of opinions and attitudes. However, in using these it is important to recognize that the verbal responses of persons—what they say they do—may be at variance with their actual behavior in a particular situation. For example, on a public opinion poll a large proportion of persons may indicate opposition to segregated housing, yet these same individuals

prescriptive and proscriptive norms

We can conclude from the above [studies of Robert Straus and Selden D. Bacon, *Drinking in College,* Yale University Press, 1954] that normative systems play a role in the consumption of alcoholic beverages, and that pathological reactions to drinking tend to be greater for certain ascetic Protestant and Mormon groups, as compared with other religious groups. We would hold, in general, that pathological drinking behavior is associated with a relative absence of directives for the act of drinking alcoholic beverages itself. The important question then is: What is there about the nature of the normative systems of the ascetic Protestant and Mormon groups that predisposes their deviants to greater pathological reactions and, consequently, their structure to great strain?

We have indicated above that there is an absence of directives regarding drinking behavior among the ascetic Protestant and Mormon groups. In contrast to the prescriptive norms associated with drinking by Jews, for example, the ascetic Protestant and Mormon norms may be characterized as primarily proscriptive. Total abstinence is the norm for these groups. Hence, deviation from the abstinence pattern, even in what is ordinarily recognized as socially approved drinking in the larger society, e.g., before dinner, at parties, and like occasions, is associated with an almost complete absence of directives. As Straus and Bacon have pointed out in discussing the drinking behavior of Mormons, "If drinking behavior is adopted, variation must be the rule since there is no norm. Extremes are likely since the behavior itself represents rejection of social rules."

Jewish drinking, as Charles R. Snyder has shown [in *Alcohol and the Jews,* The Free Press, 1958], is patterned by an elaborate system of explicit directives as to what, when, where, with whom, how much, and why one is expected to consume alcoholic beverages. The norm is predominantly prescriptive in nature, and deviation from the drinking norms is associated with gradual and predictable patterns of deviant behavior. Thus Snyder's statistics show that tendencies to alcohol pathology increase in "step like" fashion from Orthodox Jewish drinking, which is associated with the relative absence of signs of pathology, to the Reform and Secular drinking pattern in which pathology is relatively high. Nevertheless, the highest rate still tends to remain lower than rates for the Protestant group. (Mizruchi and Perrucci, 1962:395–396.)

would not sell their homes to blacks, live in racially mixed residential areas, or support—financially or otherwise—groups organized to integrate neighborhoods or laws designed to protect the housing rights of minorities.

Another yardstick for determining standards is the actual behavior of persons under conditions in which they live. For example, the prevalence of gambling, commercial or social, can be taken as an objective indicator of the limited relevance of this phenomenon as a social problem. But it should be emphasized that from a social-policy perspective even these behavioral indicators are subject to change and may quickly become dated.

Using reality as the gauge for estimating norms raises another pertinent question: Whose reality? In other words, how reliable are the sources of data? Many of our judgments regarding deviant behavior and undesirable community conditions are based on official statistics and reports. Our ideas about housing in America come, for the most part, from either census data on housing conditions or municipal reports of housing code violations. In almost every instance, the processing and labeling procedures, which operate differentially in American communities, distort and bias official statistics. Sometimes we are aware of the partial or biased character of official statistics, such as in the area of crime statistics (Short and Nye, 1957; Biderman, 1967); at other times, we are not. (*See* Documentation 4.) Consequently, official statistics need to be handled with great sensitivity in order to extract the relevant data regarding particular types of deviant behavior and conditions. (*See* Documentation 5.)

Finally, the perspective of history can often help bring discontinuities into focus. By understanding the genesis of a possible social problem and the community's response to it, one can make estimates of the extent to which it represents a moral or objective social problem. For example, certain forms of behavior now identified as mental or physical illness are considered social problems primarily because of the way they were initially presented to and subsequently perceived by community members. An historical analysis of the discrepancy between reality and the community's standards is useful, therefore, in estimating the objective or moral basis of the problem. Erikson (1962:310) points up the importance of an historical perspective in the following comment:

> A social norm is rarely expressed as a firm rule or official code. It is an abstract synthesis of the many separate times a community has stated its sentiments on a given issue. Thus the norm has a history much like that of an article of common law: it is an accumulation of decisions made by the community over a long period of time which gradually gathers enough moral influence to serve as a precedent for future decisions. . . . Each time the community censures some act of deviance, then, it sharpens the authority of the violated norm and re-establishes the boundaries of the group.

In most instances, of course, there is insufficient data of any type available to state with certainty the extent of a discontinuity or to identify the problem as exclusively moral or objective. Few discontinuities are one or the other type; in fact, in many cases the moral and objective standards are congruent. Admittedly, many estimates of social problems are not much better than educated guesses, and this limitation should always be kept in mind. Nevertheless, a perspective of judging behavior

uniformity and cooperation in crime statistics

A [continuing] problem with crime statistics is that of uniformity and comparability and the difficulty of obtaining the cooperation of thousands of independent agencies. In spite of the great effort made by the Uniform Crime Report section of the FBI, uniformity is a constant problem of police statistics and this is true to a much greater extent for court and correctional figures. In addition, there is considerably less effort being made to obtain the cooperation of agencies working with parolees and minor offenders.

This difficulty is, in part, a result of the necessity of obtaining information from thousands of independent local agencies. If a large number of such agencies cooperate, it may then become extremely difficult to audit and check reports for uniformity and adherence to standards set down by the collecting agency. When large numbers of agencies fail to report, or different sets of agencies report at different times, comparability becomes a serious problem. These problems of comparability and uniformity plague all present statistical reporting systems but are, of course, of less importance for police statistics than court statistics. They remain important barriers to the development of better crime statistics.

The fragmented and uncoordinated nature of the present approaches to crime statistics may also be classified as a major problem of crime statistics in the United States. Perhaps the most important effect of this fragmentation is the practical impossibility of following individuals through the system to learn what happens to them at each stage in the process and why it happens. The absence of such information dooms any attempt to reconcile the sta-tistics produced by each of the systems and makes it almost impossible to describe the operation of the larger system of justice with any accuracy. The fragmented effort has also resulted in the development of systems reflecting uneven amounts of statistical expertise. Both developments work against uniformity, comparability and the improvement of some of the separate systems.

Problems of crime statistics which are of particular importance for criminological research have not been emphasized in this review in the belief that the most persistent general problem of crime statistics are also the most serious limitations of statistics for criminological research. For example, the existing fragmented systems provide very limited information on the characteristics of persons involved in the several stages of the criminal process. This fragmentation also makes it particularly difficult to study problems of recidivism or to assess effectiveness of various treatment programs. In similar ways, the problems of interpretation, uniformity, and those resulting from self-evaluation limit the research utility of current statistics.

A tentative solution is the establishment of what might be called a national center for crime statistics. Such an agency could reasonably be expected to work in two directions. First, it could be given sufficient resources to undertake independent internal programs to improve criminal statistics. In addition, it could be given the task of providing assistance in the development of criminal statistics to federal agencies and state and local governments when requested. (Chilton, 1968:91–92.)

in comparison with norms is essential in order to maintain a scientific frame of reference for analyzing and understanding social problems.

the relevance of moral and objective standards

The apparent discontinuities between conditions or behavior and community standards (moral and/or objective) are numerous. The investigator, therefore, is faced with the task of determining which of the various discontinuities have significance in the functioning of the social system,

---

DOCUMENTATION 5

delinquency and socio-economic status

TABLE 1. INSTITUTIONALIZATION

Socio-Economic Status	Training School		High School	
	(N)	(%)	(N)	(%)
I (Lowest)	73	50.0	112	13.3
II	48	32.9	333	39.6
III	19	13.0	282	33.5
IV (Highest)	6	4.1	114	13.6
TOTAL	146	100.0	841	100.0

TABLE 2. SELF-REPORTED BEHAVIOR

Socio-Economic Status	Most Delinquent		Least Delinquent	
	(N)	(%)	(N)	(%)
I (Lowest)	42	16.0	69	12.0
II	101	38.4	233	40.4
III	91	34.6	191	33.1
IV (Highest)	29	11.0	84	14.5
TOTAL	263	100.0	577	100.0

Recent empirical investigations by the writers suggest a further weakness of official delinquency statistics, viz., that such data are uneven in their biases. For example, a comparison of the reported delinquent behavior of boys and girls in different socio-economic categories finds few statistically significant differences in the incidence of such behavior. The traditional assumption of a higher incidence of delinquent behavior among members of the lower socio-economic groups, based upon official statistics, is not substantiated.

The above show the extent of socio-economic bias in the institutionalized population as revealed by data obtained from high school students in three contiguous western cities (ranging in size between 10,000 and 25,000) compared with students in this state's training schools for committed delinquents. Table 2 shows that there is little if any difference in delinquent behavior by socio-economic level, while Table 1 shows that a full 50 per cent of all institutionalized boys come from the lowest socio-economic category which comprises only 13 per cent of the high school population. This raises serious questions not only for the study of socio-economic status and delinquency but for any variables correlated with socio-economic status. (Short and Nye, 1957:208–209.)

'that is, which have important consequences for the social order. The task is further complicated by the necessity to determine whether the basis of the social problem is the particular community condition or behavior per se, the criteria or standards against which the deviance is measured, or the means employed to make this evaluation.

It is perhaps easiest to conceive of social problems as undesirable conditions or behaviors. Almost all sociologists would agree that particular types of behavior or social conditions require amelioration. But the standards themselves may also be a major basis of the problem (Becker, 1963:157). For example, laws prohibiting child labor were passed to prevent the exploitation of minors. Now the community is interested in stimulating an interest in work among low-income children, and elaborate measures for work permits have been instituted to allow children under sixteen years of age to engage in gainful employment. One could argue that in circumventing these child labor laws the employer of underage children, the children themselves, or their families are behaving in ways inconsistent with one of the objective norms of the community. But these laws were passed at a time when we were concerned with preventing exploitation. This is no longer our major concern. The sociologist might well argue, therefore, that where a standard is no longer pertinent, one way to solve the problem is to shift the definition of what is appropriate.

To illustrate the possibility that the means of evaluation may be the basis of the social problem, one can cite the differential rates of illegitimacy between white and nonwhite populations. (*See* Documentation 6.) These statistics are based on numbers of children born to mothers who are not legally married. But were the criteria for evaluation to include common-law marriages or long-term faithfulness between cohabiting partners as legitimate, then the assessment of the extent of the problem may be appreciably reduced.

VALUE JUDGMENTS

In order to determine the relevance of discontinuities in behavior and social conditions, the sociologist must exercise certain value judgments about the requirements of the social order and the goals of the individuals participating in it (Merton, 1966:781–782). Of course, requirements and goals may not always be congruent and the sociologist, in making his judgment, must strike a balance between the desirable and undesirable aspects of the discontinuities (Mills, 1959:8–9).

These value decisions and commitments involve both description and explication and, it should be noted, they have been confounding men of goodwill for a long time. The difficulty is not so much one of specifying requirements in general terms as it is one of delineating particular substantive areas of conduct and of drafting specific empirical statements of

Another generalization also related to family breakdown is met so often that by now it threatens to attain the status of "fact," namely, the number of births out of wedlock has soared. In 1965 the number was 291,000 as compared with 176,600 in 1954. This is a tremendous number, and the more distressing since there has been no services explosion to keep pace with the population explosion. However, in terms of people's behavior, the only relevant index of increase in illegitimacy is rate, that is, the number of births out of wedlock per 1,000 unmarried women of childbearing age.

The rise in rate (as differentiated from numbers) was relatively steady over several decades. This rise represents a long-term trend and not a sudden upsurge. Moreover, in the last eight years reported (1958–1965) the rate has oscillated within about two percentage points, at about the same level rising or falling one point or less annually, but in effect representing an eight-year plateau. Since all national illegitimacy figures are based on estimates, with a number of States not reporting, very slight changes should not be regarded as significant. Thus, the current picture is a large rise in numbers and a leveling off in the rate of nonwedlock births. (The ratio—the proportion of live births that are out of wedlock —has risen for both white and nonwhites. However, ratio is far less meaningful than rate as an index of change.)

The recent relative stability of rate does not diminish the problems caused by nonwedlock births but it should affect the conclusions drawn from the statistics, the measures taken to act on those conclusions, and the attitudes of those who ponder the meaning of the figures.

Over half the children born out of wedlock are nonwhite, although only 12 per cent of the population are nonwhite. The reasons for this difference have been much discussed and need only be mentioned here. They include (1) less use of contraception, (2) less use of abortion, (3) differences in reporting, (4) reluctance to lose a public assistance grant by admitting to a man in the house, (5) the expense of divorce and legal separation. It seems probable that, even if discount could be made for these and other factors, a difference would remain. It would be a much smaller difference, however, and conceivably could still relate more to income than to color.

If further evidence were needed on this virtually unchallenged relation between income and illegitimacy rates, figures on the in high- and low-income tracts should be sufficient. . . . [In a study of out-of-wedlock births in New York City] Pakter and associates, for example, found that the proportion of births varied from a high of 38 per cent in the (predominantly black) Central Harlem district to a comparative low of 9 per cent in the (predominantly white) Pelham Bay District.

Attitudes toward illegitimacy and toward marriage are clearly linked with the economic position of the Negro male. A male head of house who is not a breadwinner and provider is a hazard to the happiness of the marriage, and his loss of economic status is so great a hazard to his intrafamily status that he may decamp, either to protect his own ego or to make his family eligible for support from AFDC (aid to families with dependent children). Some recent changes in the AFDC program are aimed against the latter reason for family desertion. (Herzog, 1966:5–7.)

community conditions. For example, the maximization of psychological and physical gratification, the minimization of pain and mental discomfort, and the full utilization of one's capacities are virtually unchallengeable as goals for individuals participating in the community.

But the question arises: Who is to say what constitutes maximum gratification, minimum discomfort, full utilization? The arguments supporting the "good life" of the Negro under conditions of slavery or of the factory worker during the era of paternalistic industrial operations suggest that these kinds of criteria are not sufficient. Rather, they must be coupled with a set of other requirements, namely, the opportunity to achieve these goals unrestricted by irrelevant social characteristics. Further, recognition must be given to the physical and psychological needs of community members who, for one reason or another, are unable to participate fully or well in the social sector (Goode, 1967).

These views on the individual and his rights are clearly a matter of values. When specific issues need to be evaluated, there is nothing approximating a consensus among sociological analysts. For example, the desegregation of the public schools and, in northern urban centers, the forced busing of primary school children from their neighborhood point up the conflict. Although it may be argued that these measures are undertaken to meet the social-policy requirements of maximizing intellectual growth without reference to an irrelevant status, nevertheless, it is difficult to counter the impression that such integration efforts raise considerable psychological and emotional problems for both white and black students, as well as for their families. As a second illustration, consider the level of economic support for the physically handicapped, the mentally retarded, and the unemployed breadwinner. To what extent should such an individual be supported if he cannot participate well and fully in the social system? In the utopian society it should be possible for all community members to participate fully in the life of the community, to have the opportunity for complete physical and psychological gratification, and to be judged according to individual capacity as well as individual effort in the assessment of one's contribution to the community. Unfortunately, Utopia is hardly around the corner.

Consideration of these elements raises fundamental questions which most sociologists would agree are largely matters of values rather than areas of potential investigation. One of the issues about which there is considerable controversy is the extent to which the community must be stratified vertically. In other words, is it fundamental to the maintenance of the social order for individuals to be classed above and below each other on some scale of ranking (Tumin, 1967)? Whether a horizontal social structure is possible or desirable is a subject for continuing debate (Moore, 1963).

A related question has to do with the concept of equity. Should the

possible distributions of family income

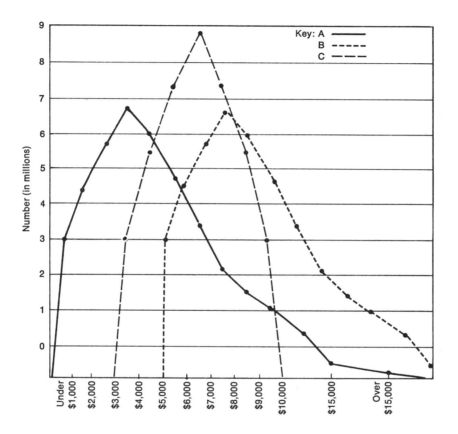

The distribution of families by income in the United States in 1955 is shown by curve A. It ranges from less than $1,000 to well over $15,000, with a peak at about $3,500. Now the question is, what is equity? One argument would be that if the minimum income in the United States were $5,000 and everyone else kept his same place, as in curve B, this would be a fair distribution. But some would argue that there is too much difference between the lowest and the highest family income. Thus, if no one earned less than $3,000 and no one earned more than $10,000, as in curve C, the difference would be much less. The second curve (B) demonstrates pulling everyone up a notch; curve C demonstrates clustering more people about the mean. Each of these constitutes a different definition of equity.

objective of the community's collective activities be to raise the lot of all members while maintaining the same relative distribution, or should it be to maintain the place of the average man but reduce the extremes of the distribution—i.e., reduce the number of very rich and very poor? This can be most easily illustrated graphically in terms of earned income. (*See* Documentation 7.)

In practice, of course, the desirable social goal may be a combination of both alternatives. In terms of the improvement of education in low-income areas, for example, neither of these models is strictly applicable. It would be equally bad to suggest that the improved education of some should be achieved at the sacrifice of others, or that a mere increase of two years of education for every student would meet the desirable objectives in terms of individual goals. Rather, one would specify both a shift upward of the mean as well as a general raising of the entire curve. In viewing the problems of individual goals and the requisites of the social system, therefore, the sociologist must be concerned not only with his position on the requirements of vertical differentiation but also on his meaning of concepts such as equity.

In discussing goals for the individual in terms of the requirements of the system, we have not pointed out the virtues of conformity based solely on an acceptance of the prevailing moral belief system and the Judeo-Christian code of ethics. These permeate the teachings and socialization of virtually all community members. Pragmatically, conformity —at least to some extent—with such a code of ethics is indeed a requirement for the individual. It can be argued that the development and maintenance of a psychological identity requires a set of moral prescriptions against which the individual can measure himself.

PRIORITY OF CONCERNS

Even if the frequency and duration of particular acts of deviant behavior were known with precision, there would still remain the issue of the importance that people assign to the various deviations. For the most part, the sociologist must estimate their critical character from what he presumes represents the views of community members and also what he believes is the impact of the deviance on the orderly functioning of community life. Merton (1966:781–782) points up the matter very well:

> Furthermore, the frequency of deviant acts—whether counted in absolute or relative numbers—is of course not enough to measure the social significance of the discrepancy between standards and behavior. Social values and their associated standards differ greatly in the importance people assign to them. They are not all of a kind. Everyone knows that petty theft—the very term includes an evaluation of significance—differs in its moral and social significance from homicide, this

difference being partly registered in the currently different punishments meted out to the two classes of offenders. But how are these two classes of deviant behavior to be compared as to the degree to which they constitute a social problem? Is one homicide to be equated with 10 petty thefts? 100? 1,000? . . .

In short, there are no agreed-upon bases for rigorously appraising the comparative magnitude of different social problems. In the end, it is the values held by people occupying different positions in society that provide the rough bases for the relative importance assigned to social problems. . . .

The link between the goals of the individual and his integration into the social system does, in fact, consist of a set of norms that might be referred to as the moral order. For the most part, individuals in their day-to-day conduct and in their attempts to minimize physical discomfort and psychological conflict behave in ways that are consistent with norms. This is true not merely because of their concern for sanctions and punishments or for the presence and actions of social-control agents, but because it is the way they have always done things. This process is often referred to as the *internalization of norms and values*. Indeed, a basic individual goal should be the opportunity to internalize the moral constructs of the community.

For the sociologist to make judgments that require choosing between one mode of behavior or condition and another or between individual and community goals, he must take into consideration the total requirements of the social order. These include continuity—the requirement that the social order afford a degree of stability and predictability—and consistency—the assurance that at least some of the values will hold from one moment to the next.

For the social system to function well, it must be adapted to utilize the influence of the majority of its population, but at the same time it must be respectful of minority opinion, views, and values. Further, it must be so organized that even as it provides stability, it allows some degree of flexibility and opportunity for change in its value system (Brim and Wheeler, 1966). Indeed, deviation can be a normal product of stable institutions, a vital resource that is guarded and preserved by forces found in all human organizations. As Erikson (1962:313) notes:

Perhaps two different (and often conflicting) currents are found within any well-functioning system: those forces which promote a high over-all degree of conformity among human actors, and those forces which encourage some degree of diversity so that actors can be deployed throughout social space to make the system's boundaries. In such a scheme, deviant behavior would appear as a variation on normative themes, a vital form of activity which outlines the area within which social life as such takes place.

As is true of individual goals, the various objectives of the social order are sometimes incompatible. To the extent that the social order is preoccupied with the maintenance of the current social structure, then the opportunities for modifications that might alleviate some of the social problems may be minimal or nonexistent. For community life to endure, a balance needs to be struck which will permit the work of society to get done and still provide for innovation and change in community conditions, in the behavior of its members, and in the normative patterns themselves (Merton, 1966:819). In a sense it is possible to portray man's relationship to his social environment as a struggle to actualize his individual goals within the limitations placed upon him by the social order, which at any point in time guides human conduct and limits the ways that man can function. The fundamental problem to be solved by an enduring society, then, is training individuals to be responsible and at the same time assuring the development of free and creative persons.

the process of socialization

The process by which persons acquire knowledge, skills, and dispositions that make them more or less able members of the community is referred to as *socialization*. While one often thinks of socialization in terms of the period from birth to late adolescence, clearly the process of being socialized continues as long as one lives. In our culture, certain experiences are not open to persons until they reach a particular age or until they have achieved certain prerequisites, such as income, education and social recognition. In addition, shifts and changes in the normative patterns of the society require adjustment and adaptation on the part of community members throughout their lives.

SOCIALIZATION AND SOCIAL PROBLEMS

One way of thinking about the genesis of social problems is to regard them as products of a socialization process that is not or cannot be entirely successful. The lack of success is related in part to inadequate mechanisms for socialization or a failure by community agents and organizations to socialize fully the individual community member and, in part, to the competition between agents of socialization who hold conflicting—or at least not fully congruent—normative values. Identification of discontinuities between norms and community behavior or conditions as social problems presupposes that activities of the community at large need to be directed to the amelioration of inadequacies of the socialization process. Such community efforts may be oriented to modifying the normative structure, to strengthening the moral order of the community, or to restructuring the socialization mechanisms so that the individual's actions and those aspects of community life over which he exercises some control are made more consistent with the normative structure (Dentler and Erikson, 1959; Bensman and Gerver, 1963).

The only alternative to adequate socialization that can be used with any success is the partial or full isolation of certain community members or community areas. In almost every case the use of isolation is evidence of the community's inadequacies to deal with its social problems. The imprisoning of a man for life or the restricting of passage through certain parts of large American cities because of riots are manifestations of the inability of the community to cope with social problems. Today, the majority of social-control efforts seek to minimize the use of isolation and exclusion and to focus, instead, on the socialization and the resocialization of individuals. Familiar programs such as remedial education courses, sex education programs, and religious instruction, to name a few, are among the many mechanisms that are used to develop an individual's understanding and discernment of the normative standards of behavior expected of community members and to provide him with the tools for further social growth. Training schools for delinquents, mental hospitals, and landlord-tenant courts illustrate resocialization mechanisms that are intended to bring individuals back into line with the normative standards of their community.

While the subject of socialization is extremely complex, it is not possible to provide a sociological analysis of social problems without some consideration of the socialization process.

SOCIALIZATION AND SOCIAL CONTROL

In any enduring community, the socialization process is "organized" in the sense that the interpersonal relationships which provide the socialization for the individual do not come about through random encounters. A person is born into a family; attends school and, sometimes, church; engages in some kind of work; and is exposed to a finite range of the mass media. Through all of these systematic and organized encounters, he learns. He learns how to conduct himself when in specific places, how to behave with specific people, and how to perform when engaged in specific tasks. In the terms of the sociologist, the individual learns that, when placed in a certain "role," his behavior is expected to be of one sort or another (Cottrell, 1942). Much of this learning experience provides him with not one but a series of alternate modes of expression and behavior (Lemert, 1967). Aside from the problems of innovation and social change, minimal social problems are accorded the community in which there is maximal socialization, that is, where community members have internalized its norms to a high degree (Williams, 1960). Community members under these conditions know what is right and proper and behave accordingly because it is the "thing to do" and not because of explicit awareness of sanctions (Williams, 1960).

Successful socialization also concerns the internalization of strategies, or approaches, which the individual may use to cope with the day-to-day situations to which he has not previously been exposed. Socialization includes the adoption of styles of thinking, utilization of intellectual schemes, and the balancing of one desired end against another. Both the learning and internalization of specific norms and the development of particular postures are equally critical for a person living in today's society.

In a complex urban society, a great amount of energy is constantly being expended to maximize the socialization potential of individuals. In the process, much specialization of effort takes place. One way to understand the "work" of the community is to dissect community life into the components that are responsible for various aspects of socialization, i.e., into social-control systems. Such an approach acknowledges that while a large part of an individual's social conduct involves anticipating social roles, a large part of socialization consists of efforts to resocialize or, if you will, to extinguish those behavioral responses that are deemed inappropriate by community norms. These efforts rest on the systematic development of mechanisms of social control, and these mechanisms, of course, are of major concern in the analysis of social problems.

One of the reasons that so much energy needs to be devoted to social control by community members is the difficulty of implementing control models in a complex and diverse urban society. Lemert (1967) points this out very clearly in discussing the problem of drunkenness in the United States. As he notes, no model of social control has been evolved which has effectively diminished the cause of excessive drinking. In large societies such as ours, with our mixtures of ethnic minorities, diverse localities, and occupational groups, it is unlikely that any single model will have general applicability across the board. So various programs of prevention and amelioration are developed with the result that conflicting social-control programs are sometimes put into effect which either cancel each other out or combine to deliver a negative impact (Rein, 1967).

Clearly, the socialization and social-control processes regarding behavior are highly informal and, indeed, virtually invisible, but not entirely. Many social-control mechanisms in urban society are bureaucratically developed and systematically delegated to institutionalized groups.

There is, of course, considerable ambiguity and diffuseness in the specialization that exists within the social structure; nevertheless, it is possible to separate out aspects of the social system and look at them as discrete elements (Wilensky and Lebeaux, 1965:13–23). Characteristically, these elements—sometimes called social institutions—are relatively independent in function and contain inherent mechanisms of social control.

the major social-control systems

Sociologists do not fully agree on what is the best or most valid delineation of the socialization or social-control systems of the community. For heuristic reasons we have fixed upon six distinguishable entities which can be thought of as social-control systems: (1) the family, (2) education, (3) health and welfare, (4) social structures, (5) political-economic institutions, and (6) community ecology or environment. These systems are not aligned horizontally; rather, they represent a vertical differentiation of the social order of the society.

THE FAMILY

There is at least one distinction that should be made between the family system and all others. It is a system that exists largely without formal organization or corporate structure. With the possible exception of certain family-oriented societies and a few unusual family dynasties that have maintained interlocking control in the business and political world, the family system is essentially responsive to the mandates of the other social-control systems. Moreover, to a much greater extent its social-control mechanisms are informal; that is, the sanctions are personally derived from the individual's role relationships within the family system rather than from legislation or other formal means.

This does not means that the importance of the family system should be underrated. The social-control functions of the family are many. To a large extent the early socialization—and resocialization—of community members takes place within this system. Parents are accorded special recognition in this respect, an illustration being their right to reward or deprive their children in many areas without sanctions, a fact which is recognized in a variety of laws. For example, in the Commonwealth of Massachusetts it is illegal for anyone except his parents to serve alcohol to a minor. Finally, many of the normative descriptions of the community with which we shall be concerned stem directly or indirectly from the individual's mode of conduct as he operates in the community in his role as a family member.

EDUCATION

The educational system has become an important system of social control with the development of the modern urban community. Given the complexities of the contemporary world, the educational system fills the need to formalize the important communication task for the community, namely, the maintenance of continuity in the cultural and technical bodies of knowledge.

Many sanctions are accorded the educational system by society. First, the political-economic system provides a series of formal rewards for persons whose performance in the educational system is of an advanced and superior quality. This is evident in terms of minimum job requirements, promotions, licensing criteria, and the educational prerequisites of most professional groups. Moreover, many of the manners and styles important for successful engagement in the political and economic system are derived from exposure to the educational system. The concept of "Ivy League schools," for example, refers not to vine covered buildings but to certain educational institutions that socialize their students to dress and talk and, perhaps, think in particular ways. Second, there are strong links between an individual's place and activities within the social structure and his educational background. Despite concepts of equal opportunity, who a person is and where he can go to be educated represent important limitations in terms of his activities within the social and political-economic systems. While the G.I. Bill provided educational support for great numbers of returning World War II veterans, it apparently did little to upset the traditional rankings regarding who obtains the most and best education (Duncan, 1967).

HEALTH AND WELFARE

Perhaps more than anything else the development of an organized health and welfare system marks the urban community today. Such a system encompasses not only the organized practice of health care, including many community and national public health and insurance programs, but also a large number of functions that formally were accorded to either the family or religious institutions. Among these latter functions are the responsibility for developing and financing treatment programs for the mentally and physically ill, care of dependent children, and the economic support of individuals who, for one reason or another, do not participate fully in the world of work. It has been suggested that the existence of such a broad and active health and welfare system is an indicator of the many discontinuities that exist in the urban community and the lack of efficacy of the other systems.

This perspective, that the health and welfare system is a residual one, is challenged by a number of persons (Beck, 1967). They offer considerable evidence that the system functions for more than society's down-and-outers and serves goals other than merely to pick up the pieces for malfunctioning community members. Instead, they see the health and welfare system as providing the social-development function in the community. They note that our public health laws and regulations benefit the rich as well as the poor and that so-called welfare benefits are used and enjoyed by large segments of the population. For example, the social security insurance program which provides financially for the postwork years focuses not on the indigent but on the productive worker. Likewise, the vast sums spent for research on various aspects of health, leisure, recreation, and the like, fall within the province of the health and welfare system. From this point of view, health and welfare is a developmental system rather than a residual one and operates because the others do not function well.

This conflict in perspective—residual versus social-development—raises a number of conflicting issues for the planner and, indeed, for the analyst of social problems as well. On the one hand, many specialists in this field hold that to focus on residual activities invariably ends up with the health and welfare system degrading the client and creating essentially a second-class citizen isolated from the mainstream of American life. On the other hand, these same people who embrace fully the social development point of view which holds that the system should function across the board, acknowledge that this concept often fails to provide a fair share of the resources for those people in the community who need them most. For example, a public health program that makes no reference to financial or medical indigency is likely to be overused by the middle-income community members and, as a consequence, to be of minimal utility in dealing with the health problems of the poor. This criticism is also aimed at family counseling agencies in many suburbs and in a number of large cities.

In a sense, the health and welfare system needs to strike a balance between the two concepts. It needs to promote activities for those individuals whom the other systems—family, educational, economic—have failed while at the same time acting as a purveyor of the good life for all community members (Beck, 1967).

SOCIAL STRUCTURE

The social structure or system is composed of those elements that give individuals a set of particular positions and, to a large extent, a particular style of life within the community. There are three different aspects of the social structure that need to be discussed: class ranking, "heritage" or family background, and membership groups.

As we all know, there is a wide body of sociological literature and many popular conceptions concerning social class or social stratification. The vertical distinctions occupy a predominant place in the structural system. It is not critical here that we engage in the debate current among sociologists about whether there are discrete classes in American society, or a uni- or multi-dimensional ordering, or which characteristics most account for one's social position or class ranking. We do know that styles of life, ways of behaving, manners of dress, and prestige are accorded to individuals differentially. Although characteristics of social class are rooted in the political, economic, and educational systems and, to some extent, are still derived from family background, nevertheless, one's position in the structural system is important in its own right. Certainly we know that much conforming behavior takes place because of community members' regard for their social position.

Included in and obviously linked to the general class ranking are those structural delineations into which individuals are born. These include race, religious outlook and, except for a few groups, status as a native born and multi-generational American. With the possible exception of religious affiliation, most of the sanctions of the other dimensions are negative. That is, normal behavior that marks one as belonging to a particular ethnic group or racial minority or of being a first-generation immigrant is looked upon unfavorably and often occasions sanctions from other community members.

Finally, included in this system are the large membership groups that are a predominant characteristic of the urban community. To a large extent memberships in such associations as the country club, the missionary society, or a civil rights group stem from and are related to other characteristics in the structural system, i.e., social class, religious affiliation, racial or ethnic background, etc. Other affiliations result from participation in the political-economic system: the Jaycees, Kiwanis, Lions, Rotary, and other less well-known business groups. Of somewhat minimal influence today—perhaps fortunately—are the college fraternities and other "snob" organizations. So many associations within the political-economic system have their social aspects that it is sometimes hard to distinguish where one leaves off and the other begins.

POLITICAL-ECONOMIC SYSTEM

Many sociologists conceive of the political-economic system as two separate entities although in the complex urban community there is so much overlapping in function and activity that for our purposes it is sufficient to regard them as a single unit.

The main function of the political system is the formalization and legitimization of the normative sanctions of all other systems, and its social-control features are clearly inherent in the large number of law enforcement and regulatory bodies. We have already referred to the concept of legal norms. The political-economic system and the elements in it have severe responsibilities in this sense. Many of these responsibilities involve negative sanctions, that is, punishment; but rewards also constitute a major portion of their authority.

The economic aspect is as critical to the community as is the political, for man's work—his occupational position—is not only vital to his functioning but also involves him with the social-control characteristics of the other systems. The opportunities to obtain the rewards, comforts, and psychological and physical gratifications are accorded the individual almost exclusively through his participation in the world of work.

If one looks at the political-economic system in its interaction within itself, one finds conflict and accommodation as well as cooperation. Unlike the family structure, the political-economic system specifies formal sanctions and is clearly characterized by bureaucratic methods of social control.

COMMUNITY ENVIRONMENT

Perhaps the most diffuse and embracing system is the community ecologic system which concerns the interrelationship of man with his environment. Individuals articulate their behavior within certain boundaries of space and time. Some of these boundaries are a function of cultural norms, such as the sixty-minute hour; some are the result of physical and environmental conditions, such as outside temperature or the length of the day.

Environment, of course, can be and is being modified, sometimes successfully and sometimes with unexpected and disastrous side effects. Man has extended his habitat by building up as well as out; he has increased the amount of useful land by filling and draining and irrigating. He has learned to control temperature and light artificially, to overcome distance, and to harness the elements. Still, many of the norms of the community are related to particular ecological characteristics which in themselves operate to provide mechanisms of social control. Children who live by the ocean learn to fear the undertow; residents of the plains learn to cope with tornados; inhabitants of the desert and the mountains learn to adapt their life styles to the geographic realities.

In one respect the ecological system differs from those previously discussed: it is the only system that man has tried so resolutely to modify and dominate. Nevertheless, the system is basically a passive one. Like the frame of a picture, its presence is unnoticed until it is damaged or removed. The social-control functions of the ecological system are more subtle and indirect than those of the other systems, and they are closely meshed with man's attempts to manipulate and control. The use of a particular body of water for shiploading docks or stretches of land for superhighways, for example, specifies to a considerable extent who is going to be living in the areas surrounding these physical properties. The reverse is equally true, for the restriction of land and shores from commercial ventures may also determine a community's life style. In such decisions lie the mechanism of social control. In this sense, the community ecological system articulates with all of the other systems we have considered.

RELATIONSHIPS BETWEEN SYSTEMS

It should be emphasized that the systems which provide the socialization and social-control functions are always changing and being modified. Moreover, the social-control efforts that occur within a system have their effect on the activities of other systems. Preventive programs adopted within the health and welfare system, for example, may have a profound impact upon the entire political-economic system, and changing family norms may place added burdens on the educational system or significantly modify the social structure.

We have taken the time here to point up some of the social-control aspects of the various systems of socialization because it is these functions which provide the genesis for the normative structure of the community. By having a system concept available, it makes feasible the analytical job of reviewing social life and assessing the social-problem potential of discontinuities between behavior and conditions and the norms that are provided in the community.

the sociologist's responsibility

Essentially, then, we are taking the view that what the sociologist does is to look at individual and group behavior within existing community conditions and, correspondingly, to look at sets of normative standards that are current in the community. Where there are departures from these norms, the analyst must make some evaluation of the extent to which these discrepancies are barriers to the fulfillment of basic goals of individuals or to the functioning of the social system.

Perhaps it is academic nit-picking, but the issue could be raised whether it is possible to regard something as a social problem when there is no discrepancy or discontinuity between behavior or condition and the existing set of standards in the community. Using our perspective of social problems, it would indeed be difficult to arrive at such a judgment. One could, however, acknowledge the social-problem potential of some particular type of behavior or activity. A case in point is the value, in both moral and objective terms, placed by society on maintaining life and increasing longevity. To the extent that this goal is fulfilled, certain serious problems of overpopulation and surpluses of persons too old for the work force may be expected to arise. The general stance, however, would be to regard the resulting discontinuity, rather than the prior condition, as the social problem.

Even when social problems are looked at in all of these ways, there still remain a number of specific considerations that the analyst must take into account, including the interpretation of empirical data, the extent to which discontinuities are known, and the degree to which they are open for public and private judgment. In the final analysis, of course, the question of the importance of one social discontinuity in comparison with another rests with its meaningfulness in terms of the goal-achievement opportunities of community members and the functioning of the wider social system.

BECK, BERNARD.
1967   "Welfare as a moral category." Social Problems 14(Winter):258–277.

BECKER, HOWARD S.
1963   Outsiders: Studies in the Sociology of Deviance. New York: Free Press.

BENSMAN, JOSEPH AND ISRAEL GERVER.
1963   "Crime and punishment in the factory: the function of deviancy in maintaining the social system." American Sociological Review 28(August): 588–598.

BIDERMAN, ALBERT D.
1967   "An overview of victim research." Paper presented at the American Sociological Association Meeting, San Francisco (unpublished).

BRIM, ORVILLE G., AND STANTON WHEELER.
1966   Socialization After Childhood. New York: Wiley.

CHILTON, ROLAND J.
1968   "Persistent problems of crime statistics." Pp. 89–95 in Simon Dinitz and Walter C. Reckless (eds.), Critical Issues in the Study of Crime. Boston: Little, Brown.

CLARK, KENNETH B.
1965   Dark Ghetto: Dilemmas of Social Power. New York: Harper and Row.

COTTRELL, LEONARD S., JR.
1942   "The adjustment of the individual to his age and sex roles." American Sociological Review 7(October):617–620.

DENTLER, ROBERT A. AND KAI T. ERIKSON.
1959   "The functions of deviance in groups." Social Problems 7(Fall): 98–107.

DUNCAN, BEVERLY.
1967   "Education and social background." The American Journal of Sociology 72(January):363–372.

ERIKSON, KAI T.
1962   "Notes on the sociology of deviance." Social Problems 9(Spring):307–314.

GLOCK, CHARLES Y., AND BENJAMIN B. RINGER.
1956   "Church policy and the attitudes of ministers and parishioners on social issues." American Sociological Review 21(April):148–156.

GOODE, WILLIAM J.
1967   "The protection of the inept." American Sociological Review 32(February):5–19.

HERZOG, ELIZABETH.
1966   "Is there a 'breakdown' of the Negro family?" Social Work 11(January): 3–10.

LEMERT, EDWIN M.
1967   "Four models of social control." Pp. 472–480 in H. Gold and F. Scarpitti (eds.), Combatting Social Problems. New York: Holt, Rinehart and Winston.

MERTON, ROBERT K.
1966 "Social problems and sociological theory." Pp. 775–823 in Robert K. Merton and Robert A. Nisbet (eds.), Contemporary Social Problems. Second Edition. New York: Harcourt, Brace and World.

MILLS, C. WRIGHT.
1959 The Sociological Imagination. New York: Oxford University Press.

MIZRUCHI, EPHRAIM H. AND ROBERT PERRUCCI.
1962 "Norm qualities and differential effects of deviant behavior: an exploratory analysis." American Sociological Review 27(June):391–399.

MOORE, WILBERT E.
1963 "But some are more equal than others." American Sociological Review 28(February):13–18.

NETTLER, GWYNN.
1961 "Good men, bad men, and the perception of reality." Sociometry 24 (September):279–291.

REIN, MARTIN.
1967 "The social service crisis." Pp. 526–533 in H. Gold and F. Scarpitti (eds.), Combatting Social Problems. New York: Holt, Rinehart and Winston.

SHORT, JAMES F., JR., AND F. IVAN NYE.
1957 "Reported behavior as a criterion of deviant behavior." Social Problems 5(Winter):207–213.

TUMIN, MELVIN.
1967 Social Stratification: The Forms and Functions of Inequality. Englewood Cliffs, New Jersey: Prentice-Hall.

WARRINER, CHARLES K.
1958 "The nature and functions of official morality." The American Journal of Sociology 64(September):165–168.

WEINBERG, S. KIRSON.
1960 Social Problems In Our Time. Englewood Cliffs, New Jersey: Prentice-Hall.

WILENSKY, H. L. AND C. N. LEBEAUX.
1965 Industrial Society and Social Welfare. New York: Free Press.

WILLIAMS, ROBIN M., JR.
1960 American Society: A Sociological Interpretation. New York: Knopf.

CHAPTER 3

cause and
control

THE PRECEDING CHAPTERS have been concerned with elaborating
the social-policy perspective that will guide our analysis of social problems. Certainly the posture of the sociologist in the identification of
discontinuities in behavior and community conditions represents one of
the major thrusts in his role as an analyst of social problems. His task is
much broader than that, however, and the value of his effort is dependent upon the demonstration that his use of the scientific point of view
can lead to an understanding of the phenomenon at hand that is satisfying or, at least, acceptable to those within the community—an explanation of cause is another way of putting it. Further, his sociological
acumen should permit the development of intervention techniques and
strategies that will control or reduce the identified discontinuities, in
short, the practice of social engineering.

a scientific view of social phenomena

Consideration of the sociologist's role as the discoverer of the causes of
social problems and as the developer of hypotheses of intervention requires us to discuss, however briefly, some of the fundamental issues involved in the application of the scientific method to problems of social
life. We have pointed out that the sociologist, in analyzing discontinuities, utilizes a particular approach in his effort to understand the social
problems that plague the community. He follows, basically, the same
rules that govern the work patterns of both life and physical scientists. Before defining and discussing in detail the concepts of cause and amelioration as they apply to social problems, it will be helpful to review certain
fundamental positions regarding the way the sciences look at phenomena
under investigation. Of necessity, certain procedural considerations in-

volved in scientific inquiries must be omitted from this cursory review.

Scientific inquiry begins with an interest in a particular phenomenon, usually referred to as a *variable* or *dimension*. The description, prediction, and understanding of this phenomenon or variable constitutes the work of the investigator. In its fullest sense, understanding of a phenomenon requires that one know both what causes the behavior and what methods or techniques will permit it to be modified and redirected. Each of the tasks of science—description, prediction, and understanding—are important. It is fair to say, however, that as sociologists we are strongly oriented to the understanding of causes, for we are seeking to maximize our ability to intervene. Nevertheless, it must be admitted that considerable effort and energy must be expended in sheer description and prediction of those phenomena termed social problems.

DESCRIPTION

Description implies that a full and communicable portrait of the phenomenon is available. Certain biological scientists and medical researchers spend their working lives developing descriptions of particular diseases. This has not been the case in the social sciences. One of the real problems in the field of social relations is the paucity of adequate descriptions of the phenomena under investigation. Although most of the sociological terms used to describe deviant behavior and inadequate community conditions are known to the general public and bantered about by them, the terms are often grossly defined, and similarities in usage obscure differences in meaning. The concept of mental illness is a good illustration. For some, the term includes virtually all types of deviant conduct; for others, it is confined to a particular set of systemic manifestations such as hallucinations, delusions, and extreme withdrawal; and for a few, including some psychiatrists, the concept is of no utility. They argue that mental illness describes neither personal conduct nor a behavioral syndrome but is rather a label put on some people but not on others for reasons extraneous to their conduct (Szasz, 1961).

Descriptions of social problems are limited not only by the lack of consensus about what should be included in a particular definition but also by the differences in observability and visibility of various phenomena. Certain types of deviants just do not come to the attention of the sociologist in systematic and unbiased ways. Practically speaking, the investigator must often work with incomplete enumerating and less-than-representative samples in developing definitions. The phenomenon of juvenile delinquency is illustrative of the problem. The question arises whether the types of delinquency which are reported to legal or related authority (and are thereby easily available for study) represent in either proportion or substance the range of delinquent acts that are common and typical among an adolescent population. Adequate description, then, is fundamental to the study of social problems.

PREDICTION

Prediction refers to the specification of social phenomena or variables that permits one to state the differential likelihood of the incidence and prevalence of social problems. In the jargon of statistical researchers, the social-problems variable is referred to as the *dependent variable,* the thing one wishes to predict; the *predictor variables* are independent measures (Selltiz et al., 1959). Frequently, investigators undertaking a descriptive study will also include predictor variables to give the inquiry added dimension.

The notion of prediction in the behavioral sciences is important in two ways. First, studies of a predictive character may lead to causal hypotheses about a particular phenomenon. Second, prediction is useful in the intervention process and the amelioration of social problems. For example, an investigator concerned with school dropouts (the dependent variable) might find that one out of one hundred girls leaves high school in her senior year compared to five out of one hundred boys. This knowledge may stimulate a series of causal hypotheses to explain school dropouts as well as suggest that any resources available for the amelioration of this problem might better be concentrated on one sex rather than the other.

CAUSAL STUDIES

It should be emphasized, of course, that the mere documentation of a relationship or association between two variables is not sufficient grounds to regard the predictor variable as a cause of the dependent one (Selltiz et al., 1959). Students of social relations recognize that predictions are usually stated in terms of probabilities, for perfect relationships between variables are not likely to be found. Nevertheless, predictive information often provides the leads to the causal understanding of phenomena (McCord and McCord, 1960). Also, the availability of predictor variables, by suggesting likely solutions to problems, makes possible the development of a strategy which, at the very least, conserves resources in the application of particular treatment or intervention programs.

A number of considerations inhibit causal studies of social phenomena. One is our basic revulsion to using human subjects for experimentation, especially if the experiment may endanger life or cause undue mental or physical suffering. The grisly details of Nazi experiments using concentration camp inmates have only served to reinforce this reaction. Another deterrent is the sheer magnitude of the administrative problems.

These include the financial costs and manpower resources needed for conducting broad-scale experiments as well as the difficulties of obtaining the necessary and usually long-term cooperation of the subjects (Freeman and Sherwood, 1965).

Of necessity, therefore, causal statements have often been extrapolated from predictive studies and the information so gained treated as if it were causal. Particularly pertinent examples are the epidemiologic investigations into the relationships between human pathology and social behavior which have been undertaken by medical and public health researchers. For instance, health authorities who now choose, and with considerable reason, to regard smoking as a social problem of health have sought to identify characteristics of teen-agers who do and do not smoke. Studies among high school populations show, for example, that the presence in the household of parents or older siblings who smoke and the occupation of the father are associated with the likelihood of a student's smoking in high school (Salber et al., 1968). In this way epidemiologic investigations of smoking, mental illness, and other deviant conduct serve as the basis for causal hypotheses and for programs of intervention.

Causal studies have at their root, however, one particular element that distinguishes them from predictive ones. This factor is the ability, either naturally or through man's ingenuity, to introduce modifications into the study. By adding or removing, strengthening or weakening the independent variables, investigators can establish their relevance to the dependent variable—in our case, deviant behavior or undesirable community conditions. The model for such studies, of course, is the laboratory experiment. Cause implies that one can make predictions about the dependent variable which can be tested either by observing natural variations or by manipulating the independent variables. For example, if one were concerned with mental retardation as a social problem, one could learn from predictive studies that there is a higher rate of mental retardation in families whose diets are deficient in protein. Given this predictive finding, an investigator could undertake an experiment in which groups of newborn children are provided with protein supplements while other groups are allowed to subsist on their regular diets. If there is an opportunity to select at random from the same pool large enough groups of children whose environmental circumstances other than diet remain constant, it is possible to evaluate whether the problems of nutrition and protein intake are linked *causally* with mental retardation.

Because there are many areas in which it is simply not possible to undertake well-conceived experimental investigations, the student of social problems is often forced to settle for less-than-ideal research designs. Many times he will be faced with having to look at predictive relationships as if they were indeed causal investigations. Largely through statistical manipulations he will seek to persuade his peers—and the practitioners and policy-makers as well—that until more dependable results can be achieved, studies of relationships and associations should be regarded as causal.

THE STATE OF KNOWLEDGE

The social-policy analyst who seeks to study problems of discontinuity is always plagued by the limited amount of information and the partial understanding of social life that characterizes the social sciences. Some years ago, for example, Foote and Cottrell (1955), in providing an analysis of contemporary family life and in specifying hypotheses for the improvement of interpersonal competence, explicitly noted that the time was past when sociologists could avoid declarations on such problems because of the limitations and omissions in the available data. Their position is consistent in many ways with the orientation of this volume. It becomes a form of academic pussyfooting to refrain from examining current conditions and the prospects and approaches for amelioration on the grounds that more information is needed. While such an orientation may enjoy a certain type of respectability among academic persons of a scholarly ilk, the fact is that community life continues and, in most cases, the best approximation at any point is at least as justifiable as an apathy occasioned by the decision to wait (Foote and Cottrell, 1955). A part of the constantly changing orientation, of course, is related to improved technology derived from scientific inquiry into physical and social life.

concepts of cause

Views on causality and causal models are quite varied, and no attempt will be made here to develop a comprehensive coverage of all of them. It is useful, however, to suggest at least several different ways of thinking about the problem of cause. There is no need to deal in an extended fashion with the philosophical problem that there is always an unknown level of cause and that man never finds the ultimate cause of a particular behavior or condition. Pragmatically, the cause of a phenomenon is said to be identified when no important question is raised to challenge the explanation as demonstrated by man's power over the phenomenon and control of its manifestation. We are told, for example, that a particular virus causes measles and we are satisfied with this explanation because it has been demonstrated that an immunization program can ameliorate the disease. Certainly one can ask why this particular virus causes measles. Such a question is not entirely irrelevant but, for our purposes, the question of the ultimacy of cause is beyond the scope of this discussion. However, it is important to point out that a variety of models may be used to help understand and comprehend the problems with which we are concerned. Three such orders of models are pertinent here.

ONE-FACTOR EXPLANATIONS

The first model is a one-factor explanation based on the predictive assumption that a particular precondition, or independent variable, is thought to be the cause of a dependent variable. Such a model derives its impetus from laboratory investigations in which it is possible, through genetic breeding of subjects, the sterility of conditions, and the randomization of subjects into experimental and control groups, to rule out all other possible explanations of cause (Freeman and Sherwood, 1965). In practice, however, one-factor explanations rarely hold in real life, or even in the physical sciences. Honesty demands that most one-factor explanations be followed by the statement, "all things being equal."

MULTI-FACTOR EXPLANATIONS

In terms of social behavior, most of the types of dependent variables with which we are concerned require taking into account many independent influences. Thus, the second model of causality to be explicated involves a number of variables. When we think of multi-factor explanations, we conceive of a dependent variable that is sensitive to a series of independent variables, each of which may result in a certain amount of change. To complicate this model one begins to specify what is technically referred to as the *interaction between independent variables*. In other words, the presence in varying quantities of one variable in relation to another may intensify or diminish the impact of the cluster of independent variables. In the case of many social problems, a large number of variables which by themselves are insufficient to cause a particular phenomenon, when taken together, may yield the resultant discontinuity.

This second type of model is often used by public health researchers and is referred to by them as an *epidemiologic model* (MacMahon et al., 1960). These investigators conceive of three domains of influence upon a particular disorder, namely, the agent, the host, and the environment. The battle against malaria is a good illustration of this approach. Malaria is caused by a microscopic parasite (the agent) which is transmitted by the bite of a female mosquito (the host) which lives in tropical and subtropical swamps (the environment). The utility of such a model becomes apparent when one begins to think about possible ways to control the problem. For example, if the task is to prevent malaria, oil can be poured on the swamps to get rid of the mosquito larvae, DDT can be used to kill the adult mosquitoes, or a vaccine can be developed to immunize against the parasitic organism.

Often, and with considerable utility, the epidemiologic concept of agent, host, and environment can be applied directly to the types of social problems being considered here. Let us use an aspect of juvenile delinquency—car theft—to demonstrate how the epidemiologic model can suggest ways of ameliorating social problems. Suppose, for example, that a group of young teen-age boys has been arrested for stealing cars. The youths, viewed here as the "host," could be taught not to take cars or, alternatively, could be directed to a more constructive use of their free time. Or the police—the "agent," in this case—might be persuaded to redefine the problem as joy-riding, thus removing the offense from the category of car theft. Finally, the unprotected car, the "environment," might be made less accessible by urging owners to remove ignition keys and to lock all unattended cars. Each of these solutions implies a different "cause": delinquent boys, inaccurate definition of the problem, or careless owners. A comprehensive intervention program would, of course, be directed at all three.

SEQUENTIAL EXPLANATION

A third and still more complex model suggests a sequential or chain reaction influence of one or more variables on another set of variables which culminates in the phenomenon that is viewed as a social problem. This causal model has also been referred to by some as the *specification of sufficient or necessary conditions*. Howard Becker (1953) has provided us with a concrete illustration in his analysis of the use of marijuana. He argues that a series of definite preconditions are essential for a person to become a marijuana user: he has to smoke, he has to enjoy smoking, he has to inhale, he has to find the reaction to marijuana pleasurable, and so forth. According to Becker, therefore, for a particular behavior or condition to come about it must be preceded by series of conditions, each of which is essential and all of which are linked by immutable bonds.

One can go on in great detail to specify variants of different causal models. The important point to remember, however, is that to understand the etiology or cause of social problems the investigator cannot confine his thinking to either a one-factor or even a multi-factor approach that merely exemplifies a number of alternative variables linked to a phenomenon. As we shall emphasize later, one of the limitations of the present state of knowledge concerning social problems is the barrier created by the lack of explicit models to explain various phenomena.

In the development of intervention strategies, a number of different approaches are possible and at least two are of interest to us here. The first is based on an understanding of the etiology or cause of the discontinuity; the second considers intervention in terms of the impact of the problem on the community.

Investigators who would develop an etiologic perspective would again do well to look to the public health field for models. Quite often, when talking about problems of control, public health people refer to primary, secondary, and tertiary prevention (Leavell and Clark, 1965:7). Tertiary prevention involves direct therapeutic intervention to treat the individual's symptoms; secondary prevention concerns the modulation of the disease's immediate causal elements; and primary prevention undertakes to shift the basic structures or environment to reduce the incidence of the etiologic agents. In the case of mental illness, for example, the following strategy might be developed. As tertiary prevention, the patient would be given appropriate drugs to help alleviate the symptoms; as secondary prevention, he would be advised to modify his life style to avoid precipitating situations; and finally, as a primary strategy, the community might be persuaded to change aspects of its social order that are deemed to cause the individual's problems (Suchman, 1968:94).

In terms of the kinds of social problems that we wish to discuss, there is considerable variety in the way intervention strategies are used. For example, Cloward and Ohlin (1960) argue that the reduction of delinquency requires drastic modification of the occupational and social-class structure in order to open up opportunities for individuals to achieve within the American society. Contrast this with programs of group work and recreation in high delinquency areas or with the utilization of training schools for adjudicated delinquents. Like the problem of cause, many of the remedial actions and activities currently in vogue are undertaken without awareness of or explicit rationale for their intervention strategy. It is now held by most students of social problems that intervention strategies require an impact model as well as an etiologic model. This impact model and the notion of it leads to the other observation that should be made here.

Frequently intervention approaches must be substantively different from the actual etiologic or causal models that explain a particular phenomenon. For example, the Gluecks (Glueck and Glueck, 1962) found that adolescent delinquency was highly correlated with a poor relationship between the boy at age five and his mother. Obviously nothing can be done about a fifteen-year-old's relationship with his mother ten years earlier. Intervention programs to meet the current problem must be formulated on other bases than etiology. Moreover, a delinquency prevention program for five-year-olds today would have to be based on the unsupported assumption that conditions have not changed in the intervening years or that they would not change drastically in succeeding years.

The development and implementation of intervention strategies to ameliorate or modify deviant behavior and conditions of social disorganization involve the application of a number of different techniques. In the actual analysis of programs of intervention, it is often difficult to unravel the particular theoretical positions on which such programs are based. In broad outline, however, the various etiologic frames of reference for the study of social problems and the various modes of intervention designed for their amelioration stem mainly from two theoretical orientations. One focuses on the individual, the other on the social order.

In contemporary thinking, a partial integration of views has been achieved, particularly in the development of the cultural or communication perspective. Persons who advocate an individual orientation recognize and acknowledge the relevance of the social structure in molding the behavior of individuals; those who hold a structural perspective recognize that the outlines of the social structure are the product of the actions and activities of individual men, whether or not organized into collectivities. Many theorists in both camps are sensitive to the matter of cultural values and their transmission through communications.

individual-oriented theories

Logically, if not pragmatically, it is possible to argue that the solution to all social problems consists in directly engaging the individual so that his values as well as his behavior conform to existing community norms. Several views can be formulated on the way individuals may be modified, and these constitute distinct approaches to the solution of social problems.

BIOLOGICAL EXPLANATIONS

One frame of reference focuses on the biological and physiochemical makeup of man. Although many mystical and prenaturalistic views about the relationship between the individual's biological characteristics and his social-role behavior have been abandoned, we have considerable evidence that genetic differences do exist and that they influence the way individuals respond to community norms.

Although the span of performance potential is quite wide within individuals and open to environmental influence, each of us is born with varying capacities to perform in certain ways. Not only are there individual differences in physical structure, but there are differences in, for example, genetic potential for long life, intellectual capacity, and the ability of certain glands to function effectively, given the range of conditions to which the individual is exposed.

Certain social problems are directly traceable to the biological and physiochemical bases of the individual. Among these are certain types of mental retardation, certain modes of expression defined as mental illness, a number of physical handicaps such as blindness and deafness, and a range of somatic diseases including cardiac conditions and obesity. Numerous techniques have been advanced by physical scientists for intervening in social problems occasioned by an individual's biological and constitutional limitations. Recent examples include fluoridating the water supply to control tooth decay, prescribing low-cholesterol diets for incipient cardiovascular disease, publicizing the relationship between smoking and cancer, relieving mental tension with tranquilizers, and chemically regulating fertility by birth-control pills.

The social significance of these and other developments in the life sciences cannot be ignored by the sociologist interested in social problems. Indeed, a resurgence of interest in the relationship between biology and social life is apparent, and in the next decade one may expect an increased concern in *sociobiology,* as the field is beginning to be called (Russell Sage Foundation, 1968:16).

PSYCHOLOGICAL VIEWS

For the past generation, the most intense interest in causal explanation and intervention strategy has been at the level of individual psychology. The influence of Freud and the early proponents of psychoanalytic theory has been the basis of program developments and practice principles for the treatment of a wide variety of conditions and behaviors characterized as social problems, including the neuroses, the psychoses, juvenile delinquency, drug addiction, alcoholism and, indeed, at some level the majority of all social ills.

Even today there exists no unitary psychological framework with respect to psychodynamic theory. Early psychodynamic concepts were tied to a biological perspective of behavior, and therapeutic techniques sought to modify the individual's basic instincts or status. Later thinking emphasized the impact of experience, particularly during early childhood, on the psyche and future development of the individual. A subtheory held that frustration is the cause of deviant behavior because it leads to aggression. Both of these views suggest that to ameliorate many social problems the individual must first increase his insight into and be able to rationalize better the underlying basis of his behavior. More recently a new school has evolved that seeks to deal not with the individual's basic psychological processes but with his inability to cope with society's stresses and strains. Cure is not the main task of the therapist; rather, it is to strengthen and support the patient so that he can "once again participate in the interactions that make up the warp and woof of life" (Smith, 1968:20).

WIDESPREAD INTERVENTION

The largest proportion of social-control agents, however, are still engaged in activities that are rooted in the general psychodynamic viewpoint. These range from psychoanalytically oriented psychiatrists, who regard long-term therapy as the only proper intervention technique, to a wide variety of professionals such as social caseworkers who deal more with environmentally confined areas of behavior rather than with the totality of the individual's emotional life.

Other practitioners make use of group-process techniques, variously called group psychotherapy, sensitivity training, psychodrama, and so on, having in common the goal of modifying the individual's psychological system through group interaction. Still others, taking their framework from community psychiatry and public health, have used concepts such as crisis intervention and community consultation to describe their efforts to reach larger populations. The crisis concept refers to immediate and special intervention in the case of individual or community crises, such as natural disasters, death of relatives, and so forth. Consultation involves working not with clients or patients but with the caretakers or gatekeepers who are responsible for particular programs. For example, a trained community consultant, usually a psychiatrist or psychiatric social worker, counsels a schoolteacher about the behavior problem of a student or advises a visiting nurse responsible for recently released mental patients.

Widespread criticism of the more individualized approaches to intervention have been voiced in many circles. These stem from the prohibitive cost of one-to-one therapy, the critical shortages of trained professionals to man such programs, the mounting evidence that these interventions are more appropriate to middle-class clients and available only to the more affluent sections of the community. (*See* Documentation 1.) The most telling criticism, however, is the limited evidence from experimental research of the efficacy in terms of outcomes of the various psychotherapeutic approaches, although there are some reports of partial success (Sheldon and Jones, 1967).

Another concept of individual intervention that has found some ac-

individual vs. community

The distinctive departure which Freud undertook in his psychotherapeutic practice was to consider himself the patient's agent. In this way he tried to do what he could for the individual patient, and repudiated his obligation to the patient's family and society. Evidently, he felt that he could not do justice to both parties, since the two were so often in conflict. He must also have believed that the family and society were not helpless; if they needed assistance, they would seek and obtain help of their own.

This is, of course, a fundamental tenet of the democratic-liberal ethic, and more especially of the ethic of autonomy. When two or more parties conflict, their differences should be openly acknowledged; each should have free access to help from his own agents to promote his own interests and welfare; lastly, those involved in the conflict . . . should not also be its arbiters.

It is not surprising that these principles are completely ignored by all the modern schools of psychiatric treatment: milieu therapy, family therapy, group therapy—these and many other practices attempt to achieve the impossible, that is, to "help" the patient and at the same time "do justice" to his family, friends, employers, and government. I say that this development is not surprising because analysts themselves have failed to hold fast to what I have called their moral mandate. Freud himself spoke hopefully of a future, when a demand for "the large-scale application of our therapy will compel us to alloy the pure gold of analysis with the copper of direct suggestion." In this way, a "psychotherapy for the people"— that is to say, for the "poor" and the "uneducated"—will be brought into being, which will be suitable "for treating a considerable mass of the population" (Sigmund Freud, "Lines of Advance in Psycho-Analytic Therapy," 1919). But what kind of help, or therapy, does a "considerable mass of the population" need?

The poor need jobs and money, not psychoanalysis. The uneducated need knowledge and skills, not psychoanalysis. Furthermore, the poor and the uneducated are also often politically disenfranchised and socially oppressed; if this is the case, they need freedom from oppression. For the kind of personal freedom psychoanalysis promises can have meaning only for persons who enjoy a large measure of economic, political, and social freedom. (Szasz, 1965:19.)

ceptance, especially among educators, is based upon learning theory. Practitioners who subscribe to a learning-theory approach argue that the basic stimulus-response process can be extrapolated to intellectual and social aspects of behavior. There are diverse theories for explaining the learning process and a variety of intervention approaches to the internalization of specific responses and the maximization of learning generalization or *set learning*. This approach uses conditioning techniques that reward correct behavior or punish incorrect behavior and may involve highly complex teaching machines and the use of computer simulation.

From the standpoint of both intervention and etiology, it is fair to say that there is no clear-cut ranking of the appropriateness of various theoretical perspectives or of the efficacy of different intervention technologies. There are only various impressions based upon limited evidence. Fortunately, well-designed experimental studies are on the increase (Freeman and Sherwood, 1965). While no definitive studies have been completed at this time, there does appear to be a trend away from a psychodynamic orientation and toward a more behavioristic approach based on a social or a learning perspective.

A recent analysis by Cohen (1966:59–62) specified seven serious limitations that adhere to concepts of intervention which focus on the individual. Although perhaps most applicable as criticisms of the psychodynamic point of view, they also hold for the whole array of individual-oriented intervention efforts.

1. Such control theories take too dismal a view of conformity. Appropriate as well as inappropriate behavior can provide psychological satisfaction and gratification to the individual, and neither deviance nor conformity has an exclusive claim on the impulse life—"doing what comes naturally."

2. Individual-control theories tend to identify deviant impulses as always being egocentric, self-seeking, shortsighted, hostile, and so on. Frequently, however, deviance represents a means of achieving the goals of the organizations with which the individual is affiliated or the objectives of the community to which he belongs rather than being behavior that the individual adopts because of his own personal stake in things.

3. Deviant behavior is often looked upon as being closer to original or unsocialized human nature, but there is little evidence that deviant behavior has any more affinity with instincts and basic impulses than with conforming actions.

4. In the development of individual-oriented intervention theories, the independent variables remain unmeasured and unobserved and are inferred from the acts themselves, a situation which lays such theories open to accusations of being tautologous—"delinquents are people who commit delinquent acts; delinquent acts are the behavior of delinquent people."

5. A theory that conceives of personality as a totality divided into compartments that are somehow interconnected raises major difficulties, chiefly by diverting attention from other possible interpretations of behavior. While conforming acts are interpreted as being closely linked to the immediate situation and ongoing activities, normatively forbidden acts are subject to speculations about subconscious motivations and internal dynamics of personality. There is no reason to assume, however, that

the meaning of deviant behavior is any less varied or subject to "surface phenomena," which can be observed, described, and verified, than is conforming behavior.

6. Since frustration is a most commonplace and everyday experience which only occasionally precipitates outward aggression and, conversely, since many aggressive acts appear not to be related to any frustrating experience, the frustration-aggression theory becomes insupportable unless the definitions of aggression and frustration are tailored to fit each situation—a practice difficult to defend.

7. Most of the formulations in this area stress that deviant acts are committed by "kinds of people" who have special or peculiar personalities, which view completely overlooks the fact that so-called deviants frequently behave perfectly normally and otherwise normal people occasionally indulge in deviant behavior.

In addition to Cohen's criticisms, the social-problems analyst finds another limitation to intervention theories that focus on the individual. Too often the behavior with which we are concerned and the social problems which we wish to control are not related to deviant acts of individuals but rather are community conditions brought about by the actions or lack of action of groups or classes of community members— slum landlords, unscrupulous industrialists, dishonest businessmen, corrupt union officials, venal politicians—or the operations of large-scale institutions or the structures of entire social systems.

structural approaches

Sociologists have always been concerned with the relationship between an individual's behavior, or its outcome in terms of community conditions, and the structural characteristics of the relevant social system. This tradition goes back to the nineteenth century French sociologist, Émile Durkheim, who observed in his classical study of suicides that the phenomenon increased not only in times of depression but also in times of rapidly increasing prosperity (Durkheim, 1897). According to Durkheim, when the social order is unstable and marked with an absence of coordination and solidarity between social groups and an increase in group conflict, there is likely to be an increase in at least certain forms of deviant behavior. In the decades since Durkheim's original work, his conception of a lack of cohesion and integration in society—termed *anomie*—has found considerable use among social theorists and, as a consequence, has suffered a diffuseness of meaning.

In the late 1930s, Robert Merton (1938) elaborated upon the concept of anomie to distinguish several modes of social-role response. He assigned the term *cultural goals* to those aspirations and expectations which man learns through living in a community with a particular set of values and norms which specify the means by which he may legitimately pursue these goals. Merton also distinguished between the ways facilities and opportunities for achieving cultural goals in a manner compatible with the norms are distributed among persons occupying different positions in the society, i.e., the concept of differential access to institutionalized means. The terms *structural stress* or *structural strain* are used to describe the discrepancy between the cultural goals of community members and the means accessible to them for realizing these aspirations. In other words, when the institutionalized means are not distributed in a manner that permits certain groups or certain community members to make use of them, other actions take place. According to the structural point of view, therefore, community members are adaptive and conforming in their behavior when the cultural goals and institutionalized means are congruent; they tend to become deviant when goals and means are inconsistent.

Merton (1957), as well as other structural theorists such as Dubin (1959), have specified alternatives to conformity and have indicated a number of outcomes or modes of behavior that would constitute social problems or at least deviance. Such outcomes develop when cultural goals are undefined, conflicting, ambiguously defined, or the institutionalized means are absent. By these standards, one mode of deviant conduct is innovation; professional thieves, white-collar criminals, and cheaters in examinations are cited as examples of individuals who adhere to the goals but reject or do not have available to them the normatively prescribed means. A second mode of deviation is an overconformity that amounts to ritualism. It can be seen in individuals, especially bureaucrats, who rigidly follow the rules without regard to the ends for which they are defined, who make a virtue of overconformity to institutionalized means at the price of underconformity to prescribed cultural goals. A third category, described as retreatist, is exemplified by the psychotic patient who withdraws from the rat race by abandoning both the goals and the means. Finally, there are the rebels, the revolutionaries, who withdraw allegiance to the culture and the social system they deem unjust and seek to reconstitute the society anew, with a new set of goals and prescriptions for attaining them.

USE IN ACTION PROGRAMS

It must be acknowledged, of course, that no fully integrated structural theory exists, and much of the thinking regarding intervention techniques depends on a partially developed point of view and the questionable results of the OEO Poverty Program (Moynihan, 1969). Nevertheless, the concept of anomie, with its emphasis on normlessness and alienation, and its elaboration by the structural theorists have led to major programs of intervention. Indeed, stemming from this point of view are many of the broad-spectrum community-action and antipoverty programs currently being supported by the federal government through the Office of Economic Opportunity. A structural interpretation is useful for dealing with social problems that involve either individual behavior vis-à-vis one of the major control systems or the overall character of the community. For example, it could be argued that a cultural goal in the United States is for the adult female to have and rear children and to express love and affection via sexual relationships. The institutionalized means is rather clear: marriage and a stable sexual relationship with one partner. But it could be argued that this opportunity is not open to all women in the community because the potential pool of partners either reject, do not understand, or are unable to conform to either the cultural goal or the institutionalized means. Such a point of view may partially explain the high rates of illegitimacy, one-parent homes, and the stereotype of the unmarried mother on welfare, especially among low-income blacks.

Government has placed a great deal of emphasis at the policy level on the problem of structural deficiencies with reference to the political-economic system. Some years back, Cloward and Ohlin (1960) published a volume dealing with problems of delinquency that had a major impact on the development of many large-scale intervention programs. The authors held that many problems of low-income youths were related to their knowing and accepting the cultural goals but lacking the institutionalized means for achieving them because of a failure by the community to make such means available. This opportunity theory contends that the social structure must be modified to permit a greater congruence between institutionalized means and cultural goals for the poor, the minority group member, and others to whom the social system has denied such opportunities.

In recent years, intervention programs have been developed that emphasize broad aspects of the social structure which engage many persons in the community. To a certain extent these efforts have overshadowed more minute social-control and social-change programs which either deal with highly specific types of social discontinuities or seek much smaller modifications in the structural order. Of course, many of the more limited programs are being carried out by local officials, usually without their having any systematic understanding of the rationale behind their work. The premise of necessity is the basis for many of these programs of intervention and social control which operate in a variety of situations ranging from mobilization of the military to caring for the aged. Needs not filled by existing institutionalized mechanisms also provide the spur for such lay programs as Parents Without Partners, a collective organization for the divorced and widowed, and the many other voluntary groups that are formed to deal with specific social needs and problems.

LIMITATIONS

One of the interesting dilemmas for the structural theorist is the time-ordering of events. Do changes in the social roles of individuals and in the types of behavior and disorganization that confront us stem from structural innovations and modifications or do the changes in behavior lead to changes in the structural means available? Nam, for example, argues that the GI bill, which brought so many veterans to college and provided legitimate opportunities for many Americans, was a consequence not a determinant of community conditions. As Nam (1964:32) concludes:

> It would be fair to say, however, that the GI programs were not so much prime movers in the continued educational progress of the country as they were responses to the growing demand for formal education in a society where social organization and value complexes were undergoing change.

The notion of structural intervention, the concept of anomie, and the emphasis on strains and stresses within the social structure provide useful explanations for many social problems, but they have their limitations. Some analysts of the contemporary American community criticize the perspective often advanced by sociologists regarding the inevitability of particular structural arrangements (Tumin, 1963). They contend that equality of access to legitimate means is not enough. For them the solution lies not in reworking the existing social order but in shifting the orientation of American community members away from the present vertical structure toward a more horizontal one. Others have taken this position to task and maintain that a vertical structuring is endemic to the social order (Moore, 1963).

Other limitations center in the implementation of social intervention models. Modification of institutionalized means has to be undertaken with the realization that such developments often run counter to the well-established relationships between institutionalized means and cultural goals that exist for large segments of the community. A good illustration of the complexity of the problem can be found in the attempt, particularly in Northern cities, to increase the quality of education for lower socio-economic and minority group children. The intervention has consisted largely of efforts to redistribute either students or teachers (on the grounds that the most experienced and competent teachers seek out the better schools) in different parts of the city. In order to provide educational settings in which there are high expectations and aspirations for both teachers and students, some redeployment has been deemed necessary. The effect of this strategy on the quality of education is still being debated; the effect on the social structure has been profound.

Parents, particularly white middle-class parents, have recognized the value of excellent schools as an institutionalized means for achieving for their children the cultural goal of upward occupational mobility and entrance into the professions and high-prestige work roles. The efforts to change the mode of operations of school systems by introducing a racially and economically mixed student body has not only resulted in considerable conflict and strife but, in almost every major city, has triggered an exodus of the highly educated and professional families to the suburbs or spurred the development of a system of private schools. So we see that intervention techniques designed to maximize institutionalized means often raise barriers or conteractions that limit their utility. Competing points of view regarding racial "integration" of city schools exist, of course. The counterargument, heard increasingly often among upwardly mobile middle-income Negroes, is that they do not care what color the students are, so long as the best education possible is provided. Or, to put it more directly, they do not want their children to attend schools with lower-class, lower-achieving children—black or white.

communication views

The concept of structural intervention presupposes, in part, that the development and amplification of institutionalized means occurs in a system in which there is clarity of cultural goals as well as an understanding of the manipulative and coping skills required to utilize the institutionalized means. A number of persons in the social-problems field argue that intervention techniques are also needed to provide for the learning and acceptance of the cultural goals and for the development of requisite skills so that individuals and groups can maximize their use of institutionalized means (Cloward and Ohlin, 1960). Various theories have been advanced regarding social problems that are related to a deficient knowledge of both the cultural goals and the interpersonal and technical processes needed for understanding and utilizing institutionalized means. One view stems from the ideas of early criminologists such as Shaw and McKay (1942) and suggests that deviant rather than normative goals are transmitted to some in the community via primary group socialization. The result is the clustering of deviant individuals in groups that have acultural goals. This point of view, particularly among crimi-

differential association

Sutherland was among the first to perceive that the concept of social disorganization tended to obscure the stable patterns of interaction among carriers of criminal values. . . . [H]e had been influenced by the observation that lower-class areas were organized in terms of both conventional and criminal values, but he was also impressed that these alternative value systems were supported by patterned systems of social relations. He expressly recognized that crime, far from being a random, unorganized activity, was typically an intricate and stable system of human arrangements. He therefore rejected the concept of "social disorganization" and substituted the concept of "differential group organization." . . .

Having freed observation of the urban slum from conventional evaluations, Sutherland was able to focus more clearly on the way in which its social structure constitutes a "learning environment" for the acquisition of deviant values and skills. In the development of the theory of "differential association" and "differential group organization," he came close to stating explicitly the concept of differentials in access to illegitimate means. But Sutherland was essentially interested in learning processes, and thus he did not ask how such access varies in different parts of the social structure, nor did he inquire about the consequences for behavior of variations in the accessibility of these means. (Cloward, 1959:170–171.)

nologists, has led to the development of a theory of differential association usually attributed to E. H. Sutherland (*see* Documentation 2). The core of this theory is that deviant conduct is learned in a process of communication with other people in small intimate groups. These learnings include the techniques of committing the deviance and the specific direction of motives, drives, and rationalizations, or attitudes, that support acultural or noncultural goals.

Other individuals who focus on the communication process use such concepts as *self* and *role*, which are derived from the theories of the early social-psychologist George Herbert Mead (1934). Mead and his students emphasized the importance of understanding the process by which the actor labels, classifies, and judges himself. How he feels about himself, conducts himself, tries to do with and about himself depends, in their view, on what sort of object he thinks he is or wants to be. According to the structural viewpoint considered earlier, if the individual's self-image is of limited congruence with the cultural goals, then the likelihood of his behaving in ways conforming to the normative structure of the society is doubtful.

A similar set of limitations exists with respect to one's ability to make use of legitimate means, even when the community makes them available to particular groups of citizens. It has been observed, for example, that access to many of our treatment programs requires information and a degree of sophistication that is not characteristic of large segments of the population. In order to be accepted for treatment, the client must be able to project the appropriate image to the therapist (Hollingshead and Redlich, 1964). Typical social welfare agencies have been accused, and in some cases quite rightly so, of maintaining programs that are almost impossible for the poor to participate in because of their lack of requisite interactional skills. This problem is well-recognized and has resulted in attempts to create new procedures for the delivery of health, legal, and employment services in poverty-striken areas by such agencies as the Office of Economic Opportunity. The communications perspective has relevance for the solution of social problems because intervention efforts require not merely the provision of institutionalized means but also the development and socialization of individuals to make proper use of them.

APPLICATION IN PROGRAMS

Although there is a strong emphasis today on structural intervention efforts, it is important to take into account deficits in communication and in individual characteristics. One reason structural efforts are insufficient is that conformity to cultural goals sometimes is not as physically or emotionally gratifying as nonconformity; sometimes legitimate means are too complicated or demanding in comparison with illegitimate ones. It is important to remember that man, even in his encapsulated status within a complex urban environment, still responds in rather basic ways to sexual stimulation, hunger, pleasurable sensation, and so on. Structural changes may have little impact if the process of conforming to cultural goals interferes with such highly satisfying and gratifying behavior. Proponents of structural change fail to recognize that motivation to accept cultural norms is often easier for groups of individuals whose exposure to nonnormative behavior has been minimal. They fail to reflect, when dealing with the so-called disadvantaged groups, that there are elements of the life styles of poor or minority groups that the interventionists, too, would find pleasurable (Miller, 1958). Where acceptance of cultural goals requires the sublimation of such behavior, one may anticipate great, indeed sometimes practically impossible, barriers to successful implementation.

Along the same lines, there are many instances where it requires much more effort to use institutional means to obtain the cultural goals than to use noninstitutional ones. Although children are taught otherwise, crime sometimes does pay. As we all know, many white-collar criminals and certain individuals engaged in the vices do not necessarily end up in either jail or the gutters of skid row. In terms of the cultural goals of economic status and prestige, they may be doing very well indeed. Such individuals sit on the boards of private colleges, are appointed regents of state university systems, are recognized as important figures in voluntary groups and even seek and win political office.

The structural approach, then, cannot be implemented in all cases. Certainly a realistic understanding of both the interaction between individual needs and gratifications and individual motives and behavior, and of the appropriateness of structural intervention are required; also, strategies must be promoted with a worldly understanding of the competition between cultural goals and intrinsically satisfying experiences for the individual. In the past decade the pendulum has swung much more to the side of structural intervention. Proponents of any particular intervention approach or particular etiologic stance must recognize the need for integration of various viewpoints. The problem, of course, is that all intervention efforts face competition for scarce resources. Thus the risk is always present that a unitary approach is advocated on the grounds of economy and as a means of avoiding the chaos of a program that seeks to use a multiplicity of approaches. No illustrations of broad-scale programs combining various intervention strategies are available even today. Integrated programs that take into account both individual characteristics, communication deficiencies, and structural opportunities exist only on the drawing boards of social planners and in the ideologies of students of social problems.

format of the book

In both the development of intervention strategies and the search for causal factors associated with particular social problems, it is necessary to have a perspective on the particular segments of the community that are affected by the problem. The targets—or victims, if you will—of particular social problems are rarely found in an entirely random fashion throughout the community. For each particular social problem, of course, it is possible to utilize a virtually infinite number of characteristics of individuals, or of parts of the community in which they are found, to differentiate those persons affected or most likely to be affected by a particular problem from those who are not threatened or represent a low risk.

In an orderly analysis of the social problems faced by the contemporary urban community, one cannot progress without a framework that takes into account a few distinctive characteristics that pinpoint the incidence and prevalence of the various problems. The selection of such a limited set of initial characteristics has to be made on practical as well as theoretical grounds. Our approach is to seek to differentiate individuals on the basis of selected characteristics which sociologists almost always cite in describing community members and which the agents of social control, i.e., the various social-control systems, use in reporting incidence and prevalence of social problems. Many of these characteristics are already embodied in the definition of the problem. In presenting our formulations of social problems, we will use two distinct perspectives. The first will consider discontinuities that are pervasive throughout society; the second will deal with those problems that are peculiar to a particular age group or cycle of life.

PERVASIVE PROBLEMS

There exists a series of social problems that can only be described as pervasive. We have arbitrarily identified six which we will discuss in detail in Part II: persistent poverty, inadequate economic participation, discrimination and prejudice, urban deterioration, involvement and alienation, and corruption and community life. Admittedly, these problems may have a greater impact on persons at certain ages than at others, but their presence can be found in all age groups and they are therefore considered superordinate to the particular problems of the life cycle. These problems are rooted in the social order itself and by one means or another affect rather directly community members of all ages. Moreover, to a large extent, these discontinuities are the immediate precursors of the problems of role performance and social conduct that are tied to the life-cycle stages.

Indeed, the very organization of the book from this point on reveals our sociological bias. We attempted to indicate earlier that the sociologist's position with respect to structural influences needs to be integrated with the views of those who emphasize individual characteristics, and that problems of communication, or what is sometimes called culture, also need to be incorporated. Nevertheless, and despite the obvious circularity of individual factors' influencing cultural or communication ones that in turn influence structural variables, it is our position that the thrust of intervention needs to be at the structural level. Not only is the social structure the most appropriate starting point for developing efficacious programs of intervention, but it is equally pertinent for finding parsimonious explanations of the genesis of social problems. Thus our concentration on the pervasive social problems as the initial point of departure.

LIFE-CYCLE PROBLEMS

Without a doubt, age is the variable most commonly viewed as relevant in the development of theories of social-role behavior (Cottrell, 1942).

Its use as an identifier on practically every public reporting form is testimony that the general public, as well as behavioral scientists, regard it as a major distinguishing attribute within the American community. Age constitutes a key variable with respect to the norms of the community regarding what is right and proper as well as to the expectations and self-image of community members. Many of our legal codes are structured in terms of age, as are many of the formal entitlements of public programs. Certainly a wide range of political and economic activity is similarly restricted.

We choose to think about age in terms of a life-cycle development. Our position with respect to the identification of social problems makes it mandatory for us to approach the analysis by expressing certain judgments—in part, value judgments—about the appropriate conduct of people. The use of an age distinction allows us to paint a portrait of what one may regard as appropriate conduct and reasonable entitlement within age categories. In some instances, of course, a number of acceptable alternatives need to be presented, but such a portrait must take into account the moral order, the objective responses of community members, and the sensitivity of the sociologist regarding what is desirable.

We have divided the life cycle into seven stages and a discussion of these will comprise Part III of this book. The stages are infancy and early childhood (birth through five years), childhood and preadolescence (six through twelve years), adolescence (thirteen through seventeen years), young adulthood (eighteen through twenty-two years), marriage and parenthood (twenty-three through forty-five years), middle age (forty-six through sixty-four years), and old age (sixty-five and over). Admittedly these age breaks are arbitrary and, at times, we will take license to vary somewhat the ages within each period. Not only is this necessary because of an overlapping in social roles in the urban community but because many times the age groups discussed in the literature with respect to the specification of appropriate conduct or related deviations vary from the arbitrary ranges we have selected.

Simply put, what we are suggesting in Part III is that certain social problems of the community, in incidence and prevalence, can be related most distinctly to the age of individuals; thus, a person's place in the life cycle is a useful way of approaching the differentiation of social problems as they affect particular target populations.

REFERENCES

BECKER, HOWARD S.
1953 "Becoming a marihuana user." American Journal of Sociology 59 (November):235–242.

CLOWARD, RICHARD A.
1959 "Illegitimate means, anomie, and deviant behavior." American Sociological Review 24(April):164–176.

CLOWARD, RICHARD A. AND LLOYD OHLIN.
1960 Delinquency and Opportunity: A Theory of Delinquent Gangs. New York: Free Press.

COHEN, ALBERT K.
1966 Deviance and Control. Englewood Cliffs, New Jersey: Prentice-Hall.

COTTRELL, LEONARD S., JR.
1942 "The adjustment of the individual to his age and sex roles." American Sociological Review 7 (October):617–620.

DUBIN, ROBERT.
1959 "Deviant behavior and social structure." American Sociological Review 24(April):147–164.

DURKHEIM, EMILE.
1897 Suicide. Translation by John A. Spaulding and George Simpson. New York: Free Press (1951 edition).

FOOTE, NELSON N. AND LEONARD S. COTTRELL, JR.
1955 Identity and Inter-personal Competence. Chicago: University of Chicago Press.

FREEMAN, HOWARD E. AND CLARENCE C. SHERWOOD.
1965 "Research in large-scale intervention programs." Journal of Social Issues 21(January):11–28.

GLUECK, SHELDON AND ELEANOR GLUECK.
1962 Family Environment and Delinquency. Boston: Houghton Mifflin.

HOLLINGSHEAD, AUGUST B. AND F. C. REDLICH.
1964 Social Class and Mental Illness. New York: Science Editions.

LEAVELL, HUGH R. AND E. G. CLARK.
1965 Preventive Medicine for the Doctor in His Community. Third Edition. New York: McGraw-Hill.

MACMAHON, BRIAN ET AL.
1960 Epidemiologic Methods. Boston: Little, Brown.

MCCORD, WILLIAM, AND JOAN MCCORD.
1960 Origins of Alcoholism. Stanford: Stanford University Press.

MEAD, GEORGE HERBERT.
1934 Mind, Self and Society: From the Standpoint of a Social Behaviorist. Edited by C. W. Morris. Chicago: University of Chicago Press.

MERTON, ROBERT K.
1938 "Social structure and anomie." American Sociological Review 3 (October): 672–682.
1957 Social Theory and Social Structure. New York: Free Press.

MILLER, WALTER B.
  1958 "Lower-class culture as a generating milieu of gang delinquency." Journal of Social Issues 14(January):5–19.

MOORE, WILBERT E.
  1963 "But some are more equal than others." American Sociological Review 28(February):13–18.

MOYNIHAN, DANIEL PATRICK.
  1969 Maximum Feasible Misunderstanding: Community Action in the War on Poverty. New York: Free Press.

NAM, CHARLES B.
  1964 "Impact of the 'GI Bills' on the educational level of the male population." Social Forces 43(October): 26–32.

RUSSELL SAGE FOUNDATION.
  1968 Annual Report. New York: Russell Sage.

SALBER, EVA J., HOWARD E. FREEMAN AND THEODOR ABELIN.
  1968 "Needed research on smoking: lessons from the Newton study." Pp. 128–139 in Edgar F. Borgatta and Robert R. Evans (eds.), Smoking, Health and Behavior. Chicago: Aldine.

SELLTIZ, CLAIRE, MARIE JAHODA, MORTON DEUTSCH AND STUART W. COOK.
  1959 Research Methods In Social Relations. Revised Edition. New York: Holt, Rinehart, and Winston.

SHAW, CLIFFORD R. AND HENRY D. McKAY.
  1942 Juvenile Delinquency and Urban Areas. Chicago: University of Chicago Press.

SHELDON, ALAN AND KENNETH J. JONES.
  1967 "Maintenance in the community: a study of psychiatric aftercare and rehospitalization." British Journal of Psychiatry 113 (September):502.

SMITH, M. BREWSTER.
  1968 "The revolution in mental-health care—a 'bold new approach'?" Transaction 5(April):19–23.

SUCHMAN, EDWARD A.
  1968 Evaluative Research Principles and Practices in Public Service and Social Action Programs: Russell Sage.

SZASZ, THOMAS S.
  1961 Myth of Mental Illness. New York: Harper and Row.
  1965 "The ethics of psychoanalysis." Transaction 2(May/June):14–19.

TUMIN, MELVIN.
  1963 "On inequality." American Sociological Review 28(February):19–28.

PART TWO

PERVASIVE PROBLEMS

persistent
poverty

IN THESE TIMES the temptation is great to explain the social problems of the American urban community by focusing on the problem of poverty to the virtual exclusion of all other characteristics of individuals and of the social structure. There is, certainly, good grounds for the view that the most pervasive and embracing condition in the current spectrum of social problems is the economic status of community members and the related characteristics found among individuals in the population.

the illusive character of poverty

While the solution offered by Karl Marx and his socialist and communist disciples is rejected, at least in part, by most community members and commentators on the American social scene, it is apparent that there is much cogency to the position that deviant behavior and undesirable community conditions are closely tied to inequities in the economic structure. When one begins to pursue the etiology of virtually any social problem in the United States, a major variable to be considered is the socio-economic status of the community member or social group under analysis. Although measures of socio-economic status often include other factors besides financial status, it is certainly evident that the position of the individual within the economic structure determines to a large extent his image in the community, his own values and style of life, and his prospects for maximizing his potential both for self-gratification and for contributing to society. Investigators of specific social problems have pointed out that economic status may be a consequence rather than an antecedent of certain social afflictions (Antonovsky, 1967:66–68). Nevertheless, it is important to emphasize the critical role of economic resources in today's urban community and to explicate the inevitable bond between the problem of poverty and the role of inadequate economic resources, for here lies the cornerstone of social problems in the United States.

Poverty is as much a moral problem as an objective one. The history of American communities shows great concern with the problem of poverty, and much overt social conflict has ensued because of the reactions of community members to an inadequate income. Nevertheless, values concerning what is right and proper in terms of economic resources for all community members stem as much, if not more, from the views of experts within the several social-control systems as from any consensus within the general population. The social unrest in the United States that is reflected in industrial strife, picketing, demonstrations, protest marches, sit-ins, and riots, as well as in the Great Society orientation to the problem of poverty of the Kennedy-Johnson administrations, undoubtedly represents the views and feelings of many poor people within the community. But it is fair to say that essentially the national response to poverty in the midst of affluence is a commitment to a set of moral values. Whether this commitment is advanced because of political expediency, concern with the eventual consequences of failing to engage in modifications in the social order, or a basic sense of humanitarian concern is quite immaterial. While the present views on what is economically right and proper are undoubtedly motivated by the particularistic interests of persons in the political-economic system and by the professional outlook of leaders in the health and welfare system, these represent a reasonably consistent set of values that are accepted throughout the various systems that constitute the sources of influence within the community.

YESTERDAY'S POOR

In examining the current value orientations regarding the availability of economic resources in the American community, one may take a historical perspective, such as Brenner (1964) provides, on the changing concepts of poverty in the United States. Poverty is not a new condition, but the definition of poverty has shifted. During the country's first two centuries of development, it was taken for granted by most Americans that the majority of people would always be poor. This was certainly the state of most immigrants in their native land. Not until the nineteenth century, when the ouput of farms, factories, and mines climbed to higher and higher levels, did Americans begin to question the assumption that poverty was the normal condition of the masses. As increased industrialization and urbanization intensified the human suffering and economic inequalities among certain segments of the community while the gross national product (GNP) continued to grow, a few social leaders began to argue, from either a moralistic or economic viewpoint, that want in America was inexcusable. Their definition of *want,* however, meant lacking sufficient resources to ward off starvation, to provide the most basic medical care, to supply a minimum of clothing and shelter, and to survive a reasonable number of years as an adult.

The community's response to starvation, to the death of persons refused medical treatment because of inability to pay, to the high mortality rates among the poor was demonstrated in a series of progressive developments: in order to ameliorate such obvious conditions of human suffering, the United States moved from a system of personal philanthropy to the development of charitable and social welfare institutions, including a network of settlement houses, privately supported bath facilities, and charity wards in voluntary hospitals. As the theme of poverty became commonplace in the literature and artistic productions of the country, and as attempts at quasi-social surveys became the vogue, increased responsibility for the care of the poor began to be lodged in government, first at the local and then at the federal level. These activities included laws that reformed, to a certain extent, conditions in the tenements of the large cities, that prohibited child labor, that regulated women's hours of work and wages, that gave limited protection to unions, and that developed programs of workmen's compensation.

Public welfare programs for the support of the unemployed and the unemployable, food supplementation, and the development of public works projects characterized the concern with poverty from the middle of the nineteenth century until the era of World War II (Brenner, 1964). It is true that one can find parallels in the presidential messages of Roosevelt during the 1930s and Johnson during the 1960s, but certainly there are qualitative differences in what each meant by poverty and what, during the intervening years, the nation came to regard as its social responsibility to do something about these conditions.

TODAY'S POOR

Many in the political and economic power structure have considerably modified their concept of who the poor are and of how their lot can be remedied and their numbers reduced. Michael Harrington (1968) has pointed out that, in contrast to the old poverty of the immigrants who came to this country with high hopes to work as unskilled or semiskilled laborers in an expanding economy, today's poor are eternal aliens in the affluent country of their birth. To quote Harrington (1968:vii):

> They are the rejects of the past. They are the people who have been driven off farmlands, workers displaced by technological advancement, old folks who face poverty in their declining years, women left alone to raise their children, unemployed teenagers and youths who

have dropped out of school but cannot find jobs. This is a new kind of poverty in a new kind of society. This is the first poverty of automation, the first poverty of the minority poor, and a poverty that under present conditions could become hereditary, transmitted from generation to generation unless the typical cycles of poverty are broken.

Harrington is only one of a number of contemporary analysts of the social scene who argue that poverty today is different from what it was in the past. It is not the temporary condition of the immigrant searching for a better life; it is not the transitory state of the young family whose breadwinner has not yet achieved success in his work career; and it is not the lot of the lazy and indolent or of the physically and mentally incompetent.

THE PERIOD OF FALSE COMPLACENCY

With respect to the availability of economic resources, the period between 1940 and 1960 can be described as one of false complacency. Not only was the country enjoying great economic prosperity, but unions had become a stable and respected force in the American economy and there was widespread belief that the social legislation of the Roosevelt era would provide sufficient governmental involvement for a sustained economic advance by the common man. Writing in *The Affluent Society,* Professor J. K. Galbraith (1958) states that poverty in this country is no longer a massive affliction but merely an afterthought. According to Galbraith, and echoed by many, the poor have dwindled to two hardcore categories. One is described as the "insular poverty" of those who live in the rural South or in occupationally depressed areas such as West Virginia. The other category is "case poverty" and includes individuals afflicted with old age, mental deficiency, poor physical health, alcoholism, and so on.

The prosperity following World War II understandably created a feeling of complacency with respect to poverty. However, in recent years not only has our definition of poverty shifted, but the "facts" upon which our complacency was based have been shown to be untrue. For example, critic Dwight MacDonald (1968) points out that while the average family income increased from $2,300 in 1929 to $7,000 in 1961, the rise in the average was largely the result of gains in income of families who already were earning over $7,500. Michael Harrington (1963), whose writings have had a major impact in molding contemporary norms of poverty, held that in 1963 between 40 and 50 million Americans—about one-fifth of the population—were living not just below the level of comfort but in real old-fashioned poverty. They were hard put to get the bare necessities of life, beginning with enough to eat.

Faulty and inappropriate use of statistics is a criticism that can be directed with some justice to even the most scholarly writers. For example, Professor Galbraith in his *The Affluent Society* used a cut-off point of $1,000 which, when adopted in 1949 as part of a congressional study, was probably too low and, to quote MacDonald (1968), ". . . in 1958, when *The Affluent Society* appeared, was simply fantastic." Of course, the issue of income still occupies a predominant place in any evaluation of poverty. Obviously man's ability to obtain goods is related to his individual gratifications and his physical and psychological well-being. The adage that anyone—at least anyone over thirty—can be happy without money just does not hold up, according to empirical sociological studies (Bradburn and Caplovitz, 1964). A more accurate observation would be that money isn't everything, but everything it isn't, it will buy. Whether hippies and flower children can continue to be happy on handouts and a shared loaf of day-old bread, only time will tell.

ABSOLUTE AND RELATIVE STANDARDS

In discussing the problem of income, one must take into account not only the amount of income necessary for survival (or some other arbitrary cut-off point), but also the question of relative inequities. Both points have been pursued in considerable detail during the past decade. As Orshansky (1965:3) has noted, in a rapidly changing pluralistic society, ". . . there cannot be one standard universally accepted and uniformly applicable by which it can be decided who is poor. Almost inevitably a single criterion applied across the board must either leave out of account some who should be there or include some who, all things considered, ought not to be classified as indigent." With due caution she argues that in 1965, on the basis of cost analyses of basic necessities, an urban family of a father, mother, and two children needed, on the average, a minimum of $3,100 a year to live. Orshansky points out that in 1963 approximately one out of seven families containing two or more persons and almost one-half of all persons living alone had incomes too low to enable them to enjoy an adequately nutritious diet and still have money left over to pay for all living essentials. As she notes, "By almost any realistic definition, individuals and families with such income—who include more than one-fifth of all our children—must be counted among our undoubted poor." She and other analysts of the problem of poverty point out that a somewhat less conservative, but by no means generous, standard that calls for about 90¢ a day for food per person and a total weekly income of $77 would add 8.8 million adults and 6.8 million children to the rosters of the poor. Thus, in terms of a moderately liberal set of criteria for minimal living standards, a total of 50 million persons, 22 million of whom are young children, exist within the bleak circle of poverty, or at least hover around its ragged edge.

In terms of relative inequity in standard of life, the poor not only represent an impressive numerical proportion of the total population but they also constitute a group that is becoming increasingly removed from the more affluent mainstream of American life. It is a well known economic fact that as family income increases the expenditures for basic essentials such as food and housing decrease proportionate to total expenditures. Therefore, the wealthier three-quarters or four-fifths of the population spend proportionately less of their gross income on necessities, leaving increasingly large surpluses to spend on other things. In the average community, members of the middle class enjoy not only more luxuries—second cars, better clothes, color TV sets, and the like—but also opportunities for higher quality medical care, better schools, and more advanced education for their children. All of this is not lost upon the poor in our midst.

Proportionate to their income, the poor pay more for goods and services than do the rich (Caplovitz, 1963). For example, it has been calculated that a family in the under-$2,000 category is expending approximately 28 per cent of its income for taxes, while the tax bite for those in the $10,000 to $14,000 bracket is only 24 per cent. Of course, some of the highest income earners in the country manage, through tax shelters, depletion allowances, and other loopholes, to pay no income tax at all. When it comes to the acquisition of capital goods—furniture, appliances, automobiles, and the like—the poverty-striken consumer, in American slang, "gets taken." As noted in a recent study by Caplovitz (1963), people with small incomes lack not only the ready cash for discount purchases of major durables but also that popular substitute for cash—credit. Because many of these families have highly mobile residential patterns and poor work histories, they do not meet the requirements for obtaining good credit, that is, a stable job, home ownership, and friends who can vouch for them. The result, of course, is a high markup on low-quality goods, the major device merchants use to protect themselves against the risks of doing business with low-income clients. In virtually every low-income area one sees a proliferation of no-money-down, easy-credit type stores. This policy, according to Caplovitz' study, represents a marked departure from the normal marketing situation in which competition between merchants results in a pricing policy roughly equivalent with the quality of the goods. Apparently merchants in poverty-striken areas do not see themselves as competing with stores outside the neighborhood. Ironically, this means that the people who are least able to afford the goods they buy must pay the highest prices relative to quality and receive the lowest return on their dollar. Moreover, since their customers do not meet the economic requirements of the larger marketplace, these merchants have a captive market and offer service on a take-it-or-leave-it basis.

But this is only the beginning. In addition to being exploited or, at the very least, subjected to unusual and inequitable business practices, the poor are frequently at the mercy of the customer peddlers or canvassers who abound in low-income areas. The customer peddler operates as a sort of poor merchant's Dun & Bradstreet, providing store owners with information on who is likely to meet his financial obligations and who is not. The peddler's prime asset is his personal relationship with the customers; through visits to the home, he gets to know the entire family, its habits, and its wants. In many instances, store owners employ such peddlers as salesmen on a commission basis, and merchants report that peddlers are apt to charge five and six times the amount the store charges for relatively inexpensive items.

It has been documented that in low-income areas even the local outlets of some chain-store supermarkets either charge higher prices or sell inferior quality merchandise at advertised prices. In so many ways, then, the system not only forces persons to live at the brink, literally, of starvation but imposes conditions under which persons with marginal and minimal incomes are increasingly excluded from the consumer opportunities enjoyed by the rest of the population. Even today, apparently very little is being done about the problems of discrimination against consumers. According to an article by the staff of *Consumers Union* (1967:52), some six of the twenty largest cities in the United States do not include even token programs of consumer education in their welfare or housing departments. Although efforts at consumer education are increasing, the article notes, they are small in comparison to the effort needed; there is little coordination and exchange of information; and programs vary widely in method, content, and overall philosophy.

COMPLEXITIES AND CONSEQUENCES

Other characteristics of poverty need to be noted briefly, for they will be the subject of separate analysis in later chapters. It is of major concern that many of the poor are black. The interaction between discrimination (see Chapter 6) and poverty complicate both sets of problems. Consideration of the ethnic character of the poor involves more than an accumulation of individual situations that violate the general norm. As evidenced by the rioting and destruction in our core cities during the past several years, the combination of discrimination and poverty represents a threat to the lives and property of all community members, both those living in the pockets of poverty and those living outside. These conditions of unrest and violence have further hastened the departure of middle-income families from the centers of our major cities. The problems of the inner city are further compounded by the association—if not outright causal link—of poverty and lower socio-economic status to many forms of individual deviant behavior, including crime, delinquency, mental illness, and so on.

Furthermore, virtually every institution of social control is faced with deficiencies having immediate bearing on the problem of poverty. While the nation as a whole suffers from tremendous shortages of manpower resources in many fields, the poor suffer from high rates of unemployment and underemployment. If the community is to meet its need for manpower, reduce the rejection rate for military service, and increase the ability of individuals to cope with employment opportunities that require literacy skills, creativity, and some technical knowledge, it must concern itself with the problems of poverty and the poor. For not only do the poor constitute an expendable pool of manpower, but their presence in the community drains existing human and financial resources to maintain their present minimal standard of living. Welfare expenses make up an increasingly large part of local and state budgets, and the personnel needed to administer such programs represent an important segment of the public and private work force. Estimates of the total budgets for health and welfare services run as high as $70 billion, while total manpower involved in the delivery of such services may run as high as four million. It has been estimated that the cumulative man-hours devoted to treatment and prevention programs directed at the problems of poverty are roughly equivalent to one man-year of employment for each five persons in the poverty group. In other words, as much as 20 per cent of the labor force in the United States is directly or indirectly working on the conditions of poverty in this country.

THE CYCLE OF POVERTY

The overwhelming characteristic of the current poverty problem is its tendency to persist over time, a situation that has been referred to as the *cycle of poverty*. (*See* Documentation 1.) It is difficult to argue that poverty today is a transitory thing that affects individuals only temporarily during parts of their lives or strikes sporatically during periods of dramatic shifts in the economy. Rather, thousands of people are born poor, live poor, and die poor. Even worse, their children have little hope of escaping and many will be doomed to repeat the cycle. This is more than a matter of humanitarian concern or simply a problem of the distribution of manpower and financial resources within the community. This massive number of people, including high concentrations of blacks and other minority groups, represents large segments of the population who do not participate in the social or the political life of the country, who are not related to the upward mobility pattern common in society, who are unusually susceptible to the unscrupulous influences of some charismatic leaders, and who constitute among their number a potentially

the vicious cycle of poverty

THE POVERTY CYCLE

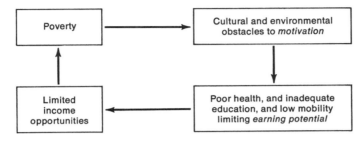

The sources of poverty are not listed in chronological sequence. The vicious cycle, in which poverty breeds poverty, occurs through time, and transmits its effects from one generation to another. There is no beginning to the cycle, no end. There is, therefore, no one "right" place to break into it: increasing opportunities may help little if health, educational attainments and motivation are unsuitable; making more education available may bear little fruit unless additional employment opportunities exist; altering adverse environmental factors may not be feasible or effective unless access to education and . . . job opportunities is enhanced.

Programs to attack each of the three principal stages in the poverty cycle may be directed at one or more of three levels: (1) prevent the problem from developing, (2) rehabilitate the person who has been hurt, and (3) ameliorate the difficulties of persons for whom prevention or rehabilitation are not feasible. Each type of "treatment" is associated generally with a separate stage in the life cycle. Prevention of poverty calls for attention principally to youngsters (and to their parents, insofar as parents' attitudes and values affect the children). Rehabilitation of those missed by preventive efforts, or for whom these efforts were ineffective, seems best designed for adults in their productive work years. Amelioration of poverty seems called for in the case of the aged, the physically and mentally disabled, and those for whom prevention and rehabilitation are ineffective. (Moynihan, 1969:9.)

destructive group in the community. It is clear to most social planners, who may disagree about the methods of intervention, that unless the community mobilizes efforts to break the cycle of poverty, the risks are great that the poor may indeed be organized in ways that result in chaos and massive destruction and disorganization within the community. Witness the riots of the past several summers.

Concepts about the causes of poverty have changed considerably since leaders in the economic, political, and health-and-welfare fields first became concerned with the problem. Cultural and individual characteristics accounted for many of the problems facing the early poor—the European immigrants—and the "case" poor—Galbraith's term for the aged, the handicapped, etc. Where these characteristics are still operant, the problems remain.

CULTURAL DIFFERENCES

Certainly in the 1800s, and even into the early 1900s, rapid industrialization and expansion created a need for manpower and labor, especially in the large cities. The "staging areas" for this industrial onslaught were the poverty-ridden tenement slums where individuals lived largely unrelated and unsocialized to the complexities and styles of urban society. Cultural differences and a limited command of English restricted their full participation in the economy.

Today these limitations are minimal and, with the possible exception of Cuban refugees and emigrant Puerto Ricans, contribute little to current problems of poverty. Contemporary poverty is no longer open to the ready solutions of evening language classes and multilingual foremen in industrial plants. Deficiencies of culture and communication continue as major explanations for the present problem of poverty but in a different sense from that which prevailed during the period of mass emigration.

INDIVIDUAL CHARACTERISTICS

Although Galbraith's estimates and projections regarding poverty in the United States have been questioned, certainly everyone will grant that those persons he describes as "defectives" continue to exist, representing one of the plaguing problems of poverty. There are, first of all, groups of individuals whose physical or biological condition limits their economic participation. These include the mentally retarded, the physically handicapped, and those with emotional illnesses. In many of these cases, the etiology of the particular handicap is not solely a biochemical condition but is also a problem of distorted attitudes and values toward traditional concepts of work and workers. Nevertheless, as long as some citizens are not provided an opportunity for participation in the worlds of education and work because they are unsocialized or mentally or physically unfit, the defective will continue to account for a significant proportion, but by no means the majority, of the poverty group.

Another important category for whom poverty is, at least to some extent, the result of an individual characteristic as well as of biological and physiological processes is the growing number of individuals of advanced age in our culture. In a later chapter we will discuss the aged as a stage in the life cycle. Although our concept of old age is changing and man's years of useful life are being extended, nevertheless, the concomitants of aging, i.e., poor health, loss of energy, and so on, have produced a significant number of persons who are poor primarily because of their debility. It should be noted that persons of advanced age—75 years and older, to use an arbitrary limit—constitute one of the fastest growing population groups in the country. Although many of these were highly productive and well-paid during their work years, they entered the job market at a time when public provisions for social security were either absent or minimal and, consequently, few are eligible for anything but the minimum social security benefits. Moreover, with the constantly rising cost of living in the United States, those private retirement and pension plans which may have been relatively munificent during the 1930s represent a small pittance in terms of today's inflated dollar.

STRUCTURAL CAUSES

In large measure, however, the emphasis in the search for causes of poverty has shifted from the individual to the social structure of the community. In all of the social-control systems we have discussed, there has been a reluctance, indeed a definite failure in some instances, to accord any—let alone equal—opportunity for the poor to participate. This deficiency is most apparent in the world of work, and no doubt this area is the most significant and should receive the focus of our concern. But we have come to realize that the deprivations of the poor also extend to educational opportunities, health-and-welfare resources, recreational facilities, stable marital and family relationships, political participation in community life, and even to fair and equal treatment before the law.

The inequities faced by the poor because of the way legal justice is currently administered has been the occasion for increased concern. As Carlin, Howard, and Messinger (1966:85–86) note:

> The law is, above all, a means of creating and protecting rights. We must inquire more fully into the extent to which it performs this essential function for the poor. For example, to what extent do potential recipients of public assistance have recourse through law when they are denied assistance, or when benefits are reduced, or are less than the recipient is entitled to? To the extent that the law provides determinate criteria for eligibility decisions and regular procedures for challenging these decisions, the benefit takes on the character of a "right." To the extent that the criteria are vague—or to the extent that

the law fails to require public assistance administrators to make their criteria known—the benefit remains a "privilege." We know something of the conditions under which "privileges" are transformed into "rights"—this has happened, for example, to benefits for the aged.

The idealized concept of the "respectable poor" that dominated an earlier period of American thought is becoming increasingly irrelevant, if it ever did reflect reality. The romantic view of the respectable poor is of an intact family of several children, a hardworking mother who strictly disciplined them and planned for their future, and a husband who did a dollar's work for a dollar's pay. Perhaps he drank a bit too much, but otherwise the head of the house was content to come home at the end of the day, take off his shoes, smoke his pipe, and doze over the newspaper. Did these families ever exist? Probably not, because even steady employment at low wages precludes much respectability given the conditions of slum housing and corruption that surround the low-income worker living in the core city.

THE WORKING POOR

It is important to emphasize that the poor are not limited to those who are unemployed, to unwed mothers who must care for their illegitimate children, or to the aged and infirm. Their numbers are swelled by a cadré of employed individuals whose occupational careers make no provisions for increases in income or upward mobility. As Tyler (1961) of the International Ladies' Garment Workers' Union relates, even union members can be counted among the indigent. He points out that sources of poverty are generally sought among the ranks of the unemployed and the unorganized low-income worker, with little attention paid to the poor who are employed in marginal industries covered by union contracts. Tyler argues that where there is a high concentration of competitive industry, such as in New York City, wage structures do not meet minimal standards of living. He describes New York, the richest city in the world, as a sector of poverty. The impression that union workers are reasonably well off, or certainly not poor, is based upon the wage scales of workers in mechanized, monopolistic industries. Workers in wage-oriented competitive industries may be poverty striken even in the midst of affluence, and many of them make up a significant part of the one-fifth of the nation who are ill-fed, ill-clothed, and ill-housed.

The Bureau of Labor Statistics' figures on unemployment do not include any of these working poor. In recent years the bureau has experimented with an index that would be more sensitive to the underemployment rate (U.S. Department of Labor, 1967). This index reflects not only the unemployed who are out of work and actively seeking a job but also the unemployed who have given up looking, part-time workers who desire full-time employment, and employees who are receiving less than the legal minimum wage. These last may be working in jobs not covered by the law, but more often they are being exploited by unscrupulous employers who knowingly violate the law. The seasonal aspects of much employment is an additional element in below-standard incomes. Workers may be paid a legal wage for full-time work, but the work lasts for only a few weeks or months during the year. All of these underpaid and seasonally paid groups contribute their numbers to the swelling army of the poor.

the subculture of poverty

One aspect of poverty about which there is controversial evidence is the concept of a subculture of poverty. In terms of etiology it is important to know whether the subculture exists because the institutionalized means for achieving normative cultural goals are lacking or because the cultural goals themselves are unknown to the poor. American folklore implies that the poor, or many of them, lived happy, fulfilled lives. Cowboy stories describe the life of the migrant ranch hand as one of independence, high adventure, and good-fellowship capped by a stimulating sense of risk and danger. In a similar vein, we have the image of the Italian laborer returning from Sunday mass to enjoy a game of bocci on the neighborhood green, or of the Jewish garment worker surrounded by his warm and boisterous family with its strong attachments to the teeming ghetto-like neighborhood.

ACHIEVING CULTURAL GOALS

A number of writers, such as Walter Miller (1958) and Oscar Lewis (1966), hold that the way of life, the values, and the characteristic patterns of behavior represent aspects of a distinctive social system, and that lower-class persons hold deviant cultural goals and values rather than institutionalized ones. Miller claims that lower-class culture is a distinctive condition, many centuries old, with an integrity of its own. Not many analysts of poverty in America subscribe fully to this orientation (Valentine, 1968); however, as we shall discuss when we turn to intervention approaches, to break the cycle of poverty may require an intensification or innovation of cultural goals as well as development of institutionalized means. Regardless, it is evident that few would subscribe to the "joys and satisfactions" of poverty.

While it is probably true that there are gratifications open to the poor in their day-to-day life which the middle-class person does not experience, accusations of middle-class bias aside, there appears to be little that is charming or romantic about the current way of life in the slum. Admittedly the poor have their roots in the peasant class from which they came or in the rural Southern traditions of their parents and grandparents; nevertheless, from the structural point of view, the problems of the poor stem primarily from a lack of opportunity and knowledge of institutionalized means to achieve cultural goals.

The difficulties with the culture-of-poverty approach are summed up well by Roach and Gursslin (1967:387–388):

> . . . studies show that most of the poor do have a relatively homogeneous socio-economic background, share a common set of life conditions, and live in close proximity in residential enclaves. The presence of these attributes has no doubt been instrumental in leading many writers to the conclusion of a culture of poverty. But these attributes are not in themselves sufficient for the emergence and maintenance of a viable subculture. Of more critical importance would be characteristics of the poor pertaining to their social psychology and the nature of their social relationships. Most writers, whether treating specifically the culture of poverty or other types of subcultures, appear to assume that these requisite characteristics are present.
>
> Relevant empirical findings do not support this assumption as it relates to the poverty group. Evidence from many studies describes various social-psychological handicaps of the poor; notably, cognitive restrictions, limited role skills, apathy, and a general state of "psychic exhaustion." Granting that knowledge is limited concerning the requisites of an adequate social actor, it seems questionable that persons with such handicaps can form and maintain the types of cultural systems implied in writings on the culture of poverty.

In an attempt to place the concept of a subculture of poverty in a useful perspective, Rodman (1963) has suggested the concept of "the lower-class value stretch." He holds that the consequence of a life of poverty is not simply an absence or loss of middle-class values. Rather, he suggests that the lower-class person typically shares the middle-class values, at least to a degree, while at the same time holding deviant values that may be regarded as unique to the lower class. Given the availability of both sets, the lower-class individual is able to adapt to his circumstances without necessarily becoming a revolutionary or an extremely deviant individual. Rodman uses the phrase "lower-class value stretch" to refer to the process by which the lower-class person places himself in a better adaptive position by providing himself with a wider range of values with which to operate. In other words, what some analysts argue is a separate set of values, Rodman sees as a response of the person in poverty to his life situation. Such characteristics as "promiscuous" sexual relations, "illegitimate" children, "deserting" husbands and fathers, and "unmarried" mothers are frequently viewed in a gross manner as simply *problems* of the lower class. Rodman has pointed out "that it makes more sense to think of them as [attempted] *solutions* of the lower class to problems they face in the social, economic, and perhaps legal and political life."

The widespread lack of opportunity to utilize institutionalized means relates to Galbraith's notions of insular poverty and the potential impact on the poor of cultural isolation and communication barriers as contributory influences in the etiology of poverty. In *The Affluent Society,* Galbraith (1958) refers to pockets of poverty that exist in the rural South and in states, such as those in Appalachia, with geoecological deficiencies. What he failed to consider is the fact that pockets of poverty exist in every large city as well as in the cotton fields of Mississippi and the hills of West Virginia. He failed to recognize that inadequate schools, differential treatment by police, distasteful experiences with voluntary agencies, apathetic interest of public welfare workers, and general repugnance by middle-class community members, as well as geography and ecology, can function to produce insular poverty.

Clearly, within such islands the lack of institutionalized norms is not the only cause of poverty. The problem is compounded by the inadequate socialization of individuals which prevents them from using and manipulating the normative means that are available.

intervention and control

In our discussion of etiology we readily admit our bias in support of the contention that the major social problems of the poor are associated with aspects of social structure. Certainly it is true that most of the massive efforts being undertaken today are consistent with this point of view. As suggested in Chapter 3, any discussion of intervention techniques must differentiate among primary, secondary, and tertiary strategies, that is, prevention of the causal conditions, control of the etiologic factors, and amelioration of the afflicted group. (*See* Documentation 2.)

INDIVIDUALIZED APPROACHES

Under the influence of concepts of individual causation, considerable effort has been expended to alleviate some of the underlying causes of poverty. This is particularly true for the significant number of poor whose status is related to health problems and biophysiological inadequacies. We have learned ways of preventing such deficiencies, at least

intervening variable model

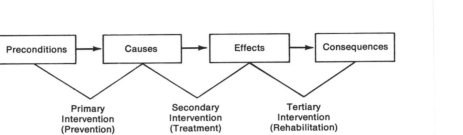

We may view a social action program as a form of intervention which attempts to prevent certain undesirable effects or consequences from developing by a deliberate attack upon causes or antecedent events. Employing the analytic model of intervening variable analysis, we may conceptualize the intervention process largely as one attempting to alter the causal nexus between the independent and dependent variable through manipulation of the intervening variables by means of which the cause leads to the effect, or which modify or condition the effect.

Three such major independent-intervening-dependent subgroupings exist: (1) the relationship between the precondition and causal variables, (2) the relationship between the cause-and-effect variables, and (3) the relationship between the effect and the consequence variables. Each of these pairs of relationships may be analyzed in terms of the intervening variables occurring between the two, and each pair offers a conceptually different possibility of prevention through intervention with the intervening variable. These three possibilities may be diagrammed as follows: We may briefly note some significant difference

for certain specific pathological conditions. Take, for example, the incidence of mental retardation among children whose mothers suffered certain illnesses, such as German measles, during pregnancy.

At the primary level, effective public health programs have served to reduce somewhat the incidence of new cases of retardation by providing better prenatal care for indigent mothers. At the secondary level of treatment, extensive programs have been introduced in recent years to combat and control mental retardation. These programs will be discussed more fully in later chapters on life-cycle problems, but they include physical therapy and special training in the early years. Even more elaborate programs have been undertaken at the tertiary level of intervention. Mechanisms for treating those already afflicted by physical and mental handicaps include vocational rehabilitation and counseling for the young and programs of medical care and expanded social security insurance for

in the three major areas of social action programs today—health, education, and welfare—in regard to both traditional and future activities. Traditionally, the field of health or medicine is largely concerned with the treatment process; physicians provide medical care to patients who have already developed the causes of illness and the objective of medical "intervention" is to prevent the full effects of the disease—death or disability—from developing. Thus, the current emphasis of medical programs is predominantly upon secondary prevention. However, with the increasing importance of the chronic degenerative diseases (such as heart disease or diabetes) where medical treatment offers little promise of any cure, the shift of future programs is toward tertiary prevention or rehabilitation of the patient who has already suffered the effects of the disease or disability, and to a lesser degree, upon primary prevention to decrease the probability of the development of causes. . . .

In regard to education, the traditional emphasis has also been upon secondary intervention, the major objective of educational programs being to decrease the negative effects of a lack of education by intervening with teaching and training programs aimed at preventing the effects of ignorance or a lack of skill. Today, there is increasing emphasis, on the one hand, upon tertiary intervention designed to reduce the consequences of a lack of education by providing adult education and training programs, and, on the other hand, upon primary intervention with preschool programs aimed at overcoming some of the preconditions of the culturally disadvantaged which interfere with their exposure to the desirable effects of educational intervention.

Finally, in the field of welfare, we find social work overwhelmingly concerned with meeting the *consequences* of poverty and misfortune in what might be called tertiary intervention or the amelioration of social ills that have already occurred. Here, too, however, traditional programs are being increasingly challenged by those progressives in the field of social work who argue that what is needed is a greater emphasis upon primary intervention, or an attack by social work upon the preconditions of social problems, and secondary intervention or social work intervention to prevent existing social conditions from developing their full negative effects. (Suchman, 1968:173–174.)

the aged. It is all too evident, however, that such individualized intervention techniques, at whatever level, are not going to remove the major causes of the cycle of poverty that plagues so many people.

STRUCTURAL APPROACHES

The most promising efforts being undertaken today and projected in the future are primarily structural ones. In many cases, these efforts include the added component of an attack on the cultural limitations of the poor by maximizing their knowledge and manipulative skills with respect to normative cultural goals (Gordon, 1967).

Before discussing these structural intervention techniques, it should be noted that the influence of persons whose orientation is based primarily on the motivation of community members and on the individual-

DOCUMENTATION 3

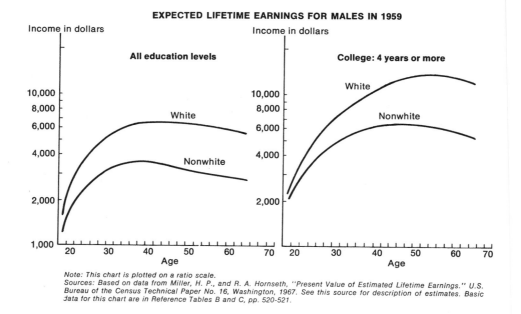

EXPECTED LIFETIME EARNINGS FOR MALES IN 1959

Note: This chart is plotted on a ratio scale.
Sources: Based on data from Miller, H. P., and R. A. Hornseth, "Present Value of Estimated Lifetime Earnings." U.S. Bureau of the Census Technical Paper No. 16, Washington, 1967. See this source for description of estimates. Basic data for this chart are in Reference Tables B and C, pp. 520-521.

ization of care remains very strong. There is still considerable argument in many circles about the need for highly professionalized persons and the great utility of psychotherapy and individual casework in dealing with these populations. This influence continues even though there is little evidence, for example, that professional social workers have more success than untrained personnel, or that treated groups show more improvement than untreated control groups in achieving academically (Meyer, Borgatta, and Jones, 1965), in getting off welfare rolls (Brown, 1968), in preventing juvenile delinquency (Walter B. Miller, 1962; Tait and Hodges, 1962; Ikeda, 1967), or in maintaining successful employment (Office of Juvenile Delinquency and Youth Development, 1966). The trend, however, is clearly in the direction of structural interventions that provide institutionalized means for involving the poor in the economic sector, in developing their acceptance of normative cultural

In 1959, young white males could expect their earnings to rise to a peak about twice that of a nonwhite. For equivalent education levels (nominally equivalent, i.e., without regard to quality differences) white college graduates could look forward to an even higher relative difference in income growth than a nonwhite. Equally important, according to our conjecture on the significance of growth with maturation, is the fact that income for a white person continues to rise for a number of years after the earlier peak is reached for a nonwhite. The longer period of income growth with age is even more marked for white college graduates compared with their nonwhite counterparts. Clearly, however, both white and nonwhite college graduates could look forward to substantially more growth in income than their corresponding group average.

The data in the chart [opposite] are intended to illustrate only broadly the different patterns of expectation of income growth. They are by no means precise for several reasons. First, of course, a cross-section for 1959 may not fully reflect changes over time. Second, no adjustment is made in these figures (although data are available in the original source) for differences resulting from economic growth. This factor has been discussed earlier. Third, no adjustment was made for the difference between whites and nonwhites in their evaluation of the future. It seems reasonable to suppose ...that nonwhites discount the future at a higher rate (in other words, value it less) than whites. A higher discount rate for nonwhites than for whites, in order to show the present value of expected earnings, would widen the relative differences between whites and nonwhites. . . .

By way of summary, the examination of data on income in relation to age has shown that this growth with age is far less evident for the disadvantaged than for others. More specifically, . . . it is far more marked for whites than nonwhites for each level of education completed. This was particularly evident in the measure of earning power as indicated in the figure on lifetime earnings. . . . College graduates have a much more pronounced growth in income with age than those with less schooling, but the difference between white and nonwhite is greater at this level than at lower education levels. (Moss, 1968:475–477.)

goals, and in teaching them strategies to integrate institutionalized means with cultural goals. This has been the promise of federal poverty programs.

The current efforts at the federal level to deal with the one-fifth of the nation involved in the cycle of poverty involve a number of related objectives. The core of the problem is, of course, the modification of the opportunity structure with respect to the world of work to enable persons from families on welfare or households with low income to have a much greater chance to participate in the occupational affluence of the country. It follows, of course, that such programs heavily emphasize education and vocational training and, in a variety of ways, seek to provide the range of intellectual and technical competence necessary to compete in today's world of work. Education is in many ways the key to higher earned income. (*See* Documentation 3.) Engagement in this almost overwhelming task involves both the modification of existing institutional-ized means by which people succeed educationally and occupationally, and modifying the industrial and economic structure in ways that permit the acceptance and integration of such individuals into the economic mainstream of American life.

MODIFYING THE MEANS

Attempts to modify institutionalized means involve both changing existing means and supplementing them with new approaches. For example, efforts have been directed at modifying the philosophies and practices underly-ing the operation of most vocational high schools so that their students are more realistically prepared for the job opportunities that actually exist in the community. At the same time, vocational curricula must be enriched so that attendance at such schools does not entirely cut off the opportunities for university and advanced technical education. In addi-tion, the educational climate must be modified so that no stigma or nega-tive identification attaches to students attending such institutions. It is also necessary to supplement such changes, even if they can be accom-plished, with new types of apprenticeship, work-study, and part-time job programs for these students. As we shall discuss subsequently, there are many barriers to these efforts, and one cannot be entirely optimistic about their ultimate, or even immediate, success.

MODIFYING THE STRUCTURE

The corollary task of modifying the opportunity structure also raises major problems. Galbraith's observations about insular poverty are applicable to the core of a large city. For example, low-income areas lacking adequate transportation to adjacent industrial complexes are as much "islands" as are towns that do not constitute attractive sites for new industry. Modification of the opportunity structure involves much more than transportation and ecology, however, for it necessitates reforming or forsaking many requirements that now characterize the economic sector of the community. To cite only a few examples: Many large cities re-quire applicants for such civil service jobs as garbageman to have a high school diploma; a number of craft unions demand character references or devise other discriminatory means to restrict apprenticeship positions to relatives or friends of persons already in the craft; and many large industrial companies make employment dependent upon scoring high on written intelligence and aptitude tests which reflect middle-class value orientations, particularly for positions with opportunities for upward mobility. It is fair to observe that efforts to modify the opportunity structure in even trifling ways in order to accommodate some of the characteristics of people from low-income areas have proved difficult and, in many instances, impossible to accomplish (Bredemeier, 1964). In this regard it must also be noted that many public agencies at federal, state, and local levels are as reluctant to change their ways and thinking as are unions and industrial corporations (Carlin, Howard, and Messinger, 1966).

Planners and interventionists engaged in poverty rehabilitation recognize that the mere provision of education and occupational training and the accomplishment of changes in the opportunity structure will not and cannot break the cycle of poverty in the terms we are discussing. Important areas of interpersonal life outside the world of work present critical needs for legal, medical, psychological, and recreational services which must be provided if the low-income person is to have fundamentally the same opportunities to acquire social habits, to care for his body and mind, and to protect his good name as have the more affluent members of the community.

To cite just one example, it is widely recognized that under our present judicial system the lower-class individual has much less opportunity, given the same set of circumstances, to press his claims and to receive equitable treatment under the law (Carlin, Howard, and Messinger, 1966). While it is true that certain recent rulings of the Supreme Court make it the responsibility of the courts to assure counsel for individuals in criminal cases, such cases constitute a very small portion of the interaction between community members and the legal system. Many transactions of a felonious nature, such as swindles and fraudulent contracts, are settled through compromises and informal mechanisms before they even reach the courts.

By far the greatest involvement of individuals with the legal system takes place not through criminal proceedings but through civil contests. These include conflicts between landlord and tenant, merchant and consumer, and public regulatory bodies and their clients. Undoubtedly millions of letters are written each year by irate customers to merchants, large corporations, and public officials threatening legal action if satisfactory consideration is not given to some matter. Admittedly, most of these threats are not carried out, certainly not by the poor who lack access to a lawyer to press their cases. The individual community member, when similarly harassed by business or financial agents, need not be unduly alarmed if he knows the legal mechanisms and has the financial means to obtain professional advice. But what of the low-income family or the family on welfare? Do they have the same opportunity to engage as an adversary in such situations? To fill this need, efforts are being made to establish systems of legal aid that will allow the poor to participate, at least to some extent, in the legal interactions that comprise day-to-day community living. Similar innovations can be found in the areas of medical and dental care, psychiatric treatment, and even in public services such as police protection, garbage collection and sanitation, health inspection of public facilities, enforcement of building code violations, and so forth.

involvement of the poor

Efforts at the restructuring of services and the development of more equitable utilization patterns cannot be accomplished solely by legislative efforts or by outside interventionists acting as "inspector-generals" to make certain that reasonably equal entitlement becomes a way of life throughout the community. During the 1960s, legislation was passed at the federal level which for the first time provided a major mechanism for breaking the cycle of poverty, namely, collective actions among the poor themselves. Supporters argued that it is important for community members in low-income areas not only to share in the decisions relating to the amelioration and control of their own social problems, but also to perceive themselves as having a voice and role in community life. Provisions called for representatives of the poor to sit on the boards and advisory councils of the various community-action programs designed to improve conditions, to stimulate and develop mechanisms for increased activity in the community's political life, and to provide opportunities for social action outside the ghetto areas.

TACTICS AND STRATEGIES

In the development of the poor's role in effecting social change, a number of different tactics or strategies have been advocated. Perhaps the most extreme one to gain wide acceptance was devised, or at least promoted, by Saul Alinsky. Riessman (1965:34) provides an analysis of the Alinsky model:

> Alinksy's Industrial Areas Foundation, functioning on a low budget without government support, has two major objectives in the communities it helps to organize: eradication of local grievances such as consumer fraud, and the development of independence and dignity on the part of the presumably apathetic, dependent peoples.

In the same article, Riessman is properly critical of the limitations of Alinsky's approach, and he quotes the observations of S. M. Miller and Martin Rein on its extremely localistic character:

. . . only some of the problems of the poor can be solved through neighborhood, or even city, changes. Increasingly, national action is needed. Consequently, the poor have to be organized on a continuing and wide basis in order to gain the political clout that will produce sweeping reforms (Riessman, 1965:35).

Riessman concludes with a consideration of alternatives, including the Alinsky model, for effective social action:

The Alinsky Model. Despite the limitations we have discussed, it suggests one extremely important possibility: namely that the various Alinsky-organized communities could, in fact, be brought together. They could be united around larger issues of relevance to the poor thus increasing their political clout and removing them from their over-emphasis on local concerns. This could provide the potential for a larger social movement. Such an undertaking obviously presents many difficulties as social movements have rarely been built in this way. The question arises immediately as to what are the larger issues that would unite these diverse local groups.

The Labor Movement. Its potential unity with community organization groups and with the war on poverty creates a possibility for social action. Walter Reuther has spearheaded the Citizen's Crusade against Poverty (CCAP) which could play a powerful role in developing community action, and conceivably at a certain point, could articulate with the civil rights movement and the Alinsky community groups.

The Civil Rights Movement. There are numerous possibilities for expansion in the present period. It could develop neighborhood-based community action programs (CORE is planning such a project) and could unite further with the growing youth movement. It could unite with the Alinsky forces, and it could unite with the intellectuals, who are searching for new forms of citizen involvement. What we are suggesting is that the civil rights movement could use its clout best in support of well-developed, well-thought-out economic, political, and social programs related to housing, education, integration, employment, anti-poverty measures. Intellectuals, because of their isolation from the power forces in the society, could benefit enormously by being stimulated to develop programs in these areas. Through the demand of civil rights forces, intellectuals would recognize that they had an audience and a power force behind them to implement these programs—a new and exciting unity might emerge. Similarly, intellectuals might work together with the Alinsky groups and with community action organizations led by the labor movement. Both the intellectuals and the groups they work with might profit enormously from this form of involvement—the movements could achieve far greater breadth and theoretic focus from such a coalition (Riessman, 1965:36–37).

In addition to encouraging the poor to participate in social action at the policy level, efforts are being initiated to use indigenous workers in some professional roles. This is being done not only to meet the shortage of professional personnel but to test the theory that the poor may be best able to deal with certain problems of poverty. As Gordon (1967: 539) notes, if the existing structure of professions is failing to meet the need, it seems foolish to treat the problem by increasing the dosage of the same medicine. He goes on to cite a number of sound reasons why the indigenous person may indeed be a more powerful agent of individual and social change in ameliorating conditions of poverty:

> The indigenous leader can communicate instantly to the suspicious and distrustful client, avoiding noblesse oblige, in a way that many middle-class professionals cannot do when dealing with disaffected, hostile, anomic youths who see the middle-class agency worker as part of the system against which he is fighting. In the long run, disparities between the class castes of counselor and client might make no difference in the outcome of the counseling, if the long run is long enough and the counseling approaches psychotherapy in its depth and intensiveness. But the kind of work which will be most common in the various phases of the Anti-Poverty Program is not likely to use the long run, and in brief contacts, first impressions can be all important in determining whether the client will be relaxed and receptive, or on his guard and defensive. Indigenous personnel who "speak the client's language" can form an extremely effective bridge between the milieu of the client and the milieu of agency; they can make important contributions to the counseling team in contacting the clients to be served, in maintaining them through their agency contacts, and may be particularly effective in follow-up work with the clients in their home, community, and on the job. A client is more likely to be able to report continuing difficulties, after his counseling contacts, to an indigenous worker, than he is to the professional interviewer toward whom the ethic of mutual cooperation and courtesy requires that he affirm the success of the counseling and deny continued problems (Gordon, 1965:340).

These programs, supported by hundreds of millions of dollars and staffed by a large number of dedicated individuals throughout the country, have proceeded for the past several years despite a large number of inherent difficulties that have minimized their effectiveness or at least rendered them less than satisfactory from the standpoint of efficiency and speed of implementation. We have already alluded to some of the basic difficulties in effecting changes by adapting institutionalized means or shifting the modes of economic operation to accommodate such proposals. Some criticisms of these efforts are unfounded, including remarks that question the motives of the participating poor or the innovators from the outside who engage in action programs. Some criticisms are the inevitable consequence of the mass mobilization of efforts, the development of a new federal bureaucracy, and the attempt to launch programs in the face of severe shortages of qualified, competent personnel. In addition, there are some basic issues that have not been confronted satisfactorily.

Perhaps the major concern of those social scientists who accept the basic philosophy of current efforts to break the poverty cycle is the appropriateness of the programs in terms of the recipients' level of cultural adaptation and competence in communication. Many of the programs flounder because the low-income person just does not have the requisite means and knowledge to engage successfully in them. Even when needed services, such as those of dentists, optometrists, and physicians, are made available and paid for, their use requires participation in interaction patterns that are often foreign to low-income persons. Lack of so-called middle-class habits, such as keeping appointments, taking initiative, dressing appropriately, speaking correctly, behaving in a mannerly way, represent major difficulties in carrying out such programs. Among the poor there are persons who are unaware of the importance of carrying change to make a telephone call for an appointment with a prospective employer or a pencil to write down the interview time, who do not know how to get from one place to another by public transportation, who are unable to check the calculations of the drugstore clerk when purchasing a number of items, or who have no idea of what is appropriate attire for work. In seeking to solve problems of this order, important attempts have been made to socialize individuals in ways that permit them to use the institutionalized means provided. Many of the concepts we discussed under learning theory, as one form of individual approach to the solution of social problems, are being undertaken, including classes in speech improvement, literacy skills, and deportment and personal care.

THE ISSUE OF SEPARATE PROGRAMS

There is a recognition in many places that these learning-theory programs for the poor cannot—at least not immediately—be modeled after their middle-class counterparts. This is, indeed, a dilemma. In these times the phrase "separate but equal" has invidious overtones. Yet, can we expect the poor, who have had literally no experience with, for example, the use of private physicians for preventive health services, to be receptive to such care (Lambert and Freeman, 1967)? Or must we accept the concept of the large, noisy, sprawling city hospital, and devote our efforts to making it not like a private group practice center or private voluntary hospital, but a place where high quality medical care can be provided in ways more consistent with the past experiences of the poor?

A similar situation prevails with respect to educational programs. Can the child living with seven siblings in a four-room flat in a noisy tenement be expected to have a quiet place to study, or is it necessary to build study halls or extend the school day for these children to provide the functional equivalent of the family study or private bedroom in which the middle-class, suburban child does his homework?

Many of the programs operating under the War on Poverty also seek to make provisions for the employment, on a paid or volunteer basis, of members of the community who are themselves being served by the programs. This is done, it is held, not only to increase the involvement of the poor in such activities but to ensure more effective handling of the problem of communication (Bredemeier, 1964). Some proponents have gone so far as to argue that poverty programs should be of the poor, by the poor, and for the poor. Critics of this view point out that specialized efforts, which in a sense serve to differentiate the low-income person from his more middle-class community peers, have the consequence of further encapsulating the poor. Such critics feel that the motives of individuals who emphasize this approach are similar to those of Southerners who pridefully point to the modern all-Negro high school or the well-equipped wing of the charity hospital for blacks. This is an unsolved problem in terms of the current poverty efforts. While ideologically and philosophically separation of services for low-income community members does limit opportunities for interaction with more fortunate peers, contact with relevant role models, and so on, the fact remains that many low-income individuals just do not have the repertoire of cultural and communication skills to enable them to engage fully at this time in the larger community. The dilemma sometimes is approached by compromising and adopting some of both approaches, but few are fully satisfied with the outcome of such compromises.

ALLOCATION OF RESOURCES

Another major issue that confronts those responsible for policy decisions is the relative allocation of resources. Should monies be used for long-term gains or short-term treatment? One suggestion of long-range planners is to devote all efforts and energies to the newborn among the poor and, if you will, to sacrifice the current generation. Proponents of such a philosophy cite the relatively limited success achieved by programs dealing with the aged, the middle-aged, or even the late adolescent. Such persons advocate concentration of virtually all resources at the preschool and early childhood level, with the barest minimum of efforts going to ameliorate the problems of the current generation of poor adults.

On the other side are the strong arguments that children in their early years are still influenced primarily by their family upbringing, and that the prospects are dismal for long-term impact without strenuous efforts to ameliorate current conditions. These social planners are the promoters and advocates of adult education, job training, cultural enrichment, new approaches to teaching in the ghetto schools, and all the other programs designed to reach all ages of poor. Implicit in their views is a concern that unless action is forthcoming throughout the poor community, social unrest and seduction to extremist behavior may make efforts at dealing with the next generation an impossibility. Certainly it is difficult to hold out prospects for young children whose streets are, and indeed sometimes must be, guarded by policemen with riot guns and by soldiers carrying rifles and tear gas bombs.

Bredemeier (1964:7) summarizes well the need to be concerned with the adult poor:

> Young and middle-aged adults among the poverty striken are important foci of concern for several reasons. In the first place, they beget, socialize, and control children whose life chances are thereby drastically reduced. In the second place, they may represent to children vivid images of the futility of ambition or of effort along the lines advocated by middle class school teachers. In the third place, they are poor.
>
> At the same time that they are important, the adult poor present the most formidable difficulties for rehabilitation. Their very existence is evidence of the failure, in their cases, of the conventional channels— the family, the schools, and the whole network of social service agencies. To think of their returning to them, is, then, idle. Moreover, these people have acquired certain investments, stakes, defenses, identifications, mistrusts, and suspicions that make most of the existing entrances to the job world (correspondence school courses, night classes) impractical and far too socially and psychically costly.

discrimination and poverty

Any discussion of current problems for the poor must mention the difficulties encountered because of the extremely large proportions of individuals within the poverty category who are also discriminated against because of their skin color. These include not only Negro Americans, but Puerto Ricans, Mexican Americans and American Indians. While it should be pointed out that many white community members are within the ranks of the poor, and that efforts at the prevention and amelioration of their condition face extreme barriers, the problems of poverty and discrimination represent a double condition of inferiority and raise additional obstacles to the efficacious implementation of programs of economic improvement.

Indeed, there are some who argue that the civil rights movement actually perpetuates the economic status quo (Willhelm and Powell, 1966). Such persons hold that as long as the issue is split along racial lines, divide and rule prevails, and there is insufficient questioning of the economic ideology that justifies existing patterns of production and consumption. If the problem is presented as one of race rather than economics, then the power elite in the community who are interested in maintaining the economic status quo have much to gain, for then the question becomes one of discrimination rather than inequitable distribution of wealth.

> In short and in summary, the historical transition for the Negro is not occurring in a civil rights context; it is instead a movement out of the Southern cotton fields into the Northern factories and then to the automated urbanity of "nobodiness." The issue becomes a question of human—not only civil—rights and involves white and Negro alike. For the Negro is merely a weathervane for the future. *His* experience will be a common one for many whites now deprived of some sort of usefulness; *his* frustrations will become those of many others the longer we hesitate to confront the meaning of human dignity in an automated society (Willhelm and Powell, 1964:6).

PROFESSIONAL RESISTANCE

Misunderstanding and resistance within the economic sector of the community are not the only obstacles to current efforts to attack poverty through structural change. Many types of programs now under way also meet with considerable opposition from the general population and, particularly, from professionals of various kinds. Many professionals from doctors and lawyers to social workers and politicians, are concerned with reinforcing their own roles and avoiding any threat—real or suspected—to their place in the existing scheme of things. Community members, particularly those who live on the fringes of poverty, also may challenge and fear efforts which they believe will modify the existing economic and social rankings in the community. Earlier in this book we referred to the two concepts of equity. Here we have convincing evidence that efforts to reduce the distance between points on the lower end of the continuum by eliminating some of the differentials in income or social status raise problems for those in the slightly higher category. It has been observed not only in the South but in many Northern cities, for example, that much of the hostility and aggression against programs dealing with the poverty problems of the Negro are related to the attitudes and behavior of students, unemployed youth, and blue-collar white workers who are only slightly better off. Then, too, many professionals who engage in well-financed and successful community efforts with "nice" people are reluctant to look with favor upon any change that might undermine their position. For instance, recreation programs that are well-established in middle-income neighborhoods or that draw support from predominately middle-income families in the community are difficult to modify in ways that would lead to the recruitment and active participation of the poor.

To recognize this aspect of the problem is to be realistic. A youth-service agency, for example, that acquired the image of catering to blacks and lower-class whites would indeed run the risk of losing its upper- and middle-class supporters. The same is true of many voluntary groups offering a variety of services such as family counseling and treatment of emotional problems. It is easy enough for the social-problems analyst concerned with issues of poverty to take a stand against such particularistic and selfish orientation; however, the fact remains that many sectarian and voluntarily supported programs have little choice but to limit their participation to token efforts if they are to continue to receive financial support from their middle- and upper-class memberships. It has taken much public pressure and, on occasion, the coercive action of government to increase the participation of such groups in current programs. One of the cherished values of American society is the extensive free choice of association between individuals and the considerable independence in the development of collective actions. How to maintain this freedom and yet accomplish the basic restructuring necessary to break the cycle of poverty is one of the dilemmas facing current reform efforts.

POLITICAL CONSIDERATIONS

Finally, it must be noted that large-scale, effective and, particularly, publically financed programs for the amelioration and elimination of poverty must consider the political as well as the economic problems involved in these efforts. While a President of the United States can offer ringing declarations about the glories of the Great Society or Black Capitalism, the support of congressmen, governors, and local officials is needed to implement any such proposals. One of the most telling arguments for increasing the community involvement and political participation of the poor is the astute and realistic appraisal that the poor will be assured successful programs only when they can wield as much political or economic power as the business associations, the church groups, and the professional societies. Any speculation about the probabilities of success of the current massive efforts at poverty control must take into account that the future of the current programs, their expansion, and their increased efficacy, depends as much on the climate of political opinion as on the technical development of program efforts.

Despite the promise of recent innovative efforts, by far the most common arrangement for handling the problem of poverty is public assistance. At the present time, the public-assistance programs in the United States represent a hodgepodge of legislation, administered in various ways, and with different levels of benefits from state to state and locality to locality. Although many of the programs are supported by federal funds, to a large extent the administration of welfare remains a state and, in many cases, a local responsibility. Since the administration and part of the funding is usually handled locally, the political orientations of local officials and the economic character of the locality have much to do with the level of payments and the eligibility requirements for welfare benefits. It is fair to say that no state provides sufficient welfare benefits for most of its recipients, that is, enough money to enable them to participate meaningfully in the good life that characterizes the living style of most Americans. Some states, such as New York and California, may be regarded as generous when their welfare payments are contrasted with those of Mississippi or Arkansas. But even in the "progressive" states, the level of assistance hardly provides for the barest necessities let alone for such commonplace pursuits as recreation, leisure, reading, or the arts.

WELFARE ESTIMATES

The number of individuals on public welfare is difficult to estimate. Contrary to the popular stereotype, many families require public assistance only sporadically. Other families are only partially supported, since someone in the household is gainfully employed even though the income is insufficient to meet the basic needs of the family. By far the two largest categories of welfare recipients are the aged and the one-parent household in which one or more young children reside. (*See* Documentation 4.) According to Herman Miller (1964:80–93) there are probably 2.5 million fatherless families in the U.S. who can be regarded as poor. Since these estimates are almost five years old, the numbers have undoubtedly increased. From time to time, many of these families find themselves on welfare under a system that fails, in perhaps two-thirds of our states, to cover adequately their basic needs.

Martin Rein (1965) in considering the problem of public welfare, suggests that we need to modify radically our accepted concepts. He maintains that the principle of socially accepted dependency must be extended to include the poor. Much of the population currently on public assistance could be removed if such a change could be realized. The

DOCUMENTATION 4

the poorest of the poor

COMPARISON OF POVERTY RATES (IN PERCENTAGES)

Type of Unit	MALE HEAD		FEMALE HEAD	
	Incidence of Poverty at the Economy Level	Income of the Poor as Proportion of Required Income	Incidence of Poverty at the Economy Level	Income of the Poor as Proportion of Required Income
Total	14	64	46	53
Unrelated individual	34	57	50	58
Family	12	65	40	49
With no children	12	64	19	62
With children	12	65	55	47
1 or 2	8	68	42	53
3 or 4	14	66	72	45
5 or more	36	62	92	41

About $5 billion of the total deficit [between the basic requirements of the poor and their actual income] represented the unmet needs of families headed by a woman. About three-fifths of the total ($6.6 billion) represented the shortage in income of families with children under age eighteen and about 60 per cent of this shortage was in the income of families with a man at the head. It is estimated that $600 million represented the deficit of poor [farmers]....

Even among the needy, there are some who are worse off than others, and in dollar terms the families consisting of a mother and young children must rank among the poorest. Such families as a group had less than half the money they needed, and the greater the number of children, the greater the unmet need: poor families with a female head and five or more children, including altogether about 1,650,000 children, as a group were living on income less by 59 per cent than their minimum requirement. Of the total family units of this type in the population—that is, of all families with female head and five or more children—nine out of ten were poor. As the above figures show, for both male and female units, those families with the highest poverty rate—the families with several children—tended also to include the poorest poor. Unrelated individuals, including a large number of aged persons, also have both high rates of poverty and substantial income deficits. (Orshansky, 1965:14.)

elements in the revised concept are summarized from the program developed by the esteemed British publication, *The Economist:*

> *Unemployment pay* should be increased so substantially that, for a short time, a man thrown out of a job should actually get more than he did while on the job to compensate for the pain in looking for a new job.
>
> *Mustering out pay* (or pension) for men displaced by technological

change, to be drawn for short periods (five years) even after they accept other jobs.

Housing subsidies to be attached to tenants rather than to houses— that is, a redistribution of subsidies to people rather than to structures.

Income guarantees unrelated to previous wages earned, so that the retired can maintain a standard of living much higher than known during their working years; an income consistent with the changing standard of living resulting from economic growth which will permit the poorest section of the old-age population to maintain a decent and adequate standard of living without recourse to public assistance.

A graduated social security tax which would be sharply progressive and have an income redistributive effect (i.e., take more from the rich and give more, proportionately, to the poor) .

Higher family allowances, even above the guaranteed income level (or the prevailing wage scale) , for poor parents with very large families (Rein, 1965:23).

RECEIPT OF PUBLIC ASSISTANCE

It is important in examining the welfare programs that exist in the United States to recognize not only that most programs are inadequate but that, at any given point in time, a relatively small proportion— Morgan and his associates (1962) estimate less than one quarter— of poor families are receiving public assistance. Thus, in the opinion of many, current welfare programs represent a stopgap intervention strategy that is inadequate in both breath of coverage and magnitude of payments for persons it is designed to help.

Theoretically the public assistance programs in the United States, particularly those oriented toward families with dependent children, are designed to be *habilitative*. According to this concept, an adequate number of social workers, occupational and social training programs, counseling services, and the like, should be able to develop large groups of productive community members from among the poor. This apparently has not happened. There are several situational explanations offered for the current state of affairs with respect to welfare. The common stereotype of the welfare recipient is a shiftless, lazy, ne'er-do-well living off the fat of the land at the expense of the middle-income taxpayer. In fact, it is not possible to do more than barely survive under the terms of most public assistance grants, and the evidence suggests that a large proportion of welfare clients want desperately to escape from their current way of life. Numerous investigations have shown that the number of "welfare chiselers" is exceedingly small; most able-bodied men who can find work support their families and resort to welfare assistance in only the rarest instances (Matza, 1966).

The recent resurgence of interest in the problems of the poor has

a proposed income allowance plan

INCOME ALLOWANCES PLAN: LAMPMAN. BASED ON A FOUR-PERSON
FAMILY AND A BREAK-EVEN POINT OF $3,000 PER YEAR

Earned Income	Amount By Which Income Is Below Break-even Point	Rate of Subsidy	Amount of Subsidy	Total Income, Including Subsidy
None	$3,000	50%	$1,500	$1,500
$ 500	2,500	45	1,125	1,625
1,000	2,000	38	750	1,750
1,500	1,500	33	500	2,000
2,000	1,000	25	250	2,250
2,500	500	25	125	2,625
2,800	200	25	50	2,850
3,000	0	0	0	3,000

Source: *Business Week*, November 13, 1965. Based on data supplied by Robert Lampman.

The various proposals of [Professor] Robert Lampman [of Wisconsin] specify different rates of subsidy to be added to earnings as reported under the income tax, such subsidies being designed to bring each individual or family up to some predetermined minimum income level. The subsidy scales are regressive, in the sense that as earnings increase the rate of subsidy declines. This is designed to afford greater assistance to very low-income earners. The matter of the level of any subsidy involves two questions—that of disincentives and the political and ethical problem posed by people receiving government subsidies and ending up with incomes as large or almost as large as those who do not. These two considerations—incentives and equity—are inherent in all of the plans we are considering.

[The above table] illustrates the operation of one of Lampman's plans, which was prepared in 1965 as an unpublished study for the Office of Economic Opportunity and which uses the Social Security Administration poverty lines . . . for determining the break-even point.

As indicated, a family with no income would be $3,000 below the break-even point. At a 50 per cent subsidy rate, the family would be paid $1,500 by the government, giving it a total income of $1,500. But if the family earned $500, the subsidy rate would fall to 45 per cent. Applied to the $2,500 difference between income and break-even point, this would produce a subsidy of $1,125 which, when added to the income earned, would give the family a total income of $1,625. The family thus keeps $125 of the $500 it earned: in effect, it pays a tax on earnings of 75 per cent. At higher earning levels, the subsidy rate declines, as shown; so does, of course, the effective tax on earnings.

Depending on the standard chosen for the break-even point and the rate of subsidy selected, the costs of Lampman's different plans vary between $2 billion and $11 billion annually, based on 1963 statistics. The proposals are predicated on keeping OASDI [Old Age Survivors and Disability Insurance] but eliminating some existing welfare programs. (Vadakin, 1968:142–144.)

spotlighted the rehabilitative efforts of welfare programs, and more careful scrutiny has brought many elements of the system into question. In terms of the normative values of the American community, current welfare programs may be regarded as fundamentally contradictory to the American way of life. The welfare recipient's privacy is invaded by the public aid department investigator; his freedom to allocate his funds as he wishes is denied; and his feelings of dignity and self-respect are negated. During the middle and late 1960s, a number of responses to the current welfare program have developed and found wide acceptance. One approach has been to organize welfare recipients so that they, like employed workers, may have a voice in the formulation and administration of programs that affect them. Participating in such organization efforts not only provides a source of influence to protect the welfare client and improve his lot but frequently engenders a shift in his attitudes, enhancing the recipient's self-esteem and encouraging his ability to move ahead economically and socially.

income-maintenance programs

An approach, which has been suggested by persons of a variety of political persuasions, is a guaranteed minimum income for every family or individual. The two most frequently advocated plans are a negative income tax (Friedman, 1962), and a children's allowance (Burns, 1962). The negative income tax involves setting up, at the national level, a standard of minimum income and providing a mechanism whereby individuals who are earning less than the minimum receive monies from the government rather than pay the government in the form of taxes. (*See* Documentation 5.) The children's allowance, currently used in some form in almost every Western country, provides payments to all families with dependent children. Where family incomes are above the poverty level, the grants are recovered through regular income tax schedules.

ADVANTAGES OF PLANS

In many ways both systems appear attractive. They minimize the intrusion of investigative personnel, the unwarranted invasions of privacy, and the stigma currently attached to receiving public assistance. However, the implementation of either scheme would involve problems.

If the only objective of an income-maintenance program were to raise the annual income of every family above an arbitrary poverty level, then the most efficient means would be a direct subsidy to close the gap between current earnings and the standard minimum income. Measured against the Social Security Administration's standard, the amount of the gap was only about $10.4 billion in 1965 (Eckstein and Harris, 1966: 35–37). However, other objectives must also be met if a program is to be acceptable. Briar (1969) recently identified five program objectives: (1) efficient reduction of the income deficit; (2) preservation of incentives to work; (3) human dignity; (4) strategic viability; and (5) benefits for the nonpoor.

The negative income tax would probably be the more economical method; but if some incentives to work were included, such as allowing a family to keep a percentage of what it earns above the poverty line, the cost could quickly double. The children's allowance would better satisfy the incentive criterion because the grants, while paid to every family with dependent children, would not be sufficient in themselves to support the family. However, this scheme makes no provision for those poor who are childless or whose children are no longer dependent.

Both programs could be administered in ways that would maximize human dignity. Each avoids the economic means test, which is the most negative element in the present public assistance program. The viability of the negative income tax is restricted by the fact that it is proposed as a single program to replace all existing welfare benefits. Our pluralistic approach to problems—adding programs as conditions dictate—makes the children's allowance more acceptable, since existing programs could be continued or revised and new ones added. The children's allowance offers the most benefits for the nonpoor and the near-poor. Unless a plan provides strong inducements to a large segment of the population, it can never be politically feasible. In addition, this plan should reduce the alienation and separation of the social classes and create conditions of greater harmony by blurring the arbitrary line between the poor and the nonpoor.

LIMITATIONS OF PLANS

Each of these proposals fails to satisfy some of the criteria; however, they are not the only income-maintenance schemes that could be designed. Combinations of these and other plans can still be created which will more perfectly realize the social and human objectives of our highest social-welfare perspective. The U.S. is bound to move in the direction of income maintenance because of the failure of our current welfare system. (*See* Documentation 6 for a discussion of payments under a guaranteed-income plan.)

It would be naive to consider eliminating the current public-assistance program without substituting an alternative, such as the negative income tax or family allowance. On the basis of evidence available, however, it seems reasonable to suggest that more—even better—public-

payments under guaranteed adequate income

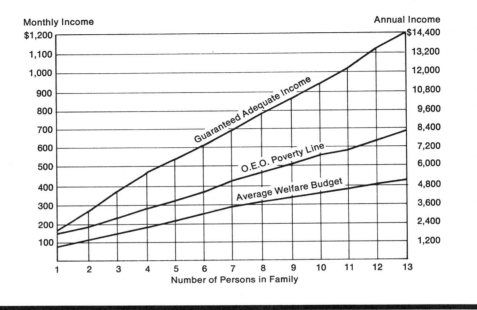

assistance programs in the form of a dole are not the solution to the problems of poverty that face the United States. Given our experience with public-assistance programs, it is quite clear that the poverty cycle is not going to be broken without considerable structural modification. While it is important not to minimize the utility of programs that train, educate, and motivate the welfare client, such programs, in themselves, are not enough. The structural barriers to economic opportunities that currently exist for many of the poor are too formidable.

Here, as in the case of many other social problems, considerable evaluation must be undertaken, for the range of programs is vast. (*See* Documentation 7.) There are, of course, certain groups such as the aged and the emotionally and physically ill whose needs can be met without structural change. For them the concept of a social insurance program seems to be a reasonable solution. Certainly the broadening of benefits under the Social Security Act would indicate that the United States is moving in this direction. Beginning with minimal benefits for a rela-

The Bureau of Labor Statistics of the U.S. Department of Labor says that a family of four needs at least $5,500 a year for the basic necessities of life, not counting medical care. We call upon the General Government to guarantee every American this minimum income.

The National Welfare Rights Organization's guaranteed adequate income is based on the Bureau of Labor Statistics (BLS) "Lower Living Standard Budget." This is the Labor Department's "minimum standard for the maintenance of health and social well being, the nurture of children and participation in community activities."

The so-called "poverty line" is not an adequate income budget, but a level below which everyone is desperately poor. It is based upon the U.S. Department of Agriculture's "economy food plan" on which it is only possible to survive with adequate nutrition for "short emergency periods of time" and only under very special circumstances. (Poverty Line income is $3,335 for a family of four.)

The so-called "low income poverty line" is based on the USDA's "low-cost food plan." It sets an income of approximately $4,400 a year for a family of four. Government surveys show, however, that only 23% of the families with food budgets equivalent to the low-cost food plan actually have nutritionally adequate diets.

The National Welfare Rights Organization's adequate income budget therefore uses the USDA "moderate food plan" which would ensure the average family an adequate income as the only sure way to combat hunger. . . .

The adjusted budget excludes the basic costs of hospital and doctors care since it is assumed that free medical care would be available through national health insurance or Medicaid or some other program. It should also be noted that this budget includes no money for cigarettes (regarded by BLS as a health hazard), non-prescription drugs or medical supplies, out-of-town travel, long-distance telephone calls, dry cleaning, or use of laundromat. It Is Therefore a Bare Minimum Budget! (National Welfare Rights Organization, 1969:7.)

tively modest proportion of the population, the Social Security program has been expanded to include large numbers of the aged, as well as the disabled and their children, who now live in a modest but dignified fashion, thanks to this program.

the role of the social scientist

A word, finally, should be said about the role of social scientists in current poverty efforts. The structural approach that has been implemented during the 1960s has raised a challenge and a dilemma for many sociologists and other professionals involved or interested in the problem. While they bemoan the lack of empirical research and objective evaluation of the goals and results of the experimental programs, they nevertheless fear the results of their research and evaluation which may

schematic design of poverty intervention

GOVERNMENTAL AND PRIVATE POVERTY REDUCTION RATES

Program Objective	STRATIFICATIONAL DIMENSIONS			
	Economic: Incomes, Basic Services, Assets	*Political:* Participation in Decision-making	Education and Social Mobility	Status
Improving social conditions	Guaranteed Annual income	"Maximum feasible participation"	Consumer education	Open housing
	Medicare-Medicaid	"Black Power"		Income guarantees without stigma
	Social Security	"Parent participation in school decision-making"		"Black is beautiful"
	Concentrated employment program			
	Housing			
Promoting social mobility	Job training	Negro separatist movements	New careers	
	Manpower programs	School integration	Headstart	
			Upward Bound	

To gain a better understanding of the objectives of various poverty programs and the relationships between these goals, we can look at efforts to reduce poverty in terms of (1) what aspect of poverty is the program aimed at, for example, the economic, political, educational, and social mobility, or status dimensions of stratification; and (2) what means does the program intend to employ; for example, is the program aimed at improving the social conditions of those who are poor (that is, jobs, income, housing, health, self-respect) or at moving some of those who are poor out of poverty into other niches in society (that is, via educational programs)? The above table may help the reader to think through these various objectives with us.

This typology can aid social scientists in program planning by pointing out the diverse and frequently conflicting goals of programs and by highlighting the relatively neglected aspects of poverty. The typology may also assist in program evaluation by providing a framework for pinpointing the goals of programs in question and for showing the relationship among goals of various programs—first steps in any evaluation. The typology leads policy makers dealing with the poor to ask what kinds of responsibilities and burdens we wish our society to have. For example, to what extent do we wish to improve the conditions of the aged or the future conditions of today's youth? To a large extent, these are not narrow technical issues, but value issues that may be expected to produce acrimonious debate. (Miller and Roby, 1969:65–66.)

slow down, impede, or even reverse the current resurgence of remedial action. It is fair to observe that many analysts of social problems consider it a definite defect that so little attention has been paid to problems of research and evaluation of the poverty efforts.

So far, accusations that current efforts are little more than a repetition or enlargement of programs already proved ineffective are only being whispered by a few critics. But there is indeed a strong risk that the well-intentioned efforts of many practitioners and interventionists will come to naught because of their lack of intellectual curiosity and critical skepticism about what specifically is being undertaken, for what ends, and with what measurable results. This lack of determination to improve the means for implementing and developing programs and the political uncertainties that threaten these efforts raise boldly the unanswered challenge to the future: How can we prevent, treat, and ameliorate poverty in the United States?

ANTONOVSKY, AARON.
1967 "Social class, life expectancy and overall mortality." Milbank Memorial Fund Quarterly 45(April):31–73.

BRADBURN, NORMAN M. AND DAVID CAPLOVITZ.
1964 Reports on Happiness. Chicago: Aldine.

BREDEMEIER, HARRY C.
1964 "New strategies for the war on poverty." Trans-action 2(November/December):3–8.

BRENNER, ROBERT H.
1964 From the Depths. New York: New York University Press.

BRIAR, SCOTT.
1969 "Only children's allowances." Social Work 14(January):5–12.

BROWN, GORDON E. (ED.).
1968 The Multi-Problem Dilemma: A Social Research Demonstration with Multi-Problem Families. Metuchen, New Jersey: Scarecrow Press.

BURNS, EVELINE.
1962 "What's wrong with public welfare." Social Service Review 36(June):111–122.

CAPLOVITZ, DAVID.
1963 The Poor Pay More. New York: Free Press.

CARLIN, JEROME E., JAN HOWARD AND SHELDON L. MESSINGER.
1966 "Civil justice and the poor." Law and Society Review 1(November):9–89.

CONSUMERS UNION.
1967 "Consumer education for low-income families, a limited survey of programs and resources." Pp. 51–57 in H. Gold and F. Scarpitti (eds.), Combatting Social Problems. New York: Holt, Rinehart and Winston.

ECKSTEIN, OTTO AND ROBERT HARRIS.
1966 Income and Benefit Programs (October). Washington, D.C.: U.S. Department of Health, Education and Welfare.

FRIEDMAN, MILTON.
1962 Capitalism and Freedom. Chicago: University of Chicago Press.

GALBRAITH, JOHN K.
1958 The Affluent Society. Boston: Houghton Mifflin.

GORDON, JESSE.
1965 "Project Cause, the federal antipoverty program, and some implications of subprofessional training." American Psychologist 20(May):334–343.

HARRINGTON, MICHAEL.
1963 The Other America: Poverty in the United States. New York: Macmillan.
1968 "Preface." Pp. i–xi in Louis A. Ferman and Joyce L. Kornbluh (eds.), Poverty in America. Revised Edition. Ann Arbor: University of Michigan Press.

IKEDA, TSUGUO.
1967 Effectiveness of Social Work with Acting-Out Youth. Seattle: Seattle Atlantic Street Center, Mimeograph.

LAMBERT, CAMILLE, JR. AND HOWARD E. FREEMAN.
1967 Clinic Habit. New Haven, Connecticut: College and University Press.

LEWIS, OSCAR.
1966 La Vida: A Puerto Rican Family in the Culture of Poverty, San Juan and New York. New York: Random House.

MATZA, DAVID.
1966 "Poverty and disrepute." Pp. 619–669 in Robert K. Merton and Robert A. Nisbet (eds.), Contemporary Social Problems. New York: Harcourt, Brace and World.

MACDONALD, DWIGHT.
1968 Pp. 7–24 in Louis A. Ferman and Joyce L. Kornbluh (eds.), Poverty in America. Revised Edition. Ann Arbor: University of Michigan Press.

MEYER, HENRY J., EDGAR F. BORGATTA, AND WYATT C. JONES.
1965 Girls at Vocational High. New York: Russell Sage.

MILLER, HERMAN.
1964 Rich Man, Poor Man. New York: Crowell.

MILLER, S. M. AND PAMELA ROBY.
1969 "Poverty: changing social stratification." Pp. 64–84 in Daniel P. Moynihan (ed.), On Understanding Poverty: Perspectives from the Social Sciences. New York: Basic Books.

MILLER, WALTER B.
1958 "Lower class culture as a generating milieu of gang delinquency." Journal of Social Issues 14(March):5–19.
1962 "The impact of a 'total community' delinquency control project." Social Problems 10(Fall):168–191.

MORGAN, JAMES ET AL.
1962 Income and Welfare in the United States. New York: McGraw-Hill.

MOSS, MILTON.
1968 "Consumption: a report on contemporary issues." Pp. 449–521 in Eleanor B. Sheldon and Wilbert E. Moore (eds.), Indicators of Social Change: Concepts and Measurements. New York: Russell Sage.

MOYNIHAN, DANIEL P.
1969 "The professor and the poor." Pp. 3–35 in Daniel P. Moynihan (ed.), On Understanding Poverty: Perspectives from the Social Sciences. New York: Basic Books.

NATIONAL WELFARE RIGHTS ORGANIZATION.
1969 "NWRO proposals for a guaranteed adequate income." Washington, D.C.: NOW (July):7.

OFFICE OF JUVENILE DELINQUENCY AND YOUTH DEVELOPMENT.
1966 "An evaluation of the San Francisco youth opportunities center." Washington, D.C.: U.S. Department of Health, Education and Welfare.

ORSHANSKY, MOLLY.
1965 "Counting the poor." Social Security Bulletin 28(January):3–26.

REIN, MARTIN.
1965 "The strange case of public dependency." Trans-action 2(March/April):16–23.

RIESSMAN, FRANK.
1962 The Culturally Deprived Child. New York: Harper and Row.
1965 "Self-help among the poor: new styles of social action." Trans-action 2(September/October):32–37.

ROACH, JACK L. AND ORVILLE R. GURSSLIN.
1967 "An evaluation of the concept 'culture of poverty'." Social Forces 45(March):383–392.

RODMAN, HYMAN.
1963 "The lower-class value stretch." Social Forces 42(December):205–215.

SUCHMAN, EDWARD A.
1968 Evaluative Research: Principles and Practices in Public Service and Social Action Programs. New York: Russell Sage.

TAIT, C. D., JR. AND E. F. HODGES, JR.
1962 Delinquents, Their Families and the Community. Springfield, Illinois: Charles C Thomas.

TYLER, GUS.
1961 "Marginal industries, low wages, and high risks." Dissent 8(Summer):321–325.

U.S. DEPARTMENT OF LABOR.
1967 "Sub-employment in the slums of [selected cities]." A series of pamphlets based on special surveys. Washington, D.C.

VADAKIN, JAMES C.
1968 Children, Poverty, and Family Allowances. New York: Basic Books.

VALENTINE, CHARLES A.
1968 Culture and Poverty: Critique and Counter-Proposals. Chicago: University of Chicago Press.

WILLHELM, SIDNEY M. AND EDWIN H. POWELL.
1964 "Who needs the Negro?" Transaction 1(September/October): 3–6.

inadequate economic participation

ALTHOUGH POVERTY represents a singularly critical concern in America today, several aspects of economic participation constitute pervasive social problems for other segments of the population as well. The plight of the one-fifth of the citizenry who live at or below the poverty level does not detract from the problems of economic participation that plague the rest of the adult population. In a number of ways, the four-fifths of the nation's inhabitants who are themselves employed or dependent upon employed breadwinners are also confronted with a broad spectrum of problems that have consequences for the individual and for the social order.

The problems of economic participation for the more affluent members of the community represent objective social concerns that demand public attention. The saliency of the problems is evidenced by the responses of community members in their attempt to ameliorate them. Few will deny that the settings and conditions under which a person works are closely related to his emotional and psychological well-being and to his self-perception as a human being. Moreover, a person's place within the occupational structure strongly affects the rest of his social life.

the rise of affluence

Seen in perspective, certain dominant factors have helped to shape the current economic-political order in the United States and the present problems and prospects of the individual and his society. While a lengthy historical discussion is impossible here, it is important to indicate in broad outline some of the economic and industrial changes that give background to present conditions. Perhaps of greatest importance is the fact that most Americans have achieved a level of affluence not possible in other parts of the world. The consequences of this fact are pervasive and far-reaching.

Historically, America's growth and development, punctuated by successive waves of immigration, reflect the individual's aspirations for economic achievement and his motivations for a better life for himself and his family (Rubin, 1966). At least by objective world standards, most Americans today are well-off economically and, measured by the number of work-hours it takes to buy a loaf of bread or rent a modest six-room house, the American worker's standard of living is the envy of the world, with the possible exception of a few countries in Western Europe. Automobiles, dishwashers, and television sets are common luxuries available not only to professional and white-collar workers but to many skilled and semiskilled laborers with steady jobs. Most Americans, on the surface at least, have more purchasing power and suffer fewer material deprivations than do their counterparts in other countries. This is as true for university professors as it is for assembly-line workers. Indeed, as suggested in the last chapter, some of the problems of the poor and some of the perspectives we hold on poverty are attributable to the disparity between the living standards enjoyed by those regularly employed and the relative deprivation experienced by those who lack the entitlements to be gained from economic participation.

THE INDUSTRIAL ECONOMY

The superficial affluence of dollar earnings in terms of purchasing power available to many Americans is a function, to a large extent, of the highly industrialized character of the economy, the great wealth of our natural resources, and the technological sophistication of U.S. production. Moreover, until recently, the American worker profited from the favorable balance of trade that accrued to this nation as the primary source of much of the world's industrial goods. This last advantage is rapidly being challenged by competition from Western Europe, Japan, and even from some emerging nations.

Some of the problems encountered through economic participation are endemic to the types of industrial structure that have developed in this country. At the outset it is important to note the bureaucratic nature of American production. This applies not only to the giant corporations and the enormous industrial empires that characterize the business world but also to organized labor, which competes effectively with management in terms of resources and influence. Concepts believed to typify the American way of life, such as the small businessman or the independent craftsman, are, to a large extent, vestiges of a romanticized past. Most American craftsmen today are organized, and much of their activity is framed by the cooperative, if not collusive, leadership of union and management. Furthermore, the contemporary successful small businessman is most likely to be the franchised representative of a syndicate that provides him with managerial resources, financial assistance, employee training, and other accoutrements of big business. In the private sector of the economy, expansion and diversification of large established companies and the development of consortiums of franchised dealers, who provide services ranging from installation of automobile mufflers to nursing care for the aged, represent most of the large-growth areas in recent years.

LABOR AND MANAGEMENT

Many of the traditional images of labor and of management have to be modified in the light of current employer-employee relationships. The historic industrial conflicts between independent unions led by indigenous and often charismatic leaders and powerful, reactionary, and often unscrupulous business magnates no longer describe industrial relations in most urban communities. Admittedly, one still sees vestiges of the conflicts of the 1800s and of the confrontations of the 1930s in some attitudes of both union and management. But today, a growing rapprochement exists between nominally opposing sides, and the objectives of labor and management have converged to a large extent. Unions are highly organized and their day-to-day affairs are run by skilled professionals who in many ways hold positions of prestige and respectability commensurate with those of their peers in the world of management. Most industrial corporations and their executives no longer look upon the worker as an inanimate object to be used, worn out, and eventually tossed aside. By the same token, many workers now hold what Purcell (1960) refers to as "dual allegiance." Purcell concludes from his ten-year study of 800 packinghouse workers that the attitudes of the workers are highly favorable toward both the company and the union. This dual allegiance is also shared by plant foremen, who were shown to be generally favorable to the union, and to union leaders, who were almost as favorable towards the company as were the rank and file.

Certainly, basic labor-management conflict occurs occasionally in American communities. Groups of workers, particularly in the service fields, still fight violently and against great odds to obtain recognition and bare living wages. But many of the industrial unions, and certainly those organized along craft lines, are not struggling for the bare necessities of survival but rather to participate more equitably in the affluence that surrounds four-fifths of the nation. While the problems of poverty that beset one-fifth of the population have become explicitly more severe from an economic standpoint, the lot of the average man has vastly improved. Why, then, is participation in the economic sector of critical concern to the analyst of social problems? Morse and Weiss (1955:198), who interviewed a national sample of employed men, provide a simple answer in the summary of their study:

> The results indicate that for most men working does not simply function as a means of earning a livelihood. Even if there were no economic necessity for them to work, most men would work anyway. It is through the producing role that most men tie into society, and for this reason and others, most men find the producing role important for maintaining their sense of well-being.

The social problems surrounding economic participation are the by-products or side-effects of America's considerable economic abundance. This prosperity is due in no small measure to the highly efficient and rationalized industrial situation and to recent rapid technological changes, both of which may be expected to continue in the future. Current problems of economic participation are interrelated, although subsequently it may be useful, for analytical purposes, to separate them. Initially, however, a gross, overall picture is indicated.

the world of work

Two approaches are possible in discussing the problems of economic participation. One can either take the perspective of the individual in the community or examine the occupational structure and its links to the rest of the social order. For most men and for many women, the hours spent on the job constitute the modality of their life in terms of time and place. At the level of psychological gratification, it is often held that the satisfaction gained within the world of work is paramount for the individual, and often for his family, in terms of the rest of his life space. Indeed, some analysts of social problems regard the lack of such gratification as the key consideration, not only in terms of economic participation but in terms of the individual's entire repertory of social relations. It is important here to differentiate between the psychological gratifications derived from the successful fulfillment of one's occupational role and the extrinsic gratifications obtained from the prestige and material rewards made possible by one's particular job. Of course, the two are closely related.

THE IMPORTANCE OF MONEY

At the most elementary level, there is the matter of economic or monetary return for work. Considering the rewards that accrue to those with

mental-health differences by occupational level

We begin by comparing occupation groups within the sample of Detroit auto workers. The overall results are clear and striking. When workers are classified into job levels by reference to skill and variety of work operations, responsibility, and pay, mental-health scores show consistent and significant correlation with the occupational hierarchy. The higher the occupation the better [the] mental health. . . .

One simple set of figures will make this evident. The table [below] compares occupations by the percentages of workers enjoying good mental health—that is, having "high" mental-health scores. The cutting point for "high" is of course, arbitrary, but constant; it . . . represents the upper one-third of all workers. Jobs were assigned to the levels or categories by reference to three criteria: the official job title

(clarified when necessary by consultation with automotive "insiders"); the worker's own description of his duties, job operations, and training time required; and the rate of pay. The occupational classification of workers and the derivation of mental-health scores were completely independent operations, each carried out with no reference to the other. Consequently, nothing in the procedure could have spuriously contributed to the obtained mental-health differences by occupation. Inevitably there were borderline cases and ambiguities but since these occasional errors of occupational classification would tend to reduce rather than exaggerate the relationship to mental health, the differences reported between occupations may be considered minimum figures. (Kornhauser, 1965:56–57.)

MENTAL-HEALTH DIFFERENCES BY OCCUPATIONAL LEVEL

Occupational Category	YOUNG		MIDDLE-AGED	
	Proportion with High Mental Health	Number of Workers	Proportion with High Mental Health	Number of Workers
Skilled workers	58%	33	56%	45
High semiskilled			41	98
Ordinary semiskilled	35	46	38	82
Repetitive semiskilled	10	30	26	73
Total		109		298

money, the importance of financial return should not be overlooked. Not only are the goods of consumption and many of the comforts of life readily obtainable by those with money, but these rewards have a symbolic meaning in terms of one's standing in the community and one's self-image as a successful person (Mills, 1951). Cadillacs are more comfortable than Chevrolets; they are also more prestigious, connoting a stance and posture that fulfill the individual and readily suggest to him and to others something about his role in the community. A similar function is filled by dressing one's wife in designer clothes or by vacationing in Europe. Size of income is also a major determinant of who obtains high quality medical care, excellent educations for their children, an attractive spouse, and even high political office.

Americans may pretend that the best things in life are free, but studies show an unmistakable correlation between income and self-expressions of happiness, length of life, and breadth of stimulating experience (Bradburn and Caplovitz, 1964). According to surveys of the general population and among personnel of particular industries, such as the automotive industry, per capita income is a concomitant, if not a determinant, of mental satisfaction and physical well-being (Kornhauser, 1965). (See Documentation 1.) Part of the problem of economic participation for most people, therefore, is the strain induced by efforts to maximize their incomes. Only the very rich, because of the extremities of the graduated income tax, would be an exception and even they—thanks to various tax shelters and legal loopholes—may succumb to the urge to make more money.

Different individuals, given different places within the social order, vary in their concepts of what it is to be poor or well-off, poverty-striken or affluent. Some rare individuals feel quite satisfied with their income and material possessions, whatever they may be. But much of the pressure in today's economic world is related to the functional basis of money. There is little need to belabor this point. With the possible exception of the extremely wealthy, who regularly enjoy the advantages of excess income, everyone else, from high government official to factory worker, faces financial deprivation as one of the problems of economic participation. In many cases this deprivation is not so much a matter of the amount of income; rather, it is the discrepancy between income and aspirations.

WORK SATISFACTION

Psychological gratification in the world of work, of course, is not limited solely to having money to buy things. One's work provides thrills and frustrations, and persons performing various work roles may gain satisfaction from a job well done, be he a surgeon who completes a life-saving operation, a professor who gives a stimulating lecture, an architect who designs an aesthetically pleasing building, a technician who contributes to the exploration of outer space, or a laborer who successfully locates a leak in the water main. As in the case of net income, professionals and others who hold high-status occupational positions have more opportunities to achieve gratification from their work. But this is, of course, a relative rather than an absolute judgment. A professor in a mediocre college who teaches introductory courses to large freshman classes compares himself to colleagues in prestige institutions who direct stimulating seminars of honor students and graduate scholars; the surgeon who performs routine operations rates his work against that of colleagues at the frontiers of medical research; and so it goes with tool and die makers, electronic technicians, janitors, and cleaning women. Part of the problem is that, from one occupational role to the next, there exists considerable disparity in the extent to which work is valued and appreciated and to which it offers intellectual or physical stimulation and challenging opportunities. It should be emphasized that even many white-collar occupations which provide more-than-adequate incomes offer little opportunity for gratifying experiences and push the worker into a constructed and anomic life (Mills, 1951).

The concept of the worker who takes pride in his work is a part of the American ethos. Our folk literature is filled with such men: John Henry, the steel driving man; Paul Bunyan, lumberjack par excellence; Pecos Bill, king of the cowboys; Casey Jones, railroad engineer. Whether the myth squared with reality is perhaps unimportant; the ideal is there. Today, however, the sheer efficiency of mass production methods and the resulting fragmentation of work has so narrowed the occupational role for many industrial workers and technicians that the satisfactions to be gained from a job well done are severely limited. Studies are virtually conclusive in finding that the lower a worker is on the occupational scale, the less joy he experiences in his labor and the more likely he is to work simply for the money. Blue-collar workers, in particular, have limited opportunities for job autonomy and self-expression through work, although there is considerable evidence that they desire such opportunities (Lyman, 1955). Workers who feel they are being paid a fair wage take money virtually for granted and express a desire for more satisfying employment opportunities. Only when they feel they are receiving less than they deserve do workers tend to rank money foremost among the values they express toward their work (Dubin, 1958).

CAREER OPPORTUNITIES

A related issue can perhaps be explained most cogently by the concept of career. Many segments of the world of work are structured to include a series of more or less clearly defined steps that constitute a career ladder —a succession of related jobs through which persons move (Wilensky, 1964a). To illustrate: within the university setting, one moves forward through the academic ranks from instructor to full professor; within certain crafts, through progressive levels of skill from apprentice to journeyman to master craftsman. Some occupational roles, of course, never offer opportunities for a career in the sense of stages of progressive development. There have always been and always will be dead-end kinds of jobs.

Moreover, many work situations which previously offered career opportunities no longer do so, although the number of genuine careers may be increasing. In part, this increase is a consequence of the extremely technical character of the economic and industrial order, with its emphasis on formal educational requirements for many occupational roles. Contrast, for example, the young man of the 1800s who could start work as a baggage clerk and aspire to the position of railroad engineer with the contemporary young man who begins his career as an airline reservationist. The probability of his ever occupying the equivalent role of jet pilot is practically nil. It is simply not possible to occupy many of the positions at the top of various job hierarchies without considerable educational prerequisites. This is equally true in many industries, particularly those valuing creative talent, such as advertising agencies and graphic arts studios, or technical skills, such as engineering firms or computer centers.

ADVANTAGES OF ORDERLY CAREERS

Orderly careers, as a study by Wilensky (1961:535) shows, have ramifications beyond the work setting:

> Orderly experience in the economic system is associated with many social ties which range broadly and at the same time overlap. Men who have predictable careers for at least a fifth of their worklives belong to more organizations, attend more meetings, and average more hours in organizational activity. Their attachments to the local community are also stronger—indicated by support of local schools and, to a lesser extent, by contributions to church and charity.
>
> In both formal and informal contacts, the men of orderly career, more than their colleagues of chaos, are exposed to a great variety of people: the fellow-members they see in clubs and organizations represent many social and economic levels; frequently-seen relatives and close friends are more scattered in space both social and geographical, cutting across neighborhoods, workplaces, occupations, or income brackets. Finally, the total participation pattern of the orderly is more coherent: close friends tend to form a circle and they overlap work contacts.

Then, too, the structuring of industrial relations between union and management results in certain career barriers and terminal points. For example, supervisory positions, such as foreman and assistant foremen in the automotive industry, represent the cut-off point for union membership and participation. As soon as an employee assumes these work roles, he is regarded as part of management. The worker with considerable investment and identification with the union, and protected by its contract and benefits, may indeed be less motivated and more reluctant to move up the company ladder. Also, in many industries and large business organizations, specialization and competition have resulted in a major emphasis upon selection procedures and preparatory training for roles at the top of the occupational hierarchies. Thus, key executives in many consumer industries are selected for management training programs at relatively early ages, and recruits for such positions usually come from college campuses, not from the ranks of those already working for the company. "Success" often means giving up one's craft or profession. (*See* Documentation 2.)

The importance of economic participation to other matters in the external world needs to be stressed as well. We have already observed the importance of income with respect to a person's access to the good things of life. Income is not the only characteristic of economic participa-

---

DOCUMENTATION 2

staff vs. line

To be sure, business was always work with people. But when the size of enterprises was small, the head could remain a colleague among other colleagues; he did not cut connections entirely and enter a new milieu. William Allen White's autobiography shows that he was able to maintain all his life the amiable fiction that he was only a working newspaper man. Similarly, the older generation of college presidents was composed largely of men who continued to think of themselves as scholars. So, too, the older generation of business executives kept their hats on in the office, chewed tobacco, and otherwise tried to retain their connections with the shop. Today, however, the familiar organizational concepts of "staff and line" symbolize the cutting off of direct contact between the executive and the working staffs of both staff and line. To sit at his new big desk—or to get there—he has to learn a new personality-oriented specialty and unlearn or at least soft-pedal his old skill orientation.

To the point is a story of an engineer who is offered the far more lucrative job of sales manager. He loves engineering, but his wife won't let him turn down the promotion. His sponsor in the organization tells him it is now or never: does he want to be wearing a green eyeshade all his life? He reluctantly accepts. That night he has a dream. He has a slide rule in his hands, and he suddenly realizes that he does not know how to use it. He wakes in panic. The dream clearly symbolizes his feeling of impotence in a new job where he is alienated from his craft.

The executive who has moved up from a professional position can hardly help feeling that his work is air conditioned: fine only so long as the machinery below runs smoothly. Those colleagues whom he has left behind will not be slow, in their envy, to remind him that he can no longer consider himself a competent craftsman among his fellow craftsmen, that he does not fool them if, as an editor or by-line columnist, he occasionally attends a presidential press conference; or, as a college administrator, an occasional scholarly convention; or, as a sales manager, occasionally makes a mark on a drawing board. (Riesman *et al.*, 1950: 155–156.)

---

tion that is highly valued, however. In addition, there is occupational prestige and the benefits of social status it provides within the general community, including access to social networks, opportunities for social interaction with other high-status persons, and entitlement to the preferment accorded those in higher echelons (Wilensky, 1964a; Havighurst, et al., 1962). Even today, policemen and other civil servants often behave differently to upper- and middle-class persons than to blue-collar and working people. In many communities, the professional person or high-status businessman, homebound after too many martinis, is likely to be offered a ride home in a police car, while the laborer in a similar state of inebriation would find himself escorted not too gently to the local lockup. A similar pattern of discrimination is evident in the treatment of youth in the community. Destructive actions may be viewed as childish pranks if committed by the son of a respectable citizen who can pay for the damage, but if the offender's father is an unskilled laborer who cannot pay, the charge may be malicious mischief.

OCCUPATIONAL MOBILITY

Perhaps the key issue to be reckoned with is the empirical fact that all community members do not have the same chance to achieve occupationally and, therefore, are hampered in their chances to achieve within the broader outlines of social status as well. In discussing poverty, we referred to its cyclical quality and to the difficulties of moving out of such a condition of life. Studies of social mobility show that education, both quantitatively in terms of duration and qualitatively in terms of where it was obtained, is the chief determinant of upward mobility (Blau and Duncan, 1967). While findings differ as to whether opportunities for sons to move up from their father's work role have actually decreased or simply remained static since a generation ago, it is clear that chances for occupational mobility are not improving (Rogoff, 1953). A number of studies—particularly the one by Lipset and Bendix (1952a)—indicate that few Americans move on to stable employment in white-collar occupational roles if they have worked for any period of time at a blue-collar job. (See Documentation 3.)

Although many Americans remain romantically convinced of the equality of opportunity, the facts are that equality, at best, is limited and opportunity is tightly bound by educational qualifications and family status. The demand for more and better educational training aggravates the disabilities imposed on the significant number of young people who by virtue of family finances or foolhardy termination of their education are denied practically all opportunities for occupational advancement (Abramovitz, 1960). The hippie movement of the mid-1960s, with the impetus it gave to school dropouts among youths who presum-

upward and downward mobility

The interchange between manual and non-manual occupations from the point of view of social mobility can most easily be shown by contrasting the proportion of time which those who work with their hands have spent in the nonmanual occupations with the proportion of time which nonmanual workers have spent as manual laborers.

Though little confidence can be placed in the over-all contrast between 11.1 and 20.2 per cent, it is of interest that the range of variation in the two groups differs markedly. Those who hold manual jobs at present have worked for from only 9 to 13 per cent of their careers in nonmanual occupations. But those now in nonmanual occupations have spent from 5 to 29 per cent of their life-careers as manual workers. (Lipset and Bendix, 1952b:494.)

PERCENTAGE OF TIME SPENT IN OCCUPATIONAL DIVISIONS OTHER THAN PRESENT, BY PRESENT OCCUPATIONAL GROUP AND DIVISION

Present Occupational Group and Division	Number	PERCENTAGE OF TIME SPENT	
		In Manual Occupations	In Non-manual Occupations
Professional	23	5.7	. . . . .
Semiprofessional	19	13.4	. . . . .
Own business	105	26.0	. . . . .
Upper-white-collar	72	10.4	. . . . .
Lower-white-collar	67	29.5	. . . . .
Sales	42	21.2	. . . . .
All nonmanual	343	20.2	. . . . .
Skilled	169	. . . . .	9.3
Semiskilled	98	. . . . .	13.5
Unskilled	44	. . . . .	12.8
All manual	314	. . . . .	11.1

ably would have continued in college and even gone on to graduate and professional schools, is a contemporary illustration of the need to be concerned with the relationship between education and the world of work. Whatever the values and motivations that led serious young people to participate in this movement, the consequences for their adult years may be irreversible.

The temptation is great to blame the world of work for many of the strains in community life. However, if we look at the situation in perspective, we find that changes in the American family since the period of industrialization probably have been exaggerated. The system of mate selection, the marital relationship, and parent-child responsibilities in the preindustrial family all show striking similarities to the family of today. Moreover, family strains commonly attributed to industrialization were noted by analysts of preindustrial family life (Furstenberg, 1966). Certainly caution is required in emphasizing, or at least overemphasizing, the impact of the current occupational scene.

PROFESSIONALIZATION

Our observations on occupational status and mobility lead to a consideration of the issue of the socialization experiences associated with work and the resultant discrepancies that arise. Many of these differences have been attributed to the increased homogeneity of values that has taken place in our culture in recent years without any commensurate adjustments within the occupational structure. Given a situation in which most community members are aware of the dominant cultural prescriptions for personal advancement, a disproportionate amount of their energies and efforts within the occupational structure is often devoted, at least superficially, to meeting the community's expectations in this respect. As a result, to cite one illustration, there is a continual effort on the part of individuals in a variety of work roles to move their occupation into the category of a profession. This seeking of professional status is particularly applicable to occupations at the fringes of the established professions (Wilensky, 1964a). With the increase in professionalization, access to the occupational role is often further limited. In many cases, professionalization has the same monopolistic effect on occupational mobility—and, consequently, on social mobility—as restrictive membership practices by unions and nepotic employment policies by some businesses. The result is often severe shortages of manpower resources during periods of sudden and rapid expansion of the economy.

The emphasis upon professionalization is only one of the many considerations in the problem of allocating occupational resources. From the standpoint of the social order, the contemporary community faces many occupational gaps and inadequacies and operates with a less than satisfactory distribution of manpower resources. In addition to the problems of professionalization and the consequent barriers—often pseudobarriers in terms of the tasks involved—they raise, there is also considerable inequity in the financial rewards for the various positions. In many service fields, such as those concerned with the care of the aged, the poor, and the mentally ill, as well as in many skilled crafts, such as printing and the building industries, a variety of restrictions and inequities have severe consequences for the distribution of human resources.

Riessman and Pearl (1965) comment on this point in regard to the provision of social services. They argue that the expansion of services, if it is also to reduce unemployment, requires an identification of those professional tasks which can be delegated to less skilled persons. They acknowledge that such a move would, in effect, reverse the recent tendency of service industries to raise standards and increase the quality of performance by expanding their employment of professionals.

For the most part, the problem of the distribution of resources is a moral one, and citizens become concerned only when they are the recipients of the disparities in distribution. At times, certain severe problems of resource allocation do come to public attention, usually because a large enough segment of the population has experienced the inequality to make it an objective as well as a moral concern. For example, the scarcity of trained nurses in the health field, the difficulties in recruiting personnel for social-control agencies such as police departments, and the perennial shortage of school teachers for our educational systems have reached such proportions that they now represent genuine social problems of concern to the entire community (Orzack, 1967).

TECHNOLOGICAL DISPLACEMENT

Finally, the increasing problem of technological displacement must be noted. Although automation is frequently cited as the cause of technological displacement, the problem is more complicated than merely the increased utilization of electronically programmed equipment. (*See* Documentation 4.) Indeed, there is considerable controversy over whether or not automation actually reduces the total working force. But what it does do, as do many other technological advances, is minimize the opportunities for economic participation of significant clusters within the labor force. Automated equipment in heavy industries may serve to reduce costs and increase growth rates, thereby increasing opportunities for some. But the vast and sweeping technological inputs into our system have negative consequences for the undertrained and the poorly educated and, for certain persons, displacement is easy to rationalize on the grounds that retraining cannot be economically justified. Those at the lower end of the occupational ladder are most frequently affected and hardest hit by any technical innovation (Miller, 1966).

A number of questions are still unanswered regarding the ultimate impact of automation. Seligman (1966:263) has summarized the situation very well:

> Clearly, the problem is considerably more complicated than the proponents of automatic adjustment suggest. Is there some optimum rate of innovation which would cause neither disruption nor technical stagnation? What are the indirect impacts of automation, i.e., how does automation in one sector of the economy spill over into others? How do

geographic shifts stemming from automation affect people, industries, regional economies? Can demand keep pace with output? Can output keep pace with population? Will capital accumulation be employed in ways that will insure a balance between savings and investment, between capacity and demand? Or will we have to break the traditional work nexus of our society by providing incomes as a matter of right equal to the "wages" of the machine which displaces the human being in production?

It is important to note that the problems created by technological change and the proliferation of new knowledge, and the dislocations resulting from automation affect not only the production worker and laborer. Even older workers in some high-status professions such as engineering are threatened. One of the unattractive aspects of many engineering specialties is the rapid obsolescence of technical knowledge. High beginning salaries attract a constant flow of new engineers into the industry. Since the recent graduate is likely to have more advanced knowledge and be more experienced in recent technological changes than his colleague with twenty year's service, he is often hired for superior positions. Many industries face the problem of obsolescence of their old professionals.

The many forces currently pervading the world of work are viewed with varying degrees of optimism and pessimism by analysts of the American industrial scene. Even those who are optimistic recognize the volatile situation, and virtually all agree that the next decades will see a marked redistribution of the work force into new occupations and professions, with all the social and psychological stresses that accompany such shifts. These social scientists further recognize that this redistribution of manpower will place extensive demands on the educational system, and they point to the need for radical modifications of the ways our society selects and trains its workers (Miller, 1966).

causes

In looking at the various problems of economic participation found in the urban community, one is struck by the strong relationship between the development of technology and the array of problems presented. Undoubtedly, underlying all of the issues raised in this chapter are the sweeping technological changes that have taken place in the economy over the past sixty or seventy years. One may even argue that the problems of economic participation are the inevitable consequences of industrial, if not social, progress.

will our computers destroy us?

We have recently heard a great deal about the disruptive effects of computing machines on our social and economic institutions. In industry, computers mean automation, and automation is supposed to mean unemployment. The United States, with its extravagant investment in computers, is plagued by unemployment for unskilled workers; it is frequently argued that these facts are causally related. Already the computers have begun to displace workers whose tasks are simple and repetitive; clerical workers, workers on assembly lines, and the like. The variety of jobs formerly done only by humans that the machine can perform more rapidly, accurately, and economically increases with each new generation of computers. If we extrapolate this trend, say the pessimists, we are faced with the prospect of mass unemployment for all but a handful of highly trained, highly intelligent professionals, who will then be even more influential and over-worked than they are at present. Only recently a distinguished English physicist predicted that within twenty years electronic engineers might have to become conscientious objectors in order to prevent these pernicious machines from wrecking our social and economic institutions.

According to the prophets of doom, our situation is hopeless. The computer is already stirring up industrial strife as management desires and labour resists the effects of automation. Great masses of people will soon be unemployed, and the devil will surely find work for their idle hands. The gap between advanced and developing nations will increase, thus heightening international tensions. People will become demoralized when the personal identification and self-respect that work confers is suddenly withdrawn. The educational system will be unable to educate citizens for life in the Leisure State. All the industrial and commercial machinery of production and distribution of commodities will have to be taken over by the state, which will lead inevitably to tighter economic controls or even dictatorship. And so on and on runs this hopeless catalogue. I find it difficult to state these awful anticipations convincingly, because I do not believe in them, but those who do believe can make Aldous Huxley's *Brave New World* and George Orwell's *1984* sound like optimistic promises of salvation.

What can we do about it? It is foolish to dream of reversing history. We cannot pass laws forbidding science and technology. The computing machines are here, and they will not merely stay; they will grow bigger, faster, and more useful every year. They will grow because engineers want to build them, scientists want to use them, industrialists want to employ them, soldiers want to enlist them in new weapons systems, politicians want their help in the processes of government. In short, they will flourish because they enable us to accomplish tasks that could never before have been undertaken, no matter how many unskilled labourers we might have set to work. Computers will continue to amplify our muscles. The question we must ask is not whether we shall have computers or not have computers, but rather, since we are going to have them, how can we make the most humane and intelligent use of them? (Miller, 1966:109–110.)

Unlike the problems of poverty, the problems of economic participation represent some utility in terms of the functioning of the social order. It could be argued, for example, that only with the efficiencies of automation and the advancements of technological change could a general level of prosperity be maintained for the majority of community members. Americans often express pride in the number of automobiles produced in this country, and point to this inundation as an accomplishment of our assembly-line system of production. In so doing, we ignore the heavy toll that monotonous work has taken in terms of job satisfaction, and we gloss over the relative degrees of social status and deprivation existing between the more and less affluent within the community.

Most economists agree, however, that the growth curve in terms of national production and the ability of the consumer to absorb capital goods is not a consistently accelerating one. This situation is related in part to the rapid industrialization in other parts of the world and the accompanying limitation on our overseas markets, and in part to the approaching saturation of large segments of the domestic consumer market. Some economic theorists argue that there is going to be a continued decline in the rate of growth of the gross national product (GNP). It does appear that the production of certain commodities highly related to the economic participation of blue-collar workers, such as housing, is at a plateau and that our economy is likely to experience minimal growth in many industrial areas.

The rather dramatic efforts at tax reduction in the early 1960s and the imposition of a surtax on income less than a decade later have made us aware of the variety and the inconsistency of the fiscal actions needed just to maintain the status quo. We also became aware during this period of the impact of armed conflict on employment, productivity, and the general economic status of the nation. It is a simple matter, of course, to blame the problems of economic participation on the robustness of the economic structure and to accept technological unemployment, irrational professionalism, lack of job satisfaction, and the like, as the inevitable consequences of a postindustrial economy. Such fatalistic response is countered by those who can see the possibilities for genuine change in habits and ideology. New modes of consumer practices and shifts in the norms of consumption can effect remarkable change on industrial structure. Evidence is cited, for example, of the achievable ambition of two homes, two cars, and two annual vacations for every middle-class family. The charge that economics is the "dismal science" was not made without some basis in fact, and the pessimism of many economists reflects their awareness that the etiology of many problems of economic participation lies in current economic policies, the state of the market (nationally and internationally), and the monetary orientation of our society.

Many analysts of the world of work are extremely doubtful of this country's ability to meet the employment requirements of its population. Michael Harrington (1965:421) states the problem in this summary:

> According to the Department of Labor, the United States will require over 101 million jobs by 1980. Between 1964 and 1970, the labor force will grow at a rate of one-and-a-half million a year. Just to accommodate this increase—and *without* reducing unemployment—would require job generation on a scale not even achieved during the Korean War. And if one adds in the absolutely reasonable goal (it should be axiomatic with the neo-Keynesians) of reducing unemployment, as officially defined, to 3% by 1969, that would take, according to AFL-CIO Research Director Nathaniel Goldfinger, 1.9 million new jobs a year.
>
> The Government is extremely pessimistic about its ability to measure up to these extraordinary job quotas. In order to meet the 1964–1970 manpower requirements, Washington reports that an annual 4% increase in gross national product will be needed during the entire period. And it then says, "But at no time in our recent peacetime history have we been able to sustain a rate of increase in the gross national product of 4% for more than a brief period." That is to say, the welfare state and economic measures of the past are, by Administration admission, probably not equal to the labor force requirements of the future.

POLITICAL-ECONOMIC DISHARMONIES

Along with problems of industrial structure, we must recognize that the strange interaction between the political and economic aspects of our culture and their lack of integration in a coordinated system bring about discontinuities in economic participation. Indeed, some of the programs designed to foster equity and create more uniform standards have themselves contributed to the current state of affairs. It is not only the conservatives who charge that certain practices of labor unions, for example, are related to the current problems of economic participation. When meaningless and irrelevant requirements, such as kinship to a union member, are imposed as a condition for entry into a particular craft, then one is struck with the cogency of such arguments. When unions fail to recognize that certain supervisory jobs should no longer be regarded as a part of management but as progressive steps in a worker's career ladder, again one can appreciate the restrictions placed upon equitable economic participation.

The relationship between the worker and his union has changed in other ways as well. In earlier periods, the union provided an important membership group that gave the worker a sense of belonging and a measure of respect not provided by his job. Strikes often had the positive benefit of allowing him an opportunity to affirm his solidarity with his fellow workers. As unions have become stabilized and entrenched, the typical worker is apathetic about participation and takes little interest in union activities. In large industrial unions, such as the steelworkers, sometimes less than one-half of one per cent of the membership attends meetings (Seidman et al., 1958). Although unions still constitute a potentially viable force for alleviating the worker's lack of psychological gratification, their present evolution tends to contradict this possibility.

Another glaring illustration of an early solution that has become a problem is civil service. Civil service systems at the federal, state, and local levels were inaugurated with the good intention of reducing graft, nepotism, political appointments, and the like. Based upon so-called objective employment specifications and guarantees of long-term tenure, such systems have their acknowledged advantages. For many jobs, however, particularly those requiring creativity, high levels of technical skill, or strong elements of interpersonal competence, the present operations of large public systems under civil service codes tend to impede economic participation and minimize the individual satisfaction of workers. Impediments may range from unrealistic residential requirements for certain positions to the existence of practically no grounds for terminating employment or reducing responsibility of individuals incompetent to perform the tasks for which they were hired.

BUREAUCRATIC ARRANGEMENTS

In discussing economic participation, we have noted the highly bureaucratic character not only of public service but of many large industries as well. Bureaucratic arrangements should not always be disparaged; indeed, they are inevitable given the scope and breadth of many current operations. But, if as a consequence of bureaucratization, there develop insurmountable rigidities and an inability to modify or change the organizational stance, then we must be concerned with the contribution bureaucratic elements make to the etiology of problems relating to economic participation. Of special consequence is the extent to which criteria for participation become traditionalized and allowed to persist after they have become irrelevant to the actual tasks demanded of the individual on the job. Although Whyte (1956) may have exaggerated somewhat, his study of the "organization man" points up the problem well. (*See* Documentation 5.) Such matters as dress style, conformity of spouse, and type of house or automobile are often held as essential requisites for professional and white-collar workers, even though they have no relevance to the job to be done.

Another factor contributing to reduced levels of economic participa-

the organization family

Sometimes the man (recently promoted to management) cherishes the idea he's going to have it both ways, but if he does he is in for some poignant experiences. Let him pick up where he left off as if nothing at all had happened (they had to send somebody; just a fluke it was me), and he will soon be reminded by others that he and his wife are now different. He begins to notice the little edge in the joking remarks of his friends (What did that crack mean about the car? So it's a ranch wagon. So what?). For his wife, unless she is exceptionally shrewd, the disillusionment is even more cutting. More than her husband she has bucked the idea that getting ahead in the company will mean any sacrifice of the modulated life and, unlike her husband, she must suffer the ambiguities of her new status unshielded by the rules of the game and the trappings of rank that set up a buffer zone in the office.

Repeatedly, I keep running into management wives who bitterly resent (one to the extent of physically shaking me) a study I did on the subject four years ago. What they seem to resent most is the point made about the social demands of success. They actually believe in the plateau—or, rather, they desperately want to. Indignantly, they deny that becoming a boss's wife will mean any shedding of old associations. In other companies maybe, but not in this one. And why should we ever want to leave Crestmere Heights? Not the snappiest section of town perhaps, but they're real people here and none of us cares a hang about that rank stuff. Furthermore, that crowd out in Brinton Hills is not our dish of tea. You were exaggerating terribly. Weren't you really?

Husbands who have come to the fork in the road may also ponder the idea of finding the plateau, but unlike their wives, they don't really believe it. The few who still try to convince themselves that the earlier dream is possible will now find scant comfort from their colleagues, who while not cynical have become too sophisticated to keep a straight face on the matter. "The trouble with you men," I heard one young executive exclaim to two friends, "is that you're still small-town Baptists at heart."

The figures of speech younger executives use to describe the situation they now find themselves in are illuminating. The kind of words they use are "treadmill," "merry-go-round," "rat race"—words that convey an absence of fixed goals, as we remarked before, may make them seem less ambitious, less competitive than their forebears, but in the more seemingly co-operative climate of today lies a prod just as effective. They are competing; all but the fools know this—but for what, and against whom? They don't know, and there is the trap. To keep even, they must push ahead, and though they might like to do it only slightly, who is to say what slightly is. Their contemporaries are in precisely the same doubt, and thus they all end up competing against one another as rapaciously as if their hearts were set on the presidency itself. (Whyte, 1956:175–176.)

tion is the ambivalence of the American community toward concepts of planning with respect to economic resources. Despite empirical documentation of the limits of job mobility and the narrow range of "free choice" that typify most occupational careers today, many people still view with concern and, sometimes, fear the centralized control of employment markets or the guidance of people to certain educational or vocational opportunities. Although in recent years such programs have made considerable headway, it is fair to note that inadequate planning at various levels of government, imprecise specification of educational requirements, and ineffective vocational guidance have contributed to the problems of manpower shortages and economic displacement (Wilensky, 1964b).

Finally, it is to be recognized that individual factors are also related to limited economic participation. To repeat, discrimination plays a forceful rule in determining the occupational mobility of individuals and in limiting their chances for obtaining personal satisfaction from their jobs. Although largely related to race, discrimination also extends to sex, age, and physical condition. All of these attributes represent barriers to full participation (Crook and Heinstein, 1958). Discrimination, for whatever reason, is essentially a moral problem; many community members simply fail to adhere in the occupational sphere to the ideals of equality and equity which are regarded as part of the American ethic. Moreover, the worker today is subject to many influences within the social and economic structure that stimulate beliefs and behavior contrary to traditional American norms of individual initiative and private enterprise. The bureaucratic orientation of the economic system and, to some extent, the operations of contemporary health and welfare programs tend to develop attitudes not in keeping with our historic norms of self-motivation, personal freedom, and rugged individualism. Thus, the disparaties between life's realities and the nation's ideals contribute to the strains of economic participation.

intervention and control

A number of processes are currently operating to handle some of the problems of economic participation. For a number of years, certainly since the 1930s, the human relations approach has been used to deal with the problem of worker satisfaction. Essentially, this approach consists of efforts to enhance the worker's perception of his worth and to improve, via counseling programs and health and welfare services, his extraoccupational life roles. At least in the early days of "human engineering," the rationale for any attempt to improve worker morale was that it would result in higher productivity (Roethlisberger and Dickson, 1939). Today such arguments must be made with care. More recent research indicates that such efforts do not necessarily lead to the expected outcome. Management or "expert" opinion of what would improve morale is not always accepted by the workers; furthermore, even where morale may be improved by the provision of mental and physical health programs, there is no consistent evidence that the results are related to increased production (Carey, 1967).

WORK-RELATED PROGRAMS

Considering the amount of time and effort the average person devotes to his work, it could be argued that business and industry has a responsibility to provide programs for human betterment regardless of their direct relevance to productivity or even to worker satisfaction. Such efforts are widely supported and even demanded by unions—especially those for whom wages are no longer a significant issue. For example, unions such as the United Auto Workers are beginning to insist on the inclusion of mental health benefits as part of the union contract (Freeman, 1968). Farsighted leaders of both labor and management believe that provisions for leisure-time activities, pensions, and educational programs for workers' children represent the direct responsibility of the combined labor-management complex.

In brief, one approach to intervention in the problems of economic participation is to recognize that, despite wide disparities among job classifications, there is a need to minimize the possibility that these disparities will be perpetuated and carried over to other life roles. The production worker in the automobile assembly plant is entitled to psychotherapy on the same basis as the company's sales representative. The mechanic in a small machine shop is entitled to pension benefits on a par with the owner who buys his security with stock options. Efforts to develop greater equity in the extraoccupational world, regardless of one's place in the job structure, have been supplemented in recent times by the government's strengthening, extending, and broadening its retirement system—Old Age, Survivors, and Disability Insurance (OASDI), commonly known as Social Security. Social Security is an insurance scheme, contributed to by worker and management, and in no way different from that bought by a physician, for example, from a private insurance company. Recognition that inequities in life style are not inevitable and need not occur despite a highly stratified vertical occupation system is an intervention approach that holds much promise, and many future developments along these lines can be expected.

Obsolescence of human resources is another problem of economic participation which must be recognized and planned for. In many large industries, for example, programs of early retirement are now being considered and, occasionally, implemented. The rationale for early retirement, at least on a voluntary basis, is based on the considerable merit to be found in a planned displacement of workers. Increasingly, workers who live well and enjoy life will want to retire early and, by so doing, will afford opportunities for younger people to move up. If this can be done without undue financial sacrifice on the part of older workers, then the satisfactions of both age groups can be maximized (Moore and Streib, 1959).

SECOND CAREERS

A more novel, and perhaps a more promising, intervention strategy is the concept of radical shifts in work patterns and second careers as a means of maximizing the economic participation of individuals. For example, the retired engineer, no longer as technically knowledgable as younger colleagues, is still a valuable member of the community in a new role, such as a teacher in a vocational high school. The administrator of a large corporation, displaced because his job now requires more vigor and know-how, could still be a valuable staff member in a local welfare council, many of which suffer from a severe shortage of good administrative personnel. The surgeon, no longer temperamentally or physically able to stand the rigors of the operating room, can perform many important roles in health care, especially considering the dearth of public health workers throughout the world. There is already in existence an extensive organization of retired professors who go as scholars-in-residence to small colleges that could never have enjoyed their services when they were younger.

Such efforts as have been made in the field of second careers have usually approached the problem at the upper echelon of the occupational ladder. But having proved successful here, would the same program not hold for others as well? The thirty-year man retiring from the armed forces at age fifty could fill a crucial place in a juvenile delinquency prevention and control program. The mechanic displaced by automation could find a useful career in developing programs of supervised leisure or vocational training for unemployed youth. People of many ages and skills have contributed immeasurably to the success of the Peace Corps and its domestic counterpart, VISTA, and to similar volunteer programs throughout the world.

MEANINGFUL LEISURE

Another approach to the problem of worker satisfaction is the concept that, if things cannot be remedied within the occupational world, much more can be done to provide a useful and happy life during the other hours of his day. Most communities have an array of voluntary groups that are extremely active and attract a host of willing participants. For the most part, however, blue-collar workers and persons from lower-class background have little preparation for roles in such groups. Programs of leisure-time activities, early retirement, health and welfare counseling, and on-the-job training, are not enough; the economic sector must also recognize the need for encouraging and teaching people at the individual level to participate effectively in wider community activities.

At a structural level, we have already referred to the possibility of changing the values and aspirations of persons in the American community. Many of the efforts to shift the wants and desires of the typical community member are undoubtedly undertaken for self-interest as well as for altruistic reasons. Must the communication media and the recreational industries, for example, increase the distance between the haves and the have-nots within the population? Somehow these enterprises must be organized and coordinated to maximize participation by persons of different backgrounds and occupying different structural positions. There exist instances of such leveling, and the efforts have been extremely beneficial. As an illustration we cite the development of our national park system and the opportunities it offers a family of relatively modest means to enjoy the beauties of nature and to engage in the pleasures of outdoor life.

A very romantic view of the past pictures the more rural way of life as providing opportunities for free expression and extensive participation unrelated to work, regardless of one's position. Unfortunately, in these times our urban situation is unlikely to provide such pathways for expression naturally. Rather, they must be planned for and, to a large extent, publicly acknowledged if not publicly supported. The benefits of such efforts are many, for not only do they provide inputs into the economic system but they serve to ameliorate the personal problems of satisfaction and pleasure within the community.

A number of analysts who have considered the utility of introducing and expanding the leisure activities of community members warn us, however, that patterns of creative and challenging leisure are not likely to compensate for the inevitable spread of stultifying labor. They maintain that labor that requires little investment of self tends to be linked with leisure that is full of malaise. Such an assessment is probably correct with respect to many spectator sports and to much commercialized recreation.

Unless there are accompanying changes in the value orientations of community members that will break the vicious circle of dull work and dull play, the meaningless round of work to be endured and leisure time to be killed will continue.

PLANNED OBSOLESCENCE

A highly controversial concept which may have some utility in the improvement of economic participation is planned obsolescence. Usually this idea is discussed with negative or critical overtones and, as an excuse for the manufacture of shoddy merchandise with relatively short life spans, it is indeed reprehensible. However, if the emphasis is on the planning and the results are a more satisfactory replication of consumable goods in ways that will increase job opportunities, occupational mobility, productivity and, ultimately, economic participation, then the concept may have real merit. Why should houses be built to last a century and automobiles to run ten years? Slums and unsafe highways are the inevitable result. The convenience and economy of disposal products, ranging from plastic plates to paper dresses, can be extended to more durable goods. (How and where to dispose of some of these so-called disposable items is another matter.) Tax advantages in the form of depreciation allowances have already effected a revolution in the replacement of obsolete plants and equipment; such incentives can be made available to consumers as well as to business and industry.

While it is argued that style obsolescence, such as the annual changes in automobile designs, may mean a certain amount of waste and consumer expense, the overall economic advantages may well out-weigh these objections. The introduction of rigorous standards of quality control could assure that products would perform well for the time they were designed to last. Repairs and replacement parts would be things of the past. The requirement to modify some traditional American values with respect to excellence, durability, and craftsmanship in order to maximize economic participation need not be subject to greed or fraud. Better planning must include adequate controls, and programs of planned obsolescence must be accompanied by social responsibility on the part of all concerned.

OPPORTUNITIES FOR PARTICIPATION

The concept of a career ladder can also serve as an intervention technique when it serves as an escape route from dead-end or otherwise unrewarding jobs. The traditional apprenticeship system is largely outmoded, and even the newer methods of in-service and on-the-job training are no longer adequate to the task of preparing people for upward movement in the occupational heirarchy. The increased professionalization of many lines of work has broadened the area encompassed by the concept of career. Formal education, however, still retains its preeminence as the principal avenue of career advancement. Much of the recent emphasis on new careers, especially careers for the poor and the so-called indigenous workers, has not given sufficient consideration to the legitimating function of education. For positions in public agencies covered by civil service codes, almost no amount of job experience or nonacademic training can overcome the basic lack of requisite formal educational experience. Until some progress can be made in reforming the civil service system, every program that purports to advance workers in a career line must incorporate realistic provisions for school attendance.

WORK-STUDY PROGRAMS

In recent years, work-study programs have proliferated at both the high school and college levels. These programs must be broadened to include more workers and the benefits extended to cover the income needs of families. Educational leaves and released time for schooling must be built into entering job descriptions. These programs must not be cut short or curtailed at the college level but must extend to professional and graduate schools as well. Education should be viewed as a continuing and continuous process that extends throughout the work life of the individual. At present, the field of education is almost the only civilian career that provides for continued schooling, and even these programs are deficient because they usually do not include remuneration to cover tuition costs and living expenses. The military services, which emphasize a thirty-year career program with provisions for full pay and time off for study, represent a model that business and industry, as well as the professions, might emulate.

INCREASED GOVERNMENTAL PROGRAMS

The development of career ladders and, indeed, of better utilization and distribution of manpower points to the increased role of government, and public agencies in particular, in dealing with the problems of economic participation. We have seen the first attempts at this with the increased governmental support for educational programs and the recognition of the importance of education in terms of economic participation. In certain professions there have been dramatic illustrations of how inputs into the occupational system by government have served to help reduce some of the more severe manpower deficiencies. For example, financial support for the training of psychiatrists and the improvement of salaries for residents in this medical speciality has resulted in a rapid recruitment into this professional group, thereby reducing the severe shortage of personnel. In the future, one of the key modes of intervention is undoubtedly going to be the subsidization of various training programs that are geared to meet critical manpower shortages in crucial areas in both the public and private sectors.

The problem underlying all of these intervention methods is the necessity for increasing opportunities for participation on an equitable basis for all individuals within the system. This is not a simple matter, however, and alternative strategies and a wide choice of programs need to be developed. The importance of economic participation cannot be overemphasized. The discontinuities in this area are as pervasive and, in many ways, as critical as those of poverty.

REFERENCES

ABRAMOVITZ, MOSES.
1960 "Growing up in an affluent society." Pp. 158–179 in Eli Ginzberg (ed.), The Nation's Children. Part 1: The Family and Social Change. New York: Columbia University Press.

BLAU, PETER AND OTIS DUNCAN.
1967 The American Occupation Structure. New York: Wiley.

BRADBURN, NORMAN M. AND DAVID CAPLOVITZ.
1964 Reports on Happiness. Chicago: Aldine.

CAREY, ALEX.
1967 "The Hawthorne studies: a radical criticism." American Sociological Review 32(June):403–416.

CROOK, G. HAMILTON AND MARTIN HEINSTEIN.
1958 The Older Worker in Industry: A Study of the Attitudes of Industrial Workers Toward Aging and Retirement. Berkeley: Institute of Industrial Relations, University of California.

DUBIN, ROBERT.
1958 The World of Work. Englewood Cliffs, New Jersey: Prentice-Hall.

FREEMAN, HOWARD E.
1968 "Evaluation research and the explanatory power of social factors." Pp. 79–93 in Leigh M. Roberts, Norman S. Greenfield and Milton H. Miller (eds.), Comprehensive Mental Health. Madison: University of Wisconsin Press.

FURSTENBERG, FRANK F., JR.
1966 "Industrialization and the American family: a look backward." American Sociological Review 31(June):326–337.

HARRINGTON, MICHAEL.
1965 "The politics of poverty." Dissent 12(Autumn):412–446.

HAVIGHURST, ROBERT J. ET AL.
1962 Growing Up in River City New York: Wiley.

KORNHAUSER, ARTHUR.
1965 Mental Health of the Industrial Worker: A Detroit Study. New York: Wiley.

LIPSET, SEYMOUR AND REINHARD BENDIX.
1952a "Social mobility and occupational career patterns, I. stability of job-holding." American Journal of Sociology 57(January):366–374.
1952b "Social mobility and occupational career patterns, II. social mobility." American Journal of Sociology 57 (March):494–504.

LYMAN, ELIZABETH.
1955 "Occupational differences in the value attached to work." American Journal of Sociology 61(September):138–144.

MILLER, GEORGE A.
1966 "Thinking machines: myths and actualities." Public Interest 2(Winter):92–112.

MILLS, C. WRIGHT.
1951 White Collar. New York: Oxford University Press.

MOORE, E. H. AND J. F. STREIB (EDS.).
1959 The Nature of Retirement. New York: Macmillan.

MORSE, NANCY C. AND ROBERT S. WEISS.
1955 "The function and meaning of work and the job." American Sociological Review 20(April):191–198.

ORZACK, LOUIS H.
1967 "Social change: implications for welfare manpower." Pp. 557–571 in H. Gold and F. Scarpitti (eds.), Combatting Social Problems. New York: Holt, Rinehart and Winston.

PURCELL, THEODORE V.
1960 Blue Collar Man: Patterns of Dual Allegiance in Industry. Cambridge, Massachusetts: Harvard University Press.

RIESMAN, DAVID, NATHAN GLAZER AND REUEL DENNEY.
1950 The Lonely Crowd. New Haven: Yale University Press.

RIESSMAN, FRANK AND ARTHUR PEARL (EDS.).
1965 New Careers for the Poor. New York: Free Press.

ROETHLISBERGER, FRITZ J. AND WILLIAM J. DICKSON.
1939 Management and the Worker. Cambridge, Massachusetts: Harvard University Press.

ROGOFF, NATALIE.
1953 Recent Trends in Occupational Mobility. New York: Free Press.

RUBIN, ERNEST.
1966 "The demography of immigration to the United States." The Annals 367(September):15–22.

SEIDMAN, JOEL, JACK LONDON, BERNARD KARSH AND DAISY L. TAGLIACOZZO.
1958 The Worker Views His Union. Chicago: University of Chicago Press.

SELIGMAN, BEN B.
1966 "On theories of automation." Dissent 13(May/June):243–264.

WHYTE, WILLIAM H.
1956 The Organization Man. New York: Simon and Schuster.

WILENSKY, HAROLD L.
1961 "Orderly careers and social participation: the impact of work history on social integration in the middle mass." American Sociological Review 26(August):521–539.
1964a "The professionalization of everyone?" American Journal of Sociology 70(September):137–158.
1964b "Mass society and mass culture: interdependence or independence?" American Sociological Review 29(April):173–197.

CHAPTER 6

discrimination and prejudice

MORE THAN TWENTY-FIVE years ago, the distinguished Swedish social scientist, Gunnar Myrdal, pointed out that the problems of racism, segregation, and discrimination in the United States are bound up with the conflicting ideologies or discrepancies within the moral order. On the one hand, Americans are committed to individual liberty and freedom of choice; on the other hand, most Americans support the concept of equality (Myrdal, 1944). Although this analysis may be dated and incomplete, it identified a generation ago the strains and conflicts that can be observed throughout American social life today, and it placed the genesis of these discrepancies within the structures of social differentiation (Campbell, 1961).

Americans discriminate in many ways. Prestige universities admit only the highly rated applicants, distinguished professors seek out the brightest graduate students as research assistants, and influential corporations choose from among the honors list to fill their executive training programs. Young women in the marriage market usually have some ideas about the qualities they wish in their mates and so, of course, do their mothers. Discrimination, it can be argued, is to a large extent an outgrowth of the social structure and moral order that characterize the American community. There is little reason to believe, despite considerable public sentiment and verbal expressions to the contrary, that the citizens of the United States either enjoy equality or desire random choice in all segments of their social lives. While randomization of personnel would perhaps make for more exciting major league pennant races or more interesting genetic combinations in mate selection, such policies would likely arouse only ludicrous exclamations from the general run of community members and, for that matter, the experts who provide much of the guidance and influence in the various social-control systems.

Discrimination, it should be noted, becomes a moral and social issue only when the grounds for it are irrational or categorical—that is, when the discriminatory act is based not on peculiarities of individual personality but on characteristics that identify a person as belonging to a particular group. Such discrimination reaches the proportions of a social problem when its existence necessitates the extended use of community resources to control it or results in widespread expressions of dissatisfaction from community members. In this chapter we will be concerned for the most part with the problem of the Negro in contemporary American society. Although it is clear that discrimination in terms of race represents the most critical concern, it is important at the outset to indicate that race is not the only basis upon which invidious distinctions may be made, and that black Americans are not the only group that one might include in an analysis of the problem.

the phenomenon of discrimination

There still exist in the United States problems of discrimination on the basis of religion and national origin. Further, as Myrdal observed several decades ago, perhaps the greatest "minority" group in the United States is composed of women. Also, large numbers of people, by virtue of physical or mental disabilities and social or moral deviances, are also stigmatized and thus excluded from full participation in society. In addition to discrimination based upon so-called differential achievements and potential, there are other forms of discrimination that are of concern even though they are not as pervasive or as debasing as that which faces the black man.

It could be argued, of course, that virtually all forms of selective rewards that are not based upon competitive standards represent unfair and irrational modes of conduct in American society. For example, even the businessman who prefers the Phi Beta Kappa may be wrong. Recent studies suggest that the most successful adults are not always those who achieve the highest grades and recognition in college. But in this chapter we will gloss over these lesser types of discrimination. Discrimination against black Americans represents the critical problem, for it differs in both the dimension and the quality of degradation imposed. Therefore it is important to explicate its total and persistent character and to recognize the full effects it has on almost one-tenth of all Americans.

DISCRIMINATION AND PREJUDICE

At this point we should differentiate between discrimination and prejudice. *Discrimination* implies an act or practice; *prejudice* connotes an attitude or opinion. A once-prevalent view—and one still not completely abandoned—interpreted discrimination primarily as a consequence of a person's attitude toward various outgroups (Glenn, 1963). We now know from a large number of studies in various fields that there is only limited correspondence between prejudice and discrimination. Attitudes and behavior, thoughts and actions are not the same things.

While certain moral experts in the community stress the desirability of good thoughts about one's fellowman, this view has little consequence for the functioning of the social order (Linn, 1965). Many individuals work their entire lives for employers or supervisors whom they do not like and may even hate. But if, on the job, the role behavior between employer and employee is entirely appropriate and does not interfere with job performance, then there is little reason to consider such an anomoly as a social problem. Many times the power of the social structure, the internalization of norms, or an irrationality between feelings and behavior minimizes the impact of prejudice on the functioning of the community. Citizens prejudiced against Catholics voted for Kennedy; patients prejudiced against Jews choose Jewish physicians; and individuals prejudiced against certain manufacturers may still buy their products. While we do not want to dismiss the link between prejudice and discrimination, our concern here is not with reduction of prejudice but with the minimization of discrimination. The blending, if not the conscious amalgam, of these two concepts in the term *racism* may account in part for the argument and even anger that have attended its use in recent years.

THE NATURE OF DISCRIMINATION

The problem of discrimination against blacks, however labeled, is an extremely critical concern because of its nontransistory character. Many individuals at different periods in their lives are discriminated against. This is particularly true with respect to age and sex roles, as well as to the temporary incompetence of individuals to understand or represent the attributes of certain roles. Girls in their early teens usually go through a period in which they are discriminated against by boys seeking dates, for the latter are not quite sure whether the girls represent eligible potential conquests. Many individuals who move to the United States from other countries, or even from one region of the United States to another, are temporarily discriminated against until they learn the codes of conduct and the expectations of others, or until they lose the identifying characteristics that enable the natives to single them out as different.

Whether because of group-identification or unfortunate individual characteristics, many persons are never completely integrated into society, and many areas of community life exhibit varying degrees of fragmentary discrimination. Such "parttime" practices of discrimination are often by-products of the more intensive but transitory discrimination that has marked the history of ethnic and religious groups in the United States. For example, one finds that informally, if not formally, membership in certain fraternal and social organizations is restricted to white Anglo-Saxon Protestants, or what the Sunday-supplement sociologists have termed WASPs.

While there are clearly dysfunctional aspects to fragmentary discrimination, and the parties concerned are often deeply affected as individuals, the problems in contemporary America are much less severe for virtually every group except the Negro. (It should be pointed out that other groups, such as Mexican-Americans, American Indians, and Puerto Ricans, also find a large proportion of their life space restricted to a subordinate status.) In some ways, a degree of transitory discrimination may be functional in the development of community life and, therefore, not entirely irrational. To the degree that there are dominant norms regarding modes of conduct and social mechanisms provided by the community for the eventual integration of minority group members, then such temporary discrimination may be interpreted as the sanctions that provide the impetus for the continued socialization of minority members into the larger community.

COPING WITH DISCRIMINATION

Minority groups, particularly those of an ethnic or national character, often have been able to cope with problems of discrimination by establishing functional equivalents of the institutions that serve majority members of the community. This process has developed into an effective mechanism of social control to minimize the problem of discrimination for many groups. The history of Jewish organizations in America is perhaps the most explicit illustration of the utilization of such a mechanism. In many moderate sized communities, the discriminatory practices of the admissions committees of most social and cultural organizations led to the development of Jewish country clubs, for example. Often these "substitute" facilities have finer golf courses, better food, and more interesting social programs than those available for their Gentile counterparts. Discrimination in appointments to medical staffs resulted in the development of a network of sectarian hospitals, particularly Jewish and Catholic. The rise of parochial schools was in large part a response to the predominately Protestant orientation of the public schools. Most college campuses which maintain Greek societies even today have one or two fraternities or sororities that are identified as "Jewish," even though most Greek-letter groups have liberalized their pledging practices regarding Jewish students.

Either because they tend to lessen the effects of discrimination or because they offer needed quality service, many institutions that began as functional equivalents have been adopted into the larger community network or, at least, are regarded with a certain amount of civic pride. This process is particularly apparent in the medical care field where many Jewish-sponsored hospitals are now fully integrated into major medical complexes. Boston's Beth Israel Hospital is one of the important teaching institutions of Harvard Medical School and New York's Mount Sinai Hospital not only provides top quality intern and resident training but has recently established its own school of medicine. Fierce competition exists among all medical graduates for admission to their residency and intern programs, and certainly there is little reluctance on the part of anyone in the community to use their services. Except for the blacks, most other minority groups, either through "separate and equal" or "separate and better" community resources, have been able to minimize the fragmentation of their group life by utilizing separatist institutions that are coordinated with those of the larger community through a network of influence and power.

The Protestant denominational university, for example, that solicits financial contributions from Catholics and Jews and recognizes their importance to the university by appointments to the board of trustees finds it difficult to maintain religious discrimination in the employment of faculty or the admission of students. Industries that sell to companies dominated by members of ethnic groups find it expedient, at least at the visible level, to minimize discriminatory employment practices or other actions that may be interpreted as being directed against a religious or ethnic group. In certain industries, marked changes in employment and promotion practices have occurred when management was made explicitly aware that discrimination limited business prospects and reduced profits.

RELIGIOUS-ETHNIC DISCRIMINATION

There is no attempt here to minimize the problems of discrimination faced by many members of minority groups in the United States, but it is necessary to acknowledge that much fragmentary discrimination is, generally, of limited importance in terms of the total social lives of individuals. Moreover, many of the problems are matters of attitude and psychological sensitivity rather than serious limitations on the minority individual's participation in community life. Many Americans, in their day-to-day relationships, do not even observe the ethnic or religious identification of the persons or groups they meet. Few Americans hesitate to shop in stores such as Gimbels; few investors avoid stock offerings underwritten by Lehman Brothers or notes secured by W. Heller and Company; and homeowners of all kinds have purchased houses built by Levitt and Sons, although it has probably been called to their attention that the founders, if not the current owners of these corporations, were Jews.

This is not to deny that minority groups or many members of such groups have a substantial investment in maintaining, at least in some spheres of life, separation from others in the American community. In the case of the Jew and the Catholic, particularly, part of the motivation for fragmentation rests with the religious identification of the individuals involved and their emphasis on maintaining endogamy—marriage within the group—and not fully assimilating into the larger community. By and large, Jewish and Catholic fraternities, sororities, and social clubs exist today not because they are required for the full participation of youth in community life, but rather because of adult concern over the eventual loss of a separate religious identity. The socialization process and the transmission of culture have provided a positive reinforcement of subgroup identities for many minority members, and these identities are maintained and fostered by fragmentation, at least at the level of social activities. Italians, Eastern Europeans, and Chinese, for examples, maintain group pride and are reluctant to give up entirely what they regard as the gratifications that come from group interaction, specialized dietary habits, and identification with the old country or with a particular national heritage (Gans, 1962; Hughes, 1963). Much analysis of American society has concentrated on the relative strains induced by the melting-pot value as compared to the development of overlapping islands of cultural homogeneity. While the final word certainly has not been written about the problems of psychological identification and the pros and cons of total assimilation versus national and religious heterogeneity in the United States, for many ethnic groups there has developed a meaningful rapprochement with the larger society (Glazer and Moynihan, 1963).

the uniqueness of black discrimination

No rapprochement has occurred in the case of the Negro. On all grounds, in every sphere of activity, the black has reason to be concerned with his status in the larger community. Considering the attention paid to the problem, there is no need here to detail the problems of economic survival and economic opportunity for the Negro. He has great difficulty in obtaining loans or mortgages at reasonable interest rates in the business world. Discrimination still limits his admission in any significant numbers into many educational institutions and professions. The black stands less chance of living as long as a white American and his annual death rate is significantly higher than that of his white counterparts.

DOCUMENTATION 1

white and nonwhite death rates

In the United States, over-all mortality has been consistently higher in the nonwhite population. In 1900, the death rate for the white population was 17.0 per 1,000; the death rate for the non-white population, 25.0 per 1,000. . . . By 1963, the rates for the white and nonwhite segments of the population had declined to 9.5 and 10.1, respectively. The relative difference between the two groups—47 percent in 1900—had been reduced to only .6 percent by 1963.

At first glance, the wide differential in mortality between the white and nonwhite groups which existed in 1900 has been largely eliminated. But such is not the case. Death rates are affected by two important factors: the mortality prevailing at specific ages and the age distribution of the populations for which they are computed. (U.S. Department of Health, Education and Welfare, 1965:28.)

AGE	1900		1963	
	White	Nonwhite	White	Nonwhite
All ages	17.0*	25.0*	9.5*	10.1*
Under 1	159.4	333.9	22.3	41.7
1-4	19.4	43.5	0.9	1.8
5-14	3.8	9.0	0.4	0.6
15-24	5.7	11.5	1.0	1.6
25-34	8.1	12.1	1.3	3.2
35-44	10.1	14.8	2.6	6.5
45-54	14.8	24.3	6.8	13.2
55-64	27.0	42.1	16.2	27.9
65-74	56.2	68.9	37.5	52.9
75-84	123.3	120.9	85.8	74.6
85 and over	262.0	215.2	215.8	145.7

* Rates per 1,000 population in each age group

(*See* Documentation 1.) He must always remain anxious and concerned about his reception by hotels and restaurants when he is traveling, about where he may build or buy a house, about whether he should accept a social invitation, and about how to explain to his children why they were not invited to a birthday party. In the past, in such areas as FHA-insured private housing, government policy has encouraged the perpetuation of discriminatory practices (Abrams, 1955).

As we noted in the chapter on poverty, many of the problems faced by blacks confront all individuals in the American community who are poor or are considered lower class. But two important points need to be noted: first, the cycle of poverty is much more rigid and difficult for the Negro to escape; second, and perhaps more important, the problems of discrimination do not end for the Negro with relative economic affluence, graduation from the "right" university, or the adoption of acceptable speech patterns.

Certainly anyone who reads a newspaper is aware of incidents in which highly educated and professionally well-regarded Negroes have suffered the indignities of burning crosses and the dangers of dynamited homes. Blacks with considerable income, social presence, and all the other genteel qualities that, it is argued, represent the entrée to participation in the good life of the community still find it difficult—and sometimes impossible—to do such simple things as rent a cottage at a beach resort or attent a charity ball. And there are less obvious ramifications of discrimination that place an unfair burden on the community member who happens to be black: he abstains from that extra drink which everyone else is having; he manifests overly polite behavior in mixed company; he oversocializes his children to conform to community norms because of anxieties and concern over his particular identification. Moreover, the black also develops stereotypes of the white world, and he may minimize the opportunities of contact with the larger community that *are* open to him (Williams, 1964).

PROSPECTS FOR REDUCTION

Some social analysts have argued that, given enough time and the emergence of a significant Negro middle class, discrimination against blacks will become a transistory phenomenon, with only slightly more fragmentation than that experienced by other minority groups in the United States. Unfortunately, the evidence for such a position is not entirely convincing and the argument is, at present anyhow, untenable. It is not only the lower-class, uneducated Negro who has economic problems. As Duncan (1967:102) has pointed out, it is the middle-educated group which suffers the most:

> It is not, therefore, the high school "dropout" who feels the greatest force of occupational discrimination, but the high school graduate or the man who completes some college work short of graduation. To be sure, the college graduate may have to render his professional or technical services in a segregated setting; but he is not prevented to the same degree as the college "dropout" or high school graduate from achieving the occupational level for which his training purportedly prepared him. At the other end of the scale, poorly educated Negroes do not suffer as much relative deprivation as those who attain the minimum standard of elementary schooling.

Right now, racial discrimination in America not only subjects a large group of citizens to suffering and deprivation because of their skin color

armed forces failures by race

The ultimate mark of inadequate preparation for life is the failure rate on the Armed Forces mental test. The Armed Forces Qualification Test is not quite a mental test, nor yet an education test. It is a test of ability to perform at an acceptable level of competence. It roughly measures ability that ought to be found in an average 7th or 8th grade student. A grown young man who cannot pass [it] is in trouble.

Fifty-six percent of Negroes fail it. This is a rate almost four times that of the whites. . . .

Although service in the Armed Forces is at least nominally a duty of all male citizens coming of age, it is clear that the present system does not enable Negroes to serve in anything like their proportionate numbers. This is not a question of discrimination. Induction into the Armed Forces is based on a variety of objective tests and standards, but these tests nonetheless have the effect of keeping the number of Negroes disproportionately small. (U.S. Department of Labor, 1965:41–42.)

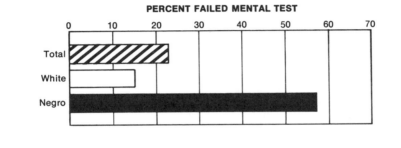

PERCENT FAILED MENTAL TEST

but it imposes an inordinate drain on the community's resources. Efforts to reduce discrimination require great expenditures of funds and, to the extent the Negro fails to become a participating member of society, the burden of supporting him represents an additional cost to the community. Despite the contribution made by blacks to the operations in Vietnam, fully one-half the Negro males of draft age are rejected for physical defects, illiteracy, and lack of education. (*See* Documentation 2.) In these times of severe shortages of skilled craftsmen, thousands of Negroes are unemployed or engaged in extremely low-skilled jobs simply because they lack the educational and vocational opportunities to fit them for these better jobs.

In addition to the waste of human and community resources, the race problem has had disastrous effects on the development of urban life. In many cases, discrimination by the white community and the forced segregation of the Negro in the core city has resulted in virtually un-remediable problems for many urban centers (Miller, 1965). The exodus of white families, particularly middle-class families who provided the tax base and social leadership, is a problem that confronts almost every eastern and midwestern city. The "pressure cooker" atmosphere of ghetto slums that can explode at any moment into disorders, riots, and armed uprisings is an inevitable consequence of the current situation. (*See* Documentation 3.) Watts and Newark will have special meaning for most Americans for a long time; and, it is fair to say, unless the prob-lem of discrimination against the Negro is handled expeditiously, the United States is threatened with similar and recurring disorders through-out her major cities (Blauner, 1966).

Finally, discrimination against blacks has had immediate repercus-sions throughout the nonwhite world and threatens to compromise the leadership role of the United States. In an era of developing black na-tions, it is wise to remember that white people constitute a minority of the world's population. Is it possible for sincere, well-intentioned govern-ment officials to praise the United States and our system of government when our internationally circulated periodicals and satellite-beamed television news reports dramatically display the racial strife we face be-cause of discrimination? How easy is it for the successful American busi-nessman to tout our economic system to potential Asian and African business associates, given the present plight of the American Negro? Dis-crimination against the Negro represents the major moral problem facing the American people today. It is also the burning objective social problem of this generation (Rose, 1965).

causes of black discrimination

In examining discrimination, particularly that directed at blacks, one is confronted with a variety of competing explanations. Etiologic inter-pretations range across a spectrum, from those emphasizing individual characteristics, through those stressing discontinuities in socialization and communication, to those focusing on structural qualities of the com-munity. In the space of this chapter, it is necessary to be less than com-plete in examining these explanations, for each has been the subject of voluminous investigation.

INDIVIDUAL DIFFERENCES

With respect to individual differences, the literature abounds with studies that purport to short that there are—or are not—biological differences in intelligence and intellectual capacity between blacks and whites (Jensen, 1969). Most of the early studies found differences between the races and suggested that they were due to genetic factors. Over the years, and particularly in recent decades, most of the new research and the re-analysis of earlier studies have led experts in psychometrics to take the position that the differences that appear in both standard testing situations and in day-to-day observation of Negroes are probably the result of differential opportunities largely created by the process of discrimination itself.

The scientific appraisal of this debate is that the data are insufficient to prove either argument. The definitive research must await a racially integrated America in which opportunities are the same for both races. The conclusion based on present data is that *if* there are any inherent distinctions, they are inconsequential. Even now, differences in IQ scores within each race greatly exceed differences between the races. Race is simply not a meaningful consideration upon which to judge an individual's intelligence (Pettigrew, 1964). Even if significant genetic differences between the races were firmly established, this would not be a rational justification for discrimination because by definition *discrimination* implies an irrational response. Treating persons differently on the basis of objective differences is not discrimination in the sense we are discussing.

THE NEGRO AS A TARGET

This is not to say that Negroes are not at the present time relegated to a socially inferior position in comparison with whites. Indeed, the problem of discrimination represents a circular process. Inadequate intellectual development and limited educational opportunities are reflected in the way individuals achieve with respect to formal tests, educational performance, and day-to-day social interaction in the larger community. The process of discrimination, then, forces and maintains differentials in social competence. These differences, some believe, make the Negro a ready target for the feelings of anger and frustration vented by white members of the community (Dollard et al., 1939). At a socio-psychological level, the Negro serves as the scapegoat or victim of the aggression that stems from frustration. Even today, the individual black remains relatively unprotected and, therefore, presents a "safe" target for hostility on the part of other community members. In this respect, it is often maintained that white community members who are low on the social-prestige and occupational scales are the ones who manifest the most intense and disruptive types of discrimination.

Among the explanations offered for the intense resistance and frequent violence exhibited by whites of lower socio-economic status toward

ghetto police

When economic and social institutions fail to provide the life-chances that a substantial part of a population wants, and when political institutions fail to provide a remedy, the aspirations of the people begin to spill over into forms of activity that the dominant society regards either as unacceptable or illegitimate—crime, vandalism, noncooperation, and various forms of political protest.

Robert M. Fogelson and Robert D. Hill, in the *Supplemental Studies* for the riot commission, have reported that 50 percent to 90 percent of the Negro males in ten cities studied had arrest records. Clearly, when the majority of men in a given population are defined as criminals—at least by the police—something more than "deviant" behaviour is involved. In effect, ghetto residents—and especially the youth—and the police are in a state of subdued warfare. On the other hand, the police—devoted to the racial status quo and inclined to overlook the niceties of mere law in their quest for law and order—have found a variety of means, both conventional and otherwise, for countering the aims of Negroes. In doing so, they are not only adhering to the norms of their institution, but also furthering their personal goals as well. The average policeman, recruited from a lower- or middle-class white background, frequently of "ethnic" origins, comes from a group whose social position is marginal and who feel most threatened by Negro advances.

The high arrest rate in the Negro community thus mirrors both the push of Negroes and the determined resistance of the police. As the conflict intensifies, the police are more and more losing authority in the eyes of black people; the young Negroes are especially defiant. Any type of contact between police and black people can quickly lead to a situation in which the policeman gives an order and the Negro either defies it or fails to show sufficient respect in obeying it. This in turn can lead to the Negro's arrest on a disorderly conduct charge or on a variety of other charges. . . .

The police often resort to harassment as a means of keeping the Negro community off-balance. The riot commission noted that: "Because youths commit a large and increasing proportion of crime, police are under growing pressure from their supervisors—and from the community—to deal with them forcefully. 'Harassment of youths' may therefore be viewed by some police departments—and members even of the Negro community—as a proper crime prevention technique." The Commission added that "many departments have adopted patrol practices which, in the words of one commentator, have 'replaced harassment by individual patrolmen with harassment by entire departments.' "

Among the most common of the cops' harassment techniques are breaking up streetcorner groups and stop-and-frisk tactics. Our study found that 63 percent of the ghetto police reported that they "frequently" were called upon to disperse loitering groups. About a third say they "frequently" stop and frisk people. Obviously then, the law enforcer sometimes interferes with individuals and groups who consider their activities quite legitimate and necessary. Black people in the ghetto—in the absence of adequate parks, playgrounds, jobs, and overcrowded houses with rats and bugs—are likely to make the streets their front yards. But this territory is often made uninhabitable by the police.

Nearly a third of the white policemen in our study thought that most of the residents of their precinct (largely Negro) were not industrious. Even more striking about the attitudes of the white police working in these neighborhoods is that many of them deny the fact of Negro inequality: 20 percent say the Negro is treated better than any other part of the population, and 14 percent say he is treated equally. As for their own treatment of Negroes, the Campbell-Schuman survey reported that 43 percent of the black men, who are on the streets more than the women, thought that police use insulting language in their neighborhoods. Only 17 percent of the white males held this belief. Of the Negro men, 20 percent reported that the police insulted them personally and 28 percent said they knew someone to whom this had happened; only 9 percent and 12 percent, respectively, of the whites reported the same. Similarly, many more blacks than whites thought that the police frisked and searched people without good reason (42 percent compared to 12 percent); and that the police roughed up people unnecessarily (37 percent as compared to 10 percent). Such reports of police misconduct were most frequent among the younger Negroes, who, after all, are on the receiving end most often.

The policeman's isolation in the ghetto is evident in a number of findings. We asked the police how many people—of various types—they knew well enough in the ghetto to greet when they saw them. Eighty-nine percent of the police said they knew six or more shopowners, managers, and clerks well enough to speak with, but only 38 percent said they knew this many teenage or youth leaders. At the same time, 39 percent said that most young adults, and 51 percent said that most adolescents, regard the police as enemies. And only 16 percent of the white policemen (37 percent of the blacks) either "often" or "sometimes" attended meetings in the neighborhood.

The police have wound up face to face with the social consequences of the problems in the ghetto created by the failure of other white institutions—though, as has been observed, they themselves have contributed to those problems in no small degree. The distant and gentlemanly white racism of employers, the discrimination of white parents who object to having their children go to school with Negroes, the disgruntlement of white taxpayers who deride the present welfare system as a sinkhole of public funds but are unwilling to see it replaced by anything more effective—the consequences of these and other forms of white racism have confronted the police with a massive control problem of the kind most evident in the riots.

In our survey, we found that the police were inclined to see the riots as the long range result of faults in the Negro community—disrespect for the law, crime, broken families, etc.—rather than as responses to the stance of the white community. Indeed, nearly one-third of the white police saw the riots as the result of what they considered the basic violence and disrespect of Negroes in general, while only one-fourth attributed the riots to the failure of white institutions. More than three-fourths also regarded the riots as the immediate result of agitators and criminals—a suggestion contradicted by all the evidence accumulated by the riot commission. The police, then, share with the other groups—excepting the black politicians—a tendency to emphasize perceived defects in the black community as an explanation for the difficulties they encounter in the ghetto.

The state of siege evident in many police departments is but an exaggerated version of a trend in the larger white society. It is the understandable, but unfortunate, response of people who are angry and confused about the widespread disruption of traditional racial patterns and who feel threatened by these changes. These is, of course, some basis for this feeling, because the Negro movement poses challenges of power and interest to many groups. To the extent that the movement is successful, the merchants, for example, will either have to reform their practices or go out of business—and for many it may be too late for reform. White suburbanites will have to cough up funds for the city, which provides most of them with employment. Police departments will have to be thoroughly restructured. (Boesel et al., 1969:29–31.)

integration, especially of schools and housing, are the precariousness of their own economic situation, the insecurity of their social position, and the frustrations of their existence. Homeownership, for example, is a status symbol to such people, and they vigilantly guard their urban neighborhoods against any element that poses a threat to their hard-won possession. Because many such people see the bussing of black children to schools in their neighborhood as a step toward breaking down the housing barriers, they cling to the neighborhood-school concept as an "acceptable" defense against integration.

EARLY SOCIALIZATION

The problem of discrimination in schools and housing takes on added significance when one observes that these issues frequently expose young children to the negative racial attitudes of adults in the community, including their own parents. This early socialization serves to perpetuate acts of discrimination that positive experiences and interactions with Negroes would help to reduce. While there are marked discrepancies between attitudes and behavior—in this instance, between prejudice and discrimination—it must be acknowledged that the experiences of some community members are transferred into actions by others. Hostility and aggression toward the Negro and the maintenance of stereotyped views of his competence and potential are unquestionably transmitted from individual to individual within the community (Williams, 1964).

While frustration, aggression, and the marginal status of many whites may account for some of the discriminatory behavior of some community members, they do not explain sufficiently all such actions. They do not, for example, account for the serious and sometimes violent opposition of at least some residents to Negroes' moving into middle-class neighborhoods or even upper-class suburbs. At best, blacks can expect an uneasy neutrality from their white neighbors regardless of their social characteristics. (*See* Documentation 4.) Perhaps it is most useful to regard insecurity and frustration as contributing factors and not as complete explanations.

SOCIAL AFFINITY

Social rejection and economic loss are two other factors frequently cited as causes of racial discrimination in the areas of housing and employment. Persons often state, whether it is true or not, that they have no objection to living on the same street with a Negro except that his buying a home there would lower property values. Or businessmen will maintain that while they would be glad to hire Negro salesmen, the customers would object and take their business elsewhere. In fact, several studies have documented instances where Negroes have moved into suburbs or middle-class urban areas without any appreciable reduction in property values (Laurenti, 1960). Likewise, numerous experiences in the business world indicate that the employment of Negroes generally has no negative impact on the sales or profits of a company.

Some analysts argue that all claims of potential economic loss are simply rationalizations and serve to cover up deeper prejudices. Some of these fears, particularly in the area of housing, have been realized in the vicious practice of blockbusting. When a black family moves into a formerly all-white neighborhood, unscrupulous operators urge residents to sell their houses, often at a substantial loss. The houses are then resold at inflated prices to house-hungry Negroes, making a quick and tidy profit for the speculator. In other situations, the arrival of a few black families has resulted in a mass exodus of white residents and a consequent reduction in property values because of a sudden excess of available housing. Such neighborhoods frequently begin to deteriorate and may well result in further spreading of slums. While local laws and realtor codes have sought to correct panic-selling abuses, the economic explanation—fear of declining property values—has at least some basis in fact, and this aspect of the situation cannot be minimized (Laurenti, 1960). Recent court actions have sought punitive damages for losses resulting from real estate malpractices, and ethical realtors have made serious efforts to combat these trends.

BLACK VISIBILITY

The heightened visibility of the Negro makes him a more obvious candidate for discrimination than his white peers. While not all white Americans can be remolded into fashion models or other "ideal" types, they nevertheless have more opportunities than most blacks to disappear into the larger community. There is evidence from the recent past that light skin color and Caucasian features were often more highly valued, at least among middle income blacks, than Negroid characteristics, even among Negroes (Freeman et al., 1966).

The new emphasis on Negro identity and the recognition that "black is beautiful" has probably negated if not reversed this trend. However, the inability of blacks to disguise their minority status is a problem faced by no other group except perhaps those with marked physical handicaps.

If we accept the view that the development of attitudes and the internalization of norms are guided by the processes of communication and interaction, and if we acknowledge that skin color can represent a barrier to communication and interaction, then visibility cannot be dismissed as a possible explanation for the operation of discrimination.

DOCUMENTATION 4

attitudes of white residents to mixed housing

Half of the sample [of Kalamazoo white residents] expressed themselves as being indifferent toward life in a mixed neighborhood and this did not vary greatly in subcategories except with those of less than a high school education of whom more than half were frankly hostile to mixed housing and only 31 percent neutral; and the professional and business executive group of whom 75 percent were neutral and only six percent hostile. . . . The professional and business executive group is highly sensitive to the changing currents of community opinion and it would be expected that the majority of its members would espouse the type of attitude which is socially correct. The group of less than grade school education is both less sensitive to currents of thought in the community and is under less pressure to express attitudes which are considered socially acceptable in middle class circles. There was little variation in the percentage of the two groups who favored integrated housing, indicating that the professional and business group does not have many members who take a stand in advance of public opinion

on a controversial question.

The desirability of mixed housing was a subject on which the individuals in the area who might be assumed to be most sensitive to the currents of community opinion tended to refrain from expressions of either acceptance or open hostility. Insofar as they deviated from a non-committal stand it was more apt to be in the direction of acceptance, while those whose age or social status might make them less sensitive to a changing climate of opinion were more inclined to express hostile sentiments. The general attitude of neutrality or acceptance was most marked in those above eighth grade education who had occupational status above the rank of laborer, who lived in a home costing more than $8,000, and who were in the age bracket between 20 and 40. These differences, however, are not sharp enough to alter the statement that the prevalent attitude toward a Negro entering a mixed housing area was one of uneasy neutrality with occasional sharp expressions of hostility and slightly less frequent expressions of friendship and welcome.

BLACK IDENTITY

Perhaps an even more powerful explanation of discrimination can be found in the basis of the Negro's existence in American society. His roots in human slavery and, at least in the South, the hostility engendered by the War Between the States provide convenient rationalizations for placing limitations on the Negro's full participation in community life. Unlike other national or religious groups who suffered oppression and discrimination at various times in this country, the African "immigrants" did not share a common ethnic and cultural identity. Differences in tribal language and custom were utilized to prevent the development of a sense of solidarity among the slaves and, more important, reciprocity within the group which would enable them to meet collectively the

Acceptance or rejection of mixed housing appeared to be a matter of conformity to general Kalamazoo opinion rather than the result of specific social patterns which might be thought to affect racial prejudice. Although there was a variation in the proportion expressing hostility and acceptance, the mode in all but one of the sub-groups was a statement of indifference or neutrality. (Hunt, 1960:206–207.)

FACTORS RELATED TO MIXED HOUSING ATTITUDES OF WHITE RESIDENTS

		Percentage Taking Designated Positions		
	N	Favor	Neutral	Hostile
Proximity				
Next door to Negro	63	24%	44%	32%
Not next door	70	17	54	29
Entry in Area				
Before Negroes	95	16	50	34
After Negroes	38	32	47	21
Education				
Beyond high school	34	14	52	34
9th to 12th grade	69	24	54	22
8th grade or less	30	17	31	52
Occupation of Chief Wage Earner				
Professional, business executive	17	19	75	6
White collar, small business	27	11	56	33
Labor	89	23	47	30
Age				
40 plus	82	14	46	40
Under 40	51	34	53	13
Price of House				
Under $8 000	73	18	44	38
Over $8,000	61	25	59	16
Total Sample White Residents	133	20	50	30

challenges of oppression. Emancipation provided freedom from bondage but did not stimulate strong in-group identity that allows a minority people to resist the hostile forces in the dominant society. Only in the last few years has the Afro-American begun seriously to search for his cultural identity and to develop a racial pride and cohesiveness similar to that exercised by other minorities in America.

FAMILY ENVIRONMENT

Whether or not the roots of the problem lie in the background of slavery, it is quite clear that, in many instances, the contemporary Negro family represents an environment that creates difficulties for each new generation. Moynihan (1965) points out that today, as in past generations, slave and free, a large number of Negro children are reared in one-parent matriarchal households. Even where both parents are present, the role of the wife and mother in many poverty-striken households reveals important differences in comparison with her counterpart in middle-class families. In many black households, these differences are even more striking.

Moynihan's views, while challenged on many counts, are based on his interpretation of existing deficiencies in the black family. These include: the unavailability in the home of appropriate male role models, especially for boys; the dominance of the mother in the rearing of children; and the occupational structure that provides many more job opportunities for women than it does for men. According to some sociologists (Rainwater and Yancey, 1967; Valentine, 1968), these interpretations shift the focus of responsibility, and even blame, for the plight of blacks back upon themselves rather than placing it squarely on the larger community and the racist orientation of American society. The Kerner Commission Report (National Advisory Commission, 1968a) and a number of supporting studies (National Advisory Commission, 1968b) have documented the extent of white racism in our society, and this current ideology denies the supposed implications of Moynihan's position, even when it does not question his facts.

The thesis that opportunities for blacks in the world of work are dependent on the structure of the family raises many discouraging issues. It is clear that the economic and political structures have encouraged and perpetuated the female-based black household. More low-level service type jobs are available for women than for men. This creates a different relationship between the sexes, with accompanying strains and dislocations. The welfare laws, even after recent improvements, still discriminate against families that include an able-bodied but unemployed or underemployed male. In the recent past, if not today, the father in such a household was literally required to abandon his family before it would be eligible to receive welfare aid. In many states, these requirements have been applied differentially to the two races and thus the impact on black families has been increased. In recent years, black welfare recipients have begun actively to oppose the welfare establishment in its entirety; it would seem, therefore, that many of the people the system supposedly serves no longer support it. (*See* Documentation 5.)

BLACK OR POOR?

The argument that lack of progress by blacks is due solely to the systematic denial of institutionalized means for their advancement and to the structural barriers raised against their full participation in American society remains in dispute. Explanations that draw their substance from

social workers and the welfare establishment

Public welfare is another area in which old ideas have been perpetuated beyond their time. The roots of the present welfare-department structure lie in the New Deal legislation of the 1930's. The public assistance provisions of the Social Security Act were designed to give aid to the helpless and the non-competitive: the aged, the blind, the "permanently and totally" disabled, and dependent children. The assumption was that the recipient, because of personal disabilities or inadequacies, could not make his way in life without outside help.

The New Deal also provided work (e.g., the W.P.A.) for the able-bodied who were assumed to be unemployed only temporarily. But as the Depression gave way to the war years and to the return of prosperity, the massive work programs for the able-bodied poor were discontinued, leaving only those programs that were premised on the notion of personal disability. To a considerable extent today's Negro poor have had to rely on the latter. Chief among these programs, of course, is Aid for Dependent Children, which has become a mainstay of welfare. And because of racial discrimination, especially in education and employment, a large part of the Negro population also experiences poverty as a permanent state.

While most of the social workers in our survey showed considerable sympathy with the Negro cause, they too felt that the root of the problem lay in weaknesses in the Negro community; and they saw their primary task as making up the supposed deficiency. A hefty majority of the respondents (78%) thought that a large part of their responsibility was to "teach the poor how to live"—rather than to provide the means for them to live as they like. . . .

The social workers, however, are unique among the groups surveyed in that they are quite critical of their own institution. The average welfare worker is not entirely at one with the establishment for which she works. She is likely to be a college graduate who regards her job as transitional. And her lack of expertise has its advantages as well as its disadvantages, for it means that she can take a more straightforward view of the situations she is confronted with. She is not committed to bureaucracy. . . .

The disparity between the welfare establishment and the average welfare worker is evident in the latter's complaints about her job. The complaints she voices the most deal *not* with her clients, but the welfare department itself and the problems of working within its present structure—the difficulty of getting things done, the red tape, the lack of adequate funds, and so on. Of the five most-mentioned difficulties of welfare work, three dealt with such intra-agency problems; the other two dealt with the living conditions of the poor.

There is a good deal of evidence to support the social worker's complaints. She complains, for example, that welfare agencies are understaffed. The survey indicates that an average caseload is 177 people, each client being visited about once a month for about 50 minutes. Even the most conscientious of caseworkers must be overwhelmed by such . . . ratios.

As in the case of the schools, welfare has engendered a countervailing force among the very people it is supposed to serve. Welfare clients have become increasing hostile to the traditional structure and philosophy of welfare departments and have formed themselves into an outspoken movement. The welfare-rights movement at this stage has aims: to obtain a more nearly adequate living base for the clients, and to overload the system with demands, thus either forcing significant changes or clearing the way for new and more appropriate institutions. (Boesel et al., 1969:27–28.)

differences in cultural backgrounds and value orientations and from individualized problems of adaptation have been advanced to augment and frequently counter the structural thesis. Do there exist group characteristics of black culture and individual differences in life styles that mitigate against the integration and assimilation of Negroes? Evidence from research in this area is ambiguous and contradictory. The so-called culture-of-poverty school postulates a similar life style for all low-income minority groups, especially those residing in ghetto areas. Some analysts, such as Oscar Lewis (1966), tend to view this situation critically; others, including Miller, Riessman and Seagull (1968) and Coles (1965), take a more positive view and recognize social values that exist even among the most deprived. Still other analysts, among them Thomas Gladwin (1963) and Hylan Lewis (1960), argue that the life styles of the urban poor represent not a system of culturally evolved social patterns but rather a disjunctive series of adaptations to the stress and strain of everyday existence that is viewed as capricious and uncontrollable (Herzog, 1967).

The concept of a culture of poverty had a vogue which distorted its usefulness and now tends to obliterate even its limited utility. A reasonable use of the analogy between lower-class life styles and culture is to think of poverty as a subculture within the larger American culture. This distinction was made by Oscar Lewis in his paper presented at the 1961 National Conference on Social Welfare. In our urban society, everyone, including the poorest, belongs to more than one subculture. At different times and in different situations an individual may respond to one influence and not to another. While we find important regularities in the behavior of persons sharing a common set of circumstances, we also find individual differences and subgroup variants that coexist with the prevailing patterns.

VALUE DIFFERENCES

Even in the larger culture there may be conflicts and contradictions that force the individual to choose among several equally acceptable courses of action. At least two sets of values—those we cherish as ideals and those we live by every day—are held by most individuals. The classic example is the parent who admonishes the child, "Do as I say, not as I do." This duality of values (Rodman, 1963) explains some of the apparent inconsistency between what people, including poor blacks, say they do—or believe they ought to do—and what they actually do. In a research interview, a respondent who is black and poor may subscribe to the common American middle-class culture and its value orientations, and may even prefer them, without any thought to their relevance to his everyday behavior. The poorest black mother may have high, even unattainably high, expectations and aspirations for the educational and occupational achievements of her children. Is this ambition to be applauded as laudatory or criticized as unrealistic?

Very often, as Herzog (1967) points out, an individual may pay homage to two conflicting values but recognize only one choice. Black families may value stable happy marriages but recognize that a fatherless household or an illegitimate child are acceptable, if less valued, alternatives. Because a much larger proportion of black families are poor, the confounding of race and socio-economic status has resulted in many research findings being attributed to the influence of race when, in fact, the association is due largely to social class which has not been accounted for in the correlation.

The high priority given to lack of institutionalized means as an explanation for the problems of discrimination has tended to blur the influence of social and cultural differences and to underemphasize the manipulation of these more individual variables in suggested solutions. Many of the current problems faced by the American community, from swollen welfare rolls to crime in the streets, are interpreted as the outgrowth of inadequate institutionalized means that limit severely the participation of blacks in the life of the community (Pettigrew, 1964).

STRUCTURAL RIGIDITIES

The extreme viewpoint implies that the problems of discrimination would be solved if by some magical means it were possible to remove all barriers to participation in the educational, political, and occupational world and to make available every sort of opportunity to blacks. Such a conception suggests that at least part of the Negro community no longer wishes to persist as an identifiable group. It further supposes that the value system of all blacks is congruent with the dominant American culture. This point of view has been criticized on several grounds. Some, such as Handlin (1957), maintain that few minority groups disappear entirely into the larger American scene; moreover, neither the social order nor the psychological well-being of minority groups is best accomplished by utter and complete assimiliation.

Perhaps of even greater consequence is the different distribution, at least at the present time, of the life space of blacks compared to that of their white peers. In fact, the wider community continues to be guilty of keeping the Negro confined both socially and residentially.

> The programs suggested for overcoming Negro concentrations face great obstacles. They arouse the ire of the ignorant and the prejudiced. They are disquieting to even the fair-minded and the sophisticated who live good lives and who perform their civic duties conscientiously. And

they will be bitterly opposed by a wide range of people: owners, mortgagers, and others who profit from the present patterns of land use; political leaders in the central cities, including Negro leaders, who fear the dissipation of established constituencies, as well as political leaders of other areas whose tenure will be disturbed by the incursion of new voters into their districts; old residents of suburbs and the better central-city neighborhoods who hold strongly to their comfortable social situations and established shopping, social, and educational patterns (Grodzins, 1967:150).

To combat discrimination, it would seem, requires not only improvement of the institutionalized means but also consideration of more effective techniques of value-orientation, communication, and interaction. Evidence of this is reasonably clear; in a number of cities, recent dramatic improvements in the institutionalized means at the disposal of blacks have not altered appreciably the basic problems of discrimination. Studies indicate, for example, that even when housing is available in predominately white suburbs and a number of black ghetto families have sufficient economic resources to afford such a way of life, there is no mass rush to take advantage of such opportunities (Watts et al., 1965). Ignoring for the moment the problem of subtle psychological fear, it is reasonable to ask why a family possessing considerable status in a predominately black ghetto, living within easy access by public transportation to the resources of a major metropolis, and commanding sufficient purchasing power to assure decent, although restricted, housing would want to move twenty miles from where they now live and work and where they are held in considerable esteem by their less fortunate neighbors.

BLACK CULTURE

While it can be argued that the Negro has been denied the culture of the larger society, he is certainly not cultureless. The earlier statement that blacks do not have the kind of national or religious identification that has supported other minority groups does not mean that blacks have no community leaders or no cultural institutions. Furthermore, these functions are in no sense limited to the Martin Luther Kings and the NAACP. Every community has its ministers, editors, and educators, its churches, social clubs, and fraternal organizations.

On balance, the judgment that discrimination is due primarily to the lack of institutionalized means would seem to be a one-sided view of the etiology of this problem. Clearly, the nexus between individual and group differences and the lack of institutionalized opportunities has to be recognized, namely, the past failure of the community to provide adequate opportunity for interaction, communication, and socialization of black people.

intervention and change

The approaches to the problems of discrimination have undergone marked changes during the last decade. Researchers and planners have advocated new intervention strategies and, for the most part, they have been accepted on the political scene. Prior to World War II, the underlying strategy of most intervention programs was predicated on a link between attitudes and behavior. Such programs assumed that changing people's attitudes towards the Negro would eventually lead to a reduction in the problems of discrimination. This approach has been largely abandoned, however.

LEGAL TACTICS

The slowness and ineffectiveness of the attitude-discrimination approach was largely responsible for its demise. We now have learned that behavioral change may precede rather than follow attitude change, and this knowledge has opened up new possibilities for action. Perhaps the most successful illustration of this new approach was the integration, by fiat, of the armed forces. A presidential order almost overnight provided opportunities for Negroes—in our terms, legitimate means—that were not thought possible the day before. While there is no pretense that blacks in the armed forces do not still face problems, particularly in the social aspects of military life, all of the evidence supports the effectiveness of regulatory mechanisms that promote nondiscrimination.

> Although the military was until recent times one of America's most segregated institutions, it has leaped into the forefront of racial equality in the past decade. What features of the military establishment can account for this about-face? There is a combination of mutually supporting factors that operate in the successful racial integration of the armed forces. For one thing, the military—an institution revolving around techniques of violence—is to an important degree discontinuous from other areas of social life. And this apartness served to allow, once the course has been decided, a rapid and complete racial integration. The path of desegregation was further made easier by characteristics peculiar or at least more pronounced in the military compared to other institutions. With its hierarchical power structure, predicated on stable and patterned relationships, decisions need take relatively little account of the personal desires of service personnel (Moskos, 1966:147).

Efforts at development and enforcement of legal statutes provided opportunities in the early 1950s for blacks to participate politically by voting and to engage in a wide range of educational and occupational

DOCUMENTATION 6

voting behavior of blacks

Results from an intensive nationwide survey of the 1952 presidential election, conducted by the University of Michigan Survey Research Center, [show that three out of four citizens voted]. Among Negroes, however, only one out of every three eligible persons reported voting in 1952. . . .

Despite the paucity of reliable information on Negro voting, two nationwide studies allow us to contrast the above finds with turnout in the 1960 presidential election. Both were conducted by NORC, one in May, 1963, and the other directly after the assassination of Presi-

dent Kennedy in November, 1963. In each study, the following question was asked of respondents: "Did you happen to vote in that [the 1960] election or were you unable to for some reason?" The above table is a comparison of these findings with those of the 1952 study. Looking first at the proportion of voters in the samples, we observe little change from 1952 to 1960. By contrast, the proportions of Negro voters show a dramatic positive trend. Indeed, the NORC figures indicate that Negroes were almost twice as likely to vote in 1960 as in 1952. (Orum, 1966:39–40.)

PERCENT OF VOTERS IN TWO ELECTIONS

Voter	1952 %	1952 N	1960-MAY %	1960-MAY N	1960-November %	1960-November N
National Sample	73	1,614	72	1,505	71	1,358
Negroes	32	157	57	162	53	163

opportunities formerly closed to them. (*See* Documentation 6.) One would have suspected that during this period the problem of racial discrimination would have diminished as a major issue on the American scene. This has certainly not been the case. Several explanations can be offered for the continued concern with discrimination in addition to the obvious problem of enforcing rules and laws in many areas, including employment (Weaver, 1964).

First, and perhaps inevitably, as discrimination was reduced and more opportunities became available more often to more blacks, many of them began to perceive the true dimensions of the "good life" of the white world and were motivated to press for more rapid improvement and change in their own lot.

Second, as the areas of concern were broadened, more and more whites began to comprehend the implications of discrimination. The original areas of change were well-clarified and involved rights belonging to all American citizens. Since in many ways these changes affected the South to a greater extent than they did the North, the majority of the country's population was supportive, or at least undisturbed by them. Legal segregation of schools, for example, was not an issue in northern cities such as New York and Chicago. It was possible during this period, therefore, for whites, particularly in the North, to tacitly support the intervention of the National Guard at Little Rock or the federal marshalls at the University of Alabama.

Throughout the 1950s, the southern states continued to be the main target of the regulatory mechanisms instituted by the federal government. Not until the 1960s did the concept of de facto segregation gain prominence. With the Supreme Court's ruling that de facto, as well as legal, segregation was unconstitutional, the consequences of discrimination became indeed a nationwide concern. Moreover, the expansion of federal programs to wider areas of social life, such as housing, forced many white citizens to examine critically local patterns of segregation; this accounts, in part, for the increased community concern with the process of nondiscrimination (Bressler, 1960; Hunt, 1960). Then, too, the recognition and support of legislation to provide more equitable opportunities in terms of institutionalized means—for example, the widespread efforts of the Office of Economic Opportunity and the Office of Education at the federal level—have made apparent to large segments of the white community not previously affected that they, too, are guilty of supporting discrimination and denying equal opportunity to all community members.

VIOLENT TACTICS AND WHITE OPPOSITION

There is a growing fear of black rebellion. Fed up with the squalor of their living conditions, frustrated by their lack of redress, impatient with the pace of programs designed to extend the range of their legitimized means, many young blacks have turned to violence. Beginning with Watts in Los Angeles, the list of cities torn by rioting and destruction continues to grow. After analyzing the cause of rioting in the United States, the National Advisory Commission on Civil Disorder (1968a) concluded that most of the more than one hundred incidents reported in 1967 involved blacks acting against local symbols of white American society.

That the implementation of programs to meet the legitimate needs of the Negro has not been entirely successful is so obvious that it needs little documentation. At the root of most failures is the ambivalent attitude of the white community. Residents of all-white neighborhoods, whose children attend all-white neighborhood schools, may be complacent about or even consider themselves sympathetic to nondiscrimination. But when a program is initiated which includes bussing black children into their schools or transferring their children into racially mixed schools, the reaction is often quite different. In the past, union leaders, particularly in the craft unions, have represented themselves as bulwarks of liberalism, but the facade quickly crumbles when attempts are made to provide opportunities for blacks within their specific jurisdictions.

In brief, as programs that seek to open up opportunities for blacks have touched a broader base of the American population, and as challenges to the power of de facto segregation have increased, clear evidence is available that a majority of the white community is opposed to the massive changes that are required to modify quickly the lot of the Negro. The term *white backlash* has become a common description of the reactions of white community members toward the liberal programs designed to develop further opportunities for blacks and speed their assimilation into the political, economic, educational, and social life of the community.

"MAKING IT" IN THE LARGER SOCIETY

One of the limitations of current efforts that must be recognized is the relevance of communication and interaction to the problem. The simple provision of opportunities is not enough. For example, the reduction of barriers to federal employment and the guarantee of equal job opportunities for blacks does not by itself improve the lot of many people. True, secretarial, clerical, and maintenance positions may be filled more often by blacks, but the shortage of individuals with professional and technical training severely limits the opening of many legitimate avenues for blacks in the world of work. It is clear that much more than the occupational sphere requires modification, and the obvious point of entry is the educational system. From this rather incontestable view regarding the primary target spring many of the dilemmas facing the American community in terms of black-white relations.

THE EDUCATIONAL ISSUES

If the educational problem is dealt with first, there is the question of whether any progress can be accomplished without providing schools that are racially balanced or at least racially mixed. In 1967, the U.S. Civil Rights Commission asserted—admittedly without clear-cut evidence —that black children learn more in schools where they have the opportunity to interact and relate in a social setting with teachers and pupils of both races. Such an assumption, of course, is consistent with the views of those who hold that transmission of values, as well as knowledge, is critical for the development of the individual. Recent findings, however, are tending to challenge the Commission's theory that integration itself results in higher achievement by black students, although the evidence is still inconclusive. Some educators are beginning to postulate that the quality or kind of educational experience may be more important than an integrated setting. Creative, innovative, "quality" education is certainly the selling point for the top-rated suburban public high schools and better prep schools. But, as Coleman and his associates (1966) have pointed out, few if any "separate but equal" educational settings exist for blacks in the United States today.

This inequality is due to class and social status as well as to skin color. There is no doubt that in most of the major cities in the United States, the middle-class children receive the better education. Generally, school teachers, like most community members, would rather relate to and deal with individuals whose codes of conduct and value systems are consistent with their own. In addition, their energy and efforts in the classroom have a more visible impact if they do not have to struggle with the problems of inadequate home life and economic deprivation of their students. Most college professors prefer to teach in schools with the brightest students and the most prestige, and there is no reason to assume that grammar and high school teachers feel any differently. Faced with the pragmatic difficulty, if not impossibility, of providing equal educational opportunities in racially separate schools, black leaders and their white colleagues turned their major efforts toward developing programs for integration. The Supreme Court decision with respect to school desegregation is being carried out formally in the South by the gradual—sometimes very gradual—dissolution of the dual school system and in the North by a variety of efforts, including open enrollment, redistricting, and bussing. Many of these programs have met with considerable resistance from both white backlashers and black separatists (Tretten, 1968), and practical as well as political considerations have limited their scope (Decter, 1964). However, programming is not the prime difficulty in promoting nondiscrimination; the real problem is to develop some regulatory mechanism to deal with the moral issues.

> Certainly it could be argued . . . that some rather massive restructuring of our educational system is needed. As a minimum, it would seem that no great increase in achievement can be expected from *only* providing better school buildings and equipment or shifting Negro students from segregated to less segregated schools unless special and powerful programs directed at overcoming educational deficits are also instituted. This is not to deny that desegregation may improve the average test scores of Negro and other minority group students: the survey presents evidence that those Negro students who first entered desegregated schools in the early grades generally obtain slightly higher average test scores than those who entered in the higher grades. Moreover, it is likely that the academic performance of particular Negro students may benefit (or suffer) as a result of desegregation, depending on the conditions, including the degree of segregation, in a given school. Nor is it to assert that there are no other benefits to both minority and

majority group students which flow from school desegregation. Rather, it is to argue that desegregation alone is likely to be too little and too late to overcome the handicaps with which most Negro children are burdened by the time they enter school (Sewell, 1967:478).

THE PESSIMISTIC FUTURE

The seriousness of the educational situation and its links to other social determinants is widely recognized on the part of black families, particularly those whose ambitions are centered on the dominant-value scheme. Given these circumstances, there is increasing pressure to implement the 1968 nondiscrimination-in-housing ruling as well as to push for improvements in the educational and occupational sphere. In addition, opportunities for freedom of movement within the social life of the community are on the agenda for reform. It is such efforts as these that have provoked the reaction of entrenched whites against further reduction of discrimination.

The countermovement in the black community toward separatism and the severing of all ties with the white majority is a further cause for pessimism with respect to the immediate future. Middle-class blacks with access to and influence in the dominant society are reducing their interracial contacts and avoiding the kinds of communication and interaction upon which good intergroup relations strongly depend.

INTEGRATION vs. SEPARATISM

Some social observers feel that emotionally, and perhaps even objectively, the concepts of integration and nondiscrimination are so similar that they have to be exercised simultaneously; however, this is certainly not essential from a logical standpoint. Many students of American culture point out that other minority groups have attained records of achievement through legitimate means without widespread integration. The Jew is a case in point, as is the Irish-Catholic, although perhaps to a lesser extent. The argument of whether or not integration is an essential element in the reduction of discrimination brings one back to the basic dilemmas and conflicts in the American value system. The history of legislation, particularly at the local level, and the reactions of community members point to the fact that a large proportion of the white community does not want integration, at least in housing and in certain types of social activities. The issue of whether or not a strategy is realistic which deals simultaneously with the problems of integration and nondiscrimination is open to question. Certainly, there is considerable disenchantment on the part of many blacks who doubt this will ever be accomplished.

Proponents of the integration movement argue that integration is the only solution to the problem. They contend that discrimination against the Negro will not end, nor will his feelings of inferiority and inadequacy be overcome, without integration. The alternative concepts of Black Power and black separatism have gained wide acceptance among a large segment of the Negro leadership. Black Power has, of course, its emotional basis and in many ways represents the rallying cry of a long-term dissatisfied and protesting group:

> And power—not desegregated lunch counters, not integrated schools, no, not even equal (or for that matter, preferential) access to jobs—is what the Negro revolt is all about.
>
> Indeed, the Negro revolt cannot be understood except as a long-suppressed reaction against an imbalance of power—an imbalance which whites take for granted, but which Negroes have always resented. Negroes have never had the sense of controlling their own destinies; they have never had the feeling that they were making or even participating in, the decisions that really counted, the decisions that affected their lives and fortunes (Silberman, 1965:123).

From an extremist perspective, this kind of approach suggests the likelihood of a significant segment of the American population—the blacks—mobilizing and using force and violence as well as block voting to obtain their ends. However, a more moderate view holds that the concept of Black Power does not differ significantly from the separatism that has proved useful to other minority groups in establishing their place in the American community. The Black Power movement may be a means of reducing the dependency of the black leadership on the "style" of the white power structure in the community (Thompson, 1963).

BLACK POWER

Many black leaders view Black Power from this moderate stance. They argue that the eventual diminution of discrimination is not going to come about by forced opportunities for integration, not when the movement of a single family into a formerly all-white area of a Pennsylvania suburb results in riots and draws 500 screaming whites to the doorstep of the home bought by a black man with his own money in ways consistent with the legal code of the Commonwealth of Pennsylvania (Bressler, 1960). Integration is not going to be accomplished, they maintain, when white families move away in droves from the core city because the rezoning of school boundaries places their children in contact with a relatively large number of Negroes. Integration is not the solution when many of the social clubs that include judges, legislators, and prominent businessmen among their members refuse to accept Negroes who have achieved importance within the black community.

black power

The adoption of the concept of Black Power is one of the most legitimate and healthy developments in American politics and race relations in our time. . . . It is a call for black people in this country to unite, to recognize their heritage, to build a sense of community. It is a call for black people to begin to define their own goals, to lead their own organizations and to support those organizations. It is a call to reject the racist institutions and values of this society.

The concept of Black Power rests on a fundamental premise: *Before a group can enter the open society, it must first close ranks.* By this we mean that group solidarity is necessary before a group can operate effectively from a bargaining position of strength in a pluralistic society. Traditionally, each new ethnic group in this society has found the route to social and political viability through the organization of its own institutions with which to represent its needs within the larger society. Studies in voting behavior specifically, and political behavior generally, have made it clear that politically the American pot has not melted. Italians vote for Rubino over O'Brien; Irish for Murphy over Goldberg, etc. This phenomenon may seem distasteful to some, but it has been and remains today a central fact of the American political system. (Carmichael and Hamilton, 1967: 44-45.)

The concept of Black Power, if looked at objectively and employed with reason, represents an alternative solution to integration—forced or otherwise. (*See* Documentation 7.) It is an argument that raises the possibility of increased group pride as a mechanism for the attainment by blacks of more of the good things of life and, at the same time, recognizes the probable impossibility of accomplishing full integration, particularly where segregation is a de facto rather than a legal phenomenon.

In addition to its potential for destructive and violent activity, Black Power raises several political-legal concerns. Many of the programs designed to improve the lot of low-income families, which includes the vast majority of urban blacks, are either government-sponsored or government-financed. Ironically, the success of the earlier drive to end discrimination in federal programs has put separatist activities beyond the pale of government support. The expenditure of federal funds for any program that has a for-blacks-only emphasis is open to question on legal grounds. Also, there is the pragmatic problem of political feasibility.

> "Black Power" and New Left spokesmen have argued—and, evidently, convinced some liberals—that the only way in which Negroes could wrest anything from the power structure was by violence and rioting. They say that only after the riots in Watts did the federal government pay any attention to Negroes in that area. Now it is true that some special programs were initiated in Watts, though actually there was a

minimum of money expended and a maximum of rhetoric. (The programs, by the way, were not funded with new appropriations but came out of the money that had already been earmarked for antipoverty programs in other Negro ghettos. In that sense, the Watts riot merely led to a redistribution of inadequate funds.) To be sure, Chicago Negro communities got sprinklers on their fire hydrants after the riots—but not much else.

The definitive answer to those who see riots as a "creative" strategy came, however, in the 1966 elections, with the election of men to Congress pledged to cut back the entire poverty program. In Bakersfield, California, the scene of several days of racial violence last May, the voters decided overwhelmingly on November 8 not to participate in the federal antipoverty program. According to the *New York Times,* "Most of the benefits of the poverty programs now in effect . . . go to Negroes." Those who still argue that violence and riots help the Negro cause had better think again (Feldman, 1967:79).

It is one thing to hold that all children in the United States are entitled to the highest quality of education and to argue that the way of achieving this is to promote the integration of all public schools. It is another thing to say that programs of nondiscrimination can be developed only through the collective—and sometimes violent—actions of blacks themselves and, moreover, that such activities are a proper and legal function of federal expenditure. Several disadvantages can be seen in the implementation of the Black Power concept. First, it may tend to maximize white backlash. Second, it may eventually result in all-black programs competing with government-sponsored ones which for political or legal reasons cannot use this approach. Finally, it would seem to promote, at least temporarily, a further polarization of the races.

Clearly, massive integration in housing or the elimination of de facto school segregation is not going to be accomplished in the near future. It is equally foolish to assume that the mere opening of employment opportunities is going to have a dramatic impact on the problems of discrimination. The remedy requires more than increasing the number of Equal Opportunity Employers or persuading unions to accept Negro members. Given the climate of the white community today, it is doubtful that their values will change to the extent required to promote integration and freedom of choice in education, housing, and social relations, federal laws and programs notwithstanding. While gains undoubtedly will be made, they will remain small and sporadic, with the continuing risks of violence and the proliferation of radical movements (Clark, 1965). Perhaps the application of rational Black Power will trigger the solution, but one cannot be completely optimistic about the chances for ending discrimination in the contemporary American community.

REFERENCES

ABRAMS, CHARLES.
1955 Forbidden Neighbors. New York: Harper and Row.

BLAUNER, ROBERT.
1966 "Whitewash over Watts." Transaction 3(March/April)3–9.

BOESEL, DAVID, RICHARD BERK, W. EUGENE GRAVES, BETTY E. EIDSON AND PETER H. ROSSI.
1969 "White institutions and black rage." Trans-action 6(March):24–31.

BRESSLER, MARVIN.
1960 "Successful racial invasion." Social Problems 8(Fall):126–142.

CAMPBELL, ERNEST Q.
1961 "Moral discomfort and racial segregation—an examination of the Myrdal hypothesis." Social Forces 39(March): 228–234.

CARMICHAEL, STOKELY AND CHARLES V. HAMILTON.
1967 Black Power. New York: Random. (1968, New York: Vintage Books.)

CLARK, KENNETH B.
1965 Dark Ghetto: Dilemmas of Social Power. New York: Harper and Row.

COLEMAN, JAMES S. AND ERNEST Q. CAMPBELL, CAROL J. HOBSON, JAMES McPARTLAND, ALEXANDER M. MOOD, FREDERIC D. WEINFELD, ROBERT L. YORK.
1966 Equality of Educational Opportunity. Washington, D.C.: U.S. Government Printing Office.

COLES, ROBERT.
1965 "It's the same, but different." Daedalus 94(Fall):1107–1132.

DECTER, MIDGE.
1964 "The Negro and the New York schools." Commentary 38(September): 25–34.

DOLLARD, JOHN, L. W. DOOB, N. E. MILLER, O. H. MOWRER AND R. SEARS.
1939 Frustration and Aggression. New Haven: Yale University Press.

DUNCAN, OTIS DUDLEY.
1967 "Discrimination against Negroes." The Annals 371(May):85–103.

FELDMAN, PAUL.
1967 "The pathos of 'black power'." Dissent 14(January/February):69–79.

FREEMAN, HOWARD E., J. MICHAEL ROSS, DAVID ARMOR AND THOMAS PETTIGREW.
1966 "Color gradation and attitudes among middle-income Negroes." American Sociological Review 31(June):365–374.

GANS, HERBERT J.
1962 The Urban Villagers: Group and Class in the Life of Italian-Americans. New York: Free Press.

GLADWIN, THOMAS.
1963 "The anthropologist's view of poverty." Pp. 73–86 in Social Welfare Forum, 1961. New York: Columbia University Press.

GLAZER, NATHAN AND DANIEL P. MOYNIHAN.
1963 Beyond the Melting Pot. Cambridge: M.I.T. Press.

GLENN, NORVAL D.
1963 "Occupational benefits to whites from the subordination of Negroes." American Sociological Review 28(June): 443–448.

GRODZINS, MORTON.
1967 "The metropolitan area as a racial problem." Pp. 141–151 in H. Gold and F. Scarpitti (eds.), Combatting Social Problems. New York: Holt, Rinehart and Winston.

HANDLIN, OSCAR.
1957 Race and Nationality in American Life. Boston: Little, Brown.

HERZOG, ELIZABETH.
1967 "Is there a 'breakdown' of the Negro family?" Pp. 185–197 in John Scanzoni (ed.), Readings in Social Problems. Boston: Allyn and Bacon.

HUGHES, EVERETT C.
1963 "Race relations and the sociological imagination." American Sociological Review 28(December):879–890.

HUNT, CHESTER L.
1960 "Private integrated housing." Social Problems 7(Spring):196–209.

JENSEN, ARTHUR R.
1969 "How much can we boost I.Q. and scholastic achievement?" Harvard Educational Review 39(Winter):1–123.

LAURENTI, LUIGI.
1960 Property Values and Race: Studies in Seven Cities. Berkeley: University of California Press.

LEWIS, HYLAN.
1960 "The changing Negro family." Pp. 108–137 in Eli Ginzberg (ed.), The Nation's Children. Part 1: The Family and Social Change. New York: Columbia University Press.

LEWIS, OSCAR.
1966 La Vida: A Puerto Rican Family in the Culture of Poverty, San Juan and New York. New York: Random.

LINN, LAWRENCE S.
1965 "Verbal attitudes and overt behavior: a study of racial discrimination." Social Forces 43(March):353–364.

MILLER, LOREN.
1965 "The protest against housing segregation." The Annals 357(January): 73–79.

MILLER, S. M., FRANK RIESSMAN, AND ARTHUR SEAGULL.
1968 "Poverty and indulgence: a critique of the deferred gratification pattern." Pp. 416–432 in Louis Ferman, Joyce Kornbluh and Allen Haber (eds.), Poverty in America. Ann Arbor: University of Michigan Press.

MOSKOS, CHARLES C.
1966 "Racial integration in the armed forces." American Journal of Sociology 32(September):132–148.

MOYNIHAN, DANIEL P.
1965 The Negro Family: The Case for National Action. Office of Policy Planning and Research, U.S. Department of Labor. Washington, D.C.: U.S. Government Printing Office.

MYRDAL, GUNNAR.
1944 An American Dilemma. New York: Harper and Row.

NATIONAL ADVISORY COMMISSION ON CIVIL DISORDERS.
1968a Report of the National Advisory Commission on Civil Disorders. New York: Bantam Books.
1968b Supplemental Studies. Washington, D.C.: U.S. Government Printing Office.

ORUM, ANTHONY M.
1966 "A reappraisal of the social and political participation of Negroes." American Journal of Sociology 72 (July):32–46.

PETTIGREW, THOMAS F.
1964 A Profile of the American Negro. Princeton, New Jersey: Van Nostrand.

RAINWATER, LEE AND WILLIAM L. YANCEY.
1967 The Moynihan Report and the Politics of Controversy. Cambridge: M.I.T. Press.

RODMAN, HYMAN.
1963 "The lower-class value stretch." Social Forces 46(December):205–215.

ROSE, ARNOLD M.
1965 "The American Negro problem in the context of social change." The Annals 357(January):1–17.

SEWELL, WILLIAM.
1967 "Review symposium." American Sociological Review 32(June):475–479.

SILBERMAN, CHARLES E.
1965 "The deepening crisis in metropolis." Journal of Intergroup Relations 4 (Summer):119–129.

THOMPSON, DANIEL C.
1963 The Negro Leadership Class. Englewood Cliffs, New Jesey: Prentice-Hall.

TRETTEN, RUDIE.
1968 "Black power and education." School and Society 96(November):428–430.

U.S. DEPARTMENT OF HEALTH, EDUCATION AND WELFARE.
1965 "White and nonwhite mortality differentials in the United States." Health, Education and Welfare Indicators (June):27–38.

VALENTINE, CHARLES A.
1968 Culture and Poverty: Critique and Counter-Proposals. Chicago: University of Chicago Press.

WATTS, LEWIS G., HOWARD E. FREEMAN, HELEN M. HUGHES, ROBERT MORRIS AND THOMAS PETTIGREW.
1965 The Middle-Income Negro Family Faces Urban Renewal. Washington, D.C.: Housing and Home Finance Agency, Department of Housing and Urban Development.

WEAVER, ROBERT C.
1964 Negro Labor. New York: Harcourt, Brace and World.

WILLIAMS, ROBIN M., JR.
1964 Stranger Next Door. Englewood Cliffs, New Jersey: Prentice-Hall.

CHAPTER 7

urban deterioration

THE DECISION TO EMPHASIZE the urban community throughout this book is more than a matter of taste and interest. Contemporary American social life is centered in and about the city. Individuals who conceptualize broad areas of the country—ranging from Boston to Washington, from San Francisco to San Diego—as single megalopolises know that space exists within each metropolis and, of course, in the regions between them (Gottman, 1961). Their conceptualization, however, portrays quite dramatically the present style of life in the United States. From a primarily rural country, with a few large cities as centers of transportation, we have moved to a pattern of community development in which urban life predominates.

the meaning of urban life

Traditionally, city size is reckoned by the absolute number of persons living within a politically circumscribed area. But such statistics by themselves are misleading, for many individuals intensely involved in urban life now live in communities adjacent to the big cities and must be characterized as urbanites. (*See* Documentation 1.) Indeed, as we shall stress later on, because of their contiguous relationships with the core city, the suburbs and exurbs of the metropolis share many of the problems of deviance and disorganization associated with the inner city.

Urban identification, it should be noted, does not require that a person live in a large community. Many cities of 50,000 to 100,000 population are considered "urban" because of the characteristics of the problems found there, the style of life of community members, and the orientation of their citizens. By an urban way of life we are referring essentially to a system of social relationships in which a person's place of

urbanization

At the time of the first United States census, in 1790, the largest city in the land, Philadelphia, had but 44,000 persons. New York was the new nation's second largest city with 33,000 inhabitants. Boston, which ranked third, had only 18,000. Levittown, New York, which didn't exist before World War II, was nearly 50 percent larger in 1960 than the country's biggest city was in 1790. Levittown had over 65,000 inhabitants at the time of the 1960 census.

Despite the many detractors of suburban life and the massive effort to renew city cores, the nation's speediest growth is expected to continue to take place in the suburbs. The United States suburban population is expected to triple between 1960 and 1980 while the population for the nation as a whole climbs less than 50 percent. In the decade to 1960, suburban populations increased 56 percent while the nation's largest cities rose less than 5 percent. Chicago's suburban population, which was only slightly smaller than the city's in 1960, is expected to be nearly twice as great as the city's in 1990. Among the nation's three largest cities, only New York will be entering the 1970's with most of its daytime work force still resident within city limits. The nation's major metropolises thus are turning into urban dinosaurs. They may prove just as ungainly. (Gordon, 1963:16–17.)

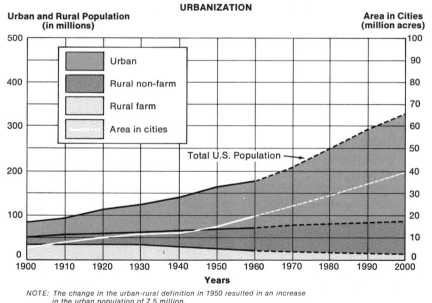

URBANIZATION

NOTE: The change in the urban-rural definition in 1950 resulted in an increase in the urban population of 7.5 million.
Source: Census Reports.

residence is independent of a wide range of other activities, including his work. It specifies a grouping of people in which the residential unit is fundamentally a consuming rather than a producing unit.

The enormous growth of urban life cannot be overemphasized. Mitchell Gorden (1963) notes that as late as 1880 the population of Los Angeles stood at 10,000 inhabitants; it rose over 2,000 per cent between 1900 and 1950. It is estimated that at the present time over 70 per cent of America's population lives in centers that can be characterized as urban and, Gorden maintains, by 1980 over 90 per cent will be living in urban areas. Every year, for example, metropolitan New Yorkers give birth to roughly one-third of a million babies, most of whose lives will be lived out in metropolitan areas. Urbanization is perhaps an inevitable consequence of industrialization and the country's economic and political structure. While few would urge that we "keep 'em down on the farm," this does not deny the critical problems faced by the American community with its high degree of urbanization.

PROS AND CONS OF CITY LIFE

Many urban problems are intrinsic to the difficulties of the ecological community-control system regulating city life. Problems of transportation, of air pollution, of space for recreation and self-expression are glaring consequences of building upward rather than outward, of pavement rather than grass, of impersonal social relationships rather than primary group relationships. From both the objective and moral perspective, it can be seen that the physical and bureaucratic arrangements of city life determine many of the major social ills confronting the community member today. The very character of the city shapes the strategies and conditions the choice of intervention methods. Urban life is responsible in part for changing the norms that surround many contemporary social activities and for defining certain conditions and behaviors as undesirable. Driving in rural areas from one small town to another along scenic winding roads is a pleasurable adventure; negotiating one's way by subway from the Bronx to Brooklyn or by freeway from the San Fernando Valley to Hollywood Boulevard is a traumatic experience. Rural teen-agers who gather twigs and branches to build a bonfire in an empty Pennsylvania cornfield are engaging in wholesome fun; city kids who strip fences and billboards to start a fire in an empty lot in Chicago may be charged with delinquency. In any number of ways, urban life enforces constraints that minimize opportunities for the enjoyment of routine tasks and activities and that restrict free expression and interpersonal relations (Greer and Orleans, 1962).

There is certainly a great deal that is attractive about city living, including opportunities to attend exhibits, theaters, and operas, to mingle and interact with individuals from a variety of backgrounds and interests, to pick and choose one's pleasure from a vast cafeteria of exciting events, to savor the food of many different nationality and ethnic groups, and to enjoy the anonymity of the city, free from concern about "what the neighbors will think." The city can be truly a glamorous place, but for many the romance is far overshadowed by the problems that appear to be concomitant with burgeoning urbanization.

THE CORE CITY

At the center of the major urban problems—indeed, of the metropolis itself—is the core city from which all else radiates. Problems abound in the core city. A major one, of course, is the provision of adequate housing in terms of public health criteria and aesthetic standards. The shame of our cities, however, refers to more than the ugliness of our Harlems, Wattses, Roxburys, and Lawndales. While perhaps too much has been made of the impact of bad housing on such social ills as delinquency, mental illness, and crime, there are sufficient and compelling reasons for decrying the extreme physical discomforts of cold in the winter and heat in the summer, of unbelievable overcrowding, of smells, dirt, and smog with which core-city residents are plagued.

Experimental studies undertaken in cities such as Baltimore show that physical health problems, and possibly psychological ones as well, are intensified by the conditions that are endemic to the overcrowded, decrepit housing of core cities (Wilner et al., 1962). Further, the various attempts to renew and rehabilitate such housing have not been overwhelmingly successful. Many of the massive high-rise public-housing projects that were built to replace deteriorating brownstones have simply become vertical slums, where the high concentrations of population put the same burdens on inadequate city services and facilities and where the elevator and stairwell supplant the alley and vacant lot as sites for robbery and rape. Moreover, land clearance procedures are often responsible for the disruption of long-term friendships and the interpersonal identification of residents forcibly relocated. Italian immigrants, for example, who had lived in the North End of Boston since their arrival in this country found themselves in their old age removed from their familiar haunts (Gans, 1962). Even ten years after this uprooting, their response was described as still "grieving for a lost home" (Fried, 1963). Small store owners, who through personal acquaintanceship and intimate dealings have managed to survive in low-rent districts, find it impossible to relocate and compete with the large supermarket chains; they are literally forced out of business by urban renewal. One of the frustrations of dealing with the problems of the inner city is the feeling that you are damned if you do and damned if you don't. Action or inaction:

neither course is without human anguish and the exacerbation, if not the further proliferation, of social problems.

THE URBAN BLACK

It would be ducking the issue not to acknowledge that a major problem of the core city is the concentration of nonwhite populations. (*See* Documentation 2.) White Americans, unless they are too poor to do otherwise, are generally unwilling to live in truly racially mixed areas (Fishman, 1961). The continued concentration in the central city of black ghettos and the consequent compounding of the problems of discrimination and isolation of the poor seem far from solution (Goldblatt and Cromier, 1962). Meyer (1963:91) describes vividly the plight of the Negro in our nation's capital:

> Lack of moral standards and lack of self-control make the recent immigrants from the South all the more dangerous when they are huddled together in overcrowded ghettos without the guidance necessary to help them adjust to city life. Discrimination in housing in the entire metropolitan area is firmly enforced by the real-estate interests. There is little decent low-cost housing within the city limits. To all intents and purposes, the Negro population lives in drab concentration camps without hope of escape. The barbed wire that fences them in may not be visible to most white people. But it is there.

At one time, the city expressed a vitality and a robustness that gave it a soul of its own. But today it is the home of the oppressed, the aged waiting to die, and the poor blocked from equal participation in the institutionalized means that lead to the good life. The current state of the city has severe consequences for the business community and the economic health of the country. As the middle-class and more well-to-do residents desert the core city for the suburbs, the remaining population faces the problem of supporting needed services in the face of a narrowing tax base. The poverty of the city reflects not only the helplessness and failure of individuals but it represents a breakdown in the business and industrial community as well. Industries are reluctant to expand within the city limits for fear of increased real estate, sales, and municipal income taxes, which they oppose (Sexton, 1964). Most school systems in the core city, particularly those with high proportions of blacks, are saddled with aging, poorly lighted, depressing buildings surrounded by broken asphalt and rusting fences, staffed by inexperienced teachers without enough seniority to be either well paid or eligible for transfer, and overcrowded with pupils lacking in discipline, incentive, and "middle-class" background and values. (*See* Documentation 3.) The protective and social services are equally inadequate, providing increased impetus

the black man and the city

In this century the Negro has become an urbanite. Three out of every four Negro Americans today reside in cities, while only one in four did so as recently as 1910. This shift represents a process of massive migration involving many millions of uprooted people. The dimensions and character of this historical process provide the larger perspective within which we must view current racial issues in urban America. Significant Negro migration to the city began during World War I. European hostilities simultaneously provided large war orders for American industry and stemmed the vast tide of immigrant labor, thereby opening up new employment opportunities for those Negroes willing to migrate. Labor recruiters encouraged the process, and young Negroes in vast numbers began what one demographer describes as "the greatest and most significant sociological event of our country's recent history."

Not all of this human surge, however, was stimulated by the attractive pull of new jobs; there were significant "push" factors as well. The high birth rate among rural southerners, the mechanization of southern agriculture, the boll weevil, government programs limiting agricultural production, and, finally, the shift of cotton cultivation to the Southwest and West—during the past half-century these factors literally almost starved the Negro off the southern farm.

The migration increased to enormous proportions in the 1920's. The pace slowed during the depression years, but accelerated rapidly again with America's entry into World War II and continued during the 1950's. Between 1950 and 1960, over a million and a half Negro southerners broke their home ties and left the region. More than a half million went to the Northeast, a like number to the Midwest, and over a third of a million to the West. Thus, Negro migration has involved not only a movement from farm to southern city but also a movement out of the South into nonsouthern cities. This wider distribution of Negro Americans throughout the nation has made absurd the time-honored segregationist claim that race relations are a southern problem and should be left exclusively to the South to solve. Now that virtually as many Negroes live outside the ex-Confederacy as in it, race relations are clearly a national concern.

It is a national concern, however, with a strongly urban cast. Today the Negro American is more urban than the white American and is especially concentrated in our largest metropolitan centers. Twenty metropolitan areas, only half of them in the South, contain 40 percent of the nation's Negroes. Our five largest cities dramatically illustrate the point. Between 1940 and 1960, the central-city nonwhite proportion of the population more than doubled in New York City and Philadelphia and approximately tripled in Chicago, Los Angeles, and Detroit. Today more Negroes live in the New York metropolitan area than in any single southern state, about as many Negroes live in metropolitan Chicago as in the entire state of Mississippi, and more Negroes live in metropolitan Philadelphia than in the entire states of Arkansas and Kentucky combined. (Pettigrew, 1969:47–48.)

for those who can manage to move. Their leaving creates further problems for the core city and, ultimately, for the entire urban metropolis.

THE SUBURBAN EXODUS

In many ways the decline of the core city and the exodus to the suburbs represent related concerns. Shifts in population and, particularly, changes in the socio-economic and other characteristics of city residents have consequences in terms of the economic structure. New approaches need to be implemented to handle the difficulties of transportation, the provision of medical services, and the ways in which people participate in the political and social life of the community. Much has been written about the

---

DOCUMENTATION 3

educational segregation

In 1962 John E. Coons, Northwestern University law professor, prepared for the United States Commission on Civil Rights a report on segregated schools in Chicago. Ten schools in each of three groups were selected—white, integrated, Negro—and the findings [for pupils, appropriations, teachers, and books are shown in the table below].

In 1963 a *Handbook of Chicago School Segregation* claimed that 1961 appropriations for school operating expenses were almost 25 per cent greater per pupil in white than in Negro schools, that teacher salaries were 18 per cent higher, that nonteaching operating expenses—clerical and maintenance, salaries, supplies, textbooks—were 50 per cent higher, and that only 3 per cent of Chicago's Negro population finishes college. . . .

Despite the fact that the median income in Chicago is higher than in New York, Chicago in one recent year spent $410 per pupil while New York spent $761.52.

Inequalities and the compensatory formula now being advocated—reverse inequality—produce only one kind of conflict, one which may be more easily resolved than other disputes because it involves simply the redistribution of money. The "concept" of equality itself seems far less susceptible to change—the notion that, with proper attention, the abilities of have-not children may prove roughly equal to those of haves and that, therefore, they should not be separated, sent off at an early age on different tracks, or given disproportionate access to higher education. (Sexton, 1964: 100–101.)

1961–1962	White	Integrated	Negro
Number of pupils per classrooms	30.95	34.95	46.8
Appropriation per pupil	$342	$320	$269
Number of uncertified teachers	12%	23%	27%
Average number of books per pupil	5.0	3.5	2.5

dullness and conformity of life in the suburbs where, according to the contemporary folk song, people live in little boxes made of ticky-tacky that all look just the same. Other criticisms have been aimed at the undesirable consequences of the suburbanite's snobbery in interpersonal relationships, his pseudo-ethnocentricism in social identification, and his failure to equip his children with the life experiences necessary for their adult roles in the wider community.

The innocent country bumpkin of the last century is being replaced by the naive resident of suburbia who grows up unaware that there are people who do not have enough to eat, who gesture differently and speak with an accent, who pick the pockets of the unwary, and who may even have different standards of sexual morality. It is possible, for example, for many white suburban children to go through elementary and even high school without ever seeing a teacher or fellow student of a different race. Often their only interracial contact is a once-a-week cleaning woman from the city who rides the subway or interurban bus for an hour and a half to earn a few dollars a day plus carfare and to receive, periodically, the family's castoffs and hand-me-downs for which she is duly grateful despite a nagging resentment at having to accept such charity to make ends meet.

In many ways the structuring of the urban community represents the glaring rigidities that are apparent in the socio-economic system and emphasizes the discrepancy between the haves and the have-nots. The less affluent inner city dweller experiences the "reality" of the suburbs only through the TV screen. The typical suburbanite sees life in the core city filtered through the pages of the daily newspaper or the hermetically sealed windows of the commuter train. The point where the city transportation system ends, where telephone toll charges begin, where suburban police and fire departments take over represents a wall that shields suburbia from the problems of the core city and its residents. The isolation, both physical and psychological, of the suburbanite is increased and reinforced by segmentation within the core city itself: high-rent Gold Coast areas and, in some urban centers, remarkably persistent bohemian enclaves represent islands in the ecological structure where people can live worlds apart on the same street.

causes

It has already been observed that many of the problems of the urban community are a consequence of the economic and industrial development of the United States. These trends have been intensified by the decline of the core city and the mass movement of middle-class families to the suburbs. Each wave of migration from the city leaves fewer individuals with energy, interest, and competence to engage in the political and social affairs of the community.

With the exodus of skilled workers, many industrial plants have also left the core city. This is particularly true of technical and automated industries. The turnpikes and major highways servicing almost every large city are now lined with small electronics plants and regional offices of insurance companies and foreign car distributors. Why should the executives of a publishing house, for example, spend an hour commuting to the heart of the metropolis when they can live within easy driving distance of their office located in a suburban industrial park? There they can employ their neighbors' daughters as secretaries, thus assuring themselves of well-educated and socially compatible personnel. Also, by moving a few miles out, companies can often obtain long-term tax benefits, a strong inducement to a company that is faced with increasingly higher real estate taxes in the city. Suburban communities delight in having light industry within their borders; not only do such companies help maintain the wall between core city and suburb, but they also provide a good portion of the tax money for the fine schools and services which the residents of the locality have come to expect.

ECONOMIC RELOCATION

With the decline of the railroad as the major mode of transportation between cities there is little reason for many industries to remain in the core city. Airports are usually located on the perimeter of the metropolis. The local shopping center has supermarkets, specialty shops, and branches of most of the major downtown department stores which fill the wardrobe and household needs of the suburban housewife. In fact, many of the branch stores are more aesthetically laid out and tastefully decorated than the parent store in the city.

Certainly the big city and its bustling center will persist, for there is still a need for certain types of businesses to remain in an easily accessible location. The out-of-town jewelry buyer, for example, would rather walk down Manhattan's 45th Street than find his way to Westchester; the fisherman needs the docks of San Francisco to unload his catch; and the stockyards of Kansas City logically are located adjacent to one another. The facts of our economy dictate that the core city will continue, but primarily as a service area to be exploited and used by the suburban fringes. Technological advances and the increasing affluence of many community members are responsible, in part, for the flight to the suburbs. Given the mass production of the automobile, the development of an excellent network of expressways, and the economic ability of many individuals to own one or more cars, it is inevitable that many community members will desert the life of the cliff dweller for the green lawns and quiet streets of suburbia.

LURE OF THE SUBURBS

Some people romantically believe that almost all Americans want a bit of land and a house or, if they cannot achieve this, a garden apartment out of the city. For many, suburban life represents an expression of prestige and success. Formerly, only the affluent banker could arrive at his office at ten o'clock and only corporation presidents stopped off for a cocktail before taking the suburban train home to the "country." These are role models that perhaps many community members aspire to emulate. The degree to which they have succeeded is closely related to such unromantic developments as improved transportation patterns, modern credit arrangments, and new methods of building and construction. The ability to mass-produce homes—even entire communities—complete with heating systems and modern appliances is a postwar phenomenon attested to by the many Levittowns and similar tract-home developments sprawled throughout the United States. It is thoroughly American to prefer an automatic washing machine to a commercial laundry service and a barbecue on the patio to a formal dinner party.

It is not only middle-class affluence and the attractiveness of the suburbs that have shifted U.S. living patterns. Many of the activities within our economic system designed to promote an increase in the gross national product are also connected with the shift in the residential character of the country. The federal government has a large responsibility for promoting economically the movement of people away from the core city. This is most readily apparent in the benefits granted armed forces veterans. The GI Bill of Rights, first passed in 1944, included loan guarantees that made possible home ownership for many families who previously did not qualify under conservative banking practices which required large down payments and an established credit rating. Today, houses can be bought and sold quite readily despite cycles of tight money and easy money. Veterans' legislation and the Federal Housing Authority have revolutionized the norms regarding homeownership. Bankers no longer look askance at a worker with a reasonably steady income who asks for a no-money-down, thirty-year mortgage. Even the most conservative businessman, who loudly protests government interference in every other area, is entirely supportive of these programs (Foard and Fefferman, 1960).

There is no doubt that the participation of government in the development of suburban living has provided a vital stimulus to the growth of many industries, to the increased production of automobiles, appliances, and other capital goods, and to the general inflationary momentum of economic life (Haar, 1960). This and the relative ease of becoming a home-owning suburbanite represent some of the determinants of the present problems of urban life (Rapkin and Gringsby, 1960). It is probably academic to ask why, during the 1940s and 1950s, policy-makers did not focus more on low-income families in the central city instead of developing programs and concentrating resources to meet the needs of middle-income workers in the suburbs. Politically astute, they perhaps reasoned that, after all, those too poor to participate in this way of life constitute only one-fifth of the population.

DECLINE OF URBAN NEIGHBORHOODS

Families who can afford to leave the core city are motivated by more than a desire for a bit of grass and another half bath (although overcrowding in itself is deleterious to all animals—*see* Documentation 4). The breakdown in interpersonal styles of life in the core city are another important factor. To some extent, the reduction in ethnic identity among city dwellers needs to be taken into account. At one time the term *neighborhood* had a meaning; living there was purposeful for the residents who strongly identified with each other in terms of common language, customs, and food habits, and whose social and religious lives were centered around a particular church or synagogue. The neighborhood was highly protective and in many ways similar to a small town. Gans (1962) titled his study of Boston's Italian North End *The Urban Villagers*. Such people were proud to live in Greenpoint or Flatbush or the East Bronx, and many suburbanites still reminisce about their childhoods in Dorchester, the South End, or Mattapan.

CONSEQUENCES FOR CITIES

Most cities whose core had not yet been strangled by the tentacles of the suburbs were fragmented. Neighborhood shuls, delicatessens, kosher markets, and the ability to communicate in Yiddish whether one was Hungarian, Polish, or German made the city a convenient and homelike place for the immigrant Jew. Similarly, the corner saloons, the priests from the old country, friends from the same county or town, and the pleasant sound of the brogue prompted the Irish immigrants to cluster together. One still sees some of this in certain Eastern cities, but the phenomenon is rapidly disappearing.

Today the grandchildren and great grandchildren of the European immigrants are predominate in the population. Largely as a result of our system of universal public education, the third and fourth generations are thoroughly Americanized. Although raised by bilingual parents, many of the present generation have not bothered to learn the mother

consequences of crowding

What are the effects of the social behavior of a species on population growth—and of population density on social behavior?

Some years ago I attempted to submit this question to experimental inquiry. I confined a population of wild Norway rats in a quarter-acre enclosure. . . . By the end of 27 months the population had become stabilized at 150 adults. Yet adult mortality was so low that 5,000 adults might have been expected from the observed reproductive rate. The reason this larger population did not materialize was that infant mortality was extremely high. Even with only 150 adults in the enclosure, stress from social interaction led to such disruption of maternal behavior that few young survived.

With this background in mind I turned to observation of a domesticated albino strain of the Norway rat under more controlled circumstances indoors. The data for the present discussion come from the histories of six different populations. Each was permitted to increase to approximately twice the number that my experience had indicated could occupy the available space with only moderate stress from social interaction. In each case my associates and I maintained close surveillance of the colonies for 16 months in order to obtain detailed records of the modifications of behavior induced by population density.

The consequences of the behavioral pathology we observed were most apparent among the females. Many were unable to carry pregnancy to full term or to survive delivery of their litters if they did. An even greater number, after successfully giving birth, fell short in their maternal functions. Among the males the behavior disturbances ranged from sexual deviation to cannibalism and from frenetic over-activity to a pathological withdrawal from which individuals would emerge to eat, drink, and move about only when other members of the community were asleep. The social organization of the animals showed equal disruption. Each of the experimental populations divided itself into several groups, in each of which the sex ratios were drastically modified. One group might consist of 6 or 7 females and 1 male, whereas another would have 20 males and only 10 females.

The common source of these disturbances became most dramatically apparent in the populations of our first series of three experiments, in which we observed the development of what we called a behavioral sink. The animals would crowd together in greatest number in one of the 4 interconnecting pens in which the colony was maintained. As many as 60 of the 80 rats in each experimental population would rarely eat except in the company of other rats. As a result extreme population densities developed in the pen adopted for eating, leaving the others with sparse populations.

Eating and other biological activities were thereby transformed into social activities in which the principal satisfaction was interaction with other rats. In the case of eating, this transformation of behavior did not keep the animals from securing adequate nutrition. But the same pathological "togetherness" tended to disrupt the ordered sequences of activity involved in other vital modes of behavior such as the courting of sex partners, the building of nests and the nursing and care of the young. In the experiments in which the behavioral sink developed, infant mortality ran as high as 96 per cent among the most disoriented groups in the population. Even in the absence of the behavioral sink, in the second series of three experiments, infant mortality reached 80 per cent among the corresponding members of the experimental population. (Calhoun, 1963:33–35.)

tongue of their ancestors. Those who do choose to retain an ethnic identity can do so without living in the old neighborhood, for special foods, newspapers, and foreign-language magazines are easily obtainable in many areas of the city. Except in isolated instances, therefore, the fragmented pluralism of the last century has largely disappeared, and with it, much of the concept of neighborhood.

POSTWAR DEVELOPMENT

With the advent of World War II and the tremendous industrial expansion during and following the war, the Far West developed huge population centers. Since the style of life there was relatively new and the ecology more permissive, building was outward rather than upward as was the style in the urban centers of the East. Consequently, California architecture found its way not only to the valleys of Los Angeles but to the suburbs of Detroit, Cleveland, and Baltimore. The ranch-style house became the fad in New England as well as in Texas.

In some ways the development of the new industrial centers such as Houston, Phoenix, and Seattle which are supported primarily by jet-age industries has drastically changed the norms of what is considered desirable, good, and worthy of emulation in terms of a style of life. The requirements of the business world demand considerable moving about by young families from one metropolis to another. This mobility has been charged with reducing the cohesiveness of the extended family and shifting the reference-group identification from a neighborhood and ethnic group to work associates and peer groups (Litwak, 1960). While this interpretation has been challenged, there is no question but that *neighborhood* has become a demographic, if not a specifically geographic, concept. The only exceptions are the segregated ghettos of the poor, particularly the black poor, and the transient retreats of hippies, artists, and the castoffs of society. In these areas, the neighborhood continues to provide interpersonal relationships for the residents.

It is only realistic to concede that in the suburb the child receives a better academic education, the housewife has an easier time keeping her house clean and providing recreation for her children, and the husband has more facilities for playing tennis or golf and more space for pursuing his hobbies. Many suburban families have several TV sets, at least two cars, separate telephone listings for the children, and one or more pets. Most of these amenities are available in the city, but usually only the very rich can afford them. Progressive governmental programs made suburbia possible. Through hindsight we now know that these very same programs also created the conditions for the deterioration of the inner city. The plea of nolo contendere may forestall the placement of blame; it cannot excuse a failure to search for a solution to urban blight.

intervention and amelioration

The intervention programs developed to handle urban conditions vary markedly from stopgap to long-range, from fragmented to coordinated, from local to regional. The most visible and most common approach used during the depression years and the postwar period was the construction of public housing, particularly for the poor. Public housing was promoted partly on the grounds that it would alleviate many of the social ills associated with poverty in the core city. Major efforts in virtually every city were concentrated on the destruction of entire blocks, and often whole neighborhoods, of slum housing. After the land was cleared, massive high-rise apartment buildings were constructed on the sites. Most social planners still acknowledge the importance of public housing—or at least public subsidy as an underlying remedy to the housing problem—but they now feel that the massive destruction which took place in the major cities of the United States has proved relatively futile in improving urban conditions (Schorr, 1964).

HOUSING REHABILITATION

Public housing has often led to the further ghettoization of the city, and it has not brought about any noticeable decrease in the rates of crime, delinquency, school dropouts, and the like. Public housing has not influenced the middle-class American to remain in the city. Moreover, the maximum-income requirement for admittance to most public-housing developments is so restrictive that it has resulted in a homogeneous tenantry of very low-income families. There is considerable evidence that these large masses of people, either through ignorance or apathy, are largely unconcerned with the maintenance of the housing provided for them; also, such concentrations of the poor do not make for an environment in which appropriate socialization in terms of the middle-class value system is feasible or practical. There is evidence in a number of cities that the public-housing programs have destroyed more than they have built, that they have reduced, not increased, the total quantity of standard or above-standard housing available to the poor. This is due in part to the fact that deterioration has outdistanced redevelopment and in part to the extensive use of "renewed" land for stores and highways which act as buffers between lower and middle-class neighborhoods, thus increasing the isolation of the poor. More and more, public-housing programs which call for massive destruction and limited rebuilding are being looked upon as a last resort (Jacobs, 1961). Such programs have brought about further segregation of the poor, particularly the black poor. Current thinking is centered on programs which provide planned recreation areas, increased resources for schools, multiple use of facilities and, ideally, selective redevelopment rather than widespread demolition and the construction of more skyscrapers for the poor (Greer, 1962). All plans have their faults, however. (*See* Documentation 5.)

The concept of selective redevelopment stresses rehabilitation rather than renewal. Such a concept implies, first of all, that programs should be undertaken while it is still possible to refurbish and renovate existing housing. Such renovation should not be confined to the worst areas of the community but should include dwellings for persons of moderate income as well. Since prevention of new slums is considered as important as rehabilitation of the old ones, the programs must be started before the onset of massive deterioration (Epstein, 1966). Such approaches have been undertaken in several major cities and the results seem promising. Success is most likely where programs are designed to attract the support and participation of residents and influential groups within the community.

The idea of selective neighborhood redevelopment represents both a response to the homogeneity of low-income public housing and an application of the pluralist concept of redevelopment advanced by such planners as Herbert Gans and Jane Jacobs. Berger (1966:89-90) summarizes their views:

> [T]here is the pluralist alternative, an alternative perhaps best expressed in the recent work of Herbert Gans, and, to a lesser extent, of Jane Jacobs. Whatever reservations one may have about the work of either, each of them projects an unambiguous image of the kind of human solidarity they would like to see fostered by urban planning. This solidarity is loose and heterogeneous, composed of more or less autonomous groups and neighborhoods formed on the basis of ethnicity and social class; communities attached, perhaps, to the notion that good fences make good neighbors, but necessarily related to one another through those political and economic accommodations long characteristic of urban life. If they are open to criticism as "romanticists" (although it is not clear to me why a preference for dense street life, or an insistence that an ethnic working-class neighborhood is not necessarily a slum, renders one vulnerable to such criticism), it should at least be said in their defense that they obviously care enough about the *quality* of urban life to evoke a strong and clear image of it (something their critics do not always do)—strong enough in Mrs. Jacobs' case and clear enough in Professor Gans' case to make it easy for a reader to be for or against them.

MIDDLE-CLASS URBANITES

In many cities, particularly New York and some of the West Coast communities, great effort has been made to provide publicly supported—or

the costs of segregation

Today's wide-scale patterns of segregation and the prospect of their further expansion have several extremely important consequences for the nation as a whole. One of the most dramatic of the current ramifications is the fact that the problems long associated with the Negro ghetto because of generations of discrimination—educational deficiencies, high rates of illness and social disorders, low employment rates, and predominantly low incomes even among those who are employed—all press with increasing force upon the cities as the ghettos continue to grow. At the same time, the financial and leadership resources of the cities have been severely depleted by the middle-class white movement to the suburbs. As a separate political entity, the city has, with growing force, been deprived by the expanding rings of suburbia of the resources it needs to set its house in order.

The newly emergent residential patterns have thus transformed segregation from a parochial concern largely confined to the South (though posing a moral dilemma for the entire nation) into the hardest kind of practical economic problem affecting all the urban centers of America.

But the problem no longer stops at the city line. Today, segregation increasingly threatens the rational planning and development of entire metropolitan areas—a consequence of profound significance in light of continued population growth and the scarcity of urban land, which make it essential that future generations be housed in a less haphazard fashion.

In recent years choice land on the periphery of the larger cities has been devoured at a ferocious rate. In metropolitan Philadelphia, for example, while the population of the "urbanized" or heavily built up area grew by 24

at least publicly sponsored—middle-class housing as well as lower-class dwellings. The rationale for such an approach is the importance of maintaining within the environs of the city persons of various economic and social status. Unfortunately, the programs have not proved too successful. Even when low-income and middle-income housing are located contiguously, it is apparent in both the architecture of the buildings and the interaction of the residents that a wall exists. So far neither social programs nor efforts to increase interpersonal involvement have been able to break it down (Schorr, 1964).

Rent subsidy, or rent supplement, is another alternative to urban renewal which is now being advocated. As Glazer (1967:154–155) notes, these programs are still in the demonstration stages.

> [T]he government has put its hope for low-income family housing into rent supplements. . . . Yet while Congress has accepted the principle, it has resisted the appropriation of funds required to put a large rent-supplement program into effect. Rent supplements them-

per cent during the 1950's, its geographic spread doubled. This reckless consumption of land cannot continue much longer. Municipalities are already grappling in various ways with the challenge of making more efficient use of the land which is still within feasible commuting distance. The aim of their plans is to keep the metropolitan areas fit places in which to live, with a satisfactory balance of the various elements that together constitute an adequate human environment: homes, commercial and cultural centers, adequate transit facilities, industries, parks. . . .

In metropolitan Washington, regional planning agencies recently devised a "Plan for the Year 2000." This plan is essentially a general set of principles for meeting the needs of a population that is expected to grow to more than twice its present size before the end of the century. The plan suggests that future growth be channeled along six radial "corridors" extending outward in star fashion from the central city. Highways and transit lines would run alongside the corridors; centers of commerce and various service areas would be located at appropriate intervals. To preserve as much as possible of the green countryside, parks and open recreation areas would be placed between the corridors.

The plan, however, fails to take into account one vital consideration: the effect of race. If the movement of the city's population continues in its present directions, three of the planned corridors will be heavily Negro. They will have their central origins in neighborhoods which currently are Negro and which already are expanding outward in the directions proposed by the plan. The other three corridors will be almost exclusively white, since they originate in the only white residential areas that remain within the city. Thus segregation will be extended for an indefinite period into the new suburbs. If, on the other hand, Negro expansion is cut off along the three corridors which are presently "open," the future population growth will be forced back into the city, thereby intensifying dangerous pressures which already exist. (Grier and Grier, 1966:87–89.)

selves raise a host of intriguing problems for the sociologist of the future; for if the homeowner and the middle-income renter have resisted the low-income housing project coming into their neighborhoods, how will they feel about the subsidized low-income family? What stigma will it bear? How will its relations with unsubsidized (or less subsidized) neighbors be affected? If there is stigma, will it be because of the program under which the family is subsidized, the low income which makes it necessary, or some social or cultural attributes correlated with low income?

The concept of a heterogeneous, pluralistic urban community as an alternative to the homogeneous, dualistic metropolis where the have-nots are concentrated in the core city and the haves live in the suburban fringes is based on a comparatively simple presumption, namely, that the middle-income city dweller can be persuaded that urban living is the best deal for him—more fun, more exciting, more convenient than the suburbs. The city must, however, be able to provide more opportunities for him and his children, better places to enjoy leisure and cultural activities, and stronger guarantees of adequate government services. Assured of sufficient police protection, good educational facilities for his children, and minimal risk of property loss, a faculty member at the University of Chicago, for example, would be foolish to spend several hours a day commuting to the Midway when he can live on Chicago's South Side, walk to work, enjoy the excitement and satisfaction of living near his colleagues and many people of many different backgrounds, and have easily accessible the cultural resources of a great city.

Often tagged with catchy phrases such as "planning with people," these programs to provide quality urban living are not only expensive to establish but open to the risk of eventually reverting to single-class communities. As the middle-income residents begin to exert their power and influence, they literally buy out the low-income families. To some extent, this has been the history of such attractive bohemian areas as Greenwich Village, Beacon Hill, Old Town, Nob Hill, and the like. These communities have pointed with pride to their heterogeneity: poor students, striving artists, and biracial couples living side-by-side with successful publishers, affluent advertising executives, and vice-presidents of large corporations, all sending their children to the same public schools, reading the neighborhood newspaper, and demonstrating, if need be, to preserve their neighborhood. There is a romance and charm about such areas which attracts upwardly mobile people. Inevitably, the rapid in-migration of more affluent residents results in the exodus of those families who stood to benefit the most from such arrangements.

GEOPOLITICAL CONSIDERATIONS

Although broad-scale neighborhood rehabilitation offers the greatest promise for progressive urban redevelopment programs, their long-term success is dependent upon the maintenance of the tenuous balance between the demands of pluralism and the motivation of individuals. On the one hand, it is essential that these areas be made as desirable to live in as possible which, of course, requires money and human resources. On the other hand, it is important that there be planned control over their development and maintenance lest, with their increased desirability, the pluralistic character is lost.

The provision of services in the core city demands considerable economic participation by community members and, in many places, it already requires more than the residents can afford. One solution has been for the federal government to finance initial inputs. Unfortunately, most of these expenditures have gone to pay for stopgap measures in emergency situations rather than broad programs of prevention. It is with extreme reluctance that urban residents are willing to provide the taxes that are necessary for reconstituting the core city.

The only feasible approach is a realignment of political subdivisions by legislative fiat. There are simply too many independent villages, towns, and suburbs to permit the kinds of social planning and economic efficiency required in these times. Every major city is surrounded by ten, twenty, possibly thirty separate municipalities. Most of these maintain separate police forces, fire departments, garbage collection and public health services. With consolidation, one public health physician might be able to supervise the activities for all these communities. As it is now, the ones who need his services the most are least able to support him. Consequently, such towns frequently have as a public health officer a political appointee without training for his tasks.

Certainly, when we think about the complexities of modern police technology, we must admit that multiplying one chief and four or five patrolmen twenty times over is an ineffective way of providing protective services. The same can be said for municipal purchasing agents, building inspectors, and fire departments. This duplication of services exists in many metropolitan areas. While a large number of these subdivisions can afford to pay for such services, the transfer to unified systems of control would free money for better use in the core city without any increase in the total tax load and would allow a more meaningful interchange of services between suburb and core city. Such matters as code uniformity also need to be undertaken:

> To achieve a broader approach to urban expansion and to insure more effective and expeditious regulation, metropolitan areas increasingly will need to devise and experiment with new ways of collaborating on a metropolitan-wide basis. Such ordinances as zoning, subdivision control, building, housing, fire and other similar codes, regulations of open space easements and airport approaches, and rules governing mapped streets and future transportation corridors will need to be brought together and reorganized into one *urban development code* (Chapin, 1963:84).

BROADENING THE URBAN BASE

In a few areas, metropolitan districts have been established to provide some services. But this does not meet the issue of broadening and increasing the tax base which is necessary to furnish the poor and other marginal groups with adequate services and the funds required to maintain good schools and clean, efficient government.

Some cities, recognizing the need for political subdivisions balanced economically as well as in other ways, have pursued a policy of annexation as the city population moved outward. (*See* Documentation 6.) Perhaps the most meaningful example is the city of Atlanta. Its reputa-

modifying city limits

Annexation activity has been increasing in the United States practically every year since the end of World War II. In 1945, 152 cities of over 5,000 population accomplished an annexation of some kind. The following year, the number rose to 259. It passed the 300 mark for the first time in 1949, the 400 mark for the first time in 1952, and the 500 mark in 1955, and soared straight to 712 in 1961; it has climbed further since. The 1,083 square miles annexed in 1960 was the largest ever, 68 percent above the previous peak of 64 square miles annexed in 1956. A survey by the American Municipal Associa-tion showed that in the seven years from 1951 through 1957 there was hardly a state in the Union whose cities did not carry through at least some significant annexation. The territory they annexed in those seven years contained more people than the 1960 census showed for five states put together: Nevada, Wyoming, Vermont, Delaware, and New Hampshire.

Champions of annexation are convinced of the urgency of this act as a lifesaving measure for cities which have not yet been strangled nearly to death by surrounding municipalities. (Gordon, 1963:368–370.)

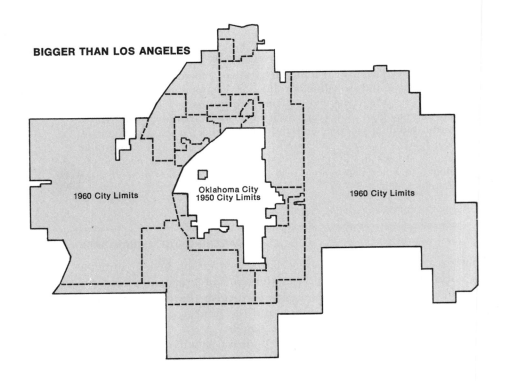

BIGGER THAN LOS ANGELES

1960 City Limits

Oklahoma City
1950 City Limits

1960 City Limits

urban renewal

Urban renewal is like a lady with a past who has been unable to live it down. Her early sins consisted of large-scale displacement of Negro families, inadequate relocation of the evicted families, the ousting of small businesses, and the demolition of buildings whose sites have never found buyers. Though the lady sins less often and has recently demonstrated some creditable virtues, her past excesses continue to be cited. . . .

Contrary to the original intention of its congressional sponsors, urban renewal has veered in its motivation from slum clearance to city regeneration. It is now reclaiming downtown store areas, building middle- and high-rent housing, getting industries to stay in the cities, drawing back those that have left them, and getting new ones to come in. This shift in emphasis has paralleled a recent concern about the plight of cities by the President, by Senate committees, and by the big-city press.

While urban renewal is helping a number of cities with some of their problems, it is not meeting the main problems and is even diverting public attention from them. The cities are in deep financial and social trouble. They can no longer afford to educate and train their underprivileged, support their unemployed and elderly poor, police their streets, mend their

sick, or operate their courts, jails, utilities, and garbage plants. The reason is simple. A city's tax jurisdiction ends at its borders. As long as it grows within these borders, generating more tax-paying sources and increasing its revenues, it can remain solvent. But when more of its good taxpayers leave and a poorer population enters, revenues decrease and costs simultaneously rise. This forces the city to borrow more, which in turn adds to its maintenance costs. Taxes are raised to meet these maintenance costs, further accelerating the exodus of its paying customers. But an urban society in which there is freedom of movement and which sees thirty-five million people moving annually from house to house, city to suburb, and state to state, including millions of poor people in search of a better education and life for their children, cannot put up a "No Entry" sign as many suburbs have done. The metropolis must remain a free port open to all and must be equipped to educate the nation's poor as well as pay the soaring costs of city life. It cannot do this, however, under theories devised for a nineteenth-century economy. The United States has successfully weathered the shift from an agricultural to an industrial society but has not coped with the urban revolution that came in its wake. (Abrams, 1969:38–39.)

tion as a relatively good place to live, its liberal policies in combating discrimination, and its popularity as a center for national and regional corporate headquarters have been the result of the far-sighted ideas of an exceedingly liberal mayor who served during the 1940s and 1950s. He did not permit suburbs to spring up autonomously and independently. With the movement of the more affluent, middle-class individuals to the suburbs, he instituted a policy of annexing these lands into the central city. Through this maneuver the city maintained a relatively strong tax base and retained control over such departments as education, health, fire, and police, which were manipulated to meet the differential needs of different groups of citizens.

Until the political character of most metropolitan areas is realigned to create meaningful ecological units to replace the artificial boundaries that now separate the suburbs from the city, there is little hope of accomplishing major long-term changes (Wheaton, 1967). The solutions to the problems of urban life eventually rest in the hands of the politico-economic social-control system. A few new schools, the enforcement of antidiscrimination laws, and public-housing projects are not going to dent the fundamental problems, nor will more rapid transportation, better highways, or larger parking structures. *(See* Documentation 7.)

Suburbanites have certainly not exercised their responsibility in this respect. They have been reluctant, for example, to develop exchange programs with core city schools, to institute joint training programs for their police and firemen, to unify their welfare services, or in any other way to recognize the need for interaction between suburbia and the core city. The shifting of boundaries represents perhaps the only long-term solution to the problems of urban redevelopment and the prevention of continued deterioration of urban life.

REFERENCES

ABRAMS, CHARLES.
1969 "Housing policy—1937-1967." Pp. 35–45 in Bernard J. Frieden and William W. Nash, Jr. (eds.), Shaping an Urban Future: Essays in Honor of Catherine Bauer Wurster. Cambridge, Massachusetts: M.I.T. Press.

BERGER, BENNETT M.
1966 "Suburbia and the American dream." The Public Interest 2(Winter):80–91.

CALHOUN, JOHN B.
1963 "Population density and social pathology." Pp. 33–43 in Leonard J. Duhl (ed.), The Urban Condition: People and Policy in the Metropolis. New York: Basic Books.

CHAPIN, F. STUART.
1963 "Taking stock of techniques for shaping urban growth." Journal of the American Institute of Planners 29(May):76–89.

EPSTEIN, JOSEPH.
1966 "The row over urban renewal." Pp. 197–206 in Judson R. Landis (ed.), Current Perspectives on Social Problems. Belmont, California: Wadsworth.

FISHMAN, JOSHUA A.
1961 "Some social and psychological determinants of intergroup relations in changing neighborhoods." Social Forces 40(October):42–51.

FOARD, ASHLEY A. AND HILBERT FEFFERMAN.
1960 "Federal urban renewal legislation." Law and Contemporary Problems 25(Fall):635–684.

FRIED, MARC.
1963 "Grieving for a lost home." Pp. 151–171 in Leonard J. Duhl (ed.), The Urban Condition: People and Policy in the Metropolis. New York: Basic Books.

GANS, HERBERT J.
1962 The Urban Villagers: Group and Class in the Life of Italian-Americans. New York: Free Press.

GLAZER, NATHAN.
1967 "Housing policy and the family." Journal of Marriage and the Family 29(February):140–165.

GOLDBLATT, HAROLD AND FLORENCE CROMIER.
1962 "The effective social reach of the fair housing practices law of the city of New York." Social Problems 9(Spring):365–370.

GORDON, MITCHELL.
1963 Sick Cities. Baltimore: Penguin Books.

GOTTMAN, JEAN.
1961 Megalopolis: The Urbanized Northeastern Seaboard of the United States. New York: Twentieth Century Fund.

GREER, SCOTT.
1962 The Emerging City. New York: Free
Press.

GREER, SCOTT AND PETER ORLEANS.
1962 "The mass society and the parapolitical structure." American Sociological Review 27(October):634–646.

GRIER, EUNICE AND GEORGE GRIER.
1966 "Equality and beyond: housing and
segregation in the great society."
Daedalus 95(Winter):77–106.

HAAR, CHARLES.
1960 Federal Credit and Private Housing,
The Mass Financing Dilemma. New
York: McGraw-Hill.

JACOBS, JANE.
1961 The Death and Life of Great American Cities. New York: Random.

LITWAK, EUGENE.
1960 "Geographic mobility and extended
family cohesion." American Sociological Review 25(June):385–394.

MEYER, AGNES E.
1963 "The nation's worst slum: Washington, D.C." Atlantic Monthly 212
(August):89–92.

PETTIGREW, THOMAS F.
1969 "Issues in urban America." Pp. 47–94
in Bernard J. Frieden and William
W. Nash, Jr. (eds.), Shaping an
Urban Future: Essays in Honor of
Catherine Bauer Wurster. Cambridge:
M.I.T. Press.

RAPKIN, CHESTER AND WILLIAM G. GRINGSBY.
1960 Residential Renewal at the Urban
Core. Philadelphia: University of
Pennsylvania Press.

SCHORR, ALVIN L.
1964 "Slums and social insecurity." Divi-
sion of Research and Statistics, Social
Security Administration, Department
of Health, Education, and Welfare.
Research Report No. 1. Washington,
D.C.: U.S. Government Printing
Office.

SEXTON, PATRICIA CAYO.
1964 "City schools." The Annals 352
(March):95–106.

WHEATON, WILLIAM L.
1967 "Operations research for metropolitan
planning." Pp. 207–217 in H. Gold
and F. Scarpitti (eds.), Combatting
Social Problems. New York: Holt,
Rinehart and Winston.

WILNER, DANIEL M., R. P. WALKLEY, T. C.
PINKERTON AND MATTHEW TAYBACK.
1962 The Housing Environment and Family Life. Baltimore: Johns Hopkins
Press.

involvement
and alienation

LEISURE IS A TERM USED to describe the nonproductive activities of community members; that is, the time they spend away from their jobs or, in the case of the housewife, away from the care of the home and children. It represents, in the thinking of many, the periods of time in which individuals have fun, rest, and restore themselves psychologically and physically from the frustrations, anxieties, and toil of their work and familial responsibilities. But if leisure is to be used in this sense, then it is necessary to employ other concepts to round out the description of the individual's participation in the total life of the community.

A vital part of the normative standards associated with democratic community life include the concept of responsibility; every community member is expected in some degree to contribute to the stability of the community and to participate in appropriate programs of innovation and social change. In the contemporary urban community it is difficult, if not impossible, to separate those segments of nonwork time that primarily maximize the psychological gratification and physical restoration of the individual from the time he spends engaged in the tasks essential and relevant to the conduct of the life of the community and by which he develops an identification with his community and its social groups. Without such an identification, it is unlikely that the individual can maintain a self-image of personal worth or work within the normative structure of the community to realize his ambitions and contribute to orderly social change (Wilensky, 1961).

social and political participation

A series of pervasive social problems are related to the variations in participation by community members and to the social and political roles they choose to play. As a consequence, there is an interplay of disparities and incongruities in social and political participation for the individual and for the community. For the individual, marginality in the social and political life of the community raises barriers in the communication of the values and moral norms for him, his family, and others with whom he has close relationships. Further, such marginality spills over and affects his psychological frame of reference with consequent impact on personality and attitudes.

INTEGRATION IN THE COMMUNITY

Sociologists, from the early days of Émile Durkheim, have employed his concept of anomie to refer to the individual's lack of integration into the structure of the community. Contemporary sociologists refer to anomia as a social-psychological characteristic reflecting feelings and attitudes of individual disorientation, anxiety and isolation (Seeman, 1959; Dean, 1961). Both anomic behavior and feelings of alienation, as observed in earlier chapters, characterize the lot of the poor and those who are discriminated against (Neal and Seeman, 1964). Recognition is given in many of the intervention programs to the need for increased social and political participation in order to reduce psychological feelings of anomia and to modify the conduct of community members, although the relationship between social participation and alienation is not conclusive (Erbe, 1964). (*See* Documentation 1.)

Variations in the means, types, and extent of social and political participation of community members are related, of course, to the maintenance and modification of norms and values in the community and to the degree of rigidity of its social structure. At the present time, there are a number of recurring problems of social and political participation. Perhaps the most obvious is the extent to which an individual's economic status represents a barrier to such participation and to the opportunities of personal gratification from such interaction. A basic example is voting behavior—the minimal citizen responsibility of going to the polls and in other formal ways registering one's favor or disfavor with the activities going on in the community (Sykes, 1951). Although there are exceptions, such as the strong turnouts of particular ethnic groups concentrated in parts of some of the urban centers, in general the poor vote less often than the more affluent. Certainly the political sector of the community has been less concerned with their participation. As Leonard Riessman (1954:83) notes:

> [I]t can be said that the middle class, on the whole, tends to dominate the organizational activity, the intellectual life, and the leadership of the community. Secondly, it was found that the higher class is

organizations and alienation

Studies that have dealt with the relation between alienation and organizational involvement either have treated involvement as a cause and alienation as an effect, or have finessed the matter by simply referring to the two as "correlates." But one can well argue that alienation is a cause of organizational involvement: persons . . . who are in retreat from the world, are relatively unlikely to participate energetically in formal associations.

I have no data to test the effect of organizational involvement on prospective alienation, but I do have a variable that will provide a rough test of the propensity of the alienated to become organizationally involved. The interview schedule contains a list of "imaginary organizations," all but one of them very political in nature, about which questions were asked concerning the respondent's level of interest. In addition, respondents were asked if there were any other organizations, like those described, that they would consider joining if such an organization existed. The number of organizations we asked about specifically, in which the respondent indicated he was "very interested," was added to the number of organizations he mentioned spontaneously, to obtain a total number of "organizations of interest." My hypothesis here is that, if alienation is a cause of organizational involvement, and thus antecedent to it, alienation ought to be negatively associated with the number of organizations of interest.

A look at the table [below] discloses only

NUMBER OF PROSPECTIVE ORGANIZATIONS OF INTEREST BY ALIENATION, SOCIO-ECONOMIC STATUS, AND PERCENTAGES

	Alienation			Socio-Economic Status		
	High (189)	Med. (192)	Low (198)	High (203)	Med. (188)	Low (207)
Three or more	33%	31%	34%	41%	30%	27%
One or two	41	47	48	49	49	38
None	25	22	18	10	20	35
		$d = -.041$			$d = .194$	

slight, if any, association between alienation and interest in new organizations. But there is a discernible association between interest in new organizations and socio-economic status, a known predictor of organizational involvement. When the effects of socio-economic status and alienation are partialled, the association with status remains constant (.177), while the association with alienation shifts erratically to a *positive* .018, meaning that, with socio-economic status controlled, the most alienated have a miniscule tendency to be more interested in new political organizations.

This test is not entirely conclusive, of course, since no roster of existing organizations or imaginary "sociable" organizations was offered for comment, but such evidence as we have certainly does not support the contention that alienation is antecedent to organizational involvement. (Erbe, 1964:212–213.)

more realistic in its aspirations, as seen by its greater willingness to recognize the necessary steps for an upward occupational move. The lower class, on the other hand, shows a startling lack of ideals in this matter, part of which might be traced to a lesser degree of involvement in and knowledge of the affairs and social mechanisms of the community.

VOLUNTARY GROUPS

There are even more subtle differentiations in the mechanisms that promote the activities of political parties and of voluntary groups in the religious, fraternal, and health and welfare fields (Rein, 1964). Certainly, it is a pragmatic strategy for national organizations concerned with health problems, recreation, citizenship training, or whatever, to orient their programs to the clients who also provide the resources for their support. Much criticism has been offered of the middle-class orientation of such groups, ranging from the Boy Scouts to the American Legion, and from the Heart Association to the Episcopal Church. In the scheme of things, when the economic support of segments of the community is essential to continuance and expansion of such activtities, clearly differential participation by economic status is the result.

Since many of the important voluntary groups, as well as community organizations with an explicit political purpose, have considerable power in shaping community life, the differential place accorded the individual of limited economic means is correlated with his inability to occupy positions of power within such organizations or to exert any meaningful influence on issues in which he has a stake (Riessman and Miller, 1964). As a matter of fact, the economic affluence of the individual is associated with the roles he takes across the network of voluntary groups and the whole spectrum of political activities (Bell and Force, 1956; Bell and Boat, 1957). The limited participation of the less affluent determines the degree of personal gratification he obtains in this manner and thus a cycle is maintained of further isolation from these activities.

PARTICIPATION OF THE POOR

The apathy of persons from limited economic backgrounds toward so-called civic organizations that focus on particular problems of illness, community disorganization, and politics is a result, many would hold, of the individuals' lack of opportunities for expression. A number of studies (Rein, 1964; Bloomberg, 1966) stress that the middle-class orientation of voluntary health groups has influenced public policy with respect to the mentally ill and the mentally retarded, for examples. *(See Documentation 2.)* This bias is perhaps most obvious in terms of the orientation of the established religious bodies in the typical community.

As we noted in discussing poverty, recognition of this problem is evidenced in current massive community efforts being supported by federal funds. One of the striking developments was the concept embodied in the 1964 federal anti-poverty legislation that created the Community Action Programs under the Office of Economic Opportunity. This law requires "significant representation" and "maximum feasible participation" on the part of the recipients of such programs. As Ali Akbar notes (1966:4):

> It is now being realized increasingly that without the active cooperation of the target population, program goals are difficult to achieve. It is gradually being accepted that for the realization of program goals, as well as for the promotion of social harmony, there should be adequate linkage and consistent communication between the beneficiaries and the organizers of services. This is sought through "maximum feasible participation" by the beneficiaries of services in policy-making, in program planning, and even in administration. The principle of participation is regarded as a desirable social goal as well as a tool to further program goals.

LAYMAN AND PROFESSIONAL

There is another related problem that is also of considerable concern: not only is there a strong risk of influence and participation, socially and politically, being centered on an economic elite, but there is the question of concentration of power in a technical or professional elite as well. Given the complexities of organizational management and the size of the population base of many organizations, there has grown up on the American scene an extensive cadre of individuals and commercial enterprises that cater to the needs of the voluntary organization. For example, there is a professional structure within organizations such as the YMCA or the Boy Scouts of America, with paid executives handling organizational affairs from a network of national, regional, and local offices. In many ways these can be likened to the bureaucratic structure of national companies. Even relatively autonomous organizations, such as an individual church, a local civic club, or a chamber of commerce, frequently have executive officers or administrators who actually run the organization. As in many other areas of community life, bureaucratic arrangements in the organizational enterprises that reflect social and political participation are inevitable. Neither time, interest, nor competency permits a community to accept such roles as avocations or trust them to amateur management.

The concern here is whether such professionals do not in the end

participation and performance

Are these two conditions—low participation and poor performance in solving problems—related? No simple answer to this question can be validated directly. What we can do is examine more carefully those who participate and then see whether the most and least active are also the most and least successful in having their needs met through community institutions.

For example, compared with those who vote, take sides, try to persuade others, and the like, those who do not even vote tend to be from the younger, less educated, less residentially stable, lower-income segments of the society —the "problem people." These correlations, however, are far from strong enough to prove the point by themselves. What about voluntary associations? Manual workers participate less than nonmanual, women less than men, Catholics less than Protestants; membership is correlated with education and with socio-economic status in general. Although the total number of lower-middle- and lower-class individuals participating in associations is undoubtedly greater than the total number from the much smaller upper-middle- and upper classes, the latter are proportionately represented much more heavily. Moreover, those associations most likely to become involved in defining and

solving community problems not only attract the smallest numbers of members, but also recruit much more heavily from the upper than the lower rungs of the socio-economic ladder. And males and those of higher social standing also tend to be heavily overrepresented among officers and informal leaders in voluntary associations, especially ones likely to have some impact in community affairs.

The most extensively organized segments of the community are the upper and upper-middle classes. From this group come those who comprise the majority in the professional and business associations, who provide most of the leadership for the more prestigious civic and service clubs, and who normally dominate the boards of private welfare and medical agencies. When their wives also participate in voluntary associations, they are much more likely to hold office or serve in some special task than members from lower strata; and the upper-class women are much more likely to hold top offices or wield real power on an agency board than their middle-class associational counterparts. For most of these upper- and upper-middle-strata associational activists, vocation, civic duty, and maintenance of family social standing are all quite nicely interwoven with their organizational contacts and programs.

take over completely the roles supposedly reserved for the lay representatives of the community. Does the executive director of the local mental health association serve only as an administrator and resource consultant to the lay public who supports such a group, or does he in fact develop policies, strategies, and points of view that become the programs of his group and, in turn, establish the values and norms of the community? Does the public relations corporation running a political candidate's campaign seek merely to promote his views and policies, or do they tell

The case now seems stronger. But what about the people whose authority and influence most directly shape the community-organizing decisions within the major institutional sectors? By and large they are individuals who combine many of the social characteristics typically valued in an American urban community: most of them are upper-middle- and upper-class, male and married homeowners; they tend, though less clearly, to exclude those who derive from the newer or less "accepted" ethnic groups and who are identified with religious minorities; but they are somewhat less "local," by place of birth and pattern of family residence, than the general public (except in suburbs). This overall pattern varies from one institutional sector to another. Persons from low-status ethnic groups and families appear as leaders only where organized labor dominates. However, upwardly mobile ethnics who come from low-status families in other communities are likely to turn up in technical and professional roles in areas of government such as public housing—indeed, technical experts and professional administrators in such fields as housing, planning, education, and welfare often change cities a number of times while seeking career advancement. On the other hand, where those who make the institutional decisions are in mercantile, legal, or real estate enterprises, or are elected government officials, they are likely to be quite local in origin or background. For the most part, women partici-

pate extensively only in decisions concerned with culture, health, or education.

The actual decision makers in the local community, although varied in social background, are clearly a highly selected and very small segment of the total adult population. Those whom the city at present serves best—the well-to-do, the professionals, the highly educated, the suburbanites—predominate. Those for whom life in the city is most difficult and who are often seen as "problem people"—the poor, the still-derogated minorities, many of the youth, those with little formal education, the new arrivals with little means—such people almost never appear among the ranks of the decision makers. Although it is true that some of those who do participate directly in community decision making desire and actually attempt to act as partisans of the deprived and the neglected, it is equally true that *most* local resources allocated by community decision makers without the intervention of the state or federal government have been used to make the life of the already "advantaged" members of the community ever more advantageous. Present patterns of community organization fail to bring existing problems effectively to the attention of most citizens, fail to motivate citizens to action even when problems are recognized, and fail to involve . . . in community decision making those whose needs are met least well by the established uses of community resources. (Bloomberg, 1966:387–390.)

him which platform planks he can or can't get by with and what promises will win the votes of one group or another? There is, then, considerable risk that a professionalized elite may be developed which will be just as effective as a social or economic elite at barring the participation of the ordinary citizen and convincing him of the futility of his contribution, thereby limiting his interest and creating apathy. The layman's functions in these circumstances are mere window dressing and all he has left are modest bits of prestige accruing from his name on a letterhead, his picture in the newspaper, and the receipt of thank-you notes signed by other esteemed individuals in the community.

radical groups

Given the scheme of things in which economic barriers or a professional elite minimize the participation of large segments of the community, one of the other risks—a real one today on the American scene—is the development, maintenance, and intensification of dangerous extremist activities. The violence and hate that characterize many of these groups are attractive to the disaffiliated and the disenchanted. They are often led by unscrupulous demogogues who are aware of the social-psychological needs of large numbers of community members to participate and who make capital of the citizen's marginal place in many traditional organizations. Such organizations abound on the right and left of the political spectrum and they have fostered the development of innumerable splinter groups that take up and abandon, almost at random, a host of tasks and issues that confront community members.

The range of extremist activities is wide and involves many areas and segments of community life. In the field of race relations, the Black Panther Party represents a quasi-military force that frequently clashes with police and the National Guard. Disruptive tactics, which occasionally spill over into violence, have been used by militant groups demanding reparation payments from American church groups under terms of the Black Manifesto, by the National Welfare Rights Organization seeking radical restructuring of the welfare system, by Students for a Democratic Society (SDS) attempting to radicalize and revolutionize the university establishment.

Numerous student groups, including black separatist and interracial radical organizations, have demonstrated, protested and, on occasion, wreaked havoc on campuses across the country. Among their demands are educational reform, curriculum revision, and a significant role in school policy and campus control. (*See* Documentation 3.) Their objectives range from increased relevance of their studies to outright rebellion. The immediate results vary from compromise to capitulation, from repression to representation, from stalemate to significant change. (*See* Documentation 4 for a particularly dramatic account of the problem on one college campus.)

It must be recognized, however, that in many instances those characterized as extremists may operate as important forces for innovative social change. In a historical perspective, their presence often has proved valuable in modifying norms, restructuring values, and redirecting some of

DOCUMENTATION 3

left and right, black and white

The radical student rebellion has not yet affected the central functions and character of the university. It is still dominated by departments, and by a specialist-minded faculty. Research and publication are still the chief means by which faculty members gain status. Undergraduate teaching gets less attention than either graduate teaching or research and writing. Most students are interested primarily in jobs, careers, and credentials in colleges and universities, and no one has suggested how to change this, short of reversing the entire trend to mass higher education. The increasingly large support universities need comes from states, the federal government, parents, corporations, and alumni, on the assumption that they are a good thing for society, and help increase its wealth and solve its problems. Out of this massive support, the functions of the university that traditionalists and radicals alike would like to see increased—social criticism and the liberal arts—are supported on a scale they have never known up to now. But one can see little prospect that the modern university can be transformed into the school of the revolution, though one sees rather that there is a greater possibility that some universities will be destroyed in an effort to do so.

Interestingly enough, in the past few months the rebellion of black students has had much greater impact on the universities than the years of disorder by white student radicals. The explanation is simple. As I have suggested, the student radicals don't quite know what they want to do with the university, and many of their demands (for student participation, for example), can be accommodated without major upset. Radicals are to be found on many faculties, as they always have been, and Marx and his successors are in the curriculum. All this does not make them happy, because the academic

tone changes all, but they have found no means to affect this, and their major thrust has been to such peripheral matters as to who recruits on campus and the university's formal relation with defense institutions.

On the other hand, the demands of the black students have been concrete, and have gone directly to curriculum and university organization. They want specific courses on American Negro history and culture, and African history and culture. They want programs to recruit more black students, tutor them, and support them. They want more Negro faculty. Whereas the impact of the white student radicals has been met by administrators as that of an external invading army, which they have tried to appease with educational changes which scarcely interested them, the attack of black students has been directly on educational issues, and can be met to some extent by changes in curriculum, and by student and faculty recruitment. Not that there are not critical dangers to the university developing in the black demands—there are. They are the implicit demand for quotas of students and faculties, the sometimes voiced demands for separate living quarters and separate and exclusive courses for black students, and involved in both is a potential attack on the ability of the university to maintain standards. But whereas the white radical students have fundamentally been interested in the university as a base for an attack on society, or as a surrogate for their attack on society, the black students, whatever their rhetoric, are fundamentally interested in changing it so it can do a better job of getting them *into* society. The university has to fight the first, but it can respond positively to the second. The problem here is the illusions of many black students as

(continued to next page)

to just what is involved in getting into society. White radical students have convinced a good number of them that it is all or only a game unrelated to ability and effort.

There is a second reason why white radicals have not been able to change the university: their faculty allies on political issues have been split and, on the whole, have been conservative on university issues. Even Herbert Marcuse has partially exempted the university, or at any rate the San Diego Campus of the University of California where he teaches, from the devastating critique to which he subjects the rest of society. Many a faculty member who has said "yes" to getting out of Vietnam or getting military recruiters off campus has said "no" to greater student participation in the shaping of the curriculum, or in the advancement and selection of faculty members.

But there is a third reason why the radical students have not reshaped the university: there is no image or vision, no outline or guide, no philosophy available, that tells us how to shape the university. The traditional liberal arts curriculum is dead. It can excite little loyalty from anyone, except for academic deans and the humanities faculty. Those parts of the university that prepare people for the more concrete and obviously meaningful tasks in the

world remain relatively unaffected by student disorder—engineering; the sciences, the law and medical schools. Their students and faculty generally do not get involved, and do not see that the university needs reforming—or, if they do, they have rather positive and manageable proposals as to who and how to reform it. It is the social sciences and the humanities that supply the rebels, student and faculty, and of these it is the "softer" rather than the "harder" fields, sociology rather than economics, English literature and history rather than foreign languages. The crisis of the university is a crisis of those areas. How should students in these fields be educated, for what functions, what resources should be devoted to education in these areas, to what ends? It is the traditional liberal arts areas of the curriculum that are the sources of discontent and unhappiness—and in this sense, sociology, which provides by far the most student militants, is no exception, for it is not the technicians that sociology trains, but rather the social critics it forms, who become the rebels. Nor can the radicals be appeased, either by the university or the society. They insist that both must be overturned and transformed—to be replaced by what, remains vague, and to most people frightening. (Glazer, 1968:17–19.)

DOCUMENTATION 4

conflict on the campus

ITHACA, N.Y., May 27—What happens to the great university when its faculty is divided over its president's actions on fundamental and highly controversial issues?

Here at Cornell, the battle lines are sharply drawn. A group of 10 senior professors has started a campaign to remove the president, Dr. James A. Perkins.

They charge that freedom to teach has been

compromised by a series of incidents that began last year, 12 months before the traumatic crisis of April 19 and 20, 1969, when black students seized the student center, brought in guns, and forced the university administration to capitulate.

The 10 professors make up a small minority of the faculty, but it is regarded as unusual that a group of senior professors should publicly call for the ouster of their college president. . . .

At least a dozen other senior members of the faculty have announced their intention of leaving this hauntingly lovely campus for less scenic but calmer universities. Others in the 1,300-member faculty are job-hunting. Cornell is threatened by a wide erosion of faculty members, especially in the College of Arts and Sciences, where two departmental chairmen are resigning.

Dr. Perkins insists that the majority of the faculty members are with him.

Typical of his supporters is Dr. Hans Bethe, a Nobel Laureate in physics, who said that while he wished Dr. Perkins "hadn't given in so quickly," the president could be "extremely useful if we manage to break into a calmer situation."

"I believe Perkins does have a flexibility of mind and that he does want to innovate," Dr. Bethe said. "If the students will let him do it slowly and at his own tempo, I think the results will be very good."

Professor Ernest F. Roberts of the Law School, who is secretary of the faculty, said: "On the whole, I'm one of his fans. The actions relative to the Willard Straight incident were the only sane decisions that could have been made.

"Looking back, I would not alter one decision. I think the right thing was done."

Professor Roberts said he thought Dr. Perkins was being blamed unfairly for every administrative action during the crisis.

A leader of the opposition is Dr. George H. Hildebrand, who said of Dr. Perkins: "He's an adroit man, and I'm afraid he can waffle through this crisis.

"One-quarter to one-third of the faculty support his attempts to politicize the campus. One-quarter to one-third see through him, and know what's going on. The rest are the soggy middleground professors that want to keep peace in the family and believe 'Perkins means well.' "

Other professors have organized a group called "Concerned Faculty," consisting of 40 to 70 faculty members who generally support the demands of the militant Black Liberation Front and the radical white Students for a Democratic Society. They are inclined to defend Dr. Perkins.

Another group, the Committee of 41, . . . believes Cornell will survive the onslaughts of student power. But it has reservations about Dr. Perkins.

This group warned the president that it might resign in a body if academic freedom was abridged. Some of its members are especially disturbed over the autonomy that has been conferred upon the new Center for Afro-American Studies.

The crisis has provoked deep personal enmities. Professors who used to regard each other with good-natured tolerance now refuse to shake hands. Some professors with painful memories of the Senator Joseph R. McCarthy era suspect that their lectures are being monitored by black militants for any suggestion of "racism."

Others, determined to stay, proclaim that teaching will remain free. They speak scornfully of departing professors as summer soldiers and sunshine patriots.

With the spring term ending, students and faculty members are still talking about and reviewing the hectic days of crisis at Cornell. . . .

The June issue of The Cornell Alumni News is devoted entirely to the crisis.

John Marcham, the editor, sums up:

"Emotion, not reason, controlled much of what went on. Universities have tried to operate on reason, and this university fell apart when faced with unreason.

"It had constructed elaborate systems of student discipline and academic management, and they all appeared to come apart at once when faced with the dazzling rhetoric and resoluteness of about 100 of the campus's 250 American blacks." (Bigart, 1969:1, 30.)

the well-established, traditional modes of expression. We have already commented on the use of power, in this case Black Power, as a means of effecting social change. Whether or not this struggle proves to be a useful approach to handling the problem of discrimination, it certainly has shaken the thinking, the party lines, and the status quo orientation of other groups. But this does not mean that the risks of such extremist movements and radical notions in politics are always fruitful. In many cases they impede rather than serve as a source of healthy stimulation to activities within the community. It is apparent, for example, that the various activities of splinter groups in many cities have literally drained the poverty program of funds, forced unhealthy compromises, and moved off-target the work that needs to be done. In recent U.S. elections a number of high-level candidates were defeated because of white backlash against legislative desegregation. The 1969 mayoralty contest in Los Angeles between incumbent Mayor Samuel W. Yorty and black Councilman Thomas Bradley is a recent example. (*See* Documentation 5.) Campus violence has prompted state legislatures and the U.S. Congress to consider drastic and repressive measures against student activists.

Extremist movements often provide appropriate stimuli and meaningful expression for individuals who are dissatisfied with the pace and extent of social change. Such groups, however, can become threats to progress, and their destructive functions, their ruthless behavior, and the revolutionary excess of their programs are major problems for the community. This was certainly true of the youth movements in Nazi Germany and in Red China, of vigilantes in the early history of the West, and may also be true of certain highly aggressive groups engaged on one side or the other in the disputes that are rocking the American scene.

mass culture

Finally, it is important to consider the phenomenon of mass culture. We have alluded previously to problems that arise from the sameness that seems to descend on communities that suffer from an overexposure to mass media. The total number of hours spent watching TV far overshadow other cultural activities and usurp the time and leisure that might be devoted to social and political participation. Strong monopolistic trends in the field of journalism have concentrated newspapers in the hands of a few powerful owners. Even in many of the largest cities, community members are offered only one opinion or a single perspective on the news. Rising costs and the economies of size have put many with differing or conflicting views out of business. In a number of commu-

DOCUMENTATION 5

LOS ANGELES, May 27—Los Angeles voters turned out in record numbers today (May 27, 1969) in a mayoral election with national implications.

The two contenders were Mayor Samuel W. Yorty, seeking his third term in City Hall, and City Councilman Thomas Bradley, trying to become the first Negro Mayor of the nation's third largest city. . . .

About 18 per cent of the city's 1.27 million voters are Negro. Mr. Bradley thus had to poll a sizable white vote to stand any chance of winning.

Two recent polls agreed that Mr. Bradley, who spent 21 years on the Los Angeles police force, was leading Mr. Yorty in the nonpartisan election but differed sharply on the margin.

A poll conducted Saturday by *The Los Angeles Times* gave Mr. Bradley a lead of 53 per cent to 36 per cent, with 11 per cent undecided. A poll bradcast by television station KNXT, however, showed Mr. Bradley leading by only 43 per cent to 38, with 19 per cent undecided.

The election ended an exceptionally angry and often highly personal campaign that saw both candidates impugn each other's character and honesty.

After the April 1 primary, in which Mr. Bradley led Mr. Yorty by more than 100,000 votes, the Mayor immediately accused his fellow Democrat of running a "racist" campaign by appealing for the "bloc vote of black militants and left-wing extremists."

Mr. Yorty made a big issue of the fact that one Bradley staff member had once been a member of the Communist party.

The Mayor also alleged that Los Angeles was "one big campus," ripe for takeover by radical elements. He accused Mr. Bradley of being "anti-police" and predicted that hundreds of policemen would quit their jobs if the City Councilman was elected. . . .

Mr. Bradley retorted that the Mayor was running a "campaign appealing to fear and the darker side of man's nature." Several of the Mayor's own Commissioners resigned to protest Mr. Yorty's campaign tactics. . . .

A smooth and low-key speaker, Mr. Bradley, who is a lawyer, sought to convince people that he was an unflappable and trustworthy man in a time of great turmoil and confusion not only in Los Angeles but in urban centers throughout the country.

The widespread unhappiness with Mr. Yorty showed itself in the diverse character of Mr. Bradley's support. Every major Democratic leader in the state, and many from outside, endorsed Mr. Bradley except Mrs. Carmen Warschaw, the national committeewoman, whose husband works for Mayor Yorty.

About 90 per cent of organized labor not only supported Mr. Bradley but contributed workers and money to his campaign. Mr. Bradley was also able to draw on thousands of volunteers, many of whom got their first political baptism working for either Senator Robert F. Kennedy or Senator Eugene J. McCarthy in last year's California primary.

Even some members of the Los Angeles business establishment, long a strong supporter of the Mayor, endorsed Mr. Bradley on the grounds that Mr. Yorty had undermined the business climate in the city.

However, the Mayor was still able to draw on a reservoir of goodwill built up over eight years in office, particularly in the San Fernando Valley, the largely white, middle-class suburb where he makes his home, and among Mexican-Americans. (Roberts, 1969:24.)

[Mayor Yorty won by a 53 per cent majority.]

nities, single owernship extends to radio and television as well as to newspapers. Strong arguments can be raised with respect to the benefits that accrue to mass culture in terms of the collective understanding of the dominant values of the society. The assimilation of everyone to a particular point of view or set of policy positions has grave risks, of course, and the healthy community should be aware of these dangers.

SELECTIVE IMPACT

This discussion suggests that the cultural deviant or the representative of a minority opinion may be limited in his ability to make known his views and to function in the larger society as an agent of social change and innovation. Mass media serve to reinforce and create stereotypic images of appropriate conduct and standards of aesthetics. They reduce opportunities for the individual to find gratification and feel pride in subgroup affiliations and accomplishments that, while modest in terms of the larger culture, are major accomplishments for the individuals involved. Mass culture serves to reinforce and create perceptions of inadequacy in children toward parents and in community members toward each other if they lack the economic means, the intellectual capacity, or the time, energy, and motivation to participate in the ways described by the Hollywood columnist or the New York disk jockey. Can the child in the family of extremely modest income take pride in the family's first car if it is a used one, especially when full-page ads tell him that even last year's models are already obsolete? Can a father's gift of an inexpensive or homemade toy compete with the smoking rifles and battery-operated sewing machines featured on the television commercials? Can a teen-ager take pride in the songs and dances of his ethnic background when the pleasures of the discotheque and the attractions of Las Vegas or Palm Beach are portrayed so vividly by the media (MacDonald, 1957; Gans, 1966)? The pervasiveness of this mass culture is such that there is relatively little variation across educational, professional, or socio-economic lines. (*See* Documentation 6.)

FUNCTIONAL EQUIVALENTS

Related to the production of a mass culture and the tremendous impact of the commercial communications media is the entrepreneurial nature of most leisure-time activities in this country. With their regulatory mechanisms, they undeniably limit the gratification that can be derived from relaxation, fun, and enjoyment. Indeed, the complex urban community has developed, for some, functional equivalents consistent with city life: the bowling alley for the bocci game in the park, the zoo for a walk in the woods, the deep-sea fishing party for the dropline in the

who watches television?

A recent nationwide survey of TV-viewers, sponsored by CBS, reports that those with more than four years of college average about 3 hours a day of viewing compared to the 4.3 hours of those with only grammar school education. Admitted prime-time viewing is unrelated to education. When the CBS survey asked them to name their favorite programs (those watched regularly), over half of those at the top of the educational range named light entertainment shows, the overwhelming preference of everyone else. . . .

Unfortunately, the actual record of viewing —in diaries, for instance—reveals even fewer differences. Education has a lot more to do with how people *feel* about TV than what they *do* with it. College graduates criticize TV programming, but they choose to watch extensively, and in doing so, find themselves in Mr. Minow's wasteland, unable, because of the limited high-brow fare available, to exert much more selectivity than the general population. They clearly display more signs of guilt and uneasiness at this state of affairs, but apparently it's not so punishing that it makes them flick the dial to "off."

Perhaps the most telling data demonstrating the interpenetration of brow level, not merely in television viewing but also in reading, come from Wilensky's study in the Detroit area (*see* Table). . . .

. . . The typical professor crosses one or two levels of TV exposure. The engineers and executives, middle mass, and the underdogs on relief are quite similar in their TV-viewing habits. Television, again, appears to be a powerful force for cultural standardization, since these groups include men making more than $100,000 and others who have been unemployed for years. The department chief at GM, his foremen, and the unemployed autoworker on relief are bound together in the common culture of Huntley-Brinkley, "Restless Gun," and Mr. Clean. (Wilensky, 1964:193–194.)

EFFORTS TO BE DISCRIMINATING IN MEDIA EXPOSURE BY OCCUPATIONAL GROUP AND STRATUM (IN PERCENTAGES)

	MIDDLE MASS					UNDERDOGS		
	Age 21–29		Age 30–55		Total	Negro	White	Total
	WC*	BC*	WC*	BC*				
N=	(69)	(54)	(251)	(304)	(678)	(81)	(105)	(186)
Cultural, Educational, Special TV Shows								
No favorite	83%	83%	75%	83%	80%	96%	91%	94%
One favorite	7	8	10	12	11	4	5	4
Two or more	10	9	15	5	9	0	4	2
Indiscriminate TV-viewing								
Never	28%	41%	37%	29%	33%	15%	19%	17%
Seldom	35	33	36	33	34	36	30	32
Often	17	9	11	15	13	16	19	18
NA†	4	6	4	3	3	4	12	9

* WC = white collar; BC = blue collar
† "No TV" *and* "never watches"

Adapted from Wilensky, 1964: Table 3.

local pond, and the catered cocktail party for the backyard picnic. It would be foolish to argue that the Jet Set do not have fun, that the upper-middle-class family does not enjoy the summer in Europe arranged by the travel agent, or that the suburban girl does not shine at her "sweet sixteen" party at the country club. Certainly we have no evidence that these types of activities are less gratifying to the people involved than were those of another generation, although one often hears statements to this effect. There is nothing to show that one does not receive as much spiritual uplift from the singing of a professional church choir as from one composed of neighbors, or as much gratification from serving in a fund-raising drive organized by Ketchum, Inc., as from working on one run by an indigenous committee.

INDIVIDUAL AND COMMUNITY CONSEQUENCES

The point to be made, however, is that many of the barriers that exist in the world of work and many of the problems of economic participation spill over into the management and enjoyment of recreation and leisure today. For the most part, leisure of virtually all sorts requires both a middle-class orientation and an adequate income; thus severe inequities result for those who do not belong or are not so fortunate. What is there to do on a hot summer evening if you live in Harlem, or on a cold winter afternoon on Chicago's South Side? What are the prospects for a good life for everyone and the chances for occupational and social achievement and gratification if all physicians are supposed to look and act like Dr. Kildare, lawyers like Perry Mason, and politicians like Ronald Reagan (to mix the metaphor only slightly)? It is only since the 1960s that television and the movies have stopped portraying servants as Negroes, pawnbrokers as Jewish, and gangsters as Italian. Even today, a person need only look at a few reruns on the Late-Late Show to recognize the congruence between community stereotypes and the presentations of the mass media.

For the community, the problem of social and political participation involves many diverse and pervasive elements. (*See* Documentation 7.) Among them are the strain of getting the community's work done, of reflecting the majority view, of respecting the successful and talented who influence these workings. There is the need for making certain that control of community life is not left by default to the economically affluent nor relegated by indifference to a professional elite, that individual participation in the organizational structure by which work gets done is not restricted, that personal gratification is not too dependent upon economic and social characteristics. Finally, there is the positive obligation to maintain and foster the healthy aspects of diversity and heterogeneity. A large order for any urban community.

political involvement

Hypothesis: Of those individuals classifiable as Isolates, Neighbors, or Community Actors, political involvement will be directly related to social participation type, with Isolates being least involved and Community Actors being most involved. (This reflects involvement in the organization of the parapolitical system.)

This hypothesis was tested through comparing types of social participators by scores on the [Political Involvement Scale: (1) voted in an election, (2) took a position on local government issues, (3) tried to persuade others, and (4) attended meetings]. From the table, it is clear that different types of social participators vary greatly in their political involvement.

The proportion totally unpolitical ranges from a quarter of the Isolates to 11 per cent of the Community Actors in the city, and 29 per cent of the Isolates to 10 per cent of the Community Actors in the suburbs. At the other end of the scale, the proportion of social participation types with scale scores of 3 or 4 ranges from 14 per cent of the Isolates to 24 per cent of the Community Actors in the city, and from 14 per cent of the Community Actors in the suburbs. Thus the hypothesized order holds in each part of the metropolis, but there is a stronger relationship between political involvement and the parapolitical system in the suburbs. (Greer and Orleans, 1962:641–642.)

PERCENTAGE DISTRIBUTION OF POLITICAL INVOLVEMENT SCALE SCORES FOR THREE TYPES OF SOCIAL PARTICIPATORS IN CITY AND SUBURBAN SAMPLES
[in areas of Metropolitan St. Louis]

Political Involvement	TYPE OF SOCIAL PARTICIPATOR*					
	Community Actors		Neighbors		Isolates	
	N	%	N	%	N	%
City sample						
none (0)	11	11	17	25	40	25
low (1–2)	62	65	42	61	96	61
high (3–4)	23	24	20	14	22	14
TOTAL	96	100	69	100	158	100
Suburban sample						
none (0)	11	10	14	23	29	29
low (1–2)	59	49	36	58	57	57
high (3–4)	49	41	12	20	14	14
TOTAL	119	100	62	101	100	100

Source: Greer and Orleans, 1962: Table 3.

* Social Participators: (1) Community actors, who are members of voluntary organizations based in the local community, and who are informed with respect to the affairs of the area; (2) Neighbors, who participate in the small world of the neighborhood, but who are not involved in the larger world of the local community; and (3) Isolates, who are involved at neither level.

We have already stressed the relationship between industrialization and urbanization and the various pervasive problems that face the contemporary urban community. To a considerable extent, these properties underlie the issues of individual social participation and political action. Since community life requires a great deal of bureaucracy in the world of work and in the functioning of government, it is apparent that political and social participation must be developed under similar arrangements. It is also quite clear that the power and prestige of individuals in the economic sector are correlated with their performances in social and political activities. The active participation of the insurance agent in Kiwanis, the contractor in his local political club, or the industrialist's wife in university activities represents a means-end situation of great relevance to continued success. Even where the gains are not explicit and direct, such activities serve to reinforce and enhance the participant's prestige and ancillary power, which in turn tends to motivate and stimulate further intensification of such behavior.

INEQUITIES IN OPPORTUNITY

In addition to the link between economic affluence engendered by the world of work and the opportunities and motivation of participation, it must be recognized that various strata within the community are subjected to differential demands on their time and energy. The executive who can announce an emergency board meeting by having his secretary call the members is in a far better position to participate than is the blue-collar worker who has to make these calls himself from a pay phone during his lunch hour. The academician who can attend an afternoon meeting with the mayor is in a much more convenient situation than the truck driver who must complete a daily quota of deliveries. The doctor's wife who can afford a baby sitter while she attends a coffee for a local candidate and the salesman who can drive comfortably to a regional party convention are more likely to engage in the community's political life than are those who lack these amenities (Slater, 1960; Moore, 1961).

Then, too, it should be pointed out that a considerable part of the communication and interaction process of different groups stresses to varying degrees the role of the individual in community responsibility. The student who is exposed during college to a variety of political opinions, confronted with role models who are deeply committed individuals, and even, perhaps, influenced by courses in the behavioral and social sciences is a much readier candidate for social and political experiences and activities of a meaningful nature.

Women also play a special role. Discriminated against in the world of work and relegated to a relatively subordinate status as young mothers, modern suburban women frequently compensate by becoming intensively engaged in the community's political and social life. These concerns may correctly, if cynically, be regarded by some as substitutes for other activities and a means of keeping their brain cells working, as efforts to relieve the boredom and frustration of being with crying babies, of facing only the challenge of the automatic washer and the frozen-food locker. Whether the roots of much of the participation of middle-class women in the activities of the community are in a sense "compensatory" is beside the point; there is no question but that a large proportion of a community's social and political tasks is accomplished through the efforts of women. Studies indicate that they monopolize most of the national and local health and welfare organizations, constitute the largest block of workers in political activities, and dominate the programs of religious groups (Slater, 1960; Moore, 1961).

DIFFICULTIES IN IDENTITY

It is only fair to point out that in an earlier, less industrialized era conditions in the United States may have been different and concerns with the problem of social and political participation and the effects of mass culture may have been less pertinent. The romantic view is of the early New England town meeting in which the citizenry walked through the snow, collected in the schoolhouse, and decided after unlimited debate what was right and proper for the community. But one does not need much data to recognize that each individual did not necessarily operate as a free agent. Debtors were responsive to the values of those to whom they owed money and farmhands to the wishes of their employers, special-interest groups operated to achieve their own particular ends and, ultimately, choices were made with the stakes of individuals well in mind. Nor were business, church, or even leisure time as democratic as all that. Wealth, position, and education set off an elite that dominated rural as well as urban affairs. With the possible exception of those types of recreation that depended solely upon nature, such as hunting and fishing, equal access to the good things of life has been an ideal fervently held but infrequently realized in America.

Essentially, the cultural use of leisure has always been a luxury, a phenomenon of the rich of whom there have always been very few. However, in our contemporary society, most community members have considerable time away from the job and a majority of the people have the capacity for creativity and independence in activity. Yet we are a society blunted by what Shils (1960) refers to as the "brutal culture," with a coterie of professionals and a few key individuals dominating the scene in our voluntary community organizations and civic and political life.

To suggest that, as problems arise, people discuss and formulate viewpoints on them, that these viewpoints are organized and compete, that the best one wins and is promptly implemented by the people or their representatives is, as Mills (1963) notes, a fairy tale. According to Rosenberg and White (1957), the ogre that destroyed this land of make-believe was the Industrial Revolution. They point out that industrialization and technological innovation have made for a high degree of standardization in both products and ideas. The elongation of the chain of organizational command has enhanced the possibilities of an oligarchic control as local and informal groups become less visible, less viable and, hence, less resistant to control. Many of the traditional categories—extended family, ethnic identity, and so on—have lost much of their significance. The structural characteristics of large bureaucracies and the widespread inequalities of opportunities have undermined the functions of associations in inculcating values and transmitting political norms. Rank and file identification with the organizational leaders has diminished, particularly for the member whose life is peripheral and whose participation is tangential to the economic aspects of the community. In brief, both structurally and psychologically, the social and political alienation of many persons in the community is a function of the disintegrating influence of mass society on the ties of sentiment and loyalty to specific groups that characterized the social structure of democracies in an earlier period. Without attachment to primary or intermediate structures, the individual has no bonds, no motivations to participate socially and politically in the life of the community. The managers and the elite exercise power and control, despite our equalitarian value system, and they and their colleagues, through the power of the media, set the tastes, habits, fads, and fashions that pervade the value structure of the community (Gusfield, 1962).

intervention approaches

Lack of motivation, or apathy, on the part of large groups of individuals and the structural constraints that lead to these characteristics are not the only aspects to be considered in developing concepts of intervention in the problems of social and political participation and the contemporary use of leisure time. Equally relevant is the recognition that many of the traditional styles of community participation are fundamentally inconsistent with the urban industrialized way of life. The electronic computer is essential to maintaining the membership lists of the lodge, the "Y," or the big city church. The paid public relations expert is usually better able to develop a successful political campaign for the city councilman than are his ordinary friends and neighbors. In these times it must be acknowledged that, in many ways, the expert is not only more available but better equipped and, on the average, more likely to make advantageous decisions for the people he represents—and sometimes for the entire community—than are the community members themselves. Contemporary history provides some glaring examples of erratic community behavior.

ALLOCATION OF DECISIONS

One particularly appropriate illustration that has been the object of considerable study by social scientists is the implementation of fluoridation programs for improved dental health (Gamson and Lindberg, 1960). It is a well-established and virtually indisputable scientific fact that the addition of small quantities of fluoride to the drinking water of communities naturally lacking the chemical reduces the number of cavities that develop in children's teeth, and probably in adults' as well. Except in the case of patients using artificial kidney machines, there is no known medical evidence that such a procedure is detrimental to health. Further, its cost is extremely low, adding at most a few pennies a year to the average tax bill. Nevertheless, in a large number of communities in which the issue has been placed on the ballot, a majority of community members have voted against it (Coleman, 1957; Metzner, 1957).

These defeats have been explained in a number of ways. Some contend that the responsibility rests in the susceptibility of most Americans to the emotional pleas of highly charged minorities. Others argue that the negative vote represents an idiosyncratic attempt to demonstrate one's independence from the character of life in our mass society. Only a very few opposed it on conservative medical grounds, arguing that the dangers of its long-term use had not been evaluated. (These latter may, in the end, be proved right, a fact that would demolish the illustration but would not destroy the point it makes.) Whatever the reasons, as a result of community decision, hundreds of thousands of children suffer needless dental decay, and hundreds of thousands of parents are required to pay for dental treatment that should not be necessary.

Other less clear-cut instances of lay intrusion into areas of professional competence are available. For example, parent groups have thwarted the orderly development of educational programs—sex education is a subject area currently under attack—on the grounds that they know best what and how their children should be taught. As a result of such activities, many wise educators, public officials, and professionals in voluntary groups resort to all kinds of techniques to control public participation in their programs. They build up personal power blocs and try to influence the choice of lay persons to fill leadership roles. The professionals invent busywork, including many of the self-surveys that various groups march around taking, and they focus lay attention on meaningless and minor issues while they make the major decisions. Whether we like it or not, there are many areas of modern social life about which the expert and the professional do indeed have more knowledge and intelligence. It is fallacious to assume that if community members are given the facts they will always act upon them and that, furthermore, the action will represent the wisest decision.

Rather than play the game of community involvement on every issue, it would be wiser to recognize the responsibility of professionals and to develop social-control techniques that regulate their behavior and keep them in line. The hospital that develops a board of overseers composed of deans of medical schools to supervise its activities and makes membership on its lay board purely an honorific role is an illustration of such an action. One of the paramount considerations in the development of intervention techniques is to recognize explicitly the changes in ways of life and the styles of doing things and not to hold too closely to antiquated and unworkable norms.

SOCIALIZATION FOR URBAN LIFE

A reasonable alternative with great potential for effectiveness in at least some areas of community life is education. The greatest promise lies in efforts to educate the public so that they can deal adequately with technical matters and know appropriate methods of coping with the complexities involved in social and political participation today. These efforts include more than teaching people how to operate a voting machine. They involve the extension of programs of serious education throughout the community (Clark, 1956; Liveright, 1967).

A number of significant efforts have been undertaken in the field of adult education which has a wide range of participants. (*See* Documentation 8.) In order to make such opportunities more equitable, recognition must be given to the time and energy differentials as well as to the economic considerations that preclude the full participation of many people. For example, it may be necessary to shift somewhat the voluntary character of such programs. In a few urban centers there are illustrations now evident, such as the provision of babysitting services during class hours and full-tuition scholarships for adult education courses. But much more has to be done along these lines, including leave from employment for the blue-collar worker to give him an opportunity to share in such efforts, tuition payments where necessary for low-income students, sabbatical leaves not only for university professors but for secretaries and truck drivers as well. The concept of a career ladder must be made

In 1959 most people attending adult programs in institutions of higher education were primarily vocationally oriented. In the urban evening colleges the largest number ranges in age from 20 to 35 and represents men and women who are continuing interrupted education. Hundreds of thousands of these young men and women are attending evening colleges and extension classes for special programs in business, industry or engineering, or to complete the Bachelor's degree essential for promotion. . . .

Second only to this group are the many teachers taking courses to qualify for promotion, or to complete state-required certificates. But John Dyer, in *Ivory Towers in the Market Place,* makes the point that there is no typical student: "Perhaps the first characteristic of the evening college is heterogeneity. One finds here many students who already have college degrees and others who have only finished high school. The age range is from eighteen to sixty-five or seventy, with the median age being thirty plus. One-third is under twenty-five; 10 per cent over forty-five."

Dyer emphasizes the variety of motivation among these students, but suggests that there are two major ones: one growing from "life space" areas (the nonacademic motivation) and the other from "life chance" areas (rational, economic motivations).

John R. Morton, in his study of university extension services, has identified the extension student as one who attends extension classes, resident centers, or one who uses correspondence techniques, conferences or extension library services. He observes that men constitute a slight majority, with the educational status of all students "considerably above the average for the nation as a whole. Only 5 per cent of the users of university extension services had failed to complete high school, with 37 per cent completing under-

graduate college work and more than 10 per cent being engaged in graduate study." Morton further reports that more than three-fourths of participants in extension activities hold full time jobs. The age of the extension student is near that of the evening college enrollee, with the median age being 34 years, although the older student (median age, 35) is more likely to be enrolled in conference and institute programs while the younger student (25 year median) registered in the correspondence program. Morton reports that one out of three students is a professional educator; the second largest group is composed of workers in business and industry.

Although no comparable data are available we know that many thousands of doctors, lawyers, engineers, teachers and other professional persons return every year to college campuses for refresher or advanced training. And even though very many of these are not registered in evening college or extension divisions, they represent a sizeable number of people who count upon colleges and universities as sources of continuing education. As far as junior college adult clientele are concerned, we have no representative figures, but it appears that these people tend to be younger and more directly interested in technical and recreational programs.

As a result of special programs and recruiting efforts it seems likely that during the next ten or twenty years these institutions will attract an increasing number of older persons interested in continuing their education; professional groups desiring to keep in touch with recent scientific and technical changes; specialists wishing a broader general education; women stimulated to continue the education they abandoned for careers as housewives; college graduates wishing to continue or renew intellectual interests. (Liveright, 1967: 103–104.)

relevant for many more occupations, by providing built-in mechanisms and facilities for continuing education.

Social and political participation needs to be defined, not only as an obligation of the citizen but also as an obligation of the social structure to make provision for opportunities to participate. This is common practice today only among the intelligentsia and the economic elite, college professors and business executives, for example. The manager of the large plant does indeed get "credit" within his company for assuming an active role in the chamber of commerce; the university professor can get leave to run for the legislature. Even the high-level union official is allowed time off to participate in governmental planning programs and the like, but this idea needs to be extended to include more people across wider strata of society.

Perhaps the most promising of such attempts have been the efforts of the Office of Economic Opportunity and the regulatory statutes that provide for the participation in the policy-making of individuals in the areas concerned (Burke, 1968). What is essential is that such programs do not become only symbolic window dressing, that there be explicit recognition of the two areas of responsibility: the professional elite who make decisions in highly technical areas and the program participants who share on a basis of equality the essential policy decisions.

Voter registration efforts, particularly among formerly disenfranchised groups such as Southern Negroes and Puerto Rican or Mexican-American minorities, have had widespread effect in shifting the balance of political power to a more representative base. Organized efforts to get out the vote have also been highly effective among many nonparticipating groups, especially blue-collar union members. The proposal to finance political campaigns from public funds (possibly collected along with income taxes) instead of private contributions would make more equitable the participation of all community members in the political life of the nation.

THE MASS MEDIA

With respect to the mass media, it is often held that allowing the marketplace to determine the form and substance of radio and television programs is highly undesirable. The inability or unwillingness of the industry to regulate itself has been the subject of congressional investigation with the implied threat that further regulatory efforts might be required. Current federal regulations on the scheduling of educational and cultural programs on commercial broadcasting time and the laws that require equal time for all major political candidates are some indication of reasonable controls imposed at a minimal level. For the most part, the marketplace dominates the mass media and, as a result, the brutal culture apparently takes precedence over just about anything else. Realistic compromises are available; the final alternative may be to socialize or subsidize completely radio and TV as is done in Great Britain. Nevertheless, recognition of different "levels of cultural interest," as exemplified in British broadcasting, is a real possibility. In our society, it is often suggested that there should be public competition with commercial ventures; such competition should be more than the token one offered today by educational television (Schramm, 1963).

RISKS OF INTERVENTION

The problem with the development of effective techniques of intervention in terms of social and political participation, radical groups, and mass culture is the conflict between the ideals of individual liberty and the repressive hand of arbitrary control or the deadening effect of culture standardized at the lowest common denominator. In a sense this conflict represents a moral and aesthetic problem. While experts may deplore both the stodginess and inflexibility of bureaucratic control and the vulgarity and monotony of low-brow tastes, many social critics consider it illogical to counter the majority's apathy and indifference in these areas by instituting regulatory measures or imposing social controls that require intervention by professional elites. Nevertheless, more and more people are beginning to feel that the risks of noninvolvement are too great and the dangers of alienation are too serious not to continue the quest for democratic means of modifying conduct and increasing participation.

ALI, AKBAR.
  1966 "New trends in client participation in urban development: a view from a developing country." Paper presented at Brandeis University (unpublished).

BELL, WENDELL AND M. BOAT.
  1957 "Urban neighborhoods and informal social relations." American Journal of Sociology 62(January):391–398.

BELL, WENDELL AND M. T. FORCE.
  1956 "Social structure and participation in different types of formal associations." Social Forces 34(March):345–359.

BIGART, HOMER.
  1969 "Cornell bears scars of conflict/faculty divided over Perkins." The New York Times May 28:1, 30.

BLOOMBERG, JR., WARNER.
  1966 "Community organization." Pp. 359–425 in Howard S. Becker (ed.), Social Problems: A Modern Approach. New York: Wiley.

BURKE, EDMUND M.
  1968 "Citizen participation strategies." Journal of the American Institute of Planners 5(September):287–294.

CLARK, BURTON R.
  1956 Adult Education in Transition: A Study of Institutional Insecurity. Berkeley: University of California Press.

COLEMAN, JAMES S.
  1957 Community Conflict. Glencoe, Illinois: Free Press.

DEAN, DWIGHT G.
  1961 "Alienation: its meaning and measurement." American Sociological Review 26(October):753–758.

ERBE, WILLIAM.
  1964 "Social involvement and political activity: a replication and elaboration." American Sociological Review 29(February):198–215.

GANS, HERBERT J.
  1966 "Popular culture in America: social problem in a mass society or social asset in a pluralist society?" Pp. 549–620 in Howard S. Becker (ed.), Social Problems: A Modern Approach. New York: Wiley.

GAMSON, WILLIAM A., AND CAROLYN G. LINDBERG.
  1960 "An analytic summary of fluoridation research: with an annotated bibliography." Community Aspects of Fluoridation: Working Document 21. Cambridge: Harvard School of Public Health.

GLAZER, NATHAN.
  1968 " 'Student power' in Berkeley." The Public Interest 13(Fall):3–21.

GREER, SCOTT AND PETER ORLEANS.
  1962 "The mass society and the parapolitical structure." American Sociological Review 27(October):634–646.

GUSFIELD, JOSEPH R.
1962 "Mass society and extremist politics."
American Sociological Review 27
(February):19–30.

LIVERIGHT, A. A.
1967 "Adult education in colleges and
universities." Pp. 95–108 in H. Gold
and F. Scarpitti (eds.), Combatting
Social Problems. New York: Holt,
Rinehart and Winston.

MACDONALD, DWIGHT.
1957 "A theory of mass culture." Pp. 59–73
in Bernard Rosenberg and David M.
White (eds.), Mass Culture: The
Popular Arts in America. Glencoe,
Illinois: Free Press.

METZNER, CHARLES A.
1957 "Referenda for fluoridation." The
Health Education Journal 15(September):168–178.

MILLS, C. WRIGHT.
1963 "Structure of power in American
society." Pp. 23–38 in Irving Lewis
Horowitz (ed.), Power, Politics, and
People. New York: Oxford University Press.

MOORE, JOAN W.
1961 "Patterns of women's participation in
voluntary associations." American
Journal of Sociology 66(May):592–
598.

NEAL, ARTHUR G., AND MELVIN SEEMAN.
1964 "Organizations and powerlessness: a
test of the mediation hypothesis."
American Sociological Review 29
(April):216–226.

REIN, MARTIN.
1964 "The social service crisis." Trans-
action 1(May):3–6.

REISSMAN, LEONARD.
1954 "Class, leisure, and social participation." American Sociological Review
19(February):76–84.

RIESSMAN, FRANK AND S. M. MILLER.
1964 "Social change versus the 'psychiatric
world view.'" American Journal of
Orthopsychiatry 34(January):20–38.

ROBERTS, STEVEN V.
1969 "Turnout sets record as Los Angeles
picks mayor." The New York Times
May 28:24.

ROSENBERG, BERNARD AND E. M. WHITE (ED.).
1957 Mass Culture: The Popular Arts in
America. Glencoe, Illinois: Free
Press.

SCHRAMM, WILBUR L.
1963 The People Look at Educational
Television. Stanford: Stanford University Press.

SEEMAN, MELVIN.
1959 "On the meaning of alienation."
American Sociological Review 24(December):783–791.

SHILS, EDWARD S.
1960 "Mass society and its culture."
Daedalus 89(Spring):287–314.

SLATER, CAROL.
1960 "Class differences in definition of
role and membership in voluntary
associations among urban married
women." American Journal of Sociology 65(May):616–619.

SYKES, GRESHAM M.
1951 "The differential distribution of community knowledge." Social Forces
29(May):376–382.

WILENSKY, HAROLD L.
1961 "The uneven distribution of leisure:
the impact of economic growth on
'free time.'" Social Problems 9(Summer):32–56.
1964 "Mass society and mass culture: interdependence or independence?" American Sociological Review 28(April):
173–197.

CHAPTER 9

corruption and
community life

OF THE SEVERAL PERVASIVE social problems that we have discussed in this volume, corruption is the most difficult to estimate in prevalence and incidence, for it is largely invisible and unobserved. Its roots lie in the development of innovative patterns of social behavior—that is, illegitimate means to obtain desired ends—to achieve highly valued cultural goals. In the process, institutionalized means may be circumvented and participation in certain aspects of community social life forsaken (Cressey, 1954). From the standpoint of objective criteria, much, if not most, corrupt behavior is normative in an objective sense. It becomes a social problem only when the consequences are judged to be detrimental to the functioning of the social order.

One of the characteristic aspects of corruption (in contrast to the other pervasive problems discussed) is the extent to which it is interwoven into the lives of all community members. Unlike true crime or violence, corruption cannot be considered an interaction between perpetrator and innocent victim; rather, it represents a rapprochement among the various parties involved. The bribe-giver and the bribe-taker are both guilty; the code violator and the code enforcer who agrees to overlook a violation must share the responsibility for wrongdoing. Indeed, the community's general concealment of corrupt acts, thereby rendering them unobservable, is just as important as the individual's attempt to hide his corrupt practices by operating in an invisible way.

the nature of corruption

In terms of total impact on the social order or return for the parties involved, much of the corruption in the American community is petty: the professor who buys the secretary of the buildings and grounds department a box of candy and obtains a sticker that allows him to park anywhere on the campus; the traveling salesman who avoids long-distance toll charges by using fictitious code names in placing person-to-person telephone calls to which the recipient replies, "He is not in"; or the businessman who charges a dinner for himself and his friends as an entertainment expense on his income tax return. It is difficult to argue that, in and of themselves, such deceptions undermine the basic social order. Most of us can think of hundreds of little acts of this type in which we have been involved, and it is easy to rationalize such behavior as inconsequential and harmless. One may argue, however, that the existence of such conduct reduces the possibility of consistent regulation of social behavior among community members and indicates strongly the proclivity of individuals to ignore normative standards in the face of possible personal benefit.

Another kind of corrupt act that is often defended as inconsequential is that undertaken because of the irrationality and rigidity of the norms. Such acts frequently represent connivance between parties to enhance the so-called effectiveness of community life. In some universities, for example, professors are permitted to authorize salary payments to students only at specified levels; rather than engage in a tortuous process of obtaining special permission, administrator, professor, and student collude to falsify the number of hours worked so that the student may receive a justifiable wage. Government departments, faced by a rigid, often unrealistic, civil service salary schedule, often supplement the salary of certain key professionals by allowing them time off illegally to pursue private activities for profit. Airline personnel occasionally let a person with a tourist-class ticket occupy a first-class seat without bothering to upgrade the ticket and make the additional collection because of the paperwork involved. The list could be extended indefinitely. In the view of the participants—and of many others in the community—these actions simply represent more effective ways of dealing with rigidities within the system and of avoiding the difficulties inherent in approaching the problems head-on and in conformity with the norms.

SERIOUS CORRUPT PRACTICES

Finally, there is corruption that can be regarded as serious, involving as it does actions that clearly result in personal gain for one or both, and usually both, of the parties involved, but which, nevertheless, fails to have serious consequences on the overall social order of the community. Large Christmas gifts by suppliers to corporation purchasing agents are justified on the grounds that the suppliers would have obtained the business anyway, therefore the gifts have no import beyond the expression of friendship. The traffic cop who accepts a cash payment equal to the amount the curbed driver would be fined may reason that the impact is exactly the same, with the possible exception of the time the offender would have to spend in court. The fashion model, who regards "dates" with out-of-town buyers as her personal choice, and the industrial magnate, who sponsors a debutante ball for the daughter of an important government official, reject notions of corruption, arguing that such conduct is not harmful and represents personal decisions on their part. Clearly, in judging the motivation underlying such conduct, one confronts a thin line between "right" and "wrong," and the impact of such actions on the functioning of the community is equally difficult to appraise. Would the supplier have continued to obtain the business of the corporation without the Christmas gifts? Is the accident rate any higher in communities where policemen do not take bribes? Would the model keep her job if she did not date buyers? And would the government official rule the same way had his daughter not been feted? On balance, of course, the only considered answer is, "maybe." It is the ambiguity in role relationships in these actions that leads one to regard them as part of the social problem of corrupt practices. Such behavior is often indistinguishable from that which does have an impact on the various social-control systems and on the moral order; they also impede regulatory approaches designed to minimize those types of corruption that clearly are risks in terms of the social order. If one could clearly and consistently separate the harmless types of behavior from those that are more serious, the former could be ignored. The ambiguous character of such behavior makes this a difficult if not impossible task.

DESTRUCTIVE CORRUPTION

There is, however, much corruption that cannot be rationalized or justified in the terms just presented. It is found in all sectors of life and affects the norms governing virtually all behavior. We have compiled a partial list of corrupt practices which are periodically uncovered and documented, although in truth they remain of only passing interest within the general community:

1. Collusion in the setting of prices for both consumer goods and items purchased by competitive contract is known to exist, even among very large companies. Community members pay for this through higher prices and increased taxation.

2. Payoffs to police by individuals and organizations engaged in such activities as bookmaking minimize legal control of gambling.

3. Bribes to housing inspectors and officials of other regulatory agencies limit the application of construction and building standards and the enforcement of housing codes, public health regulations, etc.

4. Fee-splitting among physicians and other medical personnel influences referral policies and may deny the patient the most appropriate practitioner for a particular type of care or treatment. Such activities minimize the utility of standards of performance and frequently serve to conceal incompetence (Garceau, 1966).

5. Improper influence of judges and court clerks occurs through indirect payments or contributions to their political parties. Particularly prevalent in child adoption cases and the assignment of executors of estates, such practices prevent the equitable adjudication of cases and the implementation of professional standards in the legal process.

6. In the entertainment industry, payoffs to disk jockeys and movie theater managers often determine what records and movies are played and the extent to which they are pushed. Cultural taste thus becomes a function of the frequency and extent of such corruption rather than the aesthetic or entertainment value of the product. Similarly, roles in the legitimate theater, movies, and nightclub revues may go to the actress or singer most willing to offer sexual favors and not necessarily to the person most qualified for a particular role or part.

7. The placement of government contracts, the passage of special-interest legislation, and the inclusion of exemptions to regulations such as zoning are influenced strongly by either direct payoffs to legislators or excessive contributions to their political campaigns.

8. The location of state universities, federal projects, interstate highways, and the like are as often determined by political clout or private corporate influence as by the exigencies of the situation. Another favorite technique is to employ consultants and other so-called unbiased decision-makers who are informed of the expected outcome in advance.

9. Superintendents of schools, public health officials, police chiefs, and city purchasing agents frequently are selected not on the grounds of their professional competence but on the strong prediction that their tenure in office will not interfere with ongoing activities and financial arrangements.

10. Political appointments to the judiciary, the regulatory agencies, and key government positions are often made on the basis of the size of an individual's campaign contribution rather than on the basis of his qualifications. Politicians also arrange promotions for relatives and friends of large contributors, and buying off a political opponent with the promise of a choice appointment is not unknown.

11. Union officials sometimes lend pension and health-and-welfare funds under their jurisdiction to companies in which they have a private financial investment. Such discretionary powers permit these officials to acquire business partnerships and controlling interests without risking personal capital.

These illustrations are hardly exhaustive of the wide range of corrupt

An essential ingredient in Irv Stern's Wincanton operations was protection against law enforcement agencies. While he was never able to arrange freedom from Federal intervention. . . . Stern was able in the 1940's and again from the mid-1950's through the early 1960's to secure freedom from State and local action. The precise extent of Stern's network of protection payments is unknown, but the method of operations can be reconstructed. .

Two basic principles were involved in the Wincanton protection system—pay top personnel as much as necessary to keep them happy (and quiet), and pay something to as many others as possible to implicate them in the system and to keep them from talking. The range of payoffs thus went from a weekly salary for some public officials to a Christmas turkey for the patrolman on the beat. Records from the numbers bank listed payments totaling $2,400 each week to some local elected officials, State legislators, the police chief, a captain in charge of detectives, and persons mysteriously labeled "county" and "State." While the list of persons to be paid remained fairly constant, the amounts paid varied according to the gambling activities in operation at the time; payoff figures dropped sharply when the FBI put the dice game out of business. When the dice game was running, one official was receiving $750 per week, the chief $100, and a few captains, lieutenants, and detectives lesser amounts.

While the number of officials receiving regular "salary" payoffs was quite restricted (only 15 names were on the payroll found at the numbers bank), many other officials were paid off in different ways. (Some men were also silenced without charge—low-ranking policemen, for example, kept quiet after they learned that men who reported gambling or prostitution were ignored or transferred to the midnight shift; they didn't have to be paid.) Stern was a major (if undisclosed) contributor during political campaigns—sometimes giving money to all candidates, not caring who won, sometimes supporting a "regular" to defeat a possible reformer, sometimes paying a candidate not to oppose a preferred man. Since there were few legitimate sources of large contributions for Democratic candidates, Stern's money was frequently regarded as essential for victory, for the costs of buying radio and television time and paying pollwatchers were high. When popular sentiment was running in favor of reform, however, even Stern's contributors could not guarantee victory. Bob Walasek, later to be as corrupt as any Wincanton mayor, ran as a reform candidate in the Democratic primary and defeated Stern-financed incumbent Gene Donnelly. Never a man to bear grudges, Stern financed Walasek in the general election that year and put him on the "payroll" when he took office.

Even when local officials were not on the regular payroll, Stern was careful to remind them of his friendship (and their debts). A legislative investigating committee found that Stern had given mortgage loans to a police lieutenant and the police chief's son. County Court Judge Ralph Vaughan recalled that shortly after being elected (with Stern support), he received a call from Dave Feinman, Stern's nephew. "Congratulations, Judge. When do you think you and your wife would like a vacation in Florida?"

"Florida? Why on earth would I want to go there?"

"But all the other judges and the guys in City Hall—Irv takes them all to Florida whenever they want to get away."

"Thanks anyway, but I'm not interested."

"Well, how about a mink coat instead? What size does your wife wear?"

In another instance an assistant district attorney told of Feinman's arriving at his front door with a large basket from Stern's supermarket just before Christmas. "My minister suggested a needy family that could use the food," the assistant attorney recalled, "but . . . how could I ask a minister if he knew someone that could use three bottles of scotch?"

Campaign contributions, regular payments to higher officials, holiday and birthday gifts— these were the bases of the system by which Irv Stern bought protection from the law. The campaign contributions usually ensured that complacent mayors, councilmen, district attorneys, and judges were elected; payoffs in some instances usually kept their loyalty. In a number of ways, Stern was also able to reward the corrupt officials at no financial cost to himself. Just as the officials, being in control of the instruments of law enforcement, were able to facilitate Stern's gambling enterprises, so Stern, in control of a network of men operating outside the law, was able to facilitate the officials' corrupt enterprises. As will be seen later, many local officials were not satisfied with their legal salaries from the city and their illegal salaries from Stern and decided to demand payments from prostitutes, kickbacks from salesmen, etc. Stern, while seldom receiving any money from these transactions, became a broker: bringing politicians into contact with salesmen, merchants, and lawyers willing to offer bribes to get city business; setting up middlemen who could handle the money without jeopardizing the officials' reputations; and providing enforcers who could bring delinquents into line.

From the corrupt activities of Wincanton officials, Irv Stern received little in contrast to his receipts from his gambling operations. Why then did he get involved in them? The major virtue, from Stern's point of view, of the system of extortion that flourished in Wincanton was

that it kept down the officials' demands for payoffs directly from Stern. If a councilman was able to pick up $1,000 on the purchase of city equipment, he would demand a lower payment for the protection of gambling. Furthermore, since Stern knew the facts of extortion in each instance, the officials would be further implicated in the system and less able to back out on the arrangements regarding gambling. Finally, as Stern discovered to his chagrin, it became necessary to supervise official extortion to protect the officials against their own stupidity. Mayor Gene Donnelly was cooperative and remained satisfied with his regular "salary." Bob Walasek, however, was a greedy man, and seized every opportunity to profit from a city contract. Soon Stern found himself supervising many of Walasek's deals to keep the mayor from blowing the whole arrangement wide open. When Walasek tried to double the "take" on a purchase of parking meters, Stern had to step in and set the contract price, provide an untraceable middleman, and see the deal through the completion. . . .

Protection, it was stated earlier, was an essential ingredient in Irv Stern's gambling empire. In the end, Stern's downfall came not from a flaw in the organization of the gambling enterprises but from public exposure of the corruption of Mayor Walasek and other officials. In the early 1960's Stern was sent to jail for 4 years on tax evasion charges, but the gambling empire continued to operate smoothly in his absence. A year later, however, Chief Phillips was caught perjuring himself in grand jury testimony concerning kickbacks on city towing contracts. Phillips "blew the whistle" on Stern, Walasek, and members of the city council, and a reform administration was swept into office. Irv Stern's gambling empire had been worth several million dollars each year; kickbacks on the towing contracts brought Bob Walasek a paltry $50 to $75 each week. (Gardiner, 1968: 75–76.)

practices that are common in American communities. When, on occasion, community reaction becomes severe enough to render the corruption visible and observable, one can find in the mass media empirical evidence of the types of behavior just noted. Bredemeier and Toby (1960:250–286) characterize a wide range of corrupt practices as "relentless bargaining." For example, they describe a young college graduate whose first job was selling typewriters. The young man quit the first day when he learned that the machines were not sold at a uniform price but were haggled over, with the best bargainer sometimes paying only half the asking price. His next job was selling sewing machines. Here he found that one machine costing the company $18 was to be sold for $40 and that another costing $19 was to go for $70. He quite that job and finally obtained a third in the used-car business. He soon learned this business "had more tricks of fleecing customers" than either of the other two.

We know with considerable definiteness that corruption is rampant throughout the business world, government, the health and welfare sector, the educational system, and at many other levels. (*See* Documentation 1 for a discussion of "protection" paid in one community.) The millionaire, the middle-class professional, the unemployed poor—all have some stake in corruption. While the extent of corruption is virtually impossible to estimate with any accuracy, its prevalence cannot be denied and, as a mechanism for circumventing the accepted norms of honesty and probity, it represents one of the most pervasive problems for the community.

causes

A simple way to dismiss the pervasive problem of corruption in contemporary American society is to argue that it existed throughout history and that Americans are no more afflicted than any other society. Undoubtedly historians could point to other ages in which community life was equally corrupt, but it is difficult to deny that our present pattern represents corruption in its severest form. Several years ago, the owners of the Playboy Clubs, for example, were only mildly discomfited over the disclosure that they had attempted to bribe the state licensing commission in order to obtain permission to serve liquor in their New York City establishment. Policemen in some large cities apparently feel perfectly at ease in sending out printed thank-you notes for "tips" received for performing tasks that are really part of their jobs, such as locating stolen property. In other large cities, it is possible to hire an off-duty policeman to direct traffic and keep order at private parties; that such "overtime" is split between the officer and his superiors is common knowledge. To convey the uniqueness of corruption in the United States and its integration into the functioning of the social order, the social analyst is forced to use examples rather than statistics because of the difficulty of obtaining quantitative information.

CORRUPTION FOR ACHIEVEMENT

Why does corruption come about? The underlying cause is relatively easy to specify. With the heavy emphasis on upward mobility and the value placed on high levels of aspiration, "innovation"—to use Robert Merton's descriptive—represents an illegitimate way of dealing with problems of day-to-day life. It is a mechanism by which those who are blocked from or who are without knowledge of legitimate means attempt to attain commonly accepted goals or ends. In many ways, the roots of the problem are inherent in the early development of the country and in the coping behavior of successive waves of American immigrants. Our society's emphasis on personal goal attainment without sufficient legitimate means for attaining these goals tends to induce high rates of innovative behavior designed to achieve the goals by whatever means. Since more attention is paid to crimes and criminal behavior than to corruption—that is, practices that are marginally legal or difficult to detect— there exists a disproportionate amount of political corruption and organized crime in the lower status ethnic groups in our society (Wheeler, 1966). Wilson (1966:30–32) identifies three theories of political corruption:

> There are at least three major theories of government corruption. The first holds that there is a particular political ethos or style which attaches a relatively low value to favors, personal loyalty, and private gain. Lower-class immigrant voters, faced with the problems of accommodation to an unfamiliar and perhaps hostile environment, are likely to want, in the words of Martin Lomasney, "help, not justice." If such groups come—as have the Irish and the Sicilians—from a culture in which they experienced a long period of domination by foreign rulers the immigrant will already be experienced in the ways of creating an informal and illegal (and therefore "corrupt") covert government as a way of dealing with the—to them—illegitimate formal government. The values of such groups are radically incompatible with the values of (for example) old-stock Anglo-Saxon Protestant Americans, and particularly with those members of the latter culture who serve on crime commissions. Whatever the formal arrangements, the needs and values of those citizens sharing the immigrant ethos will produce irresistible demands for favoritism and thus for corruption.
>
> The second theory is that corruption is the result of ordinary men facing extraordinary temptations. Lincoln Steffens argued that corrup-

tion was not the result of any defect in character (or, by implication, in cultural values); rather, it was the inevitable consequence of a social system which holds out to men great prizes—power, wealth, status—if only they are bold enough to seize them. Politicians are corrupt because businessmen bribe them; this, in turn, occurs because businessmen are judged solely in terms of worldly success. The form of government makes little difference; the only way to abolish corruption is to change the economic and social system which rewards it. (Steffens admired Soviet communism because it was a system without privilege: "There was none but petty political corruption in Russia," he wrote after visiting there. "The dictator was never asked to do wrong.") A less Marxist variation of this theory is more familiar: men steal when there is a lot of money lying around loose and no one is watching. Public officials are only human. They will resist minor temptation, particularly if everyone else does and someone is checking up. They are not angels, however, and cannot be expected to be honest when others are stealing (no one wants to be thought a fink) and superiors are indifferent. The Catholic Church, having known this for several centuries, counsels the young in its catechisms to "avoid the occasion of sin." The solution to this sort of corruption is to inspect, audit, check, and double-check.

The third theory is more explicitly political and has the advantage of seeking to explain why governmental corruption appears to be more common in America than in Europe. Henry Jones Ford, writing in 1904, observed that in this country, unlike in those whose institutions follow the British or French models, the executive and legislative branches are separated by constitutional checks and balances. What the Founders have put asunder, the politicians must join together if anything is to be accomplished. Because each branch can—and sometimes does—paralyze the other, American government "is so constituted that it cannot be carried on without corruption." The boss, the machine, the political party, the bagmen—all these operate, in Ford's view, to concert the action of legally independent branches of government through the exchange of favors. The solution to corruption, if this is its cause, is to bring these various departments together formally and constitutionally. This, of course, is precisely what the National Civil League and other reform groups have attempted by their espousal of the council manager plan for municipal government, and what advocates of strong and responsible political parties have sought with respect to state and national government. If the chief executive, by virtue of either his constitutional position or his control of a disciplined majority party, is strong enough to rule without the consent of subordinates or the intervention of legislators, then no one will bribe subordinates or legislators—they will have nothing to sell. The leader himself will rarely be bribed, because his power will be sufficiently great that few, if any, groups can afford his price. (This is how Ford explained the lesser incidence of corruption in American national government: the president is strong enough to get his way and visible enough to make bribe-taking too hazardous.)

In terms of the economic means for achieving the good life, the innovative proclivities of persons of lower socio-economic status may be more observable, but the success-orientation of American society yields temptations and motivations throughout all strata. In fact, "innovation" may serve as a great leveler. Whyte (1955:146) illustrates the point well:

> The rackets function in Cornerville as legitimate business functions elsewhere. The racketeer patterns his activity after the businessman and even strives to gain respectability so that he may become accepted by society at large as he is accepted in Cornerville.

THE CONTINUITY OF CORRUPTION

It is not known whether the quantity of corruption varies with socio-economic status; however, the historical tradition of the country would indicate it is pervasive across the board. The development of the United States rests on a Puritan heritage that not only condemned or sought to control by legal means many personal activities but also removed from public practice a wide range of behaviors offering hedonistic satisfactions (Herman, 1967). At the same time, the settling of the vast country required innovation, strength, aggressiveness, and a willingness to take high risks. (*See* Documentation 2.) The economic and the social history of the United States indicates that many of the most successful men lived outside the letter of the law. Among those who settled in this country were many who did so to escape past histories of failure or deviance; moreover, it can be argued that the conditions necessary for the successful expansion and settlement of this country were not conducive to a strict adherence to legitimate means in order to attain cultural goals.

Henry G. Manne (1962:58) has stated:

> Businessmen of an earlier era are regularly alleged to have been a lawless breed. And, although there is good reason to discount many of these stories, charges of larceny, sabotage of competitors, conspiracy, and other flagrant derelictions of lawful activity permeate the reports of our early business history. But, surely, we know far too little about trends and causes in criminal activity to conclude that businessmen are better people today.

In other words, as a number of writers have made clear (Lemert, 1951:61–62), graft and corruption, as well as vice and crime, are natural outgrowths of our social organization. In fact, it has been argued that there is a necessary interdependence between the system of social control and corruption (Block, 1951). The political party, for example, is essentially an extralegal development but obviously a very indispensable one; in the past, it has provided large portions of the population with a variety of different types of help. (*See* Documentation 3.) It is the politi-

the pioneer and tradition

Life on the Western frontier presented many variations. Opening up the fertile prairies was a relatively calm and peaceful business. There was, however, sufficient inland banditry and enough piracy in the steamboat trade to lend color and vitality to the tranquility of the Ohio and Mississippi valleys. The opening up of the great agricultural states of the North Central area was, in the main, dependent upon orderly men willing to assume the necessary routine tasks. Men engaged in wresting a living from the soil have little occasion for sharp disputes or violent combat. Hence the great agricultural Middle West, Ohio, Indiana, Illinois, Iowa, Minnesota and Wisconsin, took on the general orderliness of life characteristic of New England. In these regions the strong motif of Puritanism developed. At the same time the folkways, mores and laws of New England were transplanted to the Western scene. Thus Iowa and Eastern Kansas became more New English than New England.

Those who were seeking a fortune in the Far West and especially those who invaded the mining sections of the Rocky Mountains were pioneers of different character. It is true that many sturdy and courageous men of honor were tempted by considerations of the economic opportunities and advantageous climate to participate in the development of Colorado, Montana, Wyoming, California and the Oregon Country. But here also came the flotsam, outlaws from Eastern states, ex-convicts made bitter by real or fancied injustice, desperadoes. The Western frontier became in fact the haven of refuge for the horse and cattle thief of Nebraska and Kansas, for the escaped burglar from an Eastern penitentiary, for the counterfeiter who might have new opportunity to ply his illicit vocation. Paroled convicts came from Australia, while Mexican outlaws swelled the numbers.

In fact the background of many of our pioneers was so disreputable that a special code of etiquette arose for conversing with strangers. As one Westerner put it:

"Never ask a stranger where he came from or he may draw a trigger. He may very well have come from jail."

Indeed too much inquisitiveness, as Everett Dick expresses it, was "an invitation to gunplay."

In California the signs of the times were well expressed in a song of the day:

cal parties that supply the important unity and dynamics that give positive movement and a sense of equilibrium to government. Over the years, the political party has come to depend for financial support upon campaign contributions, and favors or preferments are the lures that politicians hold out to those who would join them.

Given America's puritanical heritage, as expressed in the legal suppression of gambling and illicit sexual pleasures, large segments of the population, intent upon personal gratifications, are drawn into the network of corruptive behavior. Many legitimate businesses and enterprises profit from such activities. Some of this profit is direct; for example,

> "Oh what was your name
> in the States?
> Was it Thompson or Johnson
> or Bates?
> Did you murder your wife
> And fly for your life?
> Say, what was your name
> in the States?"

Legal, religious and educational institutions and controls were virtually nonexistent in the mining camps and mountain frontiers. Here, too, there were few women. This meant there was little of the conserving influence of good women or the stabilizing values of family life. The distorted sex ratio in the almost exclusively male population was undoubtedly a factor in the frontier crime rates. This distorted sex ratio brought the inevitable influx of scarlet women who became the hostesses of the gambling dens and night clubs. . . .

Shooting scrapes and jealous quarrels over the attentions of these willing ladies were a frequent accompaniment of strong liquor, frustrated impulses and the code of the times. According to the latter, no red-blooded man was expected to take silently the curses and insults of his rivals. Personal insults, however much deserved, demanded immediate action. If a mountaineer was denounced as a liar, a thief, or by less mentionable epithets he did not hesitate to annihilate his slanderer. The mountaineer was quick on the trigger, aimed well, and without remorse. Thus we may ac-count for the emotional origins of many a mountaineer murder. Life was cheap, but honor was long on the Western frontier.

Climate, we may say parenthetically, may have added to the murder rate. At least high altitude is said to be irritating, and may have contributed to the resentment occasioning explosive murders.

A large share of frontier crimes were economic in motivation. Vast sums of money were afloat in the West and this, too, stimulated an invasion of outlaws and hoodlums. It was common practice in the cattle country to drive thousands of cattle up the long trail from the Southwest to the markets. First these markets were in Illinois, Missouri and Arkansas, but later as the railroads pushed west, they were in Abilene, Great Bend and Fort Dodge, Kansas, and finally in Utah, Nevada, Colorado and Wyoming. When the cattle were delivered, payment was made in cash and thousands of dollars were turned over to the rangers because of the lack of banking facilities. Often the rangers were forced to protect the gold and silver in their saddle bags with their lives, and many a life was lost. Sometimes the life was that of a cattleman, sometimes it was the quick-shooting outlaw's.

Even the United States Marshalls appointed to preserve law and order often had no other recourse than to shoot it out. (Elliott, 1944: 188–189.)

telephone and telegraph companies make large profits through leasing special wires to bookmakers, and many landlords receive handsome rents from call girls and proprietors of houses of prostitution. Other businessmen turn to corrupt practices to maintain their competitive position in the marketplace.

In these times, given the efficient operations of big business, the relatively small entrepreneur could hardly compete were he not able in one way or another to innovate in terms of legitimate means. Such innovation may take the form of engaging in unscrupulous deals with customers; providing favors or special services, including the purchase of stolen goods; or making some kind of pay-off to the appropriate regulatory and tax bodies. As such behavior moves upward throughout the system, it provides a rationale and a justification for those who perhaps would not ordinarily engage in such practices. For them, it comes to represent the way things are done in a particular specialty.

The medical specialist who lacks credentials from an esteemed residency contends that fee-splitting with established physicians is the only way he can involve himself in the medical care of the community. The small manufacturer who pays off the union representative in order to be assured of a steady supply of skilled employees argues that this is his only guarantee that he can have the functional equivalent of the on-the-job training program of his large competitor. The small store owner who offers a 20 per cent discount on cash purchases so he can dodge payment of income tax says that this is the only way he can compete with the large discount house.

THE COMPLEX SCENE

The increased complexity of urban life and the trend toward bureaucratic organization maximizes the likelihood of corrupt practices. In simpler societies, where more of the dealings are on a primary-group, face-to-face level, the exchange of goods and services is subject to the systematic development of reciprocal, or quid pro quo, relationships. Such bartering and trading in a more formally oriented social order becomes redefined as corruption. Favors become bribes; family loyalty is viewed as nepotism; and political agreements are termed deals. In the past, when small independent businesses were the major consumer outlets, grocery store owners, for example, discussed and informally agreed among themselves on the prices of many staples; the jobber or wholesaler served as an intermediary and sometimes as an agent of social control in order to avoid ruthless competition. Today, when marketing managers of large chains make similar arrangements over cocktails in a dimly lighted cafe, the matter is interpreted differently. When it is done by the vice-presidents of great corporations, it is a violation of the antitrust laws and a federal crime.

Before the era of civil service, the local politician who arranged for a cousin to obtain a city job by talking to the mayor was following accepted procedure; the politician who uses his power to change test scores on a competitive examination for a similar position today is clearly acting illegally. Formerly, the town policeman who issued a license on the father's word that his son could drive a car was not regarded as seriously out of line; today, the motor vehicle examiner who accepts tickets to a sporting event from a boy's father for the same purpose is indeed guilty of taking a bribe.

the politician social worker

The ways in which immigrant political support was purchased are familiar and need no elaborate review here. They had at least three kinds of needs which the ward heeler could fill on behalf of the party leadership. Above all, they needed the means of physical existence: jobs, loans, rent money, contributions of food or fuel to tide them over, and the like. Secondly, they needed a buffer against an unfamiliar state and its legal minions: help when they or their offspring got in trouble with the police, help in dealing with inspectors, in seeking pushcart licenses, or in other relations with the public bureaucracy. Finally, they needed the intangibles of friendship, sympathy, and social intercourse. These were available, variously, through contact with the precinct captain, the hospitality of the political clubhouse, the attendance of the neighborhood boss at wakes and weddings, and the annual ward outing.

As has often been noted, these kinds of services were not available, as they are today, at the hands of "United Fund" agencies, city welfare departments with their platoons of social workers, or through federal social security legislation. The sporadic and quite inadequate aid rendered by the boss and his lieutenants thus filled a vacuum. Their only rivals were the self-help associations which did spring up within each ethnic group as soon as available resources allowed a meager surplus to support burial societies and the like. The fact that the politicians acted from self-serving motives in distributing their largess, expecting and receiving a *quid pro quo,* is obvious but not wholly relevant. At least it was not relevant in judging the social importance of the services rendered. It was highly relevant, of course, in terms of the political power base thus acquired. (Cornwell, 1964:30.)

The point, of course, is rather evident, namely, that in a community characterized by highly formal and secondary relationships, the workings of the society require ethical neutrality on the part of community members, for community machinery cannot make judgments in a particularistic fashion. Many of the opportunities for innovation that, on a highly personal level, do not challenge the system could become serious detriments to the continuity of social life. Most significant, perhaps, is the indistinguishable line between harmless and rational "special" relationships between parties, and those relationships that lead to high degrees of inequity.

Some politicians, for example, maintain their ethical stance by setting limits, such as $5 or $10, on the value of gifts that they will accept; some purchasing agents regard it proper for suppliers to entertain them, but not their families; and some school principals allow teachers to accept homemade Christmas gifts but nothing of monetary value. However, the line between such expressions of respect or friendship and activities that represent efforts to gain special favors is thin.

This danger is not limited to business and politics. Take the public welfare worker, for example, whose client bakes him a cake to express her gratitude. Not to accept it would be regarded, in most municipalities, as immature and unreasonable. Yet the same worker who allows his client to baby-sit for his children or help his wife with the housework is regarded as taking advantage of his client. It is socially acceptable to tip the maître d' for a good table in a nightclub but not the ticket seller at the ball park for saving some box seats. With the growth of vertically structured organizations and the anonymity of urban community life, tasks that formerly were regarded as personal relationships have become impersonal. Under these circumstances, grey areas are bound to develop concerning what is appropriate and inappropriate conduct. University professors, for example, often retain their friendships with former colleagues who hold responsible positions in federal agencies which grant research funds. When such persons come to town on "site visits" to review grant applications, there is often considerable ambiguity about the appropriateness of invitations to cocktails and dinner or to stay with the old friend. Persons formerly employed by advertising agencies frequently move into key marketing positions or take jobs as advertising directors of large corporations. Whether or not it is consistent with normative standards for such persons to favor former employers who may have been instrumental in their career development is certainly an open question. Even today, union officials may still have risen from the ranks. Should a former colleague on the production line receive special consideration for minor infractions of union rules? It is certainly difficult to judge.

Finally, one must face the fact that despite the greater efficiency of many bureaucratic elements in the contemporary community, there are still a great number of decisions and actions that are guided by uncertain criteria. In these cases, marginal behavior is essential in order for the work of the community to be accomplished. While most corruption can be subsumed under Merton's category of innovation, the counterrisk of blind adherence to the norms imposed by bureaucratic arrangements is equally damaging. Many public health clinics, for example, have income restrictions. Should the public health official enforce them rigorously and deny free dental care to the younger children of a city fireman who has two older children in college because the fireman's annual income is $50 or $100 over the maximum? Is it corrupt to rig the bids for building construction at the state university to favor a contractor currently completing one building on the campus and who could begin work immediately on the next, thus completing the job six months earlier than a lower bidder who must first assemble a crew and equipment? Is it not sometimes virtuous to show favoritism in placing certain individuals in public jobs, such as a son whose father and grandfather before him were principals of the local high school or members of the police force or fire department? Is the issue appreciably different when it is a craft union recruiting new members to an apprenticeship program? Should the federal government require a new supplier to purchase his goods in the free market when for forty years he has been doing business with and obtaining his materials from the same company? Again, it is difficult in day-to-day life to make judgments between corruption and efforts that avoid highly ritualistic behavior.

intervention and control

It would be unrealistic to suggest that sweeping modifications in the style of economic relationships between community members are going to be accomplished overnight. Indeed, as we tried to point out in the discussion of etiology, the risks of ritualistic behavior may be as severe as those of innovation. This does not mean, however, that programs are not and cannot be implemented to deal effectively with the growing problems of corruption in American society.

We have described some of the arrangements at a political level that are responsible for many of the practices that are abhorrent to the norms of the community. A major one is the dependence of politicians and political parties upon donations and subscriptions to finance campaigns and to supplement what are often token salaries attached to highly responsible jobs, whether elective or appointive. This has been recognized most recently by the movement for federal legislation to provide for public support of the campaigns of presidential candidates. A one-dollar deduction from the income-tax return of every American citizen, for example, would overcome the dependence of presidential candidates on $100-a-plate dinners with their requisite reciprocities. If extended to all political campaigns, such funding would make possible a realistic restriction on the token payments now contributed from private sources. Moreover, realization of the responsibilities of the political office holder and recognition of this in terms of an adequate income would reduce sharply the temptation to accept bribes or other "gifts" of questionable propriety.

This problem, of course, is not limited to political office but holds as well for a large number of corporate and public positions. Given a social structure in which law enforcement officers have incomes significantly lower than those of most community members (*see* Documentation 4), in which judges receive a pittance in comparison with the fees of the trial lawyers whose cases they hear, in which a tax adjuster earns less per year than the entertainment deduction claimed by many of the business-

Policemen complain, and the experts tend to agree, that police salaries are not high enough to attract college-educated or other highly-skilled persons, and that policemen are not adequately compensated for the hazards and responsibilities they are asked to accept. Painters, carpenters, electricians, mechanics, firemen, for example, tend to earn as much or more than policemen in the South and Midwest and in the smaller eastern cities. Only on the West Coast do policemen have [an edge]. . . .

These statistics are minimum and maximum pay figures for patrolmen as of January 1, 1969, except for Chicago and Philadelphia estimates, which include pay raises to take effect July 1, 1969. A retroactive pay hike, which will place them just below San Francisco in the big-city standings, is expected for New York patrolmen early in the year.

These figures do not reflect pay differentials based on longevity, . . . paid holidays, . . . or uniform allowances. Nor do they reflect cost of living variables, which tend to reduce the apparent gap between metropolitan police salaries and the pay scale for smaller cities, particularly in the South. (Lipset, 1969:81.)

Top 10 Cities, 500,000 or more	Minimum Base Pay	Maximum Base Pay	Lowest 5 Cities, 500,000 or more	Minimum Base Pay	Maximum Base Pay
San Francisco	$9935	$10,535	San Antonio	6000	7200
Chicago	8710	11,000	Memphis	6120	7440
Los Angeles	8580	10,105	Kansas City	6180	8150
Philadelphia	8480	9000	Atlanta	6210	8220
Seattle	8340	9600	Boston	6345	8320
San Diego	8150	9900			
Cleveland	7935	8935	*Lowest 5 Cities, 100,000–500,000*		
New York	7930	9380			
Detroit	7500	10,300	Knoxville	4500	5700
Houston	7200	8100	Mobile	4910	6120
			Little Rock	5100	6120
Top 5 Cities, 100,000–500,000			Portsmouth, Va.	5400	6900
			Chattanooga	5520	6480
Oakland	9875	10,535			
Berkeley	9385	10,345			
Torrance	9240	10,190			
San Jose	8665	10,535			
Fresno	8410	9840			

men whose returns he audits and you have a ripe breeding ground for corrupt behavior.

SPECIFYING GUIDELINES

In addition to the problem of the economic reward system, there are a number of other areas where current practice fails to spell out with any clarity the limits of what is ethical and appropriate. Only very recently have federal officials and consultants been asked to follow certain broad guidelines with respect to corrupt practices and been required to indicate their financial interests in large corporations or other holdings. Such regulatory procedures do not apply to congressmen, however, and only a few have volunteered to divulge their financial affairs. School systems remain ambiguous about the propriety of gifts to school personnel; many companies still condone kickbacks to suppliers and expensive Christmas gifts to customers; professional lobbyists continue to be well-paid to wine and dine legislators who are in a position to block or push through preferential legislation.

One requirement for the development of responsible bureaucracy is the formulation of more definitive and explicit rules and guidelines concerning appropriate behavior. Such sanctions and controls will be workable only if there is a reasonably honest appraisal of the forms of reciprocities and gratuities that indeed represent the functional equivalents of practices which existed in the days when life was more primary-group oriented. It is unrealistic to suggest that a viable bureaucracy can be built solely on a formal rewards system. However, it should be possible to develop more explicit criteria for determining what constitutes the difference between perquisite and corruption, between fringe benefit and graft. Such guidelines should be available not only for the development of relationships between adults, but in the socialization of children as well (Thau, 1962; Miller, 1966).

REDUCING HYPOCRISY

In addition to salary adjustments and control of reciprocal arrangements, our analysis of corruption must take into account the "pleasure principle" that underlies much of human behavior. This is difficult to do in a community system that conceals many of its hedonistic outlets from nonparticipants or those who are regarded as the enforcers of the moral order. If gambling were legalized, for example, bookies would become respectable, graft would be reduced, and the process of gambling could be regulated. A senior New York City judge has written:

> Gambling is essentially the poor person's means of satisfying a normal human instinct. It puts a spark in his daily existence—an important item when you think of the boredom and the lack of home life of the underprivileged. In a recent policy trial, the prosecutor sought to discredit a defense witness. To a question as to whether she ever played policy, the witness replied with commendable frankness: "Why, sure, man; everyone in Harlem play the numbers." The policy racket is reputed to be a billion dollar a year business. It has been estimated that the American public spends 20 billion dollars a year—most of it

the bookie business

The odds at the track are calculated after deducting the 15 to 18 percent of the total betting pool which goes to pay taxes and other expenses. The bookmaker pockets that amount.

But he is not a man of unlimited resources. He must balance his books so that he will lose no more on the winner than has been bet on the other horses in a race, after his percentage has been deducted. He cannot control the choices of his customers, and very often he will find that one horse is the favorite choice of his clientele. His "action," as he calls it, may not reflect the action of the track. Therefore, he must reinsure himself on the race in much the same way that a casualty insurance company reinsures a risk that is too great for it to assume alone. To do this, the bookmaker uses the "layoff" man, who, for a commission, accepts the excess wager.

The local layoff bettor also will have limited funds, and his layoff bets may be out of balance. When this occurs, he calls the large layoff bettors, who, because of their funds, can spread the larger risk. These persons are gamblers who comprise a nationwide syndicate or combine. They are in close touch with each other all the time, and they distribute the bets among themselves so that an overall balance is reached on any horse race.

With a balanced book at any level—handbook, layoff, or syndicate—the edge is divided, and no one loses except the men and women who placed the bets. As an indication of the volume of business I am talking about, one of the largest operators in the combine does a layoff business of $18 million a year. His net

illegally—on horse races, football pools, slot machines, and the policy game.

I decry a Las Vegas, but I believe in the legalization of gambling under public control. Bring gambling out in the open. Give the public a chance to satisfy its desire. Then, by appropriate regulatory legislation, extend it in one direction or another, or confine it, as developments warrant (Murtagh, 1960: 53).

Certainly there are limits to what is possible in the way of restructuring illegitimate activities to legitimize their hedonistic gratification. It is doubtful that sex mores can be modified to remove the bartering of sexual favors from the economic market. Nevertheless, even here suggestions about the legal regulation of prostitution have relevance. Parimutuel betting, for example, has the advantage of allowing the big winner to be spotted and income taxes collected on his gains. But since off-track betting is allowed only in Nevada, a flourishing illegal gambling empire is the result. (*See* Documentation 5.) Legalized abortion would remove some of the corruption from medical practice and eliminate the

profit is $720,000 a year. This is a 4 percent return on volume, with relatively no risk, as a result of balancing his books on each event.

The term "gamblers" is a misnomer for these persons. They accept money that the small gamblers wager, but they do not gamble at all. This is further illustrated, graphically, by what we know as the numbers racket.

A man purchases a ticket with three numbers on it, paying a dollar for the ticket. Since there are 999 such numbers, he should reasonably expect the odds to be 998 to 1. The numbers bank usually pays 600 to 1 on such a wager— or less—so you can see that the only gambler in this situation is the man who makes the bet. The operator pockets forty cents of every dollar bet—that is, if the game is run honestly. That, however, is too much to expect from this group. If the play is too high on any one number, they manage through devious means to ensure that a number on which the play has been small will be the winner.

While we do have great problems in estimating the total amount gambled illegally, we can get some idea from significant records made available by the Internal Revenue Service through raids.

For example, the records of an Indiana bookmaker indicate that for a three-day period he received a total of $1,156,000 in wagers. A check of the gross receipts of a large department store in the same city indicated its gross for the same three days as $31,863. A Chicago bookie's records showed he took in $6,400,000 in total wagers for one year, while a chain grocery store in Chicago showed total gross receipts of only $293,000. While, actually, these comparisons may be unfair, in that the bookmakers probably are doing considerable layoff betting from smaller bookies in other cities and other states, these two instances are not unusual, as the following Internal Revenue figures indicate: A Los Angeles bookmaker, Jack Rosen, took in $4,511,000 in one year. A Miami bookie received $1,594,000; a Virginia bookie, $1,221,000 for an eight-month period; and a Tennessee bookmaker, $1,689,000 for five months. (Kennedy, 1962:77.)

need for even well-intentioned and highly ethical doctors to circumvent the rules and regulations. Programs permitting the legal prescription of narcotics for drug addicts would minimize some of the corruption associated with the international illicit drug traffic. The legalization of homosexual relationships between consenting adults would frustrate the blackmail rings that now prey on sexual deviants.

Finally, it should be emphasized that bureaucracies must be constantly aware and sensitive to the rigidities that apparently are characteristic of organizations over time. Flexibility is often difficult to implement when administrations are oriented to large groups and when programs and practices are difficult to individualize. This presents a major challenge to present-day life in the American urban community. It is impossible to rework the social order so that it becomes once again the friendly, open community that existed in the preindustrial era. Rather, it is critical to build, to plan, to develop, to "program" (in a computer sense) mechanisms that minimize the functional rigidities of bureaucracies and enhance their powers for individualization. This is the challenge and the approach to the minimization of many current problems of corruption.

It is important, of course, not to lose sight of the underlying problem, namely, the emphasis on aspiration and achievement that runs through all our community life. Admittedly it is unrealistic to suggest that the equation of success with affluence, which characterizes the philosophy of most Americans, is likely to be changed now or in the near future. Nevertheless, this should not deter us from emphasizing values, goods, and prestige that are unrelated to economic status, gratifications that are uncorrelated with material possession, and respect that is unassociated with financial reward. Only by so doing can the community minimize the attraction of corruption. All other approaches represent essentially stopgap measures or palliatives.

CITIZEN RESPONSIBILITY

Perhaps the cynic will say, considering the nature of the American community, that the situation is one that will have to be lived with. The point has been noted relevant to gambling:

> Individual citizens, by working to elect honest public officials and raise policemen's pay, can make a major difference in this matter. But in the last analysis it depends on the business executive, the factory worker, and the housewife who have been financing big-time crime with their two-dollar bets and their ten-cent wagers. If they would stop patronizing the illegal bookie, the numbers runner, and the sports-pool operator, they could take the profit out of gambling and bring organized crime down to size quicker than all the combined efforts of the federal and local law-enforcement agencies (Kennedy, 1962:79).

Corruption, like the other pervasive social problems discussed in the preceding chapters, cannot be dismissed; it is linked to virtually all the specific social problems connected with the life cycle. It is important to be aware of the pervasiveness of such disorganizing elements in the character of American communities and to take this into account when analyzing the problems inherent in the life cycle.

REFERENCES

BLOCK, HERBERT A.
1951 "The sociology of gambling." American Journal of Sociology 57(November):215–221.

BREDEMEIER, HARRY C. AND JACKSON TOBY.
1960 Social Problems in America. New York: Wiley.

CORNWELL, ELMER E., JR.
1964 "Bosses, machines and ethnic groups." The Annals 353(May):27–39.

CRESSEY, DONALD R.
1953 Other People's Money: A Study in the Social Psychology of Embezzlement. Glencoe, Illinois: Free Press.

ELLIOTT, MABEL A.
1944 "Crime and frontier mores." American Sociological Review 9(April): 185–192.

GARCEAU, OLIVER.
1966 "The morals of medicine." The Annals 363(January):60–69.

GARDINER, JOHN A.
1968 "Wincanton: the politics of corruption." Pp. 61–79 in President's Commission on Law Enforcement and Organized Crime: Appendix B. Washington: U.S. Government Printing Office.

HERMAN, ROBERT D.
1967 "Gambling as work: a sociological study of the race track." Pp. 87–104 in Robert D. Herman (ed.), Gambling. New York: Harper and Row.

KENNEDY, ROBERT F.
1962 "The baleful influence of gambling." The Atlantic Monthly 209(April): 76–79.

LEMERT, EDWIN M.
1951 Social Pathology. New York: McGraw-Hill.

LIPSET, SEYMOUR M.
1969 "Why cops hate liberals—and vice versa." The Atlantic Monthly 223 (March)3:76–83.

MANNE, HENRY G.
1962 "Corporate responsibility, business motivation, and reality." The Annals 343(September):55–64.

MILLER, ARTHUR.
1966 "Business morality: some unanswered (and perhaps unanswerable) questions." The Annals 363(January): 95–101.

MURTAGH, (JUDGE) JOHN M.
1960 "Gambling and police corruption." The Atlantic Monthly 206(November):49–53.

THAU, THEODORE L.
1962 "The business ethics advisory council: an organization for the improvement of ethical performance." The Annals 343(September):128–137.

WHEELER, STANTON.
1966 "Delinquency and crime." Pp. 201–276 in Howard S. Becker (ed.), Social Problems. New York: Wiley.

WILSON, JAMES Q.
1966 "Corruption: the shame of the states." The Public Interest 2(Winter):28–38.

WHYTE, WILLIAM FOOTE.
1955 Street Corner Society. Chicago: University of Chicago Press.

PART THREE

LIFE-CYCLE PROBLEMS

CHAPTER 10

infancy and early childhood

ACCORDING TO THE STEREOTYPE, the years from birth to six are years of contentment, happiness, spontaneous gratification, and joy. Certainly, it is a period when the child is relatively unencumbered and unconcerned with the trappings of society. With the exception of the family and the health-and-welfare systems, most of the activities within the community neither involve the young child nor devote much energy to his problems. This does not mean, however, that all children live their first five or six years in the American community unexposed to exigencies or that the period is one of equity in risks for all of the same age.

Most important, it is held with considerable conviction that the stance and posture of the individual during the subsequent years of his childhood, his adolescence, and his adult life are framed and shaped by this initial period of life. Virtually without exception, students of social behavior argue strongly that the prospects for educational and occupational achievement and participation in the good life of the American community, as well as the development of his temperament and ability to withstand a lifetime of emotional conflict and stress, depend on the individual's experiences in these very early years. The successful engagement of the child with his environment during this period represents the key to his future competencies and opportunities for subsequent gratification and productivity.

Calendars and magazine illustrations almost always portray the infant as smiling and rosy-cheeked, the three-year-old as curious and bright-eyed. Most children in this age group, when seen at play in nursery school, on the playground, or on TV, appear carefree and unburdened. But a myriad of problems, ones that have particular consequences for the family and health-and-welfare sector, confront the very young. In Part III we shall discuss problems of the life cycle; however, an exhaustive review is not intended. Only the most critical problems will be surveyed, and even here it is necessary to examine some of them less than fully.

Not all of the social problems that face the young child are interconnected to the same degree, although the portrait we paint should reveal some of the links that exist between the various problems. In this and the subsequent chapters, our approach in discussing social problems differs somewhat from earlier chapters in matters of organization. For clarity, the various problems will be taken up one at a time, with each discussion including a description of the concerns, their causes, and the various intervention approaches.

infant mortality

The first issue of consequence is the sheer survival of the newborn child, particularly during the first week of life. One of the distinctions between population growth in previous eras and now is the sharp reduction during the first half of this century in the death rate among newborn children. Although data earlier than the 1930s is rather inaccurate, conservative estimates suggest that between 10 and 15 per cent of newborn babies died in infancy at the beginning of the century. By the 1930s, the mortality rate had been cut at least in half. Between the mid1930s and 1950, the rate was further reduced, the annual decline being almost 5 per cent. Since 1952, the infant-mortality rate has been leveling off, community efforts apparently having failed to result in further marked reduction. Certainly the reductions between the 1950s and 1960s are infinitesimal in comparison with the changes that occurred earlier in the twentieth century. Shapiro (1965) estimates that over the entire period 1951–62 the rate of decline averaged only 1 per cent a year, a small fraction of the annual rate of change in the preceding period. Further, some of the year-to-year fluctuations represent important increases, rather than decreases, in the rate (Shapiro, 1965:3).

A significant aspect of the problem is the differential risks of infant mortality among various groups within the population. In 1962, for example, the infant-mortality rate in the United States was 25.3 per 1,000 live births; over 40 per cent of the deaths were concentrated in the first twenty-four hour period, and another 24 per cent occurred during the balance of the first week of life. But infant-mortality rates differ among regions of the country and, in particular, between whites and nonwhites (a category which includes Negroes, American Indians, and various oriental extractions). The available data on race and the findings of several smaller studies that include economic variables suggest strong socioeconomic differences in infant mortality rates. (*See* Documentation 1.) Among whites, the range in rates by geographic region is quite small, despite variations in economic composition, degrees of urbanization, and available medical resources. The Mountain states have the highest infant mortality for whites, the rate being somewhat less than 26 per 1,000, and the West North Central states have the lowest rate, being about 22 per 1,000. In comparison, rates for nonwhites range from somewhat over 30 per 1,000 in the Pacific states to almost 49 per 1,000 in the Mountain states. For the United States as a whole, infant deaths among whites during the first year of life are 22 per 1,000 compared with 41 per 1,000 for nonwhites.

There are a number of reasons why race and, at least by inference, socio-economic status are correlated with infant mortality. Although data on cause of death among infants are often not reliably or fully reported, most of the information suggests a relationship with the age of the mother; consequently, children who are the fruit of late pregnancies in large families are more prone to death (Mechanic, 1962). The data further indicate that part of the differential in death rates is related to the distributions in quantity and quality of medical care and, in particular, the availability of prenatal treatment (Yankauer and Allaway, 1958). It should be noted that certain countries in Western Europe have lower infant-mortality rates than the United States. The Netherlands stands in a special position with respect to infant loss (Curran, 1966). It is generally held that Holland's low rate of less than 20 per 1,000 is related to a long tradition of basic infant care in the family, supplemented by district nurses and welfare centers, and supported by a rising standard of living for virtually all of the population. The data on The Netherlands suggests that the United States has not yet reached the point where only minor additional reductions are possible. The attainment of a maximum infant-mortality rate of 20 per 1,000 would seem to be a realistic goal for the United States.

REDUCING INFANT MORTALITY

General conditions that can contribute to the goal of reducing infant mortality are improvements in the standard of living, expansion of medical and hospital resources, and the control of births, particularly for women in their later childbearing years. Through community-action programs, specific efforts to reduce mortality should be directed at the high-risk groups which can be identified in general by their concentration in economically depressed areas, their high rate of illegitimacy, their record of loss from prior pregnancies, and their racial origin. Certainly many questions remain in the development of these programs, including more precise ways to identify high-risk populations and to overcome some of the personnel shortages in the obstetric and child-health fields.

During the last decade, particularly at the federal level, there has been major concern with the problems of infant mortality and of pre-

DOCUMENTATION 1

race, income, and prenatal mortality

NEONATAL MORTALITY RATE PER 1000 LIVE BIRTHS AND SOCIO-ECONOMIC STATUS BY ETHNIC AND RACIAL NEIGHBORHOODS, SYRACUSE, 1950-56

Neighborhood	Live Births	Neonatal Deaths	Mortality Rates	Average Socio-economic Score
Negro	1,442	46	32	96
Native White	1,749	52	30	91
Italian	3,226	66	20	90
Polish	2,208	33	15	91
TOTAL	8,626	197	23	92

For the total city, (of Syracuse), principal causes of death during the neonatal period are congenital malformations, complications associated with prematurity, and injuries at birth. There are 34,700 live births and 658 neonatal deaths in the total city for the seven-year study period, resulting in a neonatal mortality rate of 19 per 1,000 live births.

As seen in the above table, socio-economic status is fairly similar for all neighborhoods. The neonatal mortality rate for the four racial and ethnic neighborhoods combined is only slightly higher at 23 than the total city rate. By individual neighborhoods, however, there is great variation with the Negro and Native White rates of 32 and 30 respectively, being significantly higher than the rates of 20 and 15, and

in that order, in the Italian and Polish neighborhoods. It should be noted that Negro and Native White neighborhoods consisting of two different racial populations have similar, almost identical, rates. At the same time, neonatal mortality rate in the Native White neighborhood contrasts with and differs significantly from the mortality rates found in neighborhoods populated by white persons of Italian and Polish ancestry.

The analysis, thus far, demonstrates that Negro and Native White populations, though different racially, have similar neonatal mortality rates when socio-economic status is held constant. Also, it demonstrates that the neonatal mortality rate of white native-born persons in a lower socio-economic neighborhood differs

mature birth. Part of this concern is based on a general desire to conserve human stock and part on the discovery that a relationship exists between inadequate prenatal care and mental retardation. Many of the same types of programs associated with reducing the incidence of mental retardation are viewed as mechanisms for lowering the infant mortality rate. Dr. Arthur J. Lesser, deputy chief of the United States Children's Bureau, has emphasized repeatedly the need for better medical care facilities for low-income families. He holds that there is a positive association between family income and infant mortality, and he maintains that the situation is worsening in cities with populations in excess of 500 thousand. Dr.

from rates of other Caucasian populations in neighborhoods of similar socio-economic status. Because the Native White and Negro neighborhoods with different racial populations have similar rates, and because the neighborhoods of white native born and white foreign born have different rates, though racially similar, doubt is cast upon any hypothesis that racial factors directly contribute to variations in the distribtion of neonatal mortality by residential neighborhoods.

Since socio-economic status as defined in this study and family income are not interchangeable variables, the family finance factor is introduced into the analysis at this point to see if it helps to explain the wide variations in neonatal mortality rates among different neighborhoods. Family income data are reported by census tracts and include the total earnings of all family members in one household for a single year. As seen in the table below, income is unequally distributed among the racial and ethnic populations included in this study. Median family income varies from a low of $1,584 in the Negro neighborhood to a high of $3,121 in the Polish neighborhood. The Italian and Native White populations are second and third, respectively, following the Polish in the hierarchy of annual family income by racial and ethnic neighborhoods.

Using all 15 census tracts in the racial and ethnic neighborhoods, a Spearman rank correlation coefficient was computed because of the small numbers of units in the analysis. For the variables, median family income and neonatal mortality rates, a correlation coefficient of $-.75$ gave definite evidence of a significant negative association. As median family incomes decrease, neonatal mortality rates increase. The Negro and Native White populations in the lowest socio-economic area of the city have similar high neonatal mortality rates notwithstanding their racial difference. It would appear that the similarities in high neonatal mortality rates is explained by the low-income status of families that populate these two neighborhoods. More than half of the families in the combined census tracts of these two neighborhoods received less than $40 per week in 1950. As a contrast, the Polish neighborhood has a low infant mortality rate of 15 and a median family income of $3,121, indicating that half of its families received incomes of $60 per week or more in 1950. (Willie and Rothney, 1962: 524–525.)

ANNUAL MEDIAN INCOME OF FAMILY BY RACIAL AND ETHNIC NEIGHBORHOODS, SYRACUSE, 1950-56

Neighborhood	Median Family Income
Negro	$1,584
Native White	2,101
Italian	2,676
Polish	3,121

Lesser notes that with the influx into the larger cities of groups with lower incomes and a higher risk of infant mortality there is a corresponding increase in the number of people dependent upon tax-supported medical services (Lesser, 1963).

PRENATAL CARE

Compounding the problem is the fact that prospective mothers who are deprived invariably do not seek prenatal care or do so only late in pregnancy. This group gives birth to a higher proportion of babies with low birth weights, usually associated with premature delivery. Moreover, hospitals that typically care for the poor have become even more overcrowded, and many have had to shorten the period of postpartum care. In response to this worsening situation, the federal government has appropriated approximately $25 million. These and other funds have been used to build maternity and child-health clinics that offer family planning and prenatal care in addition to more adequate facilities for obstetrical care. It is widely held by experts in the health-care field that a solution to the problems of organization and delivery of services, particularly for the poor, is as much a requirement to remedy the situation as improved medical knowledge.

The entire period of infancy and early childhood is dominated by rapid maturation and the struggle for survival; however, the first several months and, particularly, the first week after birth are the critical periods in the life of the young child. Although deaths do occur after the first several months of life, the level of medical care—and perhaps the robustness and resiliency of the children who survive this initial period—results in minimal mortality after the first few days of life. But there are several conditions, literally social diseases, that represent severe physical and mental handicaps.

mental and emotional problems

Many hold that the earliest years are critical determinants of the child's emotional status throughout the remainder of his life. In this view, severe mental illness, such as psychosis, as well as less serious neurotic conduct are functions of parent-child relationships and the early socialization of the infant (Brim, 1959). The discussion of the relationship between early child-rearing practices and subsequent problems of mental disorder will be reserved for later chapters, when the prevalence of such illnesses brings them to the attention of the community.

FAMILY RELATIONS

The general subject of early parent-child relationships and their impact on the future development of the individual is a subject that has received most specialized consideration in the fields of psychology and physiology of human growth and development (Ausubel, 1958). Most of the research on parent-child identification and the learning of social roles by the young child points to the primary impact of the family. From the very beginning, parents are associated in a benevolent and altruistic light with the satisfaction of the child's visceral needs, biological survival, and emotional security. They therefore wield tremendous power in regulating the child's motivations, satisfactions, and standards, and in influencing the course and outcome of his ego development. Further, students of child development argue that in the unstructured attitudinal environment of children, from which most competing influences are excluded, the specific behavioral differentiations and value systems of parents soon become relatively preemptive in their influence. The tendency to use existing orientation and habits rather than acquiring new ones gives parents a great edge in structuring the values of the young child.

In addition to parental influence, much emphasis is given to the relationship between siblings in families, and a considerable literature exists concerning sibling rivalry and the influence of other sibs on the newborn child. Such matters are too complex to be considered here except to note that these relationships are believed to account for the wide variations in adult, preadolescent, and adolescent behavior of individuals. In our society, children play not only with their siblings but with other children at very early ages. When with their peers, children are concerned with achievement, self-actualization, self-expression, and spontaneity in an environment that is as benevolent as possible. The child seeks a highly personal identity in the group, an identity that is congruent with his fundamental personality trends and temperamental predispositions. Some of the variability of his subsequent career may indeed stem from the nature, quantity, and quality of these early play groups.

AUTISM

A problem usually evidenced during the first six years has to do with the matter of speech. There are, first of all, a small number of children who fail to learn to communicate at all, or who do so at such a minimal level that their ability to relate socially is severely impaired. The problem of autism is relatively rare and is more common in boys than in girls (Clarke and Clarke, 1966). An autistic child usually exhibits one of two behavioral patterns: either he is highly aggressive, noisy, and displays unruly behavior or he rejects social contact almost entirely, centering his life around himself, peering from behind furniture, and avoiding all group activities. The prognosis for childhood autism is very poor (*see* Documentation 2). One study (Bender, 1955) reports that of sixty children between the ages of two and six who were diagnosed as autistic, over one-half were in institutions; of the older ones still at home, approximately one-half were regarded as unimproved or manifesting severe problems. Other writers are also pessimistic about such childhood disorders (Kanner and Eisenberg, 1955). While the problem is statistically rare, autism is a major concern for the families involved and for psychologists and psychiatrists who study child development.

To come face to face with a "schizophrenic" child is one of the most awe-inspiring experiences a psychotherapist can have. It is not the bizarreness of the child's behavior which makes the encounter so immediately challenging, but rather the very contrast of that behavior with the appeal of some of these children. Their facial features are often regular and pleasing, their eyes are "soulful" and seem to express deep and desperate experience, paired with a resignation which children should not have. The total impression first goes to the heart and immediately convinces the clinical observer, even against the better knowledge of previous experience, that the right person and the right therapeutic regime could bring the child back on the road to coherent progress. This conviction has the more or less explicit corollary that the child has been in the wrong hands and, in fact, has every reason to mistrust his "rejecting" parents. (We saw how far Indians and whites would go in accusing one another of doing deliberate harm to their children; our occupational prejudice is "the rejecting mother.")

I first saw Jean when she was almost six years old. I did not see her at her best. She had just made a train trip, and my house was strange to her. What glimpses I could catch of her (for she was frantically on the move through garden and house) showed her to be of graceful build, but tense and abrupt in her movements. She had beautiful dark eyes which seemed like peaceful islands within the anx-ious grimace of her face. She ran through all the rooms of the house, uncovering all the beds she could find, as if she were looking for something. The objects of this search proved to be pillows, which she hugged and talked to in a hoarse whisper and with a hollow laugh.

Yes, Jean was "schizophrenic." Her human relationships were centrifugal, away from people. I had observed this strange phenomenon of a "centrifugal approach," often interpreted as mere lack of contact, years before in the behavior of another little girl who was said to "notice nobody." When that little girl came down a flight of stairs toward me, her glance drifted in an absent way over a series of objects, describing concentric circles around my face. She focused on me negatively, as it were. This flight is the common denominator for a variety of other symptoms, such as the preoccupation with things far away and imagined; the inability to concentrate on any task at hand; violent objection to all close contact with others unless they fit into some imaginary scheme; and immediate diffused flight from verbal communication, when it happens to become more nearly established. Meaning is quickly replaced by parrotlike repetition of stereotyped phrases, accompanied by guttural sounds of despair.

The observation that Jean, on her mad rush through my house, again and again paused long enough to concentrate her attention and to lavish her affection on bed pillows seemed

STUTTERING

A more common communication problem among very young children is stuttering (Lemert, 1951). Considerable work has been done by physiologists and speech therapists to distinguish various types of stuttering.

significant for the following reason. Her mother had told me that Jean's extreme disorientation had begun after the mother had become bedridden with tuberculosis. She was permitted to stay at home in her own room, but the child could speak to her only through the doorway of her bedroom, from the arms of a good-natured but "tough" nurse. During this period the mother had the impression that there were things which the child urgently wanted to tell her. The mother regretted at the time that, shortly before her illness, she had let Jean's original nurse, a gentle Mexican girl, leave them. Hedwig, so the mother anxiously noticed from her bed, was always in a hurry, moved the baby about with great energy, and was very emphatic in her disapprovals and warnings. Her favorite remark was, "Ah, baby, you stink!" and her holy war was her effort to keep the creeping infant off the floor so that she would not be contaminated by dirt. If the child were slightly soiled, she scrubbed her. . . .

When after four months of separation Jean (now thirteen months old) was permitted to re-enter the mother's room, she spoke only in a whisper. "She shrank back from the pattern of the chintz on the armchair and cried. She tried to crawl off the flowered rug and cried all the time, looking very fearful. She was terrified by a large, soft ball rolling on the floor and terrified of paper crackling." These fears spread. First, she did not dare to touch ashtrays and other dirty objects, then she avoided touching or being touched by her elder brother and gradually by most people around her. Although she learned to feed herself and to walk at the normal time, she gradually became sad and silent.

Maybe the child's frantic affection for pillows had to do with that period when she was prevented from approaching her mother's bed. Maybe, for some reason, she had not been able to take the separation, had "adjusted" to it by a permanent pattern of fleeing from all human contact, and was now expressing her affection for the bedridden mother in her love for pillows.

The mother confirmed that the child had a fetish, a small pillow or sheet which she would press over her face when going to sleep. For her part, the mother seemed desirous of making restitution to the child for what she felt she had denied her, not only during those months of illness, but by what now seemed like a general kind of neglect by default. This mother by no means lacked affection for the child, but she felt that she had not given Jean the relaxed affection she needed most *when* she needed it most.

Some such maternal estrangement may be found in every history of infantile schizophrenia. What remains debatable is whether the maternal behavior such as the mother's relative absence and the nurse's total presence could possibly be a "cause" for such a radical disturbance in a child's functioning; or whether such children, for some intrinsic and perhaps constitutional reasons, have idiosyncratic needs which no mother would understand without professional help—and professional people, until very recently, could not even spot these children when they were young enough to be (supposedly) saved with special dosages of well-planned mother love. (Erikson, 1963: 195–198.)

Specific classifications, while useful for diagnostic purposes, need not concern us here. Essentially, as Lemert notes, stuttering is any disruption of speech rhythm following or associated with blocking of lips, contraction of the tongue, spasms in the vocal cords, and tension of the diaphragm which disturbs the breathing process. To a large extent stuttering is a transitory problem and, with maturation, many children outgrow its handicapping character. It is estimated that between 10 and 12 per cent of young children have speech handicaps of one sort or another, most of which fall into the category of stuttering. About 1 per cent of the adult population, or approximately 4 in every 100 persons, stutter to a degree that marks them as deviants. As in the case of autism, male children apparently are more prone to this disorder, and it is estimated that there are anywhere from two to ten male stutterers for every female so afflicted.

To a large extent, stuttering has very low social visibility, particularly in small children. Much of the behavior is regarded as just a peculiar quality in the speech of the young. Stuttering is considered here as a social problem because, given the emphasis in the modern world upon the processes of communication and the attractiveness of highly verbal persons, a child with any language problem faces difficulties in self-acceptance and in the development of his self-identity. Young children who have been rejected by family and peers because of speech impediments exhibit a high incidence of extreme shyness, seclusiveness, moodiness, depression, and anxiety. The problems of stuttering and speech deformity, it is held, often have their genesis in emotional problems.

Interestingly enough, speech defects in young children go relatively untreated in the typical American community. Unlike the physical abnormalities of blindness and deafness, which are researched and treated by a wide variety of public and voluntary agencies, speech problems, particularly ones of young children, are often ignored. Although little is known of the extent to which the young child is tormented by such afflictions, the relevance of verbal interaction at every age suggests that this problem warrants more attention.

mental retardation

Emotional problems and speech defects are minor, however, in comparison with the problem of mental retardation. It is estimated that nearly 200,000 persons are confined to public institutions for mental defectives in the United States and that their maintenance costs nearly $500 million a year. In addition, an unestimated number of children with various levels of mental retardation are found in the community, many of them living in custodial or semicustodial circumstances with parents or other relatives. Such defectives contribute in disproportionate numbers to the population of the poor. Mental retardation is a good illustration of the transformation of a social problem from a moral to an objective concern. It shows how, when experts and community leaders become involved, considerable attention may be paid to a problem that formerly went unnoticed. In the case of mental retardation, it was the concern of President John F. Kennedy and his family that stimulated interest in the problem and resulted in the expenditure of considerable government resources, including the establishment of a new institute among the National Institutes of Health charged with research and program development to remedy the problem.

As research and treatment of the mentally retarded has become more sophisticated, and the problem has become more visible and observable, awareness of the complexities involved has increased (Ehlers, 1964). It is important to note the difficulty of differentiating the problem of mental retardation from that of cultural deprivation. The latter is a consequence of the failure of large groups of children to engage successfully in the educational process of the community. For a long time there has been a tendency to underestimate the impact of social interaction and, particularly, the educational process on the mental development of individuals and to overestimate the more hopeless genetic causes of much mental retardation.

COMMUNITY REACTION

The problem of the mentally retarded is illustrative of the way a community handles deviants whom they are unable to rehabilitate in large numbers. Tizard (1966) points to analogous circumstances between the early treatment of the blind and the current handling of the mentally handicapped. He points out that in both instances social relief was first confined to residential centers which eventually, if not at the outset, became custodial institutions remote from the affairs of ordinary life and physically separated from the community. They became, to use Goffman's (1961) phrase, "total institutions," places where inmates ate, worked, lived, and slept; where large numbers of individuals were herded together in common wards, mess rooms, and day rooms; where they were regimented and disciplined by a small staff who maintained wide social distance from them. Institutions for the mentally retarded became self-perpetuating, and less equipment, less staff, and harsher treatment became commonplace. Only recently has the conception of institutional care for the mentally retarded shifted to include therapy or rehabilitation. Even today, it should be noted, treatment of the retarded is often based on criteria such as social class rather than on patients' needs. (*See* Documentation 3.)

Part of the change in orientation is due to an awareness that mental deficiency or mental retardation is not a single disease or entity. It is, rather, a term applied to a condition of subnormal mental development present at birth or appearing in early childhood and characterized mainly by limited intelligence. In the past, IQ scores have represented the major distinction between various types of mental retardates; in general, those with IQs under 25 are referred to as idiots; between 25 and 50, as imbeciles; and from 50 to 80, as morons.

With the growth of mental testing, an extremely large number of dull or moronic persons have been identified in the population. It is difficult to obtain precise figures regarding the prevalence or incidence of mental deficiency because such estimates are generally based on IQ tests that are heavily influenced by education and culture. The problem of mental retardation is an interesting one. Although the symptoms of organically related retardation are often manifested at birth or soon after, the discovery of them within the community usually occurs only after school age. Once the child "disappears" into the adult population, the so-called prevalence figures become reduced; for example, three studies cited by O'Connor (1966) show a 50 to 100 per cent reduction in mental retardation after the age of fourteen. It is doubtful if any of this reduction is due to recovery; more likely it is the result of differential visibility and observability within the population.

CAUSES

The question of etiology is complicated by the unreliability of tests and instruments, especially for early identification and differential diagnosis of mental retardation. Norms of intellectual growth are rudimentary and do not distinguish the late bloomer from the truly retarded or the organically damaged from the socially deprived. Recent concern with poverty and social disadvantage has emphasized the heredity-environment dilemma in differentiating between biological and cultural causes. Admittedly, individual differences are largely the result of genetic variations and, as Clarke and Clarke (1966:123) note, it may be assumed that heredity plays an essential part in determining the limits of intellectual development. However, these limits are considerably wider than was formerly thought, and the social interaction and environmental situation may be more determinative of the child's retardation than his physical condition.

The retarded, more than any other group in Western culture, have been reared in the most adverse circumstances, often spending years in residential schools and institutions with all that implies or living at home under conditions of neglect and misunderstanding. Given these circumstances, it would seem likely that the feebleminded individual would function at the lower limits of his potentiality whereas individuals with normal intelligence living under ordinary conditions would approximate more closely their upper limits. According to the interaction theory of nature-nurture, where environment is adequate, observed differences between children are probably genetic in origin; where it is inadequate,

speed of hospitalization of retardates

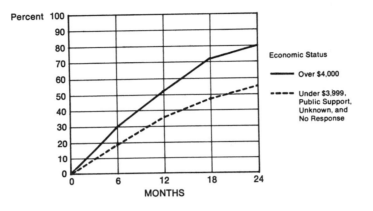

[Extremely retarded] patients whose families have a higher socio-economic status, whether measured by parents' education, father's occupation, or family income, tend to be hospitalized earlier and at a significantly higher rate than patients who come from a lower socio-economic milieu. The most noticeable difference in admission rates, however, was for family income. Cumulated admission rates for six-month periods since application for two categories of family income are shown in [the accompanying figure]. Lower income includes not only those families making less than $4,000 a year but also those that are partially or fully dependent on public support, while higher income families were those making $4,000 or more a year. It is clear from this figure that patients from better-off families are admitted more rapidly than those from a more economically deprived environment. For the first six months, the respective per cents were 30 and 17. By the end of the twenty-four month period, 79 per cent of patients with a yearly family income of $4,000 or over had been admitted as compared to 56 per cent for patients from poorer families . . . .

With respect to the socio-economic status and structure of applicants' families, it would seem reasonable to assume that prospective patients who come from a more deprived environment would be admitted more swiftly than those who are more fortunate. The opposite is true. Indeed, the single most significant findings pertain to the effect of family income on the speed of hospitalization.

The lack of published data on differential admission rates for other hospitals for the retarded precludes an assessment of the seemingly unusual findings of this study. Such findings take on a wider meaning, however, when seen in the light of the many studies on social class and psychiatric treatment. These studies have indicated that, on the whole, upper class patients are much more likely to receive psychotherapy and stay longer in therapy than lower class patients. Furthermore, there is some indication that the poor are less likely to receive continuing service from private or even some public social service agencies than the rich. (Sabagh et al., 1966:121–122, 126.)

environmental influences are superimposed on genetic differences. When this occurs, it is often difficult to separate the cultural effects from the biological. Nevertheless, it is not unreasonable to assume that large segments of the population designated as retarded are in fact underfunctioning to various degrees. Certainly the army's success with rehabilitating draftees with marginal intelligence scores would bear this out.

Technical problems of research make conclusions about the biochemical and organic origins of mental retardation most difficult. In nearly every case of gross mental defect, organic disease or congenital pathology is a causative factor. Clinical evidence of cerebral malfunction or brain damage is found in many persons with severe mental abnormalities, and postmortem examinations of mental defectives reveal a wide variety of cerebral pathology. Certain abnormal metabolic manifestations and congenital anomalies which are known to cause injury to the brain or to interfere with its function are genetic in origin. However, many other adverse factors are nongenetic, including prenatal traumas, birth injuries, pre- and postnatal infections, protein deficiency and malnutrition in general, and social deprivation. These acquired or accidental anomalies are frequently associated with poverty and parental neglect. Unfortunately, programs of restoration and rehabilitation too often take the conservative bias of assumed genetic cause and overlook the social factors that might be more amenable to amelioration. Many experiments, particularly those using operant conditioning or stimulus-response approaches, have pointed to the possibility that even retarded adults can be provided with sufficient intellectual resources to contribute to community life.

INTERVENTION STRATEGIES

Intervention strategies include the development of training and treatment centers for the retarded that will emphasize maintenance of children in the community; early, preschool identification of those with organic problems and an evaluation of their trainability; and assessment of inadequate family environments that may lead to cultural deprivation and social retardation. Research into biochemical and physiological causes must continue in order to develop more effective prevention programs. A case in point is the discovery of the high incidence of mentally retarded and physically handicapped children born to mothers who were exposed to German measles during the first trimester of pregnancy. This finding has spurred the development of a measles vaccine and, more important, has prompted many mothers to expose their daughters to the disease at an early age so that a natural immunity can develop. The potential of premarital counseling for prospective mates who represent a high risk of compounding genetic problems has recently been demonstrated in the case of hereditary harelip, and the technique has obvious merit for controlling some aspects of genetically caused mental retardation.

Community attitudes toward mental retardation, and particularly the stance of the educational system, must and can be changed so that the social stigma attached to mental deficiency is decreased and opportunities for the afflicted are increased. Our current stress on intellectual excellence too often results in discrimination against the less bright. If our communities would be willing to make even slight concessions at reorganizing activities and practices in order to accommodate the less verbal, less intelligent individual, many retardates could probably function adequately in society (Dexter, 1962). At least part of the solution rests with modifying the system of family and community agencies that provide care and work-training programs in home and community settings. Total programs for the retarded are needed, including residential units, state schools, counseling services, and sheltered workshops, and involving all levels of government.

illegitimacy and parental deprivation

Illegitimacy and parental deprivation are discussed together because, at least in the case of the very young child, illegitimacy is a major explanation for his being reared without an adult male in the household. A generation ago, Malinowski formulated the rule of legitimacy which asserts that in every society the common modal pattern is for each child to have a legitimate father who acts as protector, guardian, and representative (Goode, 1966). Of course in the American community, as in all others, this is not always the case. A small number of children, by virtue of the unexpected death of a parent or the more common practice of separation or divorce, are reared during their formative years without the presence of both parents in the home. By far the most common reason for deprivation of this sort, however, is the lack of a legitimate father, a phenomenon magnified by the high rate of illegitimacy in American communities (Department of Health, Education, and Welfare, 1960:9).

Illegitimacy figures per se are, of course, difficult to verify since it is estimated that one out of five marriages in the United States takes place after conception (Christensen, 1958, 1960). We are not concerned here with the problems of sexual conduct. Such a discussion is reserved for a subsequent chapter in our life-cycle analysis. What is important is that in the United States at least one in twenty and perhaps as many as one in ten of all children are born without an acknowledged father.

The status of illegitimacy in the history of American society, as well as of Western Europe, is in itself an interesting topic. The laws and values of the American community have shifted markedly regarding the illegitimate child. With respect to inheritance, for example, he is no longer stigmatized but regarded as an equal heir with the child born in a legal marriage. Many states no longer issue birth certificates identifying illegitimacy or require the name of the natural father. Quite apart from any moral considerations, however, illegitimacy is a social problem in terms of the formal status-structure of the community, and the illegitimate child, particularly the young child, is highly vulnerable on a number of grounds. The choice is clearly one either of the mother's rearing the child by herself or in an extended family network, or the community's making provisions for its foster care or adoption. (Meyer et al., 1956; Jones et al., 1962; Witmer et al., 1963).

Today, at least in the larger urban centers, the illegitimate child who is white, and whose mother is Protestant or Jewish (particularly) and is willing to give him up for adoption, probably faces a life no different from his legitimate counterparts. Programs of adoption and the desire to adopt children on the part of educated, usually prosperous, couples who cannot have children of their own have provided a source of adoptive parents for white Protestant and Jewish children. Indeed, it could be argued that many of these adopted children are reared in environments and have life opportunities much better than would have accrued to them if the pregnant mother had married the child's natural father. Among children of Negro or racially mixed backgrounds and, to some extent, lower-income white Catholics, the problem is severe. It is estimated, perhaps overestimated, that anywhere from one-tenth to one-third of Negro babies are born out of wedlock. The provision of substitute parents has not been a solution for them. This is due both to the apathy of the American public toward adopting such children and to the requirements for racial and religious matching often imposed on adoption agencies by community customs or the legal system.

CONSEQUENCES OF ILLEGITIMACY

Neither the moral problem nor the stigmatizing labels constitute the major social concern with respect to the illegitimate, fatherless child; rather, it is his limited opportunities for normative early development at a point when the process of identification within the family is so important. Although there tends to be a movement towards overlap between the maternal and paternal roles in the typical American family today, and the differentiation between the functions of each sex in the family is less sharp, the male in a typical middle-class family has a special role as the authority figure, moral arbiter, and disciplinarian. And of course he influences the mother's childrearing practices, at least to a certain extent. The father also has a somewhat different role, depending on the sex of the child. He helps the girl to find her biological and social sex roles by acknowledging her femininity, and he serves as a model of masculinity for the male child. The father usually subjects his son to more rigorous disciplinary control than he does his daughter and so influences his son's identity in terms of readiness for peer group educational experiences. Although admittedly we do not know fully the dynamics of the identification process between parent and child in the American family situation, certainly the matriarchal household in which fathers are not present represents a difficult socialization situation as well as a difficult economic one. This is particularly true in many black households where poverty is a way of life. As Riessman (1962) points out, illegitimacy becomes an important concern not so much because of the illegitimate status but because of the role differences accruing to the young child in such circumstances.

CONTROL

The historical solution to this problem has been to provide foster parents when legal adoption seems unlikely. Programs of foster care have been the subject of several analyses, all of which point to the difficulty of obtaining responsible surrogate parents whose interest extends beyond the temporary economic reward from child-support payments (Weinstein, 1960). Most foster care represents either inadequate home conditions or a continual shifting of the child from one home to another, thus denying him consistent love and affection and a chance to develop his identity. (*See* Documentation 4.)

A number of studies point to the undesirability of institutionalized childrearing in orphanages and suggest the need for more intimate home situations (Weinstein, 1960). As a consequence of these findings, there has been considerable investment in programs to provide economic means to enable the unmarried mother to retain her child. Federal funds distributed by AFDC (Aid for Families with Dependent Children) provide minimal levels of economic subsistence for mothers and children in fatherless situations (Wiltse, 1964). This solution has not been without criticism, however, for such households often represent the extremes of parental deprivation, and multiple illegitimacies have further complicated the problem.

In addition to the problems created by the one-parent household, there is also concern with parental deprivation resulting from immature or conflict-ridden relationships between mother and father living in the same household. It is commonly held that the young child's experiences vis-à-vis his parents shape and mold his personality and temperament, with particular consequences for his attitudes regarding sexual behavior, moral responsibility, and occupational aspirations. Some researchers have attempted to trace the impact of early childhood on

Clearly, the promise has not come to pass. When social workers can speak of children in foster-family care by such terms as Beatrice Malone's "the child in-between world" or by Joseph Reid's "orphans of the living," it is obvious that the profession assuming major responsibility for foster-family care is sorely troubled about the children receiving care. What are the facts?

Do the children return home or move into adoptive homes? All of the evidence indicates that permanent homes are not being achieved for most children in foster-family care. Maas and Engler, on the basis of their study of all children in foster care in nine different communities of various size, geographical location, and cultures, predicted that better than half the children in foster care at the time of the study would live "a major part of their childhood in foster families and institutions." The report further stated that adoption or return home was not occurring to an encouraging degree except, perhaps, in one community; in most of the communities, about 20 per cent of the children were leaving care in a six-to-nine-month follow-up period.

The evidence of the failure to achieve permanent plans for children was even more overwhelming in a 1961 study by the Children's Bureau in collaboration with the Child Welfare League of America; a sample of over 62,000 children, representing a population of 425,000 children, was used. Of all children receiving foster care under the auspices of public agencies, return home was anticipated for only 12 per cent and adoptive placement for another 13 per cent; voluntary agencies were having better success with placements for adoptions —25 per cent—a reflection of the larger proportion of infant children of unmarried mothers in their case load. Their success in reuniting parents and children was comparable to that of the public agencies—13 per cent. Remaining in their present placement or moving to another foster-care facility was the plan for 71 per cent of children in foster care under public auspices and for 57 per cent of children cared for in foster care by voluntary agencies.

Another index of the failure to provide some permanent plan for children, other than foster care, is the length of time children stay in foster care. The Children's Bureau found that 22 per

subsequent emotional and behavioral development. Although clear-cut relationships between the interpersonal processes and later outcomes are not always apparent, investigators have found that a broken home is much more prone to be an economically deprived one. Consequently, a child reared in such a home is more likely to live in a community environment in which deviance, utilization of illegitimate means, and lack of community responsibility are endemic. In this sense it could be argued that illegitimacy and other types of parental deprivation place children in an environment in which their future growth and development are handicapped, given the orientation of the American community (Jenkins, 1958; Robbins, 1966).

cent of the children in public foster care had been served from six to eleven years and that 9 per cent had been served twelve years or more. Maas and Engler found that the average (median) years in foster-family care ranged from 1.2 years in one community to 8.0 in another; the percentage of children in foster care for more than 5.5 years ranged from 7 to 46 per cent. Many of these children are truly "orphans of the living," rootless, unhappy, without close ties to anyone.

There are sound reasons why many of the children in care are not returned home or placed for adoption. There is a sizable proportion of children whose parents are interested in them, maintain continuing contact with them, but, for one reason or another, cannot or do not plan for them to return home. Other children, for whom adoption would seem to be the answer, are frequently the children most difficult to place—children emotionally disturbed, intellectually or physically handicapped, older, or from minority groups. Many times, too, outmoded laws stand in the way of legally freeing children for adoption.

Do the children who must grow up in foster-family care—a number running high into the thousands—have a sustaining and continuing relationship with one family? Many do, but many others do not. The Children's Bureau found that 58 per cent of the children in foster care under the auspices of public agencies had had more than one placement; of this group, 16 per cent had had four or more placements, and "in the rare case the child had been placed 22 times!" Do they maintain close and meaningful ties with their own parents? Again, the answer must be "no." Maas and Engler found that in approximately half of the cases parents visited infrequently or not at all.

Are the children who do remain in care achieving the emotional and social development that seemed promised by foster-family care; are they overcoming the many problems that they brought with them to care? Again, the answer for many children is "no." Maas noted that "forty to fifty per cent or more of the children in foster care in every one of our nine communities showed symptoms of maladjustment." Many child welfare workers have noted, along with Maas and Engler, that children without close and continuing ties with responsible adults are the children who have a confused sense of identity, relate shallowly, and are unable to learn to trust others. All other studies seem to indicate that for many children foster-family care has not provided the conditions that would allow for normal growth and development and for overcoming the effects of prior deprivation. (Lewis, 1964:36–37.)

extrafamilial encounters

In our previous discussion we focused on the interaction between parent and child and the outcomes in terms of future life course. At the close of the period under discussion, that is, at about five or six years of age, the child becomes involved in his first formal engagements and encounters with the larger community. In American society, this exposure may take place as early as three or four years if the child participates in nursery school and prekindergarten programs or at the age of five in the many parts of the country where kindergarten represents the first year of the child's school life.

There is considerable debate about the desirability of taking very young children away from the home for large parts of the day. Such programs are not uncommon in other parts of the world, however; the Scandinavian countries, for example, have much more inclusive programs. Most experts agree that when such programs represent rational extensions of the home and provide situations for continued maturation and growth, intellectually and physically, they are probably neutral in their impact. Points of view differ, however, when such programs are looked upon as remedial, to overcome the deficiencies of family life. It is commonly held that pre-school programs in low-income areas are not of the same caliber as those in middle-class and suburban communities. Thus the child penalized in his home life likewise finds himself penalized at school:

> The middle class child arrives in school readied by his parents and society for the kind of education we provide for him. The lower class child, the culturally deprived, the in-migrant to our urban American culture, is not prepared. He is already faced by difficult tasks in kindergarten and early primary school. This statement may, at first, sound ridiculous. What difficult tasks are demanded of kindergarten children? Yet, if one thinks of all the work that a middle class mother goes through to involve her child with books, toys, and other objects, one realizes how much effort goes into the pre-education of middle class children. The lower class child also gets a pre-education, but it is an education which, unfortunately, does not prepare him for the kind of education that our schools provide (Duhl, 1964:16).

On these grounds, the Office of Economic Opportunity has placed great emphasis on Head Start programs. The child's outlook on the world, the way he plays, what he plays with, the variety of new experiences he achieves, and the like, are emphasized in ways to substitute for the low-income child the normative childrearing practices of the middle-class family. Whether such efforts equalize the future opportunities of the child for successful community life is difficult to assess. While such extrafamilial encounters may promote intellectual development, they may also raise additional problems for the young child in terms of his psychological development, attitudes toward his parents, and difficulties in coping with his familial setting. Only time will tell which of these views is correct.

child accidents and child abuse

Although the problems of infant mortality and congenital malformation are the largest health risks for the newborn in today's urban community, two other phenomena need to be mentioned briefly—child accidents and child abuse. Extended discussion is virtually impossible here since little is known about the prevalence, incidence, or etiology of these problems.

Child accidents refer to severe or permanent disablement of children due to a wide variety of accidents both in and outside the home. Such accidents are usually uncovered through the reports of medical practitioners with considerable experience in pediatric medicine. Approximately 3 per cent of those persons unable to work or to engage in adult careers are in such a status because of disfiguring or disabling accidents that occurred during early childhood. It is not certain whether this is a new social problem or whether better reporting techniques have provided us with a fuller picture of the incidence of such occurrences; however, the social-problem aspects should be noted (Gil, 1968). Most experts believe that the phenomenon of childhood accidents represents social defects and not random occurrences or physical differences among the children concerned. Such social defects, it is implied, reflect to a large extent differences in the outlook of parents and their conscious and unconscious regulation—or lack of it—of the child's life and environment.

The problem of child abuse is of equal concern. Although its prevalence cannot be accurately determined at present, we do know that a significant proportion of children who come in contact with the medical-care system show evidence, as revealed by X-ray and physical diagnosis, of abuse by adults, presumably their parents or others in the household. Recently, the Children's Bureau has sponsored the development in all states of reporting procedures that require physicians to report suspected cases of child abuse (as they are now required to report gunshot wounds). Such efforts not only will provide opportunities to intervene in cases of individual children but also will make available objective information for epidemiologic studies and other research on the problem.

Some tentative findings are indicated from a preliminary report on these data (Gil, 1968). First, more than a third of the reported cases do not, upon investigation, seem to involve abuse (although they may represent child accidents). Second, many of the reported injuries were not serious and apparently were due to somewhat excessive disciplinary measures on the part of caretakers. Third, 2 per cent of the injuries were fatal and 6 per cent involved serious head injuries. Finally, the age distribution is surprisingly wide—birth to 21 years of age—and more uniform than previous reports have indicated. (*See* Documentation 5.)

CAUSES

There is a tendency to assume that child abuse and child accidents, like many of the other social problems discussed here, are found in greater than expected proportions in low-income families; however, these two problems represent instances in which visibility, at least, may not be

age distribution of abused children

Many investigators observed that children involved in incidents of abuse tend to be very young. A recent study of 85 abuse cases by Schloesser in Kansas found 70 per cent to be under three years of age and 32 per cent under six months. McHenry et al. at Children's Hospital in Pittsburgh studied 50 cases of multiple skeletal trauma seen over 10 years. They found that 60 per cent of the cohort were under nine months of age at the time of injury. Boardman studied 12 cases at Children's Hospital in Los Angeles all of whom were under three and one-half years old. De Francis reports that 56 per cent of the 662 cases from the 1962 press survey were under four years old. Simons and Downs report that of 313 children in the New York City study cohort 28 per cent were under one year, 41 per cent one to under five years, 23 per cent five to under ten years, and 8 per cent ten years and over.

Kroeger reports that of 52 children in the Chicago hospital survey 33 per cent were under one year and 66 per cent were under three years. Less than 20 per cent were over five years of age.

Johnson in a recent study of 107 abused children served by the Department of Welfare in Denver, Colorado, found that 33.7 per cent were under one year, 56 per cent were under three years, 68 per cent were under five years, and 32 per cer.t were between six and thirteen years. None were over thirteen years old.

An analysis of the age of 483 children reported to the Illinois Central Registry during the first year of mandatory reporting (1965–66) shows that about 15 per cent were under six months, about 25 per cent under one year, about 40 per cent under two years, about 62 per cent under four years, about 25 per cent from four to under ten years, and about 13 per cent ten years and over.

An analysis of the age of 201 children reported to the New York Central Registry during the five last months of 1964 shows that about 27 per cent were under one year, about 65 per cent were under four years, nearly 25 per cent from four to under ten years, and about 9 per cent ten years and over.

As can be seen, the age distribution of abused children reported in accordance with mandatory reporting legislation to the Illinois and New York Central Registries is nearly identical. The age distribution of the 48 children reported through the Brandeis University —NORC [National Opinion Research Center] survey and the 504 children reported through

differentially distributed among economic classes. Little is known about either the etiologic bases of childhood accidents and abuse or what constitutes appropriate intervention strategies. We do know that with the control or virtual elimination through immunization techniques of such early childhood diseases as measles, influenza, scarlet fever, mumps, whooping cough, and polio, these new "social" diseases have become of considerable concern.

According to one group of researchers who have studied preschool children, accidental injury is one of the leading causes of death during

the Brandeis press survey is shown [below].

Data from the NORC and press surveys, as well as data from the Illinois and New York Central Registries and from the citywide studies in New York and Denver reveal age distributions which are less skewed towards the very young age groups than the age distribution of abused children observed in hospitals such as those reported in the Pittsburgh, Los Angeles, and Chicago hospital studies. One partial explanation of this difference may be that children seen in hospitals may, as a group, have suffered more severe abuse than children reported through more broadly based surveys, and that children upon whom more severe physical injuries were inflicted tend to be younger than those upon whom less severe injuries were inflicted. The different age distribution of the fatal and non-fatal cases reported through the Brandeis press survey supports this explanation. Further support is suggested by the fact that among the children reported through the NORC survey 6.25 per cent were fatally injured and 8.33 per cent suffered permanent damage, whereas 33 per cent of the children reported through the press survey were fatally injured. The age distribution of the children reported through the press survey is more skewed towards the younger age groups than the distribution of the children reported through the NORC survey. (Gil, 1968: 28–30.)

AGE DISTRIBUTION OF CHILDREN REPORTED IN NORC AND PRESS SURVEYS

| | NORC Survey | | Press Survey | | | | | |
| | | | Fatal Incidents | | Non-fatal Incidents | | All Incidents | |
Age	No.	%	No.	%	No.	%	No.	%
Under 6 months	1	2.08	26	15.9	46	13.5	72	14.3
6 to under 12 months	3	6.25	15	9.1	27	7.9	42	8.3
1 to under 2 years	6	12.50	33	20.1	36	10.6	69	13.7
2 to under 3 years	4	8.33	19	11.6	38	11.2	57	11.3
3 to under 5 years	7	14.58	20	12.2	57	16.8	77	15.3
5 to under 8 years	} 15	} 31.25	22	13.4	43	12.6	65	12.9
8 to under 10 years			8	4.9	17	5.0	25	5.0
10 to under 12 years	5	10.42	1	0.6	18	5.3	19	3.8
Over 12 years	7	14.58	5	3.0	28	8.2	33	6.5
Not reported	0	0.0	15	9.1	30	8.8	45	8.9
TOTAL	*48*	*99.99*	*164*	*100.0*	*340*	*100.0*	*504*	*100.0*

the childhood years, as well as the frequent cause of future disability (Meyer et al., 1963). These investigators report that the preschool child appears particularly subject to risk from the human and physical forces that combine to produce accidents. Another study indicates that for children under five, the major causes of injury and death are motor vehicle accidents and fire burns, followed closely by drowning and poisoning (Haddon et al., 1964). Foote (1964) has attempted to provide a sociological approach to childhood accidents by analyzing some of the institutional factors involved. For instance, he points out that automobile speed limits and laws regulating the use of swimming pools and beaches are hard to enforce. Yet accidents in these areas account for a significant proportion of childhood injuries. With respect to accident repeaters, studies have identified two types of children as being particularly accident-prone: the gregarious, aggressive, active, uninhibited, adventurous child (Krall, 1964) and a minority type represented by the extremely withdrawn, cautious, and inactive boy (Mellinger et al., 1963).

CONTROL

Investigators engaged in the study of accidents among young children acknowledge the high incidence of the problem and the great public concern; at the same time, they recognize the exploratory character of their work and the difficulties of separating the causative individual personality characteristics of parent and child from the socio-structural ones. Such lack of knowledge, of course, hinders the specification of appropriate intervention techniques and presents an unsatisfactory causal explanation of the problem.

role of the family

The theme underlying our consideration of the young child has been the maximization of physical survival free from injury and disease and the preparation for future life roles. Although there is considerable controversy over which dynamic qualities of family life represent the key determinants of the child's future course, the importance of these early formative years in terms of developing emotional status and temperament and patterns of aspirations and morality is clear. In the complex urban community today, efforts within the political and the health and welfare social-control systems are directed toward mediating the difficulties encountered by many children because of inadequate personal socialization. Without knowing quite how it is accomplished, most analysts of social behavior would agree that some families are more successful than others in helping the young child to develop a stance and posture that will equip him for his roles in the larger community.

In discussing these early years in the life cycle, the student of social problems will be wise to avoid the fallacy that a return to traditional forms of family structure and relationships will solve the psychological puzzles that constitute the mystique of the socialization process. One of the arguments often raised is that if the family were strengthened—and by this is usually meant "more traditional" in the sense of the farm family of the last century—many of the problems of psychological gratification and identification would be handled. Such a position is a highly emotional one and, by placing it against the fabric of current community life, one can easily perceive its illogical character. The maintenance of traditional family life, with the division of labor of adult members based on sex roles and the expectations toward the child based upon the maintenance of a broadly functional nuclear unit, is inconsistent with the current economic structure and the allocation of contemporary work and community roles.

From the standpoint of social problems, the remedy (and the intervention strategy) requires a modification of the norms regarding early upbringing and role relationships rather than more strenuous efforts to bring the child's functioning and behavior back into line with traditional norms. For example, in terms of the matriarchal family in which the mother either dominates or is the only adult present, the normative standard of the society perhaps should be one that promotes the early and sustained provision of alternatives to the family as the basic unit with which the child is expected to identify. Considerable controversy, of course, reigns about the applicability of organizational mechanisms, such as round-the-clock nursery programs, to replace the family. Many sociologists, even though they reject the traditional concept of the family, including its present structuring, acknowledge that the primary group remains the most appropriate setting for the child. They recognize, as Litwak (1960) maintains, that bureaucracies function well only when the goals are clearly defined and the techniques reasonably rigorous for meeting these goals. In the case of childrearing, our lack of understanding, particularly of the psychological dynamics, raises serious questions as to whether such functional equivalents to the family represent a reasonable solution. This does not mean, however, that the only alternative is to return to the past role relationships within a traditional family structure. Rather, some hold that the key to the future functioning of the child lies in restructuring the norms of the family and in developing primary groups that embody different values. These new norms would insure that the child's learning of behavior patterns and internalizing of attitudes would be more consistent with the place we aspire for him in the world.

The traditional norms regarding the sacredness of the family have been so powerful that the social thrust has been toward customary and consistent behavior rather than toward experimentation and remolding. Such innovation, however, may represent the future, and perhaps only, hope of maximizing these early years of the child's life.

AUSUBEL, DAVID P.
1958 Theory and Problems of Child Development. New York: Grune and Stratton.

BENDER, LAURETTA.
1955 "Twenty years of clinical research on schizophrenic children with special reference to those under six years of age." Pp. 503–515 in G. Caplan (ed.), Emotional Problems of Early Childhood. New York: Basic Books.

BRIM, ORVILLE G., JR.
1959 Education for Child Rearing. New York: Russell Sage Foundation.

CHRISTENSEN, HAROLD T.
1958 "The method of record linkage applied to family data." Marriage and Family Living 20(February):38–43.
1960 "Cultural relativism and premarital sex norms." American Sociological Review 25(February):31–39.

CLARKE, ANN M. AND A. D. B. CLARKE (EDS.).
1966 Mental Deficiency: The Changing Outlook. Second Edition. New York: Free Press.

CURRAN, ELIZABETH.
1966 Report of the International Conference on the Peri-natal and Infant Mortality Problem in the United States. Vital and Health Statistics Series. Series 4, No. 3. Washington: U.S. Department of Health, Education, and Welfare.

DEPARTMENT OF HEALTH, EDUCATION, AND WELFARE.
1960 "Illegitimacy and its impact on the aid to dependent children." Report of the Bureau of Public Assistance. Washington, D.C.: U.S. Government Printing Office.

DEXTER, LEWIS A.
1962 "On the politics and sociology of stupidity in our society." Social Problems 9(Winter):221–228.

DUHL, LEONARD J.
1964 "K-4/a new school." Trans-action 1(March):16–17.

EHLERS, WALTER H.
1964 "The moderately and severely retarded child: maternal perceptions of retardation and subsequent seeking and using services rendered by a community agency." American Journal of Mental Deficiency 68(March):660–668.

ERIKSON, ERIK H.
1963 Childhood and Society. Second Edition, Revised. New York: Norton.

FOOTE, NELSON.
1964 "Sociological factors in childhood accidents." Pp. 448–458 in William Haddon Jr., Edward A. Suchman and David Klein (eds.), Accident Research: Methods and Approaches. New York: Harper and Row.

GIL, DAVID G.
1968 "Incidence of child abuse and demographic characteristics of persons involved." Pp. 19–39 in Ray E. Helfer and C. Henry Kempe (eds.), The Battered Child. Chicago: University of Chicago Press.

GOFFMAN, ERVING.
1961 Asylum. New York: Doubleday.

GOODE, WILLIAM J.
1966 "Family disorganization." Pp. 479–552 in Robert K. Merton and Robert A. Nesbet, Contemporary Social Problems. New York: Harcourt, Brace and World.

HADDON, WILLIAM, JR., EDWARD A. SUCHMAN AND DAVID KLEIN.
1964 Accident Research. Methods and Approaches. New York: Harper and Row.

JENKINS, WESLEY W.
1958 "An experimental study of the relationship of legitimate and illegitimate birth status to school and personal and social adjustment of Negro children." American Journal of Sociology 64(September):169–173.

JONES, WYATT C., HENRY J. MEYER AND EDGAR F. BORGATTA.
1962 "Social and psychological factors in status decisions of unmarried mothers." Marriage and Family Living 24(August):224–230.

KANNER, LEO AND LEON EISENBERG.
1955 "Notes on the follow-up studies of autistic children." Pp. 227–239 in Paul H. Hoch and Joseph Zubin (eds.), The Psychology of Childhood. New York: Grune and Stratton.

KRALL, VITA.
1964 "Personality characteristics of accident repeating children." Pp. 427–437 in William Haddon, Jr., Edward A. Suchman and David Klein, Accident Research: Methods and Approaches. New York: Harper and Row.

LEMERT, EDWIN M.
1951 Social Pathology. New York: McGraw-Hill.

LESSER, ARTHUR J.
1963 "Current problems of maternity care." The First Jessie M. Bierman Annual Lecture in Maternal and Child Health presented at the University of California, Berkeley, May 10.

LEWIS, MARY.
1964 "Foster-family care: has it fulfilled its promise?" The Annals 355(September):31–41.

LITWAK, EUGENE.
1960 "Geographic mobility and extended family cohesion." American Sociological Review 25(June):385–394.

MECHANIC, DAVID.
1962 Medical Sociology. New York: Free Press.

MELLINGER, GLENN D., DEAN I. MANNHEIM AND BARBARA F. WOLFINGER.
1963 "A comparison of the personal and social characteristics of high and low accident children." Paper presented at the meeting of the Society for Research in Child Development, Berkeley, California, April 12.

MEYER, HENRY J., WYATT C. JONES AND EDGAR F. BORGATTA.
1956 "The decision by unmarried mothers to keep or surrender their babies." Social Work 1(April):103–109.

MEYER, ROGER J., H. N. ROELOFFS, JOANNE BLUESTONE, AND SANDRA REDMOND.
1963 "Accidental injury to the pre-school child." Journal of Pediatrics 63 (July): 95–105.

O'CONNOR, NEIL.
1966 "The prevalence of mental defect." Pp. 23–43 in Ann M. Clarke and A. D. B. Clarke (eds.), Mental Deficiency: The Changing Outlook. Second Edition. New York: Free Press.

RIESSMAN, FRANK.
1962 The Culturally Deprived Child. New York: Harper and Row.

ROBBINS, LEE N.
  1966 Deviant Children Grown Up. Balti-
        more: Williams and Wilkins.

SABAGH, GEORGES, RICHARD EYMAN, AND
        DONALD N. COGBURN.
  1966 "Speed of hospitalization: a study of
        a preadmission waiting list cohorts in
        a hospital for the retarded." Social
        Problems 14(Fall):119–128.

SHAPIRO, SAM.
  1965 Infant and Peri-natal Mortality in
        the United States. Vital and Health
        Statistics Series. Series 3, No. 4.
        Washington, D.C.: U.S. Department
        of Health, Education and Welfare.

TIZARD, JOHN.
  1966 "Individual differences in the mentally
        deficient." Pp. 166–187 in Ann M.
        Clarke and A. D. B. Clarke (eds.),
        Mental Deficiency: The Changing
        Outlook. Second Edition. New York:
        Free Press.

WEINSTEIN, EUGENE A.
  1960 Self-image of the Foster Child. New
        York: Russell Sage Foundation.

WILLIE, CHARLES V. AND WILLIAM B. ROTHNEY.
  1962 "Racial, ethnic, and income factors
        in the epidemiology of neonatal
        mortality." American Sociological Re-
        view 27(August):522–526.

WILTSE, KERMIT T.
  1964 "Aid to families with dependent
        children: the basic service." The
        Annals 355(September):75–81.

WITMER, HELEN L., ELIZABETH HERZOG,
        EUGENE A. WEINSTEIN, AND MARY
        E. SULLIVAN.
  1963 Independent Adoptions. New York:
        Russell Sage Foundation.

YANKAUER, ALFRED AND NORMAN C. ALLAWAY.
  1958 "The relation of indices of fetal and
        infant loss to residential segregation:
        a follow-up report." American Socio-
        logical Review 28(October):573–578.

CHAPTER 11

childhood and preadolescence

PSYCHOANALYSTS OFTEN REFER to the age of seven through twelve years as the latency period. Compared with the problems faced by adolescents and adults in the contemporary American community, this period is a relatively quiescent and untroubled time. Excepting fatal accidents, death rates for this age group are extremely low; involvement with the legal-political system is limited; and severe problems of emotional illness are relatively rare. But in a sociological sense, it is perhaps more accurately described as a learning-the-ropes period rather than a latent period (Geer et al., 1966). It is the time when the child first begins to cope with a considerable degree of autonomy and to engage in activities on his own with the larger community. It is the period in which the child's world is continuously expanding. Previous to this time, he is essentially a homebody, with his culture largely confined to the family and perhaps to his informal friendship groups. After entering school, the child comes into contact for sustained periods with persons other than his immediate family, and he cannot escape the need to learn more and with greater speed in order to facilitate his relations with strangers (Hawkes and Pease, 1962). Unlike his earlier years, the preadolescent spends considerable time away from home, mostly in school. The classroom is usually his first constant and highly organized group experience, and the teachers he meets there profoundly affect his future. He becomes sharply aware of the necessity for learning and communicating and of the need for interpersonal, intellectual, and physical skills. One study suggests that fully a third of the child's time is spent in public (White, 1956).

The future orientation of this age level needs to be emphasized. According to one account of suburban life, this is the period during which children are prepared for the work habits of later life. In middle-class communities, it is the time when they learn that they will have to put in many long and arduous hours if they wish to attain a high material standard of living (Seeley et al., 1956). Punctuality and responsibility are emphasized, and the community takes serious and formal steps to develop the qualities that are felt to be prerequisites for success in adult occupational and social life within the community. Children are "institutionalized" in the sense that they internalize the community norms about the value of education, the importance of material possessions, as well as the prevailing ethos on the use of leisure; they learn when to tell a joke, when not to "horse around," and how to manipulate objects and human beings (Seeley et al., 1956). Preadolescence is also the age when the first signs and early warnings of social inadequacies stemming from the home life become evident and visible to others in the community. During this period, many children reveal for the first time the physical and behavioral problems that lead to their being tagged as "good" or "bad," "smart" or "dumb," labels that may stick with them throughout their lives. For example, in a study of adult sociopaths, Robbins (1966) found that among individuals who violate seriously the legal and ethical norms of the society, the most common period for the onset of reported behavior problems is the first five years of school. The appearance of these problems at this early age apparently differentiates those who in adult life will show sociopathic behavior from individuals who are more conforming to the norms of the community. As she notes, the absence of psychiatric and behavioral symptoms in childhood virtually guarantees that a child will not be sociopathic as an adult (Robbins, 1966). In the child's experience with the larger society, the educational process occupies a dominant role and is a crucial factor in his "learning the ropes."

education of the child

According to the child-development experts, "School is the child's business—his job" (Breckenridge and Vincent, 1960:546). They contend that the attitudes which the child learns on this job not only determine much of his early success or failure, but also influence the rest of his educational career and his adult attitudes toward work, responsibility, himself, and his later life in general. Students of human development who attempt to classify the periods of individual growth are virtually in agreement about the importance of these early years for enabling the child to establish an identification with the norms of the community. A distinguished psychoanalyst describes the period that begins at about age six, and extends for the next five or six years, as the crucial one for the development of a "sense of identity" (Erikson, 1963) or, as other analysts put it, a sense of duty and achievement (Witmer and Kotinsky, 1952).

School, with its increased participation in group activities, offers many children their first exposure to standards of moral conduct and ethical behavior different from those of the parental home. Some of these experiences are supportive and serve to widen the child's horizon of what is acceptable. Frequently, by broadening his notion of the norms, such contacts increase the child's tolerance. Some of his experiences, however, are unsatisfying and raise conflicts. Against these he needs to develop an immunity in much the same sense that his body struggles with the viruses he picks up. In school and, of course, elsewhere, the pre-adolescent child really begins to understand the key cultural distinctions held in the modern urban community. He becomes acutely sensitive to social differences between male and female. He learns the importance of being a regular guy, of looking out for himself, of knowing when to stop. The elementary-school age is also a period in which, interestingly enough, the interpretation of children's behavior begins to single out those who constitute "problems." Parents and, to some extent, teachers become concerned with the child who is overaggressive, boisterous, and silly, who is careless, disorderly, disrespectful, and rebellious. On the other hand, most professional practitioners, particularly those oriented towards psychodynamic views, are most seriously concerned with the child who is shy and withdrawn, who daydreams and passively fails to cooperate, who is nervous, fearful, and retreats from activities. Indeed both types of problems may be behavioral in nature, but in general it is the latter type that children fail to outgrow and that represents diagnostic signs of future problems in psychological functioning, school performance, and occupational success.

The educational system and the academic socialization of the child represent a major social problem of which the American community is now aware. The impact in terms of the child's relationship to social-control agents in the community is not usually visible until after childhood. It has been observed by many, however, that the failure of the educational system to promote, particularly with equity, the intellectual and motivational development of children during this period is related to many of the pervasive social problems existing today. The problem lies partly in the rigidities of the educational process itself and partly in the middle-class orientation of the educational system. Schools in general fail to be aware of the wide range of variations in the social status, life styles, and familial regulatory mechanisms of children.

THE NEED FOR EDUCATION

Early in the history of the American community, and certainly in less differentiated societies than ours, education was blended with other activities of the family and with the larger social life of the tribe, clan, and state (Shostak, 1967). Education was an undifferentiated part of the general socialization of the child. The emergence of education as a separate institution is related to the division of labor in the world of work. In these times, with the increased technology of modern society, everyone must be at least functionally literate, that is, have the reading ability necessary to comprehend employment forms, job placement tests, and blueprints (Clark, 1964). As Clark notes, with the advance of industrialization, the education threshold for employment rises throughout the labor force, and educational preparation is markedly lengthened. An approximation of this inflation of educational requirements would equate a baccalaureate degree of today with a high school diploma of a generation ago. Not only has the level of schooling been extended, but the amount of knowledge to be learned has increased, especially during the early grammar-school years. No matter how long the individual remains involved in the web of the educational process, he can never adequately assimilate—nor can the educational system adequately present—the virtually endless amount of material required in these times. The fact is that today educationally incompetent people are characterized as much by inadequate schooling as by too little schooling. Brainwork, as Clark (1962) points out, is the primary economic need of advanced industrial societies. Education rarely overtrains persons for our type of economy, but it can undertrain them. It is important, therefore, to look at what grammar-school education fails to do for the child and to try to understand some of the reasons why it fails.

THE EXTENT OF ILLITERACY

We have already noted the severe difficulties faced by individuals who lack the basic skills of literacy. It must be acknowledged that the American child is not particularly literate, at least when compared with children in other advanced technological countries. There tend to be great geographic variations in the literacy of adults in the United States. Even today, discounting for the moment the retarded and the psychologically disturbed, perhaps 10 per cent of American children sit through grades one through six without learning much more than to write their names and to comprehend street signs. Rejection rates for the armed forces clearly indicate the pervasiveness of illiteracy in our country. Estimates of its prevalence vary greatly by region and state, but current figures indicate that between 5 and 10 per cent of the draftees fail to achieve the fourth- or fifth-grade reading level required by the armed forces because they lacked an adequate grammar-school education.

Ideally, in addition to literacy, these early educational years provide the child with a concept of the breadth of the community, with an appreciation for the persuasiveness of the moral order, with an understanding of the links between one social-control system and another, and with some recognition of the interrelatedness of social life. Even more important, however, is the opportunity this period offers for many children to overcome any marked deficiencies of their early home environment. Outside of the family, the grammar-school experience provides the most important of the intersecting social environments that shape and motivate the young learner. Many students, unfortunately, are exposed to a system that allows them to think that, because of familial background and the occupational and social status of their parents, they are frozen into a particular caste for the rest of their lives. All too frequently, the school system tends to reinforce attitudes and confirm patterns that open doors of opportunity and achievement for some but not for others.

CURRENT CRITICISM

Education's broadest function has been to act as the caretaker and dispenser of the cultural funds of society, but not as its critic (Clark, 1964). The content of education, even at the lower levels, is heavily involved in transmitting uncritically the components of the general culture and, in these times, more and more of this cultural transmission is seriously disturbed. Nor is this culture conserve transmitted evenly and uniformly. Instead, it is selectively handled, with sociability often being given priority over intellectuality, racial prejudice and class discrimination over equality, and achievement in certain technical areas over development of strategies for integrating new experiences. The way the teacher evaluates the child apparently may influence not only his school work but his performance on so-called IQ tests. (*See* Documentation 1.)

In past decades, the failures of the school were mostly viewed in terms of truancy and, perhaps, the rate of runaways among very young children. In terms of a clinical orientation, attention was most frequently directed toward the manifestation of problems characterized as school phobias. But only a small number of children at these early ages play truant, and most school-phobia problems, particularly among middle-class children, resolve themselves. Today, while the new critics recognize the academic incompetence of the schools, they are much more concerned with the fact that the early school years condemn to mediocrity or destroy as a resource for the American community a significant proportion of its future adult population.

In his *Death at an Early Age* Jonathan Kozol (1967) gives a poignant sense of the "destruction of the hearts and minds of Negro children in the ghettoes of Boston." John Holt (1964) contends in *How Children Fail* that learning is inhibited in the best "progressive" schools by the climate of fear. Paul Goodman (1964) asserts in *Compulsory Miseducation* that the present school system is leading straight to *1984*.

This problem of intellectual mediocrity is particularly acute for the black child for whom vocational training is still being advocated. Tumin

self-fulfilling prophecies in the classroom

A recent experiment was designed to test the hypothesis that, within a given classroom, those children from whom the teacher expected greater growth in intellectual competence would show such greater growth.

Within each of the six grades of the elementary school, there were three classrooms, one each for children performing at above-average, average, and below-average levels of scholastic achievement. In each of the eighteen classrooms of the school about 20 percent of the children were designated as academic "spurters." The names of these children were reported to their new teachers in the fall of 1964 as those who, during the academic year ahead, would show unusual intellectual gains. The "fact" of their intellectual potential was established from their scores on the test for "intellectual blooming."

Teachers were cautioned not to discuss the test findings with either their pupils or the children's parents. Actually, the names of the 20 percent of the children assigned to the "spurting" condition had been selected by means of a table of random numbers. The difference, then, between these children earmarked for intellectual growth and the undesignated control children was in the mind of the teacher.

Four months after the teachers had been given the names of the "special" children, all the children once again took the same form of the nonverbal test of intelligence. Four months after this retest, the children took the same test once again. This final retest was at the end of the school year, some eight months after the teachers had been given the expectation for intellectual growth of the special children. These retests were not, of course, explained as "retests" to the teachers but rather as further efforts to predict intellectual growth.

For the school as a whole, the children of the experimental groups did not show a significantly greater gain in verbal IQ and mental age than did the control-group children. However, in total IQ and mental age, and especially

(1962) notes in his review of Conant's (1961) *Slums and Suburbs:*

> One can no longer treat American Negro youth as though, with rare exceptions, some form of practical vocational education was the best thing for them. However "unrealistic" other educational perspectives may seem, from the viewpoint of the stark realities of early drop-outs and unemployment of Negro youth, it is altogether unrealistic, from the viewpoint of democratic commitment and Negro self-images, to advocate different education for Negroes and whites. There are, in short, *several* sets of harsh realities which must be confronted, and there is little question as to the reaction of the Negro community to proposals to provide primarily vocational education for Negro boys and girls (Tumin, 1962:421).

By relegating the black, lower-income child to a "second-class" education,

in the reasoning IQ and mental age, the experimental children gained more than did the control children. Even after the fourth-month retest this trend was already in evidence though the effects were smaller.

Toward the end of the school year of this study, all teachers were asked to rate each of their pupils on the following variables: the extent to which they would be successful in the future, and the degree to which they could be described as interesting, curious, happy, appealing, adjusted, affectionate, hostile, and motivated by a need for social approval. A comparison of the experimental and control children on each of these variables was thought to be valuable to obtain some idea of the effect of the experimental treatment on behavior other than intellectual-test performance. In addition, it was thought that differences in teachers' perceptions of the experimental and control children might be suggestive of the mechanism whereby a teacher communicates her expectation to her pupils. There is, of course, no way to be sure that the children's behavior was accurately described by the teachers. If it were, and if the experimental- and control-group children differed in their classroom behavior, we would know at least that changes in intellectual ability were accompanied by changes in other classroom behavior. If the teachers' descriptions of the children's behavior were not accurate, any differences in the descriptions of the experimental and control children could be ascribed to a kind of halo effect. Such a halo effect might suggest the possibility that altered perceptions of children's behavior might be associated with differences in teachers' treatment of the children, such treatment differences leading to differences in intellectual performance and remaining to be discovered.

The children from whom intellectual growth was expected were described as having a significantly better chance of becoming successful in the future, as significantly more interesting, curious, and happy. There was a tendency, too, for these children to be seen as more appealing, adjusted, and affectionate and as lower in the need for social approval. In short, the children from whom intellectual growth was expected became more intellectually alive and autonomous, or at least were so perceived by their teachers. (Rosenthal and Jacobson, 1968: 230–233.)

the schools destroy his motivation and fail to equip him with the knowledge needed to procede further along the educational route so important for adult success. To a certain extent, the current educational process shortchanges all children because it develops essentially antiintellectual, anticreative attitudes and, in many ways, draws an unrealistic picture of the requirements for success in the adult world.

CORE CITY ISOLATION

Any discussion of the problems of the young child in school today needs to take into account the sweeping geographic and residential trends of the country. We have already referred to the population shift from the core of a metropolis to its suburbs. We have argued strongly that this movement tends to further separate and isolate the blacks, the poor, and other minority groups from the mainstream of the society. Before pursuing this problem, however, it must be noted that the school system has not been able to keep pace with either the technological or residential changes that have taken place in our society (Corwin, 1965). Part of the problem has to do with the sheer numbers of children involved. As Corwin points out, elementary school enrollments have doubled since 1900 and are expected to double again by 1975. The population explosion raises problems for the educational systems of the suburbs as surely as it has for those in the core city.

The problems within and without the city differ greatly in type and degree. In the core city, as we shall discuss subsequently, the monogeneity of lower-class neighborhoods results in great difficulties for teacher and student alike. The tendency is for the city school to become a holding operation. There is frequent turnover of staff occasioned by the reluctance of many teachers to work in the core city when more manageable students can be found in the suburbs, along with higher pay or at least a better life (Becker, 1961). Also, as we noted in Chapter 7, the problems of finance arising from the tax situation in the core cities have severely reduced expenditures for meaningful experimentation, for the development of new physical plants, and for the introduction of the specialized programs that are common in many suburban schools. As Marburger (1963:320) notes:

> In spite of the fact that more youth are finishing high school and going on to college, increasing numbers of young men and women, including a good percentage of the most able and most intelligent youth, do not find what they need in school, do not learn, lose purpose and direction, and drop out. They are abetted by indecisive parents, tolerated by an apathetic community, often tacitly disestablished by the school.

"Old-fashioned" education is the order of the day in most city schools more through default than choice. Lacking sufficient funds, the school system cannot attract the creative young teachers to work there; many of them cannot even afford new textbooks, let alone language laboratories, teaching machines, closed-circuit TV, and many of the other physical and mechanical aids available in the middle-income suburb. The suburban school systems, spurred partly by the tremendous increases in enrollment and partly by the availability of educational funds, have experimented extensively with such·concepts as team teaching, master teachers, special art, music, and language programs, coordinated curricula, and the like. Given existing conditions, it is not surprising that the lower-income child in the core city is subjected to an early education that inhibits the imagination and utilizes less individualization of instruction (Chandler et al., 1962). Without such individual attention, the child with high intellectual potential is bored and the one with low intellectual potential is frustrated. However, it should be noted—indeed emphasized—that schools are not often able to overcome the social and economic deficiencies of family life. (*See* Documentation 2.)

PAROCHIAL SCHOOLS

Of particular interest in these times are the core city parochial schools which are operated almost exclusively by the Catholic Church to educate the children of this faith. In many ways, these schools illustrate well the range of quality that exists and the kinds of problems that confront the educational process in the core city (Boardman, 1966). Some of the best and some of the worst institutions are represented among the parochial schools. The bad ones have come about partly because of the difficulties in obtaining qualified staff—especially members of religious orders. Many of the institutions that train the teaching sisters are badly outdated. These colleges use a normal-school approach that emphasizes the importance of penmanship and correct spelling rather than understanding and encouraging creativity on the part of the child. As a result, there is considerable concern and unrest with the current status of grammar-school education in parochial schools. Although at least one study argues that it is the economic background of the child and not his exposure to a parochial school that is related to differences in educational achievement (*see* Documentation 3), criticism both within and without the Church has increased. Jencks (1966:25) argues the case well and indicates why one sees, at the same time, outstanding parochial schools:

> Private control has several advantages in a school which serves slum children. To begin with, it makes it possible to attack the problem in manageable bites. It is inconceivable that a big city school system can be reformed all at once. Failing that, however, it may be impossible to reform it at all. If, for example, the system is geared to docile teachers who do not want and cannot handle responsibility, how is it to accommodate the enterprising minority who have ideas of their own and want freedom to try them out? The superintendent cannot alter the whole system to deal with a handful of such teachers, even if he wants to. But if he does not alter the system, the better teachers will usually leave—or not come in the first place. Somehow the system must be broken up so that its parts can develop in different directions. Little cells of excellence must be nourished, gradually adding to their own number and excitement. Unusual talent must not be spread so thin over the whole system that no single place achieves the critical mass needed to sustain a chain reaction. Yet this is just what a conventional, centrally controlled system tends to do, for in such a system "special treatment" for a particular school is quickly defined as "favoritism." (This attitude is illustrated in the response of big cities to the

school desegregation: a reappraisal

What, then, is the present consensus about the policy implications of Coleman's survey? The answer is that no consensus exists, even among experts. My own judgments are as follows:

(1) The resources—both fiscal and human —devoted to black and white children's schooling are not dramatically different, except perhaps in certain parts of the South. Nor do we devote substantially greater resources to educating middle-class children than to educating lower-class children.

(2) Variations in schools' fiscal and human resources have very little effect on student achievement—probably even less than the Coleman Report originally implied.

(3) The report's assertion that peers have a consistent effect on achievement may or may not be correct. My guess, based on available data, is that peers do have an effect, but that it is relatively small.

None of this denies that unusually dedicated and talented individuals can create schools in which initially disadvantaged children learn a remarkable amount. But it does deny that the achievement levels of large numbers of disadvantaged children can be appreciably enhanced by spending more money, hiring better teachers, buying new textbooks or making any of the other changes that reformers normally advocate.

If improved student achievement is our goal, the Coleman Report's implication is obvious: we must alter the whole social system rather than just tinker with the schools. There is plenty of evidence that major changes in a child's social and cultural environment will affect his intellectual development, often dramatically. Bruno Bettelheim and others have chronicled the impact of the Israeli kibbutz on hitherto deprived North African and Yemenite Jews. Here in America we know that children raised on Long Island do far better, even in first grade, than those raised in Appalachia. Similarly, children raised in Jewish homes do better than those raised in Christian homes, even in the

offer of federal funds under the new Elementary and Secondary Education Act. Almost nobody wants to concentrate this money in a few places to create really good schools; everyone wants to spread it across the whole system.)

MIDDLE-CLASS SCHOOLS

In the best school systems, usually located in the suburbs, children in the third and fourth grade are taught algebra as part of "new math" and creative writing as part of language arts. Certainly not all pupils in these ideal school systems think of the experience as fun, but it does represent a challenge that far exceeds the experience given children in

same city. And the World War II draftees who grew up in the America of 1917–1941 did far better on standard tests than the World War I draftees who grew up in the America of 1900–1917. Intellectual skills are, therefore, not just a function of genetic differences. But neither are they a function of school differences. If the Coleman survey convinces us of that basic truth, it will have served its purpose.

Does this mean that we should simply let inferior schools rot? I think not. Good schools can make a difference—if we know what kind of a difference we want them to make.

Underlying the comments of most people who discuss the Coleman Report is the assumption that academic achievement is the most important objective of schooling, and if school reform does not affect achievement, it is worthless. Yet despite much popular rhetoric, there is little evidence that academic competence is critically important to adults in most walks of life. If you ask employers why they won't hire dropouts, for example, or why they promote certain kinds of people and not others, they seldom complain that dropouts can't read. Instead, they complain that dropouts don't get to work on time, can't be counted on to do a careful job, don't get along with others in the plant or office, can't be trusted to keep their hands out of the till, and so on. Nor do the available survey data suggest that the adult success of people from disadvantaged backgrounds depends primarily on their intellectual skills. If you compare black men who do well on the Armed Forces Qualifications Test to those who do badly, for example, you find that a black man who scores as high as the average white still earns only about two-thirds what the average white earns. Not only that, he hardly earns more than the average black. Even for whites, the mental abilities measured by the A.F.Q.T. account for less than a tenth of the variation in earnings.

With these observations in mind, go visit a slum school and ask yourself what the school is actually doing. You will usually find that it seems to share the employers' priorities. It devotes very little time to academic skills. Instead, the teachers spend their time in a vain effort to teach the children to behave in what they (and probably most employers) regard as the proper way. . . .

From this perspective the best index of a school's success or failure may not be reading scores but the number of rocks thrown through its windows in an average month. The Coleman survey does not speak to this question. (Jencks, 1969:43–44.)

the lower-income, core city schools. This does not mean that children in middle-class suburban schools are provided with as complete an education as possible or that all that goes on there is desirable in terms of their future development.

Two defects seem almost endemic even to the best schools. The first is an antiintellectual viewpoint that springs from the larger society's emphasis on technology and its instrumental view of education as a means to an end rather than as a value in itself. It is not the educated man whom the middle-income community promotes as a role model but the economically successful one. The child is socialized to admire the practical man, and he begins early to understand that, while it is important to succeed in school, he must not be stigmatized as an intellectual. Often

parochial school origins

A substantial literature supports the proposition that American Catholics have not contributed to the scientific and intellectual life of the country in proportion to their numbers in the population. The usual explanation for this phenomenon is that the cultural values and social organization of American Catholics impede intellectual and scientific achievement. The tight hierarchical authority of the Church, as well as its emphasis on the present life as a preparation for the hereafter, encourages the attitude that intellectual pursuits are not very important and may even be dangerous.

Such an explanation seems plausible enough, but it has never been tested empirically. Nor does it answer a prior question: why did the American Church—clergy and laity—adopt an organization and a set of values which tended to deny the validity of intellectual achievement? Our answer to this question may be very prosaic, but it explains the previous underrepresentation of Catholics among scientists as well as the apparent change recorded here. American Catholics were too poor, and had immigrated too recently, to be concerned with much beyond economic survival, and the Church was too fearful of the destruction of the immigrants' faith to worry about intellectual endeavor. With rare exceptions intellectualism is a luxury that is sacrificed when life itself—that of individuals or that of an organization—is threatened.

Ordinarily, a man does not become an intellectual unless he goes to college; nor does a group produce eminent scientists unless a substantial proportion of its members have gone to college. Higher education was quite beyond the imaginative powers of most immigrants, and in any case it was economically unfeasible. Development of intellectual and scientific concerns among Catholics had to await the preparation of an adequate social and economic base, and this did not occur until the late 1940's.

SOCIO-ECONOMIC STATUS BY RELIGION AND AGE

Per Cent:	Age 23–29		Age 30–39		Age 40–49		Age 50–59	
	Protestant	Catholic	Protestant	Catholic	Protestant	Catholic	Protestant	Catholic
Attending College	29	28	34	26	29	19	25	12
Earning More than $8,000	29	25	40	36	51	39	40	29
(N)	(907)	(352)	(167)	(653)	(169)	(691)	(97)	(352)

As the above table demonstrates, the younger generation of Catholics has now come abreast of white Protestants from the same sections of the country on various measures of economic and social status, and as their economic situation changes, the immigrants' defensive attitude of separatism has declined, while a liberal, self-critical orientation has become more common in certain crucial segments of the Catholic community. . . . [N]ot until the middle 1950's did the grandchildren of the peasant immigrants have the economic and social means for serious academic pursuits. (Warkov and Greeley, 1966:412–413.)

the ideal student, as Corwin (1965) notes, is not the one who is the best student but the one who is only slightly above average; it is this type of student who is looked upon as the "all-American kid."

The second conspicuous problem for the child in the middle-income suburb is the perspective he receives on life in the urban community—the importance of material possessions, the preoccupation with economic success, and the acceptability of illegitimate means and corruptions as part of the life style of the individual. The very basis of the educational system in American society sets a pattern leading to disrespect for persons occupying key roles in schools.

For the lower-income pupil, the teacher represents somebody unusual, somebody who wears a white shirt, who often speaks in a different manner, and who tends to have notions about conduct and morality that are different from those of his family members (Sexton, 1961; Riessman, 1962). For many children from middle-class families, the elementary school teacher represents either an occupational or a social failure. The school teacher is perhaps the lowest-status professional on the American scene. This low status is related, to a considerable extent, to the relatively low income paid teachers and to the fact that it is primarily a woman's occupational role. Teachers, particularly male ones, are not generally recruited from among top-ranking students (Wolfe, 1954; North, 1958). Many analysts of the problems of youth assert that, for all children, the low worth accorded the elementary school teacher has an impact on their perception of the school experience and their values regarding the educational process. It is also clear that, compared to the other disciplines, most schools of education are staffed by less competent faculties and the quality of education in such settings is often low (Koerner, 1963).

SOCIAL CLASS BIAS

One must come to grips with the serious inequities and problems of the educational process for the lower-class child. Most social analysts argue that the school, rather than providing a therapeutic force for combatting the rigidities of the American social-class structure, becomes a pawn of it (Corwin, 1965). Instead of equality, the student learns in the classroom the subtle practices of discrimination that are implicit in the teacher's preference for the middle-class pupils, whom she designates to receive the honors and awards. Rather than demonstrating equity and acceptance of all children, the educational process reinforces the discrepancies of which the lower-class child is already aware, at least to a limited extent. The problem, of course, is that persons in charge of schools have middle-class backgrounds and attitudes and these are reflected in the management of the school's affairs. Even when teachers do come from lower and working-class families, many may try to "escape" their backgrounds and overcompensate by adhering even more rigidly to middle-class standards. The prevalence of female teachers is also a problem. Many children in low-income families, particularly Negro boys from matriarchal homes, fail to find the appropriate male role models that are so critical to their development of an image and a perspective consistent with the demands of the adult world.

RECENT EXPERIMENTS

Concern with the impact of the educational process on the preadolescent child and recognition of the importance of the role of the school in shaping the future life course of the individual has led to a large number of experiments. Some of these have arisen within the educational establishment itself, and imaginative school administrators and pedagogic experts have endeavored to implement a variety of new concepts: team teaching, in-school training programs, teaching machines, and the like. In many ways, however, the large-scale bureaucracies that run our schools inhibit experimentation and provide an unduly conservative influence on educational policy. Jencks (1966:23–24) summarizes the situation well:

> Organizational sclerosis of this kind is extremely difficult to cure. For obvious reasons innovation from the bottom up becomes impossible and unthinkable. But even innovation from the top down is difficult. It is easy to get people to go through the *forms* of change, but it is almost impossible to get them to *really* change, because they are frozen into defensive postures based on years of stand-pattism. If the principal tells the teachers he wants them to revamp the curriculum, they immediately begin looking to him—not to their students in the classroom—for cues and clues about the kinds of changes to propose. If the teachers tell the students to think for themselves, the students interpret this as just another move by the teacher to complicate "the game," another frustration in their efforts to "give the teacher what he wants." If the school board tries raising salaries in order to attract new kinds of teachers, it must still assign them to the same old schools, where they are still treated like filing clerks. So the more imaginative and dedicated teachers leave after a year or two for other schools—often in suburbia—which treat them better. In such circumstances more money may just mean more of the same.
> A business which becomes afflicted with this kind of disease either goes bankrupt or else creates a monopoly or cartel to protect itself from more dynamic competition. The same is true of school systems. Were it not for their monopoly on educational opportunities for the poor, most big city school systems would probably go out of business. If, for example, the poor were simply given the money that is now spent on their children's education in public schools, and were told they could

spend this money in private institutions, private schools would begin to spring up to serve slum children. In due course such schools would probably enroll the great majority of these children.

A number of educational innovations have come from other social-control groups in the community, particularly the political and the health-and-welfare systems. These changes primarily relate to modifying and reworking the links between the educational system and other segments of community life.

It is often argued that the school, operating through the young child, represents an important intervention point for the entire family. Those who support a mass intervention technique hold that the school child from six to twelve years of age not only represents a malleable force in terms of his own developing identity, attitudes, and aspirations, but also acts as a bearer of social change to the adults and younger siblings in the household. In many ways, the school system, through its involvement of the young child in its programs, can lead to significant changes in the views of other family members. Despite this, or perhaps because of it, the young child is often exposed to diverse and conflicting views. We have already alluded to this in our discussion of some of the class differences between the teacher and the parent.

Even when there are no disparities of social class, there often are considerable variations in what professional educators and what parents believe constitute appropriate educational content for the six- to twelve-year-old. Much of the pressure for teaching subject matter as a means rather than as an end stems from the upward mobility and high-aspiration patterns exhibited by parents in suburban communities. Several studies record the severe conflicts between professional educators oriented towards breadth of intellectual experience and parents concerned with the number of words a child can spell correctly or the age at which he can do the crossword puzzle in the newspaper. Many of these strains eventuate in open conflict between community members, organized or individually, and school boards, professional educators, and educational administrators. Such conflicts are readily grasped by the young child and he reacts with concern over the outcome of the issues and the relative merits of the various points of view. The issue of lay versus professional control of the educational system is much too complex to discuss here in detail. Nevertheless, it should be noted that this struggle represents an input of uncertainty and conflict into the life of the child.

CHANGES IN CHILD BEHAVIOR

Finally, it should be noted that the last three years of preadolescence are marked by radical changes in educational content and also in the child's attitudes, perceptions, and motivations toward the educational process. Gesell and his associates (1956) have described the changes that are common in the tenth, eleventh, and twelfth years:

The ten-year-old. Assimilativeness is a cardinal educational trait in the ten-year-old and on into maturity. It is both a mood and a capacity. The child loves to memorize at length, to identify facts, to spot cities on a map, and he has short and choppy but numerous spans of attention.

The eleven-year-old. At eleven, he shows great concentration, and he works competitively with one group against the other. His intellectual processes become very factual. While not yet academic, his thinking is relatively concrete and specific; he begins to like extra-curricular activities. He becomes eclectic rather than reflective, and he begins to create the foundations for perceptual thinking.

The twelve-year-old. The twelve-year-old group is spirited and their enthusiasm is abundant. It rises to a boisterous pitch. Pupils begin to focus quietly on individual tasks. They begin to manifest the ability to do independent work, to become aware of political and civic issues, and to criticize the educational process itself.

As Gesell points out, although the twelve-year-old is not an adult in miniature, he has by this time captured many of the styles of thinking that he will keep with him in his future educational career. Certainly, as far as his formal exposure to education is concerned, he has learned the ropes; he has, at the very least, a capacity to mature. It is this marked shift in the thinking process that occurs between the ages of six and twelve that is so critical for future life development and that makes the educational process during these early years so significant. Yet, at the present time in many American communities this transition is not handled well. (*See* Documentation 4.)

mass communications

Closely linked to the educational experience of the six- to twelve-year-old child is his exposure to the mass media. The aspect of the problem that is of interest to us here represents an outgrowth of the communications revolution, namely, television and its wide appeal to children. One study indicates that children spend as much time watching TV as attending school (Schramm et al., 1961). Prior to television, the mass media were oriented much more to adult consumers, or at least to persons with the skill to read. Children's books and radio programs, while of some interest and influence, hardly compare with the impact of television. Certainly, as an art form, television can be directed to almost any group. Programs during the afternoon and early evening are particularly designed for the

How might we improve the process of education in America? Indeed, do we even want to do anything in this regard? While there is no consensus regarding reforms, there is widespread discontent with the educational status quo. When the Russians out-raced America into space with Sputnik, the schools were loudly blamed for inattention to the "hard" sciences. When vacationing students riot at resorts, the schools are censored for inadequate attention to moral and behavioral standards. When the Chinese Communists broke the spirit of certain American prisoners of war in Korea, the schools were held responsible for inferior training in patriotism and fidelity. When American eligibles fare poorly in international art competitions (the Moscow Music Judgments, etc.), the schools are criticized for inferior work in the fine arts. When some 68 percent of Negro youths fail to pass the Selective Service mental tests, the only screen through which all male Americans must pass, the schools are castigated for contributing to much human loss and suffering. And, at present, with Medicare, community mental health advances, and the war on poverty having exposed gaps in the available supply of "care-takers," the schools are being blamed for inattention to the "soft," or social and welfare, sciences. The picture is much the same in the non-substantive, or character-shaping, dimension of the educational status quo.

In the past 40 years the schools have adopted, adapted, and abandoned three different styles of educational approach, and the end of this searching and groping is not in sight. The 1920's saw schools and families alike endorsing the restrictive child psychology of the behaviorist associated with John B. Watson. Use of a strict upbringing meant regular schedules, sharp punishment, and generally stringent discipline in the school and the home. The pendulum went full swing in the 1930's, however, when, "under the impact of Freud (little read, but widely popularized) and of John Dewey (less read, but invoked even more often), leniency, indulgence, free expression, and uninhibited opportunity for 'learning by doing' were favored." This too produced its reaction, the free-for-all playgrounds which called themselves schools going out of style and out of business in the 1940's. Since that time and reflecting the influence of Dr. Spock, Dr. Bettleheim, and others, new attention has been paid to the urgent need for discipline and for limit-setting in home and school settings. Anger on the part of the parent, teacher, or school administrator is acceptable, from a psychological point of view, if it is in the service of firmness and consistency and does not obliterate love, a most difficult emotional balance to reach.

There is no consensus in either education or in family sociology about the direction the school-family relationship ought now to take. There is intense concern, however, among specialists who agree that "through all three fluctuations, there has been no noticeable decline in the percentage of emotionally disturbed children—or morally bewildered parents. If anything, the contrary." (Shostak, 1967:131–132.)

six-to-twelve age group, but of course many children are exposed to adult programming as well. Some critics maintain that adult programming is not particularly adult in any case. Parenthetically it should be pointed out that although many motion picture offerings are of an adult nature, particularly those shown on TV, children in this age group see them also.

During the 1940s and the 1950s, a great deal of attention was paid to the possible negative impact of different types of television and movie programming on the emotional states of children and to the media's influence on deviant and, particularly, highly bizarre acts. The findings from several studies that were undertaken seem to suggest that any view of the mass media as either the major determinant of serious deviancy by young children or the *direct* cause of frequent disreputable conduct is a faulty one (Himmelweit et al., 1958). While some critics believe that seeing particular techniques of destruction or sadism might give a few children an additional stimulus, in general, the mass media, including television, do not have the disastrous effects that many feared.

Another concern about the effect of media on this age group is perhaps less carefully studied but of greater importance. This is the extent to which the mass media serve as an influence on the values and attitudes of the young child. In particular, they subject him to an overwhelming dose of common taste and a homogeneous definition of aesthetics. The desirable values of diversity and heterogeneity in personal choice are completely obliterated. (Gans, 1964). The link between the values of a society and its comics, for example, is illustrated in a comparative study by Berger (1966:26) of American and Italian comic strips.

> Let me summarize the underlying psychological and social attitudes in these comics which I am hypothesizing might be broadly accepted cultural values.
> These Italian comics reflect a basically conservative approach toward experience and society. Authority is generally portrayed as valid and rebellion against it as futile. Social mobility must depend on miracles in a rigid and hierarchical society in which all attempts to climb are brusquely repulsed.
> The American comics described here suggested, on the other hand, an irreverential approach toward authority. Authority is often invalid, and not necessarily worthy of respect. So there is much more anti-social and rebellious activity, which is seen as possibly successful. Mickey Mouse is the only conformist of the group; but then Mickey . . . is also very popular in Italy.

In our discussion of social participation and leisure (Chapter 8), a number of comments were offered about the problems of mass culture and their potentially deleterious effects on the American community. One thing the media do is to depict images of different social roles, including occupational ones (Bauchard, 1952; Gentile and Miller, 1961). Although information is scanty, there is considerable reason to believe that during this learning-the-ropes phase values, attitudes, and orientations are fostered which make anything but a highly conforming role very difficult for the individual to adopt in the future. Studies of the impact of television and the movies and an occasional paper on current fads among the early teen-age population indicate that many in advertising, as well as elsewhere, are aware of the impact of the media in shaping the child (White and Abel, 1963). Although the point need not be labored, the relationship between problems faced by the young child and the norms stressed by the mass media are not to be overlooked (*see* Documentation 5).

moral identification

During the period of six to twelve years, the child is confronted with a range of interpersonal interactions in which the norms of what is right and proper are presented to him. This is the period when for the first time he must decide independently on the role he will take vis-à-vis others in the group and the strategies he will adopt in order to maximize his satisfactions. At this age the child acquires considerable autonomy of action, and adults do not necessarily have sufficient awareness of or supervision over his social roles to guide or countermand all of the behavioral decisions that he makes.

To understand the ethical issues and develop a morality of his own is indeed difficult for the young child in the complex urban community. To a large extent the problem of moral identification is endemic to the American community with its variety of situations and lack of consistency, all of which the child witnesses daily. The pervasive influence of manipulation and the widespread evidence of corruption in the day-to-day dealings of the adult world also contribute to the child's confusion.

This is the period in which the child begins to evaluate not only his own behavior and that of his peers but the adult world as well. Numerous illustrations can be cited of children's awareness of the willingness and proclivity of adults to violate the norms of society. The child learns that it is all right to do certain things, providing there is a low risk of being caught or the gains are sufficiently great in comparison with the potential sanctions. He learns that norms commonly held are violated under certain circumstances and that conflicting norms are concurrently espoused within the American community. The child begins to understand something of the pluralistic values held by others toward many social habits and activities, including the use of alcohol, satisfaction of

the effects of television and radio: some burning questions

Broadcast-industry spokesmen generally maintain that little is definitely known or can be proved concerning the harmful effects of television. They declare that there has been little research on this subject. This position is unacceptable to educators, mental-health clinic directors, and officials of correctional and law-enforcement agencies who test, question, and treat children every day and know that television is one of the most powerful parts of their environment. Radio and television not only can and do teach, but cannot help teaching. There is no longer any question of *whether* they teach. It is only a question of *what* they teach, whether intentionally or unintentionally.

The first careful and complete studies which dealt with such effects were the Payne Fund Studies on films and their effects on children. These investigations extended over a four-year period, from 1929 to 1932. The results were published by Macmillan in some twelve volumes between 1933 and 1935. These studies are relevant here since these films, and others like them, make up a large part of the fare offered over most [U.S.] television stations.

In 1961 UNESCO published an annotated International Bibliography, *The Influence of the Cinema on Children and Adolescents*. The data, research, and studies it cites come from several hundred correctional institutions, hospitals, schools, juvenile courts, psychiatric clinics, and mental hospitals around the world. The 491 books, articles, and journals it abstracts contain several hundred additional references in their own bibliographies. Hundreds of doctors, educators, researchers, and organized child-welfare and religious groups in many nations have spent long hours collecting and analyzing the most authoritative evidence they could find.

Research activities abroad—the studies of Mary Field and J. P. Mayer in England, of Erich Wasem and a dozen other researchers in Germany, of Enrico Fulchignoni and colleagues in Italy, and of Henri Storck in Belgium; studies at the Children's Neuro-Psychiatric Center in Paris; studies by the Czechoslovak State Cinema; and extensive studies in Japan, Russia, Australia, New Zealand, Portugal, Spain, Italy, Austria, India, Denmark, and Switzerland—refute any belief that there is a shortage of data available on this problem.

Files kept for years by German juvenile courts have been studied for clues as to causes of delinquency. The files of the Spanish Guardianship Courts have been found to yield helpful information. The reasons behind the decision of NHK (the Japanese national television system) to forbid the showing of violence, or any weapons that could be used for violence, on any of their television programs have been clearly spelled out for the sake of their fellow broadcasters around the world.

The quality as well as the quantity of recent research in the United States has often left much to be desired. Studies in the United States often quote what viewers or children say, or allegedly think. But the distinguished New Zealand scholar, Gordon Mirams, in commenting on a Danish study, noted in the March, 1961, UNESCO *Courier*: "Contrary to common belief, many cartoons and Tarzanlike films frighten very young children; some cried and tried to leave the cinema, others had nausea, and parents later reported cases of bedwetting and nightmares. Yet the same children *said* they thought the films were funny. They at first refused to admit they were scared."

The inclination of United States researchers in all too many such instances has been to quote children as saying they liked very much whatever they saw and were not frightened. Such quotations have little or no validity.

The problem attacked here is a serious and complicated one. Every new technology catches its age unprepared. Television audiences are the largest ever known in the history of communications. We have been told by the nation's greatest teachers that television teaches more powerfully than any previous instruments available to society. Senator Thomas J. Dodd, chairman of the Senate Subcommittee to Investigate Juvenile Delinquency, pointed out in the June, 1961, hearings that the excerpts of scenes of violence and sex which he and his fellow committee members viewed were from programs which had had, in effect, a cumulative audience of 66,318,000 children. . . . Many children are saturated by such programs before they can read.

Mass media used this way cease to be instruments of communication and become instruments of social control. These are totalitarian rather than democratic uses. Farfetched as it may now seem, historians of the future may conclude that never before was there a period during which control of the thinking of a nation was exercised in a more totalitarian manner, or by a smaller group, than it is now by television and radio.

There is evidence that a given program will do one person harm, and yet cause no apparent harm to another. Industry spokesmen exploit these contradictions. Since the operators of the mass media find it most profitable to define and operate these media as *mass* media, the average becomes the normal. Cases which do not conform are simply dismissed as deviant or atypical. But it is this dismissal that most educators cannot accept. A disease may leave one child unharmed and kill another. To say that the average child is left only half-dead . . . is to conceal what is really happening.

Human beings cannot be averaged as if they were numbers. A small group of children, done harm, may well be more important than a thousand times as many who are not done harm. The quantity criterion cited by industry does not hold up when human beings are at stake. It takes only one child to kill or maim another, derail a train, or burn a building.

Instances of people harmed by television will not be found in averages or statistics, but in hospitals and prisons. They are specific tragedies. Factory owners used to deny that there were significant adverse effects on children from working in mines or mills. Coroners' records and hospital visits finally lifted the veil.

To say that television is *the* cause of delinquency and mental and physical unfitness would be unfair; to say that television is not *a* cause . . . is no longer acceptable.

The late W. W. Charters, Director of the Payne Fund Studies, was a serious scholar who weighed his words carefully. Soberly he wrote in 1934: "Sexual passions are aroused and amateur prostitution is aggravated. The fast life depicted by the movie characters on the screen induces desires . . . for such a life . . . . *From all these data collected about the content of pictures the conclusion is inevitable that from the point of view of children's welfare the commercial movies are an unsavory mess.*"

Dr. Charters continued: "The Big Three among the themes in 1930 were: love 29.6 per cent, crime 27.4 per cent, and sex 15.0 per cent. . . . Under the 27.4 per cent of crime pictures were included those dealing in a major way with: blackmailing, extortion, injury, hate and revenge. . . . It is inevitable . . . that producers of motion pictures who have a love for children and an interest in their development must address themselves to the problems of children's movies as the publishers of books have attacked the problems of providing a children's literature. . . ."

Dr. Charters was not talking about films now buried. Most of the same films evaluated in the Payne Fund Studies, many of which were banned in certain areas or not shown to children, have now been repeatedly shown throughout the entire nation by television. (Skornia, 1965:143–146.)

sexual needs, and the development of particularistic and reciprocal relationships with others in the community. It is a period of transition to heterosexual social relationships (*see* Documentation 6). Finally, through exposure to the mass media, through contacts with his peers and reports of their and their families' behavior, and through his own experience in coping with adults and other children, the child comes to recognize the wide range of viewpoints represented in the world (Freeman and Scott, 1966).

ROLE OF RELIGION

With regard to the development of morality, the role of religion and the process of identification with a religious faith should be mentioned. Unlike most of the social-control agents (with which the child has minimal contact during these years), the religious system places great emphasis on his development during this preadolescent period. Concerned with retaining potential adherents, all of the various faiths and denominations provide for the religious training of children from six through twelve. By means of religious schools, indoctrination in the precepts of the faith, exposure to ritual and ceremony, and promise of future gratification and rewards, religious institutions seek to establish in the child a strong identification with his faith. The child during this period begins to hold concepts of the hereafter, of the power of God, and of the consequences of violating the basic morality of his faith. Fichter (1964) describes the process of religious identification among children attending a Catholic parochial school and emphasizes the critical nature of these years in the life of the individual. As he says, "If we may judge accurately from the statements of the children themselves, their most memorable religious experience takes place in the second grade, when they receive the three sacraments." According to one boy, "When I passed from the first to the second grade, it was a big step of my religion. I learned that I was at the age of reason and that it was bad to do wrong things" (Fichter, 1964:90).

Sociological analysts of religion have considered in detail the relationship between the religious institutions and the social order of the community (O'Day, 1966). Here it is necessary only to note that a vast majority—perhaps as high as 75 per cent—of all children have at least some formal contact with a church or synagogue. Their religious experience presents to them a set of idealized norms regarding the appropriate conduct of all community members. While there is some variation in the precepts that children are taught, for the most part the Judeo-Christian heritage provides basically similar teachings, at least for the child at this age. However, many of the normative standards learned in Sunday school are clearly at variance with the behavior the child observes among peers,

middle childhood: the period of transition

It seems probable that there has been more confusion over the course of heterosexual socialization during middle childhood than during any other period. Freud and the great majority of subsequent writers have referred to this stage as a period of sexual latency. Many have viewed it as a step backward away from heterosexuality into a haven of monosexual attachments and interactions. We have already seen, however, that both the anthropologists and the surveyors have produced evidence that this is not a sexually stagnant period, and data from the present writer's study indicate that a great deal of significant progress toward eventual full-fledged heterosexuality takes place during these years.

The data were taken from questionnaires administered to all 10- and 11-year-olds attending fifth and sixth grades in ten elementary schools throughout central Pennsylvania. Urban, suburban, and rural schools were included and the full range of social classes was involved. The full report of the analysis is still in manuscript form but the results can be summarized here.

The most significant finding was that progress toward heterosexuality appears to be achieved in a series of steps, with achievement at one level preparing the way for the next. As indicated in the previous section the foundation of subsequent progress seems to be one's attitude toward his own eventual marriage. Next came an emotional attachment to a member of the opposite sex as evidenced by reporting having a special girlfriend (or boyfriend if it was a girl). The next step was to confess having been in love. After that came an expression of preference for a cross-sex companion rather than a same sex companion when going to a movie. And finally the most advanced step for these preadolescents was going out on a date.

Each step, of course, is not an absolute prerequisite to the other, but the nature of the relationships can be indicated by the following sets of comparisons: 74% of those who wanted to get married some day reported a boyfriend or girlfriend, but only 34% of the others did; 66% of those who reported having a girlfriend or boyfriend also reported having been in love, but only 19% of the others did so; 43% of those who had been in love said they would prefer a cross-sex companion at the movies but only 21% of the others expressed this preference; and finally 32% of those who would prefer a companion of the opposite sex had actually gone out on a date, while only 11% of the others had done so.

It may be true that these specific items are not of any great theoretical significance in and of themselves, and that a similar list of different items could be developed which would represent the process of heterosexual socialization equally well. The significant point is that middle childhood is actually a period of great importance in the process of becoming a fully heterosexual adult. It seems logical to assume that the steps typical of this period build upon the experiences of early childhood and in turn determine the course of development during adolescence. (Broderick, 1966:17–19.)

siblings, parents, and other adults. Furthermore, the promises of success and rewards for adherence to the norms are at variance with what he learns from the mass media and, again, from his personal experiences of how to succeed in business—or pleasure—without really trying. Contrary to what he has been taught to expect regarding unscrupulous behavior, he sees no dire consequences befalling his fellow students who cheat or otherwise con their teachers. Moreover, he soon begins to understand that his parents may be less than diligent in the practice of their religion and may, indeed, look upon religious activities and observances as mere formalistic obligations having no particular relevance to their lives or values.

RELIGIOUS-ETHNIC IDENTIFICATION

There is another perspective of the religious system which should not be overlooked, namely, that the church, more than any other group in America, provides the formal sanctions for ethnic as well as religious segregation. The charge has been made that America is never more segregated than it is at eleven o'clock on Sunday morning. While the various religious bodies differ in the extent to which they encourage or demand in-group relationships and religious and ethnic homogeneity, even young children become aware of their special religious identification and, in many cases, are socialized to believe in the superiority of their particular religious affiliation. In urban communities, the membership of many churches is pretty well limited to individuals of similar backgrounds. Thus one finds Catholic churches which cater primarily to persons of Irish, Spanish, or Italian descent, and Lutheran churches which still hold some services in German or Swedish because of the predominance of those nationality groups in the congregation. Then, too, church membership, like the rest of the community, tends to be stratified by socio-economic status. This is related in part to residential patterns and in part to the relative responsiveness of different denominations to individuals of different status. However explained, the result is that the child is faced with a dilemma: on the one hand, he is presented with a set of ideal norms regarding his relationships with his fellowman and, on the other hand, he is expected to identify with particular groups which may exclude or be critical of others.

Almost all religious groups in these times are at least somewhat sensitive to the problems of moral identification and concerned over the consequences of providing a normative system so sharply at variance with the real world that the child is unable to reconcile the discrepancies between the two. Few, however, seem to be actively trying to remedy these discontinuities.

Recently this concern has been manifested in legal actions, culminating in a Supreme Court ruling, regarding the separation of religious observance and prayer from educational activities in the public school system. It is held, on legal grounds, that religious activity as part of the public school curriculum violates the traditions of the American community and leaves unprotected the religious minorities. But, since most of the process of moral identification takes place within the realm of informal behavior and interaction and within the domains of voluntary activities on the part of community members, little prospects for regulation and modification at the level of centrally directed intervention is likely. Many religious leaders verbally hold the position that the minute and nondoctrinal issues that separate individuals and churches of different denominations can be overlooked in the face of the desirability of less differentiation in the activities and socialization of children; however, there still is too little emphasis on such efforts. While recognition is sometimes given in religious training to the comparative ideologies of different faiths and some symbolic and ritualistic attempts are made at interfaith services and social programs that seek to unify normative orientations and values, it remains a relatively unexploited recourse.

The consequences of these discrepancies for the development of a moral imperative in later years is speculative at best. However, a number of specialists dealing with the problems of individual deviant behavior during teen-age years contend that the difficulties expressed during adolescence are fundamentally related to the problems of moral identification experienced during the ages of six through twelve.

health problems

In the chapter on the young child, we discussed in some detail the problems of congenital illnesses. Several points should be raised, however, about the relationship between such diseases and the six-through-twelve-year age group. With respect to congenital illnesses such as partial blindness and deafness, the educational system operates as a source of identification. In part, this is a consequence of planned programs of detection, such as school health examinations, sight and hearing tests, and the like (Wheatley and Hallock, 1965). Although the literature contains considerable evidence that these detection procedures are less than fully utilized, they nevertheless constitute a fundamental mechanism for dealing with some of the problems not identified earlier. These procedures serve to take up the slack attributable to parental apathy and to the failure of families to affiliate properly with the medical-care system. In many cases, defects so uncovered are remediable or at least controllable. When appropriate medical attention is paid to problems of hearing and sight, considerable improvement usually ensues in the child's educational achievement and social adjustment. And, on the opposite side, there is considerable evidence that poor academic performance and related problems which surface during this period are attributable to failure to identify effectively and treat physical deficiencies.

DETECTING RETARDATION

With respect to mental retardation, the issue is somewhat more difficult and urgent. By the end of elementary school, the incidence of retardation becomes apparent and begins to accumulate. This is true for two reasons. First, symptoms of congenital retardation become increasingly apparent with the passing years, making positive identification of such children easier. Second, during this period large numbers of children who, at earlier ages, were thwarted for one reason or another in their educational development are identified through standard testing procedures and classroom observation as failing to perform at adequate levels. Whether such children are true retardates is another question.

There are several important views on why some children perform so poorly. One is concerned with the differential impact of the formal educational system on the lower-income child. The argument here is that the problem of cultural deprivation becomes reinterpreted by the school as mental retardation or, at least, as a fundamental apathy towards the educational goals and mobility aspirations of the community. This position, strongly supported by Riessman (1962), suggests that the school's interpretation of retardation and underachievement fails to take into account the psychological effects of cultural deprivation in the lower-income family.

INDIVIDUAL DIFFERENCES

Another view holds that discrepancies in performance are due to the inflexible and rigid attitude of society with respect to the place it affords the unusual and atypical child. The argument raised is that in many cases it is not a biophysiological difficulty in the child, or even a failure of the child to be goal-directed, but rather a lack of sufficient opportunity within the community for the individual whose tastes or interests and types of initial experiences mark him as different. According to this view, such oddity in performance results in the child being identified and labeled as retarded or, occasionally (but to a lesser extent), as psychotic or as having a personality disorder. This labeling and identification process results in severe stigma and differential acceptance of the child, and such children have an increasingly difficult time of making their way in the world. Proponents of this view hold that the educational system is based upon a learning curve that, even if empirically accurate in terms of the average child, fails to provide mechanisms for the one who learns at a much earlier or later age.

In certain select urban communities, at least for the upper-middle-class child, public school systems provide educational programs as well as counseling services for the parents and their children who suffer from such discrepancies, but these not only are limited in size and scope but usually are confined to communities which have the means to pay for them. Of course, a limited number of private facilities are available but they are costly.

Both of these points of view agree that the six-through-twelve ages are critical and that the community pays a toll in later years for its incompetent handling of the unusual child, the one who is "deviant" in terms of intellectual age compared to chronological age. The point is important for, to a large extent, many of the activities, particularly for children in these ages, are truly age-graded. The public school system, for example, picks an arbitrary year—even a day of the month—at which it is no longer possible to enroll your child in kindergarten or first grade. It is a system that provides age-graded social activities, such as Cub Scouts or Boy Scouts, and makes no allowances for differences in physical or intellectual maturation. The impact of these processes results in differential identification by community members; as a consequence, the child in the course of his subsequent life is limited considerably in terms of what he does and with whom he can interact. This has an important bearing on his own self-perception, his sense of identity, and his estimate of his own worth.

ACUTE DISEASES

During the past quarter of a century, considerable advancement has been made in handling the particular physical health problems of children of this age group and in preventing many incipient problems that would take their toll later. For example, there is a whole spectrum of childhood diseases that, while usually only temporarily disabling in ages six to twelve, account for serious health conditions in adult life. These include not only such childhood diseases as mumps, chicken pox, and measles, but more subtle mechanisms such as rheumatic fever following staphylococcus infections that occur among children of this age. Today, modern therapies, when available and when used, limit greatly the liklihood of present or subsequent health problems for children in this age group. However, because of the unavailability or the selective availability of these medical services based upon income and, sometimes, race, there exist pockets of disease within the population that do debilitate children. When discussing the problem of poverty, we noted very briefly—and it should be repeated here—that in several areas of the country there are relatively large proportions of the childhood population whose lack of adequate diet, inability to remedy existing medical conditions, and failure to recognize the deprivations of home life result in intense suffering. Such communities provide unequal opportunities for the child during this period to learn the ropes in the sense that is so vitally necessary to the subsequent course of his adult career.

importance of this age period

Many clinicians hold that this is the age in which the impact of the problems of identification and socialization is related to manifestations of neurotic behavior and, in particular, to psychosomatic illnesses. Many of these psychosomatic illnesses reveal themselves only later in the individual's life, but there is some evidence that their roots lie in the experiences of children during this period. The highly competitive character of the educational experience, the intensive aspirations of parents for their young children, as well as the early struggles for sexual identity are causative factors in the subsequent development of psychosomatic problems in certain community members. One disease of interest in this respect is asthma, which is typically manifested for the first time during this phase. It is often held that the child with asthma is a consequence of a clash between the child and the personality of the parent:

> The latter invariably tries to dominate the child, but with a very well marked over-anxious and protective attitude also. During the "period of socialization," the child holds back his aggressiveness and also becomes afraid of it. Thus he becomes insecure. His frustration produces an emotional reaction which his environment forces him to control. The inhibition is reflected in abnormal reactions of his autonomic nervous system (Hamilton, 1955:207).

The end result of such a process is the symptomatic manifestations that are usually recorded by the physician as asthma. Other investigators subscribe, though perhaps more tentatively, to this position with respect to other illnesses generally viewed to be psychosomatic in nature. The strong correlations often found between one psychosomatic disorder and another tend to support the position that there is such a thing as a "psychosomatic personality," the development of which can be traced back to the problems fundamental to the preadolescent period (Hamilton, 1955).

In this review of the ages of six through twelve, we indicate the relevance of the concept that identifies it as a latency period. We have alluded to it as the period of learning the ropes. For those children who fail to learn the ropes adequately, a predisposition to certain defects and anomolies is set up which will become manifest as they approach the age of active sexual expression and adult status. Six through twelve is the age about which we know really very little and with which we probably have been underconcerned. This inattention is related primarily to the fact that, compared with the active expressions of other periods in the life cycle, this one, at least on the surface, appears to be a relatively placid one.

BAUCHARD, PHILIPPE.
1952 The Child Audience: A Report on Press, Film and Radio for Children. Paris, France: UNESCO.

BECKER, HOWARD S.
1961 "Schools and systems of stratification." Pp. 91–99 in A. H. Halsey, J. Floud, and C. A. Anderson (eds.), Education, Economy and Society. New York: Free Press.

BERGER, ARTHUR A.
1966 "Authority in the comics." Trans-action 4(December):22–26.

BOARDMAN, RICHARD P.
1966 "Public and parochial." Urban Review 1(November):16–23.

BRECKENRIDGE, MARIAN E. AND E. LEE VINCENT.
1960 Child Development. Philadelphia: W. B. Saunders.

BRODERICK, CARLFRED B.
1966 "Sexual behavior among pre-adolescents." The Journal of Social Issues 22(April):7–20.

CHANDLER, B. G., LINDLEY J. STILES, AND JOHN I. KITSUSE (EDS.).
1962 Education in Urban Society. New York: Dodd, Mead.

CLARK, BURTON R.
1962 Education in the Expert Society. San Francisco: Chandler.
1964 "Sociology of education." Pp. 734–769 in Robert E. L. Faris (ed.), Handbook of Modern Sociology. Chicago: Rand McNally.

CONANT, JAMES B.
1961 Slums and Suburbs: A Commentary on Schools in Metropolitan Areas. New York: McGraw-Hill.

CORWIN, RICHARD G.
1965 A Sociology of Education. New York: Appleton-Century-Crofts.

ERIKSON, ERIK H.
1963 Childhood and Society. Second Edition, Revised. New York: Norton.

FICHTER, JOSEPH H.
1964 Parochial School: A Sociological Study. Garden City, New York: Doubleday.

FREEMAN, HOWARD E. AND JOHN F. SCOTT.
1966 "A critical review of alcohol education for adolescents." Community Mental Health Journal 2(Fall):222–230.

GANS, HERBERT J.
1964 "The rise of the problem-film: an analysis of changes in Hollywood films and the American audience." Social Problems 11(Spring):327–336.

GEER, BLANCHE, JACK HAAS, CHARLES VIVONA, STEPHEN J. MILLER, CLYDE WOODS, AND HOWARD BECKER.
1966 "Learning the ropes: situational learning in four occupational training programs." Pp. 209–233 in Irwin Deutscher and Elizabeth Thompson (eds.), Among the People: Studies of the Urban Poor. New York: Basic Books.

GENTILE, FRANK AND S. M. MILLER.
1961 "Television and social class." Sociology and Social Research 45(April): 259–264.

GESELL, ARNOLD, FRANCIS ILG, AND LOUISE B. AMES.
1956 The Years from Ten to Sixteen. New York: Harper and Row.

GOODMAN, PAUL.
1964 Compulsory Miseducation. New York: Horizon.

HAMILTON, MAX.
1955 Psychosomatics. New York: Wiley.

HAWKES, GLENN R. AND DAMARIS PEASE.
1962 Behavior and Development from Five to Twelve. New York: Harper and Row.

HIMMELWEIT, HILDE T., A. N. OPPENHEIM AND PAMELA VINCE.
1958 Television and the Child: An Empirical Study of the Effect of Television on the Young. New York: Oxford University Press.

HOLT, JOHN CALDWELL.
1964 How Children Fail. New York: Pitman.

JENCKS, CHRISTOPHER.
1966 "Is the public school obsolete?" Public Interest 2(Winter):18–25.
1969 "A reappraisal of the most controversial educational document of our time." The New York Times Magazine August 10:12–13, 34–44.

KOZOL, JONATHAN.
1967 Death at an Early Age. Boston: Houghton Mifflin.

KOERNER, JAMES D.
1963 The Miseducation of American Teachers. Boston: Houghton Mifflin.

MARBURGER, CARL A.
1963 "Considerations for educational planning." Part V in A. Harry Passow (ed.), Education in Depressed Areas. New York: Teachers College Press.

NORTH, ROBERT D.
1958 "The teacher-education student: how does he compare academically with other college students?" Pp. 278–285 in The Education of Teachers: New Perspectives. Washington, D.C.: NEA National Commission on Teacher Education and Professional Standards.

O'DAY, THOMAS F.
1966 The Sociology of Religion. Englewood Cliffs, New Jersey: Prentice-Hall.

RIESSMAN, FRANK.
1962 The Culturally Deprived Child. New York: Harper and Row.

ROBBINS, ELAINE.
1966 Deviant Children Grown Up. Baltimore: Williams and Williams.

ROSENTHAL, ROBERT AND LENORE JACOBSON.
1968 "Self-fulfilling prophecies in the classroom: teachers' expectations as unintended determinants of pupils' intellectual competence." Pp. 219–253 in Martin Deutsch, Irwin Katz, and Arthur R. Jenson (eds.), Social Class, Race, and Psychological Development. New York: Holt, Rinehart and Winston.

SCHRAMM, WILBUR, JACK LYLE, AND EDWIN B. PARKER.
1961 Television in the Lives of Our Children. Stanford, California: Stanford University Press.

SEELEY, JOHN R., A. SIM AND E. W. LOOSLEY.
1956 Crestwood Heights. New York: Basic Books.

SEXTON, PATRICIA C.
1961 Education and Income: Inequalities of Opportunity in Our Public Schools. New York: Viking.

SHOSTAK, ARTHUR B.
1967 "Education and the family." Journal of Marriage and the Family 29(February):124–138.

SKORNIA, HARRY J.
1965 Television and Society. New York: McGraw-Hill.

TUMIN, MELVIN.
1962 Review of James B. Conant's Slums and Suburbs: A Commentary on Schools in Metropolitan Areas. American Sociological Review 27 (June): 421.

WARKOV, SEYMOUR, AND ANDREW M. GREELEY.
1966 "Parochial school origins and educational achievement." American Sociological Review 31(June):406–414.

WHEATLEY, GEORGE M. AND GRACE T. HALLOCK.
1965 Health Observation of School Children. New York: McGraw-Hill.

WHITE, DAVID MANNING AND ROBERT H. ABEL (EDS.).
1963 The Funnies: An American Idiom. New York: Macmillan.

WHITE, H. F.
1956 "Psychological development in the midwest." Child Development 27: 265–285.

WITMER, HELEN AND RUTH KOTINSKY (EDS.).
1952 Personality in the Making. Fact-Finding Report of the Mid-Century White House Conference on Children and Youth. New York: Harper and Row.

WOLFE, DALE.
1954 America's Resources of Specialized Talent. New York: Harper and Row.

CHAPTER 12

adolescence

IF THE AGES SIX THROUGH twelve represent a quiescent, latent period, the other extreme is true certainly for American teen-agers. The problems for the community occasioned by young people in this stage of their life cycle are many. If one examined all the books and articles written on social life and divided them by age groups, no doubt the literature on the teen-ager would rank first in quantity.

Obviously, a thorough consideration of the subject is out of the question here. Adolescence has been discussed in a wide range of book-length analyses, and the major social problems confronting this age group are the subject of a number of lengthy documents. Certain of the concerns identified with this age group which also transpire during the post-teen and early adult years will be reserved for later discussion. Indeed, as the educational process is extended and our definition of adulthood is changed, it becomes increasingly difficult to distinguish sharply between the teens and the post-teens.

adolescence and adulthood

In contemporary life, chronological age is becoming less and less useful as a criterion of adulthood. Voting age, once firmly set at twenty-one years, has been reduced to eighteen years in several states and the trend may soon reach the national level. When high school graduation served as the norm for adequate education, this age—usually seventeen or eighteen years—marked the beginning of early adulthood. Today, many young people are well into their twenties before completing their education. Newer concepts such as mental age and social age have usurped and, for certain purposes, replaced chronological age as a measure of maturity and readiness for new roles and statuses.

Extending the educational process may lengthen the period of dependency and postpone economic responsibility, but it also creates a situation for adolescents in which faulty decisions and unwise conduct may virtually preclude their success as adults, at least in terms of prestige and the good life. The links between education, careers, upward mobility, and general social status are such that a faulty strategy—such as not realizing that college admission officers may take first-year high school grades into account—on the part of the teen-ager may render him unable to cope with adulthood in any meaningful way. At the same time, the impact of urbanization exposes adolescents to all of the risks and hazards of city life. The notion that they can be shielded from the social problems of the community is not consistent with contemporary processes of communication and socialization. In these times, the mass media, the educational system, and most of the formal social-control systems anticipate the participation of teen-agers as full-fledged members of the community. As a consequence, a great deal of effort and energy are focused on their early development and rapid preparation for adulthood.

The concern of community members and the social-control system with the deviant conduct of teen-agers is related to more than their immediate behavior. It also represents a defense of the status quo by adults who are fearful that today's teen-age conduct will become the pattern for future social life.

The teen-age years are often referred to as the age of rebellion. The teen-ager is portrayed as an individual with rather full control of his intellectual processes who is devoted to contradicting or not conforming to the dictates and norms of the adult world. It is also described as an age of mutual anxiety in which the adult members of the community—including, of course, the parents of the teen-agers—are concerned about the prospects for the wholesome integration of the young people into community life. The adolescent's anxiety is related to the difficulties of coping with the marginal status he occupies in terms of his role definition as a community member. It should be noted that some writers disagree with the view that adolescence is a period of conflict (*see* Documentation 1).

VIEWS ON TEEN-AGERS

Friedenberg (1959; 1966) has recorded a series of views of teen-agers. He observes that many adults seem to consider the terms *teen-ager* and *juvenile delinquent* as synonymous and to regard the youth problem as falling under the heading of law enforcement or the care of emotionally disturbed children. A second view treats the teen-age peer group as a separate community or subculture within the larger American society.

> Given the existence of a large population segment permeated with anxiety arising from its ill-defined status, and communicating, however imperfectly, on a national scale, one observes elements necessary for the development of something akin to a minority group psychology: a shared sense of grievance and alienation among substantial numbers of persons readily identifiable by some conspicuous trait—in this case, being in the teen years. Listing further points of similarity between minority groups and today's teenagers, one could mention *leaders and spokesmen in* the persons of disc jockeys, young entertainers and some educationists; a distinctive set of material and nonmaterial *culture traits; sentiments of exclusiveness* toward most adults and toward "square" (i.e., adult-oriented) youngsters; and *culture heroes,* selected mainly from among entertainers and athletes.

> While the theory being presented here does not hinge on teenagers constituting a true minority group, it does assume that on a national scale there is evolving a complex of attitudes and values tending to control and motivate teenagers in ways consonant with the role implied by their position as a youthful group having leisure, relatively ample spending money and few responsibilities. The theme of this emerging culture seems to be one of an increasingly institutionalized but immature and irresponsible hedonism . . . (England, 1960:537–538).

A third view, best exemplified by Paul Goodman (1960), regards teenagers as a slandered group, separated from dignity and discriminated against in response to the tensions and frustrations of adult community members. Still another view regards the teen-ager as a nascent adult who is about to assume a status that will go with him throughout his life. Finally, a number of writers, considering the teen-ager from the psychological standpoint, see him as a ping-pong ball tossed back and forth until he can find a proper resting place (Smith, 1962).

All of these descriptions are, at least in part, empirically accurate portrayals of the teen-ager in American society. None of these appraisals can be ignored in any discussion of the problems of sexual development, juvenile delinquency, nonconformity, sociopathic behavior, and occupational choice, although each viewpoint has been criticized for its limitations (Elkin and Westley, 1955).

sexual development

Perhaps no facet of adolescent behavior is more disturbing to parents and other community members and, therefore, has received more atten-

One dominant pattern in Suburban Town is that of adult directed and approved activity. The activities of the adolescent take place almost completely within the suburban community and in view of adult figures. The adolescent, in effect, has little unstructured time. Typically, on school days, he spends his time out-of-school doing two hours of homework; helping in household activities; and participating in school organizations, directed sports, or church and "Y" activities. On weekends, with more free time, he participates in some family projects, has certain allotted household tasks, and often attends gatherings at which adults are present. In summers, he either works, attends camp, or vacations with his family. . . .

Family ties are close and the degree of basic family consensus is high. The parents are interested in all the activities of their children, and the adolescents, except for the area of sex, frankly discuss their own behavior and problems with them. In many areas of life, there is joint participation between parents and children—the boys may help their fathers build patios, the members of the family may curl together, and the parents may attend the school's athletic competitions. In independent discussions by parents and adolescents of the latter's marriage and occupational goals, there was a remarkable level of agreement. The adoles-

cents also acknowledged the right of their parents to guide them, for example, accepting, at least manifestly, the prerogative of the parents to set rules for the number of dates, hours of return from dates, and types of parties. The parents express relatively little concern about the socialization problems or peer group activities of their children.

In many respects, for this given sample of adolescents, the continuity of socialization is far more striking than the discontinuity. With future education and career possibilities in mind the adolescents discuss their choice of school courses with their parents. The parents encourage their children to play host to their friends. Also, since the parents themselves engage in entertaining, dancing, and community sports, the adolescents observe that in many respects their own pattern of social life is not very different from that of the older generation. The continuity of socialization is especially well exemplified in the organization of parties and the concern with social proprieties. Typically, when a girl gives a party, she sends out formal invitations, and her guest list includes those she *should* invite as well as those she wants to invite. The girls take great pains to play their hostess roles properly, and the boys so strongly recognize their escort responsibilities that they may privately draw straws to decide

tion, than has sexual activity. The teen-ager is fully mature sexually and can, and sometimes does, compete well in all respects with persons socially defined as adults. *The Graduate* was not the first American youth to discover this fact. Adolescence is the age when young people exercise their sexual capacities, and adults expend a great deal of effort and manifest a great deal of concern over the potential consequences. Within the adult community there is considerable reluctance even to acknowledge the pervasiveness of sexual desires on the part of adolescents,

who walks home with the less popular girls.

The adolescents themselves demonstrate a high level of sophistication about their own activities, in many respects having internalized "responsible" and "adult" perspectives. For example, they took their homework very seriously; they tended to view their household tasks as their contribution to family maintenance; some suggested that the clubs to which they belonged gave them valuable social or organizational experience; and the boys, after telling of their practical jokes in school, spoke of this behavior as "silly" or "kid stuff." Furthermore, the youth culture elements in which they participated were recognized as transitory and "appropriate for their age." Thus the "steady date" was likely to be viewed as a pleasant temporary association, not directly related to marriage, which gave a certain immediate security and taught them about heterosexual feelings and relationships. Some spoke of the dating pattern as "the kind of stuff kids do at our age."

This description of adolescence in a suburban town is not an isolated portrait; it is supported in various aspects by other discussions of upper middle-class and upwardly mobile groups. Most noteworthy is the study of Elmtown (or Jonesville) by Hollingshead, Warner, *et al.* Although Elmtown is an isolated community of 10,000 population, we find many similar patterns of behavior. In Elmtown, likewise, the upper middle-class adolescent spends much of his time in supervised extra-curricular activities; the parents know the families of their children's associates and bring pressure to bear on their children to drop "undesirable" friends; the children are taught to be polite and refined in their speech and behavior and to repress aggressive tendencies. The children of the middle and upper classes, concludes Hollingshead, "are guided by their parents along lines approved by the class cultures with remarkable success."

Similar descriptions are given in other studies which discuss the deferred gratification pattern among upper middle and mobile lower-class adolescents. The child learns to forego immediate indulgences for the sake of future gains and thus inhibits his aggressive and sexual impulses, strives for success in school, and selects his associates with care. This pattern is in direct contradiction to the implications of a strong and pervasive youth culture. The individual who internalizes a deferred gratification pattern does not act solely in terms of irresponsible pleasure seeking and conforming peer group pressures and, much as he may apparently be absorbed in dances, gang activity, and sports, he does not lose sight of his long-run aspirations.

It is to be stressed here that we have been focusing throughout on the overt and behavioral, and not the psychiatric, aspects of adolescent development. No implications of any kind are intended about the psychological health or ill health of the adolescents concerned. (Elkin and Westley, 1955:682–683.)

much less to recognize the high levels of heterosexual and homosexual activity of one sort or another in which the average teenager engages.

SEX NORMS

Typically, in the average American community adults frown on all overt sexual expression. The taboos include, besides premarital intercourse, petting to the point of orgasm, homosexual activities and, certainly in the case of girls, self-masturbation. There are, however, various and conflicting views on this matter. Some analysts, such as Friedenberg (1966), challenge the norms of the society that tries to prevent "love relationships" and to deny psychologically gratifying and enduring heterosexual relations to adolescents while at the same time failing to provide any means for preventing casual contacts or for controlling opportunities for purely physical satisfaction. As Friedenberg (1966:46–47) notes, adolescents are likely to find it far easier to have sexual intercourse than sexual relationships—or, for that matter, relationships of any kind.

From the opposite perspective, others consider the problem to be the failure on the part of adolescents to reconcile the normative views of appropriate conduct held by most adults with the level of sexual needs and the modes of expression accepted by most of their peers. Persons holding this view suggest that the disparity between community norms and the postpuberty activities of adolescents creates a situation that makes it virtually impossible to handle sexual behavior without considerable guilt, anxiety, and uncertainty.

Goldburgh (1965) provides a number of reports about late adolescence that attempt to portray these years in their own terms. The consequences do not always accrue only to the unchaste. Almost all of these accounts document the problems arising from sexual conduct and sexual control and the guilt or anxiety connected with adolescent experiences.

THE CONSEQUENCES OF THE NORMS

Analysts concerned with adolescent sexual behavior and the accompanying pressures argue that the current standards of sexual behavior within the adult population do nothing to minimize the strains of the postpuberty period. Not only do the mass media extol the delights of sex and exploit the rewards of using sexual relationships to obtain other ends, but the American community, including many parents, fails to provide a consistent standard of conduct or a workable set of mores.

> In a sense, our young people are forced to bear the brunt of the assault of the sexual revolution. If they are sexually insecure, this is perhaps to be expected in an era when sexual insecurity is so prevalent. If they are obsessed with sex, this is perhaps less than strange at a time when sex appears to many as the last frontier for human expression. . . . Because the present is a time of flux and mobility in respect to sexual attitudes and behavior, extreme confusion over sexual standards is probably inevitable. Under these conditions, the teenager's own understanding of sexual right and wrong is bound to be marked by confusion and misunderstanding (Moss, 1964:139–140).

Professionals are very much aware of the extensive preadolescent sexual behavior that can be observed in young children (Broderick, 1966). The teen-age period is subject to additional hazards. Not only do adolescents find opportunities for extended sexual activities and exhibit great ingenuity in finding ways to cope with the restrictive norms of the community, but they experience as much, if not more, physiological and psychological tension than do adults who are denied sexual gratification. Physiologically, teen-agers possess full sexual capacities and needs for sexual gratification; the community, both informally within the peer group and secondarily through communication of the cultural norms, provides intensive sources of social stimulation and places inordinate stress on the physiological and social gratification accruing to sexual activities. Although the data from numerous studies of sexual behavior and development reveal wide differences, Broderick's analysis suggests that somewhere between 50 and 85 per cent of boys engage in masturbation by age thirteen and that the vast bulk of the American population —certainly of the males—experience sexual fulfillment by intercourse or other means by age eighteen.

DEALING WITH ADOLESCENT SEX

It is easy, on the one hand, to overemphasize sexual needs, conflicts, and struggles as the underlying cause of all problems that beset adolescents in the community. On the other hand, it is unrealistic to ignore the significance of the fact that teen-agers, who possess a full repertoire of adult sexual responses, must live in communities where norms formally prohibit, or at least severely limit, all expressions of sexual behavior. Neither the preaching of churchmen, the sympathetic understanding of parents, nor sex education in the schools can reduce the sex drive. Further, while knowledge about and availability of contraceptives may reduce unmarried pregnancies, the norm conflicts are still there. These discrepancies between the individual and his society and the resulting strains between the generations represent important determinants of the continuing problems of youth. Moreover, the limited research data do not permit "objective" advice on sexual conduct. (*See* Documentation 2.)

A number of commentators such as Bell (1966) have noted a growing convergence of the sexual needs and values of teen-agers and the values and norms held by their parents and the larger society. While this closing of the generation gap has resulted in a reduction in the strain between norms and behavior, nevertheless, the discontinuity between physiological capacity and social norms remains a constant problem in the American community (Reiss, 1967). For many parents and their children, the conflict about premarital sexual expression will continue to be characterized by the parents' playing ostrich and burying their heads in the sand and the youths' efforts to keep the sand from blowing away (Bell, 1966).

As we indicated earlier, a significant segment of the American community holds the view that adolescent behavior and delinquent behavior are synonymous. *Juvenile delinquency,* like most of the other terms that describe broad categories of deviant conduct, is an ambiguous term. Strictly speaking, it is a description not of an individual but of an environment that fails to socialize the child well and to achieve in him the full internalization of its norms and values.

THE MEANING OF DELINQUENCY

The term juvenile delinquency stems from a concept in British law which holds that the state represents the superordinate parent. Therefore, labeling the child delinquent suggests that his parents, or those who take on that responsibility, cannot or do not meet their commitment to keep him in line and to socialize him according to the normative values of the larger community (Barron, 1954). This definition, as reflected in our legal process, permits a child to be adjudicated a delinquent by the assigned legal authority. In this legal sense delinquency may include a variety of activities, ranging from running away from home, failing to attend school, dressing unconventionally, or acting atypically, to failing to behave according to the legal norms that in the adult world results in police and court actions.

In considering this stage of the life cycle, it is important to distinguish between those behaviors that can be regarded as rebellious in terms of community norms and those acts that, if the individual were older, would be held to be violations of legal codes. In our discussion of delinquency we will focus on the types of adolescent behavior that are contrary to the legal norms typically enforced for adults. Subsequently, we shall consider the problems of rebellious behavior, trying to distinguish, at least analytically, between the two types of deviance.

THE EXTENT OF YOUTH CRIME

In discussing the illegal activities of adolescents, one must acknowledge that not very much is known about the extent of teen-age crime. There is a wide variety of official statistics on delinquency. These include reports of the numbers of boys who have been institutionalized because of unlawful behavior and the number who have appeared before the courts. A less precise but perhaps more realistic picture is provided by assembling police reports that include information not only on arrests but also detentions, warnings, and informal approaches to the control of

DOCUMENTATION 2

the impact of sex before marriage

WIVES' EVALUATIONS OF MAXIMUM LEVELS OF PREMARITAL INTIMACY FOR IMMEDIATE POSTMARITAL SEX ADJUSTMENT

	Kissing and Petting Above the Waist	Genital Petting	Coitus
Helping sex adjustment	33.9%	54.5%	58.4%
Not helping sex adjustment	66.1	45.5	41.6
Total Percentage	100.0	100.0	100.0
Total Number	(56)	(44)	(77)

Orgasm from premarital intercourse apparently influences the wife's rating of satisfaction of the wedding night to a much greater degree than does orgasm brought about by petting. The initial sex experience in marriage was reported as satisfying by over 81 per cent of the wives experiencing premarital coital orgasm as compared to only 46 per cent of those indicating petting-determined orgasms.

Not all degrees of premarital intimacy are considered equally conducive to early marital sex adjustment. The above table shows that the more advanced the intimacy level, the more likely the subjects considered it "beneficial"

for the attainment of early marital sex adjustment. Women whose maximum premarital intimacy levels were kissing or petting above the waist were least inclined to ascribe favorable consequences to these activities for marital sex adjustment. It is interesting to note that in spite of the fact that coitus was considered most beneficial, approximately 42 per cent of the women with such premarital experience declined to attribute a beneficial effect to the experience. Although coitus was not subjectively viewed as paying greater dividends than genital petting, the ratings of sexual satisfaction for the wedding night imply otherwise. Reluctance to ascribe positive effects to premarital intercourse may reflect guilt and regret over such behavior. On the other hand, as noted above, those women with premarital sexual episodes tend to report sexual difficulties in the early weeks of marriage. Again, expectations of sexual adjustment could be high and subsequent difficulties, even of a minor nature, might be interpreted as evidence that premarital coitus is largely void of benefit for marital sexual adjustment. (Kanin and Howard, 1958:560–561.)

---

illegal conduct by teen-agers. Finally, there are strong suspicions that many criminal acts not detected or not charged to an individual offender are a consequence of the behavior of adolescents rather than of adults in the community.

It is difficult to make any judgment about whether delinquency is increasing or decreasing among adolescents. As a rough statement, many experts accept the statistic that some 2 per cent of all children are involved with the courts for delinquent actions before they reach the age of seventeen (Cohen and Short, 1966). Delinquency is not a new problem; its persistence, abetted by the complexities and the structure of today's urban community, makes it a critical problem. Certainly, there is heightened public concern about its control—a conservative statement would be that the incidence of delinquency has remained constant or increased slightly. Contemporary crime statistics prompted the following legend for an institutional advertisement: "Most criminals have to be in bed by ten o'clock." Over one-half of all the arrests for burglary and larceny and almost two-thirds of the arrests for auto theft involve persons under the age of eighteen. A significant proportion of individuals regarded as the aggressor in assault cases—almost 20 per cent of those arrested for rape—and the same percentage of those arrested for carrying weapons are also adolescents (Luger and Saltman, 1967:120). While most of these delinquencies involve boys, some 15 to 20 per cent of court appearances for illegal activities, usually for sex offenses, are made by girls under eighteen.

The problem of estimating youth crime is not limited to assessing the frequency (incidence) of cases that come before the court. If the reports of court actions or of arrests are representative of the actual rates of illegal activities by youth in urban communities, then these data would permit a comparison of the frequencies of various types of delinquency and of the characteristics of individuals involved in each. A number of studies have shown, however, that police and court statistics are not representative of all delinquent behavior committed by adolescents. While the statistics now reported do not allow an accurate estimation of the volume of delinquent activities, they do permit comparisons of change in rates from year to year, assuming the definitions upon which the rates are based do not change. Although alternative methods of measuring delinquent behavior have not been perfected, sufficient information has been accumulated to show that certain types of offenses are drastically underreported by legal authorities. In addition, the courts, police, and citizens of many communities respond differently to illegal acts committed by teen-agers from different backgrounds (Piliavin and Briar, 1964; Luger and Saltman, 1967).

LABELING THE DELINQUENT

One of the major determinants of whether or not a teen-ager is pursued, identified, and treated as a delinquent is the social milieu and school status of the individual (Vinter, 1967). (*See* Documentation 3.) Studies suggest, for example, that the middle-class child has a greater probability of avoiding formal actions for illegal behavior than has a lower-class youth (Wheeler et al., 1968). This is related, of course, to the energy and resources his family is likely to put into assisting him and to their ability, in the case of financial loss, to provide victims with compensation. It is also related to the general reluctance of community social-control agents to jeopardize the subsequent life opportunities of a teen-ager whom they

three factors affecting delinquency

PERCENTAGE WITH ONE OR MORE ARRESTS OR COURT REFERRALS
(Numbers in parentheses are base N's)

School Performance	Negro Males	White Males	Negro Females	White Females
Success	43% (14)	38% (37)	24% (25)	0% (75)
Failure	71 (38)	61 (61)	40 (25)	23 (44)

Three rather powerful factors associated with delinquency are race, sex, and school performance. The above table summarizes the simultaneous effects of these factors on lower class youth. Each of the three factors has an independent effect, i.e., influences the delinquency rate when the other two factors are held constant. The range in these rates, from zero to 71 per cent, indicates that a considerable portion of the variation in delinquency in this population can be predicted, if not theoretically explained, by race, sex, and school performance. (Palmore and Hammond, 1964: 850.)

feel will probably participate successfully in the community as an adult.

But the socio-economic status of the potential juvenile offender is not the only determinant of his probable involvement with the formal legal system. A variety of different orientations on the part of police and courts, as well as the differential influence of other social-control agents, have a marked influence on what happens to adolescents in their jurisdictions. For example, certain judges are more oriented to a psychiatric view of adolescent behavior. In their courts, many more prospective delinquents are referred prior to official involvement to child-guidance clinics or other agencies that take a therapeutic approach to behavior problems. Police and court systems in other communities are more concerned with counting noses, and their bias towards either strict enforcement or leniency is reflected in the official statistics of arrest rates for adolescents in their jurisdiction. While it is not possible here to go fully into the data, there is good evidence that arrests and court data do not reveal the whole story of unlawful activities of adolescents.

SELF-REPORTS OF DELINQUENCY

An alternative approach to measuring the extent of illegal activities by youth is based upon self-report data obtained from teen-agers themselves. Perhaps the leading example of this sort of investigation is the work of

racial differences in delinquency

RACE AND OFFICIALLY-REPORTED DELINQUENCY (In Percent)

Officially-Reported Delinquency Scale	Caucasians	Negroes	Orientals
(High) 5	0%	8%	0%
4	4	18	0
3	16	36	3
2	37	30	21
(Low) 1	43	8	76
N =	(104)	(220)	(38)

As so many other studies have shown, race is strongly related to "official" delinquency as shown in the above table. Negroes get into the most trouble with the police, the courts, and school officials; Orientals get into the least trouble. Theta, a measure of association for comparing a nominal scale with an ordinal scale, is .46.

PERCENT OF CAUCASIAN, NEGRO, AND ORIENTAL YOUTHS WHO REPORT EVER HAVING COMMITTED SPECIFIC DELINQUENCY ITEMS

Type of Delinquency	Caucasians	Negroes	Orientals
Larceny (under $2)	33%	31%	22%
Destroying property	34	31	32
Drinking liquor	24	13	8
Driving without license	26	35	26
Defying parents' authority	44	20	45
Skipping school	12	23	5
Running away	15	9	13
Beating-up kids	20	21	18
Threatening kids	4	12	5
N =	(104)	(220)	(38)

The relationship between race and self-reported delinquency, using the combined "scale" of self-reported delinquency, is only .07. . . . In general, Oriental boys report the least delinquency, rating first on only one item —defying parents' authority. Negro boys rate first on four items: threatening kids for money, beating up kids, skipping school, and driving without a license. Caucasian boys rank first on four items: larceny, destroying property, drinking, and runaway. While there is some tendency for the Negro boys to rank highest on the items involving the most personal violence, the percentages reporting these activities are very similar to that of Caucasians. (Gould, 1969: 329–330.)

Nye and Short (1957). They developed a scale of delinquent actions and used it to test a large sample of public high school students. The scale items ranged from questions about taking things valued at less than $2, to destroying public property, to forced rape. Studies such as this indicate a much higher incidence of delinquent behavior than is reflected in official statistics and suggest that at least part of the association between illegal behavior and the socio-economic and racial backgrounds of adjudicated delinquents can be explained by the differential processing of cases through the legal system (Nye, Short, and Olson, 1958). (*See* Documentation 4.)

Many analysts, such as Wheeler (1966), prefer to regard official statistics as representing only the interaction between the social-control system and a selected group within the community, not the entire population. It is an important warning to community members and social-control agents alike that the extent of unlawful acts by adolescents cannot be fully gauged by what is represented in official reports and that the nature and target of their concern should reflect this fact. In this sense, illegal behavior by adolescents must be regarded not only in terms of its objective basis but of its moral implications as well.

RECONCILING THE DATA

Despite the problematic character of the data, a number of fairly firm conclusions can be reached with respect to illegal behavior by adolescents:

> First, crimes against property and, to some extent, violence and gang activity represent important concerns because of their total volume.
>
> Second, among adolescents, crime rates are many times higher for males than for females, a reasonable estimate being a ratio of four or five to one. Some analysts, however, suggest a decline in sex differences in delinquency rates (Wise, 1967).
>
> Third, official rates of illegal behavior by adolescents appear to be highest among the lower socio-economic groups. Studies that try to estimate the total volume of illegal activity find much less marked associations in this respect, and some investigators maintain that when unreported delinquency is taken into account, social-class differences are markedly reduced (Nye, Short and Olson, 1958). Nevertheless, many researchers maintain that acts of the most serious character may indeed be concentrated in the lower socio-economic groups in comparison with the middle and upper classes (Reiss and Rhodes, 1961; Chilton, 1964; 1967).
>
> Fourth, crime rates tend to be high during middle and late adolescence and appear to decline rapidly in early adulthood. Partly this may represent differences in legal processing, for adult criminals are identified in ways that make them highly visible to the community. Police and court officials may be more reluctant to attach the label of

criminal to a young adult. It may also be that other commitments of adulthood make for greater risk and therefore less motivation for illegal activity.

Fifth, among adolescents who are officially involved in the legal process, there is a greater likelihood that teen-agers from low socio-economic backgrounds will be institutionalized than will be youth from middle-class environments (Porterfield, 1943; Axelrod, 1952). Part of this, as we have already implied, may represent an extension of the process of discrimination that pervades the American scene. On the other hand, some would contend that different treatments are indicated by a realistic appraisal of the detrimental effects that poor environments may have on the subsequent rehabilitation of delinquents.

Sixth, it should be observed that we have very limited information on the combinations of delinquent behavior that are most frequently engaged in by adolescents from different environments. Are there certain adolescents, for example, whose illegal behavior centers around property offenses while the actions of others are concentrated on crimes against individuals? The difficulty of developing adequate typologies of delinquent behavior is compounded by this lack of adequate data (Ferdinand, 1966).

The opportunities for definitive empirical investigations in the field are limited by the differential visibility of delinquent acts and the unreliability of official information. Further, until quite recently, most of the delinquency-control efforts were at the local or state level and offered only minimal opportunities to engage in research designed to evaluate the relative effectiveness of various intervention approaches. These limitations have reduced the possibilities of making rational judgments on the utility of various intervention strategies and have curtailed the development of a systematic body of knowledge on the causes of delinquent behavior. Despite these problems, however, the interest in understanding the etiology of delinquent behavior has evoked a large number of substantive and theoretical works. These writings illustrate well the various theoretical positions discussed earlier. While all have potential relevance for understanding the problems of juvenile delinquency, in general the overriding view seeks to integrate the structural and communications or interactional approaches. However, it would be useful to look systematically at the various positions.

INDIVIDUAL VIEWS

Much of the early work in the area of delinquency followed closely the interest in individual behavior and relied heavily on psychiatric explanations of deviance. Of course, concern with delinquency has always been related to the general interest in the illegal behavior of adults. There is a tradition going back many centuries to concepts of physical and temperamental differences between the offender and the conforming community member. Many of these early views emphasized differences in body type and emotional makeup and sought explanations in these and other heredity factors. Linked to this was a concern with individual characteristics of delinquents and an effort to identify intrapsychic or socio-psychological differences between delinquents and nondelinquents. Most of these classic studies obtained information on childrearing practices and early development and found that negative characteristics in these early years were strongly related to a proneness to commit deviant acts (Glueck and Glueck, 1962).

In a landmark study, Healy and Bronner (1936) examined a series of delinquency cases and interpreted the problems faced by the children in terms of inadequate socialization. Their evidence frequently included broken homes, alcoholic parents, and emotionally distressed siblings. The causal chain usually was assumed to link the stresses of lower socioeconomic family life to the distressing psychological environments which, in turn, accounted for the volume of delinquency.

Although the communications and structural points of view have been emphasized in more recent etiologic theories and intervention programs, there is still considerable interest in documenting the role of individual characteristics and the importance of personality in accounting for delinquent behavior.

Among contemporary studies, a number undertaken by various child-guidance centers seek to determine whether the personality development of the child who commits illegal acts is a consequence or a determinant of his delinquent experience. Most social analysts today have discarded most of the theories relating to inherited delinquent tendencies (such as the criminal types of Lombroso) and constitutional psychopathic personality.

Some of the psychiatric and psychoanalytic theories, particularly those that try to integrate the individual and environmental perspectives, continue to be popular (Merton and Ashley-Montagu, 1940; McCord, 1958). This point of view holds that delinquency is a form of behavior motivated by the personality of the child in order to deal with some problem of adjustment. Delinquent behavior is interpreted as an attempt to resolve a struggle between unacceptable impulses and conflicting moral standards. In this sense, a delinquent act becomes for the child a partial resolution of a psychic battle.

This orientation has been subjected to a number of criticisms (Cohen and Short, 1966), as has the view that delinquent behavior is the symptom of a pathological state of mind, that is, a sign of mental illness. Most sociologists, even when they seek to locate the problem of delinquency in individual characteristics, have a much more interpersonal perspective that emphasizes motivation and learning.

crime and delinquency rates by economic and family status

CRIME AND DELINQUENCY RATES BY ECONOMIC STATUS AND FAMILY STATUS

Crime and Delinquency	SOCIAL AREAS			
	Low Economic Status Low Family Status	Low Economic Status High Family Status	High Economic Status Low Family Status	High Economic Status High Family Status
Crime Rate (rate per 1,000 population 18 years and older)	250.0	106.4	25.7	25.7
Delinquency Rate (rate per 1,000 population age 5–17)	54.9	29.9	16.0	8.6
Delinquency/Crime Ratio (delinquency rate percentage of crime rate)	22.0	28.1	62.2	33.5

The delinquency rates show a pattern similar to that of the crime rates, with an exception regarding family status and the fact that the rates are considerably lower than the crime rates. The highest delinquency rate (54.9) is found in the social area characterized by low economic status and low family status. The lowest delinquency rate (8.6), on the other hand, is in the high economic-high family status social area. Both of the low economic status areas have higher delinquency rates than found in the two high economic status social areas, however, and unlike the finding regarding high economic status and crime rates, delinquency rates are lowered by the presence of high family status. (Quinney, 1964:151–152.)

THE SOCIO-PSYCHOLOGICAL POSITION

The socio-psychological position is based on the understanding that the individual, through his social experiences, gains a perception of himself that impinges on the way he behaves in his various roles. This view contends that a person's life experiences represent the key forces in determining his role performance or potential role performance, in the case of the adolescent. Further, the interpersonal relationships in which the teenager engages extend or limit his internalization of values as well as his choice of strategies to handle new experiences and solve new problems. In contrast to the psychoanalytic school, which sees individual personality as interacting with situational factors, this point of view holds that the individual's various social experiences shape and mold his personality. Naturally, the same interpersonal and intersituational characteristics can be used to support either point of view. Needless to say, the sociological interpretation of personality as the product of social interaction and the interpersonal basis for role performance has not been convincing to social psychologists.

DIFFERENTIAL ASSOCIATION

Another interpretation, stemming from an earlier sociological tradition, has been referred to as the theory of differential association. This perspective assumes that children and youth from different strata of society have at least some distinctive interpersonal experiences and social relationships that provide them with a set of values and a repertory of behaviors that affords physical and psychological gratification. The basic idea has been elaborated in a number of ways. It has been viewed as a process of additive valences (the relative ability to unite, react, or interact), some of which are positive, that is, consistent with general community norms, and others which are negative, that is, opposed to normative standards. Thus, delinquency is found to be highest among poor children from unstable families (*see* Documentation 5). The delinquent adolescent is viewed as one whose behavior, resulting from differential associations, reflects an enduring accumulation of negative perspectives on right and wrong and a self-concept at variance with accepted norms of good and bad (Reckless et al., 1957; Reckless et al., 1960; Dinitz et al., 1962). (*See* Documentation 6.)

Earlier in this book, the theory of differential association and the related view of subcultures were represented as general perspectives on deviant behavior. To a large extent, both of these interpretations grew out of the work of analysts addressing themselves to the problem of delinquency (Kvaraceus and Miller, 1959).

OPPORTUNITY THEORY

At several points in this book we have referred to the means-end schema of Robert Merton and described in general terms the work of Cloward and Ohlin (1960). These authors hold that most delinquent behavior is a response to the adolescent's lack of opportunity to achieve accepted goals, which the teen-ager defines in ways similar to the population at large.

In contrast to the subculture perspective, which argues that subgroups have different goals, the views of Cloward and Ohlin focus on the lack of institutionalized means for the achievement of relatively uniform goals. They interpret delinquent activities as efforts to achieve normal social goals but by innovative, illegitimate means—almost a preparation, some would hold, for the way many individuals who are unable to achieve through conformity perform throughout their lives.

The evidence thus obtained tends to give further support to the initial thesis that self-concept may be an underlying component in delinquent or non-delinquent conduct. Perhaps one of the chief distinctions between persons who will and those who will not experience difficulty with the law in their formative and later years lies in the extent to which a socially acceptable self image has been developed.

An analysis and comparison of the "insulated" and potentially delinquent nominees revealed significant differences in the self images of members in the two groups. The "insulated" boys, unlike the potentially delinquent, did not ever expect to have to be taken to juvenile court or jail. They indicated a desire to avoid trouble at all costs and they had rarely engaged in any form of theft, and they had few if any friends who had been in trouble with the law. They liked school and rarely played "hookey." They conceived of themselves as obedient sons who did not frequently behave in a manner contrary to their parents' wishes. They evaluated their families as being as good or better than most families and the relationships in the home as harmonious and cordial. They felt that their parents were neither overly strict nor lax and certainly not unnecessarily punitive. In all of these respects they differed from the boys nominated as being potentially delinquent. Further, even within the potentially delinquent group itself important differences in self-concepts and family evaluations were found between the boys who had previous legal involvement and those who had not. . . .

Those differences between the "insulated" and potentially delinquent boys were, if any-

General interest in the problem of delinquency has increased, and a number of theoretical exercises and practical experiments have been undertaken. The principal contribution of these investigations has been to counter the doctrinaire position of those who view delinquency exclusively in terms of individual characteristics. It must be noted that today we have no single or unified theory to explain adolescent deviant behavior which is acceptable to everyone and documented by empirical evidence. The tendency, however, is to emphasize group differences in communication and value-transmission and the gap between means and ends in the structural processes of the community.

One expression of this view is the commitment hypothesis which takes its cue from the retreatist symptom that is common to many delinquents.

The uncommitted delinquent youth, it would appear, is characterized by behavioral withdrawal from school. He does not study, he

thing, magnified by their respective parents. For example, all but one of the mothers of the potentially delinquent boys thought that their sons could have selected better friends. These mothers also indicated significantly more frequently than their counterparts in the insulated group that they were often unaware of their sons' whereabouts, that they did not know very many of the friends with whom their boys associated, and that their sons did not very often bring their friends home. The mothers of the potentially delinquent boys also more often than the mothers of the insulated boys stated that the family situation was characterized by conflict and that there was not very much family participation in leisure and other activities. Finally, the mothers of the "insulated" and the potentially delinquent boys differed in their evaluations of the frequency and severity of parental punishment and in their definitions of the activity level of their respective sons. The "good" boys were less frequently punished and were much more often defined by their mothers as being quiet.

These differential perceptions on the part of both the boys and their mothers strongly suggest that one of the preconditions of law-abiding or delinquent conduct is to be found in the concept of self and others that one has acquired in his primary group relationships. It should be emphasized in support of this contention that the mothers of the potentially delinquent boys were no less often in agreement with their sons' less favorable social definitions and perceptions than were the mothers of the insulated boys with their sons' more acceptable definitions. Consequently, the boys themselves, their mothers, and the teachers in each sample group of nominees were aware of some basic component(s) which steers boys away from or toward delinquency. In the realities of social interaction, "insulated" boys seem to define themselves and seem to be thought of as "good" boys by their parents and teachers to no less an extent than the potentially delinquent boys seem to define themselves and to be defined in an opposite manner. (Reckless, Dinitz, and Kay, 1957:569).

receives poor grades, and he does not participate in activities. This withdrawal tends to be accompanied by a concomitant withdrawal from identification with pathways to adult status as well, since the educational and occupational aspirations of the uncommitted delinquent youth are lower than those of the successful and committed non-delinquent youth (Polk and Halferty, 1966:92).

Whether it is necessary to go beyond normative values and social structure to understand individual delinquents is open to question. In referring to the Moynihan Report (1965), we noted that problems of communication and structural deprivation may themselves have consequences for the personality development of particular individuals. Moynihan places considerable emphasis on the lower-income Negro male's lack of success-orientation, a lack which is fostered and strengthened by the role of the female in one-parent households. This sort of evidence suggests that any comprehensive view of delinquency must include a knowledge of maturation and personality factors as well as an understanding of those problems relating to communication and structure. The critical issue, of course, is the assumption of a causal model that relates these various domains of variables; on this matter we have not advanced beyond speculation.

MODES OF INTERVENTION

Given the current emphasis on the problems associated with the inculcation of values and the inequities of institutionalized means, programs of intervention and treatment have turned from the active delinquent to the preoffender. This is not to deny that a great deal of attention and community resources are continuing to be devoted to the social control and suppression of adolescent delinquency. Although considerable emphasis has been placed on the rehabilitation of delinquents, most urban communities maintain a network of custodial institutions for juveniles and expend a considerable volume of police and court activity in dealing with the active offender. This level of activity persists in spite of considerable evidence which indicates that legal involvement and institutionalization tend to increase rather than decrease the likelihood of recidivism—that is, repeated offenses and continual interaction with the social-control system.

CONFINEMENT

The concept of delinquency implies that the community must protect itself against those who do not conform. In many cases this means confining the offending adolescent or removing him from his environment in order to break the ties of negative associations. This period of confinement is expected to provide the offender with a different perspective on the norms of the community. Even today, however, most of the so-called training schools—little changed from the days when they were known as reform schools—constitute custodial environments which offer little more than a rudimentary education and obsolete vocational training (Ontell and Jones, 1965). Most juvenile court judges recognize the limited therapeutic value of institutionalization and try to use it as sparingly as possible. In the absence of alternate solutions, however, the distressing elements in the adolescent's environment or the risk he presents to the community if he remains on the streets dictate the continued use of institutionalization as a remedial action. (*See* Documentation 7.) Each year some one hundred thousand youths between fourteen and eighteen years of age, most of them males, spend a significant portion of their time in such institutional settings.

From a humanitarian standpoint, many of these training schools represent distressing environments, and sufficient documentation is avail-

DOCUMENTATION 7

postrelease failure rate

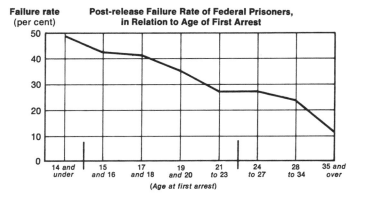

Failure rate (per cent) — **Post-release Failure Rate of Federal Prisoners, in Relation to Age of First Arrest**

(Age at first arrest)

Another indication of the need for intensive specialized treatment for youths is the vital insight gained through Daniel Glaser's study of over 1,000 Federal prisons. This study dramatically revealed the direct correlation of recidivism with initial age-arrest patterns. While the possibility of further reinvolvement with the law diminished with maturity and age, a significant proportion of the recidivists were within the 16-23 year age grouping, emphasizing the seriousness of delinquency. (Luger and Saltman, 1967:120–121.)

able about the inadequacies of their staffs to require no belaboring of this fact. The low pay scale and the lack of optimism regarding successful outcome make it difficult to develop professionalization among the personnel and to effect changes that would improve the environment of training schools. Over time, these institutions have tended to become less custodial in their physical appearance and some of the new ones have taken on the atmosphere of a boarding school (Weeks, 1958; Empey and Rabow, 1961). But even the best of these remain essentially a visible sign of the failure of the community to cope with the problems of its adolescents.

COURTS AND THEIR PROGRAMS

The criticisms aimed at the institutional settings also apply to many other elements of custodial care, including the practices of the courts and probation and parole procedures as they apply to adolescents. Some of this criticism has diminished. With less emphasis being given to the role of individual characteristics, there is somewhat less concern with individualized treatment since it is doubtful that such treatment really contributes to the alleviation of the delinquency problem. Nevertheless, it should be noted that, in addition to the corrupting influence of most custodial institutions, the legal procedures by which teen-agers are there and the scrutiny and surveillance that mark their treatment in the community while on probation or parole are also questionable.

From the outset of any delinquency proceeding, the court action represents an irrational compromise; on the one hand, the judge acts as the judicial representative of the social-control system and, on the other, as a quasi-therapist–social worker. Recent concern has focussed on the quasi-legal character of most delinquency hearings and the denial to children and adolescents of the constitutional safeguards to which adults are entitled.

WIDE DISCRETIONARY POWERS

The problems associated with the legal processing of juveniles have been examined carefully by the President's Commission on Law Enforcement and Administration of Justice (1967a). The judge has great discretionary powers in delinquency hearings. For example, he need not find that the youth committed the act for which he is brought before the court but may, on vague and general grounds, adjudicate him a delinquent and commit him to an institution. In these proceedings, delinquents are not guaranteed the right of counsel or necessarily provided with a competent attorney. In most cases, delinquency hearings are not open to the press or even to interested parties.

Some of the findings of recent studies suggest that the legal system operates in arbitrary ways that cause great distress. In one study, the correlations indicate that, contrary to expectation, judges who are more psychotherapeutically oriented are more likely to commit delinquents to an institution (Wheeler et al., 1968). Given this finding, it is easy to see how this may happen. Such a judge is aware of the detrimental environment in which the delinquent lives and is more trusting of the prospects of rehabilitation. The consequences, however, result in institutionalization of the adolescent in a place that serves an essentially custodial function. In this setting, the process of differential association is likely to increase his negative view of society and decrease his commitment to the general norms of society. Most judges dealing with such cases have little specialized training and their idiosyncratic views about the causes of delinquency may prevail with practically no rights of appeal on the part of the child or the parent.

A number of similar observations have been made about the prospects of rehabilitation through the intervention of the probation and parole systems. Placing an adolescent on probation supposedly includes an active therapeutic relationship with a trained adult who can help the youth plan his educational and occupational careers and can guide him towards social relationships and community activities that will minimize the prospects for further illegal behavior. In practice, such efforts are rarely successful. One of the reasons is the critical shortage of personnel for this job and the heavy case loads imposed by lack of adequate funds in most large cities. There is little evidence that probation programs, in the face of the general environment of the adolescent, have any impact in most cases.

Parole programs, that is, supervision of the offender after his release from an institution, are in even worse trouble, especially in terms of adequate personnel. Here, again, both the parole officer and the adolescent approach the parole process with considerable pessimism about the outcome. The central problem is the likelihood that both the institutional and the postinstitutional environment (where the adolescent lives while on parole) will not be much different from the environment in which he lived during his period of active delinquent behavior. For the most part, persons who hope to rehabilitate the juvenile delinquent are faced with conflicting demands from the community. On the one hand, the community wants the offender put away; on the other hand, it insists that he not be permanently separated from his familial setting. Thus institutionalization, or any other disposition by the legal system, represents only a semisolution.

EXPERIMENTAL PROGRAMS

Over the years there have been endless experimentations with various types of institutions and different patterns of probation and parole. These efforts have all been designed to counter some of the worst problems and to reduce the pessimistic outcome of routine procedures. Perhaps the most noteworthy have been the recent attempts to use a combination of environmental and psychotherapeutic interventions. In terms of institutional settings, the Highfields-type of institution is a good example of this approach (Weeks, 1958). Such institutions are usually small, caring for twenty to thirty boys at a time, and their programs feature a fairly structured environment. Usually, as at Highfields, this involves working during the day followed by sustained periods of group therapy. In these daily sessions it is hoped that with the guidance of a therapist the exchanges between the boys will develop an understanding of the mutual difficulties that confront many adolescents and promote a sharing of solutions and mechanisms for coping with them. This process helps the adolescent appraise himself and his situation realistically and provides him with a series of alternatives to illegal behavior.

While reports vary concerning the succcess of such settings, it is certain that with respect to recidivism they are no worse than other long-term institutionalization. When compared with traditional training schools, such settings hold considerable promise in terms of economics, manpower, and more humane custodial care. Whether they truly represent an improvement over routine probation or a system that would simply ignore the offenses and let the boys disappear into their environments has yet to be determined. Certainly we are well aware of the defects in the existing legal and judicial mechanisms of social control involving adolescents, and there is considerable pessimism regarding the prospects for meaningful innovation and stimulating change.

THE POLICE AND YOUTH

The relationship of the police to adolescents constitutes a broad topic which can be reviewed only briefly here. Many commentators have noted that the police, in all of their activities, are in an extremely delicate position in relation to the local community, and this is particularly true of their dealings with adolescents (President's Commission on Law Enforcement, 1967a). Many activities of youth are an embarrassment to law-enforcement agencies and present inherent difficulties in terms of control of illegal adolescent behavior.

We have already noted the variations in arrest rates and court referrals among different communities and the correlation between economic and social factors and the way the police act (Golden, 1963). Rates of delinquency are, to a considerable extent, a function of what the law is and how it is interpreted. (*See* Documentation 8.)

In dealing with the delinquent, the policeman is confronted with several ideological strains. On the one hand, his status vis-à-vis the middle-income segment of the community is likely to be damaged by his failure to press for legal action in a case where he has discretionary powers. On the other hand, most policemen are the product of working and lower-income families, and their encounters with juveniles from similar backgrounds evoke many images of their own adolescent experiences and engender considerable sympathy for the actions of the offenders. Thus the policeman is likely to behave differentially toward those whom he can identify by religion, nationality, or skin color. He also recognizes, to a considerable extent, the fallacy of legal involvement as a rehabilitative effort. Furthermore, in the organization of most police systems, little credit accrues to the officer whose activities center on the inhibition or

NUMBER AND RATE OF ARRESTS FOR ALCOHOL-RELATED OFFENSES, ST. LOUIS, MO., 1950–1960, BY AGE

Age Grouping	Number of Arrests		Per Cent Change	Arrest Rate*		Per Cent Change
	1950	1960		1950	1960	
10–16**	161	915	+468	240	1,240	+417
17–20	1,248	1,135	− 9	2,793	2,989	+ 7
21+	12,669	13,850	+ 9	2,071	2,826	+ 36

    * Per 100,000 of age grouping specified. Based on mean number of arrests for alcohol-related offenses, 1949–1951 and 1959–1961, exclusive of liquor law violations.

    ** The arrest rate for persons aged ten to sixteen is slightly inflated since it is based on alcohol-related offenses committed by persons sixteen and under. The contribution of persons below age ten would be negligible, however.

How can these trends be accounted for? First, the great increase in liquor law violations should be attributed not to a change in youthful behavior but to a change in definitions of illegal behavior. Periodic drifts in the attention of legislative and law enforcement officials, in which different areas of crime come under scrutiny and new measures are adopted to deal with these offenses, have their impact on arrest frequencies. A more stringent version of the liquor laws, adopted in 1959 in Missouri, made it a misdemeanor for anyone under the age of twenty-one to purchase, attempt to purchase, or *have in possession* intoxicating liquor, or to purchase or attempt to purchase nonintoxicating beer. Undoubtedly this has had its impact on the rise in liquor law violations.

Secondly, the seemingly drastic shift in juvenile behavior over the decade is related to a change in the administrative procedure of the St. Louis City Police Department, which now emphasizes formal rather than informal means of social control over this population segment. By 1953 the Juvenile Division of the Police Department had switched its emphasis from police athletic leagues to the careful recording of juvenile offenses, on the grounds that social work functions should be left to those professionally trained in this field and that the most effective police contribution would be the apprehension of offenders and accurate reporting of offenses. Taking this policy change into account, we reanalyzed 1953 and 1959 juvenile arrest statistics for alcohol-related offenses. This time the rise was only 28 per cent, in marked contrast to the 468 per cent rise previously reported [see table]. This discrepancy illustrates the impact of administrative changes in law enforcement procedures and serves as a caution in the interpretation of delinquency statistics. . . . (Sterne, Pittman and Coe, 1965:83–84.)

detection of adolescent crime. For the most part, career benefits derive from successful engagement with adult criminals and the "big arrest," not from action involving petty offenders, particularly if they are adolescents (Skolnick, 1966).

According to a recent study in which investigators observed police officers interacting with young people, the findings showed that when the teen-agers took a delinquent posture or demeanor, they frequently were handled officially as delinquents (Piliavin and Briar, 1964). Adolescents who were polite and appeared apologetic and contrite when stopped by the same officers were most often treated with leniency. If the offenders were defiant and wore their hair and clothes in ways that affronted adult norms, they were most likely to be treated very severely. These observations suggest that characteristics not intrinsically related to the offense may become the basis of an official action on the part of the police. Also, the police invariably try to evaluate whether or not this is an isolated incident for which a warning will prove sufficient to rehabilitate the adolescent.

The Piliavin and Briar findings should be interpreted in the light of another study that analyzed two police departments, one operating according to professional standards and the other on a paternalistic basis (Wilson, 1968). The investigator found that the professionally oriented department tended to recruit members on the basis of demonstrated performance and achievement and provided formal training for its men. Such departments are most likely to insist upon enforcement of the legal codes without preferential or differential treatment and to give more credit to crime prevention than to seniority or the spectacular arrest. One would assume that policemen in highly professional departments behave much differently toward the delinquent than do the officers in paternalistic departments where personal contacts, seniority, and relationships among members of the force carry more weight.

IMPROVING POLICE ACTIVITIES

The relationship between the police and the adolescent is usually one of ambiguity. Essentially, it involves pitting relatively unsophisticated, untrained individuals charged with law enforcement, ranging from the inspection of parking meters to the solution of murder, against a large number of restless, impetuous teen-agers toward whom they are expected to behave as fathers, guardians, and therapists. These unrealistic demands have led most large cities to develop a special squad of juvenile officers. In some communities such officers receive special training and are encouraged to focus their interest and attention on the prevention of illegal acts as much as on the apprehension of adolescent offenders. In rare instances, juvenile officers are specially picked from the ranks of college graduates and, occasionally, they have graduate training. For the most part, however, juvenile officers represent a special cadre in name only, being recruited from the regular ranks of patrolmen. Moreover, in some cities, such assignments are not looked upon as career advancements but rather as horizontal moves from one division to another within the department. Occasionally, such an assignment may even represent a punishment. This is particularly true for middle-range supervisors for whom further mobility, subsequent to heading a delinquency detail, is hard to come by. In some cities, such roles are often dead-end jobs, seldom sought and often actively resisted.

Because the police, to a large extent, practice their craft in privacy, there are relatively few studies of their interaction with adolescents. Some research, as well as a general knowledge of the streets, indicate that the police in most American communities do not occupy a particularly high status in the eyes of many adolescents. Policemen certainly are not viewed as role models by most teen-agers. At best, they are necessary evils; at worst, barriers to be overcome in the undertaking of gratifying experiences.

Some police departments from time to time engage in strong programs of delinquency prevention rather than concentrating on the apprehension of adolescent offenders or the surveillance of areas where adolescent offenses frequently occur or are likely to cause complaints from aroused citizens. These prevention programs often involve leisure-time or recreational activities such as those sponsored in many cities by Police Athletic Leagues. Although such ventures perhaps have strong public relations value, there is no confirmed evidence that they have any utility as preventive measures.

SCHOOLS AND WELFARE AGENCIES

In addition to community programs involving the courts and police, a number of experimental efforts by schools and social welfare agencies have sought to provide therapeutic intervention on an individualized basis. Many of these efforts take the form of individual counseling or group psychotherapy (Empey and Rabow, 1961; Empey, 1967). Some of these programs constitute collaborative efforts between, for example, a school department and a juvenile court or among groups that also sponsor and provide institutional care.

In New York City various sectarian agencies operate institutional facilities for problem youth as well as conduct extended community-based programs. These latter may be used instead of or subsequent to periods of treatment in a residential setting (Slavson, 1954). In many of the custodial settings, children diagnosed as emotionally disturbed are mixed with ones who have appeared formally or informally before the courts (Milner, 1964). While such agencies focus their attention on a relatively small number of clients, their programs do provide comprehensive treatment programs, including educational services, individualized psychological counseling, and halfway houses or other semiinstitutional settings to aid the progressive return of adolescents to the community.

To a much greater extent, these individualized programs serve preventative as well as rehabilitative functions. They often are able to reach a teen-ager who is manifesting minor problems before he has had intensive engagement with the legal system.

Because such programs have not been researched rigorously, the reports of sponsors regarding lower rates of recidivism and greater success by former clients in adult careers cannot be accepted as definitive evidence. Since control groups have not been included in the research designs of these programs, their success may be attributed to selection factors, that is, the programs may recruit better or more treatable participants. Nevertheless, such programs present a unique chance to test whether or not these special attempts are more successful than the typical training school. Among the advantages attributed to such programs is the opportunity to change the adolescent's environment and to provide treatment services for other family members. These programs recognize that the potential impact of periods of institutionalization or even of therapy as traditionally provided by most public programs is minute in comparison with the overall environment to which teen-agers are exposed.

MORAL PREVENTION PROGRAMS

Many communities have sponsored preventive programs devoted explicitly to the problem of social control of deviant and illegal behavior by adolescents. There are great variations in these efforts, but in general they can be classified into three broad groups: moral endeavors, recreational efforts, and reality-strategy programs. In practice, specific programs may adopt several of these positions in different aspects of their work, but for analytical purposes they can be separated.

The moral position assumes that increased exposure to an appropriate morality and the characteristics of good citizenship will tend to minimize the illegal behavior of adolescents. Such programs stem in part, of course, from the associations usually found between religious identification or religious participation and conforming behavior on the part of adolescents. However, most analysts dismiss these findings as concomitants of the common differences between middle-class and lower-class families. These critics maintain that the differences in delinquency rates are only reflections of other variables, such as socio-economic status, that are basic to the process of internalization of community norms. Many of these moral endeavors are sponsored by churches and other sectarian groups and often include components of reaching out into the community to obtain the participation of potential delinquents. At times, the lures of recreational facilities and social activities are included in these programs as mechanisms for stimulating and motivating teen-age participation.

Leisure-time pursuits have been and continue to be advanced as an effective delinquency-prevention program. The rationale underlying these efforts includes the untested assumption that excess energy can be expended and free-floating aggression reduced through active recreational pursuits, particularly aggressive and competitive sports for boys. Many proponents contend that such programs constitute a major preventative weapon and their arguments undergird the recreational programs of many community agencies. However, it is quite obvious from a series of reasonably careful attempts to link participation in recreational activities to delinquency prevention, that in and of themselves such efforts have little influence on illegal behavior. At the very best, perhaps, such programs may distract athletically minded youth from delinquent behavior. Apparently adolescents are able to separate their recreational activities from their illegal pursuits and, if interest in and opportunities for sports activities are high enough, they will conform and keep out of trouble, at least while they are playing.

It is argued by some observers, however, that such activities may actually be conducive to deviant activities, particularly the types of delinquency associated with youth gangs. Organized sports reinforce the highly competitive character of American life, tend to become commercialized, and frequently expose the players to rackets and illegal gambling. Even at the high school level, both adolescents and adults often consider winning the game more important than any consideration of the means employed in gaining the victory. Such competitive activities may provide a rallying point for teen-agers and supply the cohesiveness necessary for the maintenance of a more or less permanent group. When not engaged in recreation, the boys still have a structure for participating in illegal activities. Finally, sports activities often bring together boys from a variety of backgrounds who develop negative associations that may also take their toll. Both the athletic activities carried on in the sports arena and the parallel attempts at heterosexual recreation, such as sponsored dances and the like, apparently bring enjoyment and gratification to teen-agers, but there is no indication that they have any appreciable effect on an adolescent's prospects for deviant conduct.

As noted in the discussion of police programs, recreational activities are sometimes employed as a ploy to lure boys into a network that includes other types of intervention activities. Also, there is a related point of view that considers group activities, if supervised by a well-trained and properly motivated leader, an appropriate setting for therapeutic interventions of a group character. There has been considerable emphasis on the activities of group workers, usually specially trained social workers or psychologists, who attempt to use the reasonably natural relationships between teen-agers and the interactions between themselves and adolescents as a point of departure for involvement in the emotional lives of the participants. There are many variations in the approaches used, from attempting to combine simultaneously therapeutic intervention and recreational activities to the use of recreational activities as a means of establishing group identity and maintaining program appeal, with the therapeutic intervention a separate and, in some cases, supplementary activity. Again, despite the large number of programs that have employed these approaches, only a few rigorous evaluation efforts have been made and, consequently, little objective evidence of their efficacy exists.

In passing, it should be noted that many of these programs have been rightly accused of focusing their attention on groups that have the least need for preventive services. It is often observed that such preventive programs, ostensibly developed for low-income, highly delinquent-prone youth, engage as clients the most middle-class or upwardly mobile teenagers. These criticisms, and especially the acknowledged failure of such programs to avoid a middle-class bias, suggest little prospect for the utility of such intervention activities in delinquency prevention.

DETACHED-WORKER PROGRAMS

Over the last several decades, a series of efforts known as detached-worker programs have sought to provide a measure of controlled socialization for delinquency-prone youth living in low-income areas. The objective is to gradually motivate these teen-agers toward conformity with legal codes and acceptance of the values of the larger community (Powers and Witmer, 1951; Miller, 1958). These programs grew out of depression experiences that showed promise for the control of delinquency by dealing with youth in their immediate environment. These efforts employ nonthreatening and, to a large extent, nonevaluating adults who recognize the unusual character of urban life for low-income youth and appreciate its pervasive character. Such programs have been attempted in many cities, sometimes with highly trained workers and at other times with volunteers or persons with minimal formal training for their role.

The network of voluntary and publically supported detached-worker programs in most large cities presents a wide variation in the roles taken by the workers. Part of this variation represents different philosophies on which the programs are based, but a great deal depends on the individual temperament, interest, and motivation of the adult worker. Several studies have attempted to analyze the various roles and types of activities undertaken by detached workers (Kantor and Bennett, 1968). In general, however, a series of evaluations, even though limited in one way or another, tends to suggest that detached workers actually have minimal opportunity for rehabilitative approaches (Miller, 1962). The accommodations which the workers must make to the group in order to achieve even tentative acceptance by the members does not place them in a position to direct major changes in the socialization of the teen-agers. An additional handicap is created by the tendency of youth groups to compartmentalize their activities in ways that allow them to conform in the presence of adults or outsiders and still find considerable opportunity for illegal behavior at other times and places (Powers and Witmer, 1951; Miller, 1962; Short and Strodtbeck, 1963; Cline et al., 1968).

Detached-worker programs continuing on a large scale in urban centers today are looked at more realistically not primarily as delinquency-prevention efforts but rather as channels that may draw teen-agers into other networks and programs that have higher potentials for achieving this goal. For example, in a number of communities these programs serve as channels of recruitment for vocational training and employment-opportunity efforts. In the judgment of groups who have conducted evaluations of several programs, workers who are temperamentally suited and sufficiently skillful can develop warm and respected relationships with delinquent boys. In general, the main criticism of these programs is that the workers, once they have developed a meaningful relationship with the teen-agers, do not have a repertoire of resources and the necessary means to act. However, if one views such programs as channels rather than as ends in themselves, the worker, in his role of referral agent and advocate, may be the most effective recruiter for programs that, while initially less attractive to teen-agers, have a higher potential for social rehabilitation.

IDENTIFICATION OF DELINQUENTS

All of the programs that have been described, whether institutional or community-based, raise a major problem. In order to operate most effectively, all programs place considerable emphasis on the early identification of the delinquent so that resources can be concentrated on the high-risk groups within the population (Freeman and Weeks, 1956; Wilkins, 1965). Critics have come to recognize that such prediction efforts, as well as the process of court involvement, lead inevitably to negative consequences involving a labeling action and self-fulfilling prophecy. Involvement with courts and institutions often initiates processes that push misbehaving juveniles towards further delinquent conduct and make it more difficult for them to re-enter the conventional world (Becker, 1963, 1964; Freidson, 1965). The assumption is that when the adolescent becomes involved or tagged by the formal social-control process he becomes a member of a clearly defined category of deviance and, as a result of such labeling, is the recipient of differential responses from community members. This is a difficult problem and presents community-control agencies with a real dilemma.

On the one hand, minor and episodic delinquent behavior by the adolescent may result in formal identification as a delinquent with some measure of undesirable impact. On the other hand, society cannot ignore repeated offenses; moreover, denying offending youth the potential deterrent effect of court action or depriving them of whatever benefits might accrue from early identification and involvement in preventive programs may be equally harmful. Most experts agree that every effort should be made to minimize the impact of the delinquency-labeling process, and this requires selectivity and sensitivity in the use of appropriate delinquency-prediction instruments. Some delinquency experts argue, however, that the legal process would be much more fair to the adolescent offender if he had the same safeguards that are currently available to adults in court. Under the present juvenile court system, adolescents are not entitled to trial by jury, right of counsel, and many of the rights of appeal, although recent Supreme Court decisions are altering this policy. Further, since most delinquency hearings are held to be in confidence, the only information available to potential employers or others is the fact that the adolescent has been institutionalized, placed on probation, or in some other manner adjudicated a delinquent. Since many of the reasons for appearing before a court are minor or even trivial, the confidentiality of the proceedings, while perhaps initiated with good intentions, may have many more negative than positive consequences (President's Commission on Law Enforcement and Administration of Justice, 1967b).

ENVIRONMENTAL CONTROLS

Many of the troublesome and repeated illegal activities of young people could be prevented, or at least minimized, by relatively simple efforts on the part of the adult world. Many automobiles, for example, are attractive nuisances in the sense that they are so easy for teen-agers to steal or take for joyrides. While there are some sanctions imposed by the police and by insurance companies, certainly more efficient safeguards applied to automobiles would inhibit car theft. It would require little effort to devise a mechanism that would set off an alarm if inappropriate means were used to start a car, and it would take a minimum of legislative time to impose severe fines for leaving ignition keys in cars. Protective alarms on houses, better monitoring of public transportation, electronic surveillance of isolated places, such as parks at night, could remove opportunities for delinquency from the immediate environment of most teen-agers. The employment of modern technology in delinquency-prevention programs certainly makes sense, and many people argue that programs to control the immediate environment of the delinquent are urgently called for (Briar and Piliavin, 1965; Short and Strodtbeck, 1965; Cottrell and Wheeler, 1966). Some authorities maintain that these techniques do not get at the heart of the problem, and that the budding delinquent will only turn to other forms of delinquency. However, these are empirical issues that should be tested before drawing conclusions.

COMPREHENSIVE PROGRAMS

It is only fair to say that none of the approaches used and proposed has yielded demonstratively effective control of the delinquency problem. In general, evaluation studies have indicated minimal, if any, efficacy resulting from any of the techniques discussed here (Witmer and Tufts, 1954; Witmer, 1959).

As a consequence of the limited impact of these fragmented individual approaches and the rising influence of social analysts with a sociological and group perspective rather than a psychiatric orientation, the recent emphasis in delinquency control has been on comprehensive community programs. These large-scale intervention schemes seek to provide a variety of educational, occupational, and otherwise socially meaningful opportunities for the young adolescent, as well as to prepare him from birth to maturity with both the appropriate values and the intellectual and technical competencies to perform well according to the mandates of the larger society. These comprehensive community-wide programs, begun in the early 1960s under the Juvenile Delinquency and Youth Offenses Control Act, represent the precursors of more recent Office of Economic Opportunity poverty efforts and the more structured Model Cities programs of the Department of Housing and Urban Development.

STRUCTURAL APPROACH

The basic position of this structural approach is that juvenile delinquency and youth crime are two of the many symptoms that emerge from the community's failure to provide the conditions, services, and experiences that enable an individual to participate fully and competently in community life. These programs concentrated their efforts on low-income youth in the core city and their difficulties in utilizing legitimate means to obtain commonly accepted goals. A series of demonstration programs were developed that sought to increase the capability of the community and its component institutions to provide the services and conditions required by young people in order to gain the necessary competence (Cloward and Ohlin, 1960). Built into these efforts, as it was in the poverty program, were concerted opportunities for individuals living in low-income areas to make effective use of the programs. While this structural view holds that specific programs need to be directed at the control of delinquents and delinquency-prone teen-agers, and these were included in the program package, this is not the central focus of the intervention.

The major thesis is that, as the community becomes more competent in dealing with adolescents from low-income areas, it will be able to cope more effectively with all its problems, including the social control of the individual delinquent (Mobilization for Youth, 1964). In many communities, new agencies were set up to administer these programs. They focused on three principal areas: employment opportunities, education, and community organization (Palmore and Hammond, 1964).

PROGRAM ELEMENTS

The employment programs include special arrangements for school dropouts, instruction in the basic skills for the semiliterate, and the use of special techniques such as teaching machines, group counseling, and pre-apprenticeship training. One of the major thrusts of these programs was to increase work competence. Most proponents of this strategy held that perception by the adolescents of opportunities for gainful employment and useful occupational careers would effectively reduce the problems of delinquency (Willie, 1967). In line with this goal, extensive efforts were made to develop new educational services, modified to suit the needs of slum youth. Extensive evidence shows that disadvantaged youth are often below average in their educational skills, and current school programs, as noted previously, are frequently unsuited to rehabilitating or improving their learning potential.

Community resources also were developed to stimulate vocational aspirations among students and to gain family support for educational programs. In some cities, special work-study schedules were developed for potential dropouts, and neighborhood centers offered adult education, tutoring services, reading clinics, and the like. These programs were geared to eliminate apathy and lack of interest on the part of adult members of the communities. Apathy was related to feelings of alienation and to the adults' view that they were unable to cope with either their environment or their young. Among other efforts that were initiated to combat the climate of despair were the use of local residents as volunteers or as paid indigenous workers and the appointment of poor people to advisory boards and committees.

The key concept in all of this was the provision of opportunity—opportunity to develop the necessary skills and abilities to participate meaningfully in the community and to gain a sense of personal dignity and competence (Cloward and Ohlin, 1960).

In many ways, of course, these programs are not new. They go back some three decades to Chicago, where the idea developed that only through the mobilization of community efforts and the participation of community members was it possible to handle, over a long-term period, the problem of delinquency. Many of the programs of the President's Committee on Juvenile Delinquency and Youth Crime, established by Kennedy in 1961, were designed to test this hypothesis, and evaluation components were supposedly built into them. One of the formal requirements was for on-going research to test the efficacy of the overall program and the program components in reducing delinquency. This goal proved difficult to achieve, and only very limited empirical findings have been produced or are likely to become available. This was due in part to the well-meaning motives of those involved in the programs to get the job started rather than to take time to plan it in detail and to design accompanying research. Then, too, there were basic limitations in the technical knowledge available for accomplishing such evaluation without slowing down the programs and frustrating many of the efforts. Finally, these programs hardly had time to get started before the more inclusive Great Society efforts of the Johnson era were put into effect. Evaluations of program elements in some of the efforts have indicated discouraging results, as a summary of a Seattle work program indicates:

> This preliminary analysis of the Opportunities for Youth Project counsels caution to other programs using employment as a means of delinquency control. Perhaps a more intensive effort would have had a measurable impact. But it is also possible that work programs have not chosen the correct target. The assumption is that *boys* can be changed, and if *they* change the rest of the world will treat them differently. But the world may not recognize any change and may, therefore, not treat the boys differently, and the boys may know it. In New York, Mobilization for Youth may be following a more promising line of action by changing the community structure itself. Perhaps we should stop working so hard on the boys themselves and focus on the way they interact with the rest of society. In a sense, Opportunities for Youth did try to modify the interaction patterns which surrounded the boys. It attempted to modify the way a boy thinks the world sees him. We tried to provide a set of mirrors that would reflect a favorable image. Our results do not tell us what was lacking: Were the ideas incorrect? Or were we unable to manipulate the environment successfully (Hackler, 1966:164)?

In a number of the cities, the specific delinquency-control programs that operated at a structural level were co-opted by the Office of Economic Opportunity programs. In other communities, various pitfalls were not overcome by the President's Committee programs and they were either terminated prematurely or continued in such a watered-down form that evaluation would be meaningless. Certainly, the most important knowledge to come from the work of the President's Committee on Juvenile Delinquency is the great difficulty of implementing programs of structural change. Such efforts provoke resistance from professionals associated with established agencies in the health-and-welfare system and general distrust from the more affluent members of the community who fear any program described as radical or revolutionary. In reaction to the President's Committee (and also to the more recent Office of Economic Opportunity and Model Cities programs), limitations have been placed on the scope of the programs, sufficient funds have not been voted for their implementation, and other serious inadequacies in program application have gone unchecked. This is particularly true of the concept of community participation by low-income residents, which was never fully utilized. Certainly, the President's Committee programs were not implemented fully enough or for long enough periods of time, nor was evaluation research available to assess the impact of these efforts on the problem of delinquency.

Unfortunately, it appears that the fate of the President's Committee programs will also be shared by the OEO and Model Cities programs. It is very likely that the superficiality of these efforts and their eventual curtailment, in view of political reaction and the exigencies of the Vietnam war and other domestic commitments, will limit if not preclude any real test of the structural approach. However, in the light of some fifty years of fruitless experience with other approaches, it is reasonable to believe that emphasis on a structural approach that tries to deal with the problems of value-change and opportunity remains the most promising basis for dealing effectively on a long-term basis with the problem of delinquency.

adolescent rebellion

Some analysts of the contemporary American scene contend that the concept of juvenile delinquency is a value-laden and unsophisticated approach to the problems of adolescence. These critics note the arbitrariness of the meanings assigned the term *delinquency*, the differential relationship between deviant and illegal behavior from community to community, the discriminatory response of the legal system to the deviant conduct of low-income children compared with middle-income offenders, and the distinction between behaviors that are clearly illegal and those that are regarded as minor offenses because performed by minors, such as truancy or buying liquor. As Friedenberg (1966) notes, the term *delinquency* characterizes only a single type of rebellious adolescent behavior. He and other experts hold it would be more appropriate to consider the whole spectrum of supposed deviation from community norms on the part of teen-agers. Considering the limitations we have noted in the approach to delinquency, this view certainly has some relevance. It also serves to place in proper context the behavioral manifestations of adolescents across all strata of the community and allows us to understand some of the problems experienced by girls as well as boys. An approach that focuses exclusively on delinquency obscures many of the differences among teen-agers from middle- and upper-class families, and it largely ignores the problem behavior of females.

TYPES OF ACTIVITIES

There are a number of deviations other than delinquency within contemporary American society that are at least of equal concern to informed community members. Many of these deviations do not involve any confrontation with a formal social-control system; therefore, accurate data on incidence and prevalence are extremely rare and estimates vary widely. Indeed, it is plausible to argue that if the behavior of adolescents handled outside of the legal system were taken into account—that is, children referred to private practitioners or mental health centers or those who spend periods of their adolescent years in boarding schools or informally arranged foster homes—the differentials in socio-economic status reported in all delinquency statistics would be drastically reduced. Further, if such statistics were available, it is likely that the apparent differential existing between deviant conduct of males and females would also be considerably reduced.

Much of the behavior characterized as rebellious by the sensational press and other mass media certainly is of limited concern in the analysis of social problems. It seems evident that successive generations of American adolescents have chosen various collective means to display their unrest and express their dissatisfaction with their age role or, as some analysts believe, to obtain substitute gratifications for ends denied them by the adult community. Three decades ago, adolescents—particularly girls—manifested literally hysterical behavior over such singers as Frank Sinatra. More recently the teen-age population took up the Beatles only to replace them with such homegrown phenomena as the Vanilla Fudge and the Jefferson Airplane. In the Sinatra era, peg-legged zoot suits were the mark of adolescent sophistication. Today, the unisex look is in, with boys as well as girls favoring shoulder-length hair, and hip-hugging dungarees. Such behavior on the part of teen-agers can be viewed as attempts to seek an identity and a status in the community. Various explanations are given for behavior of this sort as well as for the more serious types yet to be discussed. The persuasiveness of any of the popular theories is impossible to support on the basis of empirical research.

ADOLESCENTS AS A MINORITY GROUP

One view is that rebellious adolescent behavior is associated with the minority status of youth in the community. Proponents of this view suggest that rebellion is the response of the adolescent to the restrictions placed upon his opportunities for achievement of status and the good things of life. Legal restrictions on voting, buying liquor, signing contracts, obtaining drivers' licenses, and the like thwart the adolescent at every turn. There are also realistic limitations on his ability to participate economically, both because of his inability to compete successfully with adults on the basis of technical knowledge and experience and because many suitable jobs have been eliminated by automation, unionization, or modernization. Take, for example, the job of elevator operator which used to be open to teen-agers. Today, the elevator is either self-service, operated by union personnel, or has been replaced by escalators.

Certainly an ideology of subordination besets the adolescent in his activities and roles in the community. He is eligible to go to war at the age of eighteen and is drafted at nineteen, yet most states fail to recognize his voice politically until he is twenty-one. Even teen-agers capable of gainful employment or already fully self-supporting are often required to submit to adult guardianship. American society limits severely the meaningful roles the adolescent may take in the community, literally forcing him to seek other means of gaining the recognition he may deserve and thereby reducing the hostility he may feel about his minority status.

SEXUAL EXPRESSION

We have already discussed the implications of sexual deprivation and sexual restrictions encountered by the adolescent. Social analysts who subscribe to this view usually consider sex to be a sufficient, if not a necessary, motivation for adolescent rebellion. Even many adults who reject a psychosexual interpretation of adolescent behavior are likely to view with alarm any nonconformity in this area. Such people also tend to further compound the problem by giving at least tacit approval to a double standard. Behavior that they would deplore and condemn for girls is often condoned or ignored in the case of boys.

Although a number of experts on adolescence have concerned themselves with the apparent increase of premarital sexual relations and the phenomenon of going steady and pseudocourtships during high school, there is no evidence, at least at the present, that changes in heterosexual behavior have serious consequences on the subsequent careers of community members. Perhaps the most considered opinion in this respect is that the changes in sexual conduct among adolescents mirror the modifications, which some individuals refer to as the sexual revolution, among adult members of the community. Given the greater social acceptability of early marriages and working wives, as well as the less severe sanctions on premarital and extramarital sexual activities, one would expect these changes to filter down to the adolescent population. Although some critics continue to maintain that the present modes of sexual conduct and heterosexual behavior among adolescents are an index of the extent of their conflict and unrest, evidence to support this conclusion is extremely weak.

PERCEPTIONS OF ADULTHOOD

Another view of the adolescent dilemma recognizes that teen-agers are confronted with the good things of the adult community yet are denied access to such goods and experiences by virtue of their inadequate repertoire of skills and an arbitrary limitation of opportunities. The adolescent, particularly the late adolescent, is well aware of the breadth of hedonistic pleasures and the variety of material goods that the average adult has an opportunity to enjoy (England, 1960). These range from the trappings of affluence, such as automobiles, clothes, and theater tickets, to personal conveniences, including privacy, pleasures of the senses, opportunities for meaningful participation in the community, and recognition as a useful and valued member of society.

This view holds that the lack of means to participate in the good life results in rebellious types of behavior. For example, analysts have observed that teen-agers, and particularly teen-agers in blue-collar families, have only superficial and often false conceptions of the role-behavior of adults in the community. They are much more likely to see the glamour of certain occupational pursuits but not the requirements of technical know-how and the physical and emotional risks sometimes involved. Only the frequent airline traveler is aware of the monotonous and unattractive aspects of the stewardess's job—the fact that she spends most of her time running up and down the aisle serving food and drinks and fending off the propositions of middle-aged married men. Only the family member or friend of a physician realizes the stress and harassment of a long and crowded workday and the depressions that accrue from his inability to cope with his patients' problems or, even worse, his remorse over errors in diagnosis and treatment.

In many ways the adolescent perceives adulthood as holding considerably more gratifications than actually accrue, and he fails to recognize or take into account the liabilities and problems of adult life. This view of rebellion contends that faulty communication fails to provide the adolescent with sufficient realistic information and an appropriate anticipatory socialization to allow him to place in perspective the disadvantages as well as the advantages, the requirements as well as the rewards of adult status. Such a view is similar to the frustration-aggression position (described in Part I) and it is compounded by the teen-ager's unrealistic perceptions of the adult role in the American community.

DISSATISFACTION WITH SOCIETY

Perhaps the view of adolescent rebellion most uncomfortable for adults to accept is the theory that adolescents find current life in the American community, even when perceived realistically and accurately, to be undesirable. Such a position maintains that in today's urban environment adolescents, particularly those in their late teens, become quite aware of the contradictions in values that exist both within the family and other primary-group networks and in the community as a whole. The adolescent rejects the life of the community because he perceives the hypocrisy in the accepted norms and the large degree of corruption, lack of humanitarianism, and superficiality of belief that exist among adults. Some argue, of course, that the adolescent's rejection of community life is an approach to resolving his own personal conflicts related to sexual development and interpersonal relations at an informal peer and family group level. During this decade, however, the active engagement of high school and particularly college students with the problems of discrimination and of international conflict suggests that such an explanation cannot fully explain the reactions of contemporary youth. An unbiased assessment must recognize that they are to some extent truly perceptive critics of the discontinuities of contemporary community life.

CHILDHOOD EXPERIENCES

Finally, some have attempted to explain the rebellious behavior of youth in terms of childhood deficiencies. Here one comes full circle to the view that prior inadequate socialization accounts for present rebellious adolescent behavior. Such a view, of course, suggests that the types of illegal teen-age activities previously discussed represent only a subcategory of rebellious activities and that different types of earlier socialization deficiencies are associated with the particular forms of rebellion engaged in by different categories of adolescents. The demonstration of this relationship is complicated by the fact, already reported, that the social-control systems respond as differentially to children of different social backgrounds as to adolescents of different social backgrounds and provide more serious and severe sanctions for certain types of rebellious activities than for others.

RECONCILING VIEWS

At present the level of research sophistication does not permit an estimation of the relative cogency of one explanation of rebellion in comparison with others. For the most part, the various explanations are not contradictory but rather are cumulative or at least interacting in their impact on the behavior of adolescents. For example, the faulty perceptions of teen-agers may be reinforced by their rejection of community life, for not only may adolescents be disenchanted with the community but they may also be unaware of the socially acceptable means of initiating social change and social action. Certainly an adolescent's socialization deficits and social characteristics have much to do with his opportunities for successful engagement with other young people in their attempts to handle in a meaningful manner the resultant problems of sexuality, of their new statuses within the family, and their precarious position in the larger community.

THE HIPPIE MOVEMENT

Interestingly enough, adolescent rebellion in recent years has taken on a relatively organized character. The hippie movement, for example, identifies a relatively large number of adolescents who have dropped out either on a full-time or, sometimes, a weekend basis. The movement is characterized by a specialized vocabulary, an ideal of sharing all resources, an emphasis upon nonviolence, and many symbolic expressions of love, peace, and goodwill. In many ways the hippie movement exemplifies the dissatisfaction of today's adolescents with the contemporary social order. It is possible, of course, to idealize the movement and to commend as admirable some of the outward behavior of adolescents attracted to it. In a number of ways, however, commitment to the hippie movement raises severe problems for the present and future of such dedicated young people.

Even if one does not question the obvious abandonment of certain norms with respect to dress, sexual conduct, and social interaction, there persists the difficulty of teen-agers leaving school and abandoning their training for future occupational careers. (*See* Documentation 9.) An additional danger exists in the frequently reported use of "hard" drugs by participants in the movement. Whatever may be the admirable qualities inherent in young people making their own literature, developing their own tastes in art, and confronting the adult American community with the unreasonableness of its social life, they must be assessed

At eight o'clock that evening I met Chuck at the Rising Sun Tribe's pad. . . .

The meeting was held in a 9' by 9' room—with the usual wall-to-wall greasy mattresses. When we opened the door to the room for the meeting, we found a young couple, Pete and Jay, who had admittedly just finished "making love." Steve, the leader, gave them hell. "I told you to use the 'ball room'; this room is for our meeting."

The tribal meeting went on for about an hour. It consisted primarily of various diatribes leveled at one another for not helping to paint the upstairs apartment and not participating fully in the tribe.

In one case a young fellow was chastised for sleeping out every night with a girl who had been, but was no longer, a member of the tribe. The young man, Brian, was almost voted out of the tribe for his misbehavior. His defense was somewhere in the philosophical area of "love thy neighbor." He was a persuasive lawyer and the group finally agreed that "balling anyone was a person's individual decision" and not a tribal issue.

After their formal conference, I interviewed the group about various personal matters: their views of the world and their tribal association. . . .

LY: Let me ask this question of the tribe. This is always a delicate subject with people. Maybe it shouldn't be. I'll just ask how much screwing really goes on around here? Is there more sex life around here than, let's say, back at your high school?

B: Oh, wow, ha, ha . . . I don't know that, I think there's more at my school. It isn't hidden that much here. Back at school, sex is a taboo thing. I mean the teacher's don't talk about it, the students ain't supposed to talk about it, the moms and pops don't talk about it. Nobody talks about it. If you do anything, you do it behind everybody's back. Up here it is open, it's a thing, it's part of life, and I think that it's beautiful. I enjoy it very much myself. Here, what happens is that the girls don't play so many games. They play a few, but they don't play so many. You just ask a girl and she'll say yes or no.

There are girls around here that hit on guys—two or three different guys a day sometimes. It's much freer here. When you are in a group and you and a girl want to ball and there are some guys with you and you want to get rid of them, you don't try to explain to them. Like if you were at school or something, you know, like "Would you do us a favor—go out and get some ice cream or something?" But here you just say, "Now look, I'm going in that room and that room is the 'ball room,' you know, I'm going to do 'my thing,' excuse me for a while." The way it is back home, everybody knows that girls are getting screwed and that guys are having a good time. I mean, everybody knows that. Ninety-five per cent of the girls in the school I went to were not virgins. Everybody knows that. But the first time that the fact comes out that a girl has been screwed in school, automatically she becomes a whore. Here it is different. Like I mean, back home there are lots of girls getting screwed in school, you know, and everybody secretively knows it. But the first time somebody comes along and says, "Hey, Mary got screwed last night," everybody starts on the big thing that Mary is a whore. Now here, like Mary got screwed last night and she went and did it, well, gee whiz, good enough—wow, I mean what's it to me? I mean, wow, that's the way it is here. (Yablonsky, 1968:117–122.)

in the context of the physical and mental health problems arising from the conditions under which at least some hippies live, the reported frequency of drug use and, perhaps most important, the impact of school-leaving on their future lives.

Contemporary analysts of social problems have not yet had an opportunity to pay much attention to the hippie movement (Yablonsky, 1968), but clearly its effects are considerable on the lives of those most deeply involved. As with many of the other types of adolescent rebellion and the associated problems of teen-agers, the community seems particularly ill-equipped to cope with the undesirable aspects of the hippie movement. In various large cities that have developed neighborhoods dominated by hippies, efforts to provide at least modest amounts of health care and food are being undertaken. But the approaches of religious leaders, police, and social workers to redirect the movement in ways that will minimize its undesirable effects have proved futile, and this manifestation of the alienation of youth needs to be reckoned with seriously.

LATER CONSEQUENCES OF CERTAIN ACTS

There are several additional dimensions of rebellious behavior among adolescents that ought to be noted with extended concern. Some of these represent problems not because of the immediate harmful consequences to the adolescent but because the normative standards of the community define the behavior as deviant. Such activities are likely to result in prolonged stigmatization and involvement in a web of treatment agencies from which escape is difficult. Unmarried motherhood is illustrative of a problem that is complicated by lasting stigma. The use of marijuana and other drugs characterized as stimulants or depressants may involve the adolescent in a network of legal and social agencies. Drug addiction, in the sense of heroin addiction, will be discussed in the next chapter since the prevalence of "hard" drugs is apparently a problem of this later age. However, the use by younger adolescents of marijuana and of depressants and stimulants, including alcohol, plagues our society to a considerable degree and may be related to legal entanglements (*see* Documentation 10). Becker (1953:241) argues that users of marijuana indeed do so for pleasure:

> A person, then, cannot begin to use marijuana for pleasure, or continue its use for pleasure, unless he learns to define its effects as enjoyable, unless it becomes and remains an object which he conceives of as capable of producing pleasure.

While it is a widely held belief, although one not backed up by much research evidence, that the likelihood of related deviant behavior is greater among persons who frequently expose themselves to stimulants

drinking behavior of delinquent boys

**PERCENTAGE DISTRIBUTIONS OF TYPES OF DRINKERS
BY PREVIOUS COURT INVOLVEMENT**

Types	No Previous Formal Offense	Probation or Suspension	Institution- alization
1. Abstainers	39	25	25
2. One-timers	8	10	5
3. Moderate social drinkers	33	35	30
4. Heavy social drinkers	8	15	17
5. Relief or kick drinkers	5	9	9
6. Pathological drinkers	7	6	14
N	*120*	*285*	*87*

Chi square = 23.74; 10 *df; p* < .01

On the drinking behavior of 500 delinquent boys, the data indicate that the percentage of alcohol users is about the same among delinquent boys as among other high-school boys in certain areas with a similar degree of urbanization; about 2 out of 3 teen-age boys drink beverage alcohol. On the other hand, unlike the high-school students, the frequency of excessive drinking is considerable among delinquent boys. Of the 360 boys who were users, 71% reported they had been "high," 58% that they had been drunk, 39% that they had been sick, and 23% that they had "passed out." The occurrence and frequency of these events are from 2 to 3 times greater than those reported in the high-school studies.

Since we were also interested in the extent to which delinquency is associated with alcohol use, the final example of a correlate of type of drinker deals with occurrence and disposition of previous offense. The relationship between drinker type and court involvement is presented in the above table. Boys without previous formal offenses are least likely to be found in either the heavy-drinking-without-pathological-symptoms category, in the marked-effect category or the type high-on-drinking-with-pathological behavior. Also, at least among boys in the last type, the group most predisposed toward alcoholism, there tends to be an overrepresentation of boys previously institutionalized in comparison with those either placed on probation or suspension or without previous formal offenses. This finding may be explained in part by age, since, of course, age is correlated with recidivism and probably with severity of disposition. Again, though we started out with a fairly large study group, the problems of introducing age as a control variable need to be taken into account. The known correlation between age and severity of and type of delinquency, and that between age and drinking behavior documented in this study, points to the need for study groups of extensive size, and which represent the general adolescent population, in order to develop a clear epidemiological picture. (Blacker et al., 1965:232–234.)

and depressants, the users represent social problems in their own right (Maddox and McCall, 1967; Sterne, Pittman and Coe, 1965). Unwed teen-age mothers and adolescent alcohol and drug users clearly are viewed as social problems by most community members, for they are visible indictments of a society that has failed in earlier years to prepare its near-adults to handle their postpuberty years.

unmarried motherhood

As with many other problems discussed in this book, it is difficult to estimate precisely the incidence of pregnancies among adolescent girls. This is partly due to the recentness of the attention given the problem. Public concern with sexual conduct dates only from the Kinsey reports of the 1950s, and considerable secrecy still surrounds illegitimate pregnancies, forced marriages, and illegal abortions. Therefore, the extensiveness of the problem is largely a matter of conjecture. It has been estimated that one out of every five marriages is preceded by conception; in perhaps one out of every three teen-age marriages the girl is already pregnant (Vincent, 1961).

Unmarried motherhood, of course, represents a behavioral anomaly and is looked upon as a social deviance regardless of the age of the female involved.

REASONS FOR PREGNANCY

The simple explanation that illegitimate pregnancy is related to high rates of sexual relations outside marriage and ignorance or inconsistent use of birth control measures is questioned by many practitioners with a clinical concern for unmarried mothers. Many psychiatrists and social workers believe that girls who become pregnant are not simply behaving contrary to the moral norms of the community and got "caught" but are motivated toward pregnancy as well as toward the physical or emotional gratification of sexual relations. Particularly among teen-age girls, pregnancy is viewed as a flaunting of the norms of chastity and appropriate heterosexual conduct for the age group and is evidence of rebellion and emotional disturbance.

Most researchers with a sociological orientation do not find much evidence to support these clinical impressions. For one thing, practitioners see only an extremely biased sampling of all girls who become pregnant out of wedlock. The age and social status of the unmarried mother is strangely related to the agency to which she will turn for help. Almost all of the statistics on unmarried mothers are based on studies of particular agencies and reflect the type of clients these agencies attract and accept rather than any representative sample of all illegitimately pregnant girls. The effect of this selection process on the research results is further distorted by the fact that, for each pregnant girl who gives birth to an illegitimate child, there are about fifteen others who marry while they are pregnant and approximately another eighty-five who have abortions (Gebhard et al., 1958).

INTERVENTION

If teen-age pregnancy were simply a matter of chance, resulting from random accidents, then effective contraception or accessible abortion would handle the problem of unmarried motherhood. Very few community members would ascribe to this solution. Whatever the basis of the pregnancy, the event is severely disabling, accounting in many cases for school dropouts, alienation from the family, and stigma in the eyes of many adults if not of the girl's peers.

The other solution, hiding the pregnancy and placing the child for adoption, is most commonly proposed as the best intervention approach. The difficulty it raises is twofold. As noted in a preceding chapter, there are differential opportunities for adoption, depending on the religion and race of the child. In addition, the prospective mother must carry the child to full term and, as a consequence, her status as a prospective mother becomes apparent to a wide spectrum of community members, including teachers, friends, the extended family, and so on. The labeling and stigmatization resulting from this process is frequently severe. It should also be noted that irrational formal barriers are often put into play, such as preventing the adolescent girl from attending school during her last months of pregnancy and, in some cases, requiring legal actions against the putative father. An added problem is the girl's ambivalence toward surrendering her baby because of her maternal feelings and her reaction to guilt feelings. In any event, the resulting discontinuities in the life career of the adolescent girl who becomes pregnant often lead to interpretations of adolescent sexual relations as symptomatic of mental illness. The community's reaction can be explained as a consequence of moral indignation rather than any rational understanding of the situation. Nevertheless, young unmarried mothers and other adolescent girls who act out in the sexual sphere constitute one of the major population groups frequently seen by psychiatrists in private practice and by mental health personnel associated with community clinics.

Most psychiatrists today who have considerable contact with such patients are realistic about the limitations of therapy. In most instances the treatment procedures involve considerable counseling on proper birth control procedures as well as attempts to help the girl acquire more insight into the motivations which underlie her deviant behavior.

When the adolescent girl's sexual conduct or unmarried motherhood status is the result of relationships with older men or appears to have been undertaken for money, society may intervene through its legal-control system and adjudicate the child a delinquent. By far the largest proportion of females legally classified as delinquent are girls whose precipitating offense was in the area of sexual conduct. Unmarried mothers, participants in juvenile sex clubs, and teen-age prostitutes, as well as girls who act out their rebellious behavior by indiscreet promiscuity, represent only a small portion of the total universe of girls who find themselves pregnant. Whether teen-age pregnancy is a much greater problem today or is simply more visible and therefore of wider concern because of changed attitudes about public discussion of sexual conduct is an open question. Nevertheless, its prevalence in the average American community makes it an important problem for consideration.

emotional disorders

Adolescence is the period in which one begins to find considerable manifestations of behavior that are commonly regarded both by psychiatric practitioners and the general public as symptomatic of mental illness. The prevalence of mental illness, particularly the functional psychoses such as schizophrenia, are most typically found in persons of older age. The peak period for such disorders, at least when measured by rates of institutionalization, occur in the twenty-five to forty year age group. However, the frequency of these disorders during adolescence is sufficiently great to note it here and to anticipate our discussion of this problem in the chapter that follows.

MANIFESTATION OF SYMPTOMS

Many case studies that document patient experience prior to the visibility of the illness, that is, before hospitalization or active psychiatric care, frequently report similar, though perhaps less severe, manifestations of the symptoms during the teen-age years. Adolescence also represents a period in which a significant portion of young people are diagnosed as psychoneurotic, and there are frequent comments on the manifestation of psychosomatic or psychophysiological disorders in this age group. Both of these terms are very diffuse, and the number of individuals so diagnosed and treated varies greatly, depending on the definition applied by the practitioner. Perhaps the most inclusive way of expressing the problem is to suggest that many individuals in the community fail to handle anxiety adequately or at least constructively. Both psychoneurotic and psychosomatic symptoms are frequently held to be reactions to such anxiety: a failure of the individual either to cope internally with psychological threats or to express anxiety in ways defined by the culture as meaningful and instrumental. Such neuroses take many forms, ranging from organic dysfunctions, such as paralysis and tics, to phobias (the unrealistic fear of specific objects or situations) or obsessive-compulsive reactions and the inability to control behavior that, at least to the patient if not to others, is morbid or unreasonable.

Another common manifestation is depressive reactions often associated with feelings of guilt and characterized by withdrawal, crying, fatigue, and self-depreciation. Suicide, it should be noted, is one of the most frequent causes of death during this age period. While accurate data on prevalence and incidence are not available, we do know that somewhere between 5 and 10 per cent of the young men examined for admission to the armed forces are rejected for psychoneurotic illness (Leighton et al., 1964).

Many psychiatrists hold that an even greater portion of the population at one time or another experiences psychosomatic illness. Anxiety is expressed either directly as a physical illness or as a causative factor in the development of a physical disorder. This is a common explanation for such problems as colitis and ulcers and, less frequently, of chronic sinusitis and upper respiratory infections. A popular view is that such manifestations, particularly those of a severe character, represent the cumulative defects in interpersonal relations and that early childhood experiences have a particularly important influence on the way adolescents and adults cope with anxieties, frustrations, and insecurities. The problem of neurotic behavior is raised in this discussion of adolescence because it is frequently assumed that the ambiguous status of the adolescent in our culture is a precipitating factor in the manifestation of neurotic behavior.

TREATMENT

Certainly among middle-income families there is considerable referral of adolescents to physicians and others specializing in emotional illness for behavior which the professional mental health practitioner would identify as neurotic. The middle-class child strives, often desperately, during his teen-age years for parental approval, particularly for excellence in school, recognition in sports, participation in voluntary associations, and popularity in terms of his peer-group relations. In the last area, special importance is attached to the development of normal heterosexual relationships. According to some observers, the identification of behavior among middle-class adolescents as neurotic is merely an alternate diagnosis of the behavior as delinquent; others view it as a functional equivalent. The latter group argues that while there are certainly qualitative differences between illegal behavior and neurotic behavior, such differences are the result of the cultural constraints that channel the ways adolescents from different social classes cope with their anxieties.

Another opinion is that neurotic behavior appears more visible in middle-class adolescents than in lower-class youth because of the different networks of health caretakers with which middle-class families are involved; poor families are plagued by great quantities of undiagnosed neurotic illness. Such a view is reinforced by community studies which suggest that social classes have different attitudes and different definitions of atypical and unusual behavior, particularly on the part of adolescents (Freeman and Giovannoni, 1969). In any event, whether all of these explanations hold or whether one is more pertinent than another, the urban American community provides a network of private practitioners who serve as treatment agents for a significant proportion of adolescents in the middle-income population. There is a continual expansion of public and voluntarily supported programs to render such services more uniformly across the population. The greatest impetus to these activities has come from the comprehensive community mental health programs sponsored by the federal government.

Various interpretations have been made of the utility and efficacy of psychiatric treatment of neurotic adolescents. There is very little experimental evidence to suggest that any marked benefits accrue even from long-term counseling and intensive psychotherapy. In these times, some critics question whether the manpower and economic resources expended by school systems for guidance counselors, by voluntary agencies for psychotherapists, and by mental hospitals for psychiatric personnel have appreciably reduced the behavioral problems of adolescents in comparison with teen-agers who are untreated (Meyer et al., 1965).

Regardless of the position one takes concerning the efficacy of therapeutic programs to deal with the outward manifestations of anxiety and with the neurotic behavior of adolescents, the current resources of most communities are clearly inadequate. The critical shortage of professional practitioners in most communities precludes any concerted attack on the problem if the basis of the program is a one-to-one relationship with the individual adolescent.

PREVENTION

Within the mental health field, particularly with respect to the emotional problems of the adolescent, attention has recently shifted from individual treatment to prevention. In the main, preventive efforts take on the generalized programmatic elements identified with the structural and communication types of intervention. They include, for example, providing information on mental health and mental illness as part of the school curricula, liberalizing and extending the public conception of the range of behavior that may be viewed as normal, and seeking to integrate the adolescent more fully in community affairs.

Of particular interest is the new type of program referred to as mental health consultation. Although these efforts attempt to reach all age groups in the community, they are particularly relevant to the problems of adolescents. Advocates of this preventative approach contend that professional resources should not be expended indiscriminately on individual patients but rather should serve an advisory or consultative function to persons in key roles who have sustained contact with adolescents. For example, a psychiatrist or social worker assigned to a school consults with the teachers about general problems and specific students. Except in extremely serious cases, it is the teacher, acting as gatekeeper, who has the responsibility and the contact with the students. The insight acquired by such gatekeepers—school teachers, recreation workers, and so on—will promote more meaningful relationships between them and the adolescents and will provide a basis for the adults to deal with those adolescents whose behavior problems, if more severe, would require the attention of other professionals (Caplan, 1966).

These consultative programs are sometimes part of a broader mental health effort and are tied into the community mental health system. In such cases, the consultants operate in conjunction with programs of individual and group therapy and of mental health education. The policy position of most planners and program developers in the mental health field is that such a broad approach represents the most promising solution to the psychological problems of community members and the extensive needs of adolescents in this area.

school achievement

Perhaps the adolescent problem that is uppermost in the concern of both public and expert opinion is academic achievement. Several reasons account for this interest. Many people have identified the links between illegal behavior of youth, emotional disorders, and the stress and strains of the educational process. The interrelationships between these various problems can take a number of different norms. On the one hand, as we have noted, the stress placed on academic achievement by more affluent families is related to the anxieties of adolescents which are, in turn, expressed perhaps in neurotic behavior. On the other hand, lack of parental encouragement by low-income families limits the educational achievement of their children (Alexander and Campbell, 1964; Rehberg and Westby, 1967). The failure of adolescents to find satisfactions in their educational experiences and the evidence that low-income adolescents perceive only limited opportunities to participate in higher education may be associated with delinquent behavior. This, however, is only one perspective of our concern with the educational process.

SCHOOL DROPOUTS

A second concern relates to the demands of the adult world that place the critical decision regarding an individual's total life-place in the community upon his successful completion of high school and his ability to pursue some form of advanced training. The high dropout rate now characteristic of many communities places in jeopardy the work careers of a whole generation of youth. The rate is not only excessive, but it is also disproportionately distributed among ethnic groups and socio-economic classes. In certain low-income areas of major cities, dropout rates may range from 20 to 25 per cent or more of the entering high school class. The dropout rate, however, does not reveal the true extent of the problem. Many recipients of high school diplomas are functionally illiterate; that is, they do not measure up to the minimal standards set by the armed forces, the entrance requirements for most work activities, or the normal levels necessary to render intelligent decisions and participate in the affairs of the community. As we noted in our consideration of the pervasive social problem of economic participation, ours is a highly technological society in which a repertoire of academic skills is necessary for the majority of work tasks. The completion of ten or more grades of school or even a high school diploma is meaningless for a student who cannot read, write, or do simple arithmetic.

UNDERACHIEVEMENT

These problems are closely related to the general question of under-achievement of American youth. The increasing requirements for professional and technical personnel and the shortages that exist in many fields represent in part a discrepancy between the potential of adolescents and their realization of educational opportunities. The issue of under-achievement is not limited to one social group but, at different levels, operates among youth of all economic classes. It represents a persistent deficiency in our national life and constitutes an important gap with respect to the community's requirements.

Furthermore, we are confronted with a situation in which the popular culture demands some college or university education, and virtually stigmatizes the person who has not at least set foot inside the doors of an institution of higher learning. Because of the inability of a community to maximize the learning experience during adolescence, many of the programs undertaken by students in college consist of efforts to provide skills and technical training that they should and could have obtained earlier in their educational careers. It is necessary in many instances for college freshmen to take remedial arithmetic before they can undertake a course in statistics, or rudimentary grammar before they can begin English composition. The consequences of inadequate high school achievement represent an important force that limits the upgrading of university education. These facts came to public notice and to the attention of educators through a series of surveys and investigations undertaken by Conant (1959) and his associates. They were literally appalled by the methods, approaches, and content that constitute the educational exposure of many adolescents in high school.

DEFICIENCIES OF HIGH SCHOOLS

The problems of education at the grammar school level, and particularly the difficulties faced by inner-city schools, continue into high school. With the exception of a number of suburban high schools and a few large cities that have developed elite high schools for superior students, the secondary school system can be indicted virtually across the country. The reasons for this deplorable condition have been examined and reported in detail. The difficulties include the failure of the teaching profession to attract top quality personnel because of the relatively low salary in relation to the years of required training, the low social status of the profession within American communities, and the lack of significant opportunities for advancement, increased income, and gratification in comparison with other professions.

The training of teachers is another difficulty frequently mentioned (Riesman, 1956). With few exceptions, the education of teachers is relegated to separate schools with inadequate faculties and outmoded curricula. There are noteworthy exceptions and certain schools of education have professors who are as esteemed in their fields of concentration as are those in other graduate or professional schools. But in general, the majority of high school teachers are trained, not by scholars and researchers, but by educational technicians who water down and package the information. The chemistry teacher does not learn how to be a chemist but how to be a teacher who knows something about chemistry, and courses in Freudian psychology and the development of lesson plans are given parallel status with ones that focus on substantive knowledge in the field of chemistry. Critics of high school education maintain that much of the problem is due to the perpetuation of mediocrity by inadequate schools of education that represent nothing more than extensions of the normal schools that trained teachers during the last century.

Much of the problem of underachievement and some of the problem of school dropouts is undoubtedly related to the rigidities of the high school educational system, the lack of creativity on the part of teachers, and the failure to motivate students to realize their full potential. The solution recommended by many experts is to bring schools of education into the more general orbit of the university, to recognize the need for variety and variation in teaching styles and approaches, and also to make use of new concepts for learning and innovative techniques for teaching.

Other critics of secondary schools have cited as a problem their over-emphasis on sports. Coleman (1960; 1961) has considered the problem after studying athletics in a number of high schools:

> It is indisputable that the interscholastic sports function to give the school and the community a collective identity. Few principals would seriously consider dispensing with these games. Yet, it is also indisputable that athletic contests create serious problems for schools. Perhaps the most serious problem is the change they engender in the institution itself. Their very importance to the life of the school transforms the school from an institution devoted to learning into an institution focused, at least partly, on athletics.
>
> It is useful to wonder whether another mechanism might not give the school collective goals without effecting this transformation. . . . The most obvious course is to keep the game but to change the content in the direction of educational goals. . . .
>
> There is some experience with games and contests other than athletics, the most extensive being with debate. In a number of areas where debate leagues have flourished, these contests have generated some of the same community and school enthusiasm and involvement that is evident with althletic games. In a few states, interscholastic leagues promote competition in other fields than athletics: music, drama, mathematics. Although the effects of these contests have not been adequately evaluated, they do provide examples of what might be done (Coleman, 1961:42–43).

THE MULTI-TRACK SYSTEM

Another issue that currently concerns educators is the multi-track system that has been adopted in most communities. While the American system is not as rigid as that of the British (Richmond, 1956), the young high school student is confronted with a series of alternate educational programs often labeled "college preparatory," "general," "commercial," or "vocational." Once the student (or his parents) elect or, as is often the case, is coerced into selecting one program, there is little opportunity for him to shift on the basis of changes in his interests or motivation. Middle-class children who are incapable intellectually of successfully com-

DOCUMENTATION 11

values and delinquency

RELATIONSHIP OF PEER ADMIRATION OF GOOD GRADES AND PEER-VALUE INDEX (By age, boys only)

| Peer-Value Index | GOOD GRADES ADMIRED BY PEERS | | | |
| | 10–13 Years | | 14–19 Years | |
	A Lot	Ambiva-lent	A Lot	Ambiva-lent
Low	43%	21%	55%	27%
Medium	38	48	35	30
High	18	31	9	43
N =	(76)	(71)	(65)	(60)

The table categorizes two age-groups of boys by their perception of their peers' admiration for good grades and their peer-value index scores. The responses of "some" and "not at all" were compared to the "a lot" responses. The school variable is treated as independent on the basis of the findings relating to value stability.

The table clearly reveals that association with peers who are ambivalent toward the rewards of school is likely to lead to association with peers who are attracted to deviant values. Although the relationship is strong at both ages, there is a greater polarization of peer values at the older age range. Greater consistency among peer values is accompanied by increased consonance between deviant and ambivalent school values.

The importance of assessing the peer orientation toward school in depicting the distribution of peer-value index scores is further highlighted by considering the interaction effect of individual value choices (past and present) and peer orientations toward good grades. Peer orientation toward school is strongly related to both the individual and the peer indices of values. (Lerman, 1968:232.)

pleting a university education are left entirely unprepared for jobs in the crafts and trades which they might undertake competently. Many students, particularly those of low economic status who are the victims of poor elementary schools, inadequate homes, and other environmental disadvantages, are really forced to select vocational courses in separate high schools or in separate tracks of general schools. Such programs are often criticized because they are archaic, training people for obsolete jobs or in ways inconsistent with modern technology. In addition, such programs almost invariably are given little status and low prestige in most communities. Literally, by virtue of his enrollment in such a school, the teen-ager experiences a perpetuation of his feelings of inferiority and develops a self-image of despair and failure.

The process of differential association, which we referred to as one view of the way values are developed by adolescents in our society, leads to "good boys and girls" and "bad boys and girls" by virtue of this differential school experience. The successful teen-ager, more often than not the product of a middle-class home, is found in the academic college-preparatory program where his classmates and many of the adults whom he meets by virtue of such relationships provide the sources of motivation and stimulation that direct his energies toward achievement and further education (Caro and Pihlblad, 1965; Sewell and Armer, 1966). (*See* Documentation 11.) Apparently, while teen-agers of different economic statuses differ only somewhat in occupational aspirations, they do differ markedly in educational aspirations, which serves effectively to block high-level careers for many poor adolescents (Morland, 1960). (*See* Documentation 12.)

The vocational school or the vocational program in a general high school is looked upon as a place for the educational failure, for the culturally deprived or retarded child, and for the unruly, predelinquent or actual delinquent. In such settings, the teacher often spends more time as a custodian and policeman than as an educator, and it is such programs that account for much of the problem of dropouts. Such rigid separation of programs provides few avenues for escape once the student is enmeshed in the system, even for the child with the necessary intellectual capacities and motivation. Current efforts to remedy these problems are concentrating upon eliminating the geographic separation of vocational and academic high schools and the segregation of students by tracks in different classes even for courses that are required of all students. At least a part of the solution to the problem would seem to consist in maintaining as much flexibility and integration as possible in educational programs, and the elimination or modification during high school of rigid ability grouping and the disreputable tracks.

IMPROVEMENT OF HIGH SCHOOLS

In certain large cities, the emphasis is on the development of educational parks or complexes with campus-type high schools. Here students of all ages and grades use common buildings and grounds. Serving a wider community avoids the de facto segregation of many residential areas and allows children from all social groups to share a common educational experience. This unified setting provides as many opportunities as possible for individuals to switch without stigmatization from one type of program to another, even if it means additional courses or even additional years in school. It is foolhardy to believe that the same number of hours are required by all children to grasp the curriculum. Certain children profit from individual study, additional tutorials, and sampling a variety of interests. Others can direct themselves well and adapt their interests to a particular program. Some teen-agers do not even need four years of high school, and certain colleges now have made provision for the early matriculation of students capable of university work. Others, however, need extended time before making decisions on intellectual and occupational pursuits.

adolescent educational expectations

EDUCATIONAL EXPECTATIONS, BY EDUCATION OF FATHER (IN PERCENTAGE)

Education of Father	Educational Expectations (in years)					
	16+	14	12	11−	N.R.	N
Graduate or Professional	79	9	8	2	1	(95)
Standard College or University Graduation..	65	18	15	1	1	(188)
Partial College Training (includes technical schools, etc.)	61	22	15	0	1	(280)
High School Graduates	43	23	33	1	0	(942)
Partial High School	26	24	46	3	1	(600)
Junior High School	27	23	47	2	1	(340)
Less than Seven Years of School	24	23	47	4	1	(158)
Not Reported	21	21	47	7	3	(249)

The association between educational expectations and father's education is shown in the above table. The relationship is positive, ranging from 24 percent expressing a college expectation when the father has less than seven years of schooling to 79 percent when the father has a graduate education. (Rehberg and Westby, 1967:366–367.)

For the low-income child, particularly, greater emphasis must be placed at the behavioral rather than the verbal level to convince him of his potentiality for occupational achievement. This requires not only changing the values he holds about teachers and education but also providing concrete assurance of further participation in the educational system. It is often suggested that special provision be made for small subsidies or appropriate parttime employment that will permit the student to finance his participation in the teen-age culture of his peers. This subsidization would continue into college. with scholarships, student loans, and so forth.

For students who do not do well academically and drop out of school by choice or necessity, some of the formal requirements placed on certain types of occupations must be reevaluated. The requirement of a high school diploma for employment in the sanitation department or a college education for routine clerical work is unrealistic and discriminatory. These irrational requirements have a detrimental impact upon the perceptions, motivation, and evaluation of students who cannot compete fully within the educational process, and further limit their interest and energy to achieve.

REFERENCES

ALEXANDER, NORMAN C., JR. AND ERNEST Q.
    CAMPBELL.
1964   "Peer influences on adolescent edu-
        cational aspirations and attainments."
        American Sociological Review 29
        (August):568–575.

AXELROD, SIDNEY.
1952   "Negro and white male institution-
        alized delinquents." American Jour-
        nal of Sociology 57(May):569–574.

BARRON, MILTON L.
1954   Juvenile in Delinquent Society. New
        York: Knopf.

BECKER, HOWARD S.
1953   "Becoming a marihuana user." Amer-
        ican Journal of Sociology 59(Novem-
        ber):235–242.
1963   Outsiders: Studies in the Sociology of
        Deviance. New York: Free Press.

BECKER, HOWARD S. (ED.).
1964   The Other Side: Perspectives on De-
        viance. New York: Free Press.

BELL, ROBERT R.
1966   "Parent-child conflict in sexual val-
        ues." The Journal of Social Issues
        22(April):34–44.

BLACKER, EDWARD, HAROLD W. DEMONE, JR.
    AND HOWARD E. FREEMAN.
1965   "Drinking behavior of delinquent
        boys." Quarterly Journal of Studies
        on Alcohol 26(June):223–237.

BRIAR, SCOTT AND IRVING PILIAVIN.
1965   "Delinquency, situational induce-
        ments, and commitment to conform-
        ity." Social Problems 13(Summer):
        35–45.

BRODERICK, CARLFRED.
1966   "Sexual behavior among pre-adoles-
        cents." The Journal of Social Issues
        22(April):6–21.

CAPLAN, GERALD.
1966   "Some comments on psychiatry and
        social order." Social Problems 14
        (Summer):23–25.

CARO, FRANCIS G. AND TERRENCE C. PIHLBLAD.
1965   "Aspirations and expectations: a re-
        examination of the bases for social
        class differences in the occupational
        orientations of male high school stu-
        dents." Sociology and Social Research
        49(July):465–475.

CHILTON, ROLAND J.
1964   "Continuity in delinquency area re-
        search: a comparison of studies for
        Baltimore, Detroit, and Indianapolis."
        American Sociological Review 29(Feb-
        ruary):71–83.
1967   "Middle-class delinquency and spe-
        cific offense analysis." Pp. 91–102 in
        Edmund W. Vaz (ed.), Middle Class
        Juvenile Delinquency. New York:
        Harper and Row.

CLINE, HUGH F., HOWARD E. FREEMAN AND
    STANTON WHEELER.
1968   "The analysis and evaluation of de-
        tached-worker programs." Pp. 287–
        315 in Stanton Wheeler (ed.), Con-
        trolling Delinquents. New York:
        Wiley.

CLOWARD, RICHARD A. AND LLOYD OHLIN.
1960   Delinquency and Opportunity: A
        Theory of Delinquent Gangs. New
        York: Free Press.

COHEN, ALBERT K. AND JAMES F. SHORT.
1966 "Juvenile delinquency." Pp. 84–135 in Robert K. Merton and Robert Nesbit (eds.), Contemporary Social Problems. New York: Harcourt, Brace and World.

COLEMAN, JAMES S.
1960 "The adolescent subculture and academic achievement." American Journal of Sociology 65(January):337–347.
1961 "Athletics in high school." The Annals of the American Academy of Political and Social Science 338 (November):33–43.

CONANT, JAMES B.
1959 American High Schools Today. New York: McGraw-Hill.

COTTRELL, LEONARD S. AND STANTON WHEELER.
1966 An Appraisal of the Field of Juvenile Delinquency. New York: Russell Sage Foundation.

DINITZ, SIMON, FRANK R. SCARPITTI AND WALTER C. RECKLESS.
1962 "Delinquency vulnerability: a cross group and longitudinal analysis." American Sociological Review 27 (August):515–522.

ELKIN, FREDERICK AND WILLIAM A. WESTLEY.
1955 "The myth of adolescent culture." American Sociological Review 20(December):680–684.

EMPEY, LaMAR T.
1967 Alternatives to Incarceration. Washington, D.C.: U.S. Government Printing Office.

EMPEY, LaMAR T. AND JEROME RABOW.
1961 "The Provo Experiment in delinquency rehabilitation." American Sociological Review 26(October):679–695.

ENGLAND, RALPH W., JR.
1960 "A theory of middle class juvenile delinquency." The Journal of Criminal Law, Criminology and Police Science 50(April):535–540.

FERDINAND, THEODORE N.
1966 Typologies of Delinquencies. New York: Random House.

FREEMAN, HOWARD E. AND ASHLEY H. WEEKS.
1956 "Analysis of a program of treatment of delinquent boys." American Journal of Sociology 62(July):56–61.

FREEMAN, HOWARD E. AND JEANNE M. GIOVANNONI.
1969 "Social psychology of mental health." Chapter 45 in Gardner Lindzey and E. Aronson (eds.), Handbook of Social Psychology. Second Edition. Volume 5. Reading, Massachusetts: Addison-Wesley.

FREIDSON, ELIOT.
1965 "Disability as social deviance." Pp. 80–99 in Marvin B. Sussman (ed.), Sociology and Rehabilitation. New York: American Sociological Association and Vocational Rehabilitation Administration.

FRIEDENBERG, EDGAR Z.
1959 The Vanishing Adolescent. Boston: Beacon Press.
1966 "Adolescence as a social problem." Pp. 35–75 in Howard S. Becker (ed.), Social Problems. New York: Wiley.

GEBHARD, PAUL H., WARDELL POMEROY, CLYDE MARTIN AND CORNELIA CHRISTIANSON.
1958 Pregnancy, Birth, and Abortion. New York: Harper and Row.

GLUECK, SHELDON AND ELEANOR GLUECK.
1962 Family Environment and Delinquency. Boston: Houghton Mifflin.

GOLDBURGH, STEVEN.
1965 The Experience of Adolescents. Cambridge, Mass.: Schenkman.

GOLDEN, NATHAN.
1963 The Differential Selection of Juvenile Offenders for Court Appearance. New York: National Research and Information Center, National Council on Crime and Delinquency.

GOODMAN, PAUL.
1960 Growing Up Absurd. New York: Random House.

GOULD, LEROY C.
1969 "Who defines delinquency: a comparison of self-reported and officially reported indices of delinquency for three racial groups." Social Problems 16(Winter):325–336.

HACKLER, JAMES C.
1966 "Boys, blisters, and behavior—the impact of a work program in an urban central area." The Journal of Research in Crime and Delinquency 3(July):155–164.

HEALY, WILLIAM AND AUGUSTA F. BRONNER.
1936 New Light on Delinquency and Its Treatment. New Haven: Yale University Press.

KANIN, EUGENE J. AND DAVID H. HOWARD.
1958 "Postmarital consequences of premarital sex adjustments." American Sociological Review 23(October): 556–562.

KANTOR, DAVID AND WILLIAM IRA BENNETT.
1968 "Orientations of street-corner workers and their effect on gangs." Pp. 271–286 in Stanton Wheeler (ed.), Controlling Delinquents. New York: Wiley.

KVARACEUS, WILLIAM C. AND WALTER B. MILLER.
1959 Delinquent Behavior. New York: National Education Association.

LEIGHTON, DOROTHEA C., JOHN S. HARDING, DAVID B. MACKLIN, ALEXANDER H. LEIGHTON AND ALLISTER M. MAC-MILLAN.
1964 The Character of Danger: Psychiatric Symptoms in Selected Communities. New York: Basic Books.

LERMAN, PAUL.
1968 "Individual values, peer values, and sub-cultural delinquency." American Sociological Review 33(April):219–235.

LUGER, MILTON AND ELIAS B. SALTMAN.
1967 "The youthful offender." Pp. 119–131 in Juvenile Delinquency and Youth Crime. President's Commission on Law Enforcement and Administration of Justice. Washington, D.C.: U.S. Government Printing Office.

MADDOX, GEORGE L. AND BEVODE C. McCALL.
1967 "Patterns of drinking and abstinence." Pp. 157–178 in Edmund W. Vaz (ed.), Middle Class Juvenile Delinquency. New York: Harper and Row.

McCORD, WILLIAM.
1958 "The biological basis of juvenile delinquency." Pp. 59–78 in Joseph S. Roucek (ed.), Juvenile Delinquency. New York: Philosophical Library.

MERTON, ROBERT K. AND M. F. ASHLEY-MONTAGU.
1940 "Crime and the anthropologist." American Anthropologist 42(July/September):384–468.

MEYER, HENRY J., EDGAR F. BORGATTA AND WYATT C. JONES.
1965 Girls at Vocational High. New York: Russell Sage Foundation.

MILLER, WALTER B.
1958 "Lower-class culture as a generating milieu of gang delinquency." Journal of Social Issues 14(July):5–19.
1962 " 'Total-community' delinquency control project." Social Problems 10 (Fall):169–191.

MILNER, JOHN G.
1964 "The residential treatment center." The Annals of the American Academy of Political and Social Science 335(September):98–104.

MOBILIZATION FOR YOUTH.
1964 Action on the Lower East Side. Mobilization for Youth Program Report: July 1962–January 1964. New York: Mobilization for Youth, Inc.

MORLAND, J. KENNETH.
1960 "Educational and occupational aspirations of mill and town school children in a southern community." Social Forces 39(December):169–175.

MOSS, BENJAMIN.
1964   Adolescent Sexual Behavior. Derby, Connecticut: Monarch Books.

MOYNIHAN, DANIEL P.
1965   The Negro Family. Washington, D.C.: Office of Policy Planning and Research, United States Department of Labor (March Report).

NYE, F. IVAN AND JAMES F. SHORT.
1957   "Scaling delinquent behavior." American Sociological Review 22(June): 326–331.

NYE, F. IVAN, JAMES F. SHORT AND VIRGIL J. OLSON.
1958   "Socioeconomic status and delinquent behavior." American Journal of Sociology 63(January):381–389.

ONTELL, ROBERT AND WYATT C. JONES.
1965   "Discontinuities in the social treatment of juvenile offenders." Pp. 1–16 in Robert Schasre and Jo Wallach (eds.), Readings in Delinquency and Treatment. Los Angeles: Youth Studies Center, University of Southern California.

PALMORE, ERDMAN B. AND PHILLIP E. HAMMOND.
1964   "Interacting factors in juvenile delinquency." American Sociological Review 29(October):848–854.

PILIAVIN, IRVING M. AND SCOTT BRIAR.
1964   "Police encounters with juveniles." American Journal of Sociology 70 (September):206–214.

POLK, KENNETH AND DAVID S. HALFERTY.
1966   "Adolescence commitment and delinquency." The Journal of Research in Crime and Delinquency 3(July): 82–96.

PORTERFIELD, AUSTIN L.
1943   "Delinquency and its outcome in court and college." American Journal of Sociology 49(November):199–208.

POWERS, EDWIN AND HELEN WITMER.
1951   An Experiment in the Prevention of Delinquency: The Cambridge-Summerville Youth Study. New York: Columbia University Press.

PRESIDENT'S COMMISSION ON LAW ENFORCEMENT AND ADMINISTRATION OF JUSTICE.
1967a   Juvenile Delinquency and Youth Crime. Washington, D.C.: U.S. Government Printing Office.
1967b   Task Force Report: The Courts. Washington, D.C.: U.S. Government Printing Office.

QUINNEY, RICHARD.
1964   "Crime delinquency and social areas." The Journal of Research in Crime and Delinquency 1(July):149–154.

RECKLESS, WALTER C., SIMON DINITZ AND BARBARA KAY.
1957   "The self component in potential delinquency and non-delinquency." American Sociological Review 22(December):566–570.

RECKLESS, WALTER C., FRANK R. MURRAY, ELLEN MURRAY AND SIMON DINITZ.
1960   "The 'good' boy in a high delinquency area: four years later." American Sociological Review 25(August): 555–558.

REHBERG, RICHARD A. AND DAVID L. WESTBY.
1967   "Parental encouragement, occupation, education and family size: artifactual or independent determinants of adolescent educational expectations." Social Forces 45(March):362–374.

REISS, ALBERT J., JR. AND ALBERT LEWIS RHODES.
1961   "The distribution of juvenile delinquency in the social class structure." American Sociological Review 26 (October):720–732.

REISS, IRA L.
1967   "Sexual codes in teen-age culture." Pp. 64–75 in Edmund W. Vaz (ed.), Middle Class Juvenile Delinquency. New York: Harper and Row.

RICHMOND, S. KENNETH.
1956   Education in the U.S.A.: A Comparative Study. New York: Philosophical Library.

RIESMAN, DAVID.
1956 Constraint and Variety in American Education. Lincoln: University of Nebraska Press.

SEWELL, WILLIAM AND MICHAEL J. ARMER.
1966 "Neighborhood context and college plans." American Sociological Review 31(October):159–168.

SHORT, JAMES F. AND FRED L. STRODTBECK.
1963 "The response of gang leaders to status threats: an observation on group process and delinquent behavior." American Journal of Sociology 68(March):5, 571–579.
1965 Group Processes and Delinquency. Chicago: University of Chicago Press.

SKOLNICK, JEROME H.
1966 Justice Without Trial: Law Enforcement in Democratic Society. New York: Wiley.

SLAVSON, S. R.
1954 Re-educating the Delinquent Through Group and Community Participation. New York: Harper and Brothers.

SMITH, ERNEST A.
1962 American Youth Culture: Group Life in Teenage Society. New York: Free Press.

STERNE, MURIEL, DAVID J. PITTMAN AND THOMAS COE.
1965 "Teen-agers, drinking, and the law: A study of arrest trends for alcohol-related offenses." Crime and Delinquency 11(January):78–85.

VINCENT, CLARK.
1961 Unmarried Mothers. New York: Free Press.

VINTER, ROBERT D.
1967 "Analysis of treatment organizations." Pp. 207–221 in Edwin J. Thomas (ed.), Behavioral Science for Social Workers. New York: Free Press.

WEEKS, ASHLEY.
1958 Youthful Offenders at Highfields. Ann Arbor: University of Michigan Press.

WHEELER, STANTON H.
1966 "Delinquency and crime." Pp. 201–276 in Howard S. Becker (ed.), Social Problems. New York: Wiley.

WHEELER, STANTON AND EDNA BORACICH, M. RICHARD CRAMER AND IRVING K. ZOLA.
1968 "Agents of delinquency control: a conservative analysis." Pp. 31–60 in Stanton Wheeler (ed.), Controlling Delinquents. New York: Wiley.

WILKINS, LESLIE T.
1965 Social Deviance. Englewood Cliffs, New Jersey: Prentice-Hall.

WILLIE, CHARLES V.
1967 "The relative contribution of family status and economic status to juvenile delinquency." Social Problems 14 (Winter):326–335.

WILSON, JAMES Q.
1968 "The police and the delinquent in two cities." Pp. 9–30 in Stanton Wheeler (ed.), Controlling Delinquents. New York: Wiley.

WISE, NANCY BARTON.
1967 "Juvenile delinquency among middle-class girls." Pp. 179–188 in Edmund W. Vaz (ed.), Middle Class Juvenile Delinquency. New York: Harper and Row.

WITMER, HELEN L. (ED.).
1959 "Prevention of juvenile delinquency." Annals of the American Academy of Political and Social Science 322 (March):1–145.

WITMER, HELEN L. AND EDITH TUFTS.
1954 The Effectiveness of Delinquency Control Programs. Washington, D.C.: Department of Health, Education, and Welfare.

YABLONSKY, LEWIS.
1968 The Hippie Trip. New York: Pegasus.

CHAPTER 13

young
adulthood

THE CONSIDERABLE OVERLAP in the stages of the life cycle means that chronological age, in itself, provides only a gross differentiation between community members. The increased educational experience now undertaken by a majority of young people has served to extend the adolescent period well into the eighteen- to twenty-two-year-old age group, the arbitrary boundaries set for this chapter. Only a generation ago, when high school education, or less, represented the modal requirement for the world of work, eighteen-year-olds were regarded as economically independent adults and viewed as full-fledged community members. During the past twenty years, the average level of education has risen from less than nine grades to almost twelve (Lecht, 1962:140–160; Johnston, 1963). The popular definition of adulthood has changed accordingly. Neither the parents of dependent children attending college nor the administrators of these institutions regard students as independent adults.

Nevertheless, the traditions and norms that govern individual behavior continue to recognize eighteen-year-olds as capable of considerable autonomous decision-making and responsible for their own behavior and conduct. Several jurisdictions have attempted to extend the paternalistic orientation of their legal codes to cover delinquent behavior of all young people under twenty-one years of age. In the eyes of the law and of most community members, however, individuals in this age group are regarded as adults, and many privileges and responsibilities accrue to them accordingly.

age and sex roles

All states regard the young adult as old enough to drive an automobile; most states allow him limited or complete access to alcoholic beverages. He is permitted to engage in business or commerce and often to obligate himself by contracts or pledges. In brief, young adulthood is the age of becoming a responsible community member, without protection on the grounds of incomplete intellectual or emotional development, and under norms providing for his treatment as an adult with complete responsibility for his own actions.

THE IMPORTANCE OF THIS AGE PERIOD

By the time a person completes this age period, his adult career is rather well determined. The American press likes to play up, for the comfort of its older readers, the citizen who becomes successful later in life—the grandmother who graduates from college or the athlete who gains fame in middle age. But by the time an individual reaches his twenties, it is relatively easy to predict, in broad terms, much of his future life course.

Success in an adult career, at least an occupational one, is dependent upon what happens to the individual during this period. Given the early marriage age in the United States, this is also the time for culmination of sexual motivation and the development of lasting heterosexual relationships. During these years the individual's behavior patterns are set and his values and life goals become structured. As a young adult he begins to make choices about his education aspirations and, consequently, his occupational goals. He must decide whether he is capable of or interested in undertaking tedious, long-term educational pursuits or whether he will settle for vocational training, an apprenticeship, or other routes to a work career. For the girl, the prospect of marriage and motherhood becomes a reality and, for both sexes, dating and more intimate sexual encounters come to include the possibility, perhaps the risk, of marriage.

The young woman, in particular, is confronted with the striking differentiation of the female and male roles in adulthood, and she needs to recognize and take a position (although it may be a fleeting one) on the desirability of professional or vocational achievement in a man's world in comparison with her expected role as a mother and homemaker. She begins to perceive the pressures the community exerts in terms of social prestige and the proscriptions surrounding sexual behavior to encourage marriage and discredit spinsterhood. At this point she must also reckon with the problems and conflicts that she is likely to meet in any attempt to combine occupational and family careers.

The young man is sharply confronted with the requirements of the occupational system and with his intellectual, temperamental, and economic prospects for achievement in the community. Usually by this time he understands that not everyone has an equal chance to become president of either the United States or a large corporation, that the social structure has an impact on the types of roles he may pursue, both in the world of work and in terms of wider social relations, and that suddenly other community members are judging him by a somewhat different set of criteria than heretofore. His vocational prospects and his place in the community during the next fifty years become increasingly important to him.

CONSEQUENCES OF DEVIANT BEHAVIOR

It is not surprising that this is the age during which most types of manifest deviant behavior begin to have both serious and long-range consequences for the individual. This is the age group for whom unemployment and underemployment are of crucial concern. If the community cannot cope with these problems at this age period, the prospects are slim that even the most intensive remedial or rehabilitative efforts by the social-control systems will have any impact later in his life. This is the period when rates of mental illness, particularly of schizophrenia, begin to increase. Not only is the incidence of mental illness, as measured by hospitalization, quite high for this group, but the community is faced with the possibility of increasing numbers of persons whose life will be marred by subsequent episodes of emotional illness.

While there is some evidence that earlier age groups are becoming involved with various types of intoxicants, this is the period of experimentation with "hard" drugs and the accompanying dangers of severe disability due to habitual use. Along the same lines, the use of alcohol becomes more frequent and regularized, resulting in, among other undesirable side effects, high rates of automobile accidents occasioned by irresponsible drinking.

Young adulthood is also the age at which most individuals undertake sustained sexual experience. In this area, the marked discrepancies between community norms and individual behavior become clearly apparent. For the majority of young people this experience is heterosexual and, at least in this respect, is viewed as normal. However, this is also the period when the outlines of homosexual or bisexual careers are formulated. As with the problem of mental illness, there is a considerable community concern with the accumulation of episodic and sustained homosexual conduct. This is also the time when girls become aware that the potential rewards associated with sexual conduct are not all emotional. Recruitment into prostitution is not uncommon.

Statistics from court and prison systems also indicate that this age group represents a particularly vulnerable population in terms of many categories of crime, particularly those characterized by physical aggression. Part of this, as we shall elaborate, is merely a continuation of earlier delinquent behavior that in this age category is redefined as criminal conduct. Another part, however, has to do with the meaning of money and the economic stakes involved in illegal behavior. This age group begins to contribute to the pool of individuals who cope with their economic problems by armed robbery and respond to their social conflicts by physical aggression. Such problems are not the exclusive province of young adults, but these more serious crimes begin to increase during this age period. In terms of a preventive orientation, this is the age group upon which society focuses its social-control efforts. While the earlier years, including infancy, childhood, and adolescence, still have their impact, young adulthood represents a second formulative stage to those who consider adult socialization as a set of experiences separate from childhood.

Since the serious social problems that become prevalent in this age group represent initial manifestations of deviant behavior of a persistent type, much attention has been paid to them. The problems we have discussed here, including crime and schizophrenia, constitute major fields of investigation, and the scope and quantity of available materials are overwhelming. No pretense can be made of covering fully all the available work; rather, we have been quite selective in drawing upon existing information for key concepts and relevant findings.

occupational careers

In Chapter 5, in which we discussed inadequate economic participation as a pervasive social problem, attention was given to the highly technological basis of the American economic system. The emphasis there was on the complex arrangement of tasks faced by individuals in an increasing number of work situations. In examining the changing character of work, an effort was made to point up the lack of congruence between the needs of the community and the existing supply and character of the work force. To a large extent, unemployment and underemployment constitute increasing problems among the young adult age group. With the possible exception of the very old, rates of unemployment are highest among individuals eighteen to twenty-two years of age in comparison with all other ages. The failure of individuals in this age group to participate fully and effectively in the educational system represents the key dimension of the disparity between the community's needs and the individual's potential work performance.

BLOCKED CAREERS

A number of the work problems of young adults have already been discussed in terms of racial discrimination, for this is the age of the highest rates of unemployment among blacks and other minority group members.

Except for those engaged in continued education, the community's norms prescribe work for males in this age category. This results in a stampede of high school graduates and dropouts into the labor market. This sudden, overwhelming demand for employment exposes both the defects of our educational system and the effects of automation on our industrial system. To this extent, the problem is a structural one. Young adults suddenly become aware of their limited job opportunities and low occupational potential only when it is really too late to remedy the situation. Since upward occupational mobility is typically dependent upon education, interesting and challenging positions are rarely open to those who lack a repertoire of technical skills, intellectual capacities, or apprenticeship training. A relatively large number of nontechnical job possibilities exist but these jobs offer no prestige and little possibility for future rewards. It is not so much a matter of lack of employment as lack of economic security and and social status. Young adults know that these attributes represent fundamental dimensions valued by all community members. Their attitude is that it is better to be unemployed than to embark upon a lifelong career of cleaning public toilets or stocking supermarket shelves. In line with the community's limited evaluation of these low-status opportunities, such jobs also bring limited economic returns. Menial and unrewarding jobs persist, of course, because the community needs such work done: hospitals need orderlies, apartments need janitors, universities need window washers, and industries need common laborers. Typically, these low-status, poorly paying jobs are least open to unionization since each worker is infinitely replaceable and there is little likelihood that his lot can be improved.

Eventually, however, many of the undereducated, particularly the school dropout (especially if he is a minority group member), reconcile themselves to the acceptance of this fate—low pay, lack of prestige, and risk of layoffs (Form and Miller, 1962). Such acceptance comes about not only because welfare agencies are unwilling or unable to provide economic support for individuals who will not take any available work but also because, as they grow older and move into the next age group, these people begin to get involved in a web of responsibilities that virtually exclude any other alternative. Financial responsibility for parents and younger siblings and, very often, a wife and children of his own require the acceptance of such roles. This pattern is frequently encountered among unskilled blue-collar workers. Earning marginal livelihoods, they are generally unable to participate in the good life of the society and find themselves boxed in with no possibility for future occupational growth. With population growth and increased technology, the issues become more severe. The distance between the achievements of the workers and the American promise of economic affluence and social prestige grows greater with each passing generation. The requirements of the occupational structure not only force community members to accept this disparity but at times to nurture it (Freeman and Kassebaum, 1956).

Essentially what we have in American society is a large group of individuals, particularly males, who spend a number of years after leaving school looking around for employment but resisting the limited opportunities available to them, who eventually are forced to settle for whatever job they can get, enduring it for the rest of their lives. The United States has always been confronted with the semiliterate worker who remains ignorant of or apathetic to community activities and values and who spawns numerous children who are socialized into the same lifestyle. Indeed, this portrait depicts a significant portion of the population who suffer the pervasive problems of poverty that we described earlier.

AMELIORATION

Intervention strategies designed to deal with this problem at the individual and the structural levels have proliferated in recent years. Numerous community programs, including continuation schools, evening high schools, and university extension services, have been launched. Opinions differ widely on the utility of such efforts, and there has been very little evaluative research to estimate their impact. It is reasonably certain that, in the absence of such programs, opportunities for satisfying employment would be even more limited. Whether such programs actually reach those most deficient in education and least able to achieve is a serious question. We have no precise studies, but considerable evidence indicates that large numbers of eligible workers drop out of these programs. The programs seem to succeed best with those who need them least.

During critical periods, such as the depression and the recent war on poverty, federally sponsored programs have come into vogue. These have the implicit advantage of keeping young adults off the streets, that is, providing them with some semblance of work, as was done by the Civilian Conservation Corps (CCC) during the 1930s. The more recent Job Corps, for example, was begun as a network of facilities to provide both literacy and vocational training in campus-type settings. On the surface, at least, the controlled environment of such a total institutional program appears to be a challenging way of handling the problem. However, numerous criticisms have been raised concerning the impact of the Job Corps and similar training programs. The negative stance of many individuals and groups in the local communities has made operations very difficult. In several areas major opposition to the programs has centered in local criticism of the trainees as an unsavory and discrediting element.

To some extent these programs, like many vocational high school programs, end up as dumping grounds for the social-control system. The police and courts, for example, use them as alternatives to institutional-ization and probation for young adults arrested or suspected of crime. Perhaps to a lesser extent, they are also used as a last resort by practi-tioners in the welfare and mental health fields. As in other total in-stitutional programs, the impact of such regimented attempts at mass socialization can be seriously damaging to the individual.

Another widespread alternative is the community-based program, operated on a full or part-time basis, which pays the young adult to attend. These types of vocational training programs are operated in many large cities under the aegis of the Office of Economic Opportunity (OEO) or the Department of Labor. Such programs usually function as part of a network of services. An unemployed individual in a low-income area, for example, goes to a neighborhood-based multi-service center operated under a grant from OEO where he is referred to a state-operated training program financed under the federal Manpower Training and Development Act.

INDIVIDUAL AND STRUCTURAL MODIFICATIONS

In our earlier discussion of poverty we alluded to the fact that the prob-lems faced by intervention programs were not limited to the provision of vocational skills but included the need to motivate individuals to par-ticipate in relevant programs and to acquire the necessary repertoire of social roles. To successfully hold a job, a worker must know more than how to run a particular machine; he must also understand something of the norms regarding attendance, punctuality, proper dress, peer relation-ships, response to superiors, and the like. Many observers believe that the high dropout rate from work programs is related as much to extra-vocational deficiencies as to failure to grasp vocational skills. In addition, there is considerable opposition within many unions to the acceptance of certain individuals, despite their work skills. Unions and employers often cooperate to restrict entrance to the skilled crafts, particularly if the ap-plicant is a minority group member.

The fact remains that the structure of the economic system requires a sizeable force of unemployed and underemployed unskilled workers to fill all of the dull, monotonous, low-prestige positions required by our economy. Otherwise, who would do them? Essentially, as Miller (1964) has noted, the American community defines occupational position pri-marily on the basis of two related criteria—income and the complexity of the work skills required. There are, of course, exceptions where the ele-ment of social worth enters into the community's assignment of status to a particular occupational role; the ministry and teaching are frequently so mentioned. However, given the low definitions accorded even necessary tasks that are without complexities and educational prerequisites and the limited economic returns for these activities, one can see why these positions are strenuously avoided by individuals, particularly those at the beginning of their careers. Miller suggests that community norms be modified to make these jobs more socially valued. He argues that those who accept such tedious, dirty, dull, unpleasant tasks are "heroes," and such heroes should be rewarded both in terms of status and money. Such a shift in emphasis regarding what counts within the work situation could effect a realignment that would provide considerable inducement for those without prerequisite skills to work at unpleasant but necessary jobs—something like combat pay in the military or hardship allowance in the foreign service.

A related solution is the serious reevaluation of the formal requirements, particularly those involving education, that are placed on such tasks. This suggestion is especially pertinent where the requirements represent irrational barriers to employment or are imposed in order to restrict the labor force. For example, it is utterly ridiculous that barbers and beauticians be required to have a working knowledge of physiology; yet many states require such information in their examinations for licensing. Such requirements function only to protect the monopolistic positions of individuals already in the business. Any number of job classifications have been upgraded and restricted by arbitrary requirements that limit the numbers and types of individuals who may participate in them. A really efficient bureaucratic arrangement in the world of work would avoid such artificial prerequisites, and their removal would constitute a partial solution to the employment problem raised here.

THE SPECIAL PROBLEMS OF WOMEN

Underachievement and underutilization are not problems of occupational choice faced solely by the unequipped in our society. In discussing discrimination we alluded to the many ways in which women in America are denied full participation, even today. This happens frequently in the world of work, partly because of the strains introduced into the work situation by relationships between the sexes and partly because of the belief that women are intellectually or emotionally unable to undertake certain tasks. These limitations operate for both married and unmarried women. To some extent, however, sex discrimination is based on the limited tenure of married women occasioned by intervening pregnancies or the economic success of their husbands. For example, women are frequently not considered for positions that require long periods of apprenticeship or on-the-job experience because it is assumed that by the time a woman is trained she will want to quit to start a family.

According to popular reports, this problem is being alleviated, if not by the widespread practice of birth control, at least by the public acknowledgement of such methods of family planning. Whether or not contraception has become more prevalent or more effective with the introduction of birth-control pills, open discussion of the subject is now permissible with prospective trainees and promising employees who might be upgraded. Nevertheless, if the training and potential of women in this group are compared with the available job opportunities, one finds that considerable discrimination and resulting unemployment still exist. Widespread discussion of the pros and cons of combining a career with the wife-mother role give evidence that college-educated men are less reluctant to accept such a marital relationship on a relatively permanent basis.

In line with this trend, several women's colleges, among them Radcliffe, Wellesley, Bennington, and Mundelein, have developed programs for the further education and re-education of women who, if not for their voluntary or enforced removal from the labor force during child-rearing, would be considered in midcareers. These comments on the role of the woman are raised at this point because this is the age when most young women must decide whether they are seriously interested in a long-term educational commitment, probably including training in either graduate or professional school, to prepare themselves for an occupational career or whether they view employment essentially as a stopgap measure for a short period until the right man (or any man) comes along.

EDUCATIONAL PROGRAMS

Probably the major gains in the last several decades with respect to the general problem of underemployment and occupational choice have occurred to the benefit of the male, particularly the young men from blue-collar families. One of the positive outcomes of World War II was the provision for former GI's of an opportunity for university training. Undergraduate and graduate classes were swelled by large numbers of returning veterans who might not otherwise have seen the inside of an institution of higher learning. Partly because of the impact of such programs, the expectations of American youth and their families regarding who is eligible and entitled to a university education has undergone a marked liberalization. But the impact is less than one would imagine for, in general, those who took advantage of the GI Bill were those who would have gone to college anyway (Duncan, 1967). Nevertheless, veterans' benefits, along with the development of broad networks of state colleges and universities, the proliferation of community colleges, and the increased availability of scholarships for students from lower socio-economic families, are indicative of a significant change in modern community life in the United States.

educational experience

A minimum goal for the future is the development of more effective and efficient ways to relate educational experiences and occupational roles. There are a number of ways in which improvements are possible. For example, despite the great deal of work that has been done by psychometricians in developing tests and measures, we have had only limited success in the selection of persons for university training or for job placement and have exhibited only limited ability in counseling individuals regarding particular vocational or occupational choice. As a consequence, the attractiveness of certain occupational roles and the ineffective advice of professionals in the areas of guidance and vocational counseling often result in discrepancies between the requirements of positions and the educational and temperamental characteristics of the individuals choosing to enter them.

Another frequent criticism of our educational system is its lack of flexibility in training people for dramatic shifts and changes in technology. Too much technical education today represents training for obsolescence. A young adult trained ten years ago as an expert in business practices, for example, would find himself completely unsophisticated in the new computer technologies; the engineer would find that developments in the physical sciences have moved so fast that his basic background is insufficient to allow him to keep up with current developments. The same is true of persons being prepared for careers in medicine, in education, and in virtually all of the professions. Much has yet to be learned before we can develop educational programs, particularly for professional training as opposed to a liberal arts education, that will contradict the charge of educating for obsolescence.

THE GENERAL STATUS OF HIGHER EDUCATION

A number of prestige schools have initiated programs to remedy this situation. In general, their plans involve much less emphasis on techniques and more on fundamental issues and conceptual ideas. Unfortunately, however, many of the faculty members are themselves obsolete and frequently unable to supply the inputs and innovation that would be necessary to correct this serious difficulty. Nevertheless, compared with the problems of unemployment and underemployment of those with little or no educational or technical experience, the problems of university graduates are much less severe and the effect of their inadequacies on the community is much less serious. However, long-range planners concerned with the future needs for trained manpower and the occupational distribution of workers in our society are rightly concerned about

scientists affluent, humanists militant

Federal research support has added a new dimension to the eternal class struggles within a university. To student versus faculty, assistant versus tenure professors, and faculty versus administrators has been added a new hierarchical point of tension—that between humanists and scientists. The scientists, by and large, in the federal grant universities, get promoted faster, get more space, get more income through summer employment and consulting, have more secretaries and assistants, have greater access to travel funds and expense accounts, and accumulate a greater sense of status within and outside the academic community. Some humanists obviously resent all this and consider it quite unfair, even though their own situation has improved, relative to what it used to be.

However, there is still another side to the story. The scientist who gets a series of projects going can become caught in his own apparatus. Graduate students and staff members become dependent upon him. He is committed to project deadlines and periodic contract negotiations. He is enmeshed in a web of obligations and it is very hard to break out. As a result, he often works hard at things he would rather not do—more often than need be true of the humanist.

There is some current tendency for the brightest of graduate students to prefer the sciences to the social sciences and the humanities, and this will have an impact on comparative faculty quality as between fields of study in the years to come. How much of this has been caused by federal aid and how much by the current liveliness of the different fields is not at all clear. My own impression is that the brightest students flock to the areas with the brightest new ideas, regardless of federal aid.

All this is said to have destroyed the "balance" among fields and it is generally concluded that something should be done about it. (Kerr, 1963:60–61.)

the failure of our educational system to provide the technical skills and intellectual knowledge required by the complexities of modern life.

The phenomenal growth of education beyond high school in this country and the limited flexibility of our system of higher education to accommodate such large numbers of students constitute imminent, if not current, social problems. The student unrest that pervades all academic communities and the riots and rebellions that have plagued a number of schools are symptoms of the growing pains and the inability of many institutions to adjust to the new demands placed upon them. The role of the university in the community, the participation of student groups in university administration, the ratio between teaching and research functions among the faculty, the relevance of the curriculum to current problems and student interests—all are legitimate concerns for which answers must be sought. (*See* Documentation 1.) There is a pressing need to recognize the disparities and discontinuities in our educational system and a moral demand for the entire community—faculty, students, and public—to seek creative remedies to these academic ills (Kerr, 1963).

IMPROVING SMALL COLLEGES

One of the more serious problems is the difficulty experienced by small undergraduate colleges in attracting and retaining key faculty members. Most professors are aware that research and publication are usually accomplished in large universities with excellent graduate schools. This means physical resources, such as computers, laboratories, and libraries, and the stimulation of quality students and eminent colleagues. One of the solutions to this problem has been the development of formal or informal consortiums of small colleges that not only share physical resources but allow students to matriculate in the various institutions and encourage faculties to interchange and communicate with one another. These arrangements provide trappings similar to those found in large high-quality institutions yet retain the individualization that is the strength and appeal of the small college. Perhaps the oldest and best known of such efforts is the consortium of institutions around Pomona, California, and, more recently, the development of a similar cooperative arrangement in western Massachusetts. Such plans—frequently including the construction of a single library, perhaps the development of a single graduate school drawing upon the faculties of all the colleges, and the integration of such administrative services as purchasing departments—represent an intervention technique of considerable promise.

A NEW APPROACH

There are many variations of programs seeking to solve these problems. One other program merits our consideration. This is the effort of certain major universities to "adopt" smaller schools of less prestige. This approach is one of the ways in which some of the major American universities are contributing to the upgrading of formerly all-Negro colleges in the South. Brown University and the University of Michigan, among others, have such relationships with small Southern colleges, and faculty members from the parent institution spend time teaching, consulting, and helping the small college develop its resources. In some cases, interested university students can spend a semester or a year in residence at the college to help strengthen the student body.

These and other efforts that strive for quality instruction are essential if the community goal of a college education for almost everyone is to be achieved.

The age from eighteen to twenty-two introduces a period in which community norms no longer deny the pressures of sexual expression on the normal individual whether married or single. There seems to be no reasonable way to settle the continuing debate about whether sexual intercourse outside of marriage is increasing (Reiss, 1961). Many experts, holding that premarital sex is not markedly increasing, contend that it is the more open communication about sexual matters and the increased willingness to report sexual activity that have changed. Whatever the situation, it is rather evident that the norms regarding sexual conduct have been considerably more liberal. While most community members continue to hold negative views about indiscriminate promiscuity, certainly the emphasis upon female virginity has declined. Recognition is widely given to pluralistic codes of conduct, including the possible appropriateness of sexual intimacy between engaged couples and, in the eyes of many community members, particularly those of this age group, between individuals with mature interpersonal attachments for each other whether marriage is intended or not.

SEXUAL NORMS

Deviations from the idealized norm of chastity, and the acceptance of pluralistic standards that do not assign hard and fast judgments of right and wrong to specific behavior, have not been accompanied by appropriate modifications in the communication process and in the anticipatory socialization of young people. Modern youth are not equipped at an early age to discriminate for themselves and to choose from among the available alternatives. Knowledge of birth control techniques and the availability of effective contraceptives have not kept pace with the relaxed standards of behavior. Many official and public institutions that relate to individuals of this age group, such as student health services, public hospital clinics, as well as many private physicians, fail to recognize or otherwise avoid their responsibility to provide adequate medical services for the regulation of fertility among young adults. There is, of course, considerable controversy over the appropriateness of extended programs for the provision of contraceptives. The argument by some, particularly religious leaders, is that a "free market" in birth-control materials reinforces permissive standards and contributes to increased extramarital sexual experiences. While this view is not supported by much objective evidence, the tendency of the community to avoid action in these areas undoubtedly contributes to the problem of premarital pregnancy. The prospects for any concerted systematic attack on the high

DOCUMENTATION 2

unmarried father–unwed mother mating patterns

EDUCATION OF 193 UNMARRIED FATHERS AND 193 UNWED MOTHERS, AS REPORTED BY THE UNWED MOTHERS

Unwed Mother's Education	UNMARRIED FATHER'S EDUCATION			
	College Graduate (N = 23)	Attended College (N = 44)	High School Graduate (N = 68)	Less than 12 years (N = 58)
College graduate	69.6%	6.8%	1.5%	—
Attended college	17.4	72.7	5.9	1.7%
High school graduate	8.7	18.2	58.8	19.0
Less than 12 years	4.3	2.3	33.8	79.3
	100.0	100.0	100.0	100.0

The notion that unmarried fathers are much older and much better educated than the females they impregnate is not supported by the data in the present study. This notion has not been seriously challenged as long as descriptions of unwed mothers were derived primarily from institution-type samples and as long as descriptions of unmarried fathers were either unavailable or were not reported on an unmarried father-unwed mother pair basis. For the emphasis on the age and educational superiority of the unmarried father has received support from and represents the obverse of earlier conventional descriptions, which emphasize the extreme youth, poverty, and lack of education of unwed mothers, and were derived primarily from studies of unwed mothers in [agencies and institutions] where youth and low socio-economic status were socially imposed criteria for admission.

In the above table, the educational attainment of the unmarried fathers is seen to be quite similar to that of the respective unwed mothers they impregnated. Educational differences between the unmarried father-unwed mother pairs approximate educational differences between husband-wife pairs in the population. (Vincent, 1960:42.)

rates of illegitimacy, criminal abortions, and shotgun marriages are not encouraging.

Community ambivalence towards the social acceptability of pluralistic norms regarding sexual conduct outside marriage increases the risks of illegitimate pregnancies and raises anxieties on the part of young people about "getting caught." According to many mental health practitioners, it also has consequences in terms of guilt feelings that effect the emotional outlook of individuals and, in some cases, interfere with their social behavior in other spheres such as work and academic performance. Furthermore, such experiences may have an impact on their future adult socialization and may permanently distort their life style. Despite the current so-called liberal attitudes and the permissiveness that seems to pervade the more sophisticated youth groups, the young woman who becomes pregnant is frequently regarded as degraded and the young man is stigmatized as an exploiter, although this identification of the male may not be accurate (Vincent, 1960). (*See* Documentation 2.)

THE SCOPE OF THE PROBLEM

It is, of course, difficult to assess the scope of this problem, for most of the information about such relationships stems from studies of client populations who sought help and counseling from social agencies. One can assume that this self-selection results in a biased set of informants and that the findings would tend to exaggerate the problem. But given our awareness of the current volume of premarital sexual matters, a more explicit recognition of the divergent patterns of behavior practiced by young people is required and a more responsible attitude toward birth-control information and devices is indicated.

In recent years, such recognition has been given only by certain agencies to selected groups of clients. One of the country's best-known colleges for women gives advice and contraceptives to engaged girls upon their request. The armed forces, under the guise of protection against venereal disease, provides contraceptives and information about sexual conduct to military personnel. In some communities, welfare departments have functioned in a similar capacity for their clients. There remains, however, much need for concerted action and broad-scale programs in this area.

prostitution

During this age period, many young men engage for the first time in sexual intercourse with females generically regarded as prostitutes. This is also the age group from which women, whether for short or long periods, are recruited into the ranks of prostitutes and first engage in commercial enterprises.

As is the case with premarital sexual relations, the question of whether prostitution has increased or decreased is one that cannot possibly be answered. It is often asserted that the modification of norms on sexual conduct, if not greater sexual license, reduces the motivation for males to turn to commercialized sex. This view assumes that there is a standard quantity of sexual need on the part of the male population and that if all or most of it can be gratified without a direct financial contract, there will be a reduction in prostitution. The other point of view holds that the male population has a virtually infinite and inexhaustible interest in sexual gratification and consequently will continue to demand the services of prostitutes.

CAUSAL THEORIES

A number of different theories have been put forward to account for the continued existence of prostitution. Certainly, prostitution is related in part to the availability of other sexual outlets and the patterning of social relationships within the community. One finds, for example, generally high rates of prostitution around areas that are sparsely populated and that have large numbers of unattached males, such as military bases or convention centers. Another view holds that the continued existence and the future persistence of prostitution is inevitable because of the relative attractiveness of such a means of sexual gratification; it permits sexual expression without the involvement of long-term affective relationships. As Goode (1966) points out, in many ways relations with a prostitute is perhaps less time-consuming and, in the long run, probably less expensive than the seduction process required with "a nice girl." A third proposition is that the brevity of such relationships and the financial contract itself provide the lure and provoke the interest of males in such sexual engagements.

SEX FOR MONEY

We do know, certainly, that whether or not the incidence of prostitution has changed, there have been changes in the style of operation. Except for legally sanctioned establishments in certain areas such as Nevada, the whore house as an accepted and readily identifiable institution has largely disappeared from most communities as have the overpainted streetwalkers and, some maintain, the pimp with his small stable of girls.

Some of the changes that have occurred in the character of prostitution are related to the general shift in the role of the female in our contemporary society. The unescorted girl in the modern cocktail lounge is as likely to be a virtuous young secretary as a "hooker." Moreover, since it is now socially acceptable for young ladies of this age to rent apartments by themselves, the screen of a pimp or madam is not a requisite for plying the prostitute's trade. Today, the relative sophistication of the total population makes the image of the craven city slicker luring the innocent farm girl into a career of prostitution unrealistic if not downright ridiculous. Finally, the equalitarian status accorded women and the increasing breadth of their social lives often make it difficult to differentiate between the professional prostitute and the woman who engages in casual sexual relations.

apprenticeships in prostitution

The apprenticeship is typically served under the direction of another call girl, but may occasionally be supervised by a pimp. Twenty-four girls in the sample initially worked under the supervision of other girls. The classroom is, like the future place of work, an apartment. The apprentice typically serves in the trainer's apartment, either temporarily residing with the trainer or commuting there almost daily. The novice rarely serves her apprenticeship in such places as a house of prostitution, motel, or on the street. It is also infrequent that the girl is transported out of her own city to serve an apprenticeship. Although the data are not extensive, the number of girls being trained simultaneously by a particular trainer has rarely been reported to be greater than three. Girls sometimes report spending up to eight months in training, but the average stay seems to be two or three months. The trainer controls all referrals and appointments, novices seemingly not having much control over the type of sexual contract made or the circumstances surround-

ing the enactment of the contract.

The content of the training period seems to consist of two broad, interrelated dimensions: one philosophical, the other interpersonal. The former refers to the imparting of a value structure, the latter to "do's" and "don'ts" of relating to customers and, secondarily, to other "working girls" and pimps. The latter teaching is perhaps best described by the concept of a short-range perspective. That is, most of the "do's" and "don'ts" pertain to ideas and actions that the call girl uses in problematic situations. Not all girls absorb these teachings, and those who do incorporate them in varying degrees.

Insofar as a value structure is transmitted it is that of maximizing gains while minimizing effort, even if this requires transgressions of either a legal or moral nature. Frequently, it is postulated that people, particularly men, are corrupt or easily corruptible, that all social relationships are but a reflection of a "con," and that prostitution is simply a more honest or at

---

Nevertheless, the full-time prostitute, well socialized in her profession, continues to make her way. (*See* Documentation 3.) The commercialization of sexual activity represents an interesting dilemma from the perspective of social-problem identification. Its status as a problem for community concern is based not on the judgments of experts or of most community members but on the opinions of a remarkably few moral leaders who challenge prostitution on the grounds that it either contradicts the moral norms of the community–or undermines the institutions of marriage and the family.

LEGALIZATION OF PROSTITUTION

It is held by some that prostitution becomes, or at least remains, a social problem not because of the commercialization of sexual relationships but

least no more dishonest act than the everyday behavior of "squares." Furthermore, not only are "johns" basically exploitative, but they are easily exploited; hence they are, in some respects, stupid. . . .

Training may also include proprieties concerning consuming alcohol and drugs, when and how to obtain the fee, how to converse with the customers and, occasionally, physical and sexual hygiene. As a girl trainer explains:

"First of all, impress cleanliness. Because, on the whole, the majority of girls, I would say, I don't believe there are any cleaner women walking the streets, because they've got to be aware of any type of body odor. . . . You teach them to French [fellatio] and how to talk to men.

"(Do they [pimps] teach you during the turning out period how to make a telephone call?) Oh, usually, yes. They don't teach you, they just tell you how to do it and you do it with your good common sense, but if you have trouble, they tell you more about it."

Interestingly, the specific act of telephoning a client is often distressing to the novice and is of importance in her training. Unfortunately for the girl, it is an act she must perform with reg-

ularity as she does considerable soliciting. One suspects that such behavior is embarrassing for her because it is an unaccustomed role for her to play—she has so recently come from a culture where young women do *not* telephone men for dates. Inappropriate sex-role behavior seems to produce greater personal distress than does appropriate sex-role behavior even when it is morally reprehensible:

"Well, it is rather difficult to get on the telephone, when you've never worked before, and talk to a man about a subject like that, and it is very new to you."

What is omitted from the training should be noted as well. There seems to be little instruction concerning sexual techniques as such, even though the previous sexual experience of the trainee may have been quite limited. What instruction there is typically revolves around the practice of fellatio. There seems to be some encouragement not to experience sexual orgasms with the client, though this may be quite variable with the trainer: ". . . and sometimes, I don't know if it's a set rule or maybe it's an unspoken rule, you don't enjoy your dates." "Yes, he did [teach attitudes]. He taught me to be cold. . . ." (Bryan, 1965:290–293.)

because of the necessity to limit and control its quasi-legitimate status. Prostitutes can operate only with the subrosa complicity of the police and other legal authorities. The illegal status of commercialized vice results in involvement with professional, organized crime and represents an additional source of corruption for law enforcement agencies. As with the other vices, the position of prostitution within the American social structure has the consequence of reinforcing deviant social processes within the community. It has been suggested that the control of prostitution, like the control of gambling and other hedonistic activities that occupy a place in American life, can best be accomplished by legitimating these behaviors; this, say some, is the only realistic solution to the social-problem status of such vices. But although some cities are lax in the control of prostitution —and become more so when groups such as the American Legion are holding a convention in town—legalization of prostitution is unlikely.

As a deviation from community norms, homosexuality is not confined to any particular age group but, rather, can be found among early adolescents as well as persons in later years of life. Age-specific data on homosexual behavior are probably the most difficult to obtain of any social problem discussed in this book. Homosexuality is discussed in this chapter on the young adult because offenders younger than eighteen years of age do not typically come into contact with legal authorities. Regardless of how prevalent homosexual behavior may be among adolescents, when it becomes observable, the community's reaction is to refer those involved to mental health practitioners rather than to the police or courts. In all subsequent age groups, at least some significant proportion of the individuals regarded as homosexuals come into contact with the law. In general, however, there is increasing public acceptance if not tolerance of homosexual conduct, particularly among consenting, discreet adults (Sherwin, 1961).

THE SCOPE OF THE PROBLEM

Homosexuality differs from many social problems in that, at least on the evidence available, persons involved are not identifiable by socio-economic group, profession, religion, education, or any other sociological characteristic. Wooton (1959:48) cites evidence to show that homosexuality exists at all levels of society and that homosexuals may be found not only among those possessing high intelligence but also among "the dullest oafs." There apparently are differences, however, in who becomes an overt homosexual and who is secret about it. (*See* Documentation 4.)

For the purposes of this book, homosexuality is of further interest because of the way it is popularly viewed both as a moral and as an objective social problem. It is fair to say that among the general public, homosexual behavior, at least among adults, is regarded with repugnance, and practicing individuals often are isolated from social activities in all strata of the community. Those in the fields of creative arts and letters may find some patronizing acceptance among sophisticated groups, but those among the lowest socio-economic groups become the victims of verbal and even physical assaults. Ministers and, to some extent, the medical profession and other health practitioners regard the problem as being on a different level from other social problems.

As Dr. Karl Menninger (1963:9) clearly indicates, public reaction to homosexuality is an illustration of the process whereby community members equate a crime with a sin. He holds that homosexuality represents

DOCUMENTATION 4

the homosexual community

The chief distinctions between homosexual groups correspond to the differences in the general modes of evading social controls which homosexuals have developed. Thus, secret and overt homosexuals form distinctive groups.

OCCUPATION OF 40 SECRET AND OVERT HOMOSEXUALS

Occupation	Secret	Overt	Total
Professional & Managerial	13	0	13
Clerical & Sales	9	4	13
Craftsmen	2	1	3
Operatives	1	1	2
Service	0	6	6
Artists	0	3	3
Totals	25	15	40

The distinctions between these groups are maintained by the secret homosexuals who fear identification and refuse to associate with overt homosexuals. This statement by a secret homosexual is illustrative:

"If someone who is gay wanted to be spiteful they could say something in the wrong quarter. Nobody who cared about himself would say anything. The trouble is that some don't care. I make it a rule to avoid anybody who is perfectly open about himself. It's easy not to become friendly with those people but it's hard to avoid them entirely. You certainly don't want to snub them because that might make them antagonistic. You just don't call them or see them at social gatherings. But you do meet them at bars and that's where you can be introduced to them. If they remember you and continue to say hello to you on the street, you have to acknowledge them or they might feel that you are trying to snub them."

The homosexual community thus consists of a large number of distinctive groups within which friendship binds the members together in a strong and relatively enduring bond and between which the members are linked by tenuous but repeated sexual contacts. The result is that homosexuals within the city tend to know or know of each other, to recognize a number of common interests and common moral norms, and to interact on the basis of antagonistic cooperation. This community is in turn linked with other homosexual communities in Canada and the United States, chiefly through the geographical mobility of its members. (Leznoff and Westley, 1956:260, 263.)

an affront to the moral norms held by most community members and yet such behavior is different, at least when undertaken by consenting adults, from a violation that is regarded as destructive of community structure.

SOCIAL LIFE OF HOMOSEXUALS

Indeed, there is a sense in which the common bonds that unite overt homosexuals may be regarded as a deviant social structure. Note their national magazines. Certainly homosexuals do have differentiated patterns of where to meet and how to make pickups:

There are a number of prescribed modes for establishing contact in these situations. They permit the boys and fellators to communicate intent to one another privately despite the public character of the situation. The major form of establishing contact is the "cruise," with the fellator passing "queer-corners" or locations until his effort is recognized by one of the boys. A boy can then signal—usually by nodding his head, a hand gesticulation signifying OK, following or responding to commonly understood introductions such as "you got the time?"— that he is prepared to undertake the transaction. Entrepreneur and client then move to a place where the sexual activity is consummated, usually a place affording privacy, protection, and a hasty exit (Reiss, 1961:106–107).

A significant shift in the formal handling of this problem has occurred in Britain. An Act of Parliament changed the legal statutes so that they no longer identify homosexual conduct between consenting adults as a crime but rather as a matter of individual choice. In many ways this view, which increasingly will be formalized in legal statutes, represents the informal operating principle of legal authorities in most communities. In instances where one of the partners involved is a minor, or undue pressure is exerted for participation, or indiscreet attempts are made by homosexuals to solicit in public places, the community takes action through its social-control system.

There is some evidence to suggest that homosexuals do, at least on occasion, seduce the innocent or the somewhat innocent. Reiss (1961: 109–110) describes one such encounter:

> As the boy enters adolescence and a gang of his own which takes over the corner, he is psychologically and socially prepared for his first experience, which generally occurs when the first opportunity presents itself. Lester H. illustrates this; his first experience when he went to one of the common points of convergence of boys and fellators—The Empress Theatre—to see a movie. Lester relates: "I was down in the Empress Theatre and this gay came over and felt me up and asked me if I'd go out. . . . I said I would if he'd give me the money as I'd heard they did, and I was gettin' low on it. . . . so he took me down by the river and blowed me."

THE PUBLIC CONCERN

Analysts of homosexual conduct often point out that the charged reaction of certain moral leaders and the emotional response of the general public are related to the view that sexual conduct—the rights and obligations of sexual expression—is closely integrated with the rest of the community structural system and particularly with the family and the institution of marriage. As Davis (1966:339) maintains, homosexual liaisons challenge the basic arrangements of the primary group and its monopoly as a sexual outlet. Furthermore, Americans place great emphasis upon sexual differentiation and the delineation of sex roles by appropriate dress, mannerisms, and sexual expression. To some degree homosexual activities require one partner to reject his sex, at least symbolically, and assume the behavior of the opposite sex in contradiction to the norms most of us are taught.

As with other types of deviant conduct that are held to provide hedonistic gratifications, homosexual behavior confronts the average community member with a mystique about the possible intensity of pleasurable experience and the risk that if unchecked it would become so widespread as to be truly disabling to the social order. In this respect critics frequently cite, although not always with historical accuracy, the prevalence of such activities in ancient and primitive societies. The partially sanctioned homosexual behavior found by Ford and Beech (1951:130) in 4,977 societies does not necessarily imply that such behavior had high standing in terms of desirability or that it was practiced by large proportions of the population; however, it does point to the potential emergence of more permissive standards with respect to such conduct.

Whether or not the risk of widespread homosexuality is real is relatively immaterial. (Parenthetically it should be noted that analysts of sexual conduct in the United States regard this as extremely unlikely.) However, a significant proportion of community members hold this view strongly enough to reinforce stringent informal sanctions and, in many cases, to instigate legal action against individuals who manifest such behavior.

Present community values and attitudes towards homosexual behavior are responsible for the existence of other social-policy concerns. For example, the exposure of an individual as a homosexual may endanger his job and social standing (Ruitenbeek, 1963). Also, many homosexuals are not exclusively so but also maintain heterosexual relationships, even becoming husbands and fathers. Revelations about their behavior may be destructive of such normal relationships and the threat of exposure makes them susceptible to blackmail. This is particularly true of individuals who occupy positions of responsibility and esteem. As a consequence, many public positions, particularly those in government and industry that involve access to confidential information, are not available to individuals who even in the distant past can be identified as having engaged in homosexual behavior. Allen Drury's *Advise and Consent* is a graphic fictional example.

Although precise information is difficult if not impossible to obtain, it is widely believed that in some cases the activities of homosexuals are not with truly consenting partners. The extreme image of large numbers of young children and adolescents being lured by force, money, and promises of other rewards into such activities may be exaggerated, but the dangers are patent. These also constitute grounds for community concern with homosexual behavior as a social problem.

HOMOSEXUAL SEX ROLES

That the public reacts much more negatively to homosexual behavior among males than among females is a commonly held view. Again it should be noted that the cultural norms provide for greater displays of affection, including kissing in public places, sharing apartments, and the like, between females than between males. Perhaps this differential response relates to the fact that the male who takes the opposite sex role in homosexual activities pursues a role so contrary to that performed by the male in heterosexual intercourse, which in no way involves the violation of his body orifices. Certainly with respect to both male and female homosexuality, the individual who takes the reverse role is more severely scorned:

> In purely instrumental homosexual intercourse, the male who plays the dominant role is disdained more for his coarseness than for his homosexuality; he retains his masculine character but has temporarily altered the object of his sexual drive, often to a minimum degree because the object is a youth (beardless and with other juvenile and therefore feminine characteristics) or a deliberately self-feminized man (Goode, 1966:341).

There is a widespread conception that both males and females who maintain their own symbolic sex roles in homosexual relationships find it easier to resume normal heterosexual relationships. The role-changers, on the other hand, tend to be regarded as committed homosexuals or as persons who have ulterior goals so far removed from normal relationships that they are despised even by their homosexual partners (Ward and Kassebaum, 1965:170).

CAUSATIVE FACTORS

The causal factors associated with homosexual behavior are identified only in a gross way. There are considerable areas of unexplored lore and uncharted knowledge. This absence of information is related in part to the discretion with which homosexual activities are undertaken and in part to a lack of typological data. There is no typing of homosexuals by frequency or duration of activity. We do not know how often such conduct is sporadic, intermixed with heterosexual activities, or continually and exclusively homosexual.

Most explanations credit inadequate socialization processes and inappropriate parental identification with at least a proclivity for homosexual behavior. In addition, it is believed that nongratifying and unrewarding sexual activities in the late prepuberty and early adolescent years are associated with a predisposition for such conduct. Repetition and the resulting habituation to less threatening or more satisfying homosexual experiences may account for the permanence of such patterns. There is also a growing awareness of the influence of heterosexual deprivation on subsequent conduct. The response, for example, of imprisonment on sexual behavior has been studied sufficiently to indicate that for many inmates, at least those men and women who are totally confined, homosexual behavior is transitory and represents an adaptation to an abnormal situation. In their study of a women's prison, Ward and Kassebaum (1965) carefully distinguished between the prisoners for whom homosexual activities are an expedient and perhaps sole solution to sexual gratification and the smaller proportion of inmates whose life careers are wholly or in part oriented not only to homosexual gratification but to a way of life, inside and outside the prison, in which sexual-companionship relationships are confined to the same sex.

Finally, in plays and novels and, occasionally, in psychiatric literature there is some recognition that homosexual behavior may be undertaken on an occasional or experimental basis as an innovative orgasmic experience. As a famous author wrote in a recent novel, "Friction is friction." The dominant values of the American community make it difficult to judge the extent to which homosexuality on the personal level represents an anxiety-producing role and conflict-ridden status. The behavior may be a manifestation of unresolved psychosexual problems; however, the extent to which such persons hold themselves in low esteem and view their lives with despair because of the fear of discovery or self-disclosure is not known.

INTERVENTION

In any event, homosexuality represents a phenomenon of deviant behavior for which two types of possible solutions are indicated: (1) modification of the normative standards accepted by the community and (2) ameliorative efforts directed at nonconforming individuals and groups. England's removing of homosexual activities between consenting adults from the status of criminal behavior and the consequent impact of this legal reform on the norms of the community is looked upon by most persons concerned with this problem as a progressive step. Minimizing the stigma associated with such conduct when it involves rational decisions by adult participants may encourage more individuals to become involved in various treatment programs and may also eliminate some of the more undesirable side effects, such as limitation of occupation and risk of blackmail, that currently exist.

Psychiatrists and other practitioners who treat homosexuals place varying emphasis upon developing more normative sexual patterns for their patients in contrast with counseling the homosexual to a better adjustment within his special world. Except for self-selected case studies, little is known about the success of individual therapy, particularly concerning the habitual and continual homosexual. However, since most individuals who engage in homosexual activities are not long-term and exclusive devotees of this mode of sexual gratification, counseling has a good possibility of success. An acute awareness of the strains and difficulties of sustaining a homosexual life may prove sufficient to enable some individuals to realign the target of their sexual gratification and establish new modes of conduct.

Concern with the problem of homosexuality in institutional settings has led to a number of changes in established policies although, in many ways, our prisons represent an entirely backward philosophy. Many forms of institutions, such as mental hospitals, have minimized sexual segregation and some even acknowledge the utility of intimate sexual relations between confined persons; however, few institutions would seek to promote opportunities for sexual intercourse as a public policy. But prisons, with few exceptions and contrary to procedures in most Western countries, virtually shut off the inmate from normal modes of sexual gratification. Only in recent years and among selective groups of prisoners have married inmates been permitted conjugal visits, either within the prison itself or on short home leaves. A number of prison administrators contend that their custodial duties would be lightened, homosexuality in general reduced, and rehabilitation carried forward more rapidly if the sexual needs of inmates were openly considered and some rational means developed to cope with this problem.

schizophrenia

Schizophrenia represents by far the most common and the most troublesome of the mental illnesses, being prevalent among all adult age groups. It is considered here because this is the point in the life cycle, at least in terms of hospital admissions and sustained treatment, where schizophrenia first becomes marked. It is during young adulthood that large numbers of people begin to manifest symptoms that identify them as schizophrenic. As Clausen (1966a) notes, the majority of mental patients hospitalized before the age of forty receive a diagnosis of schizophrenia.

One of the concerns with schizophrenia as a social problem is the inability at the present time to identify any efficacious means of treatment. Recent changes in treatment philosophies and the widespread use of drug therapies have shortened the average length of hospital stays and, some claim, diminished the number of readmissions. However, most mental health practitioners still regard the illness as a chronic one; that is, many if not most individuals identified as schizophrenic require either episodic or sustained care in the community or in a hospital. The tendency of most schizophrenics to require repeated hospitalizations and the need by a small number of patients for continuous hospitalization result in a high occupancy rate. It is estimated that more than 50 per cent of the beds in Veterans Administration, state, and county mental hospitals are occupied by patients with this diagnosis.

THE SCOPE OF THE PROBLEM

Although the populations of resident treatment centers have been reduced slightly from their peak in 1955, somewhere between five and six hundred thousand persons at any given time are living in institutions. Perhaps half of these patients are diagnosed as schizophrenic (Freeman and Giovannoni, 1969). As to cost, it is estimated that $3.5 billion are spent each year for the care and treatment of the mentally ill in the United States. It is reasonable to expect that between one-third and two-thirds of this expenditure is for the treatment of individuals regarded as schizophrenic. There is little question about the enormity of the problem of mental illness, and particularly schizophrenia.

A great mystique surrounds schizophrenia, as it does mental illness in general. Both terms are ill-defined and ambiguous (Jahoda, 1958; Scott, 1958). In part, the mystique is provoked by the stereotypes held by community members and by their responses to individuals whose behavior appears inconsistent and virtually uncontrollable. The mystique also stems from the ignorance of scientists and practitioners regarding the etiology of schizophrenia and the relative effectiveness of different modes of treatment. Probably the majority view today is that schizophrenia is essentially a "wastebasket" diagnostic classification. More specifically, many practitioners in the mental health field hold that schizophrenia is not a single disease entity but rather a number of different illnesses and psychological conditions that are impossible to unravel at this time. Perhaps the most reasonable way to think about schizophrenia is to view it as a family of disorders, although current attempts to classify subtypes have proved to be highly unreliable.

A part of the folklore associated with the illness is the notion that a schizophrenic is a split personality. This concept is reinforced by such novels and movies as *Dr. Jekyll and Mr. Hyde* and *The Three Faces of Eve*. Most schizophrenics, however, do not fit this characterization. Rather, they are individuals who, to varying degrees, exhibit bizarre behavior in interpersonal situations and who report a variety of distorted and delusional thoughts. Persons suffering from severe forms of schizophrenia frequently engage in conversations with themselves, hear and see nonexistent things, withdraw from all human contact, refuse to relate to other individuals in a sensible manner, and occasionally threaten to destroy themselves or others. However, most schizophrenics are neither dangerous nor crazy-acting most of the time. Their hallucinations, delusions, and withdrawal symptoms tend to be episodic and, in many instances, remain in remission for weeks, months, and even years. Szasz (1960), himself a psychiatrist, argues that there is no such thing as mental illness but only defective ways in which certain people try to deal with life problems.

SOCIAL ROLES AND MENTAL ILLNESS

An inability to perform well in work or other social situations and an incompetence in coping with the demands of day-to-day life are frequently regarded as symptoms of mental illness. Another point of view holds that the social deficiencies of individuals labeled "mentally ill" stem from the negative reactions of community members to those so identified. Whether it is the bizarre behavior of schizophrenics or merely the labeling of them as ill that accounts for the way they are perceived by the community, their opportunities for employment and other forms of social participation may be severely restricted; indeed, in order to avoid being stigmatized, persons with emotional problems may not seek needed treatment (Mechanic, 1967; Phillips, 1967). Some maintain that the inability of many schizophrenics to perform well on the job and in social situations is a concomitant of their mental disorder and, at least analytically, should not be confused with the illness itself (Freeman and Simmons, 1963). The link between the symptoms of schizophrenia and the social deficiencies that are found to occur with frequency among mental patients is the result of their stigmatization by employers, the police, and their social peers in the community (Lemert, 1962; Scheff, 1963).

Some investigators have questioned whether the stigma of mental illness is a major problem for the schizophrenic patient in terms of the reactions of persons he meets in his life roles, or whether the consequences of stigma represent mainly a residue of psychological discomfort for him (Freeman and Simmons, 1963). But it is indisputable that in many ways, such as participation in the armed forces and eligibility for jobs of responsibility and trust, the community, rightly or wrongly, has rather consistently banned the participation of those labeled "schizophrenic."

Many of the reactions towards the schizophrenic have been judged to be irrational, a result of the mystique that surrounds mental illness and the mental patient. In a number of states, for example, certain professionals, such as physicians, can have their licenses suspended for considerable periods if diagnosed a psychotic; other states suspend driver's licenses; and only rarely are such individuals given security clearances by governmental agencies. An extreme position taken by a few within the psychiatric profession holds that society is far more punitive to the mentally ill, including those judged schizophrenic, than it is to so-called normal individuals whose actions are not judged to be caused by mental illness. For example, whereas most individuals convicted of a misdemeanor or lesser felony may receive a light prison sentence or probation, individuals declared schizophrenic would be denied the benefits of due process of law and would be subject to extended periods of custody in mental hospitals (Bittner, 1967).

Some critics contend that, under the guise of humanitarian and medical philosophies, large groups of individuals are not rehabilitated or, for that matter, treated at all but rather are subjected to severe restrictions in their life roles, often being committed to total institutions without requisite legal safeguards (Szasz, 1960). (*See* Documentation 5.) Certainly the hospital experiences undergone by such patients cannot be regarded as pleasant or productive. Indeed, as we shall discuss subsequently, the very limited efficacy of most treatment programs calls into question the entire hospitalization process as it applies to schizophrenics. First, however, some comments on the etiology of the illness are pertinent.

CAUSES

The literature on mental illness abounds with persuasive discussions on the causes of schizophrenia. It is fair to say, however, that no one knows what causes this illness. The distinct possibility that schizophrenia is not a single disease entity complicates the problem and makes highly unlikely the development of any definitive theory about causation until the specific illnesses involved are isolated. Current views on etiology range from strictly biophysical—an undiscovered germ or virus or an unidentified physiological malfunctioning is the cause of schizophrenia—to faulty interpersonal relations. In addition to the important work being undertaken in the biological and physiological sciences, extensive efforts continue to document the influence of early socialization, psychosexual incongruities, inadequacies of family life throughout childhood, adolescence, and adulthood, as well as the more sociological studies that emphasize structural variables associated with communities, institutions, and groups.

All of these studies share a measure of methodological criticism. For example, the classic investigation of the relationship of social-class status to mental illness made by Hollingshead and Redlich (1958) reported much higher rates of hospitalization for schizophrenia among persons at

medical and social issues of mental illness

I have tried to show that the notion of mental illness has outlived whatever usefulness it might have had and that it now functions merely as a convenient myth. As such, it is a true heir to religious myths in general, and to the belief in witchcraft in particular; the role of these belief-systems was to act as *social tranquilizers,* thus encouraging the hope that mastery of certain specific problems may be achieved by means of substitutive (symbolic-magical) operations. The notion of mental illness thus serves mainly to obscure the everyday fact that life for most people is a continuous struggle, not for biological sur-vival, but for a "place in the sun," "peace of mind," or some other human value. For man aware of himself and of the world about him, once the needs for preserving the body (and perhaps the race) are more or less satisfied, the problem arises as to what he should do with himself. Sustained adherence to myth of mental illness allows people to avoid facing this problem, believing that mental health, conceived as the absence of mental illness, automatically insures the making of right and safe choices in one's conduct of life. But the facts are all the other way. It is the making of good choices in life that others regard, retro-

the lower end of the socio-economic continuum. Not only have other studies failed to support this finding, but a number of analysts believe that lower-class status is a result, not a cause of mental illness (Dohren-wend, 1966; Dunham et al., 1966; Turner and Wagenfeld, 1967). Another criticism leveled at investigations of family processes in relation to schizophrenia is that they have been undertaken without adequate and comparable control groups. Critics maintain that a comparison of patient groups with so-called normal individuals would reveal very few environmental differences that could be associated with the illness (Freeman and Giovannoni, 1969).

There is no way at this time to elaborate any comprehensive theory acceptable to the army of researchers and practitioners presently working on the problem of schizophrenia. The broad outlines of an interdisciplinary theory would include the recognition of a causal model that approximates to some extent the one expressed earlier in this book, that is, a series of interrelated phenomena that cut across the various domains of the life and social sciences. There is increasing evidence that different individuals have varying predispositions to mental illness (Rosenthal, 1963). Whether these are related to attacks of germs, the functioning of glands, or other physiochemical conditions is yet to be determined.

spectively, as good mental health!

The myth of mental illness encourages us, moreover, to believe in its logical corollary: that social intercourse would be harmonious, satisfying, and the secure basis of a "good life" were it not for the disrupting influences of mental illness of "psychopathology." The potentiality for universal human happiness, in this form at least, seems to me but another example of the I-wish-it-were-true type of fantasy. I do believe that human happiness or well-being on a hitherto unimaginably large scale, and not just for a select few, is possible. This goal could be achieved, however, only at the cost of many men, and not just a few being willing and able to tackle their personal, social, and ethical conflicts. This means having the courage and integrity to forego waging battles on false fronts, finding solutions for substitute problems—for instance,

fighting the battle of stomach acid and chronic fatigue instead of facing up to a marital conflict.

Our adversaries are not demons, witches, fate, or mental illness. We have no enemy whom we can fight, exorcise, or dispel by "cure." What we do have are *problems in living*—whether these be biologic, economic, political, or socio-psychological. In this essay I was concerned only with problems belonging in the last mentioned category, and within this group mainly with those pertaining to moral values. The field to which modern psychiatry addresses itself is vast, and I made no effort to encompass it all. My argument was limited to the proposition that mental illness is a myth, whose function it is to disguise and thus render more palatable the bitter pill of moral conflicts in human relations. (Szasz, 1960: 117–118.)

Throughout the course of his life experience, an individual is conditioned to ways of behaving and develops temperamental and emotional dispositions associated with the advent of this illness. Consequently, a number of different, and generally incompatible, views have been offered concerning the family and its role as an agent of socialization (Mishler and Waxler, 1966). In addition to the possibility of biological predispositions and variations in emotional resources, the individual's day-to-day life and the degree of social stress or press, as some prefer to call it, upon him is determined by his place within the social structure (Myers and Roberts, 1964). The quality and quantity of his work experience and his subjugation to various environmental problems also represent toxic elements that cause, or at least set off, the disease (Srole et al., 1962).

Although a comprehensive theory must necessarily be left in abeyance, the various therapeutic programs, while weighing differently the biological, interpersonal, and structural causal elements, apparently recognize the relevance of all of them. Also, of course, the myriad of causative factors are ascribed different social meanings by community members which call forth various social responses. In reaction to these responses, patients frequently behave in ways that result in their being labeled "mentally ill" (Clausen, 1967).

In turning to the problems of treatment and prevention of schizophrenia it is important to note that, while we may not have come very far in terms of developing efficacious treatment programs, we have made progress in implementing more humanitarian approaches. But this movement toward more humane treatment has not gone far enough. During the centuries that Western man has been concerned with the problems of mental illness, a variety of specific therapies have been advanced. Among the more recent are surgical approaches such as prefrontal lobotomy, in which a selected portion of the brain is purposely damaged; the development of a variety of chemical and electrical therapies designed to "shock" the functioning of the central nervous system; and the employment of various modes of psychotherapy, ranging from intensive, long-term psychoanalysis to group therapies of relatively short duration.

Two additional therapeutic techniques are usually held to be useful in the treatment of schizophrenia, if only for their supportive and ameliorative value. One is drug therapy, whereby tranquilizers are used to reduce the bizarre behavior and to increase the social performance of the patient. The second is the implementation of work-training and other programs directed at resocializing the patient in terms of interpersonal social participation. The rationale of these measures rests on the assumption that restoration of the individual to normal modes of conduct is important to the treatment of this illness. Many psychiatrists look upon drug therapy and the various types of vocational and social rehabilitation as necessary adjuncts to the more primary treatment procedures. Nevertheless, these supportive measures have served, for one reason or another, to reduce drastically the length of stay in public hospitals (Linn, 1959; Klerman, 1961).

INDIVIDUAL THERAPIES

It is fair to note that none of the specific therapies has been subjected to rigorous testing. Those involving surgical intervention have been abandoned as excessively cruel after reasonably adequate study failed to support their utility (Greenblatt et al., 1961). There has been a diminished emphasis on shock treatment for the same reasons, that is, limited demonstrated therapeutic effect and evidence of needless suffering as a result of the experience.

The use of psychotherapeutic techniques, particularly those of long duration, has also been minimized, but here the rationale is quite different. Many psychiatrists refuse to yield on the question of the efficacy of various modes of psychotherapy even though they cannot produce empirical evidence to support their point of view. However, most are

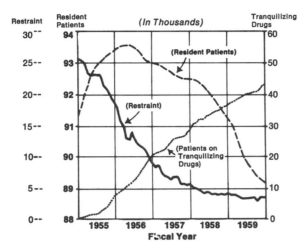

This figure shows trends in percentage of patients requiring seclusion (restraint) and in total number of patients residing in New York State hospitals in the four years following the introduction and . . . increasing use of tranquilizing drugs. (Brill and Patton, 1959:498.)

realistic enough to recognize the impossibility of providing these resources to all schizophrenics in the community. For the most part, such therapies are used only if the patient can pay for them or his treatment can serve in the training of other psychotherapists. Psychotherapeutic techniques of shorter duration, particularly those that involve participation as a member of a group, are in widespread use, and both drug therapies and work rehabilitation programs are currently in vogue. The use of tranquilizers has been shown to reduce both the number of patients requiring seclusion or restraint in hospital and the number requiring hospitalization. (*See* Documentation 6.)

One of the more inglorious chapters in the history of the treatment of mental illness is that concerned with custodial care. The virtual imprisonment of patients is rationalized on the basis that they are risks to the community or to themselves. A number of historical analyses suggest that such programs were developed and persist not because the patient presents any real danger but because the community rejects him. His containment in an institution relieves the community of the burden of having to put up with his bizarre behavior, even when it is harmless. Such institutions have existed for centuries and, undoubtedly, they contribute more to the illness than to the health of many patients. In the last several decades, humanitarian concern about the reprehensible conditions in many state hospitals and the emergence of scientific evidence to indicate an increase in the illness of institutionalized patients have brought about radical changes and amazing developments in the care of even chronic patients. This change is due in part to the work of psychiatrists and social scientists (Stanton and Schwartz, 1954) who have demonstrated that a more normal and democratic milieu will contribute to patient improvement and in part to the self-confidence expressed by patients undergoing drug therapy who have experienced remission of their bizarre symptomatology.

MINIMIZING HOSPITALIZATION

For the most part, the duration of hospitalization has become increasingly short (Gardner et al., 1964). The old view that a patient once hospitalized would always be hospitalized has certainly changed radically. Today, the hospital experience of the majority of patients can be measured in months or even weeks. This accounts for some decrease in the use of mental hospitals by community populations (Pasamanick, Scarpitti and Dinitz, 1967).

Mental hospitals have also changed their orientations. Instead of dingy, prison-like environments of complete despair, they have become environments of some hope. Hospitals built in the last fifteen or twenty years look more like hotels; physical restraints, high walls, and barred windows have been eliminated as unnecessary for most schizophrenic patients. New emphasis also has been given to the selection of better qualified aides, attendants, and paramedical personnel (Stanton and Schwartz, 1954; Caudill, 1958; Belknap, 1959; Dunham and Weinberg, 1960). This emphasis upon better qualified personnel has extended to the recruitment and training of psychiatrists. The encouragement and impetus of federal training programs, as well as the shifting orientations away from hospital care, have increased the economic rewards and enhanced the respectability of psychiatric practice. It should be pointed out, however, that these changes in the hospital treatment of mental patients are by no means universal; old-fashioned, inadequately and incompetently staffed mental hospitals still exist. A significant number of patients must continue to suffer in the back wards until these changes become uniform throughout the nation (Dunham and Weinberg, 1960).

In addition to improvements in hospital treatment, a wide variety of less custodial services have been implemented. Among these has been the development of foster-care programs and other part-time residential facilities. Besides foster homes in the community, these facilities include half-way houses and day, night, and weekend hospitals. Essentially all of these represent environments in which the individual occupies a semi-patient role, sheltered from the exigencies to total involvement in community life but exposed selectively to normal social interaction. The availability of such intermediate settings has made possible the short stay of patients in hospitals and has minimized the impact of what Goffman (1962) calls "total institutions," an impact that virtually submerges the individuality and the autonomy of the patient and constrains and restricts the staff from normal interaction with him.

COMMUNITY TREATMENT

Many persons recognize that mental institutions function to remove the patients from upsetting environments and to provide a protective setting in which restoration and natural improvement can take place. They also serve as a repository for troublesome individuals whose behavior the community is unable or unwilling to tolerate. However, for most individuals, the symptoms of schizophrenia are episodic in character. Although practitioners understand little about the length and intensity of cycles of bizarre conduct, it is known that most schizophrenics have periods, sometimes quite long ones, in which the symptoms are entirely or almost entirely in remission. At such times, hospitalization is not only unnecessary but may be countertherapeutic. Recognition of this anamoly has brought a renewed emphasis on the outpatient treatment for schizophrenics (Biometrics Branch, 1963; Mechanic, 1966). The development of community-based programs for the treatment of all mentally ill patients has been greatly accelerated during the last decade.

Even today, however, many community mental health treatment centers can be accused of neglecting the schizophrenic in favor of the treatment of children and persons exhibiting less severe neurotic disorders. Several reasons have been given for this proclivity of mental health facilities to favor such patients: the middle-class orientation of most psychiatrists has precluded their involvement with lower-class patients who constitute a large proportion of the schizophrenic population; the mental health practitioner's desire for successful results has led him to choose nonschizophrenic patients who show a greater likelihood for therapeutic change.

As with the recruitment of psychiatrists, a strong impetus from federal programs has encouraged the outpatient care of schizophrenics. These efforts have altered the role relationships of mental health professionals toward their patients and have expanded the network of persons involved in the treatment of mental illness. Not only psychiatrists but social workers, psychologists, and a wide range of other personnel, including vocational counselors and public health nurses, are engaged in the care of released patients and schizophrenics who have never been hospitalized. While such programs have not demonstrated any superiority in treating mental illness, they certainly provide functional equivalents to hospitalization, thereby minimizing admission and readmission rates to hospitals—a result considered highly desirable by most mental health practitioners. Although the environmental and interpersonal conditions within hospitals can be and, to some extent, have been remedied, practitioners believe that the institutionalization of patients represents an undesirable situation which should be prevented whenever possible.

In addition to these developments, a number of public education programs have sought to provide the general public with more knowledge about the phenomenon of mental illness. In the first burst of enthusiasm, sponsors of these programs naively presumed that they would have an impact on the basic attitudes of community members that would reduce the stigma associated with mental illness and facilitate the community's acceptance of mental patients (Cumming and Cumming, 1957). We now know from a number of studies (Scott and Freeman, 1966) that the major success of such programs consists in improving the amount of knowledge held by community members rather than in changing their basic attitudes. However, the sum of all of these developments has been a reduction in the overall antagonism of community members toward mental illness and a more sympathetic relationship between mental patients and their associates.

PUBLIC INVOLVEMENT

Regardless of whether any of the specific therapies now in use are in fact effective, the liberalized outlook of the general public and the reduced feelings of stigma should result in less resistance to treatment, particularly on an outpatient basis (Scheff, 1963). Short periods of hospitalization for mental illness will be accepted in the same way as hospitalization for physical illnesses. The current policy, again encouraged by federal programs, is to de-emphasize large state mental hospitals and, instead, to include mental health treatment facilities as part of general medical hospitals and outpatient programs. By discouraging the treatment of mental patients in any way different from other persons who need health service, such efforts preclude relegating schizophrenics to continuous care in isolated wards and, consequently, serve to minimize lengthy periods of hospitalization. In many instances, outpatient facilities make possible treatment closer to the patient's home and permit greater access to him in terms of visiting hours, consultations with relatives, and the like.

Paralleling these new treatment efforts has been an increased concern with both community organizations and political processes as they relate to mental illness. Many of those engaged in the development of mental health programs believe that understanding, acceptance, and participation on the part of the total community are essential for the success of their efforts. In most states, citizens' groups have been heavily involved at a policy-making level in the development of the community mental health facilities. In this respect, the national and local associations of mental health, although subject to criticism because of the programs they advocate, have been extremely active and influential in changing the traditional patterns of care for the mentally ill.

The main accusation against citizen groups is that they, too, are often oriented toward the treatment of children and neurotics rather than the more seriously impaired community members. This policy is explained on the grounds that most of the constituencies of these voluntary groups are drawn from the middle class in which these problems are of more concern than is schizophrenia (Davis, 1938). In recent years, these voluntary organizations and citizen groups have placed greater emphasis on recruiting members representing various strata in the community, including individuals of various ethnic and social-class groupings.

SOCIAL PSYCHIATRY

The general health field and the social sciences have experienced considerable gains from the research undertaken with respect to the cause and treatment of schizophrenia. Many behavioral research studies and a number of physiological and pharmacological investigations have been undertaken because of their potential payoff in the care and treatment of the mentally ill. As a side benefit, these accelerated research programs have made important contributions to the behavioral sciences and to the general practice of medicine.

In discussing schizophrenia as the most common of the mental illnesses, it is important to note the development of a new branch of psychiatry—social psychiatry—that is concerned with shifting and changing structural elements in the community. This social approach to psychiatry recognizes that the problems of prevention are at least of equal, if not of more, importance than the treatment of those already afflicted with mental illness.

> Prevention has to do with the quality of the interactions and the degree of effectiveness of the primary institutions of a society in providing each person with increments of ego strength and personality

robustness for coping with the "slings and arrows" of life. The nature of these interactions and experiences would be considered preventive to the extent to which such experiences enhance the degrees of psychological freedom of an individual to select behavioral alternatives and to act upon them. This preventive model and point of view was succinctly illustrated by an old Cornish test of insanity related by Woodward. The test situation comprised a sink, a tap of running water, a bucket and a ladle. The bucket was placed under the tap of running water and the subject asked to bail the water out of the bucket with the ladle. If the subject continued to bail without paying some attention to reducing or preventing the flow of water into the pail, he was judged to be mentally incompetent. Similarly, any society that attempts to provide more and larger buckets to contain the problems of that society, without simultaneously attempting to reduce the flow, might be equally suspect. Treatment, rehabilitation and incarceration are our necessary buckets to contain the flow. Prevention, however, deals with the tap, the sources of flow and the leverages needed to turn the faucets down or off (Bower, 1963:847).

For this reason, psychiatrists and other mental health practitioners have become involved in action programs that seek to reduce poverty, ethnic and racial tensions, unemployment, slum housing, and the like (Duhl, 1963). The rationales for their participation are several. Persons trained in mental health have exhibited a knowledge of social processes and an ability to understand individual motivations that have proved valuable in developing community organizations and enlisting citizen participation in a variety of social-problem situations.

In line with the view that the major conditions contributing to the development of schizophrenia are the presses or stresses that envelop individuals who experience only limited participation in the social and economic life of the community, a number of psychiatrists, often in collaboration with sociologists and anthropologists, have undertaken comprehensive studies of communities or community groups (Hughes et al., 1960). Many of these investigations, while not demonstrating a causal relationship between community structure and schizophrenia, are quite persuasive in indicating the potential link between the incidence of mental illness and deficiencies in social structure.

The prevalence of schizophrenia among low-income and minority-group members and the inordinate strains associated with certain occupational careers and other environmental circumstances have stimulated a variety of community programs. We have already discussed the mental health consultation programs for school teachers, social workers, and other "caretakers" (Caplan, 1964). A number of demonstration programs have been undertaken to increase participation of selected groups, both in the treatment process as clients of mental health or other community facilities and in the preventive educational programs of health and welfare agencies. In many ways, mental health practitioners have served as standard-bearers of a liberal and humanitarian movement to improve community conditions, and their contributions to the community's efforts to ameliorate its social problems should be recognized and applauded.

crimes against persons and property

Persons of all ages apparently commit all types of crimes, but the young-adult age group is marked by unduly high rates both of crimes against persons, that is, crimes of aggression, and of crimes against property, such as theft, robbery, and breaking and entering (Cressey, 1966). Moreover, they have the highest rates of repeated legal encounters. (*See* Documentation 7.) As noted in our discussion of delinquency, not all criminal acts result in the apprehension of offenders; further, law enforcement officials tend to hold a number of biases that determine in part who gets caught and what happens to him when apprehended (President's Commission on Law Enforcement and Administration of Justice, 1967). Nevertheless, arrest statistics reveal that young adults commit a high percentage of crimes of aggression and are heavily involved in crimes against property. Persons between the ages of eighteen and twenty-five (an age group somewhat broader than we are discussing but the age interval used in statistical reports) account for approximately 25 per cent of arrests for murder and manslaughter, 40 per cent of arrests for forcible rape, an equal percentage for robbery, 20 per cent of those for aggravated assault, 30 per cent of those for burglary, 20 per cent of those for car theft, and almost 30 per cent of those for carrying weapons. (*See* Documentation 8.)

Much of the thinking regarding the juvenile offender is relevant to our discussion here. The explanation for the high rates of criminal behavior among young adults lies not only in the offender's personal development and temperament but also in his lack of occupational and social opportunities and in the community's failure to integrate him into the social structure. As in the case of juveniles, at least of those who are arrested or convicted, an extremely high proportion of the young adults who engage in criminal activities come from lower socio-economic backgrounds, minority groups, and/or family situations which are either conflict ridden or devoid of chances for normal socialization because of the absence of one parent.

THE DIMENSIONS OF THE PROBLEM

Some authorities believe that young-adult criminal behavior represents an extension of juvenile activities and a postponement of a social ma-

post-release violation rates in relation to age at release

WISCONSIN PAROLEES		
	ADULT	
Age at release	Males	Females
	Per Cent	Per Cent
Under 20	31	40
20 to 24	37	26
25 to 29	41	13
30 to 34	40	23
35 to 39	34	29
40 to 49	29	14
50 to 59	28	50
60 and over	21	. . . .
Rates for all cases	36	23
Number of all cases	2,255	206

FEDERAL ADULT MALE RELEASES	
Age at release	Failure rate
	Per Cent
18 to 19	51
20 to 21	46
22 to 23	42
24 to 25	38
26 to 30	36
31 to 35	30
36 to 40	28
41 to 49	25
50 and over	29
Rates for all cases	35
Number of all cases	1,015

It will suffice at this point to observe that the age group which has the highest crime rates in most industrialized societies is the vaguely defined one which is in transition between childhood and adulthood. These are the people we call "adolescents." For them to become adults, in the sense that others treat them as adults, requires not just physical maturation, but the acquisition of a self-sufficient position in the adult economic and social

turity demanded by the values and cultural norms of the community. In some states this view is recognized in "youthful offender acts," an extension of the concept of the juvenile as not being fully responsible for his behavior. Such legislation usually leaves to the discretion of the courts the decision whether the youth in his late teens or early twenties is treated as a juvenile or is regarded as an adult criminal.

The extension of the juvenile-delinquency philosophy to offenders within the young-adult group is based in part on the view that the young-adult offender either is a sick person acting out the symptoms of mental illness or is a deviant individual responding to the inadequate opportunities offered him by the larger community. The mental illness explanation often is given to account for individuals who are arrested for crimes of assault and murder; the lack of opportunity hypothesis is presented to account for crimes against property.

Another view frequently expressed is that the high crime rates in this

world Prisoners tend to be persons who have failed in the past and may be handicapped in the future in achieving this transition, although most of them eventually do become self-sufficient in a legitimate adult life.

These data have two important general implications for parole policy in dealing with youthful offenders.

First is the emphasis on change. It is the consensus of both statistical analysis and personal impressions of experienced officials that youth are the least predictable of all prisoners. Although they have high rates of return to crime, this rate diminishes as they mature, and it is hard to predict when their criminal careers may end. They are in a period in which old associates and points of view may suddenly be dropped, and new ones gained. Innumerable cases can be cited where marriage, new employment, or other incidents marked a turning point which was followed by the complete metamorphosis of such offenders. Many individuals with long histories of juvenile crime, including acts of violence and drug addiction, now lead respectable and law-abiding lives.

The second implication is that youth are particularly in need of new paths to follow toward a secure and satisfying life. Frequently, they have only had gratification in delinquent pursuits, and have only felt at ease and important in a delinquent social world. Simply to release such a youth unconditionally, to give him "another chance" with no prospect that he will enter a new social and occupational world, is likely to be futile. Placing such a youth where he may have new and satisfying legitimate achievements which contribute to his self-sufficiency, and new types of contacts among his peers, is much preferable to merely "giving him a buck" by parole. A feasible school or work program, or a combination of the two, and a home in which the youth feels "at home," are ideal ingredients for rehabilitating a youthful criminal. While it is easy to state these desirable resources, their procurement is difficult. Frequently, relatives of a youth make rash promises for parole placement which they do not intend to keep, or for which neither they nor the youth are adequately prepared. This includes both home and job arrangement. (Glaser and O'Leary, 1966b:6–7.)

age group represent systematic interaction patterns between criminal and victim and that the relationship between these two participants must be taken into account in a considerable number of crimes. This is particularly true in the case of assaultive acts. It is a popular assumption, for example, that female rape victims are rarely entirely innocent. While there is little research to support this view, certainly males in this age bracket have a variety of socially sanctioned opportunities for formal and informal contacts with women who may provoke them into aggressive sexual conduct. There is considerable difference, for instance, in the tone of interpersonal relations between young adults attending a co-educational university and those living alone in a large city. As a recent study points out, many assault victims are known to their attacker:

Almost two-thirds of the 151 (rape) victims surveyed were attacked by persons with whom they were at least casually acquainted. Only 36 percent of the 224 assailants about whom some identifying information was obtained were complete strangers to their victims: 16 (7 percent) of the attackers were known to the victim by sight, although there had been no previous contact. Thirty-one (14 percent) of the assailants were relatives, family friends, or boyfriends of the victims, and 88 (39 percent) were either acquaintances or neighbors (President's Commission on Law Enforcement and Administration of Justice, 1967:81).

TYPES OF CRIMINALS

It is necessary, when considering the problem of criminal offenses in this age group, to separate various types of criminals. As we shall discuss subsequently, one of the major problems from the standpoint of amelioration is the tendency to treat all offenders alike or to make decisions regarding their "rehabilitation"—if that is what it can be called—without taking into account the nature and circumstance of the criminal act. At the very least it is important to separate those individuals whose acts are aggressive from the larger group of "ordinary" criminals, persons of this age who begin careers of regular crime with frequent and repeated offenses (Weinberg, 1960).

Certainly society needs to be concerned about those offenders whose crimes are not for economic gain, either directly or indirectly. Among this group there exists a small but troublesome proportion of mentally ill individuals who are usually characterized by the term *psychopath,* individuals whose internal controls are absent or deficient. Their single or, occasionally, series of offenses are destructive to human life and frightening to the community at large. Some of these individuals may have been in mental health treatment programs, but either the treatment failed or the offenders did not complete it. The possibility that social-control programs can be devised to reach such individuals at a prevention level is exceedingly slim.

In discussing delinquency, we noted that there are many elements within the American social structure that promote, rather than inhibit, aggressive behavior. Given this climate of community acceptance of or, at best, ambivalence toward aggression, it is inevitable that aggressive acts destructive to life and limb will be committed. Unfortunately, we do not know very much about how to identify potentially aggressive persons. Moreover, to believe that broad programs of prevention can be constructed without seriously violating the privacy, personal privileges, and freedom of large numbers of other individuals in the community is foolish.

Perhaps the key unresolved issue is whether such individuals should be treated as criminals or as mental patients. On the one hand, psychiatric care has proved only remotely efficacious in most cases. On the other

DOCUMENTATION 8

arrests of minors and young adults, 1953 and 1960

CATEGORIES OF ARRESTS

Offense for Which Arrest Was Made	Total Arrests 1960, All Ages	PERCENTAGE OF PERSONS ARRESTED IN AGE GROUPS					
		Under 18		18 to 20		21 to 24	
		1953	1960	1953	1960	1953	1960
Murder and Non-negligent Manslaughter	4,507	4.1	7.7	6.9	10.6	12.6	12.6
Manslaughter by Negligence	1,766	3.9	7.4	10.5	11.6	16.2	16.0
Robbery	29,326	18.0	27.8	18.4	19.6	20.6	18.5
Aggravated Assault	52,277	6.0	11.6	7.3	8.9	13.2	12.9
Other Assaults	134,538	5.3	10.1	7.0	8.5	14.0	13.9
Burglary	110,047	49.3	51.1	13.9	15.1	11.7	11.5
Theft (except auto)	207,548	40.1	49.2	11.1	12.1	9.9	8.7
Auto Theft	54,024	53.6	62.1	16.2	16.5	11.2	8.6
Embezzlement and Fraud	32,550	3.6	2.6	9.2	5.4	11.1	13.0
Receiving Stolen Property	10,049	24.9	27.4	11.7	13.5	12.3	13.7
Forgery and Counterfeiting	18,958	6.6	7.9	10.0	10.5	13.8	16.8
Forcible Rape	6,068	16.2	20.5	21.6	21.6	18.2	18.6
Prostitution and Commercialized Vice	25,851	1.2	1.6	9.5	8.2	28.5	22.9
Other Sex Offenses (including statutory rape)	44,532	16.0	20.7	8.1	11.2	13.5	13.8
Drug Law Violation	23,430	4.1	4.1	12.3	12.8	24.9	22.3
Carrying Concealed and Deadly Weapons	34,520	11.7	9.0	11.3	13.3	15.5	15.3
Offenses Against Family and Children	34,203	6.3	2.0	5.4	7.3	13.6	15.1
Liquor Law Violation	86,818	8.5	19.2	14.2	26.6	9.0	7.8
Drunken Driving	146,381	.5	.8	3.2	3.9	11.1	10.3
Disorderly Conduct	449,444	8.0	11.5	9.2	11.1	14.5	12.8
Drunkenness	1,326,407	.6	1.0	2.3	2.8	6.4	6.2
Vagrancy	146,105	4.1	6.3	7.9	9.9	10.2	9.8
Gambling	119,243	1.1	1.5	2.5	3.0	6.7	9.0
Arrests on Suspicion	126,782	15.1	17.6	15.2	17.9	16.6	16.5
Other Offenses	453,462	21.5	36.8	9.7	9.3	12.7	10.1
Grand Total	3,678,836	8.4	14.3	6.3	8.1	10.2	9.7

In 1960, 2,460 cities, with a total population of 81,660,735, provided information, making possible the construction of the above table. This table is presented, first of all, to show the relative volume of the different categories of crime. In that connection, it should be remembered that each arrest of a person is a unit in the tabulation so that, if a person has been arrested more than once, he will appear more than once in the totals. About 52 percent of the arrests were for drunkenness, disorderly conduct, and vagrancy, and over 3 percent were arrests on suspicion, which presumably led to no prosecution. (Sellin, 1962:20–21.)

hand, long-term custodial care, used solely as a punitive device, may contain the offender but hardly represents a humane or, for that matter, an expedient approach, considering the shortages of financial and manpower resources. We may anticipate, however, a continuance of punitive treatment for those with records of repeated aggressive acts simply because we do not know anything else to do with them.

The ordinary criminal, that is, the thief, the robber, and so on, who as a young adult begins a career of crime, raises equally troublesome problems. First, a certain portion of the crimes against property committed by persons in this age group involve the use of weapons, which is frightening to the community. Second, at least some of the crimes against property, in addition to involving force, tend to be at a level of sophistication that makes apprehension difficult and prevention by local law enforcement groups only partially successful and expensive. Third, some ordinary criminals (probably the more successful ones), as they progress through their criminal careers, eventually become involved with professional criminals and organized crime. When caught, the ordinary criminal needs legal services and possibly political favors. He requires the help of professional bondsmen, loan sharks to see him through dry periods and, upon occasion, the protection of the racketeer. Thus he is a ready source for recruitment into professional and organized crime—topics to be discussed in the next section.

POLICE CONTROL

The community faces a serious and continuous problem in its efforts to counter sophisticated criminal activities with limited police resources. As in the case of much delinquent behavior, the prevalent view today is that the most productive means of preventing ordinary crime, crimes against property and for economic gain, lies in reducing the inequities in opportunity and removing the deficiencies in socialization so that individuals can adopt more appropriate social values.

At the same time, community resources must be deployed to develop improved means of protection that will either minimize or make more difficult the activities of the ordinary criminal. It is foolhardy to believe, however, that the detection and apprehension of ordinary criminals by the police is going to eliminate crime completely in most American communities. Indeed, there is some question whether the police can achieve "high clearance rates," i.e., apprehend and convict offenders, and still conform to the principles of the law (Skolnick, 1960). The possibility of supplying sufficient police surveillance to prevent breaking and entering into homes while residents are absent, to provide protection to the many business establishments that keep on hand large amounts of cash, and to curtail automobile thefts and the robbery of delivery trucks is difficult to imagine. Probably the only realistic approach is to render the gains to be derived from criminal activities less attractive than the prospects for income and perhaps social standing that can be obtained by legitimate means.

PROSPECTS FOR REHABILITATION

With criminals in this age group, the chances for rehabilitation are very slim. (*See* Documentation 9.) Our system of criminal law imposes upon the courts dual tasks which involve diverse and often conflicting philosophies. On the one hand, the courts are confronted with maximizing the protection of law-abiding community members. Such protection frequently is accomplished only by keeping offenders isolated in a custodial setting for a long time. On the other hand, the legal system calls for the rehabilitation of the offender. Because our present penal system is primarily committed to custody, deep-seated hostility and an uncooperative attitude on the part of the apprehended and adjudicated criminal is the result. Moreover, our legal system is beset by numerous inconsistencies, including differences between states (*see* Documentation 10).

There are many similarities in the problems involving the care of mental patients and the treatment of adult criminal offenders. The numerous commentaries on the nature of the "inmate environment" apply to both groups (Irwin and Cressey, 1962; Roebuck, 1963). One can rationalize institutionalization as a mechanism for protecting the community from the offender and even, in some cases, as a convenient locus for programs of psychological treatment, work-training, and the like. But the liabilities inherent in institutional care are equally great. The pervasiveness of these settings and the resulting damage to the inmate's personality and social development have frequently been subjects of serious criticism (Garabedian, 1963). Restriction of mental and physical activity, sexual deprivation, the impact of a total institution, and the sustained contact with other deviant individuals are given as reasons for the failure of our penal system to rehabilitate adult offenders. As a consequence, high rates of recidivism are common. One out of every three persons released from custody is imprisoned again within five years (President's Commission on Law Enforcement and Administration of Justice, 1967).

> The structure of the prison is in an uneasy balance between the different functions it is designed to meet. As a prisoner expressed it: "This prison is neither harsh enough to make me repent or to fear it, nor is it good enough to make me accept society." The problem was easier some generations ago, when it was sincerely believed that the same austere treatment could satisfy as diverse functions as retribution and resocialization. But the trend today is towards an increasing belief

men, merchants, and toughs

In describing the reactions of men to imprisonment; we may be describing four basic patterns of adjustment to any situation which involves some degree of goal frustration. It is not surprising, therefore, that Parsons' "directions of deviant orientation" bears a close resemblance to these patterns: the active, aggressive use of other people as a means, both by the manipulation of verbal symbols and by violence; the use of one or the other of these methods of exploitation but not both; and the more passive, withdrawn, and conforming mode.

The maximum security prison, however, is unique in the extent of the frustrations imposed, the enforced intimacy among those who are frustrated, and the prior training in deviance possessed by inmates. The result would seem to be a social group marked by a high degree of internal exploitation where fellow sufferers are scorned as powerless victims even more than the custodians are despised as symbols of oppression. Far from being a prison *community,* men in prison tend to react as individuals and refuse to suspend their intra-mural conflict when confronting the enemy, the prison officials. Those who dominate others are viewed with a mingled fear, hatred, and envy; and the few who manage to retreat into solidarity may well be penalized in the struggle to evade the poverty-stricken existence—both material and immaterial—prescribed by the institution.

If we are correct in assuming that the more exploitative roles of the inmate social system provide practice in deception and violence, the problem of changing the custodial institution into a therapeutic community becomes in part the problem of decreasing the number of individuals who play the part of *merchant* or *tough.* Since these roles seem to be rooted in a major problem of the inmate group—the frustrations or threats of the prison environment—it might be argued that we could reduce the number of prisoners playing these roles by lessening the frustrations. Unfortunately, attempts in this direction have often failed because the patterns of exploitation have reappeared at a higher or more complex level; increases in freedom of movement, inmate responsibility, and material possessions have set the stage for more bitter struggles with higher stakes. Indeed, there seems to be some reason to doubt whether the rigors of prison life can ever be lessened sufficiently to solve the problem. There are many good arguments for improving the lot of the prisoner, but a proven increase in the number of reformed criminals is not one of them.

An alternative (and at present theoretically unpopular) solution lies in strict control by prison officials. Inmates are in effect to be forced out of exploitative roles by making it impossible or extremely difficult for prisoners to follow such patterns of adjustment. This position has many difficulties. For one thing, it opens the door to brutality or simple indifference to inmates' legitimate needs—but a serious reconsideration of its place in programs of therapy is called for.

In any event, it is evident that the inmate social system is marked by strong centrifugal forces which hamper the task of rehabilitation in that they spring from the widespread existence of force and guile in interpersonal relationships. At the same time, the fact that the inmate population does not form a closely allied group of criminals united in their conflict with the prison officials offers some hope of constructing a situation which moves the individual in the direction of reform. (Sykes, 1956:136–137.)

the sentence and treatment of offenders

OFFENSES AND TIME SERVED

SELECTED OFFENSE	STATE WITH LOWEST MEDIAN TIME SERVED			MEDIAN TIME SERVED FOR PRISONERS RELEASED FROM ALL STATE INSTITUTIONS		STATE WITH HIGHEST MEDIAN TIME SERVED		
	State	Years	Months	Years	Months	State	Years	Months
Aggravated assault	Maryland	—	9	2	—	Washington	2	11
Robbery	Massachusetts	1	8	2	9	Alabama	6	6
Burglary	Kansas	1	1	1	9	Dist. of Col.	2	8
Theft	Kentucky	—	9	1	5	Dist. of Col.	2	3

The major criticisms directed against the present complicated sentencing systems in the United States are two: one is that the wide disparity of sentences which now exist, not only from one state to another but within the same state for the same type of offense, reflect differences in attitudes of legislative bodies and judges rather than actual differences between offenders or their acts; and the other is that the time served by prisoners on various sentences is excessive and vary too much in duration.

A few illustrations may serve to point out the basis of these criticisms. In Wisconsin, for example, the maximum term of imprisonment which may be imposed for auto theft is five years; whereas, in California, with the indeterminate sentence, the statutory maximum term of imprisonment is ten years for the same offense. In the federal courts, the average sentence for auto theft in the middle district of Pennyslvania has been as high as forty-four months; in Rhode Island, the average sentence for the same offense seldom exceeds twelve months. [See table for other examples.] (Bennett, 1962:144–145.)

in rewards as superior to negative sanctions, punishment in a (re-)socialization process. And this is the fundamental dilemma: retribution points to negative sanctions, socialization (or least partly) to positive sanctions and conditions under which it is possible for the deviant to internalize a therapeutic attitude without increasing his frustrations (Galtung, 1958:139–140).

PROBATION

In most cases first offenders are placed on probation, particularly if the offense is relatively minor and does not involve weapons (Dressler, 1959). Probation implies a program of supervision and treatment designed to help the individual become better integrated into the normative systems of the community. It is difficult to evaluate the effectiveness of most probation programs. The proportion of individuals who violate their probation is great and many of them have subsequent contact with the police and the courts. A number of reasons are cited for these failures, including the lack of adequate trained staff, the overwhelming case loads of probation officers, and the limited opportunities to change the environment in which the individual spends his time while on probation.

In more progressive states, a variety of programs have been developed which experiment with limited caseloads for probation officers and provide intensive occupational training and sometimes psychological counseling under the supervision of probation departments. Such programs do hold some prospects for increased success of probation programs and, consequently, lower recidivism rates. However, the relatively insignificant differences in rates of success between well-staffed "total impact" probation programs and those with limited economic and manpower resources are discouraging. But the trend toward increased use of probation and less dependence on institutionalization is generally applauded by penologists who recognize the dire effects imprisonment has on subsequent behavior.

INSTITUTIONALIZATION

The network of institutions in our communities for the custody and care of adult offenders is extensive. They range from county farms and municipal or county jails for offenders convicted of misdemeanors (a term historically used to describe offenses not punishable by death but today variously defined and usually referring to petty crimes) to state prisons of varying degrees of security for more serious offenders and repeaters. In addition, the federal government maintains a system of institutions for various classes of prisoners.

In a number of states, efforts have been made to develop a series of graded custodial institutions, with those for young and first offenders stressing psychological guidance and occupational training with a minimal emphasis on the custodial function. Some of these rehabilitation-oriented prisons are literally without bars or fences, and their programs include opportunities for continued education, vocational training, employment in the outside community, daily or overnight leaves—all designed to avoid the complete separation of the individual from normal community activities. At the other extreme are institutions whose rehabilitative programs are perfunctory or nonexistent and whose primary concern is to keep the inmate isolated from the community. Such institutions naturally receive offenders with longer sentences and those convicted of the most serious crimes, or repeaters whose records suggest that it would be not only unsafe for the community but relatively futile to emphasize rehabilitation, at least in terms of what can be done in the limited environment of a prison.

Problems of prison administration and of the social control of offenders have been the subjects of a number of research volumes (Glaser, 1964; Ward and Kassebaum, 1965). One concern is with the extent to which the community is willing to provide resources for the care of its institutionalized prison population. In general, prisons face severe restrictions in providing humanitarian custodial care and effective rehabilitation programs (Cloward et al., 1959). Many prisons are physically harsh· and inadequately ventilated; they lack any privacy for the inmates and they provide poorly prepared, if not nutritionally substandard, food. The pay of guards, professional personnel, and administrators is notoriously low. Both an instructional staff and the necessary equipment for adequate occupational training, or for any reasonable degree of therapeutic intervention, are often missing.

Prisons have long been hotbeds of political corruption. Even today many wardens receive their appointment through political patronage with the tacit understanding that they will use some of the prison's meager funds for their personal advantage. Some wardens have been known to grant special favors to politically affiliated inmates and to hire as guards the friends of the politicians who helped them obtain their positions. Guards and other staff often supplement their salaries by providing liquor and narcotics to prisoners for a fee and by permitting cell assignments that nurture homosexual relationships. These corrupt and illegal activities on the part of prison personnel are hardly conducive to the development of different standards of conduct on the part of inmates. Several states have made amazing progress in facing these problems by adopting strong civil service hiring practices, by removing senior appointments from politics, and by developing an atmosphere of research and innovation.

In addition to the extensive federal prison system (Glaser, et al., 1966), the system most frequently characterized as progressive is that of California. Many of the attempts to evaluate new programs, to appraise various modes of training, and to experiment with different forms of custodial care are the work of criminologists and other behavioral scientists associated with this state system. Only California (and perhaps a few other states) and the federal system offer good prospects for the improvement of custodial care.

A careful consideration of the problems of prisons, and particularly of the outcome of custodial care in federal prisons, has been undertaken by Glaser (1964). This volume describes in considerable detail the inmate populations of the various federal prisons, the strenuous efforts to develop rehabilitation programs, and the relative outcomes of different types of programs with inmates of different social and psychological characteristics. Critics of Glaser's work have argued that he presents an overoptimistic analysis of the efficacy of most federal programs; other criminologists doubt that differences in outcome are related to the type of prison situation in which the person is involved (Beverly, 1965). Glaser's analysis does suggest, however, that there is interaction between the characteristics of the offender and of the type of institution to which he is sent. In his view, rehabilitation requires considerable knowledge of the most appropriate setting for particular types of offenders and judgments on whether imprisonment is primarily for protecting the community or for restoring the inmate to a useful position in society.

THE IMPACT OF IMPRISONMENT

Considerable investigation has been undertaken to identify the attributes of inmates, their environment, and their illegal behavior in relationship to various programs, although unfortunately the payoff value from such efforts has been minimal. While a number of interview and questionnaire instruments have been developed, these have only limited utility in determining differential placements, appropriate sentences, or the probability of successful tenure in the community subsequent to imprisonment. Most penologists contend that the sentencing of criminals should be based upon a carefully study of his personality, background, and experience and the nature of his offenses. Many court systems now make some effort to provide these data to the judge and his staff. The character of the American judicial system, however, limits the application of such information in many jurisdictions to the disposition-processing procedure. Crowded court calendars, minimal time, and the scarcity of trained personnel as well as, in some cases, the inability of the judge to comprehend such material are barriers to the implementation of an adequate program of social diagnosis.

The social system of the prison has also been the subject of considerable study. Beginning with the early work of Clemmer (1940), sociologists have become aware that prisons, particularly large ones that include a significant proportion of long-term inmates, represent identifiable communities, encompassing within the inmate population a social-status system with a unique set of values. The very continuity of the deviant culture that persists in many prison settings is antagonistic to the treatment and the goals that the community holds valuable and pertinent in the operations of such institutions. Some analysts of prisons have suggested that inmate life is ordered so as to ward off the deprivations of imprisonment and to provide self-esteem as well as a mechanism for gratification to members of the inmate community (Sykes, 1958).

Most recent investigations (Wheeler, 1966) stress the complexities of the prison as a social system; it is an oversimplification to portray the prison as a structure entirely hostile to the norms of the larger society or to suggest that in all cases it promotes further deviance rather than rehabilitation. Nevertheless, many penologists today believe the organization of prison life is antagonistic to rehabilitation and thus contributes to high recidivism rates. In any case, it is apparent that the day-to-day life of the prison is not determined solely by the views of the staff. Prison officials necessarily must take into account the values, attitudes and, indeed, the power of inmate populations. Wardens and staff are confronted with pressures from members of the larger community to grant special favors and privileges to particular inmates and to fill particular positions on a political basis. Also they must at times accede to prisoners' demands or run the risk of riots, strikes, and sabotage. In some ways, unfortunately, the role of the prison staff is not unlike that of a truce team, operating to maintain a careful balance between pressures from the larger community and pressures from the inmate population.

PAROLE

The key to the rehabilitation of imprisoned offenders is follow-up supervision. Such supervision, referred to as parole, supposedly provides guidance and counseling to the former inmate as he makes his way back into the community. The parole system does function as a means of social control for prisoners during the time they are institutionalized. For most offenses, either the prison sentence includes a contingency period or the legal system provides for parole after a prisoner has served part of his sentence, providing his conduct and participation in prison programs has proved satisfactory. Thus inmate behavior conforms to staff desires because of the prospect of parole.

Parole boards vary in their competence to make equitable judgments and prison staffs differ in the extent to which they employ their discretionary powers as punitive mechanisms. Parole officers, like probation officers, suffer in their inability to operate effectively (Skolnick, 1960). In part, they are limited in the technical knowledge at their disposal for dealing with former prisoners. The frequent inability of parole officers to locate inmates in meaningful employment or to place them in social environments conducive to normative behavior limits the rehabilitative impact of their efforts. In many communities, the large case loads of parole officers render supervision of released prisoners perfunctory and ineffective.

Prospects for rehabilitation and for reduction of recidivism are not high for any imprisoned groups in the population and parole violation rates are highest for young offenders of the age group considered in this chapter (Glaser and O'Leary, 1966b). Failure rates, measured by return to prison after release, differ broadly by offense and from one state to another. Within this age group recidivism rates for New York State and federal prisons are approximately 50 per cent. It has been noted that successful parole, particularly for young offenders, depends upon providing released prisoners with new paths to follow in which satisfying legitimate achievements are possible. These must include programs of continuing education and meaningful work or training, residential centers with reasonably normative values, and opportunities for consultation and counseling with sympathetic professionals. If a profile of a successfully rehabilitated inmate of this age group could be developed, it probably would show a former prisoner who changed his community environment quite radically, both in place of residence and in his network of friends; who married and started a family of his own; who obtained regular employment; and who maintained a sense of responsibility by identifying in a real sense with the norms of his adult status (Glaser, 1964).

THE LEGAL PROCESS

As noted earlier, however, there is considerable pessimism with respect to the efficacy of current parole procedures. As a consequence, penologists and court authorities strive to avoid initial imprisonment of the offender. It is obvious, too, that in American communities a prison record results in stigmatization difficult to overcome in terms of opportunities for employment, participation in the political life of the community, and enjoyment of a normal social life, including recreation, dating, and mate selection.

Much criticism has been directed at the legal procedures that surround the processing of the offender, and two issues have come to the fore that particularly affect this age group. One is the contention that both the middle-class offender and the professional criminal benefit from a legal system that maximizes the equity in the contest between accused and accuser. Their resources and legal counsel give them advantages in the adversary contest that the ordinary criminal, who usually is poor, simply does not have.

As is true with many juveniles, adult offenders are not treated equally in the halls of justice. A similar rationalization can be made for some of the inequitable treatment. The youthful offender from a moderately well-to-do family whose parents are able and willing to provide him with other types of care, such as psychiatric treatment, and with opportunities for continued education is often given a suspended or lighter sentence or is placed on probation on the grounds that imprisonment would be detrimental to the individual and of no benefit to the community. Perhaps a larger issue is the discrimination that results from the inability of the poor and indigent offender to have appropriate legal counsel or any legal advice at all. Supreme Court rulings insist that for the more serious crimes, i.e., felonies, all offenders from the first interrogation by police to the final appeal are entitled to the services of a qualified lawyer. This requirement has not been extended to misdemeanors, and many ordinary criminals do not receive the protection of legal counsel until they are actually brought before a court. Even then, such counsel may be perfunctory and inept, reflecting poor motivation and lack of interest on the part of the attorney.

As a routine procedure, some communities provide a public defender, a lawyer with a staff and salary similar to that of the prosecuting attorney who represents the accused as an equal adversary in all court procedures. For many crimes, the costs of an adequate defense include more than the lawyer's fee. There may be charges for court transcripts in the event of appeals, for investigatory services, and for travel expenses for witnesses required to present the best defense. Instead of extending the public defender concept, many communities now provide panels of lawyers who assist and defend indigent clients. Such a system is only a partial remedy, however, since in many cases these positions are undertaken on a voluntary basis or for minimal remuneration, and thus they attract only less competent members of the bar or they serve as training grounds for inexperienced lawyers. At least until recently the practice of criminal law was disdained by many of the best qualified and most promising attorneys because of the lucrative opportunities for the practice of commercial and corporation law. As a consequence, in many communities only the offender with an affluent family or the support of a criminal syndicate can offer an adequate defense. Related to this problem of differential legal services is the costs of providing bail. Again, there have been attempts to remedy the inequitable situation in which the accused who has the financial backing of either family or a disreputable organization can go free on bail while the indigent must remain in jail. Experiments in the provision of bail have been undertaken in a number of cities.

In certain cities, under the auspices of the Community Action Program of the Office of Economic Opportunity, bail has been provided to low-income and indigent persons as a "welfare" service. Other communities, in addition to such OEO-sponsored programs, have experimented with releasing persons, particularly those charged with minor misdemeanors, without their posting bail. Both types of programs suggest that a much more liberal policy than is presently in effect in many jurisdictions could be implemented. The forced incarceration of the suspect because of his failure to provide bail does a great injustice to those who are innocent and even prevents the guilty from developing the most adequate preparation of their cases. The inequities faced by the poor vis-à-vis the judicial system is a topic of great concern, given the current emphasis on equality for all citizens.

Another major issue regarding legal procedure that particularly effects the young-adult offender has to do with variations from state to state and from one community to another in the judicial processing system. These variations are related to the idiosyncracies of the laws, the characteristics of judges and court staffs, and the caseloads of the courts. There are a number of different elements in the informal processing that are of concern to students of law and of the sociology of law. One of these is the extent to which the district attorney, the accused or his counsel, and the court make a deal or, in the vernacular of the system, "cop a plea" either to reduce the work load of the court or to avoid a jury trial for a problematic case. Often the accused is given the choice by the prosecuting attorney or the court clerk of pleading guilty to a lesser offense in lieu of risking jury trial. For example, a person apprehended and liable to prosecution for a first-degree felony, which carries a sentence of perhaps five to ten years, may be allowed to plead guilty to a third-degree felony and be sentenced for a period of one to three years. The deal will permit the offender to return to the community after perhaps eight months or so (Miller and Remington, 1962).

In many cases, of course, such arrangements, particularly when the accused is guilty, may facilitate his welfare since, as we discussed, the utility of long sentences is difficult to justify. Nevertheless, there are great variations in the use of such practices from one community to another. On the one hand, innocent victims, particularly if they have been involved with the courts before, may be willing to sacrifice themselves for a short period rather than run the risk of a long prison stay; on the other hand, individuals who are going to return to crime and may commit even more serious offenses are allowed back into the community after a short time with minimal attempts at rehabilitation. Such practices are largely undertaken for expediency, in order to cut down on the work load of the courts and the prosecuting attorneys. In the same manner, district attorneys may drop cases in which a conviction might prove difficult to obtain in order to devote their energies to cases they are more likely to win, even though the offender whose case is dropped represents a risk to the community and is an individual requiring custodial care and treatment.

Then, too, the various judges within a single jurisdiction may differ considerably in the standards they apply to specific crimes and particular criminals, in their methods of reaching decisions, and even in their competence to act in this capacity. Statutes usually allow judges a considerable range of discretion in determining sentences, and similar crimes by similar offenders may result in vastly different sentences if different judges are involved (Gaudet, 1949; Glaser et al., 1966). Glaser and associates report that many lawyers feel that the best way they can serve their clients is not to study the client or the evidence, but rather to consider the judge in whose court the client will appear. In certain jurisdictions, if the defendent pleads guilty, his attorney may literally be able to pick the judge who is to do the sentencing. Lawyers in certain large cities know which judge is easy on female offenders but hard on male criminals, which gives long sentences for sex crimes but short sentences for property offenses, and so forth.

Usually it is difficult, if not impossible, in most jurisdictions to appeal the severity of the sentence, for the judge's wisdom in this respect is regarded as final. In an attempt to remedy this problem, certain jurisdictions attempt to hold sentencing clinics in which various judges discuss either actual or hypothetical cases in order to establish common ground rules for sentencing procedures. Such efforts, as well as the scrutiny of legal and sociological research groups, represent an important way of overcoming idiosyncratic discriminations within the court system (Bennett, 1962).

Another procedure, and one sometimes held to be discriminatory in terms of the social-class status of the offender as well as for various other reasons, is the judge's option in many instances not to try a case at a particular time but rather to "file" it. This action in a sense represents informal probation. The judge is implying that further involvement with the law, whether proved or not, may result in his reopening the earlier case and bringing the offender to trial. A filing is sometimes used in cases in which the accused makes restitution for property damaged or stolen. Essentially it leaves the individual, whether guilty or not, at the mercy of the court and indeed of the police. Offenders so handled are open to recruitment as police informers and spies and, in the occasional unscrupulous situation, literally may become the chattel property of an employer or an illegal group who is in a position to contrive a suspicious event that will again place the individual in the hands of the police. There is no need to prove the trumped-up offense since the judge may just as well choose to take action on the prior arraignment.

INSURANCE FOR VICTIMS

A novel suggestion made by some analysts is not to worry about the criminal but to concentrate more on the costs to the victim. Indeed, this approach has been tried and received favorable comment:

> The first modern victim-compensation programs were established in New Zealand and Great Britain in 1964. California's program, which became effective in the beginning of 1966, was the first in the United States. Only victims with limited financial resources qualify for com-

pensation under this program. New York's victim-compensation bill, enacted in 1966, also provides compensation only for those who would suffer "serious financial hardship" as a result of the crime. Various Federal victim-compensation bills, now before the Congress, have yet to receive public hearings. The Commission believes that such hearings would provide a national forum for a much-needed debate over the philosophy, assumptions, and potential advantages and disadvantages of such programs generally, and the relative merits and design of a program on the Federal level in particular.

The Commission has been impressed by the consensus among legislators and law enforcement officials that some kind of State compensation for victims of violent crime is desirable (President's Commission on Law Enforcement and Administration of Justice, 1967:83).

Many of the issues discussed here regarding prisons and the courts apply across the board to the control of criminal behavior in all age groups. However, young adults constitute a major group exposed to the legal process and to institutionalization and other community-care programs and, according to many analysts, they are the group that suffers the greatest impact from the inequities and deficiencies in the legal and penal systems. An arrest for criminal behavior involves the young adult in a web of entanglements with the law and the courts and may reinforce his already negative attitudes toward a more conforming life style. It also makes him highly vulnerable to subsequent legal violations and increases the risks of his being prosecuted for such violations (Newman, 1962).

drug addiction

Drug addiction obviously is not the exclusive problem of young adults. It deserves mention here because a high proportion of identified drug addicts are in this age group and many of the unidentified ones probably begin their experience with drugs during this period of life. In this discussion we wish to separate drug addiction from the problems of drug use noted in the chapter on adolescence. Here we are focusing on those drugs that are habit-forming and, in the United States, this refers mostly to heroin, one of the morphine derivatives (Joint Committee of the American Bar Association and American Medical Association, 1961). Certain of the barbiturates also are addictive and constitute a rather recent but not so serious phenomenon, at least in the eyes of the general public and the authorities responsible for the social control of drugs (Barber, 1968). Morphine and its derivatives are essentially depressants, and their actions, while much more extreme, are often equated with the reactions of a more common narcotic, alcohol.

There is some confusion about the use of the term *addiction,* meaning habit-forming. In a narrow sense, the delineation of a drug as addictive refers to its physiological attributes, namely that increased use builds up greater and greater tolerance for the drug so that the habitual user is able to consume much greater quantities than the average person without feeling the effects of it. In addition, elimination or curtailment of the use of the drug results in severe withdrawal symptoms of both a physiological and psychological nature, including various degrees of nausea, vomiting, diarrhea, extreme hunger, as well as hallucinations, delusions, and hysteria.

A great deal of experimental research using animals has been conducted in an attempt to delineate truly addictive drugs from those which produce primarily psychological dependency, such as cigarette smoking. There is considerable controversy about a large number of substances, including alcohol, with respect to their habit-forming qualities (Adams, 1942; United Nations Expert Committee on Drugs Liable to Produce Addiction, 1950; Ausubel, 1958; Glaser and O'Leary, 1966a). However, it is clear from both laboratory studies and reports of human experience that individuals regularly addicted to heroin or other morphine derivatives suffer severe physical withdrawal symptoms. But, as we shall discuss subsequently, the psychological needs for the drug as well as the physiological reactions impede the treatment of the addict.

Drug use apparently has increased in this country, at least it has when measured in terms of number of arrests. As the Federal Bureau of Investigation's (1967) crime reports indicate, arrests for narcotic offenses increased from some five thousand cases in 1940 to well over thirty thousand cases in 1967. Part of this increase may be the result of greater community awareness of the problem and, also, of improved techniques of detection. Nevertheless, there is considerable consensus, both among law-enforcement authorities and health practitioners, that the prevalence of drug addicts has increased markedly and is still on the rise.

THE SCOPE OF THE PROBLEM

Estimates of the number of confirmed drug addicts in this country vary considerably. Reasonable estimates, such as that cited by Clausen (1966b), place the number of addicted persons in the United States at around sixty thousand. Other analysts, however, claim that there are as many as two hundred thousand confirmed addicts at the present time. Drug addiction in the early part of the 1900s (and probably before) was primarily a phenomenon of middle and later years. The current data on arrests, however, suggest that perhaps as many as one-third of the drug addicts in the country are between the ages of eighteen and twenty-five. One of the concerns with respect to this problem is the mounting prevalence of addicted individuals in this age category.

Another trend noted is the increased use of drugs by individuals of the lowest economic status and a disproportionate use among Negroes. To a large extent, drug use is confined to large cities and, with the possible exception of Chicago and several other midwestern transportation centers, is primarily an east and west coast phenomenon. Indeed, to become a confirmed drug addict one must have an accessible and continued source for drugs. Since the supplying of drugs, as well as its use, represents an illegal activity, traffic is typically restricted to relatively large population centers in which contact with a supplier can be made while maintaining the anonymity of the user, and in which the potential clientele is large enough to afford the establishment of a trading center.

COMMUNITY CONCERN

Given the relatively low prevalence of drug addiction, it is sometimes difficult to understand the severity of the community's reactions to the drug addict and the stringent police efforts to control drug users. From the standpoint of the addict's health there is a constant danger of death through an overdose or from impure drugs. However, most of the data fail to confirm that drug addicts live any shorter lives or are more prone to physical illness than is the general population (Glaser and O'Leary, 1966b). Rather, the concern with drug use rests on a different level than bodily injury to the addict.

In the first place it is held that, without regulation, the use of drugs may indeed become widespread in the American community. The situation in the United States prior to passage of the Harrison Narcotics Act of 1914 is often cited as an example of what can happen when drug use is unrestricted. While there is no evidence to prove a relationship between physical illness and drug addiction, nevertheless, it was widely known that large numbers of American housewives doctored themselves with laudanum, an opium derivative. The Harrison Act was designed to control such self-medication and unwitting addiction by prohibiting access to opiates except by doctor's prescription. The implication is that the use of habit-forming drugs without medical supervision represents a potential for widespread addiction. Moreover, although the data are extremely impressionistic, there are some who maintain that in Middle Eastern countries, where there is little prohibition against addictive drugs, rates of use are high.

Loss of control in terms of acting out behavior, sexual conduct, and the like, are believed to be unusually excessive while under the influence of heavy doses of heroin. Many of the claims to this effect, of course, are at the level of unsubstantiated stereotypes or, perhaps more to the point, are related to selection factors of who in American society, at least, becomes the heavy user. According to Clausen (1966b), there were probably one hundred thousand addicts in the United States in 1914, many of whom were highly respected citizens. These addicts either applied to a member of the medical profession for treatment to facilitate their gradual drug withdrawal (or at least gradual withdrawal until their "habit" was a moderate one) or they purchased drugs at moderate prices from any supplier.

The popular image of the drug addict in the United States today is a person without many personal controls, disreputable in his sexual conduct, physically aggressive, and economically a noncontributor to society. All of this has some empirical relevance, perhaps, but more likely is related to the kinds of addicted persons who, given our present legal code, are apprehended. Because it is illegal, heroin commands exorbitant prices in the United States, making drug addiction an expensive habit. Those who are not affluent turn to crime and illegal activities to support their "monkey" (Ball et al., 1966; O'Donnell, 1966). Among female addicts, whose numbers are increasing, high rates of prostitution prevail. Male addicts, who still make up the great majority of the addict population, engage in a variety of criminal activities.

Not only is drug addiction found more commonly among low socio-economic and minority groups, but it is often held that drug addiction is more prevalent among the psychologically crippled. Such terms as immaturity, passivity, and dependency are used to describe addicts, although these labels tend to be rather amorphous. Current theories do suggest, however, that drug addicts tend to come from families in which parents are either overprotective or make no demands. While there seems to be little evidence of unusually high rates of psychosis among drug addicts, most who turn up in treatment centers are diagnosed as psychopathic or prepsychopathic in personality (Finestone, 1957b).

CAUSES

In terms of explaining drug addiction, even a more specific identification of the personality syndromes of the addict is unlikely to provide much understanding of the genesis of its etiology. In general, most of the recent work has focused on the process by which individuals are introduced to the drug and by which they become drug users. Contrary to popular belief, drug addicts apparently are not initially introduced to the drug through contact with a peddler (Dai, 1937; Chine, 1964). Rather, they are introduced to drugs through contact with unconventional groups, at parties in which drugs are used, or by coworkers, prostitutes, bartenders, and the like. Chine found, for example, that almost half of the drug users reported that they had personal acquaintance with another user and had experimented with drugs at a young age, before they were eighteen. He also noted that many lived in areas in which they could identify a large number of drug users.

Some sociologists place great emphasis upon the intrigue and challenge of using heroin, which shares with marijuana a social mystic because of the illegality of its use. One study suggests, for example, that the notion of achieving a unique experience and superior sensitivity are rationales for the use of drugs and that these conceptions become particularly attractive to individuals who have failed to find a place for themselves within the conventional world (Finestone, 1957a). In offering this explanation, Finestone suggests that young people, particularly those whose educational and social opportunities are blocked by delinquent careers or by dropping out of school, frequently follow such a pathway. He tries to delineate marginal users from those who are part of the "cat culture," which essentially consists of users who derive a sense of superiority and pleasure in sharing aesthetic knowledge with other addicts and in using a particular jargon.

Finally, there are individuals who take the drug because of the physical pleasure involved (Finestone, 1957a; Ausubel, 1958). Many individuals who have considerable knowledge of the process of drug addiction point out that there are stages of heroin addiction (Finestone, 1957b). The beginner, or "joy popper," has an occasional small dose and does not experience marked withdrawal symptoms. The next stage is the frantic junkie, an offender who has taken sufficient drugs to have a very clear withdrawal effect but who does not yet have a regular pattern of drug procurement. The third stage is the stable addict who takes regular doses, who usually has an adequate supply on hand to tide him over periods when he may not be in contact with his supplier, and who generally has several drug sources. It is the stable addict who is likely to spend $50 or more per day for drugs and whose physical condition resulting from the frequent use of drugs seriously impairs his ability to earn a legitimate income.

INTERVENTION

The suppression of addictive drugs in the United States has an interesting history. Prior to World War I, addictive drugs could be purchased freely from pharmacies, numerous mail order houses, and even grocery stores. In adherence to the 1912 international opium convention, the United States in 1914 passed the Harrison Narcotics Act which required all importers and handlers of coca and opium products to register and pay a stamp tax of a penny an ounce. (The Treasury Department, which was charged with enforcement, eventually refused to register any seller not affiliated with the medical profession.) Only physicians were specifically exempt from the act's provisions and then only if they prescribed the drugs to patients in the course of their professional practice. Initially, some doctors and public health clinics construed this exemption to include the treatment of drug addicts, but a subsequent Supreme Court ruling outlawed the prescription of narcotics to addicts. As a consequence, the confirmed addict turned to illegal sources.

In reaction to the increased prominence of the illicit drug traffic and the change in distribution of the user population, Congress passed the Boggs Act in 1951. This law prescribed definite penalties for the possession of narcotics, ranging from two-to-five-years imprisonment for the first offense to ten-to-twenty-years for the third. It also denied parole to those convicted of drug-law violations. In 1956 increased penalties for possession were imposed by the Narcotic Control Act. For example, the maximum possible sentence was raised to forty years. The 1956 law further provided extremely harsh penalties for the sale or transfer of drugs, including a mandatory sentence of life imprisonment for selling heroin to a minor, with the death penalty permitted upon recommendation of the jury.

Most states have their own legal codes that elaborate on the federal ones (Eldridge, 1962). In Illinois, for example, penalties for soliciting or encouraging a minor to violate the drug act include indeterminate sentences with a minimum of one to two years (Glaser and O'Leary, 1966a).

There are varying opinions on the extent to which the laws surrounding the use and sale of drugs and the attempts by the Treasury Department to limit their importation have proved successful. A pound of pure heroin, when mixed for use, can provide the addict with enough of the drug to last him for a considerable time. It is simply not possible, given the traffic with Europe, the Far East and, particularly, Central America, to intercept much of the smuggled drug. In general, only the inexperienced and amateur smuggler cannot find a way to conceal the drug; however, any attempt at more careful scrutiny of plane and ship passengers and of cars crossing the Mexican border would create customs bottlenecks that the traveler and the governments of these countries would hardly stand for. Studies in California suggest that large amounts of drugs are smuggled in and that it is impossible to control any more efficiently than we are now doing the traffic in illegal drugs. Particularly in California, as Renborg (1957) notes, it is reported that there is a constant flow of drugs to meet the demands of a profitable market; indeed evidence that the price remains relatively stable suggests that more stringent search procedures will not prove useful (Adams and Zietz, 1962).

In the United States it is virtually impossible to find treatment for the drug addict except in a few publically operated centers. Private physicians, because of the legal implications and the low success rate of earlier programs, are most loath to treat the drug addict. This is not so in other countries, or at least in certain of them. Another approach is to treat addiction as a public health problem and to deal with it in the same fashion as we handle other public health problems.

THE BRITISH APPROACH

In Britain, persons who are addicts must be registered with a central office by a physician to whom they are required to go for treatment (Schur, 1961; Lindesmith, 1965). The physician supplies the addict with the drug to which he is addicted but tries to keep the dosage to a minimum and eventually even to eliminate it. Patients pay no medical fee for the service and obtain the drug at a moderate cost in comparison with the high cost in this country (Schur, 1961). As already noted, this approach was in operation in the U.S. during the early 1920s, but neither the legal authorities nor the physicians were enthusiastic about their role, which was ambiguous at best, and this is related in part to the failure to control the problem. Persons who argue for the public health approach as exemplified by the British system point to the fact that there are very few addicts in Great Britain in comparison with the United States. Newspaper reports, however, consistently report increased rates for Britain. Critics of proposals for the legal administration of drugs to non-institutionalized addicts in the United States contend that addicts will never be satisfied with a medically prescribed dosage. They suggest that the addict will make use of these public services while seeking additional supplies from other illegal channels.

Most students of the problem argue quite strongly in favor of the British system, however. They testify to its effectiveness by pointing out that Britain has only a small number of addicts and that while they are being treated they remain gainfully employed and reasonably normal participants in the community (Schur, 1961). Certainly the known linkage in the United States between the need for funds to purchase drugs and criminal behavior has convinced many experts of the cogency of the arguments for the public health approach. Given the probable reaction among American community members and their moral views, it is unlikely that any approach such as this is going to obtain widespread acceptance or to be promoted by public bodies.

CURRENT U.S. PROGRAMS

Rather than attempting to sustain or taper off addicts in the community, treatment in the United States consists for the most part of either imprisonment or specialized hospitalization under medical and psychological supervision. A new and possibly promising approach is the employment of compulsory tests for known drug addicts to make certain they remain off the habit-forming substances. Most physicians, and indeed most criminologists and penologists, argue strongly against the use of prisons for addicts.

The current federal legislation is particularly irrational, many believe, because the provisions barring opportunities for parole for convicted addicts also prevent supervision or surveillance subsequent to their release. As a result of Supreme Court decisions releasing addicts held under improper convictions and the negative views of legal authorities and medical people, the use of prisons as a treatment setting has declined (Bennett, 1959).

In lieu of prisons, special hospitals have been developed for treatment of drug addiction. Several states and the federal government maintain such hospitals, perhaps the most famous of which is the one run by the U.S. Public Health Service in Lexington, Kentucky. Many persons in treatment in these settings commit themselves voluntarily, although some patients are sent there while under probation or while charges are being filed; in these latter cases the treatment centers do become the functional equivalents of prisons (O'Donnell, 1962). Indeed, the two federal hospitals at Lexington and Fort Worth, Texas, are constructed very much like medium security prisons.

These hospitals have proved successful in dealing with the withdrawal effects and physical problems that accompany the termination of the use of heroin. During treatment the patients are usually provided with synthetic drugs which minimize these symptoms but are not habit-forming and whose withdrawal effects, when terminated, are minimal. Most hospitals for addicts also attempt to apply intensive modes of psychological and social therapy, but the success of these types of programs has been minimal. (*See* Documentation 11.)

A series of follow-up studies reported by Glaser and O'Leary (1966a) indicates that from one-fourth to one-half of the addicts treated in such hospitals relapse after a period of six months to a year, and there is no evidence to suggest that permanent cure is the typical outcome of such hospital experiences. There is, however, a change in the amount of heroin needed to achieve the desired effect. Even if the "cured" addict returns to using the drug, the amount he needs is lower, at least until he again rebuilds tolerance to it.

It is important to recognize that in addition to the physical withdrawal problems, there are serious psychological problems as well. Most returnees to heroin do so not solely because of a need for the drug in a physiological sense to relieve withdrawal symptoms but rather because of the addict's general unhappiness, dissatisfaction, personality and social problems (Ray, 1961).

In the popular mythology, if a drug addict can manage to kick his habit, he is cured. In reality, addicts are constantly kicking and returning to drugs again. Arrest, for example, means kicking "cold turkey," which accounts for the addict's dread of arrest and perhaps for the fact that he is almost certain to go back on heroin the day he is released from prison. But there is a physical motive for the kicking-and-returning cycle which is mostly unknown to nonaddicts. I am referring to the mechanism of tolerance, whereby an addict in pursuit of euphoria builds up his daily dosage until simply to get "straight"—that is, to keep from experiencing withdrawal symptoms—he may need hundreds of times the narcotic that would kill an ordinary person. To get high the addict needs even more. Thus a habit is likely to be constantly increasing, a predicament which demands accelerating activity in begging, borrowing, burglary, shoplifting, prostitution, and all the other means by which the free-enterprise addict obtains funds.

"I guess it was sort of a lark," Dom Abruzzi said. "I was sixteen years old exactly, and I was walking with one friend on Henry Street, and he asked me, 'Have you ever smoked pot before?' I didn't know what pot was, and I had to ask him, so he told me it was marijuana, and I almost fell with shock. But then he talked about it, and he explained to me it was nothing to worry about, and three days later I was smoking my first weed. Three months afterward, I started snorting heroin. I got in on that because it was so cheap—a dollar and a half apiece to split a three-dollar bag—and everybody was getting so high and seemed so happy. A few months after that I took my first shot. That was a skin pop, and was followed a week later by a main line. But for the first few years, I would say, I was an oddity, because I kept myself in check; I didn't get a habit. I was going out with a very wonderful girl at the time, and I wanted to marry her. But in the next few years that followed, I got arrested once, then a second time, and the girl and I broke up. We had money in the bank, in a joint account. After we broke up, I took it all out and spent it on dope, and that's how I acquired my first habit.

INNOVATIVE APPROACHES

The issue of whether abstinence from heroin is possible for the formerly addicted person is currently being tested by a number of groups that emphasize programs involving intensive attempts at modifying interpersonal relationships and temperament. Perhaps the most interesting of these is an operation called Synanon, which currently has several bases of operation. Synanon is a voluntarily organized association that maintains residences in several of the major cities. In these residences former addicts live together and, through a form of quasi-group psychotherapy that continues throughout the period the addict is in residence, an at-

"I didn't even know I was hooked. I was sitting on a bench right here in the Vladeck project; I was yawning, and my eyes were tearing, and a friend came over to me and started talking to me and said, 'Dom, you know you're sick.' And for the first time I realized I was actually addicted. I had the habit, and I had to have it. So from then on it was every day, and when I ran out of the bank money, I began borrowing. I soon saw I couldn't support my habit by running around borrowing money or trying to steal money, and I started pushing. I made a lot of money pushing. I wasn't looking to make money, but it just so happened, a stroke of if-you-want-to-call-it luck, I made a lot of money. I could support my habit, I could buy clothes, I even bought a car; and odd as it may seem, I could work, just so long as I had my tools—my needle, my eyedropper, and my heroin. I would take a shot maybe three times a day while I was at work, come home, and continue selling dope. I did that for seven or eight months.

"I was young and I was small scale, actually; I guess I coulda went deeper into it, I guess I was scoring in weight an eighth, and it was costing me fifty dollars an eighth. And I would buy one eighth or two, or I would get a quarter, the equivalent of two eighths. An eighth is one eighth of an ounce. Half of it I would use for myself because I had to, and the other half I would sell, and it would bring me back three times the amount I paid for it. I did no cutting; the heroin I was getting was considered very good. Now it could have been cut a number of times, I could have made much more money, but I guess I just didn't want to cut it. The quality was terrific, and I didn't want to be bothered. I was just thinking of my habit. Today the same dope would turn over an enormous amount of money, because you don't find the same stuff anymore.

"To buy my heroin, I could go to any part of the city. At that time, I knew some people on the west end of Harlem; it was the Spanish-Italian section. It's all according to who you know at the time.

"After seven, eight months of dealing I stopped it. I was really fed up. I went to a Dr. W. on Forty-seventh Street, who supposedly will take you off the habit by lowering the shots every day. The price was sixty dollars a week, double for two weeks. But it didn't help, and the disadvantage of it was that I stopped dealing, and I found myself in a hole with money and everything. I lost my car, I lost my job, and I was back in the street with holes in my pockets and seven days of beard on my face." (Larner, 1965:75–76.)

tempt is made for the members of the group to support each other. The Synanon program is predicated on encouraging exchanges of and discussions about problems, a high degree of tolerance for unusual and deviant behavior, and group support when the individual is tempted to renew a career of drug addiction (Yablonsky, 1965). Synanon in many ways appears to be a hopeful approach to the problem of drug addiction (Volkman and Cressey, 1963). Several persons have attempted to describe group life at Synanon, but there remains a need for a careful evaluation study about whether it is any more successful than any other programs (Casriel, 1963; Yablonsky, 1965). The evidence does suggest its utility. (*See* Documentation 12.)

After the synanon sessions, the house is always noisy and lively. We have seen members sulk, cry, shout, and threaten to leave the group as a result of conversation in the synanon. The following comments, every one of which represents the expression of a pro-reform attitude by the speaker, were heard after one session. It is our hypothesis that such expressions are the important ones, for they indicate that the speaker has become a reformer and, thus, is reinforcing his own pro-reform attitudes every time he tries to comfort or reform another.

"Were they hard on you?"

"I really let him have it tonight."

"I couldn't get to her. She's so damned blocked she couldn't even hear what I was trying to tell her."

"Hang tough, man; it gets easier."

"One of these days he'll drop those defenses of his and start getting honest."

"Don't leave. We all love you and want you to get well."

At Synanon, disassociating with former friends, avoiding street talk, and becoming disloyal to criminals are emphasized at the same time that loyalty to non-criminals, telling the truth to authority figures, and legitimate work are stressed. We have no direct evidence that haircuts, synanons, and both formal and spontaneous denunciations of street talk and the code of the streets have important rehabilitative effects on the actor, as well as (or, perhaps even "rather than") on the victim. It seems rather apparent, however, that an individual's own behavior must be dramatically influenced when he acts in the role of a moral policeman and "takes apart" another member. It is significant that older members of Synanon like to point out that the "real Synanon" began on "the night of the big cop out" (confession). In its earliest days, Synanon had neither the group cohesiveness nor the degree of control it now has. Some participants remained as addicts while proclaiming their loyalty to the principle of antiaddiction, and other participants knew of this condition. One evening in a general meeting a man spontaneously stood up and confessed ("copped out") that he had sneaked out for a shot. One by one, with no prompting, the others present rose to confess either their own violations or their knowledge of the violations of their friends. From that moment, the Board of Di-

In addition to Synanon, groups similar to Alcoholics Anonymous have been organized. Although less intense than AA, these "narcotics anonymous" groups seek to provide the same sort of interpersonal milieu and group support for the addict. These programs are predicated, as noted, on a belief that the problems of psychological control are a function of the individual's lack of integration and personality needs.

An entirely opposite approach to Synanon is one which employs a specific drug, Nalline. Nalline, when injected into the arm of an addict in even minimal quantities, causes withdrawal symptoms; thus normal individuals can be differentiated from users. In parts of California and

rectors believe, the organization became a truly antidrug group; there has been no problem of drug use since.

Of the fifty-two residents described earlier, four are "graduates" of Synanon, are living in the community, and are not using alcohol or drugs. Twenty-three (44.2 percent) are still in residence and are not using alcohol or drugs. Two of these are on the Board of Directors and eleven are working part or full time. The remaining twenty-five left Synanon against the advice of the Board and the older members.

Information regarding the longest period of voluntary abstinence from drugs after the onset of addiction but prior to entering Synanon was obtained on forty-eight of the fifty-two persons. Eleven reported that they were "never" clean, six said they were continuously clean for less than one week, ten were continuously clean for less than one month. Thirty-nine (81 percent) said they had been continuously clean for less than six months, and only two had been clean for as long as a one-year period. Twenty-seven (52 percent) of the fifty-two residents have now abstained for at least six months; twelve of these have been clean for at least two years and two have been off drugs continually for over three years.

Between May, 1958 (when Synanon started), and May, 1961, 263 persons were admitted or readmitted to Synanon. Of these, 190 (72 per-cent) left Synanon against the advice of the Board of Directors and the older members. Significantly, 50 percent of all dropouts occurred within the first month of residence, 90 percent within the first three months. Synanon is not adverse to giving a person a second chance, or even a third or fourth chance: of the 190 persons dropping out, eighty-three (44 percent) were persons who had been readmitted. The dropout behavior of persons who were readmitted was, in general, similar to first admissions; 65 percent of their dropouts occurred within the first month, 93 percent within the first three months after readmission.

Of all the Synanon enrollees up to August, 1962, 108 out of 372 (29 percent) are known to be off drugs. More significantly, of the 215 persons who have remained at Synanon for at least one month, 103 (48 percent) are still off drugs; of the 143 who have remained for at least three months, 95 (66 percent) are still non-users; of the 87 who have remained at least seven months, 75 (96 percent) are non-users. These statistics seem to us to be most relevant, for they indicate that once an addict actually becomes a member of the antidrug community (as indicated by three to six months of participation), the probability that he will leave and revert to the use of drugs is low. (Volkman and Cressey, 1963: 141–142.)

elsewhere, Nalline is used on a regular basis to test addicts on probation or parole to make certain they remain off narcotics. In certain areas of known high drug use, frequent and sometimes unannounced mass testings of populations are made. The use of Nalline testing, particularly when employed in a mass-survey approach, raises considerable question of invasion of privacy and authoritarian tactics. Proponents of such an approach argue that the programs assist the former addict in staying off the drug, for he is alerted to the potentialities of these checkup procedures (Glaser and O'Leary, 1966a). Opponents argue that such tests will only result in addicts moving to areas in which controls are less rigorous. A recent study fails to support this view, however (Grupp, 1967).

Clearly, the Synanon approach of voluntary, self-help counseling programs and the authoritarian controls enforced by Nalline testing are antagonistic in philosophy. Both of these constitute new program approaches and there is little research evidence to indicate the efficacy of either or both over the long run. Perhaps the guarded proposition that each strategy may be beneficial to different types of addicts is the best that can be said for these intervention techniques (Larner, 1965).

basis of problems

To a large extent, the social problems of the young adult represent the culmination of conflicts, discontinuities, and structural inequities of earlier periods in the life cycle. The critical point that needs to be emphasized about this age group is the existence in the adult world of large numbers of young members who, instead of being contributing, productive, and responsible members of the community, are targets for rehabilitation and action.

ADAMS, ROGER.
1942 "Marijuana." Bulletin of the New York Academy of Medicine 18(November):705–730.

ADAMS, STEWART AND DOROTHY ZIETZ.
1962 "Commuting to the border: narcotics case profile." California Youth Authority Quarterly 15(Spring):3–9.

AUSUBEL, DAVID P.
1958 Drug Addiction. New York: Random House.

BALL, JOHN C., EMILY S. COTTRELL AND JOHN A. O'DONNELL.
1966 "Selected social characteristics of consecutive admissions to Lexington in 1965." Criminologica 4(August):13–16.

BARBER, BERNARD.
1968 Drugs and Society. New York: Russell Sage Foundation.

BELKNAP, IVAN.
1959 Human Problems of a State Hospital. New York: McGraw-Hill.

BENNETT, JAMES V.
1959 Report of the State of New York Joint Legislative Committee on Narcotic Study. Albany: State of New York Legislative Document Number 7.
1962 "The sentence and treatment of offenders." The Annals 339(January): 142–156.

BEVERLY, ROBERT F.
1965 An Analysis of Parole Performance by Institution of Release. Sacramento: California Youth Authority, Research Report 40.

BIOMETRICS BRANCH, NATIONAL INSTITUTE OF MENTAL HEALTH.
1963 Patients in Mental Institutions. Washington, D.C.: Department of Health, Education and Welfare.

BITTNER, EGON.
1967 "Police discretion in emergency apprehension of mentally ill persons." Social Problems 14(Winter):278–292.

BOWER, ELI M.
1963 "Primary prevention of mental and emotional disorders: a conceptual framework and action possibilities." American Journal of Orthopsychiatry 33(October):832–847.

BRILL, HENRY AND ROBERT E. PATTON.
1959 "Analysis of population reduction in New York state mental hospitals during the first four years of large-scale therapy with psychotropic drugs." American Journal of Psychiatry 116 (December):495–509.

BRYAN, JAMES H.
1965 "Apprenticeships in prostitution." Social Problems 12(Winter):287–297.

CAPLAN, GERALD.
1964 Principles of Preventive Psychiatry. New York: Basic Books.

CASRIEL, DANIEL.
1963 So Fair a House: The Story of Synanon. Englewood Cliffs, New Jersey: Prentice-Hall.

CAUDILL, WILLIAM A.
1958 The Psychiatric Hospital as a Small Society. Cambridge: Harvard University Press.

CHINE, ISADOR.
1964 The Road to H: Narcotics, Delinquency and Public Policy. New York: Basic Books.

CLAUSEN, JOHN A.
1966a "Mental disorders." Pp. 26–83 in Robert K. Merton and Robert A. Nisbet (eds.), Contemporary Social Problems. Second Edition. New York: Harcourt, Brace and World.
1966b "Drug addiction." Pp. 193–235 in Robert K. Merton and Robert A. Nisbet (eds.), Contemporary Social Problems. Second Edition. New York: Harcourt, Brace and World.
1967 "The organism and socialization." Journal of Health and Social Behavior 8(December):243–252.

CLEMMER, DONALD R.
1940 The Prison Community. New York: Holt, Rinehart and Winston.

CLOWARD, RICHARD A. ET AL.
1959 Theoretical Studies in the Social Organization of the Prison. Social Science Monograph 15. New York: Social Science Research Council.

CRESSEY, DONALD R.
1966 "Crime." Pp. 136–192 in Robert K. Merton and Robert A. Nisbet (eds.), Contemporary Social Problems. Second Edition. New York: Harcourt, Brace and World.

CUMMING, MARGARET E. AND JOHN H. CUMMING.
1957 Closed Ranks: An Experiment in Mental Health Education. Cambridge: Harvard University Press.

DAI, BINGHAM.
1937 Opium Addiction. Chicago: Shanghai Commercial Press.

DAVIS, KINGSLEY.
1938 "Mental hygiene and the class structure." Psychiatry 1(February):55–65.
1966 "Sexual behavior." Pp. 322–372 in Robert K. Merton and Robert A. Nisbet (eds.), Contemporary Social Problems. Second Edition. New York: Harcourt, Brace and World.

DOHRENWEND, BRUCE P.
1966 "Social status and psychological disorder: an issue of substance and an issue of method." American Sociological Review 31(February):15–34.

DRESSLER, DAVID.
1959 Practice and Theory of Probation and Parole. New York: Columbia University Press.

DUHL, LEONARD J. (ED.).
1963 The Urban Condition: People and Policy in the Metropolis. New York: Basic Books.

DUNCAN, BEVERLY.
1967 "Education and social background." American Journal of Sociology 72 (January):363–372.

DUNHAM, H. WARREN, PATRICIA PHILLIPS AND BARBARA SRINIVASAN.
1966 "A research note on diagnosed mental illness and social class." American Sociological Review 31(April):223–277.

DUNHAM, H. WARREN AND S. KIRSON WEINBERG.
1960 The Culture of the State Mental Hospital. Detroit: Wayne State University Press.

ELDRIDGE, WILLIAM B.
1962 Narcotics and the Law. New York: American Bar Foundation.

FEDERAL BUREAU OF INVESTIGATION.
1967 Uniform Crime Reports. Washington, D.C.: U.S. Government Printing Office.

FINESTONE, HAROLD.
1957a "Cats, kicks and colors." Social Problems 15(July):3–13.
1957b "Narcotics in criminology." Law and Contemporary Problems 22(Winter):76–77.

FORD, CLELLAN S. AND FRANK A. BEECH.
1951 Patterns of Sexual Behavior. New York: Harper.

FORM, WILLIAM H. AND DELBERT C. MILLER.
1962 "Occupational career pattern as a sociological instrument." Pp. 287–297 in Sigmund Nosow and William H. Form (eds.), Man, Work and Society. New York: Basic Books.

FREEMAN, HOWARD E. AND JEANNE M. GIOVANNONI.
1969 "Social psychology of mental health." Chapter 45 in G. Lindzey and E. Aronson (eds.), Handbook of Social Psychology. Volume 5. Cambridge: Addison-Wesley.

FREEMAN, HOWARD E. AND GENE G. KASSEBAUM.
1956 "The illiterate in American society." Social Forces 34(May):371–375.

FREEMAN, HOWARD E. AND OZZIE G. SIMMONS.
1963 The Mental Patient Comes Home. New York: Wiley.

GALTUNG, JOHAN.
1958 "The social functions of a prison." Social Problems 6(Fall):127–140.

GARABEDIAN, PETER G.
1963 "Social roles and processes of socialization in the prison community." Social Problems 11(Fall):139–152.

GARDNER, ELMER A., ANITA BAHAN AND HAROLD C. MILES.
1964 "Patient experience in psychiatric units of general and state mental hospitals." Public Health Reports 79(September):755–766.

GAUDET, FREDERICK JOSEPH.
1949 "Veterans Administration advisement and guidance program." School and Society 69(April):251–254.

GLASER, DANIEL.
1964 Effectiveness of a Prison and Parole System. Indianapolis: Bobbs-Merrill.

GLASER, DANIEL, FRED COHEN AND VINCENT O'LEARY.
1966 The Sentencing and Parole Process. U.S. Department of Health, Education, and Welfare, Welfare Administration. Washington, D.C.: U.S. Government Printing Office.

GLASER, DANIEL AND VINCENT O'LEARY.
1966a The Control and Treatment of Narcotic Use. U.S. Department of Health, Education, and Welfare, Welfare Administration. Washington, D.C.: U.S. Government Printing Office.
1966b Personal Characteristics and Parole Outcome. U.S. Department of Health, Education, and Welfare, Welfare Administration. Washington, D.C.: U.S. Government Printing Office.

GOFFMAN, ERVING.
1962 Asylums. Chicago: Aldine.

GOODE, WILLIAM J.
1966 "Family disorganization." Pp. 479–552 in Robert K. Merton and Robert A. Nisbet (eds.), Contemporary Social Problems. Second Edition. New York: Harcourt, Brace and World.

GREENBLATT, MILTON, DANIEL J. LEVINSON AND GERALD KLERMAN (EDS.).
1961 Mental Patients in Transition. Springfield: Charles C Thomas.

GRUPP, STANLEY E.
1967 "Addict mobility and the Nalline test." Paper presented at the 62nd Annual Meeting of the American Sociological Association, San Francisco, August 29.

HOLLINGSHEAD, AUGUST B. AND F. C. REDLICH.
1958 Social Class and Mental Illness: A Community Study. New York: Wiley.

HUGHES, CHARLES C., MARC-ADELARD TREMBLAY, ROBERT N. RAPOPORT AND ALEXANDER H. LEIGHTON.
1960 People of Cove and Woodlot. New York: Basic Books.

IRWIN, JOHN AND DONALD R. CRESSEY.
1962 "Thieves, convicts and the inmate culture." Social Problems 10(Fall):142–155.

JAHODA, MARIE.
1958 Current Concepts of Positive Mental Health. Joint Commission on Mental Health and Illness. Monograph Series Number 1. New York: Basic Books.

JOHNSTON, DENIS F.
1963 "Educational attainment of workers."
Monthly Labor Review 86(May):504–515.

JOINT COMMITTEE OF THE AMERICAN BAR ASSOCIATION AND AMERICAN MEDICAL ASSOCIATION.
1961 Drug Addiction: Crime or Disease. Bloomington: University of Indiana Press.

KERR, CLARK.
1963 The Uses of the University. Cambridge: Harvard University Press.

KLERMAN, GERALD L.
1961 "Historical baselines for the evaluation of maintenance drug therapy of discharged psychiatric patients." Pp. 287–298 in Milton Greenblatt, David J. Levinson and Gerald Klerman (eds.), Mental Patients in Transition. Springfield, Illinois: Charles C Thomas.

LARNER, JEREMY.
1965 "The young drug addict: can we help him?" Atlantic Monthly 215 (February):75–80.

LECHT, LEONARD A.
1962 Goals, Priorities and Dollars. New York: Free Press.

LEMERT, EDWIN M.
1962 "Paranoia and the dynamics of exclusion." Sociometry 25(March):2–20.

LEZNOFF, MAURICE AND WILLIAM A. WESTLEY.
1956 "The homosexual community." Social Problems 3(April):257–263.

LINDESMITH, ALFRED R.
1965 The Addict and the Law. Bloomington: Indiana University Press.

LINN, ERWIN L.
1959 "Patients' socioeconomic characteristics and release from a mental hospital." American Journal of Sociology 65(November):280–286.

MECHANIC, DAVID.
1966 "Community psychiatry: some sociological perspectives and implications." Pp. 201–222 in Leigh M. Roberts, Seymour L. Halleck and Martin Loeb (eds.), Community Psychiatry. Madison: University of Wisconsin Press.
1967 "Some factors in identifying and defining mental illness." Pp. 23–30 in Thomas J. Scheff (ed.), Mental Illness and Social Processes. New York: Harper and Row.

MENNINGER, KARL.
1963 "Committee on homosexual offenses and prostitution." Pp. 1–13 in The Wolfenden Report. New York: Stein and Day.

MILLER, FRANK W. AND FRANK J. REMINGTON.
1962 "Procedures before trial." The Annals 339(January):111–124.

MILLER, S. M.
1964 "The American lower classes: a typological approach." Social Research 31(Spring):1–22.

MISHLER, ELLIOT G. AND NANCY E. WAXLER.
1966 "Family interaction processes and schizophrenia: a review of current theories." International Journal of Psychiatry 2 (July):375–413.

MYERS, JEROME K. AND BERTRAM H. ROBERTS.
1964 Family and Class Dynamics in Mental Illness. New York: Wiley.

NEWMAN, DONALD.
1962 "Pleading guilty for considerations: a study of bargain justice." Pp. 24–32 in Norman Johnston, Leonard Savitz and Marvin E. Wolfgang (eds.), Sociology of Punishment and Correction. New York: Wiley.

O'DONNELL, JOHN A.
1962 "The Lexington program for narcotic addicts." Federal Probation 26 (March):55–60.
1966 "Narcotic addiction and crime." Social Problems 13(Spring):374–385.

PASAMANICK, BENJAMIN, FRANK R. SCARPITTI
AND SIMON DINITZ.
1967 Schizophrenics in the Community.
New York: Appleton-Century-Crofts.

PHILLIPS, DEREK L.
1967 "Rejection: a possible consequence of
seeking help for mental disorders."
Pp. 63–78 in Thomas J. Scheff (ed.),
Mental Illness and Social Processes.
New York: Harper and Row.

PRESIDENT'S COMMISSION ON LAW ENFORCEMENT
AND ADMINISTRATION OF JUSTICE.
1967 The Challenge of Crime in a Free
Society. (February) Washington, D.C.:
U.S. Government Printing Office.

RAY, MARSH.
1961 "The cycle of abstinence and relapse
among heroin addicts." Social Problems 9(Fall):132–140.

REISS, ALBERT J., JR.
1961 "The social integration of queers and
peers." Social Problems 9(Fall):102–
120.

RENBORG, BERTIL A.
1957 "International control of narcotics."
Law and Contemporary Problems
22(Winter):86–112.

ROEBUCK, JULIAN.
1963 "A critique of 'thieves, convicts' and
the inmate culture." Social Problems
11(Spring):193–199.

ROSENTHAL, DAVID.
1963 The Genain Quadruplets: A Case
Study and Theoretical Analysis of
Heredity and Environment in Schizophrenia. New York: Basic Books.

RUITENBEEK, HENRIK M.
1963 The Problem of Homosexuality in
Modern Society. New York: Dutton.

SCHEFF, THOMAS J.
1963 "The role of the mentally ill and the
dynamics of mental disorder: a research framework." Sociometry 26
(December):436–453.

SCHUR, EDWARD M.
1961 "British narcotics policies." Journal
of Criminal Law, Criminology and
Police Science 51(March/April):619–
629.

SCOTT, JOHN F. AND HOWARD E. FREEMAN.
1963 "The one night stand in mental
health education." Social Problems
10(Winter): 277–284.

SCOTT, WILLIAM A.
1958 "Research definitions of mental health
and mental illness." Psychological
Bulletin 55(January):29–45.

SELLIN, THORSTEN.
1962 "Crime and delinquency in the
United States: an over-all view." The
Annals 339(January):11–23.

SHERWIN, ROBERT V.
1961 "Laws on sex crimes." Pp. 626–627 in
Encyclopedia of Sexual Behavior.
New York: Hawthorn Books.

SKOLNICK, JEROME H.
1960 "Toward a developmental theory of
parole." American Sociological Review 25(August):542–549.

SROLE, LEO, THOMAS S. LANGNER, STANLEY T.
MICHAEL, MARVIN K. OPLER, AND
THOMAS A. C. RENNIE.
1962 Mental Health in the Metropolis:
The Midtown Manhattan Study. New
York: McGraw-Hill.

STANTON, A. H. AND M. S. SCHWARTZ.
1954 The Mental Hospital. New York:
Basic Books.

SYKES, GRESHAM M.
1956 "Men, merchants, and toughs: a study
of reactions to imprisonment." Social
Problems 4(October):130–137.
1958 The Society of Captives. Princeton,
New Jersey: Princeton University
Press.

SZASZ, THOMAS S.
1960 "The myth of mental illness." The
American Psychologist 15(February):
113–118.

TURNER, R. JAY AND MORTON O. WAGENFELD.
1967 "Occupational mobility and schizophrenia: an assessment of the social causation and social selection hypotheses." American Sociological Review 32(February):104–113.

UNITED NATIONS EXPERT COMMITTEE ON DRUGS.
1950 "Liable to Product Addiction: Reports 6 and 7." World Health Organization Technical Report Series Number 21. New York: United Nations.

VINCENT, CLARK E.
1960 "Unmarried fathers and the mores: 'sexual exploiter' as an ex post facto label." American Sociological Review 25(February):40–46.

VOLKMAN, RITA AND DONALD R. CRESSEY.
1963 "Differential association and the rehabilitation of drug addicts." American Journal of Sociology 69(September):129–142.

WARD, DAVID A. AND G. G. KASSEBAUM.
1965 Women's Prison: Sex and Social Structure. Chicago: Aldine.

WEINBERG, S. KIRSON.
1960 Social Problems in Our Time. Englewood Cliffs, New Jersey: Prentice-Hall.

WHEELER, STANTON.
1966 "Delinquency and crime." Pp. 272–273 in Howard S. Becker (ed.), Social Problems: A Modern Approach. New York: Wiley.

WOOTON, BARBARA.
1959 Social Science and Social Pathology. London: George Allen.

YABLONSKY, LEWIS.
1965 The Tunnel Back: Synanon. New York: Macmillan.

CHAPTER 14

marriage
and parenthood

IN MANY WAYS THE PRIOR STAGES of the life cycle can be regarded as preparatory to the vital period extending from twenty-five to forty years of age. Virtually all individuals in this age category have completed their educational training. By this time, almost all men and a large proportion of women have resolved their choice of occupational careers and are busy establishing a place for themselves within the economic structure. The majority of women have chosen a mate and most of these are well into their childbearing period. At age twenty-five, the average female has already produced two children, and the pattern of family life for both male and female is well structured.

This period can be looked upon as one of settling in. Families acquire homes and a myriad of physical goods; the presence of children accentuates concerns about housing needs and the type of community environment the husband and wife desire for themselves and their family. In the ideal scheme of things, individuals in this period of life accept full responsibility not only for their personal lives and welfare but for the shape and character of the communities in which they live.

It is also the age when personal economic hardships, emotional dissatisfactions, and feelings of futility become extremely marked for some individuals. The basic social problems characteristic of contemporary community life take their toll in many ways. Many individuals are confronted with problematic opportunities for achievement in occupational careers, with unanticipated economic insufficiencies, and with emotional deficiencies that limit their competence to perform adequately as parents. Many married couples are faced with a recognition of the inappropriateness of their selection of mates and an awareness of a less-than-satisfactory marital union. This is also a period of continued increase and development of chronic mental disorders and some deterioration in robustness and physical well-being. Further, certain individuals, typically with a background of prior illegal activities, are well established in a criminal career. Others, by virtue of their occupational roles and personal characteristics, find themselves enmeshed in corrupt business and economic practices to such an extent that they may appropriately be called white-collar criminals.

The period of settling in is characterized by efforts and activities of individuals to maximize their economic place within the community. To a large extent, the consumer market permits American families to enjoy the affluence and the good life that typifies the existence of many individuals in the United States. Here we shall be discussing the special problems that confront parents of growing children. On balance, it should be recorded that for many Americans it is a period of great fulfillment and gratification—pride in the possession of material things, accomplishments at work, the joy of watching one's children grow up, the fulfillment and gratification of community activities, the reward of recognition and prestige.

From older or younger perspectives, many of the satisfactions of this age period may seem unimportant and of little or no consequence, but for the persons involved they have great meaning. Professionals and businessmen begin to achieve recognition by being named to the boards of philanthropic community groups, their names and accomplishments are listed in *Who's Who,* and they begin to be elected to offices in fraternal and social groups. They find themselves consulted by others in the community and derive great satisfaction from serving as role models to their children and to younger community members. Some achieve political and social recognition, while others are quite content to enjoy their families, hobbies, and recreation and to secure their future through modest savings and investment programs. Both the strivers and the enjoyers may seek a continued array of new experiences in the world of work and in their interpersonal lives. Although the settling-in period is accompanied by considerable fulfillment for the majority of Americans, there are some problematic aspects of this age period, and these we will discuss in this chapter.

changes in family life

Urban Americans marry young: the average age at marriage in the United States is less than twenty-three years for males and less than twenty-one years for females. The average age at marriage has declined slightly in recent years but current practices seem to point to a reversal of this trend. Americans also dissolve their marriages at a high rate, divorce and separations frequently beginning in the very first year of marriage (Monahan, 1962). In any given year there is one divorce for each three marriages that take place. The latest figures are 2.5 divorces per 1,000 population or 9.6 divorces per 1,000 married women, which is a more refined measure since only the married are eligible for divorce. There is some question about whether the rate is increasing. (*See* Documentation 1.)

Considerable emphasis has been given to the marked changes that have occurred in the structure and function of the American family unit. Many analysts of family life seek to account for contemporary family structure and intrafamilial relationships in terms of the rather swift industrialization and urbanization that have taken place on the American scene. (These social processes are frequently associated with a number of other social problems faced by the American community.)

FUNCTIONAL CHANGES

Since most work takes place in the factory or office, the family, in its broadest outlines, has become a consuming rather than a producing unit. Neither the farmer nor the rural craftsman of a century ago exists in any numbers today. Little of the material goods that the family uses are produced at home or by the family members themselves. Ours is a community life in which commercial enterprises provide the goods; the husband, and often the wife also, engage in gainful employment in order to provide the monetary resources necessary to acquire such goods. Naturally, with the shift to industrialization and the rapid urbanization of the United States, housing arrangements and family relationships have also changed (Cohen and Connery, 1967). In general, family life in America can be characterized as a conjugal one, that is, parents and their children live as an independent unit and only a minority of households include more than one generation of adults.

STRUCTURAL CHANGES

A number of social analysts contend that some of the changes in family living arrangements have been exaggerated; multi-generation families living together do continue to exist, and contemporary conjugal units may not be any more isolated from their paternal families than they were in earlier generations. Many couples with children live in the same communities as brothers, sisters, cousins, and parents. Moreover, as Litwak (1960) has pointed out, the telephone, the airplane, and the modern highway system make feasible continued contacts and sustained affective relationships despite geographical distance separating relatively independent units. Nevertheless, the overriding image of the family is the conjugal unit. It is the husband and wife and nonadult children living together in an independent residence where each member has

the statistics of divorce

The trend of the divorce rate since 1867, the first year for which this rate was computed, showed a long-term increase that lasted 80 years, reaching a record peak in 1946. During this period, the rate increased from 0.3 to 4.3 per 1000 total population. The trend was accelerated by wars and reversed by economic depressions. During the 44 years shown on the chart, the rate first declined from the slight post-World War I peak, then resumed its upward trend (which was interrupted by the great depression) and almost doubled during the war and early postwar years—from 2.2 in 1941 to 4.3 in 1946. It declined rapidly afterwards, going back to 2.2 in 1957; since then it has remained approximately at the same level. [I]t is too early to say whether the slight increases found in 1961 and 1963 indicate the beginning of a new period of growth, but the provisional estimates of the national divorce totals for 1964 and 1965 (445,000 and 481,000, respectively, or 2.3 and 2.5 per 1000 population) suggest that the upward trend may have resumed.

The crude divorce rate, computed for the total population, depends in part on the proportion of married persons in the population, as married persons only are subject to the risk of divorce. Therefore the divorce rate per 1000 married women is a more refined measure of the incidence of divorce. The divorce rate per 1000 married women was 9.6 in 1963—slightly higher than the 1962 rate of 9.4, equal to the 1961 rate, and higher than the rates for all years from 1954 to 1960. (Plateris, 1967:3, 5.)

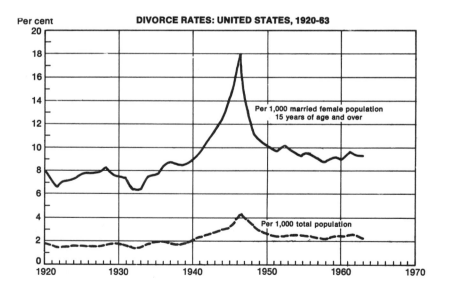

DIVORCE RATES: UNITED STATES, 1920-63

considerable control over the initiation and sustenance of interaction and relationships with other family members. Given this emphasis on the conjugal unit, naturally the community is greatly concerned with its stability and endurance.

family instability

Analysts of family life point out that problems of divorce, desertion, and separation represent only one aspect of the problem of marital stability and constitute only a single measure of the satisfactions of married life. A significant proportion of these investigators hold that there are many so-called intact families in which the relationships between the spouses are more conflict-ridden and emotionally unsatisfying than they are among couples who by legal divorce or separation or, informally, through desertion or mutual agreement have dissolved their marriage. Even with respect to the emotional development of children, intact but conflict-ridden families may provide a less desirable type of interpersonal milieu than homes broken through divorce and separation (Pollock, 1966). In discussing the rates of broken homes, it is necessary to look carefully at the alternative means by which families dissolve and to consider the influence of nonuniform legal codes upon the rates reported by various states.

Separation is often used as a term to refer to the informal breaking up of a family unit or, sometimes, as a preliminary step to divorce. But many family units undergo short and, occasionally, long separations that serve to lessen the conflicts in relationships and make possible a resumption of marital relations. All states provide for the formalization of separation, and legal separations usually involve decisions as to the distribution of property and the responsibilities, particularly of the husband, for the support of the children and his spouse. *Annulment* is a court decision that recognizes some legal flaw in the marriage which, in a sense, never existed. Some of the reasons recognized by various states for annulment include fraud, unwillingness to consummate the union, and bigamy. *Desertion* refers to one of the spouses' disappearing or avoiding contact with the family unit.

Divorce, on the other hand, refers to the legal termination of the marriage. It should be noted that the reasons for divorce and the willingness of the legal system to enter into annulments and separations differ, depending upon the state in which such actions are undertaken. For example, until a few years ago the only permissible reason for divorce in New York State was adultery. As a consequence, one of several alternative procedures was generally pursued by New Yorkers seeking a divorce: either one of the partners traveled to another state or to a foreign country such as Mexico to obtain the divorce decree; the partners colluded to set up an adulterous situation merely to provide evidence for the divorce proceedings; or finally, an annulment was sought. Annulment is used much more frequently in New York than in many other states as a means of avoiding the stringent divorce laws (Rowley, 1966). Although on a national basis, annulments represent perhaps 3 per cent of marriage dissolutions in any year, they represented approximately 35 per cent of the legal actions in New York State in a twelve-month period.

Thus, the various means employed to dissolve family units may not reflect any real differences in the underlying reasons for their dissolution. In many cases, the ways by which marriages are terminated reflect the religious orientation of the parties involved. Indeed, the actual dissolution of a marriage is associated not only with religious affiliation but with the intensity of religious views held by the mates (Freeman and Showel, 1952). Among Catholic families, particularly church-going ones, there are many fewer divorces than among Protestant families in proportion to their numbers in the total population. There is no means of calculating precisely the total family dissolution rate by religion; however, it is commonly believed that there is a higher rate of informal separations among Catholics than among other major religious groups. The assumption is sometimes made that if all types of dissolution were recorded, there would be no marked or major differences between the various religious groups.

separation and divorce

Although much of the stigma formerly attached to divorced or separated individuals has diminished, marital break up is viewed as a personal tragedy and a symptom of social disorganization. As Goode (1966:493) notes, this view is related in part to our religious heritage. In general, divorce is condemned and, until the early part of this century, it was a rare event. Our moral bias favors romantic love, and divorce suggests a mistake or a termination of this approved relationship. Some hold that the highly romantic quality attached to the husband-wife relationship in the United States and other Western countries is directly linked to the incidence of marital conflict and to the high rates of divorce. They argue that in other cultures, where there is less expectation of personal gratification in marriage or a greater emphasis on the kinship system rather than the marital relationship for such satisfactions, it is possible for individuals to maintain a marital union with less stress. Thus, while it has to be recognized that our high divorce and separation rate is bound up with our cultural values regarding marriage, nevertheless, it is a fact that the United States has the highest, or at least one of the highest, divorce rates in the world. One out of every four marriages ends in divorce.

Although most people do not accept divorce as a desirable thing, it is no longer viewed as a shameful or stigmatizing occurrence that must be hidden from others. For example, there are few occupational roles that currently discriminate against a divorced person, although this was formerly the case. This change in attitude toward divorce is related to the lessening influence of organized religion and to the increasing ability of a man to maintain himself without a wife. In a rural culture such as we had in the last century, a wife's services were critical; today, it is easy for a single adult male in the city to get along well. With the increased education of most women and their ability to compete in the job market, particularly if they are not burdened with dependent children, economic deprivations connected with family dissolution are less severe.

CAUSES OF DIVORCE

When one begins to look at the etiology of divorce and the causes of marital conflict, one becomes increasingly aware of the major function of economic problems in marital discord. Sexual incompatibility, often cited as a chief factor, appears to be of less concern (Miller, 1962). As Goode (1966:507) notes, "If husband and wife have temperamental incompatibilities and do not meet each other's *emotional* needs, they can express them in conflicts about economic matters, for economic problems pervade much of the family's life." If economics is the critical factor, then divorce should be more common among the lowest economic groups, and the evidence indicates that this is indeed the case. Contrary to popular opinion, laborers and service workers have been found to have divorce rates markedly higher than professionals or individuals in proprietary and managerial positions (Kephart, 1955) and stay married for shorter periods. (*See* Documentation 2.) The extent of an individual's education also seems to affect his chances for divorce. The lowest rates of divorce are found among college graduates and the highest among those who have not completed high school.

THE ECONOMIC FACTOR

Family income shows a similar relationship. A number of hypotheses have been raised to explain the pressures of economics upon the stability of family life. The constant irritations generated by insufficient funds erode the general well-being of the husband and wife and produce frustrations which are expressed in hostility and aggressiveness toward

DOCUMENTATION 2

occupation and divorce

**DURATION OF MARRIAGE TO SEPARATION DATE
AND TO DIVORCE DATE, WISCONSIN, 1957***

Occupational Group	TO SEPARATION		TO DIVORCE	
	Median	Mean	Median	Mean
Total	6.0	8.4	7.3	9.7
Farm	8.4	11.4	9.9	12.8
Professional	7.4	9.1	8.8	10.3
Owner-Manager-Official	10.2	11.2	11.2	12.4
Clerical and Sales	7.3	9.0	8.3	10.0
Skilled	7.5	9.3	8.8	10.5
Semiskilled	5.5	7.9	6.9	9.0
Service	5.8	8.6	7.1	10.1
Labor	4.7	7.4	6.1	8.9
Other and not stated	3.2	6.1	4.8	7.8

* The minimum number of cases in any calculation was 165.

The duration of marriages to divorce by occupational group was studied by Tarver for five selected years in Wisconsin. The manager-proprietor-official group showed the longest durations, and was followed by farmers and skilled workers. Professional and semi-professional occupations, rather oddly, along with the semi-skilled workers had the lowest median durations. A sizeable proportion of farmers (16 percent) were divorced after their silver wedding anniversary. How the occupations would differ according to the date of *separation* was not investigated.

In classifying the 1957 Wisconsin divorces according to the socio-economic classification of the 1950 United States Census, a number of arbitrary judgments had to be made particularly with reference to dual occupations and ambiguous titles such as firemen and engineers. The division of occupations, it is believed, represents the socio-economic scheme as closely as the data permitted. Obviously,

each other and the children. At the other extreme, individuals, particularly men, who work in high-income and prestigious occupations tend to find sufficient stimulation and enjoyment in their work to enable them to endure the tensions and frustrations that may exist in their family life. These advantages extend also to women who work outside the home, most of whom possess skills and training that are also related to higher education.

Finally, it is often more difficult for families in the middle and upper-income ranges to dissolve their marriages. The accumulations of possessions and capital goods, such as home, cars, furniture, and investments, make divorce, with its property settlements, alimony, and support agreements, much more complex. Unlike low-income families, higher-income

some husbands were, indeed, unemployed, retired, in military service or institutionalized. Others were students. About 12 percent of the divorces were granted to persons whose occupations were unknown or not stated.

As shown by the mean duration to *divorce* figures (the above table), the farm group has the longest mean duration followed closely by the owner-manager-official group; but, if medians are used the farming class is second. The average duration of the skilled group is somewhat exceptional in that it is slightly above the averages for the professional and clerical-sales occupations. The distribution of the divorce durations for the service class of workers gives them a relatively high mean duration also, but the median of their durations is below average. The durations drop off to below average for the semi-skilled and the laboring classes, which latter group has the lowest average durations of the eight categories.

There is a general tendency, with the exceptions noted, for the duration to shorten as one goes down the occupational scale. This holds true if one uses the median or the mean, or the date of separation instead of the date of the decree of divorce. Although 14 percent of the farmers were divorced after their 25th wedding anniversary, the figure diminishes to 10 percent according to separation date, while for other groups it was 4 percent to separation date.

The median duration in years to *separation* for farmers was noticeably less than for the manager-owner-official class, but longer than the average shown by the professional, clerical-sales, and skilled groups who shared third position. The mean duration to separation for the farm group, however, was the highest, because divorces did not drop off as rapidly in the later years of married life. The rather large group of laborers, on the other hand, showed the lowest average durations and the highest percentage separated in the first twelve months of marriage, one out of seven. The median duration to separation of the owner-manager-official group was 5.5 years longer than in the laboring group, with a difference in the means of 3.8 years. Truck drivers within the semi-skilled class showed durations equally as low as the laboring group, a median of 4.9 years and a mean of 6.8 years. Surprisingly, the mean and the median durations from separation to divorce varied very little from one occupational class to another, or less than 0.5 years. (Monahan, 1962:631–632.)

families usually enjoy a style of life that would be impossible to duplicate if the husband and wife were running separate households on the same income. Informal separations of long duration or desertions, common among low-income families, are relatively more difficult for middle and upper middle-class individuals. Not only is the deserting member traceable, but the business aspects of family life are virtually impossible to settle without a legal dissolution of the marital relationship.

These differences in divorce rates by economic group would be greater if it were possible to obtain accurate information on the number of informal separations among lower-income families. We know from data on welfare programs, such as Aid to Families of Dependent Children, that large numbers of informal separations and desertions occur in groups living at the poverty line or below. According to the 1960 census, approximately 4 in every 1,000 married women were living in households without their husbands in situations that could be described as desertions. This figure is slightly higher than the divorce rate for all married women.

The economic factor is frequently said to account for the unusually high separation and divorce rates found among blacks. Among non-whites, according to the 1960 census, the rate of households broken by separation is roughly 20 per 1,000, while the rate broken by divorce is just under 6 per 1,000. However, when occupation and education are matched, the divorce rate for blacks corresponds to that of whites. Negroes who have less than a college education have higher rates of divorce and separation than their white counterparts. Above this level, the rates are equal, or nonwhites have slightly lower rates. General fluctuations in the economy tend to affect black workers to a much greater extent than they do white workers. As a consequence, the economic factor may be an even more important influence on black family stability. The general view is that, as the economic lot of blacks is improved, their rates of marital disruption will tend to fall into line with those of white families. But some data question this view (*see* Documentation 3).

PERSONALITY AND ENVIRONMENTAL FACTORS

One should not assume that the correlation of socio-economic status and marriage dissolution reflects only problems of earning money and purchasing goods. Another generally held view is that successful marriage is less likely for those individuals who experienced stressful and unhappy childhoods. On these grounds, it has been suggested that those who come from lower socio-economic backgrounds, and thus have a greater chance of themselves being poor, are more likely to get divorced (Goode, 1951). Then, too, marriage occurs at somewhat earlier ages among those in lower socio-economic groups, and immaturity is another factor frequently cited as contributing to marital discord and dissolution.

Psychologists interested in interpersonal relations have debated the relative risks of divorce among individuals with similar characteristics and among marital partners with complementary needs. One group suggests that marital stability is higher among mates who are homogenous, that is, among those alike in personality and background characteristics (Burgess and Locke, 1953). Another group suggests that happiness in marriage is related to the contribution each spouse makes to the needs of the other (Winch, 1963). Research findings and sociological common sense suggest that each point of view has relevance for identifying the stable marriage. The couple who share similar values, whose friends and

marital instability by race and income

Per Cent

Percentage of ever-married males 25–34 years of age who were separated, divorced, or had been married more than once at the time of the 1960 Census, by income and race; based on a 5 per cent sample.

In the above figure, the inverse relationship of income to marital instability is quite unmistakable. It is also quite clear that the ratio of non-white to white marital instability grows consistently with increasing income. . . . These income data serve only to reinforce the arguments . . . that the white-non-white difference in marital instability cannot be explained solely by differences in present socioeconomic status. (Udry, 1967:673–674.)

extended family are congenial and supportive, and whose aspirations and strivings follow similar paths probably have greater likelihood of stable relationships. This is the rationale supporting much public opinion and the advice of some marriage counselors who stress marriages between persons of the same religion and race (Burchinal and Chancellor, 1963).

By way of contrast, it can also be said that individual levels of psychological gratification are more likely to be fulfilled when the needs of the man and woman complement one another. For example, the marital partner who enjoys doing things for someone else and taking care of many detailed arrangements is more likely to be happy with a partner who enjoys having these things done by another. The family system in the United States provides for a period of engagement and courtship;

couples who marry in haste have little opportunity to judge whether their psychological needs are relatively complementary and whether their aspirations and values are shared by their prospective mates.

A number of studies have sought to understand the "real"—as Goode (1966:523) puts it—complaints of husbands and wives against each other. Such reasons are difficult to analyze closely because by the time a long-term separation or divorce has ensued, conflict has pervaded virtually all areas of life. Today, however, there is considerable debunking of the view that sexual incompatibility is the chief cause for divorce (van den Haag, 1966). It is widely recognized that not only do many marital relationships endure despite major dissatisfactions in this area but, to a large extent, sexual incompatibility is a consequence rather than a cause of other interpersonal and environmental strains in the family relationship.

Most analysts of family life doubt that many families are broken as a consequence of a single event, be it the discovery of adultery or a knockdown, drag out fight. In Goode's (1956) study of divorce, he finds that the period of conflict often extends for years prior to divorce—the median time being somewhat over two years. There may be long periods of harmonious relationships interspersed with incidents of anger and disillusionment. In general, a family breakup tends to involve a gradual withdrawal of affection and warmth to the point where small matters that ordinarily would be overlooked create disharmony and conflict.

There is insufficient evidence to determine conclusively whether formal divorce decrees reflect accurately the situation regarding who is the protagonist or initiator of such action, much less who is to blame. In his study, *After Divorce,* Goode (1956) reports that it is usually the husband rather than the wife who first wishes to break up the marriage. Despite woman's improved place in the American community, men remain dominant in the family situation and in many ways have much less to lose from a divorce. This is particularly true if young children are present in the household. The husband's work role tends to provide him with a much broader range of contacts and personal relationships. After divorce, he will continue to derive satisfaction from them; also, he is relatively free to seek companionship and sexual gratification. Such satisfactions and sexual outlets are not as readily available to women.

DIFFERENTIAL INTERESTS OF SPOUSES

Although supportive research is still insufficient, analysts of family life point to several contemporary phenomena that influence family stability. One is the greater opportunity for maturity and intellectual growth available to the husband than the wife during this age period. This is particularly true for technical and professional men whose work and the contacts made there often leave them with little in common intellectually with their spouses. Men are described as growing and deepening while their wives, relegated to the role of housekeeper, stagnate and regress. The increase in the proportion of women working suggests, however, that the reversal of this trend is likely to be an increasingly important factor. Married women, even those in relatively low-status white-collar positions such as secretaries and clerks, often are employed in research laboratories, universities, advertising firms, and sales agencies. In these settings there is daily contact with a variety of individuals of diverse interests who furnish intellectual and interpersonal stimulation. At the same time, the husband may only look forward to a daily return to a rather isolated spot on a production line. Also, changing views on sexual conduct and the declining influence of the double standard permit the female to recognize that divorce or separation need not isolate her entirely from heterosexual relationships and sexual gratification. Although traditional community norms have fostered an atmosphere in which the commitment of males to the family relationship is less than that of females, the changing role of women is likely to modify this situation.

The problem of divorce is very different for couples with young children. Couples without children escape many problems of economic support and, possibly, feelings of guilt. Even community attitudes are more stringent towards divorce in which children are involved. While the average duration of marriage prior to divorce is over seven years, a significant proportion of divorces occur in the early years of marriage. Perhaps as many as 40 to 60 per cent of divorces and annulments take place in households where no children are involved (Jacobson, 1950).

THE ROLE OF THE CHILDREN

Because of the presumed sanctity of the parent-child relationship, there is little information about the extent to which children themselves represent a cause of divorce. Just as economic factors result in tension and anxiety, the problems of childrearing may be a significant element in family dissolution. An abnormal child, one with physical or emotional problems, may be the irritant that stimulates or reinforces the process of emotional disengagement that results in separation or divorce. Of course, the cause and effect relationship may run the other way: conflicts between the parents may affect the interpersonal and emotional behavior of children, resulting in a self-fulfilling prophecy. The acting-out behavior or other emotional symptoms of children may stimulate their parents to perceive the inadequacies of their own relationship. On other occasions, the love and affection that spouses normally show to each other may be displaced or transferred to a child, leaving one of the partners isolated and bereft of warmth and affection. Systematic information on the impact of children upon the relationships of adult family members is sparse; this important area of research requires further attention.

Children also present other problems when divorce occurs in the family. Among the difficulties is their appropriate socialization in one-parent families. Opportunities for outside social attachments are limited, particularly for the woman who is confined to the home by her role as mother and limited in her behavior by the norms of respectability. In recent years, a formal organization called Parents Without Partners has served to enable divorced and widowed parents to develop wider contacts and to receive support from others in a similar situation. Although adult social relationships and the opportunity to meet marriage partners undoubtedly represent part of the motivation to join, overtly the organization serves to provide substitute relationships for the children in broken homes. For example, a divorced male member may act as "foster father" to the children of a divorcee, spending time with them and taking some of the social roles of the natural father. Divorce undoubtedly puts a greater burden on the woman. Since the man can date either younger or older women, the population from which he can draw acceptable partners is considerably broader than that available to the woman, who usually looks for someone about her own age, or older. Also, since women more frequently are given custody of young children, programs such as Parents Without Partners will have greater appeal for them.

REMARRIAGE

As might be expected, the high divorce rates in the United States lead to high rates of remarriage. In about 15 per cent of all marriages, one of the spouses has been divorced. The probability that a divorced person in this age group will remarry is very high: some estimates are as high as 70 per cent for men and a somewhat lower figure for women. In general, divorced persons have somewhat lower chances for stable marriages in the second, third, and subsequent attempts. The obvious explanation, of course, is that individuals who have found it impossible to maintain a marital relationship in the first instance may not be able to maintain a long and enduring interpersonal relation with another. As previously noted, however, permanently married couples may not be any better off in terms of their satisfaction with the marital relationship. Certainly a divorced person is less likely to hold values inimicable to divorce and less likely to be committed to the maintenance of the marriage relationship "no matter what." As a consequence, the difference in attitudes and values, as well as interpersonal and temperamental characteristics, accounts for the higher divorce rates among couples in which one of the partners was previously divorced.

Perhaps the most fruitful way of viewing the problem of divorce is in terms of the period of risk, that is, the years of exposure. If American norms encouraged later marriage, in the thirties, say, rather than in the early twenties, the average number of years that people would be married would be significantly lower. Consequently it could be argued that, on a probability basis, there would be less likelihood of divorce.

Another and perhaps more practical approach to understanding the problems of divorce is to take a look at our changing attitudes toward marriage. In the past, marriage fulfilled very definite social and economic needs, particularly for the woman. Without a husband, a woman had little social standing, a limited social life, few means of financial support, no public influence, and a sparse or nonexistent sex life. Divorce spelled economic deprivation and, in the eyes of many contemporaries, moral and social degradation. Today, however, working women are being accepted into an increasing number of occupations and job situations, and the double standard of social and sexual behavior is practically aligned. Given these changes, perhaps the only strong reason for being concerned with the high divorce rate is the economic difficulties accruing to the broken family. An extreme view suggests that multiple marriage— or serial polygamy—in and of itself does not necessarily have serious consequences for community life. Rather, it is the products of early marriage and of prolonged life, i.e., dependent children and dependent adults, that make divorce a community problem.

While the concept of trading in one's spouse as one does one's car raises moral, ethical, and personal questions, these may not be, in the long run, the most important questions for community concern or, for that matter, the ones most amenable to social change. Perhaps, as some contend, it is unrealistic to think that young men and women in their early twenties can pick with unerring accuracy the kind of person with whom they wish to spend half a century. Can we really expect the vast majority of marital partners to grow, mature, and develop intellectually at the same pace and to remain compatible for such a long period? Some critics say the answer is no and that we should seek to overcome the notion that divorce is an unusual and traumatic event. Instead, we should recognize that separation, divorce, and remarriage are normal processes in the routine of community life.

INTERNAL DISSOLUTION

But what of those marriages that do stay intact, although unhappily so? It is easier to obtain information on the divorced population and to identify the problems leading to marital dissolution than it is to understand the phenomenon of marital unhappiness. As we have noted, large numbers of marriages persist for years although they fail to be gratifying experiences for the mates involved. Such a defective family life may have an impact on the children as well as on the ways adult family members perform in other spheres, such as in the world of work. Goode (1966) makes the point that, in addition to community concern about divorce and separation, it is equally reasonable to give attention to the family that is internally dissolved—that is, "an empty shell." His image of an empty shell is appropriate since many couples may remain under the same roof but seldom communicate. For reasons of prestige, economics, or religious views, such couples maintain the fiction of the stable family, but interaction in the day-to-day life of these individuals is highly superficial and solely of an instrumental sort. To quote Goode (1966:533):

> The atmosphere is without laughter or fun, and a sullen gloom pervades the household. Members do not discuss their problems or experiences with each other, and communication is kept to a minimum. Parents and children fulfill their instrumental obligations, but not their expressive ones. The husband holds a job and provides for the family. The wife takes care of the house and meals, and nurses those who become ill. The children go to school and at home do their chores. But any spontaneous expression of affection, or even of delight in a personal experience, is rebuffed by the others. Each tells the others whatever is necessary to integrate their instrumental activities—when one will be home for a meal, how much school supplies cost, or what is the next chore to be done.

Sociologists are concerned particularly about the impact of such an environment on the rearing of children. By suffering through such a marriage, the parents may not achieve any better a relationship between themselves or for their children than if they were to cut the ties and dissolve the union (Landis, 1962). In such families, adolescents find it most difficult to obtain the advice and counsel they need. Many of their deepest experiences are kept secret and their conflicts are resolved without guidance from the adult members of the family. Outside social activities involving the family as a unit are usually limited, and both adults and children are divested of expressive, emotional relationships. From the standpoint of family stability, it is important that further research be undertaken to determine the extent of such internally dissolved families. They do not appear in statistics on divorce and separation, but they contribute as much to the problem of family instability as do broken homes.

In passing, it should be noted that the likelihood of separation by death is no longer prevalent among adults of this age. The increase in life expectancy and the control of physical illness within this age group have drastically reduced the incidence of family instability because of death. However, the toll taken by wars and auto accidents is considerable and many of the problems faced by the survivors are similar to those experienced by divorced or separated families. Economic insufficiencies and the inadequate provision of both adult male and female sex-role models represent two of the more serious problems.

INADEQUATE SOCIALIZATION

Where a family is incomplete because of either divorce, separation, death, or illegitimacy, the adequacy of the family as the socialization agent of the children is a real concern. We have noted the severe economic demands created by the loss of the male breadwinner. Until this decade, only limited attention was paid to this problem. Now federal programs provide aid to families with dependent children and, in states with adequate welfare subsidies, a part of the economic burden faced by these families has been removed or alleviated. For the vast majority of broken homes, however, severe economic problems still persist. Even in 1970, less than a quarter of the states provided welfare payments or family allowances sufficient to meet minimum requirements for necessities. As was discussed earlier in the chapters on poverty and discrimination, some efforts have been made to provide substitute socialization mechanisms when one of the parents is absent from the home. These efforts have been minimal and their impact uncertain. Part-time foster parents, foster-home placements, and adoption programs operate only partially to handle the problem of adequate socialization of children from broken homes.

Undoubtedly, for those adults in the age group under consideration, the short-range solution to these problems consists of better programs of mate selection and marriage counseling. It may not be advisable or expedient to select mates by computer analysis; nevertheless, genetic counseling to forestall genetic incompatibilities and premarital counseling to determine potential temperament and personality conflicts between prospective mates should be provided. Young persons in their late teens or early twenties who contemplate marriage should typically be aware of any potential incompatibilities.

In addition to the informal consultations of clergymen and, occasionally, of physicians and school guidance personnel who offer premarital advice, the courts in some communities provide marriage counseling services to which couples seeking divorce or legal separation can be remanded prior to the granting of the decree. Neither the efforts of premarital counseling nor the programs of consultation after marriage have had spectacular success in handling problems of divorce, separation, and the "empty shell" existence of many intact families. The key probably is prevention of instability through wise mate selection.

One of the realities not faced is the extent to which early marriages are a consequence of real or presumed premarital pregnancies. A critical goal of the social-control systems should be to minimize the risks of premarital pregnancy. In our discussion of youth, we referred to the conflict that Americans face in this respect. All efforts to date have been hampered, if not rendered ineffective, by community groups that disapprove of birth-control programs directed at teen-agers. Nevertheless, many later problems of divorce, separation, and unsatisfactory marital relationships are the direct result of "shotgun pressures" imposed upon young people. Forced marriages do not allow young people sufficient opportunities to judge for themselves the reasonableness of a long life together and to assess their chances for an expressive and affective union (Christensen and Meissner, 1953).

It is unwise to believe that much can be done to postpone marriage in the United States until an age when more of the life patterns, goals, and values of the couple are firmly anchored and fixed. Neither is it likely that sex can be universally restricted to the marriage bed. The probability for increasing family stability rests at the preventive level, not at a level of intervention subsequent to marriage. If the adults in this age group are to maintain any semblance of marital stability, then community action must begin earlier in the lives of the participants.

LONG-RANGE PROGRAMS

There are many who argue that the very basis of moral relationships in the family situation must be modified in order to achieve marital stability. Many of the norms that govern family life, male and female sex roles, the relationship of parents and children, and levels of competence in family relations are drawn from an era in which views regarding the place of women in the social structure were different and in which the family was organized as a productive rather than a consumptive unit. One programmatic approach (Foote and Cottrell, 1955) suggests that family life can be improved only by building interpersonal competence prior to the years of marriage and then maintaining it. These analysts assume that stability and competence are related to such phenomena as health, empathy, autonomy, and intelligence. The community's responsibility is to maximize such attributes by the provision of needed services and appropriate programs from birth to death. The hope for dealing with the problems of family stability rests here.

A somewhat different tack is taken by Litwak (1960), who stresses the need for much less emphasis on differentiation of sex roles in the American society. The concept of the woman as primarily responsible for the care of the children in all family situations and of the husband—regardless of level of skill or temperament—as the chief breadwinner are two of the sex-linked roles he has challenged. He argues that, in many cases, the father might be the one to concern himself with the internal affairs of the family while the mother may work and be active in other community activities. Litwak stresses the need for shifts in the ways family responsibilities are delegated and in the expectations of family members with respect to the making of decisions and in participating in different family activities.

While the reversing of traditional roles is not expected in the foreseeable future, it must be acknowledged that in some ways we are moving in this direction. Certain chores formerly regarded as feminine, such as doing the grocery shopping or weekly laundry or in other ways caring for the domestic aspects of home life, are more likely today to be shared by the male. Correspondingly, the married woman is less restricted than in the past, not only in terms of gainful employment but in terms of political activities and other community ventures. Undoubtedly, the trend toward greater equality in family roles corresponds with the equalization of women's status outside the home. As remaining inequities are reduced, family stability will increase.

At present, the American family structure is being buffeted by competing pressures. On the one hand, some moralists urge a return to the good old days when the family represented a model of stability and concern for the welfare of family members, particularly the children. On the other hand, many social critics continue to pressure for a more equalitarian, democratic family life and, in many ways, their approach seems rational and inevitable. The community's ambivalence about taking a stand on these important issues is partly responsible for many of the problems of family stability. Most analysts of family life stress the relative impossibility, given our technical and industrial life style, of returning to the structure of the conjugal unit that marked the so-called good old days. However, only limited effort has yet been given to restructuring the family life of our nation although there is awareness among professionals for the need for future change. (*See* Documentation 4.)

family planning

At several points in this book we have alluded to birth control as a possible means of ameliorating some of the undesirable conditions that exist in the American community. In our discussion of poverty we indicated that the prospects for providing each child with a way of life consistent with the maximization of his social potentials are quite low for even

A rough summary follows of the properties and procedures which family-field professionals, according to their writings and researches, seem to want perpetuated in families of the future.

1. The mate-selection machinery should be reorganized to encourage couples of reasonably similar backgrounds to meet and be tested for compatibility through a prolonged courtship and engagement.

2. Premarital sex relations should be no more intimate than the consciences of the couple can tolerate and the courting relation can sustain psychologically.

3. Premarital examinations, counseling, and education should help prepare the couple for marriage, postponing and returning to circulation those who are not ready.

4. The objectives of marriage should include the continued matching and stimulating of companionship, mutual understanding, common interests and joint activities, as well as building a system of planning and problem-solving.

5. With the coming of children and the activating of the parental roles, attention to family issues of needs of dependents competes with the needs in the marital relation for which preparation is indicated.

6. The chief objectives for the family phase can be listed as mastering the family tasks of each stage, including family-size control, physical maintenance, socialization, and gratification of emotional needs, and providing the motivation and morale necessary for the stimulation and development of personality potentials of all members.

7. To attain this high plane of family achievement, an effective group organization must be built and a competent family leadership must be trained. The accent in family organization should be on integrating objectives, good internal communication, clarity of role definitions, and patterns of problem-solving and decision-making. Leadership qualities needed stress interpersonal competence, of which autonomy, empathy, judgment, creativity, and self-mastery are highly relevant to marital and family success. (Hill, 1964:28.)

moderate-income families with many children. We also suggested the utility of birth control as one solution to the problem of illegitimacy. The practice of limiting births, however, is of most crucial concern to the young family, and particularly the young adult wife. Family planning is a key way by which spouses select and structure the life styles that they and their children will follow and enjoy for years. It is important to emphasize not only the economic differentials related to family size—two can live as cheaply as one but only for half as long—but also the differentials in emotional satisfaction accruing to the smaller family, and the more extensive opportunities for social development (Rainwater, 1960).

Earlier in this chapter we noted that by age twenty-five or thirty the majority of couples who have remained married already have produced two children. By the time the parents are in their mid-thirties, the last of these children is in school most of the day, freeing the mother to pursue a career as a gainfully employed worker or as an extremely active and virtually full-time participant in community affairs. Many women, of course, move through the childbearing and the early childrearing years with little interruption in their work or community activities. There is a great difference of opinion as to the advisability of mothers with young children engaging in activities that require their absence from home for much of the day (Nye and Hoffman, 1963). However, there is little reason for a mother of school-age children to limit her activities to the care of the home. Thus, family planning introduces a measure of flexibility in a woman's community role and this, as well as the economic considerations, is responsible for the liberalization of community norms toward birth control. Many medical authorities state that family planning is also essential in terms of childspacing. Viewpoints differ concerning the desirability of building a family rapidly although most physicians believe that the physical and emotional health of the mother dictates at least a one-year hiatus between pregnancies.

BIRTH-CONTROL APPROACHES

The number of children or a particular pattern of childspacing is not really the key issue in family planning. The key issue is whether the knowledge and means of preventing conception are available to all married couples so that they can personally decide when and how many children to have in terms of the life style they plan to lead. Birth control by one means or another has been practiced throughout history. Among the methods currently in vogue are abstinence from sexual relations, confinement of sexual activity to periods of low fertility, the use of mechanical appliances such as diaphragms or intrauterine devices, and chemical control of ovulation (the pill). Not to be overlooked is the widespread practice of abortion to interrupt unwanted pregnancies. Despite the legal limitations on this procedure, it has been estimated (Ridgeway, 1966) that one in four pregnancies is terminated in this way, usually at considerable financial expense. (*See* Documentation 5.)

During a good part of their married life the majority of couples in the United States today practice birth control by either mechanical or chemical means. Many of the social differentials formerly associated with the practice of birth control, particularly the utilization of mechanical and chemical devices, have disappeared. Although research evidence is nonexistent, the impression is that birth control, except for abstinence or the rhythm method, was practiced a generation ago primarily by non-Catholic, white, middle-income families. However, recent studies of current practices indicate that religious differentials, despite Vatican

financial arrangements for abortions

ABORTIONISTS' FEES PAID

Amount Charged (x)	Number	Cumulative Percent Paid (x) or Less
None	6	5.3
Don't know	2	7.8
$ 20–$100	22	26.3
101– 200	13	37.7
201– 300	16	51.8
301– 400	15	64.9
401– 500	18	80.7
501– 600	12	91.2
601– 700	4	94.7
701– 800	2	96.5
801– 900	0	96.5
901– 1,150	4	100.0
Total	114	

Note: Mean = $337; Median = $300

Many . . . had arrangements to make before the abortion could be performed. The women found out the cost of the abortion at the time of the first contact with the abortionist. Many had a very good idea of what it would cost from the information given by the person who gave the abortionist's address. Forty-eight couples had to borrow money in order to pay the costs involved. Twelve borrowed from a bank or loan company, giving a false reason for the loan, while thirty-six borrowed from friends or relatives, of whom thirty were told the real purpose of the loan.

Even among those who did not need to borrow money, financial transactions were often complicated and time-consuming. The couples had to agree on the division of the costs between themselves, and many had to make a trip to a bank to get the necessary large amounts of cash. Twenty-two of the women paid all the costs themselves, while sixty-four shared the costs with the man involved in the pregnancy or got him to pay all the costs, and fifteen married couples paid out of their common funds. The woman's parents paid all or part of the costs in only eight cases. The fees charged by the abortionists the women actually went to are presented in the above table. (Lee, 1969:91–92.)

sanctions against the use of appliances and chemicals, have virtually disappeared between Catholics and non-Catholics. During some part of their marital careers a large proportion of couples practice family planning in ways not sanctioned by their religion (Westoff et al., 1963).

The evidence also shows that the employment of birth-control practices of all types has greatly increased among couples with less education and lower incomes, although notable differences in family size still exist when income is taken into account. Most experts on population control believe that in a country such as ours, where a large proportion of the population has sufficient education to understand and follow instructions for a variety of birth-control methods, the prospects are good for introducing such practices throughout the community. Present limitations to such a plan consist of certain archaic legal restrictions in some states; continued opposition from the Roman Catholic hierarchy, from some moral extremists and, recently, from some black leaders who interpret birth-control efforts among the poor as a form of black genocide; and, finally, the practical consideration of cost.

While a month's supply of most contraceptive products costs less than $3, this represents about 1 per cent of the take-home pay of those bread-winners in the lowest fifth of the income distribution. This is about one-sixth of the family's discretionary income available after subsistence and basic medical expenses. For those living on welfare assistance, the choice may well be between food to feed the family and contraceptives to limit the family.

Part of the opposition to implementing birth-control programs is related to the fear that authoritarian means will be used to force families to limit their size. But this is hardly a realistic danger in the American community. While perhaps sincerely held, most of these objections represent attempts to halt or impede the work of voluntary groups engaged in promoting family planning and to limit drastically the support given such programs by governmental bodies.

INTERVENTION STRATEGIES

The current emphasis on promoting freedom of choice with respect to family planning is twofold: one aspect involves strenuous efforts to remove structural barriers in the community; the other concerns effective programs to provide birth-control information and products to low-income and indigent families who request it. Income is a definite predictor of both premarital pregnancy and child-spacing practices. (*See* Documentation 6.) With respect to structural barriers, it is important to realize that until 1966 it was illegal in the state of Connecticut for a physician or anyone else to prescribe mechanical or chemical means of birth control (Way, 1966). Although there has been some breakthrough, the mass media remain extremely sensitive about providing public information on matters of birth control, and no newspaper has yet found it proper to accept advertisements for pharmaceutical products related to birth control. It is an interesting phenomenon that a practice so widely engaged in by the general public is treated with such diffidence and sensitivity by important groups in the community. Even today, many young couples are unaware until the time of their marriage of the range of considerations involved in family planning and are ignorant of the alternate techniques available to them if they wish to limit the size of their family.

In addition to present efforts to minimize or rescind legal restrictions and to make birth-control information more easily communicated throughout the community, programs are needed to educate the young people. For many, the rush into marriage begins at age eighteen, right

childspacing and family income

**PREMARITAL PREGNANCY AND DURATION TO FIRST BIRTH
BY FAMILY INCOME AND PARITY**

Parity and Family Income in 1961	Percent Pregnant Premaritally	Mean Number of Months from Marriage to First Birth	Number of Cases
1st Parity	*Percent*	*Months*	
Under $3,000	34.1	13.5	*(41)*
$3,000–4,999	25.6	17.0	*(90)*
$5,000–6,999	11.4	20.1	*(105)*
$7,000–8,999	10.8	27.3	*(74)*
$9,000 or more	4.8	32.3	*(62)*
Grand Mean	16.1	22.1	*(372)*
2nd Parity			
Under $3,000	42.8	10.1	*(28)*
$3,000–4,999	23.0	17.8	*(61)*
$5,000–6,999	23.3	21.3	*(150)*
$7,000–8,999	18.5	24.7	*(81)*
$9,000 or more	11.5	30.5	*(52)*
Grand Mean	22.0	21.9	*(372)*
4th Parity			
Under $3,000	38.1	15.0	*(21)*
$3,000–4,999	18.9	15.1	*(53)*
$5,000–6,999	24.8	17.3	*(125)*
$7,000–8,999	11.8	17.4	*(93)*
$9,000 or more	7.8	22.8	*(77)*
Grand Mean	17.9	18.2	*(369)*

after, if not during, high school. Yet many American school systems provide no information of substance on the matter and only a few have well-developed programs. Both voluntary groups and governmental agencies continue to move extremely cautiously—many believe too cautiously—in the initiation and implementation of information programs.

IMPACT OF FEDERAL PROGRAMS

For low-income families, public agencies are beginning to make available the necessary and desired products. In deference to religious leaders

The data on which this analysis is based came from an intensive interview with 1,113 women in the Detroit Metropolitan Area in 1962. Information was gathered regarding their family expectations and preferences, their pregnancy histories, and a wide range of social and economic variables. These women constitute a probability sample of all white, married women in the area who had a first, second, or fourth birth in July, 1961. As a parity sample, it represents a cross-section of families at a given point in the family-building cycle, rather than a cross-section of the urban community. . . .

Evidence from this study is in line with evidence for the nation as a whole—rapid family building is the order of the day. Half the women in our sample had their first child within the first year of marriage, and evidence from the follow-up years indicates that for many the view for subsequent births is "soon or not at all." There are important economic differentials, however, in [childspacing].

The higher the current family income, the smaller was the proportion of couples who were premaritally pregnant, and the longer was the interval from marriage to the first child and to the last child, if there was more than one child. These relationships obtain in each of the three parity groups. The differences between income groups in childspacing are substantial. For example, at second parity the percentage premaritally pregnant is 43 percent for the lowest income group and 12 percent for the highest. The lowest income group had a first child in 10 months . . . as compared with 31 months . . . for the highest income group.

These results are not a function of religious differences. Adjusting the relationships for wife's religion and church attendance . . . does not alter significantly either the direction or general magnitude of the differences between income groups. The positive direction of the relation between current income and the first birth interval was unaffected by controlling the effects of age at marriage, wife's employment history, husband's unemployment record, and a series of seven other variables sequentially.

The relationship between the spacing measures and current family income persists even when the couples have been married long enough to have four children, so the relationship is not simply a phenomenon of the first few years of marriage. Note, for example, that among those with four births, the proportion premaritally pregnant still have a strong negative relationship to current income. Whatever the cause of the association . . . it does not disappear even . . . after the birth of four children. (Freedman and Coombs, 1966:632, 634–635.)

and other power figures within the community, most public welfare systems have been reluctant to undertake such programs (Davis and Blake, 1960). However, the policies of the federal government, especially with respect to welfare mothers, have begun to have an impact on state and local agencies, both public and private, and some expansion of birth-control programs for the poor is taking place. Family planning, however, is a right of every American couple. In all cases, couples of childbearing age need to be provided with adequate information to make their own decisions. In addition, families that could not otherwise afford them should be provided with the goods and services required to implement the birth-control program of their choice.

Given the technical means to control conception, the increased educational opportunities open to women, and the needs of the community for their participation in the world of work and in its social and political life, it is hardly surprising that women have responded in large numbers. The levels of employment and participation in community affairs achieved by women in the past several decades are indeed impressive. Almost one-half of the unmarried women between the ages of twenty and twenty-four are employed; the number drops to less than 40 per cent for those between twenty-five and thirty-four years of age, and then stabilizes at about 45 per cent of the population until retirement age. While married women are represented in the work force in somewhat smaller proportions, the comparable figures are: 35 per cent for ages twenty to twenty-four, 32 per cent between twenty-five and thirty-four, and approximately 40 per cent thereafter.

In addition, much of the work of the community, that is, the day-to-day social participation in political and cultural activities, is done by women. In many ways, the levels of participation and responsibility that American women hold in their communities represent literally a revolution from past centuries. In comparison with many other countries of the world, Americans have a much more equalitarian frame of reference.

Nevertheless, Myrdall's (1944) observation of some decades ago that women constitute the largest minority group in the United States is still to be taken seriously. To a large extent women tend to be segregated in separate occupations (Gross, 1967). Further, there continues to exist, in terms of educational opportunities, a reluctance to admit women to certain types of professional training. Many occupations in commerce and industry which have little to do with physical prowess are still rarely entered by women. In virtually all areas of business, the likelihood is slim that a female will be selected for an important post or senior position. Although much of the routine work of politics is now regarded as women's work, high political office and the policy-making activities that go on in the smoke-filled rooms are still regarded as male prerogatives. The boards of directors of important foundations, trusts, and voluntary groups may have a symbolic female representative, just as they frequently include a token black among their members.

Much of the antidiscrimination legislation that has been enacted in recent years recognizes occupational discrimination against women, and a number of the adjudications made by fair-employment boards involve instances of discrimination on the basis of sex. The background of woman's limited role outside the home has been a subject of several important analyses (Komarovsky, 1953; Komarovsky and Philips, 1964).

CAUSES OF DISCRIMINATION

Historically, the division of labor and the time and energy required for homemaking and childrearing, as well as the more active roles assumed by rural women in farm work, precluded their independent participation in the world of work. Until the advent of modern technology, physical strength was a limiting factor in many tasks that might be undertaken by women. The relatively long years of childbearing and the unpredictability of pregnancies operated against women's achieving equal opportunities. For all practical purposes, however, these rationales no longer persist, although for many Americans the ideology that a woman's place is in the home remains dominant. Even in families where the wife is active in a separate career, there is considerable ambivalence on the part of both men and women as to the propriety of such activities.

Komarovsky (1953) points out that the early socialization of children stimulates the differentiation between male and female roles and that many parents perhaps unwittingly speed up a son's emancipation from the home but retard a daughter's. A similar situation exists in school, where many student activities are rigged in favor of the selection of males for the more assertive decision-making roles. The shortage of men to fill many civilian jobs during World War II provided a major stimulus for changes in occupational patterns and for opening up more opportunities for women. A majority of the physicians in the Soviet Union, for example, are women, a phenomenon related to the shortage of men during wartime and the higher male death rate occasioned by the war (Field, 1967).

INTERVENTION APPROACHES

We are witnessing today a quiet but rapid struggle for equality between the sexes. A part of the struggle is an effort to provide women with appropriate recognition by appointment to advisory committees and policy-making boards. There also are attempts at state and federal levels to engage the total community in active efforts against discrimination of all types. Considerable emphasis has been placed on testing and verifying the capabilities of women for equivalent opportunities in many work roles that were formerly delegated primarily to men. Some emphasis is also being given to providing additional and continuing educational opportunities for women who have passed the childrearing stage in order to prepare them for active roles in the world of work and for participation in community activities.

The question of woman's role is raised during this life cycle because the childrearing period realistically limits the work roles and, to a certain extent, the community participation of females. It is during this period

the protégé system and women in professions

The protégé system is typical of many professions, especially at their upper echelons. This system operates both to train personnel for certain specialties (particular areas of surgery or corporate law, for example), and to assure continuity of leadership. These fields are marked by interplay between the formal and informal relationships of the practitioners. At certain levels one must be *"in"* to learn the job. Becker and Strauss point out that "until a newcomer is accepted (in these fields) he will not be taught crucial trade secrets," much less advance in the field.

The sponsor-protégé (or master-apprentice) relationship may further inhibit feminine advancement in the male-dominated professions. The sponsor is apt to be a man and will tend to have mixed feelings about accepting a woman as protégé. Although the professional man might not object to a female *assistant*— he might even prefer her—he cannot identify her (as he might a male assistant) as someone who will eventually be his successor. He may therefore select a male candidate in preference to the female in the belief that she has less commitment to the profession and will be deflected from her career by marriage and children. When the woman is accepted as a protégé, her other role-partners—husband, father, child, etc.—may be jealous and suspicious of her loyalty to the sponsor and her dependence on him. The sponsor's wife may also resent the relationship between the sponsor and his female protégé and object to it, although we suspect that, unlike the protégé's husband, she is less often [able] to place impediments in the way of the relationship.

Upon completing her apprenticeship, the female professional faces serious problems if she does not get the sponsor's support in gaining entree to the inner circles of the profession—support which a male neophyte would expect as a matter of course. The sponsor may also exert less effort in promoting a

that many women leave the world of work and by so doing terminate their prospects for an orderly career. Lack of continuing professional education, the extended interruption of the childbearing period, and the absence of the protégé-apprentice role that is the key to professional success (Epstein, 1967), all conspire to limit or preclude a woman's return to a suitable career. (*See* Documentation 7.) The roles of wife and mother provide a full and satisfying life for many women. Certainly, this is one alternative that should remain open to all females. But we should also be aware that the traditional fragmentation of family life and the rigidity with which roles are assigned to wife or husband may constitute limiting factors on the continued stability of the family as a viable social institution.

Overt discrimination is not the only occupational barrier to be faced by American women. At a more subtle level, our society has failed to provide mechanisms whereby women may exercise their prerogatives in planning-

female student for career-line jobs. First, he may believe that she is financially less dependent on a career position than a man might be. Second, because of her presumed lack of commitment and drive, he might only reluctantly introduce her to colleagues, or recommend her to colleagues. Placement offices in professional schools also act as a filtering system in which women-students are encouraged to enter those specialties where they will presumably meet less opposition. Thus they are encouraged to seek government jobs. And, in fact, as the table below indicates, women professionals go into government service in far greater proportions to their number than do men, in this respect being much like other minority groups such as Negroes.

Moreover, we find a definite relationship between the quality of law schools and the percentage of their women graduates who enter government service. University-affiliated law schools placed only 20–30% of their women graduates in government service (though still far more than their male graduates) in contrast to the 90% placed in government service by part-time or independent schools. Similarly, women lawyers in large firms are guided into those specialties which do not normally lead to partnership. Later progress in the woman's career may be inhibited by limitations on access to fellow practitioners and peers, clubs, and associations; the circle in which job opportunities are made known and informal recommendations are made. (Epstein, 1967:13–16.)

PERCENT OF PROFESSIONAL WORKERS IN SELECTED OCCUPATIONS IN GOVERNMENT SERVICE BY SEX (1960)

DENTISTS		LAWYERS		DOCTORS		ENGINEERS	
Male	Female	Male	Female	Male	Female	Male	Female
0.03	10.0	14.0	27.0	14.0	30.0	17.0	32.0

ning for a range of adult work roles. In this respect the United States is far behind many European countries, especially Scandinavia, where networks of child-care centers and other organizational means are provided to care for children during the mother's working hours.

Moreover, American society has tended to downgrade and disparage such roles as professional homemaker and maid so that there is often a scarcity of women willing to undertake such roles and practically no provision for their training. Consequently, women who seek employment outside the home lack assurance that adequate role substitutes are available. This is particularly true for women whose earnings are limited either because they lack requisite skills or because their employment interests and opportunities are economically restrictive. Only recently has federal tax legislation allowed appropriate income-tax deductions for child-care expenses incurred by women who work. The extent of structural changes required to minimize discrimination on the basis of sex and to provide the necessary services to facilitate the employment and participation of women have scarcely been recognized, much less implemented.

occupational careers

We have already noted the critical nature of this age period in the development of orderly careers for adults in the American community. It is not rare to find persons of this age occupying positions of political and occupational prominence. A number of congressmen are under forty, as are the presidents of several large corporations and key administrators in universities and the civil service.

CAUSES OF DISCONTENT

This is the age at which an individual with a high degree of technical skill becomes concerned with the problems of occupational obsolescence and the possibility that younger men with more recent training may supersede him. This also is the period when, in many cases, the work role is so all-consuming that the individual loses touch with his family and friends and fails to participate in leisure-time activities and various cultural pursuits. We are becoming aware of how little is known about adult socialization and the various inputs that act as important change agents in terms of the way individuals in this age group look at themselves and at the world around them (Brim and Wheeler, 1966).

It is certainly obvious that not all individuals in this age group can have infinite opportunities for occupational achievement and economic success. For many individuals, this is a period of coming to recognize the limits of their work roles and to realize that they must obtain emotional satisfaction and self-actualization by performing well in spheres of life other than their work. For some, it is important to obtain additional training or retraining in order to advance or even to maintain their present positions.

INTERVENTION

One of the phenomena that we have seen emerge in the past quarter of a century has been the development of a number of formal programs directed toward persons in this age group. These programs range from doctoral training in fields in which there are severe shortages to graduate study in fields which have developed additional educational requirements for policy-making and administrative positions. In fields such as social welfare, for example, retreads (as they are called) frequently return to school for formal doctoral training after working some years in various roles in the community. Likewise, schools of public health are accepting physicians and other health workers at a masters or doctorate level. While long-term doctoral and postgraduate training is not the only type of program being offered, it is an important example of what exists at an ambitious level in training opportunities sponsored by companies and unions and community adult-education programs.

Virtually every major city provides some opportunity for graduate training in a number of fields during nonwork hours. Community colleges offer evening and Saturday programs directed largely toward the age group under consideration here. In addition, many companies and unions sponsor short-term workshops, seminars, or conferences which sometimes are partially supported by private or governmental grants. These programs are not only intellectually stimulating and personally satisfying, but they also develop people who can participate more effectively in the affairs of their communities. These programs frequently are criticized because of their middle-class orientation and because they are primarily directed at and appeal to the white-collar worker and his family. An increasing number of useful and realistically oriented programs for blue-collar workers have been developed and are being promoted with what appears to be some degree of success. For blue-collar families, however, additional remedies need to be undertaken. For example, in many cases adjustments in hours of employment, compensation for lost overtime, or other provisions for economic rewards may be required to assure worker participation.

BARRIERS TO ACHIEVEMENT

In many aspects of the occupational mobility system, however, irrelevant criteria still block achievement and, in some cases, impede and inhibit motivation for further work-oriented activities. Critics sometimes claim that many of the activities designed either to promote occupational advancement through training or to provide other modes of gratification and psychological reward represent sops to those community members whom the power structure seeks to keep in line. The legitimacy of these accusations is hard to assess, for ultimate motives are difficult to determine. Certainly the development of a nation of ardent baseball fans, happy sailboat enthusiasts, and satisfied gardners is as unacceptable a way to maintain the social order as is a population constantly aware and acutely intense about success and achievement goals in work tasks. One of the dangers of our social structure, as Weiss and Riesman (1966) have pointed out, is the tendency to make permanent those career expedients entered into on a temporary basis, particularly by those individuals in this age group who come from backgrounds that do not fully equip them for the world of work.

Opportunities for orderly career development with successive stages of advancement must be made available for as many Americans as possible. The barriers to upward mobility for working-class people are many: they seldom understand the inner workings of the occupational system; they blame their lack of success on luck or fate; and their experiences of economic insecurity, recurrent layoffs, and frequent job changes are inconsistent with the development of programs for stable careers and maximum achievement. To some extent, American communities have recognized the need for vocational guidance opportunities for adults, and many programs for this age group have been developed that parallel those offered to adolescents in school.

Although efforts to make work tasks more palatable and interesting may have some value, studies of blue-collar workers—such as auto workers—indicate that economic reward and status represent the key elements in job satisfaction (Kornhauser, 1965). Urban industrial life requires community-wide efforts to open up the opportunity structures within our society and to maximize the socialization of adults with respect to meaningful performance in the world of work. To broaden the point made by Wilensky (1964), we are in a situation in which there are tremendous demands and opportunities for literate, work-oriented employees; at the same time there are great limitations on achievement and economic return for those without educational and technical skills who find themselves unable to move ahead in a highly complex and increasingly automated environment.

white-collar crime

Since most males between the ages of twenty-five and forty are reasonably well-established in their occupational careers, two modes of occupational deviation—professional and white-collar crime—tend to predominate in this age group. It must be acknowledged, however, that this is a matter of speculation, since most white-collar crime remains largely undetected and professional crime refers to the total commitment of the offender rather than to a category of criminal activity. As a consequence, available crime statistics provide no precise data on incidence or age-specific prevalence. But somewhere in this overview of America's social problems it is necessary to discuss these two phenomena. There is an aspect of commonality that warrants our considering professional and white-collar crime together. We refer to the frame of reference which identifies both as illegal activities participated in primarily for economic gain. Beyond that, however, the two categories need to be looked at separately.

The deviant activity denoted by the term *white-collar crime* received extensive notice in the field of sociology during the 1940s, largely as a result of the work done by Sutherland (1949). The term generally is used to refer to criminal acts committed by so-called respectable persons engaged in typical occupational activities in which they often have achieved a reasonably secure and trusted place for themselves (Cressey, 1965). Sutherland (1940), in his original conceptualization of the term, suggested that persons of middle and upper socio-economic status engage in much criminal behavior; their crimes differ from those committed by persons of lower socio-economic status principally in the administrative procedures that are used in dealing with the offenders. Thus, the white-collar criminal is differentiated from the more typical offender primarily by the way he is handled by the police, the court, and the correctional system rather than by any inherent differences in the criminal acts he commits. The definition first formulated by Sutherland, that white-collar crime is crime committed by a person of respectability and high social status in the course of his occupation, has been carried over into the work of later investigators.

ETIOLOGY

As Sutherland (1941) noted a generation ago, a great deal of scattered and unorganized material indicates that white-collar crime was and is a prevalent phenomenon. To some extent we have already covered the problem in the chapter on corruption. It is important, however, to single it out for attention here and to note some of the salient points observed by Sutherland.

White-collar criminality is a frequently persistent phenomenon engaged in by individuals over an extended period of time and often in collusion with the corporate enterprises to which they belong. Illegal behavior of this type is probably underrepresented in terms of police or court actions in comparison with the more typical varieties of crime. Businessmen who violate the laws that regulate white-collar criminal activities rarely lose status among their business associates. Businessmen often are contemptuous of the laws and regulations that control white-collar illegal activities and characteristically are cynical and skeptical about the desirability of avoiding such behavior. White-collar criminals frequently do not view themselves as illegal offenders; they maintain a self-image and present themselves to others as pillars of respectability in the community.

In the chapter on corruption we indicated the high economic costs of white-collar crime and the difficulty in maintaining a legal orientation toward illicit economic exchange in which the participants were respectable citizens. To cite a clear example, twenty-nine leading electrical companies along with seven executives were convicted in 1960 for rigging

resistance to the use of criminal sanctions

As important as the practical obstacles to effective law enforcement is society's reluctance to impose criminal sanctions upon the white-collar offender. Thus despite the apparent effect of the *Electrical Equipment* cases, in which seven individual executives received and served jail sentences, since that case no antitrust defendant has been imprisoned. In seven cases since then, involving 45 individual defendants, prison sentences were imposed, but in each case the sentence was suspended. During this time the Government has recommended that, out of 58 cases in which individual defendants were charged with criminal violations, prison sentences be imposed and served in 27 cases. The recommendations covered 105 individual defendants. Similarly, Marshall Clinard's study of a variety of rationing and other controls during the second World War revealed that the sentences imposed on OPA violators after conviction were relatively mild.

While little is known of the public attitude toward white-collar crime, it is apparent that the present concern with crime is not directed at white-collar crime but at "crime on the streets." As one executive convicted and sentenced to jail in the *Electrical Equipment* conspiracy said: "[O]n the bright side for me personally have been the letters and calls from people all over the country, the community, the shops and offices here, expressing confidence in me and support. This demonstration has been a warm and humbling experience for me." But one attempt to measure public reactions to a form of white-collar crime—violations of the Federal Food, Drug and Cosmetic Act—indicated that the public would treat offenders more severely than the courts, although not as severely as persons guilty of such crimes as larceny and burglary. Consumers were asked to judge cases of food law violation in terms of how they would punish the offender. Six actual cases were selected, representing three types of violation—misbranding, distasteful but not physically harmful adulteration and physically harmful adulteration. Fifty-eight percent of the consumers felt that penalties should have been more severe than the actual court decisions, and yet within

the sale of heavy electrical equipment worth $1,750,000,000. As Clinard (1963) notes, the government and private groups who purchased this equipment were deceived about the open, competitive nature of the bids and consequently paid prices far in excess of what was reasonable. A major difference between the white-collar criminal and others is in the offender's conception of himself. The white-collar criminal does not regard himself as a criminal and considers his occasional, though persistent, criminal activities as part of another occupational role.

It is during young adulthood that many persons engaged in white-collar crime learn the techniques by which the law can be violated. They also build up a series of rationales to justify such activities, such as to be successful in business, to keep up with the competition, to support their

the maximum penalty provided by the Federal law, a one-year prison sentence on first conviction. Twenty-two percent of the sample chose penalties equal to or less harsh than the one actually imposed, while almost 20 percent felt that the violators should receive a prison term longer than a year.

The very characteristics which make white-collar criminals particularly deterrable may make it difficult to obtain the sanctions necessary to deter. They generally have families, an established place in the community, and a spotless record. They often occupy managerial or executive roles in their business and a leadership position in their community.

In the *Electrical Equipment* cases the defendants included several vice presidents of the General Electric Corporation and the Westinghouse Electric Corporation. They were described by a newspaper reporter as "typical business men in appearance, men who would never be taken for lawbreakers." Several were deacons or vestrymen of their churches. One was president of his local Chamber of Commerce, another a hospital board member, another chief fund raiser for the Community Chest, another a bank director, another director of the taxpayer's association, another organizer of the local little league.

The highest paid executive to be given a jail sentence was a General Electric vice president, earning $135,000 a year. He was married, and the father of three children. He had served in the Navy during the second World War . . . was director of a girls' finishing school, and was a member of the Governor's Temporary State Committee on Economic Expansion in New York.

Obviously there is resistance to subjecting defendants who are performing useful functions in society to criminal sanctions and especially to prison sentences. Clinard's study of OPA violators found that one reason for the light sentences imposed was "the fact that the offenders seldom had a criminal past or other circumstances which would warrant a severe sentence. As the judges on occasion stated from the bench, they 'would not make criminals of reputable businessmen.' " On the other hand Judge Skelly Wright, in considering the question of whether an income tax violator ought to be sentenced to jail, took the position that "the only real purpose of an income tax sentence is its deterrent value. Unless we use the income tax sentence as a deterrent, we are overlooking one of our responsibilities as judges." (President's Commission on Law Enforcement, 1967a:106–107.)

families well, and the like. Sutherland's (1949) point about differential association as a cause of crime and delinquency undoubtedly applies to a large extent as an explanation of white-collar criminal activities. In a rather peculiar sense, white-collar crime may also be explainable in terms of a structural point of view. A recent study of pharmacists is a good illustration.

> There are two divergent occupational role expectations in retail pharmacy—professional and business. Pharmacists adjust to this situation of structural strain by orienting themselves in varying degree to the roles, by adopting an occupational role organization. The types of occupational role organizations in turn differ in the extent to which they generate tendencies toward prescription violation. The occupa-

tional role organizations which include the professional role orientation restrain the pharmacist from violating, while the occupational role organizations which do not include the professional role orientation do not exercise this restraint on the pharmacist. Therefore, prescription violation occurs with greatest frequency among business pharmacists and least among professional pharmacists, with professional-business pharmacists and indifferent pharmacists being intermediate in frequency of prescription violation. It was thus concluded that prescription violation is related to the structure of the occupation and the differential orientation of retail pharmacists (Quinney, 1963:184).

THE LURE OF MONEY

Although many of the individuals involved would not agree, analysts concur that the not infrequent blocking or limiting of opportunities for average community members often results in their turning to white-collar crime to overcome such limitations. Here, of course, we are talking about the difference between earning $10,000 and $20,000 a year—hardly the case of a delinquent boy or an impoverished father scrounging for subsistence.

White-collar crime received special notice during World War II when many merchants and their suppliers made concerted efforts to avoid the wartime restrictions placed upon the production and sale of goods. Unethical and illegal practices were circulated in the trade as part of the definition of the situation, and rationalizations to support these violations of law were transmitted from one individual or firm to another. Clinard (1952) cites a most interesting case of two tire salesmen who organized a state-wide ring that purchased, received, and transferred new rubber tires and tubes without exchanging rationing certificates. In setting up the deal, the two offenders actually met with a number of retail tire dealers, involved them in these activities, and explained a relatively foolproof method for transferring tires without surrendering the necessary certificates. Eventually this ring involved a large number of dealers in scattered cities and towns who disposed of thousands of tires through this illegal device.

A particular form of white-collar crime, tempting and readily available to lawyers, bookkeepers, accountants, and other trusted employees, is embezzlement. Much embezzlement is of a quite ordinary nature: the retail store manager who consistently falsifies the cost of damaged goods and pockets the difference; the automobile dealer who replaces worn parts with rebuilt ones and charges his customers for new replacements; the stockbroker's representative who uses funds in a client's account to purchase stock for his own benefit. Contrary to popular views, white-collar crime cannot be explained simply in terms of gambling, high-living, or unusual expenses (Lemert, 1958). One point of view (Cressey,

1965) holds that frequently individuals who violate trusts—commonly labeled embezzlers—find themselves trapped in a financial bind that they cannot share with others; that is, they are isolated from the possibility of legitimate help. Another characteristic is that such people know, or feel they know, that their financial plight can be resolved by the illegal act, after which they will desist from their illegal behavior, or even correct it. Further, they tell themselves that their behavior is a common-place or justifiable activity in terms of the norms of their particular occupation.

INTERVENTION APPROACHES

In discussing the general problem of corruption, the difficulty of amelioration or even effective intervention was indicated. This certainly holds true in the case of white-collar crime. Given the emphasis placed upon money in the typical American community and the legal need to balance the individual's right of privacy against effective detection procedures in dealing with white-collar crime, the prospects for a reduction of such deviance by imposing criminal sanctions are limited. (*See* Documentation 8.)

Several investigations in the 1960s revealed the extent and pervasiveness of white-collar crime. Business leaders, embarrassed by repeated scandals and recognizing the economic drain of such activities, have attempted to develop normative standards and codes of ethics for their operations. Perhaps the promulgation of these guidelines and the accompanying educational campaign will improve the general situation. If the interpretation is correct that the processes of communication and differential association are the underlying explanations for white-collar crime, then better information and self-regulation within the business community may reduce illegal behavior.

professional crime

The term *professional crime* was introduced in the 1930s by Sutherland, who used it in his book, *The Professional Thief* (Sutherland, 1937). Sutherland was talking about a category of individuals engaged in illegal acts and not about the generic groups we now call *professional criminals*. This latter term, while diffuse and ambiguous, is more inclusive than *professional thief,* including not only confidence men, sneak thieves, and pickpockets (as Sutherland did) but also those who are engaged in such crimes as armed robbery, garage theft, and the protection rackets. Broadly, the term refers to criminals who engage in illegal acts that require at least a certain amount of skill, planning, and sophistication

(Cameron, 1964). Sometimes in police work there is an attempt to differentiate the "light professional criminal," whose activities rarely involve any potential of violence, from the "heavies," who present a constant threat of violence.

Partly because of Sutherland's use of the term *professional* to describe certain categories of criminal activity, sociologists have taken his work perhaps too literally and have developed a stereotype of what they mean by the professional criminal. This traditional stereotype includes the notion that the criminal becomes an expert and confines his activities to one particular type of crime, such as pickpocketing, in which he continually engages as a full-time specialty. A recent study supported by the Department of Justice (President's Commission on Law Enforcement, 1967a) suggests that this is not typically the case.

A second point that Sutherland made, which apparently is also overstated, is that professional criminals have a subculture with explicit norms that may include, as an illustration, not stooling on one another. Again, this is not entirely accurate. Professional criminals frequently know each other and from time to time develop interdependent relationships of an economic sort. But that they exist as a single, nationwide, tightly knit, organized group is not borne out by the impressions of individuals who have studied their operations in a number of cities. The report of the President's Commission on Law Enforcement (1967a) provides the most up-to-date examination of the professional criminal, but even it must be regarded as highly impressionistic.

No informed estimate can be made of the total incidence of professional crime in the United States; however, most law enforcement agents believe that only a relatively small proportion of criminals are apprehended. Many of the crimes that are committed are not reported to official agencies at all. Estimates of losses are quite variable because of the tendency of victims to overestimate the value of goods for insurance purposes and of the police to underestimate their value to make the city look better in terms of its crime problem. The general impression is that, in terms of monetary loss, professional crime is probably not as expensive as white-collar crime. Nevertheless, the dollar amounts involved are still very large, although there is considerable variation from city to city. In some cities, for example, hijacking or warehouse thefts may account for losses of hundreds of thousands of dollars; in another city, such crimes rarely confront law enforcement officials.

THE HUSTLER

Many professional criminals can perhaps best be described as hustlers, that is, they are individuals on the lookout for an opportunity to make an illegal buck. They do not have a specialty but will do almost anything that opportunity or the occasion requires. This seems to be true at least of the successful professional criminals. The more successful professionals seem to move from one type of job to the next, but exercise more care in their operations and more caution in their involvements. To a large extent, the professional criminal develops effective modes of planning and efficient techniques of operation.

Hustling is not a passive activity. For the small-time professional criminal, for example, it means moving around the bars and being seen. It means finding out what's up. It means connecting in the morning with other individuals who have a burglary set up for the evening, calling a man to see if he wants to buy ten stolen sweaters at five bucks each, scouting a street for a mark who can be conned, perhaps doing all these things in a single day and repeating them tomorrow. It means being versatile: passing a bad check, rolling a drunk, driving for a stickup, boosting a car, hitting a store window. It is not exactly planless; rather, it is a kind of unorganized existence with a purpose: to make as much money as can be made each day in whatever way can be found with practically no holds barred. If there is a norm for the operational procedures of the professional criminal it is very similar to that of the white-collar businessman, i.e., never pass up an easy buck; it just isn't right. The term *hustler* appears inadequate only for the few professional criminals who are big-time operators and whose affluence is such that they become more selective and purposeful in their activities.

Professional criminals are versatile, and for a good reason—specialization, as the stereotype holds, would simply result in too many missed opportunities. It should be noted that the professional criminal, like any other person engaged in an occupational career, needs to change with the times. For example, alarm systems and improved construction make it extremely difficult to beat most safes; so safecracking is apparently on the decline. On the other hand, the development of credit card systems and their universal acceptance has opened a new field of operations in the theft, reselling, and even forgery of credit cards.

RELATIONSHIP TO ORGANIZED CRIME

As do all individuals who engage in work, professional criminals relate to others in their business, but they do so in a strictly businesslike manner much as a small shopkeeper or salesman does to his colleagues in the field. One interesting aspect is the relationship between the professional criminal and organized crime, a relationship which seems to vary considerably from city to city. In discussing corruption, we alluded to organized crime and noted the existence, as we shall discuss further in the next chapter, of a number of individuals who run large-scale enterprises of an entirely illegal nature. The professional criminal involves himself in temporary relationships with organized crime because he needs its resources—money to buy burglary tools, a loan to pay a lawyer, or contacts to dispose of hot merchandise.

THE FENCE

The professional criminal also has contacts with intermediaries commonly known as fences. Like professional criminals, fences may engage in legal occupations as well as in their illegal operations. Many who act as wholesalers for professional criminals are otherwise legitimate businessmen whose involvement in these activities marks them as white-collar criminals. For example, after New York State increased its cigarette tax, a hustler could do quite well by renting a truck, driving to New Jersey, and loading up with cartons of cigarettes. He would then sell the cartons to New York cigar-counter operators who would resell them to regular customers for a few cents a pack cheaper than they could be purchased elsewhere in the city. Both the hustler and the cigar-counter operator make a few pennies a pack, but they add up, given our smoking habits. Reliable but unsubstantiative evidence suggests that some clothing and appliance dealers regularly augment their inventories with stolen goods and that a major outlet for stolen jewels in at least one city is known to be a legitimate jewelry merchant.

Fences, whether quasi-legitimate businessmen or full-time criminals, do not dispose of all the goods stolen by professional criminals. Many of the less successful criminals who deal in small quantities of merchandise sell directly to the public. They make their contacts in a variety of ways: in bars, through friends engaged in legitimate occupations, indeed, some maintain, through the police themselves. Many innocent and some not-so-innocent people obtain "good buys" in this manner.

THE JUICE MAN

In general, professional criminals do not do well financially and, unlike the stereotype, tend to be marginal individuals both economically and socially. One of the problems of an entrepreneurial career, as opposed to a salaried job, is the need for relatively large amounts of capital. Thus the professional criminal often finds himself dealing with loan sharks. Because of his vulnerability, the criminal finds himself paying usurious rates, sometimes reported to be as high as 100 per cent per week (President's Commission on Law Enforcement, 1967b).

The problems of economic dependence frequently put the professional criminal in the grasp of the loan shark or "juice man." This relationship begins with his first arrest or the first arrest after getting out of prison. To stay out of jail, the professional criminal has to keep working. In order to do so, he has to post bond. Since he usually cannot supply the surety himself, he turns to the bail bondsman. Most often he cannot pay the bondsman's fee, so he turns to the juice man for a loan. The professional criminal also has to retain a lawyer, who demands a fee. To pay these expensive legal costs, the criminal works even harder at his profession. This in turn means that he takes more chances, or at least engages more frequently in criminal activities. As a result, he runs a greater risk of being arrested again. Re-arrests mean larger bonds, the exact amount being related, of course, to the criminal's record as well as to the nature of the offense. His lawyer's fee goes up. He works harder, only to get caught again.

The juice man is able to extract a tremendous amount of money from his clients so it is to his benefit to pressure the professional criminal to continue his career. The operations of loan sharks and juice men are important subjects for sociological study. It is apparent that many low-economic people become involved with loan sharks or trapped by juice men because of their need for money and their reputations as poor credit risks. The illegal or quasi-legal reasons for their need of funds make them especially vulnerable. Loan companies represent a big business that is often tied to organized crime, and this connection continues to accentuate the problems of the professional criminal.

POLICE PRACTICES

Police policies and practices in many large cities are also determinants in the career of the professional criminal. If a professional criminal is arrested, he first contacts his lawyer to find out what it will take to get him out of the jam. This may include getting charges reduced or dropped or being placed on probation. But supposedly the criminal's lawyer will do whatever he can to get the criminal free. How the lawyer does this, however, is often a mystery to the professional criminal. Sometimes, and perhaps infrequently, the lawyer offers an out-and-out bribe to police officials. More often than not, a deal is made between the district attorney, the police, and the lawyer to have the professional criminal plead guilty to a lesser offense because it saves time, increases the rate of convictions, and stands the police in good stead. Or, the professional criminal may turn stoolpigeon, informing on his colleagues regarding a particular crime or on individuals involved in criminal activities which the police are particularly concerned with controlling.

THE MAKING OF A CRIMINAL

What kinds of people become professional criminals? In Sutherland's view, professional thieves typically did not come from the lower socio-economic groups in the community but from somewhat more advantaged circumstances. He reasoned that those without any intellectual training, that is, the amateurs from the slums, would not have the social abilities or contacts required to be successful professional thieves. However, this description is not consistent with what is known about the broader category of professional criminals.

The most striking impression from the President's Commission on Law Enforcement (1967a) study is the absence of any single background characteristic or pattern. In certain cities, an indication of ethnic succession has been observed. As one ethnic group begins to succeed economically in legitimate pursuits, its members tend to leave professional crime and their place is taken by a different ethnic group. In New York City, for example, Italians are abandoning professional criminal activities and Puerto Ricans and Negroes are probably increasing their participation. Professional crime requires a lot of hard work, involves specialized training not taught in schools or apprenticeship programs, and offers relatively high rewards, but only at higher risks. For these reasons, professional crime tends to devolve to ethnic groups less able to integrate into the larger economic life of the community or to individuals without the prerequisites for such integration in terms of education and social position.

INTERVENTION APPROACHES

Even the successful professional criminal who makes a reasonable living from his work is unlikely to be able to compete well in the larger community in terms of status and prestige. His position requires concealment of his illegal activities from neighbors and friends, if not from his children and, sometimes, his wife. The impression is that he tends to be undereducated, undertrained, and unlikely to be successful in a more legitimate career. Few criminals escape entanglements with the law forever, although those that are caught may often be treated leniently—a contradiction if long prison terms are considered the appropriate means of control and rehabilitation. There seems little likelihood of an individual escaping the web of professional crime once he becomes caught in it. Thus, young adults who embark on reasonably sustained professional careers in crime are unlikely to become productive members of society at any future point in their lives. It is for this reason that efforts to control their activities occupy considerable amounts of time on the part of police and other legal authorities.

From the standpoint of law enforcement, the social control and amelioration of professional crime is but one of the tasks in which police are engaged. Many law-enforcement groups rationalize their less than energetic efforts to control professional crime with the observation that, regardless of police activities, considerable crime is going to remain in all communities; the question is, who will commit it (Wilkins, 1965). These policemen contend that vigilant detection of professional punks would only mean that their activities would be taken over by better organized and perhaps shrewder criminals. Another rationalization for minimal police involvement is that many of the victims of professional crime have a bit of larceny in their hearts as well. The tourist who is conned into buying an imitation diamond bracelet with the understanding that it is "hot" is certainly not to be regarded as an innocent victim.

An obvious way of curtailing professional crime would be to reduce the willingness of the general public to profit from activities that are in themselves illegal and immoral. One suggestion is that noninnocent victims should also be subject to prosecution. A number of experts believe that a reorganization of the police departments in a number of large cities would prove beneficial to the reduction of professional crime. The competition among the various divisions within police departments and their unwillingness to communicate with each other are related problems that should be amenable to correction.

Several related innovations are also possible in the activities of courts. If some of the work pressures were removed from district attorneys it might be possible for them to develop better evaluation procedures and to clear court calendars without making deals with defendants. It is possible that a significant number of professional criminals are forced to repeat their illegal behavior in order to pay debts arising from previous charges. Some of the bail-bond reforms and legal aid programs discussed in connection with the poor might also prove helpful in shielding professional criminals from disreputable elements tied to organized crime.

On the basis of much subjective evidence, it would seem that this is the age group in which careers in white-collar and professional crime are begun and continued commitments to a life of crime are established. Both types of activity are highly vulnerable to the vagaries of economic resources in American society and both, although from very different perspectives, reflect the exaggerated emphasis placed upon monetary rewards in our culture.

importance of period

For most people, the years between the ages of twenty and forty-five represent the most viable period in the life cycle, a period during which the years of preparation by parents, the educational system, and early work experiences culminate in a stable career that determines the family's position in the community. Unless the groundwork is firmly laid in these years, the possibilities of upward mobility are quite rare. If status, prestige, and respectability do not accrue to family members in this period, there is considerable risk that later years will be marked by despair and that children reared under such conditions will have limited opportunities for either personal gratifications or significant contributions to the life of the community.

This is the age period in which families require maximum community attention and may need the most help and support. Their children are the adults of the next generation and the political and social leaders of the next several decades. The question that confronts the policy maker and community leader today is how many social development resources can be allocated to these families to assure their ability to actualize their life experiences and fulfill the so-called American dream.

REFERENCES

BRIM, ORVILLE G. AND STANTON WHEELER.
1966 Socialization After Childhood. New York: Wiley.

BURCHINAL, LEE B. AND LOREN E. CHANCELLOR.
1963 "Survival rates among religiously homogamous and interreligious marriages." Social Forces 41(May):353–362.

BURGESS, ERNEST W. AND HARVEY J. LOCKE.
1953 The Family. Second Edition. New York: American Book Company.

CAMERON, MARY OWEN.
1964 The Booster and the Snitch. New York: Free Press.

CHRISTENSEN, HAROLD T. AND HANNA H. MEISSNER.
1953 "Studies in child spacing: III. premarital pregnancy." American Sociological Review 18(December):641–644.

CLINARD, MARSHALL B.
1952 The Black Market. New York: Holt, Rinehart and Winston.
1963 Sociology of Deviant Behavior. New York: Holt, Rinehart and Winston.

COHEN, NATHAN E. AND MAURICE F. CONNERY.
1967 "Government policy and the family." Journal of Marriage and the Family 29(February):6–17.

CRESSEY, DONALD R.
1965 "The respectable criminal." Trans-Action 2(March/April):12–15.

DAVIS, KINGSLEY AND JUDITH BLAKE.
1960 "Birth control and public policy." Commentary 29(February):115–121.

EPSTEIN, CYNTHIA F.
1967 "Woman's place: the salience of sex status in the professional setting." Paper presented at the American Sociological Meetings, San Francisco (unpublished).

FIELD, MARK.
1967 Soviet Socialized Medicine. New York: Free Press.

FOOTE, NELSON N. AND LEONARD S. COTTRELL, JR.
1955 Identity and Interpersonal Competence. Chicago: University of Chicago Press.

FREEDMAN, RONALD AND LOLAGENE COOMBS.
1966 "Childspacing and family economic position." American Sociological Review 31(October):631–648.

FREEMAN, HOWARD E. AND MORRIS SHOWEL.
1952 "Familism and attitudes toward divorce." Sociology and Social Research 36(May):312–318.

GOODE, WILLIAM J.
1951 "Economic factors and marital stability." American Sociological Review 16(December)6:802–812.
1956 After Divorce. New York: Free Press.
1966 "Family disorganization." Pp. 479–552 in Robert K. Merton and Robert A. Nisbet (eds.), Contemporary Social Problems. Second Edition. New York: Harcourt, Brace and World.

GROSS, EDWARD.
1967 "Change . . . the sexual structure of occupations over time." Paper presented at the American Sociological Association meetings, San Francisco (unpublished).

HILL, REUBEN.
1964 "The American family of the future." Journal of Marriage and the Family 26(February):20–28.

JACOBSON, PAUL H.
1950 "Differentials in divorce by duration of marriage and size of family." American Sociological Review 15 (April):235–244.

KEPHART, WILLIAM M.
1955 "Occupational level and marital disruption." American Sociological Review 20(August):456–465.

KOMAROVSKY, MIRRA.
1953 Women in the Modern World. Boston: Little, Brown.

KOMAROVSKY, MIRRA AND JANE PHILIPS.
1964 Blue Collar Marriage. New York: Random House.

KORNHAUSER, ARTHUR.
1965 Mental Health of the Industrial Worker. New York: Wiley.

LANDIS, JUDSON T.
1962 "A comparison of children from divorced and non-divorced unhappy marriages." Family Life Coordinator 11(July):61–65.

LEE, NANCY HOWELL.
1969 The Search for an Abortionist. Chicago: University of Chicago Press.

LEMERT, EDWIN M.
1958 "The behavior of the systematic check forger." Social Problems 6(Fall): 141–149.

LITWAK, EUGENE.
1960 "Geographic mobility and extended family cohesion." American Sociological Review 25(June):385–394.

MILLER, S. M.
1962 "Poverty and inequality in the U.S.: implications." Child Welfare 44(November):442–445.

MONAHAN, THOMAS P.
1962 "When married couples part: statistical trends and relationships in divorce." American Sociological Review 27(October):625–633.

MYRDALL, GUNNER.
1944 The American Dilemma. New York: Harper and Brothers.

NYE, F. IVAN AND LOIS W. HOFFMAN.
1963 The Employed Mother in America. Chicago: Rand McNally.

PLATERIS, ALEXANDER A.
1967 "Divorce statistics analysis: U.S.— 1963." U.S. Department of Health, Education and Welfare. Vital and Health Statistics. Series 21, No. 13 (October).

POLLACK, JACK HARRISON.
1966 "Are children different?" Pp. 190–193 in Judson R. Landis (ed.), Current Perspectives on Social Problems. Belmont, California: Wadsworth Publishing.

PRESIDENT'S COMMISSION ON LAW ENFORCEMENT AND ADMINISTRATION OF JUSTICE.
1967a Task Force Report: Crime and Its Impact—An Assessment. Washington, D.C.: U.S. Government Printing Office.
1967b The Challenge of Crime in a Free Society. Washington, D.C. U.S. Government Printing Office.

QUINNEY, RICHARD.
1963 "Occupational structure and criminal behavior: prescription violation by retail pharmacists." Social Problems 11(Fall):179–185.

RAINWATER, LEE.
1960 And the Poor Get Children: Sex, Contraception, and Family Planning in the Working Class. Chicago: Quadrangle Books.

RIDGEWAY, JAMES.
1966 "One million abortions: it's your problem, sweetheart." Pp. 151–156 in Judson R. Landis (ed.), Current Perspectives on Social Problems. Belmont, California: Wadsworth.

ROWLEY, PETER.
1966 "Divorce, New York style." Pp. 185–189 in Judson R. Landis (ed.), Current Perspectives on Social Problems. Belmont, California: Wadsworth.

SUTHERLAND, EDWIN H.
1937 The Professional Thief. Chicago: University of Chicago Press.
1940 "White collar criminality." American Sociological Review 5(February):1–12.
1941 "Crime and business." The Annals of the American Academy of Political and Social Science 217(September): 111–118.
1949 White Collar Crime. New York: Dryden Press.

UDRY, J. RICHARD.
1967 "Marital instability by race and income based on 1960 census data." The American Journal of Sociology 72(May):203–209.

VAN DEN HAAG, ERNEST.
1966 "Love or marriage?" Pp. 170–178 in Judson R. Landis (ed.), Current Perspectives on Social Problems. Belmont, California: Wadsworth.

WAY, H. FRANK, JR.
1966 "Birth control: a new consensus." Pp. 147–150 in Judson R. Landis (ed.), Current Perspectives on Social Problems. Belmont, California: Wadsworth.

WEISS, ROBERT S. AND DAVID RIESMAN.
1966 "Work and automation: problems and prospects." Pp. 553–618 in Robert K. Merton and Robert A. Nisbet (eds.), Contemporary Social Problems. Second Edition. New York: Harcourt, Brace and World.

WESTOFF, CHARLES F., ROBERT G. POTTER, JR. AND PHILLIP C. SAGI.
1963 The Third Child. Princeton, New Jersey: Princeton University Press.

WILENSKY, HAROLD L.
1964 "The professionalization of everyone." American Journal of Sociology 70(September):137–158.

WILKINS, LESLIE T.
1965 Social Deviance. Englewood Cliffs, New Jersey: Prentice-Hall.

WINCH, ROBERT F.
1963 The Modern Family. Third Edition. New York: Holt, Rinehart and Winston.

CHAPTER 15

middle age

THE PERIOD BETWEEN forty and sixty-five years of age—commonly referred to as middle age—is the life-cycle phase that probably has undergone the most subtle modifications in style of life. The changes are related in part to shifts in age of marriage and of conception of children, matters we referred to earlier. Also, long life and robust health today characterizes the adult years of most individuals. A generation or two ago, middle-aged individuals were regarded as entering their terminal years; people in their fifties were characterized as "old." While the degenerative process accelerates during the middle years, most people in this age span have good health and the prospects of many more years of active life.

For many Americans, middle age is a time of culmination of a successful occupational career. For some, it is a period of reawakening of interest in an independent life; those children remaining in the household are teen-agers or independent young adults. By this age, many couples have achieved a modicum of economic stability and have tailored their tastes and consumer behavior to fit their economic situation. The professional person often is enjoying not only the financial rewards of career achievement but a place of prestige within his colleague group; the businessman is gratified with the power and respect that have accrued to him as part of successful entrepreneurship; the skilled worker is often highly regarded because of his level of competence; and many white-collar individuals occupy positions of trust.

This euphoria is not experienced by all persons of middle age, however. Among the more vexing problem areas that are pertinent to this age span is one that might be referred to as middle-age occupational adjustment. In addition, several other problems having a psychological component or an emotional context—often of a chronic nature—also require examination, including alcoholism, suicide, and long-term and permanent disability.

occupational adjustment

Many men, as we know, attach various and sometimes mystical meanings to their work. Work, of course, has had different meanings over history and from one culture to another (Wilensky, 1966). In the United States, work is valued in a positive sense. Until retirement age, there is a strong expectation that males will participate fully and intensively in occupational careers. As individuals progress through the life cycle, social requirements of responsibility and the need for income demand the acceptance of full-time work roles. Men in the United States during this middle-age period tend to be regularly and gainfully employed; this is the norm.

Those who fail to follow this pattern are classed as disreputable by the community and often by themselves as well. However, opportunities for new employment and occupational advancement are often limited for those in this age bracket. Their chances for learning new trades or skills and for additional career development are severely reduced. By age forty-five or fifty, most individuals who are going to reach the rank of full professor have attained tenure; physicians who are going to receive certification as specialists already have their credentials; skilled workers who are going to become master craftsmen have arrived at this occupational status; and businessmen striving for positions of leadership in commerce are well on their way.

ETIOLOGY

Some of the problems of occupational adjustment for this age group are related to a decline in the number and variety of careers open to older men. These tend to be occupational roles that are dying out or are at least declining, such as farmers, locomotive engineers, tailors, and the like (Bogue, 1959). As the demand for certain types of work diminishes or new techniques or machines provide more efficient and economical ways of doing things, individuals who have had an esteemed career in their fields may find themselves displaced or their worth devalued in the marketplace. As we pointed out earlier, some workers are plagued with problems of educational and occupational obsolescence. In the middle years, employers are reluctant to retrain or hire older workers. Either younger, better-trained men are available, or training a younger man seems a wiser investment than training a person with only ten or fifteen years of work time remaining before retirement. For the worker who has not found himself by this age, or who is anxious because of the very real risks of unemployment or devaluation of his worth, occupational adjustment has ramification for virtually all areas of life satisfaction. (*See*

social participation and job mobility

PER CENT OF RESPONDENTS WHO HAVE HIGH FREQUENCY OF VISITING

	N	Per Cent Visiting Relatives	Per Cent Visiting Neighbors	Per Cent Visiting Friends
Never reemployed	60	62	48	60
Reemployed,				
not working now	82	54	45	49
Down mobile	20	55	50	60
Stable	50	58	52	60
Up mobile	12	33	8	42
Reemployed,				
still working	118	61	41	64
Down mobile	15	60	13	53
Stable	68	60	47	63
Up mobile	35	63	43	71
All respondents	260	59	44	58

In a recent study of employed factory workers, Pope found that workers who had suffered the highest number of months of unemployment during their work careers had the lowest rates of informal social participation with kin, although rates of interacting with non-kin were

Documentation 1.) In part, as indicated before, the issue is a matter of financial reward. The pay check is important in determining life satisfaction. But there is certainly more to it than how much money one takes home at the end of each pay period.

The contented worker is identified, if not with the mission of his company, at least with his own place in it and the level of competence he has attained. A common explanation for the link between salary and work satisfaction is that the more valued individual, with the greater technical competence, is rewarded both by a feeling of satisfaction and a fatter pay check. For those in middle age, devaluation in the world of work results in a generalized alienation that has undesirable consequences for the way the individual expresses himself during his nonwork hours, the stance he takes on political issues, the ways he participates in community activities, and his interpersonal relations with his family and friends.

less affected. In this study, the ex-Packard respondents were asked a series of questions about their social participation with relatives, neighbors, and friends just before the plant shut down, and whether these remained the same following the closing of the plant. Measures of high and low social participation were constructed. Individuals with high social participation were defined as those who reported seeing relatives or friends at least once every two weeks before the plant shut down and who reported visiting them with the same or greater frequency after the plant closed. All others were considered to have low frequency of social participation.

Although they sometimes visited with neighbors, the two-time losers among the ex-Packard workers who had the lowest subjective involvement in society participated less frequently with friends and relatives than either the totally employed or the reemployed workers who were still working at the time of the interview. The most striking observation about this table, however, is that the upwardly mobile two-time losers (those workers who were re-employed at a higher wage relative to their Packard jobs and became jobless again) visited relatives, friends, and neighbors far less frequently than did any other category of workers. It was also this group of workers who experienced the greatest feelings of *anomia*. Apparently, this type of mobility experience—that is, finding a better paying job than at Packard and then losing it—had a more devastating impact on social life than any other type of mobility experience studied in this sample of displaced workers.

One can further observe from the [above] table that visiting relatives and friends is affected more strongly by losing a newly found job than is the visiting of neighbors. It could be argued that visits with relatives and friends require more expenditures of economic resources, such as the cost of transportation, than visits with neighbors. Given a second failure in the world of work, these two-time losers are more likely to withdraw from what we would assume to be more emotionally-charged relationships with relatives and friends. (Aiken and Ferman, 1966:54–55.)

Alienation in the work situation is most likely to occur when the individual has little discretion in the pace and schedule of his work, has limited freedom of choice in his activities, and senses that his career is blocked or frozen (Wilensky, 1966). Alienation increases if, in looking ahead, he sees the possibility of financial insecurity and an economic squeeze. If we could project the current picture of professional obsolescence and economic devaluation, we would probably find that the phenomena will, with increasing frequency, occur at the same time.

At virtually all technical and professional levels there are increased demands for responsible work performance. This is related in part to the way work is now done in large industrial plants and bureaucratic settings where most professionals are now employed. For example, almost all hospitals now have tissue and autopsy committees that judge the appropriateness of treatment procedures, and the success of a physician's career depends on a high level of reliable and responsible performance. The same holds for the highly skilled production worker who is employed in a plant where quality-control requirements are optimally implemented.

With advanced automation has come another tendency for jobs to be either upgraded or drastically downgraded (Buckingham, 1962). (*See* Documentation 2.) The worker in the coal field, for example, is either an oiler of machinery or a graduate engineer who runs a million-dollar automated digging machine. The skilled, middle-aged coal miner is rapidly becoming obsolete. A similar trend can be observed in managerial and administrative positions. As the organization of work has changed from the small shop to the large plant, from piecework to automated production, many tasks that were essentially administrative and managerial functions have now been converted into technical jobs. Instead of a supervisor, one needs a planner; instead of a foreman, technicians; instead of a door-to-door salesman, a sales engineer. All of these changes mean fewer opportunities for middle-range and middle-age employment.

For at least some, the present organization of work tends to increase discipline, reduce on-the-job freedom, centralize decision-making, and accentuate characteristics of reliability and precision. The hardest hit by these changes undoubtedly are those in their forties and fifties and, as we shall discuss in the next chapter, certainly older individuals in their sixties and seventies. Between the ages of twenty-five and fifty, 95 per cent of all males are in the labor force. By age fifty-five, however, the rate drops to less than 85 per cent (U.S. Bureau of the Census, 1966), indicating that a significant proportion of the labor force is not working. Some of the dislocation, of course, is related to the onset of illness or other physical disability. To a large extent, however, it is a direct result of inadequate occupational adjustment to the changing times.

INTERVENTION

What may be done about the problem? Wilensky (1966) argues that in many respects there is no ready solution. Rather, he thinks that the community must expect work dislocation for members during their middle years and must prepare them better for these possibilities. Clearly, without an extraordinary growth in the demand for goods and services, full employment for older individuals is highly unlikely while many younger persons are in need of jobs. On the other hand, there is a need for modifying the frame of reference by which middle-aged workers are viewed. Persons in the professions and in managerial roles must realize the fallacy of dumping useful individuals when, according to current life-expectancy tables, there is every likelihood of their continued robustness, energy, and intellectual competence well into their seventies.

Perhaps an equal, if not more promising, approach is the concept of second careers for the work force. We have already indicated that many

recent facts on automation and employment

Recent employment trends in certain basic American industries are especially alarming. In the electrical industry, employment of production workers dropped from 925,000 in 1953 to 835,000 in February 1961. Here was a decline of 10 per cent despite an increase of 21 per cent in production in this industry. Although there has been a large increase in the production of electrical appliances, a 50 per cent drop in employment has occurred in the production of these products since 1953. Instrument production has also enjoyed a major boom, yet today there are 30,000 fewer production workers—a drop of 15 per cent—than there were seven years ago. In the manufacture of refrigerators and washing machines, the job decline has been about 18 per cent.

The year 1960 was almost identical with the year 1950 in terms of steel production and shipments, yet in 1960 production-worker employment in steel averaged 461,800 compared with 540,000 in 1950. This was a decline of almost 80,000. In this industry, the average work week was 35.7 hours in 1960, compared with an average 39.0 hours in 1950. Because of automation and the shift from airplanes to missiles, it has been estimated that the aircraft industry alone has eliminated 200,000 production jobs in the past few years, even though the industry's dollar volume has continued to rise.

Although automation, as strictly defined, is not the only cause of employment declines in some industries, general technological change has been a major factor. For example, during the postwar period, productivity in the soft-coal industry rose by 96 per cent while employment was falling by 262,700. Railroad productivity rose by 65 per cent during the same period of time while employment fell enormously by 540,000.

During the 1960's, it will be necessary to create an even greater number of job opportunities—perhaps as many as 4 million or more job opportunities every year—to provide employment for the average yearly growth in the labor force of 1,350,000 and possible annual displacement of as many as 2.5 million or more workers from rising productivity. (Buckingham, 1962:49–50.)

women, after the childbearing age, return to the world of work and perform competently in a number of job situations in industry and commerce. As we have noted, critical manpower shortages do exist in many important sectors of the economy. It is highly feasible for many individuals with work skills and professional credentials to move rather easily from one career to another. Such shifts could mediate the problems of life dissatisfaction and fill critical manpower needs at the same time.

Male school teachers, for example, are highly sought and in short supply, particularly at the elementary-school level. Many individuals with liberal arts and technical degrees can, if given some flexibility by the educational establishment and a few specialized courses to augment their previous education, prepare for such roles. This is why it is important to orient university training not merely to a job but in ways that provide opportunities to achieve long-term life satisfaction. The individual who, after appropriate college-level training, becomes a policeman may, in many cities, retire with pension at the age of forty-five or fifty. With perhaps an additional year of education, such a person can be prepared to teach in the public school system. Such opportunities would make voluntary retirement at earlier-than-normal ages more attractive.

In this age group, the problem of occupational adjustment remains most severe for the unskilled production worker who, when he reaches middle age, is confronted not only with the dull repetitiousness of his job but with the realization that he is at the end of the road in terms of occupational advancement. The possibility of more profitably spent leisure time needs to be considered more fully. Although the problem does not seem to be of major concern to community members, planners and economists are well aware of the long-term negative effects of the current dilemma with respect to work careers for the middle-aged.

alcoholism

Most Americans drink alcoholic beverages. For the large proportion who drink only on occasion or even as part of their day-to-day lives, alcoholic consumption hardly represents a problem except, possibly, in the eyes of a few religious groups who regard any imbibing as sinful. We have already referred to the use of alcohol, particularly by young people, and its association with such negative side-effects as high rates of automobile accidents. A depressant, alcohol can impose grave risks for community members when overused in improper circumstances. For a growing number of individuals, the use of alcohol may be regarded as a disease. Through excessive drinking they have severely damaged both their physiological and their psychological health.

Even in relatively small quantities, alcohol affects the behavior of most persons. Approximately five or six ounces of whiskey taken rapidly results in the depression of sensory and motor functions sufficient to cause staggering, tongue-tripping, the impairment of dexterity, and the reduction of auditory and visual discrimination. For most persons who drink, such effects are transitory. Alcohol can also act as a sedative. It reduces anxiety, helps relaxation and, in this limited sense, may actually improve rather than impair performance of certain tasks (Straus, 1966). From a moral standpoint, some may condemn drinking on all accounts. But when consumption is limited to social situations or to circumstances where known benefits are derived, it is hard to substantiate alcohol's negative impact.

Alcoholism, however, is something else. The term admittedly is an elusive one, having no single, clear-cut, acceptable definition. Alcoholism or, as some prefer, pathological drinking is usually defined as the use of alcoholic beverages to the extent that it exceeds customary dietary or social standards and interferes seriously with the drinker's health, interpersonal relations, and economic functioning. For many alcoholics, recourse to alcohol is accompanied by characteristics of addiction very similar to morphine use. That is, once the drinker starts, he seems impelled to continue drinking until he has reached total intoxication. Blackouts, irresponsible behavior, memory loss, and similar symptoms usually accompany such compulsive drinking. If alcohol is withdrawn, severe physical reactions such as rapid heartbeat, sweating, nausea, and trembling often occur as well as hallucinations and delusions. When an individual has these drinking characteristics and manifests a compulsive inability to refrain from alcohol use, particularly under inappropriate conditions, then the term *alcoholism* is usually used.

It is difficult to estimate the number of alcoholics in the community, partly because there is no universal definition of the term and partly because much alcohol use is concealed. The best rough guess is one alcoholic for every eighteen persons who regularly consume alcohol. This proportion would identify some five million alcoholics in the United States at the present time. Of this number, over four million are men. Not surprisingly, drunkenness is currently the most frequent basis for police arrest, accounting for some two-fifths of all arrests in this age group. (*See* Documentation 3.)

Alcoholism is generally agreed to be a progressive disease that accrues over time. It is usually impossible for an individual to become addicted to alcohol without years of exposure to the drug. This is why the illness is considered in this age group, for relatively few younger persons are diagnosed as alcoholics.

ETIOLOGY

There is no definitive knowledge about the cause of alcoholism. One perspective suggests that individuals who drink excessively are characterized by special psychological traits and, from time to time, the term *alcoholic personality* is bandied about in the literature (Armstrong, 1958). Alcoholics have been characterized as suffering from extreme forms of inadequacy and chronic anxiety and requiring unusual emotional support from others. But such characteristics are rather common in the American population; certainly not all individuals who have them are alcoholics. Likewise, it is difficult to explain why such characteristics are necessarily related to alcohol consumption rather than excessive eating or narcotic addiction as the primary symptom. Moreover, one is always aware that

the chronic inebriate

The most frequent basis for arrest in the United States is on the charge of drunkenness, although it sometimes has a different designation, such as "public intoxication." A large proportion of other arrests, such as those for disorderly conduct and vagrancy, involve drunkenness. The individuals taken into custody on these charges are distinctly older than most felony arrestees. The median age of persons arrested for drunkenness in 1962 was 42, for disorderly conduct 30, and for vagrancy 37.

An analysis of the records of 187 men committed to sentences of 30 or more days in Rochester, New York, during 1953–54 indicated that the average arrestee had a record of 16.5 prior arrests, of which 12.8 were for public intoxication and the remainder for other offenses. The most frequent other offense was larceny, which comprised about a quarter of all nondrunkenness charges. These offenders, now mostly subsisting at a marginal economic level on Skid Row, usually had committed their serious felonies at an earlier age and had a greater frequency of purely drunkenness arrests when they became older. It has been suggested by Cloward and Ohlin that such men, like many drug addicts, are "double failures"; they have resorted to a "retreatist" approach to social demands, because they failed first at legitimate and then at illegitimate (criminal) means of achieving a conventional standard of living.

such psychological states may be a consequence of excess drinking rather than a cause of it. There is no real knowledge whether any set of characteristics actually distinguishes the psychological or emotional status of the alcoholic from the nonalcoholic, and whether there is any utility in the concept of the alcoholic personality.

ETHNIC DIFFERENCES

Sociologists have approached the study of the causes of alcoholism by considering the drinking customs of different groups in the community. There are striking differences in the amount and types of alcohol used by different religious, social, and cultural groups. These groups differ in their beliefs, attitudes, and values concerning alcohol and in the degree to which they sanction drinking behavior. Studies of alcohol pathology consistently place the rate of alcoholism among Irish-Americans at the top of the ethnic scale, many times greater than the rates for either Italians or Jews, both of which are strikingly low. The explanation often given is that while all three groups have high consumption rates of alcohol (or at least regular exposure to it during adult life), the use of alcohol is viewed differently by each group. For many Jews, its use is

Characteristically, these Skid Row alcoholics were found to be homeless men, who left the parental home at an early age following the death of one or both parents, or conflict with parents. This departure contributed to their failure to complete their studies or to progress in a vocational career. They seem to have then moved continually from one protective environment to another, between drinking sprees, being either in a correctional institution or in a shelter for homeless men.

Interviews by Robert Straus with 203 men in the New Haven Salvation Army Center during 1946 concluded that they were of predominantly low education and experienced only at unskilled or casual labor. Straus inferred from his interviews that heavy drinking led to homelessness in two-thirds of the cases, and the homelessness led to heavy drinking in one-third of the cases. It should be stressed, in-cidentally, that being on Skid Row is not synonymous with being an alcoholic; data indicate that, for many nonalcoholic homeless men, subsistence is more feasible in Skid Row than elsewhere—when they suffer extreme poverty, lack of family, or physical or mental defects.

Older offenders who are homeless and chronically alcoholic have a difficult time completing a parole without committing persistent rule violations. Nevertheless, their rates of serious felony acts on parole seem to decline with age. However, their drinking makes them incapable of holding a regular job or of accumulating funds. It also is difficult to provide them with a home and employment at release from prison, except as residents in a "shelter program" such as supplied by the Salvation Army or other voluntary agencies. (Glaser and O'Leary, 1966:15–16.)

---

almost a religious ritual; Italians are more likely to regard alcohol as a food; while the Irish consider it a stimulus to social and sometimes exhibitionary behavior.

This formulation suggests that there are three ways in which culture and social organization may influence rates of alcoholism (Bales, 1946). First, there are factors that operate to create inner tension, such as culturally induced anxiety, guilt, and sexual tensions. Second, there are culturally supported attitudes toward drinking and intoxication which determine whether drinking is an acceptable means of relieving inner tension. (Sometimes, the thought of drinking to relieve tension is in itself sufficiently anxiety-provoking to preclude its use.) Third, the culture provides alternative mechanisms for resolving tension. In trying to understand something about ethnic differences in alcohol use, Bales suggests that in Ireland, at least during the nineteenth century when large numbers of immigrants came to the United States, many adults were constrained by customs that delayed their maturity and social independence. For example, marriage was postponed until the later years, causing unrelieved sexual tensions. According to Bales, alcohol use was a form of social control for the potentially explosive force created by enforced dependencies, especially mother-son dependency and sexual deprivation.

The culture supported the frequent excessive use of alcohol by single males, for it provided an outlet for tension and hostility through a kind of institutionalized intoxication.

After migrating to the United States, the Irish found themselves at the bottom of the socio-economic scale. Many factors converged to reinforce the anxieties of the old country. In addition, a new culture and a new set of expectations were imposed on the adult male. Because the Irish brought with them practices and attitudes that supported the use of alcohol to the point of intoxication as a means of dealing with tension, the ready-made combination of cultural factors served only to increase pathological drinking for the Irish male in comparison with most other Americans.

Among Jews, particularly the Orthodox, drinking is a part of a religious ritual, and young Jewish boys are socialized into the use of alcohol in this way. Even though alcohol is used extensively among Orthodox Jews, sobriety is the norm and intoxication is extremely rare. In his study of Jews, Snyder (1958) found that as Orthodox practices decline and religious identification diminishes, the traditional rituals in which drinking is integrated are disrupted. As a consequence, higher rates of alcoholism are found among those Jews who are most assimilated into the larger society.

Similar studies of Italians (Straus, 1966) have identified alcohol as an integral part of their dietary beliefs and practices. Drinking and eating are inseparable activities among Italians. Their alcohol consumption usually involves wine, which not only has a low alcoholic content but is usually drunk excessively only in the context of overeating. Even when large amounts of alcohol are consumed, they are taken in slowly and in accompaniment with food that impedes the rate of absorption. Intoxication, when it does occur, is in the context of social conviviality and is accepted in much the same light as indigestion or other concomitants of gluttony.

As in the study of Jews, the investigations of Italian drinking reveal marked changes in drinking patterns according to the generation and degree of acculturation in the United States. According to Straus (1966), as alienation from the original Italian culture takes place, drinking occurs apart from the context of meals. It involves whiskey in contrast to wine or beer and takes place in settings that are not sanctioned by the ethnic religious group. Under such circumstances, the individuals involved are more prone to excessive drinking and more likely to turn into compulsive, addictive alcoholics.

Some investigators have raised the possibility that biological or physiological components need to be recognized in developing a theoretical framework for explaining alcoholism. Their contention is that people have different constitutional predispositions to become addicts. In a sense, they say, only the biologically predisposed become alcoholics when subjected to cultural patterns that sanction and promote drinking as a separate activity, apart from family and mealtime.

Certainly, such a position makes some sense, considering the character of American urban life. Admittedly much drinking occurs in family and friendship groups; however, the middle-class American stereotype of a cocktail before dinner while the husband reviews the day's events with his wife is hardly a pattern likely to lead to high rates of pathological drinking. On the other hand, much American drinking is not of this type; rather, it is engaged in by individuals away from home and in isolated and stressful situations. Individuals who are vulnerable to pathological drinking are those who live alone, who work in situations producing high levels of anxiety, who express hostility or aggression symbolically through drinking, or who view drinking as indicative of a particular status in American society. The final stop for the pathological drinker may be skid row, a section which can be found in every large American city. (*See* Documentation 4.)

INTERVENTION

There have been marked changes in the public's perception and evaluation of the alcoholic and these changes are reflected in new modes of treatment. The alcoholic formerly was regarded as a figure of despair, a weak individual without self-control, an evil influence. Alcoholics were to a large extent ignored, particularly if they came from groups with some degree of economic independence. They were and, in many places, still are treated as criminals if they come from lower socio-economic backgrounds or as insane, particularly if their behavior is disturbing to community members or intolerable to the family.

In extreme cases of alcoholism there occur degeneration of thought processes and physiological changes that result in characteristically psychotic behavior. Among the middle-aged group, a significant number of patients in mental hospitals are admitted with a diagnosis of alcohol psychosis. It is estimated that perhaps ten thousand patients at any given time are resident in public mental hospitals because of organic brain syndromes associated with alcoholism. To this number must be added large groups temporarily institutionalized in general hospitals, private psychiatric facilities, or special hospitals for the treatment of alcoholism. Approximately twelve to fifteen thousand patients classified as suffering organic illness are discharged from general hospitals in any given year with a primary diagnosis of alcoholism. An additional fifteen thousand are treated for intoxication but are diagnosed as suffering personality or character disorders.

As with the care of most individuals whose illnesses have some emo-

the drunk and the alcoholic

To be fully integrated and acculturated on skid row is to be a drunk, since skid rowers place strong emphasis on drinking, and the acculturated person is, by definition, a conformist. The drunk, however, is not to be confused with the alcoholic, although both drink to excess.

Excessive drinking on skid row does not equal alcoholism, nor do theories of alcoholism necessarily apply to the behavior patterns of the skid rower. Skid row subculture has produced a pattern of drinking rarely recognized by the literature on alcoholism. In part because of aforementioned definitional problems, traditional research into alcoholism among the homeless has used as its study population the chronic police court inebriate. On the erroneous assumption that the police court offender and the skid rowers were necessarily one and the same, theories of alienation, undersocialization, and the lack of social integration were developed to explain behavior patterns of supposed skid rowers and high rates of skid row "alcoholism" were reported.

The failure to distinguish the skid rower from the non-skid rower among the police court study population, as well as the failure to distinguish the alcoholic from the excessive drinker, has led to confusing explanations of the behavior of both skid rower and alcoholic. Recognition of the differences between the skid row drunk and the alcoholic, and of the relationship of each to skid row subculture, may lift some of the burden of confusion about the nature of skid row from the shoulders of future researchers.

Heavy drinking on skid row is a product of group norms rather than the result of individual, addictive craving for alcohol—as Earl Rubington was one of the first to point out. Characteristic skid row drinking does not take

tional bases, the treatment of alcoholics has moved from the jail to the hospital and, more recently, to the community. As Pittman and Sterne (1967) note, the number of excessive users of alcohol who require treatment is so great that it ranks fourth among health problems in the United States, outdistanced only by mental illness, heart disease, and cancer. Their view is that American communities fail to deal effectively with all dimensions of the alcoholism problem and that, in comparison with social action for other major health problems, the efforts expended on alcoholism are minimal.

Attempts to deal with the problem are, of course, not new. The temperance movement, which reached its zenith with the ratification of the Eighteenth Amendment in 1920, has a history that goes back more than a century. But Prohibition, which has been analyzed, criticized, dramatized, and fictionalized at great length, did not prove successful as a remedial approach to the problem of alcohol use. It was not until the 1930s that a large-scale movement for the treatment of alcoholics began

place alone, in the privacy of one's flophouse cubicle, or in secret. The typical skid row heavy drinker (be he "wino," "lush" or "rubbydub") is the member of a group, the bottle gang, and it is the bottle gang not only with whom he drinks but whose controls he observes and through whom he relates to his total social world, the world of skid row. It is the bottle gang which decides on the time, the place of meeting, the amount of alcohol consumed, and the conduct of the drinkers, to say nothing of who shall "go in on the bottle". . . .

The code of sharing—funds and bottle—and membership in the group, mark the skid row heavy drinker even more incontrovertibly than does his predictable appearance in court from time to time following arrest for public drunkenness. It is admittedly hard to live on skid row and not become a heavy drinker—and a more or less chronic police offender. It is not the alcoholic, therefore, but the drunk whose sacrifice of everything to the group's need marks him as a totally committed member of a deviant group. The only fully integrated and

acculturated member of skid row, the drunk is the true skid row derelict.

If the drunk represents the core status of skid row subculture, the small proportion of alcoholics stand just to one side of the center. The life of the alcoholic touches that of the drunk at a number of points: both are arrested, jailed, and incarcerated together; both spend long periods of time in bars; both often panhandle in order to secure funds for drinking; and both sacrifice all other needs to those of alcohol.

At several critical points, however, the alcoholic parts company with the drunk. He typically shares neither drink nor funds; he indulges in solitary drinking bouts; and he retains some of the community's attitudes towards the skid row drunk characteristic of his former, generally higher, status in the outside world. Because he does not identify himself with the inner-circle of the group drinker, he suffers a status loss in skid row terms. In his own terms, he is content with his acknowledged separateness from what he calls the "common" drunk. (Wallace, 1968:102–103.)

to take shape in the United States. It began with the appearance of Alcoholics Anonymous in 1934, followed by the establishment of the American Research Council on Alcoholism four years later. In 1940, the first issue of the *Quarterly Journal of Studies on Alcoholism* appeared, and this periodical continues to publish scholarly articles on the subject. There has been considerable growth in the number of official agencies dealing with alcoholism, but not all states have such programs and the emphasis on this public-health problem is often more verbal than actual.

The repeal of Prohibition in 1933 was a serious blow to the traditional moralistic view of alcohol. Attitudes that had predominated public opinion for more than a century were not easily discarded. Those who proposed the adoption of a different approach, a public-health approach, often met with strong opposition from vested-interest groups. The manufacturers of alcoholic beverages, for example, put up considerable resistance to the idea of treating alcoholism as an illness on the belief that it would dissuade people from drinking. In recent years, the liquor industry has taken a much more enlightened perspective. Distillers now actively support research and educational programs directed at the reduction of excessive use of alcohol and they promote treatment programs for the pathological drinker. The experience of Prohibition and the abandonment of the moralistic approach have stimulated the search for other means of solving the alcohol problem.

ALCOHOLISM AS A HEALTH PROBLEM

Interestingly enough, some of the resistance to treatment of alcoholics by health professionals still continues. It was not until 1956 that the American Medical Association expressed the opinion that alcoholism should come under the scope of medical practice, that hospitals should make provision for the care and treatment of alcoholics, and that interning physicians should be trained to treat the alcoholic. Although there is an extensive and increasing problem with pathological drinking in American communities today, there is still no clearly defined responsibility, either academically or clinically, for the prevention of the disorder or for the treatment of the afflicted. The alcoholic patient occupies an ambiguous role that reflects this dilemma. Some hold that it is primarily the province of the medical practitioner; others believe it belongs in the realm of the specialist in mental disorders; and still others look upon it as a community problem with its locus in the public health and welfare sectors (Plaut, 1967a).

General hospitals and social agencies base their rationalization for not accepting alcoholics on the assumption that they represent a unique problem, requiring special facilities and treatment techniques. To a certain extent this position is justified. Only a few professionals in medicine, nursing, and social work even today are trained to treat alcoholics. Furthermore, to the extent that alcoholics are regarded as personally and morally responsible for their condition, a corresponding lack of status and prestige redounds to professionals working in this field.

In the last few years, awareness of the extent and urgency of the problem has provoked marked changes; most of these, however, are still in the planning stage. A promising innovation is the development of a national commission composed of distinguished figures in medicine, law, and the social sciences, and representing a number of disciplines—forensic medicine, psychiatry, pharmacology, sociology, anthropology, and psychology—related to the prevention and treatment of alcoholism. This group has vigorously sought to integrate and synthesize the available knowledge on etiology and prevention, and to stimulate new and innovative programs (Plaut, 1967b). National recognition of the problem has prompted most states to vitalize their programs, but activity at the community level has lagged. For the most part, general hospital facilities, social agency placements, and community programs are minimal or non-existent and most of the population remain unserved.

TREATMENT APPROACHES

It must be noted that there exists no specific treatment or singularly effective way to prevent excessive use of alcohol at the present time (Bacon, 1967). Various views have been expressed regarding the proper socialization of children and the training of young people in order to minimize the possibilities of alcoholism. These range from providing them with early home experience in the use of alcohol to more stringent and rigidly enforced laws on the provision and sale of such beverages. For the most part, these recommendations represent opinions; there is little or no evidence to indicate their relative effectiveness or feasibility. Although considerable effort has been made to introduce alcohol education into the schools (Freeman and Scott, 1966), the general conclusion is that such programs have no measurable effect. The lack of any consistent norms regarding alcohol use—community standards range from total abstinence to permissive overindulgence—prevents the development of effective educational programs regarding pathological drinking.

Three rather diverse approaches have been employed to treat alcoholism, but none has achieved sustained success. One approach, used more commonly abroad than in the United States, is to motivate problem drinkers to take a drug such as Atabrine or Antabuse which reacts chemically with alcohol in such a way that the individual feels extreme discomfort. The sustained use of the drug, of course, requires the voluntary cooperation of the patient. Unless there can be a high degree of supervision, which is rare, the patient can discontinue therapy at will.

A second approach utilizes one of the various modes of individual or group psychotherapy. In general, there is no empirical evidence to indicate that psychotherapeutic intervention can prevent pathological drinking. Some case histories indicate that psychodynamically oriented practitioners may help by restructuring the life situations of the alcoholic, thereby obtaining temporary and perhaps sustained success. Such psychotherapeutic interventions often involve the family in an effort to resolve the stresses created by the presence of a pathological drinker in the household. Such approaches, however, have not been credited with marked success on a permanent basis.

ALCOHOLICS ANONYMOUS

The third treatment modality is Alcoholics Anonymous or, as it is often called, AA. Maxwell (1967) observes that more problem drinkers have found sobriety through the fellowship of Alcoholics Anonymous than through all other agencies combined. Yet he acknowledges that the AA recovery program remains an unknown quantity to many and an enigma to most. The basis of the Alcoholics Anonymous program lies in forcing the pathological drinker to understand that he cannot escape his alcoholic predicament until he faces the fact that he cannot escape it. It is only when he becomes completely disillusioned with his own ability to solve his drinking problem and abandons all hope of using alcohol as a method for solving any of his problems that he is on the road to recovery. He must, according to Maxwell, have the conviction that his drinking is not an asset but a liability; that it can only lead to more and more suffering, degradation, and perhaps insanity or death. Disillusionment must be complete. The alcoholic must be convinced that any compromise goal of safe, controlled drinking is utterly impossible.

Maxwell concludes that the key element in the Alcoholics Anonymous program is the teaming of disillusionment with hope. As he becomes involved with former drinkers who belong to Alcoholics Anonymous, the alcoholic sees evidence that alcohol can be avoided. The philosophy of Alcoholics Anonymous includes a belief in God and a view that the pathological drinker must accept the existence of a higher power which can restore him to sanity and look after him. The founder of Alcoholics Anonymous, who goes by the name of Bill, detailed the various steps to becoming a permanent member of the nondrinking community of Alcoholics Anonymous as follows:

> Admit you are licked; get honest with yourself; talk it out with somebody else; make restitution to the people you have harmed; try to give of yourself without stint and with no demands of reward; and pray to whatever God you think there is, even as an experiment, to help you to do these things.

SUCCESS OF AA

Analysts of the Alcoholics Anonymous movement recognize that personality changes do occur as a result of this conversion process, that individuals become more conforming to accepted ethical standards, including a rejection of jealousy, deceit, uncontrollable anger, and egomania. AA essentially is a close-knit primary group characterized by intimacy, mutual acceptance, and identification, and it provides exceptionally favorable learning conditions for the internalization of a new way of life. AA may be viewed as a subculture that provides its members with objective knowledge about alcohol and alcoholism; requires and facilitates their honest facing of the connection between drinking and stressful situations; helps them lead a social life that reduces their anxieties without the use of intoxicants; and makes available fellow sufferers who act as amateur therapists, listening to the individual's troubles and leading him on a path that results in his becoming the helper rather than the helped (Maxwell, 1967).

Alcoholics Anonymous has been viewed both as a romantic experiment and as a quasi-religious organization in which a few zealots represent a core of persons who admittedly have been former alcoholics. About this core, according to the second view, there remains a constantly changing fringe of pathological drinkers desperate for help, who move in and out of the arms of Alcoholics Anonymous between bouts of pathological drinking. Certainly it can be acknowledged that Alcoholics Anonymous undoubtedly serves as much of a treatment function as any of the more professionalized programs (Cain, 1963). But there is no evidence to indicate whether such an approach is useful to all alcoholics.

> Alcoholics Anonymous is not the only pioneering effort to do something constructive about alcoholism. It was, however, in the forefront of the trend to regard alcoholism as a treatable condition. Rather than moral condemnation or therapeutic hopelessness, AA has shown, beyond the slightest doubt, that an alcoholic can be rehabilitated. On the other hand, its therapy tends to be limited to those who can adjust to the intense group life of its program. Consequently, many alcoholics are not treatable via its approach. Despite this limitation, AA remains one of the chief ways of dealing with alcoholism. As a follow-up method it is unexcelled and, for thousands of alcoholics, it constitutes the main hope for a life free from the compulsive use of alcohol (Trice, 1967:511).

At the present time, the most that can be said about the problem of alcoholism is that it is receiving considerable resources in terms of basic research and experiments in therapeutic intervention. The prognosis for the pathological drinker must be guarded since there is little evidence to support one ameliorative program over another. Thus, alcoholism remains one of the more serious problems confronting our society.

suicide

As is true for most of the emotional and physical problems considered in this book, suicide is not concentrated solely in the age group under discussion. However, in the United States this age group has the highest rates of suicide and the highest acceleration of rates. The loss of life from suicide is much greater than one might suspect (Gibbs, 1966). As a rough estimate, there are somewhere between twenty and twenty-five thousand suicides in the United States each year and, like many other acts of deviance, a considerable proportion of suicides are unreported as such and remain invisible to the community. This underreporting arises because

suicide rates

In the twentieth century, the general suicide rate in the United States has risen in times of personal upheavals and financial crises—and it has consistently fallen during major wars. Although the suicide rate has leveled off in recent years, suicide now ranks among the top 10 causes of death for all Americans. About 70 per cent of successful suicides are males, but females account for about 70 per cent of unsuccessful suicide attempts. Male suicides are more often successful in part be- cause men tend to choose more violent means of killing themselves. The high suicide rate among white males is believed to be related to their higher expectations for achievement and hence their increased chances of feeling that they have failed. For this reason, the suicide rates of females and non-whites are expected to rise as they become more and more occupationally emancipated. In general, suicide rates tend to be highest among the lonely, . . . and the elderly. (New York Times, 1967:6E.)

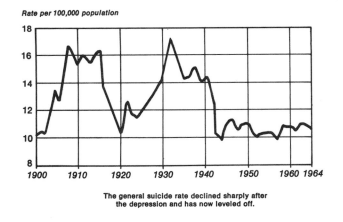

Rate per 100,000 population

The general suicide rate declined sharply after the depression and has now leveled off.

sometimes it cannot be definitely established that the person took his own life, and medical and legal officials are reluctant to so label the death. Sometimes a certain amount of connivance takes place between physician, family, and clergyman to avoid the stigma of suicide for the other members of the family.

Putting it in another perspective, suicides constitute the fifteenth most common cause of death in the United States and the rate is slightly over 1 in every 100 deaths. Among males in their fifties the rate is be-

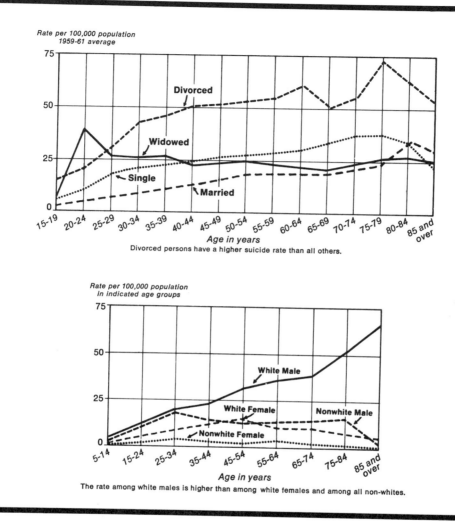

Rate per 100,000 population
1959-61 average

Divorced persons have a higher suicide rate than all others.

The rate among white males is higher than among white females and among all non-whites.

tween 30 and 40 per 100,000 population. While the rate for females is considerably lower, for this age group it is approximately 6 to 8 per 100,000 population. (*See* Documentation 5.)

CAUSES

Suicide is a social problem that has occupied the attention of sociologists for many years. This interest stems in part from the early work of the great

French sociologist, Émile Durkheim, who initiated a point of view regarding suicide that has persisted not only as an explanation for this phenomenon but also as a general framework for understanding all deviant behavior. The key concept of Durkheim's theory is social disintegration. This point of view holds that there is a low rate of suicide when a society is strongly integrated and individuals fit into it. When society is not cohesive, when discrepancies and conflicts occur between an individual's various roles, and when the social order requires a great deal of self-expression rather than dependence from the group, higher rates of suicide will prevail. Gibbs and Martin (1964) have sought empirically to demonstrate the utility of the social-integration perspective. Their approach was to develop an appropriate measure based upon occupation and age that had an inverse relationship between suicide rates and social integration. Although this point of view has been criticized severely (Chambliss and Steele, 1966), it is still the most prevalent explanation of differential suicide rates in the United States.

In addition to this social-integration perspective, a number of attempts have been made to explain suicide in terms of individual personality deficiencies or anomalies. One view argues that suicide represents the bizarre behavior of emotionally disturbed individuals. A second individual-oriented approach seeks to identify more subtle differences in the quality of interpersonal relations, regarding suicide as a result of unsatisfactory social relationships with family and other close associates. A third approach employs a psychoanalytic frame of reference. According to this argument, the suicidal person is the victim of strong aggressive impulses that he fails to express outwardly and, as a result, he turns them inward and seeks to kill himself. As with the other theories, this perspective is viewed as highly tentative, particularly since it fails to explain why certain individuals handle their aggression inwardly rather than outwardly.

While it would be foolish to ignore individual concepts in trying to understand the determinants of suicide (McCord and McCord, 1961; Hillman, 1965; Stengel, 1965), most investigators concentrate on a social-distintegration perspective and rely heavily on Durkheim's concept of anomie. Porterfield (1952), for example, holds that rifts in social relations account for suicides, and his perspective brings us back to the social-integration point of view. It is commonly believed that when solidarity is lacking, and the individual is unable to locate a place for himself within the social order either because of disparities between his background or roles and those of his associates or because of differences occasioned by interpersonal conflict, the risk of suicide is greatest. It should be noted that, while the social-integration perspective makes sense, there is a dearth of empirical data to support this viewpoint (Hagedorn and Labovitz, 1966).

There are marked social differences in suicide rates. Women, for example, enjoy a much greater immunity to suicide than men. The suicide rate increases rapidly for men as they grow older and continues to increase even into the late seventies. For women, the rate reaches a peak in their fifties and declines somewhat after that age. In general, suicide rates in terms of most social characteristics are highly variable. For example, until the 1940s, the rate for blacks was much lower than that for whites; now the rates seem to be converging. Whether this is a result of better reporting of Negro suicides or a consequence of the conflict situation in which blacks are placed in the changing world of black-white relations is difficult to determine. Another illustration is rural-urban differences. During the early 1900s, the urban rate of suicides was almost 30 per cent higher than the rural rate, but by 1960 the rate for rural areas was actually somewhat higher than that for urban areas. Again, there is the question of why. Are the rural increases due to reporting differences or to changes in the rural environment which may no longer provide as many possibilities for integration as it once did?

With respect to occupation, extremely high suicide rates generally prevail in occupations that are at the extreme ends of the income or prestige continua. Thus, high rates are found among managers and unskilled laborers, with intermediate occupations having more moderate rates. In terms of religion, Protestants have higher rates than either Jews or Catholics. Whether this represents a substantive difference or is a reflection of the relative seriousness with which Judaism and Catholicism view self-destruction (and the understandable desire of these communicants to conceal it) is unknown. The highest rates in the middle-aged population tend to be among single and divorced individuals in comparison with those who are married. All of these variations provide superficial support for the explanation that suicide is a consequence of marginal status and lack of integration into the social structure. While this theoretical perspective has been challenged, more fruitful alternatives have not been forthcoming.

In many ways, given the social-integration orientation, the rate of suicide may be regarded as an indicator of the general degree of social disorganization within a community. Several investigators have attempted to show that, where high rates of mobility prevail, individuals who are unsuccessful in occupational or career mobility tend to have the highest rates of suicide (Gibbs, 1966).

Perhaps the most systematic study of suicide is that of Henry and Short (1954), who attempted to formalize Durkheim's concept. According to these two investigators, the suicide rate of a population varies inversely with the strength of the relational system of its members; the strength of the relational system varies directly with the external restraints placed on the members' behavior; and the external restraints placed on the members' behavior vary inversely with the members' status, that is, their position on a prestige continuum. This perspective, like Porterfield's, essentially stresses role integration. Arguments over the extent to which it accounts for suicide in comparison with a more static analysis related to a status position will undoubtedly divide sociologists for some time to come (Gold, 1958). Here it is sufficient to note that, regardless of which explanation has the greater popularity at a particular time, the individual without either interpersonal or structural supports has a high predisposition to suicide.

In passing, a differentiation should be made between suicide attempts and successful suicides. The motivation of the individual who wants to attract notice to himself or who receives gratification from attempting suicide may be very different from that of the serious suicide who has every intention of taking his own life. The suggestion has been made, on the one hand, that some suicides are actually unsuccessful suicide attempts, that is, through ineptness, the person who meant only to attempt suicide unwittingly completed the act. On the other hand, some serious suicides fail because they are undertaken by people who are incompetent or otherwise unable to kill themselves. It is important in future studies to differentiate these four groups in order to understand the phenomenon more fully.

INTERVENTION

Suicide remains a very real problem and one with which society is ill prepared to cope. Since rehabilitation of successful suicides is impossible, all efforts at handling the problem must be in the area of prevention, although at various distances from the potential victim. At the proximate end are those individuals who have made previous attempts at suicide or who display evident symptoms of extreme depression. For these persons, psychiatric treatment and, occasionally, hospitalization represent one means of handling the problem. Practically, however, this approach has little to commend it. First, it is difficult to conceive of long-term institutionalization for individuals who may have been reacting to a passing mood. Second, the kind of surveillance necessary to inhibit the highly motivated suicidal individual is impossible to provide in either a hospital setting or in the community except under inhumane conditions of total restraint.

A more general and less individualized approach is provided by the suicide rescue centers which operate somewhat on the order of Alcoholics Anonymous. Sometimes these centers are staffed by professionals and other times by volunteers. The centers usually advertise a telephone number. Individuals who are depressed or who are contemplating suicide are encouraged to call the number and receive, via telephone or in person, advice, consultation, therapy and, where indicated, antidepressant drugs. Suicide centers frequently try to enlist the patient in continued therapy, and advocates believe that at least some minimum impact is made in the prevention of suicide.

Private practitioners often use a psychodynamic therapeutic approach with suicidal patients. It is difficult, of course, to evaluate the impact of psychotherapy on such individuals, for most of those so treated manifest a variety of other explicit emotional problems. The feasibility of comparing these patients with those not treated or treated differently, taking the various other factors into account, is practically impossible.

Finally, of course, at the level of broad-scale prevention, the entire gamut of programs focussed on unaffiliated individuals and less-integrated groups in the community could be viewed as plausible interventions.

permanent disability

In an earlier chapter we noted that many persons with serious mental disorders often are able to remain away from the hospital after the first episode of illness, or at least to spend most of their lives in the community with only short periods of hospitalization. This practice represents one of the marked changes that has come about in concepts of treatment and stabilization of mental illness. Nevertheless, within the age group we are discussing, a number of individuals are confined to mental hospitals, sometimes for extended periods. In part, this is a phenomenon of the accelerated incidence in this age group of serious mental illness other than schizophrenia, including organic deterioration related to alcoholism and manic-depressive psychosis.

While recent advances in the care of the mentally ill have reduced the number of long-term patients, and the use of drug therapy (tranquilizers) has provided a rationale for maintaining individuals for longer periods in their own homes, the number of chronic mentally ill patients requiring hospitalization or regular outpatient treatment continues to mount during middle age. Even where the patient suffers repeated episodes of mental illness, however, the emphasis is to minimize the amount of time spent in the hospital. Great strides have been made in reducing the proportion of mental patients requiring continual or frequent hospitalization, especially in those types of institutions which have been so accurately depicted in novels and movies as being inhuman, filthy, non-restorative environments—in many respects more like concentration camps than hospitals.

DOCUMENTATION 6

This patient, a 46-year-old white male, was admitted to the hospital after suffering a cerebral vascular accident which left him with a complete right hemiplegia and severe motor aphasia. Speech therapy progressed to the point where he could with some difficulty utter long sentences; through the efforts of physical therapy he was able to walk with the aid of a brace and cane and to climb stairs. . . .

He began to spend weekends at home and, with assistance from his wife, he was able to manage the visits quite adequately. About the time that the staff began to discuss discharge plans with the patient and his wife, ominous signs appeared. Following a long weekend at home, the patient's wife reported that he had been "worse than he was in several months." He had seemed annoyed at everyone and had complained more than was usual. During the next few months his behavior deteriorated to the point where he refused to eat, did not participate in physical therapy, and ultimately became mute and apparently unresponsive to his surroundings. He was confined to bed or a cardiac chair. However, at least early in this period, the mutism was interrupted by outbursts of psychotic speech, and at unpredictable times he would smile or grunt at certain personnel. Occasionally, he would spit his food at a nurse or kick a fellow patient. It was the general feeling of the staff that the patient was becoming increasingly depressed, possibly because of the realization that he was permanently disabled. The patient and his case were presented to one of us . . . at a weekly psychiatric conference. It was the psychiatrist's opinion that while depression may have been present, the predominant psychiatric problem was one of hostile negativism which had reached psychotic proportions. . . .

Here, then, we have a patient who apparently was making a good recovery from his cerebral vascular accident who became "uncooperative" to the point of hostile negative withdrawal.

When the patient had first become ill, his wife had genuinely attempted to help him recover; however, when she saw that his recovery would be limited and that she was destined to have even less of a provider as a husband, she apparently mobilized her own assertive and independent capacities and found to her delight that she could successfully take over his functions. At this time, she became reluctant to relinquish her new found gains (both materially and psychologically) and her chief interest seemed to be to carve out some sort of independent life for herself. Her husband was safely "put away" in a hospital because he was "sick"; her son was away at college and she was attempting to marry off her daughter. (Bursten and D'Esopo, 1965:403–404.)

The solution to the treatment of the chronically ill lies not only in greater financial outlays and better trained and selected hospital personnel, but also in provisions for a network of alternative settings and alternative treatment programs for such individuals. In our earlier discussion of schizophrenics, reference was made to the current emphasis on community mental health settings and the trend toward integrating the treatment of mental illness into the therapeutic framework of general disorders, that is, by having special wards in general hospitals. This approach, along with other innovations such as halfway houses, day hospitals, night hospitals, and the like, is equally applicable to the treatment of the chronically ill. In these settings patients receive some supervision, and the inordinate stresses that might occur in their home life are minimized. Some practitioners hold that the minimization of stress in and of itself has therapeutic advantages and constitutes an underlying rationale for such programs. Others dispute the therapeutic advantages of such intermediate settings but concur in their viability as alternatives to the disreputable chronic wards of many mental hospitals. Sometimes, however, hospitalization is regarded as a preferred solution by both the patient and his family. (*See* Documentation 6.)

Chronic mental illness is perhaps the major concern of middle-aged individuals, but other types of disability afflict them as well. Although more peculiar to the next age group, nevertheless, heart disease, strokes, and related problems do begin to occur in middle age. These disabilities, as well as accidents related to one's employment, have considerable frequency in this age group, permanently incapacitating people and preventing them from participating in the world of work (Haber, 1964). It is estimated that there are roughly three hundred fifty thousand adults in the United States who are disabled from physical or mental disease or other impairments of at least six-months duration which prevent them from being gainfully employed.

REHABILITATION AND CONTINUING BENEFITS

For many years the care of the permanently disabled was handled at the state level, with great variations in eligibility requirements, levels of support, and rehabilitation efforts. This was changed by the passage of a remarkable and foresighted program that has been continually liberalized over the past three decades, namely, the federal Social Security system. Among its many provisions is support for the permanently disabled. At the present time it is estimated that some two hundred thousand individuals are receiving benefits under the federal program, making it possible for permanently disabled individuals to exist in the community and to provide modestly for their families.

A notable feature of the federal approach is the efforts at rehabilitation. Workers who are disabled and eligible for benefits receive an evaluation to determine whether retraining or counseling might provide an opportunity for their gainful employment. This program, in collaboration with the Vocational Rehabilitation Administration and its local affiliates, seeks whenever possible to provide such training. Reports indicate a fair degree of success has been achieved.

DOCUMENTATION 7

who is eligible for disability payments?

Under the Social Security Disability Program, a person under the age of 65 can collect benefits if a physical or mental impairment keeps him from working for a year or longer. (The benefits are continued when the person reaches the age of 65 but are considered retirement rather than disability benefits.) The amount of the monthly payment to a disabled person depends on his average earnings. His dependents also receive benefits, and the total monthly payment for a family can be as much as $309 tax-free. Currently, more than one million disabled workers—plus nearly one million dependents—receive benefits. . . .

The 1965 amendments to the Social Security Disability Program extended this protection to physicians in private practice. This can be a valuable supplement to a physician's present disability coverage.

A person receives benefits only if he has an impairment which so severely limits his ability to function that he cannot do *any* work suited to his age, education, and experience. In addition, he must have Social Security work credits for at least five of the 10 years preceding the onset of his disability. Many physicians in private practice already meet this requirement because of military service or other covered work. Private physicians who have just started contributing to Social Security will be eligible for disability benefits by early 1970.

The 1965 amendments also changed the eligibility requirements by making it possible for patients whose disabilities are not permanent to qualify for benefits. Formerly, a person was eligible only if his disability was expected to result in death or to continue for a long and indefinite period—in effect, if his disability was "permanent." Now a patient can qualify if his disability has lasted or can be expected to last for 12 months or longer. (Popick, 1966:A-89–A-90.)

For certain disabled individuals, such as the chronic mentally ill, realistic prospects for rehabilitation are slim. For them, the present type of disability program helps minimize the family's financial burdens. During the 1960s, coverage for the disabled was further improved. (*See* Documentation 7.) For example, if a covered worker dies leaving minor children, or a spouse, or children who are themselves incompetent to work, the benefits of the program pass to the survivors. This type of disability program is indeed a major social gain and one that demonstrates the utility of an insurance principle for handling certain problems faced by community members.

Short-term disability is another type of problem that greatly affects individuals in this age group. Short-term disabilities are those lasting from, say, one week to six months, at which point the individual qualifies to receive benefits under the federal permanent disability program. Except for certain professional group insurance plans and costly private disability insurance, there is a conspicuous lack of progressive program development in this area. Many industrial and white-collar employees of large corporations receive sick-leave benefits, but most of these are for relatively short periods of time, perhaps five to fifteen days per year. The hourly worker, such as the self-employed domestic, does not receive even this compensation. For most workers confronted with a serious or severe illness requiring extended absences from work, there is little or no protection. Perhaps no more than one out of ten American workers is adequately covered by insurance programs, and there is considerable feeling that the expansion of such efforts is an important area for future action.

visibility of problems

The problems of middle age discussed in this chapter represent the persistent and blatant discontinuities of this age group. Others certainly exist but, in terms of community action, they remain virtually invisible. It is fair to say that the problems of middle age receive minimal emphasis and concern except and until they become extremely noticeable and observable. Ideologically, our current community emphasis upon children, adolescents, and the elderly presupposes that middle age is the period in which automony and independence characterize the life roles of individuals. One may predict, however, that as we begin to meet more adequately the problems of individuals in other age groups, more emphasis will be given to the problems of the middle-aged.

AIKEN, MICHAEL AND LOUIS A. FERMAN.
1966 "Job mobility and the social integration of displaced workers." Social Problems 14(Summer):48–56.

ARMSTRONG, JOHN D.
1958 "The search for the alcoholic personality." Annals of the American Academy of Political and Social Science 315(January):40–47.

BACON, SELDEN D.
1967 "Prevention can be more than a word." Pp. 482–493 in H. Gold and F. Scarpitti (eds.), Combatting Social Problems. New York: Holt, Rinehart and Winston.

BALES, ROBERT FREED.
1946 "Cultural differences in rates of alcoholism." Quarterly Journal of Studies on Alcohol 6(March):400–499.

BOGUE, D. J.
1959 The Population of the United States. New York: Free Press.

BUCKINGHAM, WALTER.
1962 "The great employment controversy." Annals of the American Academy of Political and Social Science 340 (March):46–52.

BURSTEN, BEN AND ROSE D'ESOPO.
1965 "The obligation to remain sick." Archives of General Psychiatry 12 (April):402–407.

CAIN, ARTHUR.
1963 Alcoholics Anonymous: Cult or Cure? Harper's Magazine 226(February): 48–52.

CHAMBLISS, WILLIAM J. AND MARIAN F. STEELE.
1966 "Status, integration and suicide: an assessment." American Sociological Review 31(August):524–532.

FREEMAN, HOWARD E. AND JOHN F. SCOTT.
1966 "A critical review of alcohol education for adolescents." Community Mental Health Journal 2(Fall):222–230.

GIBBS, JACK P.
1966 "Suicide." Pp. 281–321 in Robert K. Merton and Robert A. Nisbet (eds.), Contemporary Social Problems. New York: Harcourt, Brace and World.

GIBBS, JACK P. AND WALTER T. MARTIN.
1964 Status, Integration and Suicide. Eugene: University of Oregon Press.

GLASER, DANIEL AND VINCENT O'LEARY.
1966 The Alcoholic Offender. U.S. Department of Health, Education, and Welfare, Welfare Administration, Office of Juvenile Delinquency and Youth Development. Washington, D.C.: U.S. Government Printing Office.

GOLD, MARTIN.
1958 "Suicide, homicide and the socialization of aggression." American Journal of Sociology 63(May):651–661.

HABER, LAURENCE D.
1964 "The disabled workers under OASDI." U.S. Department of Health, Education, and Welfare. Washington, D.C.: U.S. Government Printing Office.

HAGEDORN, ROBERT AND SANFORD LABOVITZ.
1966 "A note on status integration and suicide." Social Problems 14(Summer):79–84.

HENRY, ANDREW F. AND JAMES F. SHORT, JR.
1954 Suicide and Homicide. New York: Free Press.

HILLMAN, JAMES.
1965 Suicide and the Soul. New York: Harper and Row.

MAXWELL, MILTON A.
1967 "Alcoholics anonymous: an interpretation." Pp. 211–222 in David J. Pittman (ed.), Alcoholism. New York: Harper and Row.

McCORD, WILLIAM AND JOAN McCORD WITH JON GUDEMAN.
1961 "Origins of alcoholism." American Sociological Review 26(April):290–291.

NEW YORK TIMES.
1967 Suicide in the U.S. News In Review. October 8:Section E.

PITTMAN, DAVID J. AND M. W. STERNE.
1967 "Analysis of various community approaches to the problem of alcoholism in the United States." Pp. 201–211 in David J. Pittman (ed.), Alcoholism. New York: Harper and Row.

PLAUT, THOMAS F. A.
1967a "Alcoholism and community caretakers: programs and policies." Pp. 494–503 in H. Gold and F. Scarpitti (eds.), Combatting Social Problems. New York: Holt, Rinehart and Winston.
1967b Alcohol Problems: A Report to the Nation. New York: Oxford University Press.

POPICK, BERNARD.
1966 "The social security disability program; effects of the new amendments." Postgraduate Medicine 40 (August):A-89–A-92.

PORTERFIELD, AUSTIN L.
1952 "Suicide and crime in the social structure in an urban setting: Fort Worth 1930–1950." American Sociological Review 17(June):341–349.

SNYDER, CHARLES R.
1958 Alcohol and the Jews. New York: Free Press.

STENGEL, ERWIN.
1965 Suicide and Attempted Suicide. Baltimore: Penguin Press.

STRAUS, ROBERT.
1966 "Alcohol." Pp. 236–280 in Robert K. Merton and Robert A. Nisbet (eds.), Contemporary Social Problems. Second Edition. New York: Harcourt, Brace and World.

TRICE, HARRISON M.
1967 "Alcoholics anonymous." Pp. 503–511 in H. Gold and F. Scarpitti (eds.), Combatting Social Problems. New York: Holt, Rinehart and Winston.

U.S. BUREAU OF THE CENSUS.
1966 Statistical Abstract of the United States. Washington, D.C.: U.S. Government Printing Office.

WALLACE, SAMUEL E.
1968 "The road to skid row." Social Problems 16(Summer):92–105.

WILENSKY, HAROLD L.
1966 "Work as a social problem." Pp. 117–166 in Howard S. Becker (ed.), Social Problems. New York: Wiley.

CHAPTER 16

old age

AS INDICATED IN THE PREVIOUS chapters on life-cycle problems, the chronological ages used to delineate the different age periods are arbitrary. There is considerable variation and overlap between one life stage and another. Perhaps the most difficult life-cycle stage to define is old age.

The significance of age sixty-five merits some examination. It is the customary age of retirement from business and industry. It is the general age for Social Security eligibility. Its utilization for these purposes has resulted in much more apparent uniformity in defining old age than is justified on the basis of biological development, physical and mental health, or interpersonal behavior, all of which vary markedly from individual to individual. In many ways, the problems of the aged are a consequence of a social definition of old age, a definition that results in barriers to full participation in the life of the community for many persons over sixty-five years of age.

Concern with the aged in the United States is relatively recent. Part of the concern is a matter of numbers: at least in terms of chronological years, the aged population has increased markedly during the second half of this century and it continues to increase. As Neugarten (1966) notes, at the start of the century only 4 out of every 100 persons living in the United States had reached or passed the age of sixty-five. Sixty years later, the proportion of old people in the population had more than doubled and now is almost 10 per cent of the population. The reasons for this increase are relatively obvious. In the first place, there have been expanded opportunities for effective medical intervention, particularly in the treatment of the acute, episodic illnesses that accounted for much of the death toll at earlier ages. Second, the rapid rates of migration to the United States that characterized the 1800s and early 1900s no longer obtain. With the reduction in immigration, which consisted primarily of relatively young adults, the population naturally has become older.

Do the fifteen-odd million persons in the United States over the age of sixty-five face inordinate problems? Many individuals in this age group can hardly be classified as social-problem cases in terms of either moral or objective norms. But certain phenomena can be observed which define the problems of the aged in contemporary times. There is a high rate of economic dependency among the aged; that is, large numbers of older citizens do not have the ability to support themselves. This dependency is the result of several factors: many older workers are caught in marginal industries which are subject to rapid technological and technical changes; employers frequently are reluctant to hire older applicants (Wilcock and Franke, 1963); many existing retirement programs are inadequate to meet current living costs; and, finally, the elderly are subject to recurring minor illnesses and deteriorating physical and emotional health which further deplete their limited incomes.

Coping with physical disabilities is a major problem for many older Americans. Heart disease, cancer, and stroke (rupture or blockage of the cerebral circulatory system) are common to this age group and, of course, senescence is an inevitable consequence of growing old. Senescence can best be described, perhaps, as a wearing out or running down of the body. The physiological and biological changes that take place not only effect body functions and structure but also cause intellectual deterioration and emotional instability. Also, there is the problem of morale; the older person is frequently less valued in American society than the younger adult in the community.

The problems of the aged have become visible in the community for several reasons. First, the size of the group is increasing and, second, certain pressing concerns of other age groups have been ameliorated or reduced, thus freeing the resources of the community to deal with the older citizen (Tibbitts and Donahue, 1962). For many years, there was serious neglect of the aged at all levels of government and in the work of the various voluntary, planning, and philanthropic groups. The extent to which health and welfare programs were apathetic to the problems of the aged is an interesting question for review.

general causes

The lot of older persons in contemporary society is related to changes in the occupational and ecological structure of the United States with concomitant effects on the structure and role relationships within the family. It is not necessary to elaborate in detail the marked shift from an agricultural to an industrial society that has taken place in the United States in less than a hundred years. The family unit is no longer dependent on farming or home-produced goods, hence, the extended family need not remain together physically in order to maximize their utilization of land.

Prior to the industrialization of the United States, the life of an older person who was fortunate enough to reach his sixties in relatively good health was not much different from what it was when he was younger. Admittedly his children, or perhaps his grandchildren, would take over some of the heavy work on the farm or in the family business, but there was still plenty for him to do. Many of the tasks did not require sustained effort, and age limitations in terms of strength and robustness made little difference. This flexibility in operations is not possible when work is conducted outside the family setting and the community sets the job descriptions and the types of tasks to be done (Eisenstadt, 1956).

Many of today's aged are the victims of the depression years. They were adolescents and young adults at a time when university education was rare and even graduation from high school was a difficult achievement. Theirs is a generation for whom earlier limitations for job training and educational attainment have had an impact on their eligibility for participation in today's technologically advanced work situations. The competitive pressures from younger workers further limit the occupational opportunities available to the aged. What would happen to employment opportunities for young men, for example, if most major industries and the Social Security Administration decided to make seventy the age for compulsory retirement and eligibility for old-age assistance? No doubt young and middle-aged adults would have to make considerable readjustments in their present and future economic plans. One point of view that must be respected, problematic as it may be, is that any radical revision of the retirement age in the United States would result in modified opportunities for younger population groups. But this, of course, does not mean that we can ignore the aged or avoid preventive intervention directed at the difficulties faced by community members in the over-sixty-five age group.

retirement

In our general discussion of old age we pointed out that the problems of the aged are related to recent changes in the economic structure and in the modes of work in comparison with those of a generation ago. Also, as already noted, men and women are living much longer (Dublin et al.,

1949). We have now reached the point where life expectancy for the general population has reached the seventies, and a few years longer for the average female. To give some perspective to the problem: several thousand Spanish-American War veterans, some of whom actually fought in the battle of San Juan Hill, are still alive today (Freeman et al., 1966).

In 1900, a man could expect to work, on the average, about thirty-two years. Since then, at least ten years and perhaps more have been added to his work span. At the same time, man's productivity, aided by modern machinery and computerized automation systems, has also increased. In only two decades, productivity in certain occupational fields has doubled and, in some instances, tripled. Neugarten (1966) notes a striking transformation: a century ago a man worked a seventy-hour week and had an average life expectancy of forty years; today these figures are reversed—a man works a forty-hour week and has an average life expectancy of seventy years. For women, the changes in work patterns are even more dramatic. (*See* Documentation 1.)

Moreover, with increased automation, there is good reason to think that per-unit outputs will continue to require fewer man-hours but more man-machine-hours, that is, work in which the human role is simply to monitor automatic equipment. In one sense, the requirements of the economic system demand the programming of retirement in order to provide occupational opportunities for younger members of the community. However, this method of handling work problems minimizes personal choice and decision-making for the aged and hardly squares with the concept of appropriate rewards and gratifications for contributing members of the community.

THE SCOPE OF THE PROBLEM

It is clear that the problem is one of balance, and it is in this direction that current program efforts are moving. On the one hand, some industries have developed early retirement programs, and these are often opted by the older worker. These programs represent one means of providing flexibility in decision-making while at the same time serving to increase the opportunities for younger members of the labor force. In at least a few fields, on the other hand, the potential for continued employment of older workers, sometimes on a part-time but often on a regular full-time basis, is recognized. This opportunity to extend the years of work is largely limited to the professions and to persons with highly specialized repertoires of skills. In general, the age at which individuals leave the labor force has been lowered over the past fifty years, and the proportion of workers who retire in their early and middle sixties has increased remarkably.

Studies of the interests and retirement plans of workers contradict, to

women and the world of work, 1890 and today

The pattern of labor force participation is a very different one for women than for men, as has always been true in America. In the past fifty years, however, changes in the patterns for the two sexes have gone in somewhat opposite directions. As is well known, the proportion of women in the labor market has risen dramatically in the past century; and the characteristics of women who work have changed even more strikingly. In 1890, 13 percent of the women who worked were married; in 1959, 55 percent. As recently as 1940, only one out of ten female workers had children at home under 18; by 1961, it was one out of three.

The change in age distribution is of special interest. As can be seen in the figure (opposite) where the proportions of women workers at successive ages are shown in relation to the events of the family cycle, the proportion of very young women in the labor force has increased, rather than decreased, since 1890. This is contrary to the trend for young men. It is in the middle years, however, that the change is most striking. For women aged 35 to 44 the proportion working had jumped by 1960 from 12 to 42 percent; and for women aged 45 to 54, from 11 to 49 percent.

These data illustrate the difference between the sexes with regard to the whole pattern of the work life. For most men, the trend is to shorten the total number of years spent in the labor force—for men to be older when they start work, and younger when they retire. For most women, the trend is in the opposite direction—to extend the total number of years spent in the labor force. The overall span of the work life is the same for the two sexes, generally speaking, from age 16 to 65, but within that span, women's work lives are lengthening as men's work lives are shortening.

In the present context, the implication is not that many women become economic producers and are therefore defined as economic "adults" for the first time in the middle years (although this is indeed the perception of themselves that many women hold). The implication is, rather, with regard to the age-status system. The return to the labor force brings with it for large numbers of American women, but particularly for those at higher levels of education, an increase in status that affects the relationships, not only between the sexes but between the generations within the family. It is not only the mother who works now, but also the grandmother. (Neugarten and Moore, 1968:11–12.)

a considerable extent, the view that most older Americans insist upon remaining intensely engaged in full-time employment. Indeed, many studies suggest that, with the exception of those in the professions or in highly stimulating occupations, the majority of older Americans who have sufficient economic resources want to retire at appropriate ages (Streib and Thompson, 1958). In all occupations, and particularly in the creative fields, there are some whose primary life investment is in the world of work, and these individuals are faced with the serious problem of having few other interests to occupy them were they to stop working.

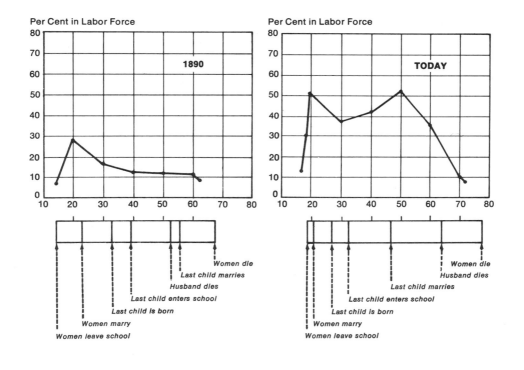

WORK IN RELATION TO SIGNIFICANT STAGES IN THE LIVES OF WOMEN, 1890 AND TODAY

Sources: National Manpower Council, *Womanpower*. New York: Columbia University Press, 1957, p. 307. Right hand portion of figure has been revised based on labor force data taken from *1967 Manpower Report*, U.S. Department of Labor, Table A-2, p. 202, and on family cycle data taken from Glick, Heer, and Beresford, 1963, p. 12. [*See* Neugarten and Moore for full references.]

The investigations of Streib and Thompson (1958), among others, strongly suggest, however, that the idea that all Americans wish to die on the job is a myth. Most people do not reject retirement if they can be economically independent.

SPECIAL PROGRAMS

In many ways the development of retirement villages, of special housing, and of social activities designed specifically for the older adult represent a response to the interests and needs of older Americans. Today it is possible for the individual who is still physically robust to enjoy a variety of recreational activities and an active social and community life without being obliged to cope with a tiring or stressing job situation. Many older Americans in retirement modify their life circumstances rather drastically, sometimes moving to another part of the country to take advantage of a milder climate or a more simple mode of living, often giving up their homes of many years to move into an apartment or other easier-to-maintain housing. Undoubtedly the current trend toward retirement housing and retirement villages, complete with medical care facilities and housekeeping services, will be extended to many more Americans, certainly to those who are economically independent. Indeed, the expansion of retirement villages and other concentrations of economically independent oldsters may well result in the eventual development of a new subculture.

> It is too soon . . . to speak of a subculture of the aged, given the fact that so small a proportion is represented in retirement communities, and the fact that on the whole the aged in the 1960's are still a relatively poor, ill-educated, heavily ethnic, and rural population. The next generation of pensioners will be different from the present one insofar as they will be less differentiated from other age groups in respect to income, education, and ethnicity. Whether or not they will become more segregated, by choice or by assignation, cannot be determined. At the same time, higher incomes, better health, and more years of retirement may well stimulate the further development of a subculture of leisure for the aged—a development which may, by making old age a less unattractive period of life, raise the prestige of this age group (Neugarten and Moore, 1968:21).

Recent federal legislation has provided important financial and programatic support for the development of such retirement communities. Although it is too early to evaluate fully their impact and utility, all observations suggest that they represent a useful innovation in the lives of older Americans. However, a problem closely tied to retirement is that of economic dependency, and many Americans still live and exist in a state of full or partial dependency.

economic dependency

Americans have always had the goal of "saving a little bit for my old age." In truth, however, most Americans reach their sixties with only a minimum of personal wealth and, for many, old age is a period of extreme deprivation and financial hardship. In addition to personal savings and investments, private annuity programs and company retirement plans have been traditional ways to finance retirement. For the most part, however, such programs are limited to professionals and other white-collar workers employed in large corporations or in highly unionized industries. Only about 20 to 25 per cent of America's blue-collar workers are covered by retirement programs of any sort. Other groups are somewhat better off: the federal and most state civil service systems, as well as a number of municipal systems, provide modest pensions in addition to Social Security benefits for their employees. Similar plans operate for large numbers of employees in the education and health fields.

SOCIAL SECURITY BENEFITS

Since its passage in the 1930s, the federally sponsored insurance program, popularly known as Social Security, has greatly benefited most American workers. It should be noted, however, that Social Security is not a welfare program but is rather a public insurance company in which virtually all American workers are policyholders. By contributing to the Social Security Administration a small percentage of his salary (along with a matching contribution from his employer), the American worker purchases retirement insurance as well as certain other benefits, including survivor and disability insurance. One might hope that eventually the extension of group and personal retirement programs, together with increased and broader coverage under the Social Security program, will make possible the financial independence of all Americans over the age of sixty-five. All retirement programs, including Social Security, suffer from the continual inflation that seems to characterize the American economy. Each year the income of retired citizens who are supposedly well-off is drastically reduced by this systematic devaluation of their retirement benefits.

MEDICARE

The current provision of medical-care insurance under the Social Security system represents a logical and meaningful extension of that program. Up until 1966, most aged Americans faced catastrophic financial burdens in the event of serious illness. A large proportion of older Americans were forced to resort to public clinics and other free (subsidized) medical services. The provision of broad health coverage under Medicare represents one way of guaranteeing some degree of economic freedom for the individual when he reaches sixty-five. Unfortunately, the costs of illness and nursing care not covered by Medicare, and the uneven benefits available through state Medicaid programs, still represent severe burdens

use of an extended health benefit program

MEDICAL CARE TYPOLOGY

Extent of care	U.A.W. retirees 1965–1966	U.A.W. retirees 1966–1967	Per cent change
No hospital or ambulatory care	39.2	26.2	−33.2
One or two ambulatory visits	10.6	11.6	+9.4
Three or more ambulatory visits	23.9	30.0	+25.5
Thirty or fewer days of hospitalization	19.2	20.9	+8.9
More than 30 days of hospitalization	7.1	11.3	+59.2

United Auto Worker octogenarians, with access to a moderate health benefit plan, have higher rates of health care utilization than those found in previous studies of persons 65 years old and older. Nearly three of every five retirees had some contact with the medical world and one of every four was hospitalized during the year. After the implementation of the broader set of health benefits, almost three quarters of the retirees had contact with the medical world and almost one of every three had hospital experience. The initial impact of the new health benefits was that more people received medical treatment, and this finding holds for all types of care. (Richardson and Freeman, 1969:229, 233.)

for many elderly people. An indication of the need for additional care can be deduced from the fact that when economic barriers to medical care are minimized, as in progressive health-benefit programs, the use of medical care increases markedly. (*See* Documentation 2.)

In terms of the present cost of living, Social Security retirement payments, even at maximum benefit, are hardly sufficient to provide the good life for the aged individual (Epstein, 1963). Currently, payments for a husband and wife, both usually covered under his insurance program, amount to less than $400 a month, not a particularly large sum for an individual whose income before retirement was $8,000 to $10,000 a year. While abject poverty is not necessarily a characteristic way of life for most aged Americans, severe problems of income restriction do exist (Palmore, 1964). Low morale and dissatisfaction among older Americans are more likely to be related to their feelings of economic deprivation and income restriction than to their concern with having a special social status. While efforts are underway to improve the economic lot of the aged, a more rational strategy is to prevent future generations of individuals in the United States from reaching old age in a dependent or partially dependent financial status.

OTHER SOURCES OF AID

At the present time, large groups of individuals, particularly those engaged in low-level, nonunionized, blue-collar work, whose sole resource for retirement is Social Security payments, have hardly enough. (*See* Documentation 3.) One of the major benefits that the worker in a unionized industry receives through collective bargaining is programatic development of retirement programs, plans that are beneficial not only in terms of sheer dollar value but also in the flexibility in retirement age allowed the worker. Thus, workers in certain major industries, such as automotive, steel, and coal-mining, have a much brighter economic future than their peers in industries with less progressive and rational union-management relations or without any unions at all. The plight of these blue-collar workers remains a most serious economic problem.

Because concern with the financial plight of the aged is so recent, many people do not qualify for the new programs and therefore are dependent upon public welfare for all or part of their subsistance. Among the gains in the last twenty years have been a revamping of the criteria for eligibility and a more realistic evaluation of minimum standards of living for the aged on welfare. While there still are some states, particularly in the South, that grant less than adequate public old-age assistance, most states provide at least a bare subsistence living for their older citizens (Steiner and Dorfman, 1957). Public-welfare allowances rarely permit funds for recreational activities or any of the luxuries available in American society, however.

NEED FOR SPECIAL HELP

Many of the elderly, while able to handle the activities of daily living, do require some special help, ranging from personal services such as cutting nails and washing hair to transportation and homemaker services. The typical American community has been particularly remiss about meeting these needs. These services are required not only by the elderly person without personal resources but also by those with modest incomes who, under ordinary circumstances, are looked upon as financially independent. In some communities, local public health departments and voluntary health and welfare agencies now regard the provision of such services as an important community program.

reducing economic dependency

SIZE OF MONEY INCOME FOR UNITS AGED 65 AND OVER:
PERCENTAGE DISTRIBUTION BY INCOME INTERVAL, 1962

Total Money Income	MARRIED COUPLES	NONMARRIED PERSONS		
		Total	Men	Women
Number (in thousands):				
Total	5,445	8,731	2,402	6,329
Reporting on income	4,719	7,709	2,173	5,536
Total per cent	100	100	100	100
Less than $1,000	5	44	32	49
1,000–1,499	10	22	25	21
1,500–1,999	14	13	12	13
2,000–2,499	13	8	11	7
2,500–2,999	12	4	5	3
3,000–3,999	16	4	6	3
4,000–4,999	11	2	3	1
5,000–9,999	15	4	6	3
10,000 and over	5	....	1	....
Median income	$2,875	$1,130	$1,365	$1,015

In order for the aged to achieve the minimum incomes currently set as the poverty levels, more than 50 percent of the families and about 60 percent of the nonmarried persons would need increases in income. Alternatively, money incomes somewhat lower than the $3,000 per family and $2,000 per individual have been suggested, in part to take account of the fact that an elderly couple has a lower cost of living than a younger family. For an elderly couple, figures of $2,800 and $2,500 have been discussed. If $2,500 for an older couple and $1,800 for a single person are taken as the poverty lines (which are the approximate amounts required for the Department of Agriculture's low-cost food plan, assuming that the elderly couple spends 27 percent of its income for food), a large proportion of the aged would still fall below these incomes. In 1962, two-fifths of the older couples and three-fourths of the single persons would not have sufficient incomes to meet the low-cost standard. Even the Department of Agriculture's economy plan, which has been priced at $1,800 for an older couple and $1,300 for an individual, is out of reach of more than one-fourth of the couples and about three-fifths of older single persons. (Kreps, 1966:152–153.)

health care

The chances of experiencing extended illness or death from acute diseases are much greater for the aged than for the general population. In recent years, concepts in medical treatment for the aged have shifted markedly.

For example, surgical procedures that would not have been attempted some five to ten years ago are now routinely accomplished. In fact, medical care for older persons with acute illnesses or conditions requiring surgical intervention is not qualitatively different from that given the rest of the population. However, one of the consequences of aging is a decline in general robustness. Moreover, the elderly are more prone to certain diseases classified as terminal, that is, there is little likelihood of reversing the disease process (Kaplan and Aldridge, 1962). The most common of these are the major "killers"—heart disease, stroke, and cancer —which are the concern of recent major federal programs (Prindle, 1968). In addition, there are other disorders, such as arthritis, that remain persistent sources of discomfort and which result in a progressively worsening physical condition. Elderly persons suffering such disabilities contribute to the significant number of aged who may be regarded as ill (Shanas, 1960). (*See* Documentation 4.)

MENTAL DISORDERS

There are a number of mental disorders peculiar to the aged, including the serious problem of partial or complete senility. Senility is the terminus of the aging process and results from metabolic and physiological changes and a reduced functioning of the circulatory and nervous system. Loss of muscular coordination, impaired sensory perceptions, and changes in the mental processes, including memory failure and disorientation, are common. Innovations and discoveries in medical care clearly represent the key to the problems of chronic diseases, many of whose causes have yet to be determined. From the standpoint of remedial action, of course, the concept of prevention at an earlier age is advocated. For example, the incidence of lung cancer among the elderly would be severely curtailed if cigarette smoking could be reduced or eliminated among younger age groups. This is equally true for emphysema, a serious respiratory disease that characteristically results from the destruction of certain membranes in the lungs and represents an increasingly serious problem as the individual increases in age.

CHRONIC DISEASES

The inevitable consequence of the strides made in curing some of the acute illnesses has been to increase the number of potential sufferers of chronic diseases. The medical condition of the chronically ill requires intensive professional intervention and, with advancing age, these treatment programs become increasingly costly (U.S. Department of Health, Education and Welfare, 1962a). We have already discussed in some detail the financial problems of medical care for the aged. While Medicare has

age and chronic health conditions

**PER CENT OF POPULATION LIMITED IN ACTIVITY AND
MOBILITY BY CHRONIC HEALTH CONDITIONS***

	Per Cent Distribution		
	All Ages	Aged 45–64	Aged 65 and Over
Total population	100.0	100.0	100.0
Persons with no chronic conditions	58.1	38.7	21.3
Persons with one or more chronic conditions	41.9	61.3	78.7
Persons whose condition limits activity	*10.9*	*18.3*	*45.1*
Hindered in going to school, working, or keeping house	5.8	10.4	22.8
Prevented from going to school, working, or keeping house	2.3	2.9	15.5
Other limitation	2.8	5.0	6.8
Persons whose condition limits mobility	*2.7*	*3.7*	*17.8*
Trouble in getting around alone	1.6	2.5	9.9
Unable to get around alone	0.6	0.6	4.1
Confined to house	0.5	0.6	3.8

(*U.S. Department of Health, Education and Welfare, 1962b:xxi.)

When people live to old age, they are likely to be unusually healthy individuals, and yet they are afflicted with chronic and degenerative diseases. This state of affairs is at odds with the popular conception of the health of the elderly. The image of old age today is as likely to be that of a vigorous, white-haired man on the golf course as it is that of the toothless grandsire in his rocking chair. Since we are focusing on the older population as a whole, we must first consider the health status of the aged in general before looking at the problems of those who are ill.

Over three-fourths of persons over 65 have some chronic health condition. Chronic health problems, however, do not suddenly appear when people pass the age of 65. Three-fifths of middle-aged persons (45 to 64) also have one or more chronic health conditions, which indicates that the elderly are likely to have lived with their health problems for a long time.

Rather than the number of persons with chronic conditions, however, a better measure of health is one that is based on limitations of function. How many people cannot perform the tasks normal for their age? How many cannot move about freely because of illness or disability?

On these points the above table shows that of every 100 persons over 65, 45 have conditions that limit their activity in some way, for example, a weakened heart, arthritis or rheumatism, or a visual impairment. Only sixteen of these persons, however, are prevented from working or from keeping house. Eighteen cannot get around as they should, but only four are confined to their homes. Figures such as these can be interpreted as good or bad, depending . . . on whether one focuses on the present instead of the past, or the achievements instead of the potentialities of the society. (Neugarten, 1966:177–178.)

minimized these financial barriers, there still exists a conspicuous short-age of personnel specializing in the health-care problems of the aged and an even more serious limitation on the availability of appropriate facilities.

SPECIALIZED PERSONNEL

The development of geriatric specialists in surgery, internal medicine, psychiatry, nursing, social work, and the like has not yet taken hold. Many health-care personnel who see the aged in their day-to-day rounds have little special training or sensitivity to their problems. Moreover, in some cases, health-care personnel reject their responsibilities or minimize them with respect to providing medical services for the older individual. It has been suggested that health-care personnel favor the younger over the older community members because the aged, both as patients and people, are regarded as relatively uninteresting. This rejection by the medical profession is partly realistic; the possibilities for successful in-tervention are limited. Although medical discoveries have been remark-able, it is a truism that everyone must die. Often the most that can be accomplished for the elderly patient from the treatment standpoint is to see that the inevitable occurs as easily and painlessly as possible.

TRAINING PROBLEMS

With the advent of the 1960s, programs have been undertaken to train social workers, physicians, nurses, and other appropriate personnel in the special problems of the aged (Falk, 1965). Federal legislation established the office of the Commissioner on Aging and authorized him to support research, demonstration, and action programs. His counter-parts at the state level are also rapidly assuming responsible roles. But given the competition for highly trained professional people from other areas of the health field and from other practicing professions and tech-nical specialities, the serious gaps in manpower are not likely to be filled in the near future. As a consequence, in addition to efforts to train and develop specialists in the care of the aged, serious attempts are being made to use less well-trained personnel and volunteers more effectively (Morris and Lambert, 1964).

Physical illness is not the only aspect of health care for the aged that needs attention. For example, physical impairments, such as hearing dif-ficulties, are neglected among this age group. There is also a conspicuous lack of adequate dental care, particularly for old people living in institu-tional settings. Programs to meet these needs require not only financial resources but personnel, who currently are not available. Programmatic efforts in caring for the aged compete, as we noted, with the needs of other populations groups for limited community resources and personnel.

If the shortage of personnel is great, the shortage of physical resources is even greater. With the emergence of chronicity as the major focus of medical care for the aged, the concept of the general hospital as an appropriate treatment setting for elderly patients needing assistance is negated. For one thing, the cost of general-hospital care is too high and, second, a general-hospital setting does not meet the realistic needs of the patients. Present medical-care resources in use for the care of the aged include the nursing home, the old-age home, the chronic-disease hospital, and the mental hospital (Lowenthal, 1964a).

Except during acute episodes or terminal phases of their illnesses, most aged individuals do not need the intensive care that general hospitals provide. On the other hand, they may routinely require some professional help. With the possible exception of the facilities operated by the Veterans Administration (which has accepted its increased role in the aging process among veterans), few public or private resources have developed integrated services for the aged. At the one extreme there is a growing number of chronic-disease hospitals, typically administered at the state level but receiving contributions of federal funds. The rate of growth of these institutions, however, is not keeping pace with the needs of the aged for professionally supervised settings. Moreover, in general, the cost of operation of chronic-disease hospitals require their restriction to patients who have some possibilities for recovery or at least stabilization of the condition so that they may return to the community.

At the other extreme is the redevelopment and reemployment of homes for the aged, a concept that has been in existence in America for hundreds of years, but one that is presently undergoing considerable modification. In the United States, homes for the aged typically developed from poor farms or other facilities for the indigent. Traditionally, sectarian groups have included among their services to the community the development and operation of such homes for the aged and recently interest in such activities has increased. These settings, sometimes restricted to members of the particular religious body, but more often not, usually provide not only living quarters but recreational facilities and, occasionally, other types of activities such as arts and crafts, discussion groups, and so forth. Many also provide medical care and treatment, usually in the form of a resident nurse, regular visits from a physician and, sometimes, collaborative arrangements with a nearby hospital. The home for the aged represents a realistic solution for the highly independent individual; the chronic-disease hospital meets the needs of the individual who requires sustained and continual medical supervision. In the middle is the nursing home.

The nursing home is a setting in which skilled nursing care and medical supervision are provided the aged individual on a regular basis. In the United States, nursing homes traditionally have been operated on a proprietary, that is, profit-making, basis with minimal contact with the more professionalized medical sector. These facilities have been criticized severely on the basis that the profit motive of nursing-home operation is incompatible with the provision of high-quality patient care. Some health-care experts maintain that such commercial institutions cannot build the necessary links to the professional medical community and to the hospitals that are required in order to provide the continuity of care regarded as optimal in the case of the elderly patient. As a practical matter, however, it is unlikely that during the next quarter century there will be adequate public and nonprofit facilities available. In order to handle the large number of aged persons who require some type of medical supervision in the last years of life, the programs of most states and the federal government have been directed toward the upgrading of proprietary nursing homes and similar facilities. Again, training of personnel, setting of standards, and attempts to assess the quality of care represent key areas for development.

SOCIAL FACTORS

Much could be written about the work of sociologists and medically trained researchers who seek to identify social factors related to the illnesses that characterize old age and which take a great toll in suffering and mortality. This area of work is not emphasized here because it represents primarily the use of sociology to solve medical problems rather than social problems. As an illustration, one can take the field of rheumatoid arthritis and indicate what seems to be a vast number of social and psychological variables associated with the illness. For example, it is reasonably clear that the disease is more common among lower socioeconomic persons and among individuals who experience status inconsistency, that is, high education but low occupational status, or vice versa. The explanation is that anger, irritation, or stress are related to this illness (Cobb and Kasl, 1966). Likewise, considerable emphasis is given to understanding social factors in heart disease (Hinkle, 1966), as well as in other chronic and severe disorders.

Some may rightfully maintain that efforts for the aged, particularly in the areas of economic assistance and medical care, represent an overemphasis on a particular population group. For example, many more states provide economic assistance for the aged at levels permitting subsistence than make such funds available to dependent children. The marked upgrading of programs for the aged reflects how energetic and intense can be the provision of services in the United States when there is an expression of interest and reasonable alertness by those involved in developing an action program.

morale

Accompanying the concern with the physical well-being of the aged is an increased interest in their psychological adjustment. As we have indicated, a number of elderly persons suffer severe emotional disorders related to organic deficiencies. In addition, there is increasing concern with the general lot of the aged. Their reduced activity because of retirement, the attitudes of younger citizens toward them, and the lack of economic wherewithal to participate in community life lead many older citizens to have a low opinion of themselves and to experience feelings of inadequacy, although whether severe mental disturbances result from the aged's social isolation is questionable (Lowenthal, 1964b). Considerable effort has been made to establish special clubs and activities for the elderly in order to counter these negative feelings and life views. A variety of publicly and privately supported golden-age and senior-citizen groups have been developed to provide activities for and interaction among the elderly and between the elderly and younger members of the community.

Some years ago a very interesting and provocative study by Cumming and Henry (1961) did much to place the problem in balance. The position of this research group, at least as originally presented, suggested that normative aging may indeed be defined as the gradual and realistic withdrawal from full participation in the life of the community and a retrenching in terms of the life space of the individual. This view was challenged by many in the gerontology field who contended that high levels of social and interpersonal activities are essential to the maintenance of psychological well-being among the aged.

Recently, there has been at least a partial synthesis of the two positions—the one arguing that curtailment of activities is a natural adjustment to aging and should not be looked upon necessarily as causative of low morale, and the polar view claiming that a high degree of activity is essential for high morale (Williams and Wirths, 1965). Simply put, the development of high morale by the aged may follow alternative patterns. For some, curtailment of activities represents an adequate mode of adjustment; for others, continued participation in a variety of social events and interpersonal behaviors is necessary, and the community must provide accordingly (Neugarten, 1965).

Perhaps even more critical is an awareness that the exigencies of inadequate financial resources and of poor health undoubtedly explain part of the relationship between levels of activity and other life circumstances of the elderly and their feelings of adjustment and happiness (Jeffers and Nichols, 1961). Therefore, in addition to recognizing that old age represents a stage in the life cycle, it is important to be aware that the very fact of its being the final stage requires concerted efforts to prevent people from entering it sooner than necessary in terms of their own values and needs and the life circumstances offered by the community in which they live (Blau, 1961).

One of the unfortunate consequences of even our more beneficial programs directed at the older citizen has been to promote the notion that to reach sixty-five years of age is automatically to be labeled "old" and, in a sense, assigned a deviant status (Rosow, 1965). This is one of the crucial problems confronting all of our intervention strategies. In our development of programmatic efforts to ameliorate some of the problems facing the older American, we have served only to stigmatize him further. Consequently, it would be useful to restrict as much as possible the undesirable labeling and stigmatization process.

dying

Death occurs, of course, at all ages, and the phenomenon of death is recognized now as an important social problem. From the standpoint of the individual, mental-health specialists have pointed to the grief reaction over the loss of a family member as one of the major crises leading to problems of severe emotional distress (Hinton, 1967). At the level of the community, also, the problem of death and dying has received attention in several ways, and there is growing interest in the phenomenon of death (Brim et al., 1970).

There has been considerable concern and popular indignation expressed recently about the commercialization of the way the dead are processed in the American community (Habenstein and Lamers, 1962). Clearly, death is a period of great stress and emotion for close family members and, at times, unfair and perhaps unscrupulous behavior has led to unwarranted funeral costs. Then, too, Americans have not developed a very consistent or sympathetic means of dealing with relatives awaiting the imminent death of a family member. And there is even greater ambiguity surrounding the communication of imminent death to the patient himself. (*See* Documentation 5.)

In a study of death in the hospital, Sudnow (1967) argues that personnel develop and organize a systematic means of handling most of

There are . . . several good reasons justifying considerable candour with people who are fatally ill. If this were to be more widely accepted in principle, how and when should such sincere conversation take place? Clearly an abrupt statement to every patient with incurable disease that he is going to die is likely to do more harm than good.

Some wish to know only a little of their illness. As with non-fatal disease, a person may be helped by simple explanations of the illness, together with a general plan of investigating or treating the condition. . . . Some dying patients want to know even less than this sort of edited version of truth. They may not want to hear a word about the nature of their condition. They may well have a hidden suspicion and gladly enter a tacit conspiracy to avoid the whole subject. They wish others to take over all responsibilities, anxieties, and decisions. This total surrender of all decision to the doctor may be somewhat less common now, especially as doctors tend to lose a little of their former authoritative manner and more patients refuse to put up with it. But when seriously ill, it can be easier for a patient to relinquish all control, all knowledge, to his doctor. If the dying person indicates openly

the deaths that occur; it is only the unusual death that raises problems. Apparently, individuals who are frequently confronted with the task of communicating the fact of death develop the skill and ability to respond to a variety of standardized reactions on the part of the bereaved.

Glaser and Strauss (1965) emphasize much more the relational qualities between individuals involved in the event of death. Death raises severe problems for many relatives in American society. In our complex system, even persons of modest property frequently become heavily enmeshed in laws and legal and fiscal roles. Moreover, the emphasis upon conjugal rather than extended families makes it difficult for children and siblings—whose affective bonds often are minimal—to respond emotionally and protectively in the mourning situation.

In these times there are rather ambiguous and unclear norms regarding the reactions of community members to the death of a kin or a close associate. With the exception of certain culturally prescribed religious rituals for subgroups, such as those practiced by religious Jews or old-country Irish, death has minimal significance in a community life oriented towards the young and the active. Neither severe grief nor blasé behavior is regarded as appropriate for those close to the deceased; yet the need to balance both moods and feelings is not only difficult but

that he does not want to know, if he shows by his manner or by his talk that he does not wish to regard his illness as fatal, it would be uncharitable to force the truth upon him. The aim is to make dying a little easier, not to apply a dogma of always divulging truth. . . . If it is unclear if an ill person desires to know the whole truth, it is possible to start by giving gentle hints. A simple explanation of the disease, mentioning the favourable aspects of treatment and touching upon the other serious possibilities, will enable the ill person to take up the aspects he wishes and ignore others. The beginnings of awareness may be started early. A surgeon before operating upon a suspected cancer will often tell the patient that if the condition is serious he will need to perform an extensive operation. The patient who has such an operation can then pursue the matter with the doctor as much as he wishes. He can apprehend the threat of the illness, or concentrate on the curative value of the treatment.

It is perhaps strange that there is so much more agreement over talking frankly to members of the family about their relative's fatal illness rather than to the patient himself, even if he shows a wish to know. It reverses the usual convention of the doctor keeping confidential the information concerning an adult and telling other people only if the patient agrees. A few doctors, if they tell the patient the serious nature of the illness, do discuss with them who else should be informed. Usually the next of kin is told, but often it is clear that some other responsible member of the family is better able to receive the information and pass on the appropriate knowledge to the rest. As with the patient, the families receiving these tidings often need more than just a bulletin of bad news. (Hinton, 1967:130–131, 133–135.)

requires a type of behavior in which there is less than full socialization and understanding. As with other programs discussed in this book, diffuseness and lack of specificity of the norms may exist even at the very end of the life cycle (Neugarten, 1965).

epilogue

The discussion of the aged concludes our review of the life cycle of the individual. In our discussion of the life cycle and our review of the pervasive social problems, we have indicated not only the discontinuities that exist in the American community but some of the current and prospective efforts to ameliorate the problems. As we noted at the outset, the strain for the development of a utopian community life persists today, as it has in the past. How well we are moving toward such an ideal form of social existence is difficult to gauge. But clearly we must realize that the contemporary American community fails to maximize the opportunities for the good life that is possible with our form of government, our technology, and our intelligence.

BLAU, ZENA S.
1961   "Structural constraints on friendships in old age." American Sociological Review 26(June):429–439.

BRIM, ORVILLE G., JR., HOWARD E. FREEMAN, SOL LEVINE AND NORMAN SCOTCH (EDS.).
1970   The Dying Patient. New York: Russell Sage.

COBB, SIDNEY AND STANISLAV V. KASL.
1966   "The epidemiology of rheumatoid arthritis." American Journal of Public Health 56(October):1657–1663.

CUMMING, ELAINE AND WILLIAM E. HENRY.
1961   Growing Old: The Process of Disengagement. New York: Basic Books.

DUBLIN, LOUIS I., A. J. LOTKA AND M. SPIEGELMAN.
1949   Length of Life. New York: Ronald.

EISENSTADT, S. H.
1956   From Generation to Generation. Glencoe, Illinois: Free Press.

EPSTEIN, LENORE.
1963   "Income security standards in old age." Research Report 3. Social Security Administration, U.S. Department of Health, Education, and Welfare. Washington, D.C.: U.S. Government Printing Office.

FALK, I. S.
1965   "Medical care and social policy." American Journal of Public Health 55(April):269–274.

FREEMAN, HOWARD E., ARTHUR RICHARDSON, JAMES F. CUMMINS AND HAROLD W. SCHANPER.
1966   "Use of medical resources by Spancos: I. Extent and sources of medical care in a very old population." American Journal of Public Health 56 (September):1530–1540.

GLASER, BARNEY AND A. STRAUSS.
1965   Awareness of Dying. Chicago: Aldine.

HABENSTEIN, ROBERT WESLEY AND WILLIAM M. LAMERS.
1962   The History of Funeral Directing. Milwaukee: Belfin Prints.

HINKLE, LAWRENCE E.
1966   "The use of a large industrial population to study the effects of social and behavioral factors on coronary heart disease." American Journal of Public Health 56(September):1470–1475.

HINTON, JOHN.
1967   Dying. Middlesex, England: Penguin.

JEFFERS, FRANCES C. AND CLAUDE R. NICHOLS.
1961   "The relationship of activities and attitudes to physical well-being in older people." Journal of Gerontology 16(January):67–70.

KAPLAN, JEROME AND GORDON J. ALDRIDGE (EDS.).
1962   Social Welfare of the Aging. New York: Columbia University Press.

KREPS, JUANITA.
1966 "Employment policy and income maintenance for the aged." Pp. 136–157 in John C. McKinney and Frank T. DeVyver (eds.), Aging and Social Policy. New York: Appleton-Century-Crofts.

LOWENTHAL, MARJORIE FISKE.
1964a Lives in Distress: The Paths of the Elderly to the Psychiatric Ward. New York: Basic Books.
1964b "Social isolation and mental illness in old age." American Sociological Review 29(February):54–70.

MORRIS, ROBERT AND CAMILLE LAMBERT, JR.
1964 New Roles for the Elderly. Papers in Social Welfare, No. 10. Waltham, Massachusetts: Brandeis University.

NEUGARTEN, BERNICE L.
1965 "Personality and patterns of aging." GAWEIN 13(May):249–256.
1966 "The aged in American society." Pp. 167–196 in Howard S. Becker (ed.), Social Problems: A Modern Approach. New York: Wiley.

NEUGARTEN, BERNICE L. AND JOAN W. MOORE.
1968 "The changing age-status system." Pp. 5–21 in Bernice L. Neugarten (ed.), Middle Age and Aging. Chicago: University of Chicago Press.

PALMORE, ERDMAN.
1964 "Work experience and earnings of the aged in 1962: findings of the 1963 survey of the aged." Social Security Bulletin 27(June):3–14.

PRINDLE, RICHARD A.
1968 "Epidemiological considerations concerning the regional medical programs: from the bureau of disease prevention and environmental control." American Journal of Public Health 58(June):1073–1076.

RICHARDSON, ARTHUR AND HOWARD E. FREEMAN.
1969 "Use of an extended health benefit program by octogenarian U.A.W. retirees." Medical Care 7(May/June):225–234.

ROSOW, IRVING.
1965 "And then we were old." Transaction 2(January/February):20–26.

SHANAS, ETHEL.
1960 Medical Care Among Those Aged 65 and Over. Research Series 16. New York: Health Information Foundation.

STEINER, PETER O. AND ROBERT DORFMAN.
1957 The Economic Status of the Aged. Berkeley: University of California Press.

STREIB, GORDON F. AND WAYNE E. THOMPSON.
1958 "Adjustment in retirement." Journal of Social Issues 14(April):1–5.

SUDNOW, DAVID.
1967 Passing On. Englewood Cliffs, New Jersey: Prentice-Hall.

TIBBITTS, CLARK AND WILMA DONAHUE.
1962 Social and Psychological Aspects of Aging. New York: Columbia University Press.

U.S. DEPARTMENT OF HEALTH, EDUCATION AND WELFARE.
1962a The Older Population. Washington, D.C.: U.S. Government Printing Office.
1962b Adapted from Health, Education and Welfare Indicators (October).

WILCOCK, RICHARD C. AND WALTER H. FRANKE.
1963 Unwanted Workers. New York: Free Press.

WILLIAMS, R. H. AND C. WIRTHS.
1965 Lives Through the Years. New York: Atherton.

Copyrighted material found on pages given in italic below are reprinted from the sources indicated with permission of the publisher unless indicated otherwise.

Pages 18–19: From the book *An Analysis of the Kinsey Reports,* edited by Donald Porter Geddes. Copyright © 1954, by New American Library of World Literature, Inc. Used by permission of E. P. Dutton & Co., Inc.

Page 26: S. Kirson Weinberg, *Social Problems in Our Time: A Sociological Analysis,* © 1960. By permission of Prentice-Hall, Inc.

Page 32: From "Persistent Problems of Crime Statistics" by Roland J. Chilton in *Critical Issues in the Study of Crime,* edited by Simon Dinitz and Walter C. Reckless, pp. 91–92. Copyright © 1968, by Little, Brown and Company (Inc.).

Page 35: Reprinted with permission of the National Association of Social Workers, from *Social Work,* Vol. 11, No. 1 (January 1966), pp. 5–7.

Pages 87 and 116: From *On Understanding Poverty* edited by Daniel P. Moynihan, Basic Books, Inc., Publishers, New York, 1969.

Pages 135, 197, 241–242, 295–296, and 300: The Public Interest, © National Affairs, Inc., 1966.

Page 187: Copyright © 1963, by The Atlantic Monthly Company, Boston, Mass. Reprinted with permission.

Page 194: From *The Urban Condition* edited by Leonard J. Duhl, M.D. © 1963, by Basic Books, Inc., Publishers, New York.

Pages 198–199: Reprinted by permission from *Daedalus,* Journal of the American Academy of Arts and Sciences, Boston, Mass. Vol. 95, No. 1.

Page 201: Reprinted by permission of the *Journal of the American Institute of Planners,* Vol. 29, No. 2, May, 1963.

Page 203: Reprinted from *Shaping an Urban Future: Essays in Honor of Catherine Wurster* by Bernard J. Frieden and William W. Nash, Jr. (eds.), by permission of The M.I.T. Press, Cambridge, Mass., © 1969.

Pages 215–216: From *The Public Interest,* © National Affairs, Inc., 1968.

Pages 216–217, 219, 296–297: © 1969, by the New York Times Company. Reprinted by permission.

Page 229: Originally appeared in *Notes and Essays,* pp. 1–23, Vol. 30, 1960, published by the Center for Liberal Education for Adults, Brookline, Mass.

Page 250: Copyright © 1969, by The Atlantic Monthly Company, Boston, Mass. Reprinted with permission.

Pages 251–252: Copyright © 1960, by The Atlantic Monthly Company, Boston, Mass. Reprinted with permission.

Pages 252–253: Copyright © 1962, by The Atlantic Monthly Company, Boston, Mass. Reprinted with permission.

Pages 266–267: Reprinted from *Childhood and Society,* Second Edition, Revised and Enlarged, by Erik H. Erikson. By permission of W. W. Norton & Company, Inc. Copyright 1950, © 1963, by W. W. Norton & Company, Inc.

Page 294: Reprinted with permission of the publisher from Harry Passow (ed.), *Education in Depressed Areas.* New York: Teachers College Press, 1963.

Page 360: Copyright © 1968. Reprinted by permission of Pegasus, a Division of Western Publishing Company, Inc.

Page 411: Reprinted from the *American Journal of Psychiatry,* Vol. 116, p. 498, 1959. Copyright 1959, the American Psychiatric Association.

Page 415–416: Copyright ©, the American Orthopsychiatric Association, Inc. Reproduced by permission.

Page 442–443: Copyright © 1965, by The Atlantic Monthly Company, Boston, Mass. Reprinted with permission.

Pages 518–519: © 1967, by the New York Times Company. Reprinted by permission.

Page 540: Copyright © 1966, by Meredith Corporation. Reprinted by permission of Appleton-Century-Crofts.

Page 542: From *Social Problems: A Modern Approach,* by Howard Becker, copyright John Wiley & Sons, 1966.

Pages 5, 12, 20, 28, 30, 70, 124, 128, 175–176, 208, 209, 210, 221, 223, 262–263, 292, 298, 322–323, 327, 329, 336–337, 372, 393, 460–461, and 476–477: Excerpts from *The American Sociological Review* are reprinted with permission of the authors and the American Sociological Association.

Pages 18, 19, 31, 33, 39, 164–165, 271, 330, 396–397, 399, 400, 423–424, 425, 487–488, 502–503, and 512–513: Excerpts from *Social Problems* are reprinted with permission of the authors and the Society for the Study of Social Problems.

SUBJECT INDEX

PRINTED IN U.S.A.